The Business Environment

The Business Environment

Seventh Edition

Adrian Palmer & Bob Hartley

London   Boston   Burr Ridge, IL   Dubuque, IA   Madison, WI   New York   San Francisco   St. Louis
Bangkok   Bogotá   Caracas   Kuala Lumpur   Lisbon   Madrid   Mexico City
Milan   Montreal   New Delhi   Santiago   Seoul   Singapore   Sydney   Taipei   Toronto

The Business Environment, Seventh Edition
Adrian Palmer & Bob Hartley
ISBN-13 9780077130015
ISBN-10 0077130014

Published by McGraw-Hill Education
Shoppenhangers Road
Maidenhead
Berkshire
SL6 2QL
Telephone: 44 (0) 1628 502 500
Fax: 44 (0) 1628 770 224
Website: www.mcgraw-hill.co.uk

British Library Cataloguing in Publication Data
A catalogue record for this book is available from the British Library

Library of Congress Cataloguing in Publication Data
The Library of Congress data for this book has been applied for from the Library of Congress

Acquisitions Editors: Leiah Batchelor/Caroline Prodger
Development Editors: Jennifer Rotherham/Stephanie Frosch
Production Editor: Alison Davis
Marketing Manager: Alexis Thomas

Text design by Hardlines
Cover design by Adam Renvoize
Printed and bound in Great Britain by Ashford Colour Press Ltd, Gosport, Hampshire

Brief Table of Contents

Detailed Table of Contents

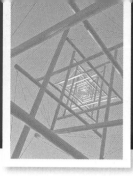

Preface

Business organizations exist in an environment that is becoming increasingly complex and competitive. The firm in its business environment is essentially similar to any living organism in the natural environment – survival and prosperity come to those that are best able to adapt to their environment. This book explores the complexity of forces that make up the business environment, and the approaches used by managers to read their environment and to respond to change in it.

The book is structured in five parts. Dividing the business environment into a number of distinct areas inevitably involves some fairly arbitrary boundaries and the chapters in each part continually seek to provide links to other chapters.

The first part provides contexts by analysing the general nature of the business environment. The key elements and forces in the environment are discussed within a systems framework.

In the second part, we focus on the external environment and explore in more detail the broad macro- environmental trends and forces introduced in Part 1. Part 2 begins with a review of the political environment. The social, technological and legal environments are explored in subsequent chapters. This part concludes with a review of the increasingly important topic of the social responsibilities of business and the ecological impacts and responsibilities of business.

Part 3 switches the focus of attention inward by looking at how organizations cope with external change. The aim here is to understand the internal factors that can facilitate or inhibit response to a changing external environment. A review is made of the different types of organization that exist in the business environment, their objectives and internal processes.

Part 4 focuses on markets, which are a means through which organizations satisfy customers' needs. Markets provide signals that should channel an organization's resources to serve groups that present them with the greatest opportunities. We begin this part with a discussion of the economic environment of business organizations, first at the micro level of market competition between firms and, second, at the macro level of national economic policy. Basic principles of micro- and macroeconomics are introduced. With the increasing globalization of business, a chapter on firms' international environment sets markets in this broader context.

The final part returns to a more holistic perspective of the business environment. In this part we look at methods of analysing a complex environment and making decisions about future business strategy. Great attention is given to the role of information gathering, data analysis and the ways in which change can be implemented. Further integration of the business environment is provided through five case studies.

This seventh edition has itself responded to changes in the business environment, with strengthened coverage of topics of contemporary concern. There is greater coverage of the impacts on business of ecological change, especially global warming. After a period of unprecedented economic growth, this book reports on change in many organisations' business environment brought about by turmoil in world financial markets following the banking crisis of 2008.

Learning throughout the book is supported in a number of ways. Each chapter contains a number of thought-provoking vignettes based on contemporary examples. In addition, each chapter has a mini-case study with review questions and a further series of chapter review questions. Key terms are introduced and defined in a glossary. Suggestions are made for further reading that will allow the reader to pursue issues raised in each chapter. The companion website provides links to relevant websites. The authors invite comments about any of the material contained in this book.

Adrian Palmer
mail@apalmer.com

Bob Hartley
bob.hartley@northampton.ac.uk

About the Authors

Adrian Palmer is Professor of Marketing, University of Wales, Swansea, and Affiliate Professor at ESC Rennes Business School, France.

Bob Hartley is Associate Dean, Northampton Business School, The University of Northampton, UK.

Specialist contributor on the legal environment: **Mary Mulholland** is Principal Lecturer in Law, De Montfort University, Leicester, UK.

Guided Tour

You are thrilled with the new Hewlett...
you have just bought, but pause to...
notebook is actually attributable to...
on the front says Hewlett-Packard, b...
the battery is made by Sony, the p...
the hard disc drive is made by Sea...
manufacturer of the disc drive woul...
its drives from other manufacturers,...
bought in raw materials. You also st...
your new laptop – not direct from He...
retailer to which you were attracte...
Then there was the DHL delivery serv...
the banking system that somehow tran...
Packard through all of the intermed...
that even simple products can invol...
relationships to bring the final pro...
complexity of these relationships is...

Opening Vignettes

A vignette begins each chapter, introducing the main topic and showing the business environment in real life.

✓ Learning Objectives

This chapter will explain:

- ✓ The nature of organizational objectives.
- ✓ The formal and informal reasons for organizationa...
- ✓ Patterns of organizational growth.
- ✓ Economies and diseconomies of scale.
- ✓ Constraints on growth and reasons behind the rece...
- ✓ Models for viewing the business environment as a...
- ✓ Methods of raising finance for expansion.

Learning Objectives

A set of objectives, summarizing what readers should learn from each chapter, is included at the start of each chapter.

◆ Thinking around t...

The tiny spy that follows you home?
Many inventions come along that have the potential to...
the excitement of a launch may be matched with scepticisr...
is one new development that has taken some time in ac...
simultaneously raising concerns among many groups ab...

RFId involves placing a small radio transmitter on...
be tracked remotely. So far, RFID has mainly been appli...
rather than individual consumer goods. The cost of ta...
to read them and process the data, means that item-lev...
But the prospect of rapidly falling costs and greater m...
to the opportunities, and some consumer groups to...
report for the EU in 2008 talked about the 'hype cycl...
new technology-based products (Schmitt and Michahe...
eventually seen as unrealistic and, eventually, adoptio...
at a much more modest level than the previous hype r...

'Thinking Around the Subject' Boxes

In each chapter you'll find additional practical examples to highlight the application of concepts and encourage you to critically analyse real-world issues.

Case Studies

Every chapter has its own case study, relating directly to the issues discussed and designed to bring the theories to life. Chapter 16, at the end of the book, provides five extra in-depth cases.

Case study:
A war of words over green airline claims

© David Joyner

aircraft ha...
fuel durin...
by the boo...
airlines su...

Actuall...
flying is r...
at first sigl...
opportuni...
more frien...
whom the...
According...
compariso...
with Ryan...
footprint...
on Alitalia...
from Lond...
footprint...
kg with A...
its 'green'...

A key issue on the mind of many businesses during the first decade of the twenty-first century has been global warming. Initially, awareness of the causes and consequences of...

Summary

This chapter has reviewed the complex nature of an orga
The environment can be analysed at three levels: the
firms and individuals that an organization directly intera
activities); the macroenvironment, comprising general f
on the microenvironment; and the internal environm
within the organization.

This chapter has stressed the interrelatedness of
environment. Although the social environment and
identified as separate elements, the two are closely link
resulted in mass ownership of cars, which has in turn af

Subsequent chapters pay attention to each of the elem
but the complexity of linkages must never be forgotten. C
elements within dynamic analytical frameworks, which can
of the future business environment.

Summary and Chapter Links

This briefly reviews and reinforces the main
topics you will have covered in each chapter, to
ensure you have acquired a solid understanding
of the key topics, as well as providing links to
information in other chapters.

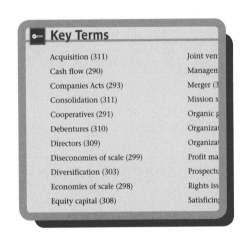

Key Terms

Acquisition (311)	Joint ven
Cash flow (290)	Managem
Companies Acts (293)	Merger (3
Consolidation (311)	Mission s
Cooperatives (291)	Organic g
Debentures (310)	Organizat
Directors (309)	Organizat
Diseconomies of scale (299)	Profit ma
Diversification (303)	Prospectu
Economies of scale (298)	Rights iss
Equity capital (308)	Satisficin

Key Terms

These are highlighted throughout the chapter and listed at
the end of each chapter for quick reference. A Glossary at
the back of the book aids revision.

Chapter review questions

1 Discuss what you understand by the term 'business
2 Suppliers and intermediaries are important stakeho
  business. Discuss the evolving role and functions of s
3 Members of an organizational set are becoming i
  examples of this interdependency, and discuss the re

Activities

1 Develop a checklist of points that you consider to b
  organization is responsive to changes in its busines
  these indicators? Now apply your checklist to three se
  manufacturing industry, the second a service-based c
  a government organization that serves the public. V

Chapter Review Questions and Activities

The questions encourage you to review and apply the
knowledge you have acquired from each chapter, while
the activities suggest practical projects for group or solo
study.

Further reading

A good starting point for understanding the competitive advar
in achieving this is provided in Michael Porter's frequently
Porter, M.E. (1985) *Competitive Advantage: Creating and Sus*
Free Press.

There is now an extensive literature on the development of
summary of the principles can be found in the following te

Buttle, F. D. (2008) *Relationship Marketing* (2nd edn), London,
Egan, J. (2008) *Relationship Marketing: Exploring Relational St*
Pearson Education Ltd.
Donaldson, W.G. and O'Toole, T. (2007) *Strategic Market Rela*
(2nd edn), Chichester, John Wiley.

This chapter has provided a general overview of the component
Suggestions for further reading on each of these componen

References

Further Reading

Each chapter includes the latest recommended reading,
covering journal articles, textbooks and other essential
sources.

Online Learning Centre

Online Learning Centre
Visit www.mcgraw-hill.co.uk/textbooks/palmer

Online Learning Centre

After completing each chapter, log on to the supporting Online Learning Centre website. Take advantage of the study tools offered to reinforce the material you have read in the text, and to develop your knowledge of business environment in an effective way.

Students – helping you to connect, learn and succeed

We understand that studying for your module is not just about reading this textbook. It's also about researching online, revising key terms, preparing for assignments and passing the exam. The website above provides you with a number of **FREE** resources to help you succeed in your module, including:

- **self-test questions** to prepare you for mid-term tests and exams
- **web links** to online sources of information to help you prepare for class
- **glossary** of key terms to help you revise core concepts.

Lecturer support – helping you to help your students

The Online Learning Centre also offers lecturers adopting this book a range of resources designed to offer:

- **faster course preparation** – time-saving support for your module
- **high-calibre content to support your students** – resources written by your academic peers, who understand your need for rigorous and reliable content
- **flexibility** – edit, adapt or repurpose; test in EZ Test or your department's Course Management System – the choice is yours.

The materials created specifically for lecturers adopting this textbook include:

- Lecture Outline to support your module preparation, with discussion topics, guide answers, teaching tips and more
- Solutions Manual, providing accuracy-tested answers to the problems in the textbook
- Case Notes with guide answers to case questions, written to help support your students in understanding and analysing the cases in the textbook
- PowerPoint presentations to use in lecture presentations.

To request your password to access these resources, contact your McGraw-Hill representative or visit **www.mcgraw-hill.co.uk/textbooks/palmer.**

Let us help make our **content** your **solution**

At McGraw-Hill Education our aim is to help lecturers to find the most suitable content for their needs delivered to their students in the most appropriate way. Our **custom publishing solutions** offer the ideal combination of content delivered in the way that best suits lecturer and students.

Our custom publishing programme offers lecturers the opportunity to select just the chapters or sections of material they wish to deliver to their students from a database called CREATE™ at

www.mcgrawhillcreate.co.uk

CREATE™ contains over two million pages of content from:
- textbooks
- professional books
- case books – Harvard Articles, Insead, Ivey, Darden, Thunderbird and BusinessWeek
- Taking Sides – debate materials.

Across the following imprints:
- McGraw-Hill Education
- Open University Press
- Harvard Business Publishing
- US and European material.

There is also the option to include additional material authored by lecturers in the custom product – this does not necessarily have to be in English.

We will take care of everything from start to finish in the process of developing and delivering a custom product to ensure that lecturers and students receive exactly the material needed in the most suitable way.

With a **Custom Publishing Solution**, students enjoy the best selection of material deemed to be the most suitable for learning everything they need for their courses – something of real value to support their learning. Teachers are able to use exactly the material they want, in the way they want, to support their teaching on the course.

Please contact **your local McGraw-Hill representative** with any questions or, alternatively, contact Warren Eels e: warren_eels@mcgraw-hill.com.

Acknowledgements

Our thanks go to the following reviewers for their comments at various stages in the text's development:

Rachel Ashworth, Cardiff Business School
Nuran Fraser, Manchester Metropolitan Business School
Olga Kuznetsova, Manchester Metropolitan Business School
Johan Lindeque, Queen's University Belfast
Carol Reid, University of Ulster
Anne Sempik, Nottingham Business School, Nottingham Trent University
Robert Webber, Leicester Business School, De Montfort University
Ying Zhang, Strathclyde University

We would also like to thank the following contributors for the material they have provided for this textbook:

Paul Cunstance, Harper Adams University College
Irena Descubes, ESC Rennes International School of Business, France
Damian Gallagher, University of Ulster
Nicole Koenig-Lewis, Swansea University
Rod McColl, ESC Rennes International School of Business, France
Alexander Moll, Visual Identity AG
Steve Worthington, Monash University, Australia

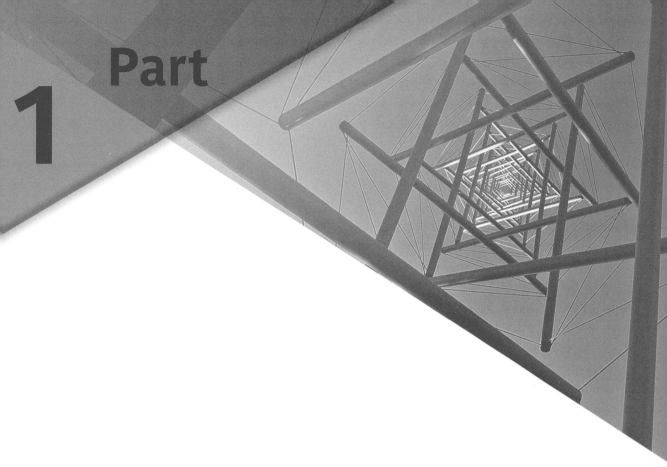

1 Part

Contexts

Part contents

Chapter 1

What is the Business Environment?

Suppose you had a million pounds to invest and wanted to achieve the maximum return on your investment over the next ten years. Where would you invest? How would you go about deciding on the best opportunities? In the past, visionary entrepreneurs have been able to read trends in the business environment, and have made goods and services that were just right for the new emerging opportunities. Billy Butlin spotted a trend for more paid holidays and achieved great success in the 1930s with his new holiday camps. The Hoover company successfully foresaw that with more women going out to work, there would be greater demand for automated household appliances such as the vacuum cleaner. In recent years, internet entrepreneurs have spotted the great desire of people to extend their circles of friends from offline to online, and the result has been the tremendous growth of social network websites such as Facebook and Twitter. Even ten years before the launch of these innovatory products, the entrepreneurs behind them might have been laughed at as unrealistic idealists, but they succeeded through a combination of good luck and good reading of the dynamic, changing environment. Looking back is easy, but predicting the next ten years is much more difficult. What opportunities will foreseeable changes in the business environment present you with? How will lots of individual changes combine with one another to influence the types of goods and services that we want to buy and the ability of firms to supply them? This chapter introduces the basic building blocks of the business environment and how organizations can make sense of its complexity so that they can improve their preparedness for the future.

✔ Learning Objectives

This chapter will explain:

✔ The elements that make up an organization's macro-, micro- and internal environments.

✔ The complex interdependencies that exist in the business environment.

✔ The concept of a value chain.

✔ Models for viewing the business environment as a system.

1.1 Defining the business environment

What do we mean by the term business environment? In its most general sense, an environment can be defined as everything that surrounds a system. The environment of a central heating system, for example, comprises all of those phenomena that impact on the system's ability to operate effectively. The environment would therefore include such factors as the external air temperature, the insulation properties of the rooms being heated, the quality and consistency of fuel supplied, etc. A business organization can similarly be seen as a system, whose performance is influenced by a whole range of phenomena in its environment. However, while a central heating system may be said to be a *closed* system, the business organization and its environment is an *open* system. For the central heating system, all elements of the system can generally be identified, but for business organizations, it can be difficult to define what makes up the system, and even more difficult to define the elements of their environment. Some elements may seem quite inconsequential today, but may nevertheless have potential to affect critically a business organization in future years. The test of a good business leader is to be able to read the environment and to understand not only how business systems and their environments work today, but also how they will evolve in the future. Society's rising expectations with regard to the ethical behaviour of business organizations is an example of an environmental factor that has emerged as an increasingly critical factor to the survival of business organizations. After studying this book, you should have a better idea of the complexity of the business environment.

Business organizations exist to turn inputs from their environment (e.g. materials, labour and capital) into goods and services that customers in the environment want to purchase. This **transformation process** adds value to the inputs, so that buyers are prepared to pay more to the business organization than the cost of resources that it has used up in the production process. This is the basis of a simple model of the organization in its environment, illustrated in Figure 1.1. This transformation process within the organization cannot be seen as a steady state, because external environmental influences have a tendency to be continually shifting, having the effect of undermining the current balance within the system. Just as the central heating thermostat has to react constantly to ensure a balance between its inputs (the energy source) and its outputs (the required amount of heat), so too organizations must constantly ensure that the system continues to transform inputs into higher-value outputs.

Of course, the organizations that form the centre of this transformation process take many shapes and forms, from a small sole trader through to a large multinational organization. The nature of the organization greatly affects the way in which it can adapt to its external environment. We will explore the great diversity of organizational types later, in the context of their ability to respond to environmental change.

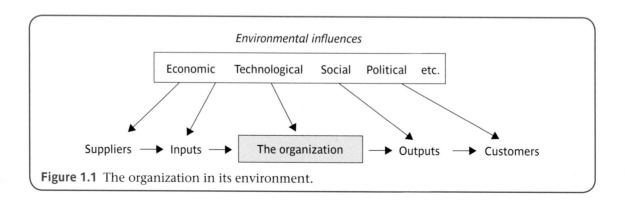

Figure 1.1 The organization in its environment.

Throughout this book, we are going to disaggregate a business organization's environment into a number of components. For now, we will introduce three important groups of components, which we will classify under the following headings:

- the macroenvironment
- the microenvironment
- the internal environment.

These are introduced schematically in Figure 1.2.

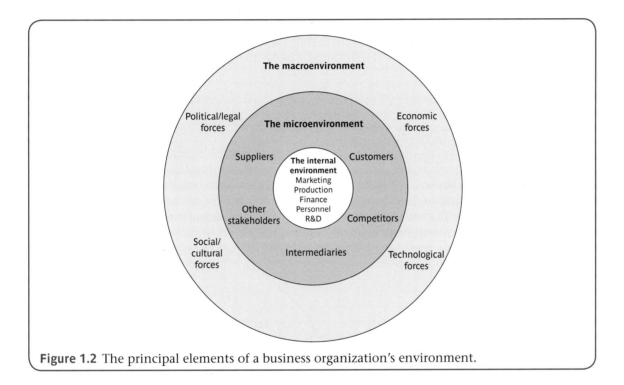

Figure 1.2 The principal elements of a business organization's environment.

The external environment comprises all those forces and events outside the organization that impinge on its activities. Some of these events impinge directly on the firm's activities – these can be described as forming an organization's **microenvironment**. Other events that are beyond the immediate environment nevertheless affect the organization and can be described as the **macroenvironment**. As well as looking to the outside world, managers must also take account of factors within other functions of their own firm. This is referred to as the **internal environment**.

The macroenvironment comprises a whole set of factors that can indirectly affect an organization's relationship to its markets. The organization may have no direct relationships with legislators as it does with suppliers, yet their actions in passing new legislation may have profound effects on the markets that the organization is able to serve, as well as affecting its production costs. The macroenvironmental factors cover a wide range of nebulous phenomena. They represent general forces and pressures rather than institutions with which the organization relates.

The microenvironment, by contrast, is concerned with actual individuals and organizations (such as customers, suppliers and intermediaries) that a company deals with. It may currently deal directly with some of these, while others exist with whom there is currently no direct contact, but who could nevertheless influence its policies. An organization's competitors could have a direct effect on its market position and form part of its microenvironment.

Why study the business environment?

History is full of examples of organizations that have failed to understand their operating environment, or simply failed to respond to change in the environment. The result has been a gradual decline in their profitability, and eventually they may cease to exist as a viable business unit. Theodore Levitt called this 'marketing myopia' and cited the example of railway companies that focused their vision on providing railway services, but failed to take account of the development of road transport (Levitt 1960). Consider the following more recent examples.

- The retailer Marks & Spencer assumed that its position was unassailable, but by the 1990s had failed to take account of the great improvements in value being offered by its competitors. The result was that many of Marks & Spencer's loyal customers deserted it, leading to a sharp fall in profitability, before a thwarted takeover bid led to new management bringing a new vision to the company.
- Healthy eating has become an important issue in the early twenty-first century. The profits of the fast-food company McDonald's fell and it was forced to close branches worldwide as consumers sought more healthy convenience food, before the company belatedly responded to change with healthier menu items.
- Music retailers such as HMV and EMI were accused of 'putting their head in the sand' and ignoring the threat to the sale of CDs posed by downloadable music sites. They adopted new distribution methods only after smaller, more aggressive companies had developed the online music market.

On the other hand, there have been many spectacular successes where organizations have spotted emerging trends in their business environment, and capitalized on these with new goods and services, or new ways of operating their business, in order to meet the new opportunities presented within the environment. Consider the following examples.

- In the airline market, companies such as Ryanair and easyJet spotted the opportunities represented by government deregulation and offered profitable low-cost 'no frills' air services, often aimed at people who would not previously have flown.
- Many supermarkets and farmers have noted consumers' concern for the purity of the food we eat, and this, combined with rising incomes, has led them successfully to develop ranges of organic foods.
- Many of the UK's pub operators have identified changing social behaviour, with fewer people using pubs as a regular venue primarily for beer drinking, but much greater levels of dining out for social purposes. This has led pub operators to increase their profits by reconfiguring their pubs as restaurants.

There is every indication that the pace of change in most organizations' business environment is speeding up and it is therefore increasingly important for organizations to have in place systems for monitoring their environment and, just as importantly, for responding appropriately to such change. There is evidence that successful organizations are not so much those that deliver value to customers today, but those that understand how definitions of value are likely to change in the future. A company may have been very good at creating value through the typewriters that it made, but it may nevertheless have failed to deliver value into the future had it not understood the impacts of information technology. In the eyes of customers, the company's traditional products would no longer represent good value when compared with the possibilities presented by the new technologies.

Of course, it is much more difficult to predict the future than to describe the past. A stark indication of the rewards of looking forwards rather than backwards is provided by an analyst who studied stock-market performance. If a cumulative investment of $1 had been invested from 1900 on 1 January each year in the stock that had performed best in the *previous* year, and then reinvested the following year, the accumulated value in 2000 would have been just $250. However, if it had been invested each year in the stock that performed best in the *year ahead*, the accumulated value would be over $1 billion. Successful companies have often been those that understand their business environment and have invested in growth areas, while cutting back in areas that are most likely to go into decline. Being first to market when trends are changing can be much more profitable than simply reacting to a market trend. However, predicting future trends can be very difficult and can involve a lot of risk. The aim of this book is to provide frameworks for making well-informed judgements about the likely future state of the business environment, based on a sound analysis of emerging trends.

1.3 The macroenvironment

While the microenvironment comprises individuals and organizations with whom a company interacts, the macroenvironment is more nebulous. It comprises general trends and forces that may not immediately affect the relationships that a company has with its customers, suppliers and intermediaries but, sooner or later, macroenvironmental change will alter the nature of these relationships. As an example, change in the population structure of a country does not immediately affect the way in which a company does business with its customers but, over time, it may affect the numbers of young or elderly people with whom it is able to do business.

Most analyses of the macroenvironment divide the environment into a number of areas. The principle headings, which form the basis for chapters of this book, are described below. It must, however, be remembered that the division of the macroenvironment into subject areas does not result in watertight compartments. The macroenvironment is complex and interdependent, and these interdependencies will be brought out in later chapters. The subheadings of the sections that follow are also those that are commonly used in macroenvironmental analysis.

Thinking around the subject

Big Mac, big business, big problem?

Business leaders have come under increasing levels of scrutiny from governments, the media and the public in general. Some people have held grudges against particular companies, and others against the system of big business in general. In 2009, anti-globalization protesters damaged a Royal Bank of Scotland (RBS) building during a G20 summit of world leaders in London; the object of the protestors was as much the world business environment in general as RBS in particular. The advent of social networking media has made it easier for groups of disenchanted individuals to connect with one another and to voice their concerns about the business environment.

Large, successful companies, it seems, just have to accept that they will never please those people who hold large corporate organizations responsible for all of the world's problems. But just how hostile is the environment to business organizations?

A report by the Future Foundation appeared to challenge the idea that young people are becoming more hostile towards big business than their parents (Future Foundation). According to a 2001 study by the organization, 16–24-year-olds have more positive feelings towards multinationals than older groups, particularly those who came of age in the 1960s, a period commonly associated with protest movements. Now in their forties and fifties, this group seemed to be the most critical of big business. The research revealed that younger generations are less inclined towards direct action than their parents and grandparents. Nearly half of all 16–34 year olds claimed they would not demonstrate if a multinational company had done something wrong. Further confounding the myth of young people wanting to change the world was the statistic that fewer than one in twenty strongly agreed that they 'would not buy the products of a large multinational company that had done something wrong'. A third of teens and twentysomethings agreed to preserving the power of multinational companies, and a further one in ten believed that multinationals are 'ultimately for the good of consumers' and should be encouraged to grow. By contrast, two-thirds of their grandparents – those aged 55 and above – claimed they would boycott goods to punish companies they considered guilty of corporate crimes. Even the issue of genetic engineering failed to provoke a strong response from young people, with only four in ten mistrusting the claims of the multinationals, compared to six in ten of their parents and grandparents.

Does this research indicate the ultimate supremacy for big business, where the golden arches of McDonald's and the Nike 'swoosh' are symbols of its global sovereignty? Should such organizations feel safe in the knowledge of this study, or do they still need to be alert to possible trouble in the future? And even if a high proportion of young people support the idea of capitalism and big business, can such firms afford to ignore the vociferous and extreme minority whose direct action and boycotts can do costly and long-lasting harm to a firm's image?

1.3.1 The political environment

Politicians are instrumental in shaping the general nature of the external environment as well as being responsible for passing legislation that affects specific types of organization. The political environment can be one of the less predictable elements in an organization's marketing environment, and businesses need to monitor the changing political environment for a number of reasons.

- At the most general level, the stability of the political system affects the attractiveness of the business environment. Companies are likely to be reluctant to invest in a country with an unstable government, for fear that the law would not protect their investment.
- Governments pass legislation that directly and indirectly affects firms' business opportunities.
- There are many examples of the direct effects on business organizations – for example, laws giving consumers rights against the seller of faulty goods. At other times, the effects of legislative changes are less direct, as where legislation outlawing anti-competitive practices changes the nature of competition between firms within a market.
- In its broadest sense, the political environment includes pressure groups and trade associations that can be influential in changing government policy.

- Government is responsible for formulating policies that can influence the rate of growth in the economy and hence the total amount of spending power. It is also a political decision as to how this spending power should be distributed between different groups of consumers and between the public and private sectors.
- Governments are responsible for protecting the public interest at large, imposing further constraints on the activities of firms (for example, controls on pollution, which may make a manufacturing firm uncompetitive in international markets on account of its increased costs).
- Increasingly, the political environment affecting business organizations includes supranational organizations that can directly or indirectly affect companies. These include trading blocs (e.g. the EU, ASEAN and NAFTA) and the influence of worldwide intergovernmental organizations (e.g. the World Trade Organization) and pressure groups (e.g. Greenpeace).

1.3.2 The social, demographic and cultural environment

Business organizations are concerned with the structure and values of the societies in which they operate. It is crucial for businesses to appreciate fully the cultural values of a society, especially where an organization is seeking to do business in a country that is quite different to its own. Attitudes to specific products change through time and at any one time can differ between groups in society.

Even in home markets, business organizations should understand the processes of gradual change in values and attitudes and be prepared to satisfy the changing needs of consumers. The 2010 edition of *Social Trends*, published by the UK's Office for National Statistics, highlighted a number of changes that had occurred during the previous 40 years:

- in 1971, the average household size in Great Britain was 2.9 people, with single-person households accounting for 18 per cent of all households; by 2009, the average household size had fallen to 2.4, with the proportion of single-person households rising to 29 per cent
- in 1970, life expectancy at birth for males in the UK was 68.7 years and for females 75.0 years; by 2008, life expectancy at birth for males had risen to 77.8 years and for females 81.9 years
- in 1970, there were 340,000 first marriages in England and Wales, but this had fallen to 143,000 by 2007
- attitudes to healthy living have changed – for example, in 1974, 26 per cent of men and 13 per cent of women in Great Britain who smoked regularly were classed as heavy smokers, but by 2008 these figures had fallen to 7 per cent and 5 per cent respectively.

These are just a few examples of detail changes that can have direct and indirect impacts on the business environment. To take the example of the decline in the number of heavy smokers, this has encouraged many governments around the world to ban smoking in public spaces. Such legislation might have been difficult to agree and implement if smokers were still a dominant group in society, but with declining numbers, the legislation has been passed. Some business sectors have been significantly affected by this, especially the hospitality and entertainment sector. As an example, in 2008 a UK-based bingo operator blamed a fall in profits on the smoking ban as many clients decided to smoke at home rather than visit a smoke-free bingo hall.

A number of general social trends with potential impacts on business can be observed in most developed economies, as the following examples illustrate.

- Leisure is becoming a bigger part of many people's lives, and businesses have responded with a wide range of leisure-related goods and services.
- Attitudes to debt have changed and there is a tendency for increasing numbers of people to buy products for experiential values rather than to satisfy basic utilitarian needs.
- The role of women in society has changed – although, worldwide, big differences in the role of women and men remain. For example, a report to the World Economic Forum in 2010 noted that,

in Nordic nations, women live longer, have high employment rates, high levels of participation in higher education, and often enjoy generous maternity and paternity schemes. At the other end of the scale, Pakistan, Chad and Yemen perform poorly. In the case of India, it was noted that women suffered from persistent health, education and economic participation gaps.

- Growing concern with the environment among many groups in society is reflected in a variety of 'green' consumer products.
- Greater life expectancy is leading to an ageing of the population and a shift to an increasingly 'elderly' culture. This is reflected in product design that emphasizes durability rather than fashionability. New services have emerged to meet the aspirations of this growing group – for example, adventure holidays and 'gap years' for older people.
- Many western European countries are becoming ethnically and culturally much more diverse. In the UK, the large number of Polish people who entered the country from 2004 has led to the development of many retail and financial services aimed specifically at this group.

In Chapter 3 we look in detail at consumers' values, attitudes and lifestyles, and the processes of gradual change in these. That chapter also explores the issue of 'cultural convergence', referring to an apparent decline in differences between cultures.

1.3.3 The technological environment

The pace of technological change is becoming increasingly rapid and marketers need to understand how technological developments might affect them in four related business areas.

1 New technologies can allow new goods and services to be offered to consumers – internet banking, mobile internet and new anti-cancer drugs, for example.
2 New technology can allow existing products to be made more cheaply, thereby widening their market through being able to charge lower prices. In this way, more efficient aircraft have allowed new markets for air travel to develop.
3 Technological developments have allowed new methods of distributing goods and services (for example, Amazon.com used the internet to offer book buyers a new way of browsing and buying books).
4 New opportunities for companies to communicate with their target customers are continuing to emerge, with many companies using computer databases to target potential customers and to maintain a dialogue with established customers. The internet, '3G' mobile phone networks and global positioning systems (GPS) have opened up new communication opportunities for many companies.

1.3.4 The economic environment

Businesses need to keep an eye on indications of a nation's prosperity. There are many indicators of a nation's economic health, of which two of the most common are measures of gross domestic product (GDP) and household disposable income. Many of these indicators tend to follow cyclical patterns related to a general economic cycle of expansion followed by contraction.

Throughout the economic cycle, the consumption of most goods and services tends to increase during the boom period and decline during recessionary periods. The difficulty in forecasting the level of demand for a firm's products is therefore often quite closely linked to the difficulty of forecasting future economic prosperity. This difficulty is compounded by the problem of understanding the relationship between economic factors and the state of demand – most goods and services are positively related to total available income, but some, such as bus services and insolvency practitioners, are negatively related. Furthermore, while aggregate changes in spending power may indicate a likely increase for goods and services in general, the actual distribution of spending power among the population will influence the pattern of demand for specific products. In addition to measurable economic prosperity, the level of perceived wealth and confidence in the future can be an important determinant of

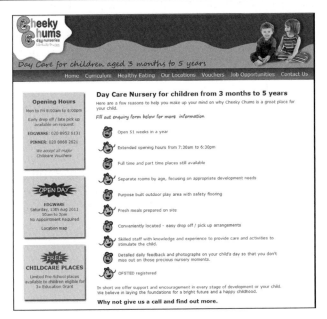

Figure 1.3 Changing family structures and growing career orientation among women have led many people to seek outside childcare services, rather than caring for children entirely within the family unit. Some cultures may regard childcare as central to family life, and would therefore provide few opportunities for a commercial childcare service. Attitudes in western countries have changed, and a growing proportion of people would regard it as quite normal to buy in professional help to look after their children. Many service providers, such as this one, have emerged to satisfy this growing market. (Photo reproduced with permission of Cheeky Chums Nursery.)

demand for some high-value goods and services. The economic cycle also affects competition for resources, with peak prices for resources such as oil and metals being reached during periods of boom, and much lower prices during periods of economic recession.

Understanding the economic environment can become particularly difficult during periods of great turbulence. During 2008, a 'credit crunch' led to the collapse of several banks and many commentators predicted that established economic patterns would change for ever. Just the existence of turbulence led many individuals and organizations to be much more cautious in the lending and borrowing decisions they made, which in turn had knock-on effects elsewhere in the economy.

Thinking around the subject

The consumer culture is dead – long live the consumer?

In September 2008 it seemed that the business environment had changed for ever, as cherished institutions collapsed, one after another. In the space of a few months, banks around the world had gone bankrupt, from the mighty Lehman Brothers down to the small savings and loans institutions that ran out of cash. Mighty retailers such as Woolworths – just one year short of its hundredth birthday in the UK – were laid to ruin. A generation had been brought up on the idea that 'greed is good' and that big end-of-year bonuses were to be celebrated, not condemned. But now greedy bonus seekers were seen as the cause of so many problems. In many circles, 'ostentatious consumption' was eclipsed by a new age of 'ostentatious utilitarianism'. At dinner parties, people who once would have boasted about how much they had paid for their Prada handbag or Jimmy Choo shoes now revelled in telling their friends how they had been so clever in 'discovering' good-value bargains in the likes of Poundland and Lidl. This coincided with a period of growing concern for the ecological environment, so any self-respecting socialite could now save their dwindling pennies and acquire street cred by convincing their friends that, by shopping at Poundland, they were helping to help save the environment. Where would all this lead? Some pundits saw an inexorable trend to an anti-materialistic world in which people felt guilty about earning bonuses (at least those who still had a job), and those who had the money felt bad about spending it. Surely the world would never be the same again and the business environment would grind to a halt as consumers' new-found values resulted in them spending less with companies, which would in turn lead to fewer people with well-paid jobs and therefore even fewer consumers able and willing to keep the economy afloat.

Reports of the death of the capitalist, consumer-led culture turned out to be premature. Some wealthy groups never stopped spending – for example, the profits of upmarket auction house Sotheby's remained strong following the financial crisis. Others appeared to have been laying low and soon came out spending again. By 2010 the profits of many upmarket retailers had begun to rise as shoppers rediscovered luxury.

Even the 'bonus culture' that had been so much maligned during the financial crisis seemed to be making a strong comeback. In February 2010, Royal Bank of Scotland, which had been brought close to bankruptcy partly as a result of its own bonus culture, announced that it would be paying £1.3 billion in bonuses to its staff.

Trying to predict the future business environment can be fraught with difficulty. In the eye of a crisis, we might think that the world has changed for ever but, as this example illustrates, systems can be resilient and the business environment, seen as a complex system, may have great self-correcting characteristics. A difficult challenge for business leaders is to distinguish transient, self-correcting changes from these that bring about fundamental change in the relationship between elements of the business environment. Maybe some things are quite constant – for example, consumers' need to adapt to the norms of their peer group – and this was just manifested in different ways at the depths of the recession, but when the peer groups' values changed, was it simply a case of back to 'business as usual'?

1.4 The microenvironment

The microenvironment of an organization can best be understood as comprising all those other organizations and individuals who directly or indirectly affect the activities of the organization. The microenvironment comprises actual people and organizations. The company may be dealing with these organizations today, or may potentially deal with them in the future. It may have no intention of dealing with other companies in its microenvironment (such as competitors), but these can nevertheless have a major impact on the activities of an organization. Also, many of these other companies and individuals may feel that they have such a keen interest in the activities of the organization that they become **stakeholders** in it. We will return to the subject of stakeholders in organizations later. The following key groups can be identified in most companies' microenvironments.

1.4.1 Customers

Customers are a crucial part of an organization's microenvironment. Quite simply, in a competitive environment, no customers means no business. An organization should be concerned about the changing requirements of its customers and should keep in touch with these changing needs by using an appropriate information-gathering system. In an ideal world, an organization should know its customers so well that it is able to predict what they will require next, rather than wait until it is possibly too late and then react.

But we need to think beyond this simplistic model of customers expressing their preferences and businesses then satisfying them. First, the people who buy a company's products are not necessarily the same people as those who consume them. Any good book on consumer behaviour will describe a range of influencers, users, deciders and 'gatekeepers' who have a bearing on whether a company's product is bought.

Second, does the customer always know what is best for them, and should organizations take a wider view of their customers' long-term interests? There have been many examples of situations where customers' long-term interests have been neglected by companies, including the following:

- fast-food companies, who have been accused of contributing to an 'epidemic' of obesity among young people by their promotion of high-fat food
- manufacturers of baby milk that failed to make mothers aware of the claimed long-term health benefits of using breast milk rather than manufactured milk products
- car manufacturers that add expensive music systems to cars as standard equipment but relegate vital safety equipment such as passenger airbags to the status of optional extras.

In each of these cases, most people might agree that, objectively, buyers are being persuaded to make a choice against their own long-term self-interest. Consumer groups have an increasing tendency to highlight the mis-selling of products that are against the best long-term interests of customers, and the results of such actions range from bad publicity to expensive product recalls and litigation. We will return to the issue of ethical behaviour in Chapter 5.

1.4.2 Suppliers

Suppliers provide an organization with goods and services that are transformed by the organization into value-added products for customers. Very often, suppliers are crucial to an organization's marketing success. This is particularly true where factors of production are in short supply, and the main constraint on an organization selling more of its product is the shortage of production resources. For example, in 2007, world steel prices rose following an increase in demand – especially from China – relative to the available capacity. Some businesses in the engineering sector were forced to reduce their production because of difficulties in obtaining supplies of steel. For companies operating in highly competitive markets where differentiation between products is minimal, obtaining supplies at the best possible price may be vital in order to be able to pass on cost savings in the form of lower prices charged to customers. Where reliability of delivery to customers is crucial, unreliable suppliers may thwart a manufacturer's marketing efforts.

Globally, many commentators have predicted shortages of key natural resources, as the demands of the rapidly growing 'BRIC' countries (Brazil, Russia, India and China) consume ever increasing resources to satisfy their growing domestic demand. This has led Chinese government agencies to seek to protect the country's future supply of scarce resources through collaborative development projects with less developed countries in Africa and South America.

There is an argument that companies should act in a socially responsible way towards their suppliers. Does a company favour local companies rather than buying from lower-priced overseas producers? (For example, many UK supermarkets have gone out of their way to highlight locally grown farm produce, which supports local farmers and has not incurred a high level of 'food miles'.) Does it use its dominant market power unfairly over small suppliers (an accusation that has been made against UK supermarkets for their treatment of their small farm suppliers)? Does it divide its orders between a large number of small suppliers, or place the bulk of its custom with a small handful of preferred suppliers? Does it favour new businesses or businesses representing minority interests when it places its orders?

Taking into account the needs of suppliers is a combination of shrewd business sense and good ethical practice. In business-to-business marketing, one company's supplier is likely to be another company's customer, and it is important to understand how suppliers, manufacturers and intermediaries work together to create value. The idea of a value chain is introduced later in this chapter.

1.4.3 Intermediaries

These often provide a valuable link between an organization and its customers. Large-scale manufacturing firms usually find it difficult to deal with each one of their final customers individually, so they choose instead to sell their products through **intermediaries**. The advantages of using intermediaries are discussed below. In some business sectors, access to effective intermediaries can be crucial for marketing success. For example, food manufacturers who do not get shelf-space in the major supermarkets may find it difficult to achieve large volume sales.

Channels of distribution comprise all those people and organizations involved in the process of transferring title to a product from the producer to the consumer. Sometimes, products will be transferred directly from producer to final consumer – a factory selling specialized kitchen units direct to the public would fit in to this category. Alternatively, the producer could sell its output through retailers or, if these are considered too numerous for the manufacturer to handle, it could deal with a wholesaler that in turn would sell to the retailer. More than one wholesaler could be involved in the process.

Intermediaries may need reassurance about the company's capabilities as a supplier that is capable of working with intermediaries to supply goods and services in a reliable and ethical manner. Many companies have suffered because they failed to take adequate account of the needs of their intermediaries (for example, Body Shop and McDonald's have faced protests from their franchisees where they felt threatened by a marketing strategy that was perceived as being against their own interests).

The internet has added to the complexity of channels of distribution. In the early days of the internet, it was widely predicted that many companies would be able to dispense with intermediaries and distribute their goods and services direct to the customer. The growth of direct-selling intermediaries such as Direct Line Insurance appeared to confirm the ability to cut out intermediaries, who were often portrayed as parasitic and delaying middlemen. The inelegant term 'disintermediation' has been used to describe the process of removing intermediaries from a distribution channel and developing direct communications. However, the reality has in many cases being quite different, with the proliferation of new types of internet-based intermediaries. Companies providing search engine optimization, affiliate marketing sites and price comparison sites, among others, have made the task of companies getting through to their final customer more complex. Some retailers have closed branches or reduced their salesforce and instead offer customers access to their product range via a website. Several UK suppliers of books, music, computer games and flowers have the logistical support to develop their business on the internet.

1.4.4 Competitors

In highly competitive markets, keeping an eye on competitors and trying to understand their likely next moves can be crucial. Think of the manoeuvring and out-manoeuvring that appears to take place between competitors in such highly competitive sectors as soft drinks, budget airlines and mobile phones. But who are a company's competitors? *Direct* competitors are generally similar in form and satisfy customers' needs in a similar way. *Indirect* competitors may appear different in form, but satisfy a fundamentally similar need. It is the indirect competitors that can be the most difficult to identify and to understand. What is a competitor for a cinema? Is it another cinema? A home rental movie? A telephone company offering videos on demand through smartphones? Or some completely different form of leisure activity that satisfies similar underlying needs?

1.4.5 Government

The demands of government agencies often take precedence over the needs of a company's customers. Government has a number of roles to play as stakeholder in commercial organizations.

- Commercial organizations provide governments with taxation revenue, so a healthy business sector is in the interests of government.
- Government is increasingly expecting business organizations to take over many responsibilities from the public sector – for example, with regard to the payment of sickness and maternity benefits to employees. In 2010, the newly elected coalition government in the UK announced its 'Big Society' programme, by which it actively sought community-based groups to take over many functions traditionally undertaken by government.
- It is through business organizations that governments achieve many of their economic and social objectives – for example, with respect to regional economic development and skills training.

Given the role of such regulators, which impact on many aspects of business activity, companies often go to great lengths in seeking favourable responses from such agencies. In the case of many UK private-sector utility providers, promotional effort is often aimed more at regulatory bodies than final consumers. In the case of the water industry, promoting greater use of water to final consumers is unlikely to have any significant impact on a water utility company, but influencing the disposition of the Office of Water Regulation, which sets price limits and service standards, can have a major impact.

1.4.6 Pressure groups

Pressure groups form part of the broadly defined political environment. Members of pressure groups may never have been customers of a company and are probably never likely to be. Yet a pressure group can detract seriously from the image that the company has worked hard to develop. Many businesses have learned to their cost that they cannot ignore pressure groups. It seems that, in Britain, fewer people may be voting in elections, but this is more than offset by a greater willingness of people to make their voice heard through pressure groups.

1.4.7 The financial community

This includes financial institutions that have supported, are currently supporting or may support the organization in the future. Shareholders – both private and institutional – form an important element of this community and must be reassured that the organization is going to achieve its stated objectives. Many market expansion plans have failed because the company did not adequately consider the needs and expectations of potential investors.

Following the **'credit crunch'** of 2008, financial institutions became increasingly important in the lives of many individuals and organizations, with reports of banks' unwillingness or inability to lend money to small businesses.

1.4.8 Local communities

Society at large has rising expectations of organizations, and market-led companies often try to be seen as a 'good neighbour' in their local communities. Such companies can enhance their image through the use of charitable contributions, sponsorship of local events and being seen to support the local environment. Again, this may be interpreted either as part of a firm's genuine concern for its local community, or as a more cynical and pragmatic attempt to buy favour where its own interests are at stake. If a fast-food restaurant installs improved filters on its extractor fans, is it doing it genuinely to improve the lives of local residents, or merely in an attempt to forestall prohibition action taken by the local authority?

1.5 The internal environment

The structure and politics of an organization can affect the manner in which it responds to environmental change. We are all familiar with lumbering giants of companies that, like a supertanker, have ploughed ahead on a seemingly predetermined course and had difficulty in changing direction. Well-respected companies such as Sainsbury's and Marks & Spencer have in the past been accused of having internal structures and processes that were too rigid to cope with a changing external environment. Simply having a strong marketing department is not necessarily the best way of ensuring adaptation to change. Such companies may in fact create internal tensions that make them less effective at responding to changing consumer needs than where marketing responsibilities in their widest sense are spread throughout the organization. Sainsbury's and Marks & Spencer eventually adapted and subsequently prospered. Others such as Woolworths either went out of business or were taken over by a more agile predator.

The internal culture of an organization can greatly affect the way it responds to organizational change. In the case of Sainsbury's, its culture was probably too much based on hierarchy and tradition, which can be a weakness in a rapidly changing external environment. **Organizational culture** concerns the social and behavioural manifestation of a whole set of values that are shared by members of the organization. Cultural values can be shared in a number of ways, including: the way work is organized and experienced; how authority is exercised and delegated; how people are rewarded, organized and controlled; and the roles and expectations of staff and managers.

For many organizations, employees are the biggest item of cost and potentially the biggest cause of delay in responding to environmental change. Having the right staff in the right place at the right time can demand a lot of flexibility on the part of employees. Many organizations have sought to improve the effectiveness of their employees by increasing their level of engagement with the organization. When the external environment calls for change, employees who share a sense of engagement with the organization are more likely to share in the threats and opportunities that environmental change presents, compared with employees who feel alienated from the organization. Change can be facilitated by a sense of teamwork, and effective communication between different groups of employees within an organization.

It is not uncommon to find organizations where communication between these different groups is characterized by distrust, and even hostility, making it difficult for the organization to respond to environmental change in a rapid and coordinated manner. In Chapter 10 we will look in more detail at the effects of internal management structures and processes on an organization's ability to respond to external environmental change.

1.6 Contextual issues in a dynamic environment

So far in this introductory chapter, we have broken down the business environment into a number of component parts. These are the basic building blocks that we will come back to throughout the book. However, the key to analysing the business environment is to see the links between these component parts. A number of these linkages have already been mentioned – for example, how the political environment affects the nature of the economic environment that the business faces. Within the microenvironment, members of the local community may also be customers of an organization. Community groups may influence government agencies, which in turn affect the activities of business organizations.

As well as taking a snapshot of the interdependency between elements of the business environment, we also need to consider their dynamic interaction. Successful business organizations have spotted trends, especially the interaction between trends in the different environments. For example, one trend in the social environment has been an increasing fear of crime, especially against children. Another trend in the technological environment has been the falling cost and increasing sophistication of mobile phones. By putting these two trends together, businesses have developed novel products – for example, mobile phones that can track children and automatically send warning messages if they stray beyond a predetermined zone.

We have introduced the main levels of the business environment in a manner that provides a foundation for the structure of this book. We will begin by looking at the macroenvironment before moving on to the micro- and internal environments. But the point cannot be stressed enough that the different elements of an organization's environment are very much interrelated and, in order to stress this interrelatedness, we will now briefly examine some common themes that run through all levels of the environment. We will focus on information and communication as two crucial elements that run through an organization's environment. We will then consider some simple frameworks that integrate the elements of the business environment, beginning with identification of the members of an organization's 'environmental set'. We will then integrate these within the concept of a 'value chain', and move on to take a dynamic look at these relationships and the emergence of power within them.

1.6.1 The interdependency of organizations in the business environment

No organization exists in a vacuum, and a crucial aspect of understanding the business environment lies in understanding the networks of formal and informal relationships that exist between a firm and its various stakeholders.

The people and organizations within a particular company's business environment that are of particular relevance to it are sometimes referred to as its **environmental set**. An example of an environmental set for a car manufacturer is shown in Figure 1.4.

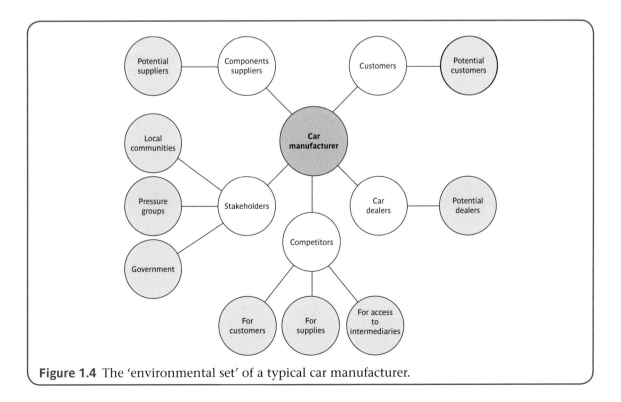

Figure 1.4 The 'environmental set' of a typical car manufacturer.

Some of these relationships between members of an organization's environmental set will be latent rather than actual – for example, a company may currently have no dealings with a prospective customer, but knows that one day they could become an actual customer. Some actual relationships with set members may be casual, infrequent and relatively unimportant for the company, whereas others will be crucial and the company will seek to develop long-term relationships, rather than rely on casual transactions. It may have power over some set members, but other set members may have considerable power over it. Although the environmental set shown in Figure 1.4 depicts a network focused on one organization, in fact networks can bring together these individual set members – for example, suppliers may have developed **strategic alliances** with the focal company's key competitors.

The relationship between set members is likely to be complex and constantly changing. Change can take a number of forms, including:

- a tendency for firms to seek the stability of long-term relationships with key members of their environmental set, rather than treating them all on a fairly casual basis
- shifts in the balance of power between members of the environment (e.g. retailers becoming more dominant relative to manufacturers)
- the emergence of new groups of potential customers or suppliers
- fringe pressure groups may come to represent mainstream opinions, in response to changes in social attitudes.

Understanding the relationship between members of an organization's environmental set is a crucial part of environmental analysis, and in Chapter 8 we will return to look in more detail at the nature of relationships that bring companies together.

1.6.2 Value chains

It was noted at the beginning of this chapter that a purpose of organizations is to transform inputs bought from suppliers into outputs sold to customers. In carrying out such a transformation, organizations add value to resources. In fact, the buyer of one firm's output may be another firm that treats the products purchased as inputs to its own production process. It in turn will add value to the resources and sell on its outputs to customers. This process can continue as goods and services pass though several organizations, gaining added value as they change hands. This is the basis of a **value chain**.

An illustration of the principles of a value chain can be made by considering the value-added transformation processes that occur in the process of making ice cream available to consumers. Table 1.1 shows who may be involved in the value-adding process and the value that is added at each stage.

Table 1.1 Value chain for ice cream.

Value chain member	Functions performed
Farmer	Produces a basic commodity product – milk
Milk merchant	Adds value to the milk by arranging for it to be collected from the farm, checked for purity and made available to milk processors
Ice cream manufacturer	By processing the milk and adding other ingredients, turns raw milk into ice cream. Through promotion, creates a brand image
Wholesaler	Buys bulk stocks of ice cream and stores in warehouses close to customers
Retailer	Provides a facility for customers to buy ice cream at a place and time that is convenient to them rather than the manufacturer

The value of the raw milk contained in a block of ice cream may be no more than a few pennies, but the final product may be sold for over £1. Customers are happy to pay £1 for a few pennies' worth of milk because it is transformed into a product that they value, and it is made available at a time and place where they want it. In fact, on a hot sunny day at the beach, many buyers would be prepared to pay even more to a vendor that brings ice cream to them. Value – as defined by customers – has been added at each stage of the transformation process.

Who should be in the value chain? The ice cream manufacturer might decide that it can add value at the preceding and subsequent stages better than other people are capable of doing. It may, for example, decide to operate its own farms and produce its own milk, or sell its ice cream direct to the public. The crucial question to be asked is whether the company can add value more cost-effectively than other suppliers and intermediaries. In a value chain, it is only value in the eyes of customers that matters. If high value is attached to having ice cream easily available, then distributing it through a limited number of company-owned shops will not add much value to the product.

The process of expanding a firm's activities through the value chain is often referred to as vertical integration where ownership is established. Backward vertical integration occurs where a manufacturer buys back in to its suppliers. Forward vertical integration occurs where it buys in to its outlets. Many firms expand in both directions.

With service being used as an increasingly important basis for differentiation between competing products, it is important that an organization looks not only outwards at the value chain, but also inwards at its own service–profit chain. The concept of the service–profit chain is based on the idea that employee satisfaction and productivity feed in to customer satisfaction and loyalty, thereby improving profitability. Profitability in turn can help create a more productive and satisfying work environment (see Figure 1.5).

The growth of the internet has led to the development of a modified form of 'virtual value chain' to try to explain how information-based industries operate a value chain that is distinct from traditional models based on raw materials, production and distribution. Getting access to web surfers can be a big challenge for many internet-based companies, such as motor insurance and electricity suppliers, who are selling a fairly generic product. Many have therefore chosen

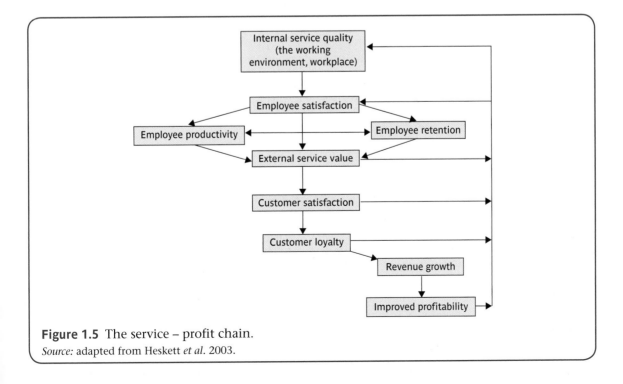

Figure 1.5 The service – profit chain.
Source: adapted from Heskett *et al.* 2003.

to pay a range of affiliate sites, price comparison sites and 'cash back' sites to help them in the task of bringing potential customers to their site.

The traditional manufacturer to customer distribution channel has also been challenged by the existence of peer-to-peer social networking websites. In many cases, a buyer's choice is strongly influenced by what their peers are saying through blogs and review sites. In this way, the peer group can create value by providing advice to buyers and information to the seller about how it could improve its product offer. The idea of 'co-creation of value' between consumers is at the heart of 'service dominant logic' (Vargo and Lusch 2008).

1.6.3 The information environment

Information represents a bridge between the organization and its environment, and is the means by which a picture of the changing environment is built up within the organization. The amount of information available to organizations seems to grow every year, as previous paper-based systems for collecting and distributing information are replaced by real-time electronic systems. Instead of a monthly printed sales report, retailers can now get real-time analysis of their sales disaggregated by type of product, time of sale, place of sale, or a seemingly endless permutations of analyses. In an age where there is a lot of information available, the key to business success is turning lots of little bits of information into actionable knowledge. It is not unknown for companies to be sitting on mountains of data, but to have no real insight into the markets they serve, the changing needs of their customers or the changing nature of the competition. Knowledge is one of the greatest assets of most organizations and its contribution to sustainable competitive advantage has been noted by many. In 1991, Ikujiro Nonaka began an article in the *Harvard Business Review* with the simple statement: 'In an economy where the only certainty is uncertainty, the one sure source of lasting competitive advantage is knowledge' (Nonaka 1991).

Information about the current state of the environment is used as a starting point for planning future strategy, based on assumptions about how the environment will change. It is also vital to monitor the implementation of an organization's corporate plans, to note the causes of any deviation from plan, and to identify whether these are caused by internal or external environmental factors. Information allows management to improve its strategic planning, tactical implementation of programmes, and its monitoring and control. In turbulent environments, having access to timely and relevant information can give a firm a competitive advantage. This can be manifested, for example, in the ability to spot turning points in the business cycle ahead of competitors; to respond more rapidly to customers' changing preferences; and to adapt manufacturing schedules more closely to demand patterns, thereby avoiding a build-up of stocks.

The internet has generated a huge amount of new information, and has challenged the assumption that an organization is at the centre of its **information environment**. The proliferation of Web 2.0 blogs, customer review sites and other social media allows customers, local communities and competitors to talk about the organization and its competitors. 'Viral marketing' has been seen by many companies as an opportunity for spreading its message rapidly, but at other times harmful messages have spread rapidly, which companies may find difficult to control. In terms of information available for planning their future strategies and operations, many companies have turned to various forms of social network 'mining' to try to build knowledge from what other people are saying in blogs and review sites. With the proliferation of information, attention is moving away from who is able to collect the most information, to who is able to most effectively turn it into actionable knowledge.

Large organizations operating in complex and turbulent environments often use information to build models of their environment, or at least sub-components of it. Some of these can be quite general, as in the case of the models of the national economy that many large companies have developed. From a general model of the economy a firm can predict how a specific item of government policy (for example, increasing the rate of value added tax on luxury goods) will impact directly and indirectly on sales of its own products.

We look in more detail in Chapter 4 at the ways in which information technology influences firms' business environment, and explore the implications of information for firms' responses to environmental change in Chapter 13.

◑ Thinking around the subject

The tiny spy that follows you home?

Many inventions come along that have the potential to change the business environment, but the excitement of a launch may be matched with scepticism. RFId (radio frequency identification) is one new development that has taken some time in achieving widespread acceptance, while simultaneously raising concerns among many groups about its privacy implications.

RFId involves placing a small radio transmitter on a product so that its movement can be tracked remotely. So far, RFID has mainly been applied to pallets and case loads of goods, rather than individual consumer goods. The cost of tags, as well as the equipment needed to read them and process the data, means that item-level tagging may still be some way off. But the prospect of rapidly falling costs and greater miniaturization has alerted companies to the opportunities, and some consumer groups to the potential threats. However, a report for the EU in 2008 talked about the 'hype cycle' that has affected RFId, like many new technology-based products (Schmitt and Michahelles 2008). The initial excitement is eventually seen as unrealistic and, eventually, adoption of the new technology settles down at a much more modest level than the previous hype might have led us to believe.

In addition to the technical issues of reducing the costs of producing RFId tags is the issue of privacy. RFId would seem like a blessing to companies keen to find out more about their products after they have left their shelves. But is its use ethical? In 2007, the EU's Information Society Commissioner called for a debate about the security and privacy issues surrounding RFId. Consumer groups and privacy campaigners have expressed concern that RFId tags could be used to build up massive databases of individuals' shopping, leisure and travel habits. These databases could be exploited by unscrupulous businesses and also become a target for cybercriminals. The fact that RFId tags track the actual items that people buy has led to fears that RFId data could be much more intrusive than the information retailers typically collect through bar code data and loyalty card programmes. As the cost of RFId tags falls and their versatility increases, they have the potential to be read at a distance without a consumer's knowledge. Would you want a bookshop 'spying' on how and where you read a book that you recently bought from it?

Not to be outdone, proponents of RFId have gone on the offensive to present the positive elements of the technology, such as its use in preventing counterfeit drugs reaching consumers; or in aviation, where tags have been fixed to aircraft spares and safety equipment. Retailers have attached RFId tags to goods to monitor thefts, and have argued that honest customers would have nothing to fear and would benefit from the lower prices resulting from reduced shoplifting.

If you were a commercial organization contemplating the use of RFId, which way do you think the privacy debate will go? Are pressure groups being paranoid about the data that companies can keep on an individual when, in reality, government agencies routinely collect much more information about us – for example, through vehicle number plate recognition? Will consumers be won over by the safety and security aspects of RFId, in much the same way as many people would readily accept the necessity for 'sinister' monitoring of their movements by CCTV? Would the most likely outcome of the EU review of RFId be a compromise, perhaps limiting how long RFId data could be kept and who would be allowed access to it?

1.6.4 The communication environment

Communications bring together elements within a firm's environmental set. With no communication, there is no possibility for trading to take place. Although we talk today about a communications 'revolution', businesses in previous centuries have faced the challenge of rapid developments in communication. Improved communication through canals, railways and steamships was an underlying foundation of the Industrial Revolution of nineteenth-century England. Today, internet-based communication technologies can be crucial for regional and national economic development. Towns and villages without access to high-speed internet services have often been passed by for economic development in much the same way as an office or factory might consider the absence of a main road or railway to be a disadvantage in terms of location.

The communication environment is changing rapidly and firms need to understand how it is likely to emerge in future. Will communication through mobile phones replace traditional landlines? What will be the business benefits of location-based mobile communication technologies that can allow communication at specific times and specific places? With the proliferation of communication media, how does a company ensure that its message stands out above the mountain of spam and unwanted communication?

More fundamentally, the question has been raised whether companies can ever again be in control of their communication in an environment of peer-to-peer social networking media. In an environment of only basic communication technologies, most of what the customer knows about a company may be based on communication from the company. Today, a customer or potential customer may rely much more on their peer groups to establish whether a prospective seller is reliable and suitable for them.

The development of social media is having profound effects on patterns of communication in the environment. We have already seen how viral marketing can rapidly build or undermine a company's position in the markets it serves. Actions taken by customers are increasingly likely to be affected by peer group communication rather than 'official' communication from the company. There are many creative examples of this effect – for example, Pledgebank is an online platform, active in 60 countries, that helps groups of like-minded people to take action. One person would sign a pledge to do something if others agree to take the same action – for example, 'I will stop eating junk food if 100 people in my town agree to do the same.' The creator of the pledge then publicizes their pledge and encourages other people to sign up.

Peer-to-peer social networks have also helped organizations in their research and development and to find answers to operational problems. It is also reported that both the EU and the White House have used social networks to generate ideas about how to solve problems such as global warming and obesity.

⟳ Thinking around the subject

Firms face up to Facebook

In the old days, companies had research departments that listened to customers, and advertising departments that sent messages to them. Although customers may have learned about a company through word of mouth, this communication channel was essentially limited to small groups of friends. The communication environment has changed rapidly in recent years and the development of 'Web 2.0' technologies has facilitated communication between customers themselves, as well as between companies and their customers. So-called 'social networking' sites, such as Facebook and YouTube, have led to many widely publicized problems for companies. For example, in 2005, the computer manufacturer Dell was hit by influential blogger Jeff Jarvis complaining about its poor customer service. Fellow consumers, no longer passive in their dissatisfaction, joined in with comments of their own, and stories of 'Dell Hell' rapidly became mainstream news. The company was rudely awoken to the power of social media and realized that simply trying to silence one individual or sue them for libel was never going to be effective. It subsequently put a lot of effort into engaging with social media, including the appointment of a 'coordinator of customer messages'.

Increasingly, companies have been mingling on social networking sites, and have sometimes created their own sites as community forums. Dell, for example, established the Dell2Dell blog, in an attempt to gain some control over communication about it. But on other occasions, companies have sponsored blogs without declaring their involvement. The retailer Wal-Mart covertly sponsored a blog that was supposedly operated by a couple camping in the store's car parks. It had hoped to manipulate content to show the company in a good light, but eventually the exercise turned into a PR disaster when news broke that the company had in fact been controlling the blog.

A significant challenge for companies is the sometimes blurred distinction between communication that is internal and external to company. Social networking sites allow employees to spread stories of dissent about the company they work for among their circle of friends. Using simpler communication technologies, a slanderous comment about a bad employer might have gone no further than a small circle of friends and family. But with their large numbers of friends linked through sites such as Facebook, dissent can spread much more widely. For example, there have been many reported cases of disgruntled restaurant workers who have told the world about the disgusting kitchens that they work in, but which customers do not ordinarily get to see. Some websites, such as www.wikileaks.com make a point of publicizing business and government policy documents that they would rather keep secret. Previously a document marked 'Top Secret' would have to have been physically stolen and copied to have an impact. Today a disgruntled employee can upload the document and have it on the screens of millions of people within hours.

1.6.5 The financial environment

There is an old saying that 'money makes the world go round', and this simple statement has continuing relevance for analysing the business environment. One important factor behind the Industrial Revolution in nineteenth-century Britain – in addition to the development of new manufacturing technologies – was the availability of finance. Financial institutions had previously been local, and largely incapable of financing the big factories and transport infrastructure that were a feature of the Industrial Revolution. Financial institutions were also needed for the transmission of money between manufacturers and their customers, who were no longer based in the local town and paid cash, but may have been located hundred of miles away and needed efficient payment systems that followed the changing patterns of trade. Financial institutions operating on a national and international level fuelled the Industrial Revolution. Today, these institutions continue to have enormous importance in the business environment. Without an efficient payment system that buyers and sellers can trust, world trade would become more costly and risky. Without funds available for investment, the construction of new infrastructure and investment in stocks would be reduced, with subsequent reduction in 'multiplier' effects on the economy. In September 2008 there was a fear that the world's banking system was in meltdown as the once mighty Lehman Brothers bank went bankrupt, and many banks around the world, including Lloyds TSB and Royal Bank of Scotland, either went bankrupt or had to be rescued by governments. Banks found themselves depleted of capital, and unwilling or unable to take risks in their lending decisions, therefore businesses found it increasingly difficult to borrow money to invest in capacity that would generate jobs and wealth. Consumers were hit not only by the effect of this on jobs and earnings, but also by banks' increasing wariness of lending to consumers to buy houses and cars, among other things. With firms and consumers unable to spend more, it seemed that, through a 'vicious circle', the economy would be in 'meltdown'.

Governments throughout the world realized that having money flowing through the system was vital for a vibrant economy, therefore on the basis that 'money makes the world go round', they resorted to creating new money and putting it into circulation through a process often referred to as 'quantitative easing'. We will return to the principles and practice of this in Chapter 13.

1.6.6 The ethical environment

All systems need rules if they are to operate efficiently and effectively. This can be observed in any marketplace, whether it is a fruit and vegetable market or a stock market. The market only functions because all participants conduct their actions according to a shared set of rules. These rules can either be informal or based on formal regulation. In many less developed economies, the dominant basis for rules is focused on embedded codes of trust. Increasingly in western societies, commercial relationships are governed by formality and regulation. Of course, informal rules in a market may not always be in consumers' best interests, as sometimes happens when suppliers have formal or informal understandings about how they can restrict the level of competition between themselves.

In western societies there is increasing concern that relationships between members of the environmental set should be conducted in an ethical manner. Ethics is essentially about the definition of what is right and wrong. However, it can be difficult to agree just what is right and wrong – no two people have precisely the same opinion. Culture has a great effect in defining ethics, and what is considered unethical in one society may be considered perfectly acceptable in another.

It can also be difficult to distinguish between ethics and legality. For example, it may not yet be strictly illegal to exploit the gullibility of children in advertisements, but it may nevertheless be unethical.

Today, ethical considerations are present in many business decisions. An example of a current issue is whether soft drinks and confectionery manufacturers should sponsor school activities – is it ethical to expose children to subconscious positive messages about junk food at a time of increasing obesity?

With expanding media availability and an increasingly intelligent audience, it is becoming easier to expose examples of unethical business practice. Moreover, many television audiences appear to enjoy watching programmes that reveal the alleged unethical practices of household-name companies. To give one example, the media have on many occasions focused attention on the alleged exploitative employment practices of suppliers used by some of the biggest brand names in sportswear.

We return to the subject of ethics in Chapter 5.

Figure 1.6 Like many bars, this one loudly promotes a 'happy hour' period during which alcohol is sold at a reduced price. For pub operators, such promotions may be vital to boost margins, especially if all bars in the area are offering equally low prices. Unfortunately, one consequence of cheap alcohol and 'buy one, get one free' offers is to increase 'binge drinking', with many town centres becoming noisy and violent areas at night time, fuelled by excessive drinking. For any individual pub, how does it balance the need for aggressive price promotion to customers with the need to appear socially responsible, for fear of further government regulation of the sector? Adverts for alcohol now routinely include warnings about the consequences for the customer of excessive drinking, but often in much smaller print than the main price information. Should a pub simply stop '2 for 1' offers and earn a higher margin on a smaller volume of sales? Although this may seem to be a responsible and profitable approach, it is unlikely to work if other pubs continue with their 2 for 1 offers – determined drinkers will simply make their way to the cheapest pub that has communicated the best offers. To illustrate the complexity of the task facing the sector, bar owners in some towns have voluntarily got together to try and agree collectively to stop price promotions that many believe lead to binge drinking. Agreement of all bar owners would be crucial, because otherwise drinkers would simply find out the cheapest outlet, and

© *lillisphotography*

other bars would be forced defensively to cut their prices to retain business. But did government see this as a benign example of socially motivated co-operation? Not the Office of Fair Trading, which gave a veiled threat to a group of Essex bar owners that they could be prosecuted for operating a cartel and illegally fixing prices.

1.6.7 The ecological environment

Issues affecting our natural ecology have captured the public imagination in recent years. The destruction of tropical rainforests, and the depletion of the ozone layer leading to global warming, have serious implications for our quality of life – not necessarily today, but for future generations. Business organizations are often seen as being in conflict with the need to protect the natural ecology. It is very easy for critics of commercial organizations to point to cases where greed and mismanagement have created long-lasting or permanent ecological damage. Have rainforests been destroyed partly by our greed for more hardwood furniture? More locally, is our impatience for getting to our destination quickly the reason why many natural habitats have been lost to new road developments?

Only a few years ago, most business organizations in western developed economies could have dismissed ecological concerns as something that only fanatical, minority groups in the population were concerned about. In the 1970s and 1980s, 'environmentalists' might have been ridiculed and associated with unrealistic dreams of the 'good life'. Today, the situation is very different, and just about all business organizations need to take the ecological environment seriously.

There are many good reasons why the ecological environment is rising up the agenda of business organizations.

■ At its simplest, many organizations face segments of customers who prefer to make purchases that they believe to be ecologically responsible. For a variety of underlying psychological and sociological reasons, some consumers may feel better about their purchase if it is perceived to be 'good' for the planet. Of course, whether it is actually good or not may be another factor, and sometimes peer-group pressure may be at variance with the technical reality. As an example, the *Independent* newspaper reported in 2007 a case, probably not an isolated one, of a London home owner who had installed a solar panel on the north side of their house. Technically, the panel would be useless, because of the lack of direct sunlight, but for the house owner, the north side of the house could be seen by everybody. A panel on the south side of the house would not be visible, and would therefore be less able to make a statement about their 'green' credentials.

■ Business organizations are dependent on the ecological environment for natural resources. If ecosystems are not carefully managed, resources that are affordable today, and taken for granted, may no longer be available, and firms will have to pay higher prices for possibly inferior substitutes. As an example, the fishing industry in Britain has been greatly reduced in size through the overfishing of the North Sea. Even companies further down the value chain of fish have been affected by this depletion of the ecological environment – for example, fish and chip shops have had to find alternative types of fish to replace increasingly expensive cod.

■ Firms can gain advantage in a market by leading in the use of alternative natural resources ahead of competitors, giving them a competitive advantage when the alternative becomes the only, or most cost-effective, source available. However, it may be difficult for firms to evaluate not only what is going to be a better use of resources for the planet, but also one that is going to be better for their organization specifically. To illustrate this difficulty, many firms have been advocating a greater use of 'biofuels', which are derived from renewable crops, rather than fossil fuels. However, there is argument about the relative size of the ecological and social impacts of fossil fuels and renewable energy sources. The dilemma for business was illustrated in July 2007, when the Virgin Group, never an organization to miss an opportunity for good publicity, announced that it would be greatly increasing the use of biofuels for its fleet of trains. However, just a few weeks later, National Express Group, another UK operator of trains and buses, announced that it was abandoning its previous plan for the increased use of biofuels. It had thought through the implications of farmers growing an increasing proportion of their crops for fuel rather than food, which could be expected to lead to progressively higher prices for biofuels and sharply increasing food prices. The consumer appeal of biofuels was also wearing thin, with the scene set for the rich western countries to benefit from this new source of fuel, while less developed countries could no longer afford basic food items because crops were diverted to fuel the West's appetite for energy. In this scenario, biofuels became less cost-effective and socially acceptable.

■ Similarly, ecological concerns may spur the development of completely new technologies, often with the support of government. Wind turbines presented a new opportunity in the early twenty-first century, which was exploited by aircraft manufacturing companies, among others. UK companies were relatively late to the scene, by which time competitive advantage had been gained by overseas manufacturers, and the one remaining large-scale wind turbine manufacturer based in the UK faced closure in 2009. However, the UK government saw advantages in being first to market with innovative 'carbon capture' technologies, and in 2010 increased funding for research and development in this area.

- Markets are often incapable collectively to alleviate pending problems in ecosystems, and political intervention may be necessary to prevent a complete failure of the ecosystem. In the example above, individual fishermen may have had no incentive to limit their own fishing, until they reached the point where only government intervention could protect fish stocks from their own individual activities, and ultimately preserve long-term employment for companies and availability of supplies for consumers. Business organizations should be able to read the political environment and be prepared for politically imposed change in their business plans. See the case study at the end of this chapter – if you were running an airline, what level of future government taxation or restrictions on air travel would you factor in to your future development plans, given current concerns about the effects of aircraft emissions?

We will return to the ecological environment in Chapter 5.

1.6.8 Systems theory, complexity and chaos

Systems theory was proposed in the 1940s by the biologist Ludwig von Bertalanffy. It is the interdisciplinary study of the abstract organization of phenomena, and investigates both the principles common to all complex entities and the models that can be used to describe them. More recently it has been applied to mathematics, computing and ecological systems. Some elements of systems theory have been applied to the modelling of relationships within the environmental sets of business organizations that we discussed earlier.

Although a number of attempts have been made to apply the principles of systems theory to the business environment, there are major differences between scientific models and the business environment. Very often, the natural sciences deal with **closed systems** in which all the parameters are known, and each can be monitored and controlled. Admittedly, this is not always true – for example, in some ecological studies it may not be possible to identify all life forms that might possibly migrate into a system. By contrast, the business environment is essentially an **open system** in which it is very difficult to place a boundary round the environment and to identify the complete set of components within the system. Elements may come or go from the system, and a researcher generally has no control over these elements in the way that a laboratory-based scientist could carry out controlled experiments.

Two developments of systems theory are complexity theory and chaos theory. Complexity theory is concerned with the behaviour over time of certain kinds of complex system. The systems of interest to complexity theory, under certain conditions, perform in regular, predictable ways; under other conditions they exhibit behaviour in which regularity and predictability is lost. Almost undetectable differences in initial conditions lead to gradually diverging system reactions until, eventually, the evolution of behaviour is quite dissimilar.

Chaos theory describes the dynamics of sensitive systems that are mathematically deterministic but nearly impossible to predict, due to their sensitivity to initial conditions. The weather is an example of a chaotic system. In order to make long-term weather forecasts it would be necessary to take an infinite number of measurements, which would be impossible to do. Also, because the atmosphere is chaotic, tiny uncertainties would eventually overwhelm any calculations and defeat the accuracy of the forecast. One of the most widely quoted examples of chaos theory is the butterfly that flaps its wings and in doing so creates destabilizing forces that trigger subsequent events, resulting in a hurricane on the other side of the world.

Many business environments may be considered as chaotic in that it can be very difficult to predict the sequence of events following an initial disturbance to equilibrium. In Chapter 15 we return to the subject of risk and turbulence in the business environment.

1.6.9 Business cycles

The business environment is rarely in a stable state, and many phenomena follow a cyclical pattern. After a lengthy period of economic prosperity during the early twenty-first century, the boom came sharply to an end in 2008 when rising levels of manufacturing output, employment levels and consumer confidence, among other things, suddenly went into reverse. Companies are particularly interested in understanding business cycles and in predicting a cycle as it affects their sector. We return to the subject of business cycles in Chapter 13. Although the business cycle is widely talked about, there are other cyclical factors evident in the business environment. The interaction between supply and demand can result in a cycle of high prices, leading to new entrants coming into the market, which leads to lower prices, which makes the market less attractive, so companies leave the market, so prices begin to rise, which attracts new entrants to the market, and the cycle repeats itself.

As well as cycles affecting tangible resources, it is also possible to identify cycles in *ideas* about how the business environment operates. There have been many studies of how ideas grow to become mainstream and the critical factors involved in this process. Chaos theory and the study of mimetics have offered an explanation of how, through random events, a small local idea can develop into a global paradigm. An analysis by Gladwell discusses how reaching a critical point is facilitated by the existence of 'connectors', 'mavens' and the 'stickiness' of an idea (Gladwell 2000). One such idea that took hold in the 1990s was 'relationship marketing' as a method of conducting exchanges between a company and its customers. It followed a long series of 'big new ideas' that have risen and fallen over time.

1.6.10 Risk and uncertainty

The business environment for most organizations is rarely in a stable state. There is no certainty that the future will follow the pattern of the recent past. For companies operating in a low-tech, low-scale environment, adaptation to change may be quite easy. But for a large organization that has to invest heavily for the future, the risks can be enormous. For very large projects, such as the construction of the European Airbus 'super jumbo' A380 aircraft, the risk and uncertainty was too large not only for one company to take upon itself, but for the consortium of companies that makes up Airbus. Apart from uncertainty about the technology, and the risk of cost overruns, there is considerable risk concerning the business environment of airlines that would be customers for the Airbus. Will passengers want to fly between a small number of very large airports in very large aircraft? Or would they prefer the alternative model of the future, which sees larger numbers of smaller aircraft flying between a much bigger network of smaller airports? What will happen to fuel prices? Will long-term real increases in fuel prices put up air fares to the point where the long-term growth rate in passenger traffic is slowed down? Will governments introduce new taxation on aviation fuel, again possibly slowing down demand for air travel? And there is always the threat of terrorism, which caused such uncertainty following 11 September 2001, and which could recur at any time.

All aspects of the business environment that have been introduced in this chapter carry an element of uncertainty. Within the microenvironment, what is the risk of a new, well-resourced competitor emerging? What if a strategic supplier goes out of business or is acquired by your competitor? What happens if government introduces new legislation or imposes new taxation? Within the macroenvironment, there is continual uncertainty for most companies about the future state of the economy and the impact of changes in disposable income on consumer expenditure. What would happen if a new government were elected with a radically different political agenda? And, in the internal environment, what is the risk of not being able to recruit the skilled employees the company needs? What would be the effect of new legislation on the recruitment and payment of employees?

There are many models for trying to comprehend the complexity of the business environment, and to attach risk levels to the different elements of it. In Chapter 15, we will look in more detail at some of these methods, including cross-impact analysis, and environmental threat and opportunity profiles. We will also discuss the development of scenarios, which is an attempt to paint a picture of the future. It may be possible to build a small number of alternative scenarios based on differing assumptions. This qualitative approach is a means of handling environmental issues that are hard to quantify because they are less structured, more uncertain and may involve very complex relationships. Scenarios may paint a picture of a major crisis or source of turbulence facing a company. For an airline, this could be a renewed terrorist threat elsewhere in the world, or the crash of one of its own aircraft. Although it may not be possible to predict the exact detail of the event, the company could establish a set of guidelines for what it should do in the event that such a scenario occurs. For example, following the abrupt collapse in confidence in the world economy in September 2008, the airline Virgin Atlantic downsized its fleet and laid off staff. It had seen a future scenario in which demand was likely to remain low for some time, and it would be better to make a rapid and decisive decision to cut capacity and costs sooner, rather than just drifting on.

1.7   The globalized business environment

Globalization has become a dominant theme for many business organizations. The number of companies that can regard their markets purely in terms of their home country is rapidly diminishing. Airlines, commercial banks and consulting engineers have for a long time seen their markets in world terms. Companies operating in sectors such as electricity supply, office cleaning and bus services would, only a few years ago, have most likely considered globalization to be something that concerned only other sectors and not theirs. However, all of these sectors have seen companies expanding outside of their domestic market.

It may be fair to say that 'going global' is no longer an additional activity that companies may decide to become involved in. The reality for more and more companies is that they are already part of the globalized business environment. Even if they are not taking their products to overseas customers, they are quite likely to be facing competition from companies that are based abroad.

At some point, many business organizations recognize that their growth can continue only if they exploit overseas markets. However, entering overseas markets can be extremely risky, as evidenced by examples of recent failures where companies failed to foresee all the problems involved.

- The mobile phone company O_2 invested over £1.5 billion in the Dutch mobile phone operator Telfort but failed to achieve higher than fifth ranking in the Dutch market. In April 2003, it admitted defeat and sold the entire Dutch operation for just £16 million.
- The grocery retailer Sainsbury's pulled out of Egypt in 2001, only two years after investing in a chain of 100 supermarkets. Sainsbury's had gone out on a limb in Egypt, which had no tradition of supermarket shopping, and the company was not helped by persistent rumours of links with Jewish owners. The supermarket's two years of involvement in the Egyptian market incurred a loss of over £100 million.
- Even the fast-food retailer McDonald's initially failed to make profits when it entered the UK market in the 1970s and had to rapidly adjust its service offer in order to achieve viability.

Nevertheless, a company that has successfully developed its business strategy should be well placed to extend this development into overseas markets. There are many examples of companies that have successfully developed overseas markets, including the following.

- The retailer Tesco successfully reduced its dependence on the saturated UK grocery market by developing outlets in the Far East and eastern Europe.
- The mobile phone company Vodafone has expanded from its UK base and now provides service in 30 countries, reducing the company's unit costs through economies of scale, and offering seamless, added-value services to international travellers.

- The Irish airline Ryanair started life with a route network that focused on Dublin. With successful expansion of this network, most of its services now do not call at its Irish base.

- Carphone Warehouse was the brainchild of entrepreneur Charles Dunstone and, after a small-scale start in London, it has successfully expanded to more than 1100 stores throughout Europe, operating under the Carphone Warehouse banner in the UK, and the Phone House in France, Spain, Germany, Sweden and the Netherlands.

Although the focus of this book is on the UK and European environment, it should never be forgotten that UK organizations increasingly have to co-exist with a global business environment. Frequent reference is made throughout this book to the global context of business.

Case study:
A war of words over green airline claims

© *David Joyner*

A key issue on the mind of many businesses during the first decade of the twenty-first century has been global warming. Initially, awareness of the causes and consequences of global warming was confined to a small part of the population, but linkages with the destructive Tsunami of 2004 and Hurricane Katrina in 2005 brought home to many people the possible long-term harmful consequences of excessive emissions of CO_2 to the atmosphere. Global warming was no longer a humorous subject where people in the developed countries of northern Europe and the US focused on the benign consequences of mild winters and the exotic new plants that they would be able to grow. Destructive winds, rising sea levels and the devastation of low-lying areas were increasingly coming to be seen as consequences of our prodigious use of fossil fuels. What will be the direct impacts on business? What might be the indirect impacts caused by increasingly restrictive government regulation? How will a company's customers expect it to act?

One industry sector that has more to be concerned about than most is civil aviation. The reduction of CO_2 emissions had already been taken on board by many manufacturing companies, the largest of which had seen reductions through a system of carbon trading initiated by the Kyoto Treaty. But civil aviation had been quite notable for its failure to embrace the principles of reducing carbon emissions. Critics of the sector pointed out that, as a result of worldwide agreements, aviation fuel was not taxed, in contrast to the steep taxation on most other forms of fuel. Although aircraft had become more efficient in their use of fuel during the 1990s, this was more than offset by the booming demand for flights with 'no-frills' airlines such as easyJet and Ryanair.

Actually assessing the ecological impacts of flying is more problematic than it might appear at first sight. The low-cost airlines have spotted an opportunity to present themselves as ecologically more friendly than the 'full service' airlines from whom they had been gradually taking business. According to analysis by Liligo.co.uk, a flight-comparison website, a couple making a return flight with Ryanair from London to Venice have a carbon footprint of 410 kg, while the equivalent journey on Alitalia would produce 977 kg. A return flight from London to Zurich with easyJet has a carbon footprint of 277 kg per couple, compared with 688 kg with Aer Lingus. Ryanair was quick to boast of its 'green' credentials, just in case potential flyers were feeling a sense of guilt as they hovered over the 'buy' button for one of its bargain tickets. The ecological benefits of low-cost airlines are based on a number of factors. First, they tend to fly with more seats occupied: according to the Association of European Airlines, in 2009 the average occupancy for an easyJet flight was 86 per cent and for Ryanair 82 per cent, compared with 73 per cent for British Airways and an average of 68 per cent on Europe's full-service airlines, Second, low-cost airlines squeeze more seats into an aircraft then their full-service rivals. For example, easyJet ('squeezyJet' to some of its passengers) fits 156 seats into an Airbus A319, whereas the average full-service airline has just 124 seats. The carbon footprint per passenger is correspondingly lower. Finally, low-cost airlines promoted the fact that they tended to fly direct between a wide range of dispersed airports, without the need to change planes at a central 'hub' airport, again reducing carbon emissions during take-off and landing.

It seemed that the budget airline companies were very effective in communicating their low price message to customers, who filled their planes, often giving more thought to a cheap weekend break by the Mediterranean than the unknown and remote possibilities of global warming. Indeed, the general public seemed to be somewhat hypocritical about the effects of global warming. Surveys had suggested that there can be a big difference between what people said and what they did - they may agree that flying was bad for the environment, but could not resist the £29.99 flight to Spain. In one survey conducted in 2007 consumers' consideration of greenhouse gas emissions came way behind other evaluation criteria when choosing a holiday, including the ease of getting a sun lounger, proximity to the beach and the range of nightlife available. Furthermore, it seemed that many people were tiring of claims about climate change and saw this as just an excuse for government to raise taxes. A survey carried out in February 2010 by the polling organization Populus for the BBC showed that 25 per cent of those questioned did not think global warming was happening, an increase of 10 per cent since a similar poll was conducted three months earlier. More people seemed to be thinking that the problem would just go away, and may have recalled previous 'scares'such as the imminent depletion of fossil fuels and the effects of 'acid rain', neither of which had really affected most people's lives, and had subsequently slipped down the news agenda.

How should airlines respond to the apparent threat to their business model that had been thrown up by the issue of global warming? Should they put their head in the sand and hope that the problem would go away? Should they concentrate on giving customers what they have repeatedly said they wanted – cheap flights – and hope that human hedonism would win out over feelings of social responsibility? Or should airlines be on their guard against possible government intervention that could undermine their business model. How could they prevent new legislation? And if it were introduced, how could they respond to it?

Politicians were becoming increasingly frustrated by the airlines' seeming lack of willingness to address issues of climate change. Already, the Bishop of London had described air travel as 'immoral', for the way that wealthy western travellers could inflict harm on people in the less developed world through climate change. Could a significant number of airline passengers really begin to feel guilty about flying away for a cheap weekend break, and cut back their purchases?

In January 2007, the communications battle was stepped up when a UK government minister described Ryanair as 'the irresponsible face of capitalism'. He had argued that while other industries and consumers were cutting down their emissions, Ryanair had expanded at a phenomenal rate, churning out more CO_2 into the atmosphere at a time when other industry sectors were reducing their emissions. Friends of the Earth, in a report entitled 'Aviation and global climate change', noted that commercial jets were adding 600 million tonnes of CO_2 a year to global warming, almost as much as for the whole of Africa. With such negative communication, would Ryanair suffer as people felt guilty about flying, and governments increasingly moved to regulate civil aviation and make it more expensive, especially for the price-sensitive segments that the no-frills airlines had been targeting?

Rarely known to be quiet, the chief executive of Ryanair, Michael O'Leary, went on a communications offensive. Dismissing the minister as 'knowing nothing', he presented Ryanair as a friend rather than an enemy of global warming. He argued that travellers should feel reassured that Ryanair used one of the world's most modern and fuel-efficient fleets of aircraft. Moreover, Ryanair's business model of filling seats at the lowest price really meant that the carbon emissions per passenger were much lower than those of traditional full-service airlines, which often flew half-empty planes. And then there was the fact that budget airlines operated an extensive point-to-point network, avoiding the costly and environmentally harmful effects of taking two indirect flights via a central hub airport.

The war of words that has ensued over airlines' contribution to global warming demonstrates the difficulty that many ordinary consumers have in evaluating rival claims. Many may have taken to heart governments' and church leaders' claims that made them feel guilty about flying. But even if hypocritical consumers were happy to carry on flying and not backing their expressed concerns for climate change with changes in their behaviour, there was certainly a possibility that governments would intervene, Both the UK government and the EU Commission had floated the idea of taxing aviation fuel, and bringing aircraft emissions within the scope of the EU Emissions

Trading Scheme. Some airlines, such as Ryanair, continued to sound off against the government, positioning them as the consumer's champion. But others, including easyJet, sensed the change in mood of the public and government bodies, and openly supported the idea of bringing aircraft emissions into the carbon trading regime. Was easyJet being philanthropic? Was it simply putting out a message that it thought its customers would want to hear, helping them salve their consciences and giving easyJet a better image than arch-rival Ryanair? Or was there a shrewd underlying commercial advantage, in which the modern, efficient easyJet fleet may use less than its allotted share of carbon emissions, which it could then sell on to less efficient 'legacy' carriers? Should the company begin planning for higher taxes on flying, and be prepared for reducing its growth plans if some marginal customers decided that a weekend break by the Mediterranean was no longer a luxury that they could afford?

Source: based on Ben Hall and Kevin Done, 'Pearson brought to earth in airline row', *Financial Times*, 6 January 2007; Charles Starmer-Smith, 'Green travel: the winners and losers', *Daily Telegraph*, 12 January 2008; Jimmy Lee Shreeve, 'Green skies?', *Daily Telegraph*, 26 June 2007; Friends of the Earth (2000), '*Aviation and global climate change*', London; 'Climate scepticism "on the rise"', BBC poll shows, *BBC News Online*, 7 February 2010, http://news.bbc.co.uk/1/hi/8500443.stm, accessed 10 October 2010

QUESTIONS

1 Discuss the possible policy options open to government to curb aircraft emissions, and assess their likely effects on 'budget' airlines.

2 The case study refers to the apparent hypocrisy of consumers who may claim to be concerned about the environment, but nevertheless continue to fly. What might bring about a narrowing of this gap between what consumers think and what they actually do? How could a company such as easyJet measure and monitor consumers' attitudes?

3 What might be the consequences for a budget airline of government policy measures that have the effect of doubling air fares in real terms? Critically discuss how a budget airline might respond.

Summary

This chapter has reviewed the complex nature of an organization's business environment. The environment can be analysed at three levels: the microenvironment, comprising firms and individuals that an organization directly interacts with (or that directly affect its activities); the macroenvironment, comprising general forces that may eventually impact on the microenvironment; and the internal environment, comprising other functions within the organization.

This chapter has stressed the interrelatedness of all elements of the business environment. Although the social environment and technological environment are identified as separate elements, the two are closely linked (for example, technology has resulted in mass ownership of cars, which has in turn affected social behaviour.

Subsequent chapters pay attention to each of the elements of the business environment, but the complexity of linkages must never be forgotten. **Chapter 15** seeks to integrate these elements within dynamic analytical frameworks, which can be used to develop holistic forecasts of the future business environment.

Key Terms

Channels of distribution (14)

Closed system (27)

Credit crunch (15)

Environmental set (17)

Information environment (20)

Intermediaries (14)

Internal environment (5)

Macroenvironment (5)

Microenvironment (5)

Open system (27)

Organizational culture (16)

Stakeholders (12)

Strategic alliances (18)

Transformation process (4)

Value chain (18)

Online
Learning Centre

To help you grasp the key concepts of this chapter, explore the extra resources posted on the Online Learning Centre at *www.mcgraw-hill.co.uk/palmer*. Among other helpful resources there are chapter-by-chapter test questions, revision notes and web links.

Chapter review questions

1 Discuss what you understand by the term 'business environment'.

2 Suppliers and intermediaries are important stakeholders in the microenvironment of the business. Discuss the evolving role and functions of stakeholders in business organizations.

3 Members of an organizational set are becoming increasingly interdependent. Identify examples of this interdependency, and discuss the reasons why it is happening.

Activities

1 Develop a checklist of points that you consider to be important indicators of whether an organization is responsive to changes in its business environment. Why did you choose these indicators? Now apply your checklist to three selected organizations: one a traditional manufacturing industry, the second a service-based commercial organization, and the third a government organization that serves the public. What, if anything, should your chosen organizations do to become more responsive to changes in their business environment?

2 Go back to Figure 1.4, which shows an environmental set for a car manufacturer. If you are studying at a college or university, repeat this diagram, but show the environmental set for your university/college.

3 Choose an industry sector with which you are familiar (e.g. mobile phones, grocery retail). Identify the elements in firms' macroenvironment that may affect their profitability during the next ten years.

Further reading

A good starting point for understanding the competitive advantage of firms and the role of value chains in achieving this is provided in Michael Porter's frequently cited book:

Porter, M.E. (1985) *Competitive Advantage: Creating and Sustaining Superior Performance*, New York, Free Press.

There is now an extensive literature on the development of close buyer–seller relationships. A good summary of the principles can be found in the following texts.

Buttle, F. D. (2008) *Relationship Marketing* (2nd edn), London, Butterworth-Heinemann.

Egan, J. (2008) *Relationship Marketing: Exploring Relational Strategies in Marketi*ng (3rd edn), Harlow, Pearson Education Ltd.

Donaldson, W.G. and O'Toole, T. (2007) *Strategic Market Relationships: From Strategy to Implementation* (2nd edn), Chichester, John Wiley.

This chapter has provided a general overview of the components that make up the business environment. Suggestions for further reading on each of these components are given in later chapters.

References

Gladwell, M. (2000) *The Tipping Point: How Little Things Can Make a Big Difference*, New York, Little Brown & Co.

Heskett, J. L., Sasser, W. E. Jr. and Schlesinger, L.A. (2003) *The Value Profit Chain: Treat Employees like Customers and Customers like Employees*, New York, The Free Press.

Levitt, T. (1960) 'Marketing myopia', *Harvard Business Review*, July–August, pp. 45–56.

Nonaka, I. (1991) 'The knowledge-creating company', *Harvard Business Review*, Vol. 69, No. 6, pp. 96–104.

Office for National Statistics (2010) *Social Trends*, 40, London, Office for National Statistics (available online at http://www.statistics.gov.uk/socialtrends/).

Schmitt, P. and Michahelles, F. (2008) *Economic Impact of RFID Report*, Zurich, ETH.

Vargo, S.L. and Lusch, R.F. (2008) 'Service-dominant logic: continuing the evolution', *Journal of the Academy of Marketing Science*, Vol. 36, 1–10.

2.2 Political systems

Throughout most of this chapter, we will be describing political systems based on the type of democracy that is prevalent in western countries. However, there is great diversity in political systems. At one extreme is a political system based on an open system of government that is democratically elected by the population of a country. The other extreme may be represented by totalitarian systems of government in which power derives not from popular representation, but is acquired by a select group. This may be in the form of communism, or may be based on the interests of sectional groups, often militarily based, that acquire power through force or tradition.

The link between the dominant political system, economic growth and the nature of the business environment is an interesting and often complex one. There has been a lot of research into the relationship between democracy and economic prosperity. The idea that autocratic regimes have an advantage in economic development was once quite fashionable. The plausibility of such a notion lies in the advantages such regimes were said to have in forcing through development in the long term. There is some evidence for this in the way that countries go about the construction of major transport infrastructure projects. In western countries with open democratic governance, a lengthy process of consultation is likely to take place before a new road is built, and there are likely to be extensive checks and balances to prevent the interests of individuals or groups being threatened or unduly favoured. In countries with less democratic traditions, government is more likely to go ahead regardless of objections. Some commentators have attributed part of the rapid economic development of South-east Asia during the 1980s and 1990s to the absence of democratic government in the western tradition.

An alternative view is that democracy is likely to foster economic development. The political institutions critical to economic development are more likely to exist and function effectively in democratic systems. These institutions include a legal system that protects property rights, individual liberties that encourage creativity and entrepreneurship, the freedom of expression that facilitates the flow of information in an economy, and institutional checks and balances that prevent the theft of public wealth often observed in totalitarian systems. There is a suggestion of a non-linear relationship in which greater democracy enhances growth at low levels of political freedom but depresses growth when a moderate level of freedom has already been attained. Improvements in the standard of living, health services and education may subsequently raise the probability that political freedom will grow.

There are many variations in political systems and their links to economic development. The Chinese system, for example, is one of district, city, regional and state government, which is similar to an electoral college. There are elections at all levels but the system is not democratic on the western model. Also it is interesting to note that there is now a split between political and economic systems. Previously communism was both a political and an economic system, but the modern Chinese system is much more subtle than this. Within a centralized state system are powerful regional governments, and individual free-market systems in many sectors.

Corruption remains a barrier to economic development in many countries. Some companies may survive and prosper by bribing government officials, but the success and growth of such companies is not necessarily based on the value they create for consumers. In many cases, they have simply bought themselves a dominant position in a market that the government is happy to allow them to exploit, in return for a payment that is made. In government systems with poor accountability, such payments may not be made for the public good, but instead just add to the private wealth of government officials.

The link between accountability and ethics is apparent in political systems. Individuals embark on careers in politics for a number of reasons, and it may be quite naive to assume that they all do so for the purpose of implementing policies for the public good that are in accordance with their personal convictions. There is often a grey area of corruption and personal benefit, which political systems have responded to with a need for politicians to be more accountable. During

2010, for example, many UK Members of Parliament were accused of abusing the system of reclaiming personal expenses, resulting in new procedures for making them accountable. Abuse of a privileged political position can also undermine public confidence in the political process. This in turn can lead to lower levels of public engagement in politics, reflected in typically low levels of voting in elections, especially among younger people.

The statistical evidence of a link between democracy and economic growth is mixed. One study of economic growth data for 115 countries from 1960 to 1980 found that countries with high degrees of political openness achieved an average annual real per capita growth rate of 2.53 per cent, compared with 1.41 per cent in more closed political systems. This implies that more democratic countries may grow 80 per cent faster than less democratic countries. However, other studies have given more ambiguous results, including some that reported a weak negative overall effect of democracy on economic growth (Barro 1996).

Table 2.1 reports data for a selection of countries, linking annual GDP per capita with an index of political freedom within the country (for example, the extent of universal voting rights), a ranking of economic freedom (for example, the ease with which new entrants can enter a market), and ranking of corruption. A casual glance at this table will reveal that many of the poorest countries of the world are associated with lower levels of political freedom and a high level of corruption.

Table 2.1 National indices for selected countries linking GDP per capita, political freedom, economic freedom and corruption.

	GDP per capita 2008	Index of political freedom 2009	Ranking of economic freedom 2009	Ranking of corruption 2009
Burundi	144	4.5	160	168
Liberia	222	3.5	163	97
Tanzania	482	3.5	97	126
Haiti	729	4.5	141	168
Pakistan	991	4.5	117	139
India	1,017	2.5	124	84
Zambia	1,134	3.5	100	99
Nigeria	1,370	4.5	106	130
Philippines	1,847	3.5	109	139
China	3,267	6.5	140	79
Hong Kong	30,863	3.5	1	12
Canada	45,070	1	7	8
UK	43,541	1	11	17
Ireland	60,460	1	5	14
Switzerland	64,327	1	6	5
Norway	94,759	1	37	11

Source: based on United Nations (1998); World Bank (2008); Freedom House (2010); Transparency International (2010); World Factbook (2009).

Note: The measure of political freedom comprises a composite of two separate indicators, political rights and civil liberties. The combined score is between 1 and 7, 1 being the freest and 7 being the least free. The organization Freedom House considers countries with scores of between 1.0 to 2.5 'free'; those scoring between 3.0 and 5.0 as 'partly free'; and those scoring between 5.5 and 7.0 as 'not free'. The ranking of Economic Freedom consist of one index, in which the freest economy (Hong Kong) is ranked 1 and the least free economy (North Korea) ranks 179. Ranking of corruption is based on data provided by Transparency International (2010), with the least corrupt country being ranked 1.

whereby it is not financially advantageous for an individual to enter employment, because the benefits that they are giving up are greater than the wages they will earn. There are a number of structural issues that governments have sought to tackle in order to improve the relative economic standing of disadvantaged groups. As an example, many single parents have found it uneconomic to enter the labour market because the loss of benefits and costs of childcare are greater than their earnings

Pursuing full employment may be an admirable goal as a means of reducing poverty. But public perceptions of government programmes to get people off benefits and into employment can very easily change from enlightenment to harassment once pressure is put on people, whether they be the well-meaning unmarried mother or the work-shy who would rather claim benefits than work.

⟳ Thinking around the subject

Will the poor always be with us?

It seems that even a socialist government dedicated to reducing social inequality cannot easily eliminate inequality. According to a report by the Office for National Statistics, the income of the richest and poorest 10 per cent of the population had each grown by around 5 per cent between 1997 (the date when a Labour government was elected) and 2003. But, in absolute terms, the gap between rich and poor had widened. The poorest 10 per cent had seen a £28 a week rise, compared to the richest 10 per cent, which had seen a rise of £119. Furthermore, the wealthiest 1 per cent of the population had prospered. In 1991, they owned 17 per cent of the nation's wealth, but by 2003 the figure had grown to 21 per cent. A large part of this growth was attributed to a rise in house prices (Office for National Statistics 2008).

It has often been argued that the surest way out of inequality is through education, but the report found that children's chances of doing well in exams depended enormously on their parents, qualifications and jobs. In 2002, more than three-quarters of children with parents in higher professional occupations achieved five or more GCSEs at grades A to C. Less than a third of children with parents in manual or clerical jobs achieved this (Office for National Statistics 2004).

Even when the government takes proactive measures to help disadvantaged groups, these may backfire. In 2001, the government abolished entrance fees to national museums, arguing that high charges were deterring poor people from sharing the nation's heritage and learning from it. After the abolition of charges, museum attendance figures rose. However, a subsequent report by the National Audit Office indicated that it was relatively wealthy middle-class parents who were now making more visits to museums, and disadvantaged groups were still underrepresented in the admission figures. Worse still, many of the middle-class parents who were now making more visits to state-subsidized museums now made fewer visits to privately owned museums, many of which were forced to cut back their expenditure and reduce the number of staff they employed.

What policies can in practice be used to overcome social inequality? Given the importance of education as a means of reducing inequality, what can governments do to encourage people from disadvantaged backgrounds to take part in higher education? Even in higher education, is government policy sometimes contradictory, as evidenced by the introduction of tuition fees, which may deter groups in society that have traditionally been afraid of getting into debt?

2.5   The structure of government

To understand the nature of the political environment more fully, and its impact on business organizations, it is necessary to examine the different aspects of government. Government influence on businesses in the UK can be divided into the following categories:

- central government
- regional government
- local government
- European Union (EU) government
- supranational government.

Most countries have hierarchical levels of government that follow a roughly similar pattern. The UK will be used to illustrate the principles of multi-level government influences on businesses, with reference to comparable institutions in other countries.

2.6   Central government

The central government system of most countries can be divided into four separate functions. The UK is quite typical in dividing functions of government between the legislature, the executive, the civil service and the judiciary. These, collectively, provide sovereign government within the UK although, as will be seen later, this sovereignty is increasingly being subjected to the authority of the EU.

2.6.1 Parliament

Parliament provides the supreme legislative authority in the UK and comprises the monarch (the present Queen), the House of Commons and the House of Lords. The House of Commons is the most important part of the **legislature** as previous legislation has curtailed the authority in Parliament of the monarch and the House of Lords. It is useful to be aware of the procedures for enacting new legislation so that the influences on the legislative process can be fully understood (see Figure 2.1).

New legislation starts life as a Bill and passes through parliamentary processes to the point where it becomes an **Act of Parliament**. Most Bills that subsequently become law are government sponsored and often start life following discussion between government departments and interested parties. On some occasions these discussions may lead to the setting up of a Committee of Enquiry or (less frequently) a Royal Commission, which reports to the government. The findings of such a committee can be accepted, rejected or amended by the government, which puts forward ideas for discussion in a Green Paper. Following initial discussion, the government would submit definite proposals for legislation in the form of a White Paper. A Parliamentary Bill would then be drafted, incorporating some of the comments that the government has received in response to the publication of the White Paper. The Bill is then formally introduced to Parliament by a first reading in the House of Commons, at which a date is set for the main debate at a second reading. A vote is taken at each reading and, if it is a government Bill, it will invariably pass at each stage due to the government majority in the House of Commons. If it passes the second reading, the Bill will be sent to a Standing Committee for discussion of the details. The Committee will in due course report back to the full House of Commons and there will be a final debate where amendments are considered, some of which originate from the Committee and some from

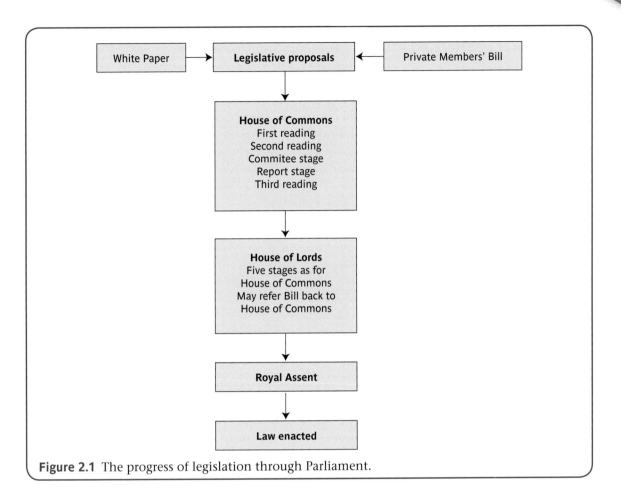

Figure 2.1 The progress of legislation through Parliament.

members of the House of Commons in general. The Bill then passes to the House of Lords and goes through a similar five stages. The Lords may delay or amend a Bill, although the Commons may subsequently use the Parliament Act to force the Bill through. Finally, the Bill goes to the monarch to receive the Royal Assent, upon which it becomes an Act 1911 of Parliament.

This basic model can be changed in a number of ways. First, in response to a newly perceived problem, the government could introduce a Bill with very few clauses and, with the agreement of party managers, could cut short the consultation stages, speed up the passage of the Bill through its various stages and provide Royal Assent within a matter of days, instead of the months that it could typically take. This has occurred, for example, in the case of a one-clause Bill to prohibit trade in human organs, a measure that had received all-party support. A second variation on the basic model is provided by Private Members' Bills. Most Bills start life with government backing. However, backbench Members of parliament can introduce their own Bills, although the opportunities for doing this are limited and if they do not subsequently receive government backing, their chances of passing all stages of the parliamentary process are significantly reduced.

The **lobbying** of Members of Parliament has become an increasingly important activity, brought about by individuals and pressure groups to try to protect their interests where new legislation is proposed that may affect them. Typical tasks for which professional lobbyists have been employed in recent years are:

■ the British Roads Federation regularly lobbies for greater expenditure on roads, and seizes opportunities presented by relevant new Bills to include provisions that are more supportive of increased expenditure on roads

- each year, prior to the Chancellor of the Exchequer's annual Budget speech (which forms the basis of a Finance Act), considerable lobbying is undertaken by vested interests that appeal for more public spending to be directed to their cause and/or less taxation to be imposed on it.

If organizations are to succeed in influencing their political environment, they need to identify the critical points in the passage of a Bill at which pressure can be applied, and the critical members who should form the focus of lobbying (for example, the members of the Committee to which the Bill is sent for detailed examination). As we will see later, much legislation that passes through the UK Parliament is enacting EU legislation. At this stage it may be too late for lobbyists to achieve significant change in the overall policy underlying the Bill, although it may still be possible to amend details of its implementation. The role of lobbying is considered in more detail later in this chapter in the context of pressure groups as forces within the political system.

Political parties typically make bold promises in their election manifestos. If elected, they may promptly enact legislation that formed the flagship of their campaign. However, after a honeymoon period, governments must set to work addressing structural issues in the economy, which will take some time to make good. This may involve painful economic measures in the short term, but the payoff is improved economic performance in a few years' time. With a five-year election cycle for Parliament in the UK, it is often claimed that voters have short memories and will forget the austere economic conditions of two or three years previously. What matters at election time is the *appearance* that economic conditions are getting better. Therefore, government economic planning may try to achieve falling unemployment, stable prices and a consumer boom just ahead of a general election. This may itself lead to structural problems that must be sorted out after the election, leading to a repeat of this cyclical process (see Figure 2.2). The existence of the political cycle frequently impacts on the economic environment, with periods of increased expenditure just before an election and reduced expenditure shortly after. Organizations may acknowledge this cycle by gearing up for a boom in sales just ahead of a general election.

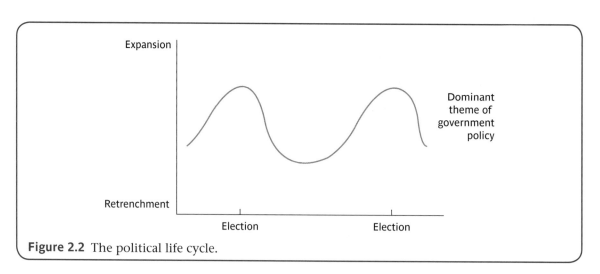

Figure 2.2 The political life cycle.

2.6.2 The executive

Parliament comprises elected representatives whose decisions, in theory, are carried out by the executive arm of government. In practice, the **executive** plays a very important role in formulating policies, which Parliament then debates and invariably accepts. In the UK, the principal elements of the executive comprise the Cabinet and ministers of state.

The Cabinet

The main executive element of central government is made up of the Prime Minister and **Cabinet** (comprising approximately 26 members), who determine policy and are responsible for the consequences of their policies. The Cabinet is headed by the Prime Minister, who has many powers, including the appointment and dismissal of ministers and determining the membership of Cabinet committees, chairing the Cabinet and setting its agenda, summarizing the discussions of the Cabinet and sending directives to ministers. The Prime Minister is also responsible for a variety of government and non-government appointments, and can determine the timing of a general election. Many have argued that Britain is moving towards a system of presidential government by the Prime Minister, given the considerable powers at his or her disposal. There are, however, a number of constraints on the power of the Prime Minister, such as the need to keep the loyalty of the Cabinet and the agreement of Parliament, which may be difficult when the governing party has only a small majority in the House of Commons.

In practice, the Prime Minister is particularly dependent upon the support of a small 'inner cabinet' of senior colleagues for advice and assistance in carrying policy through the party. In addition to this small inner cabinet surrounding the Prime Minister, recent years have seen the development of a small group of outside advisers on whose loyalty the Prime Minister can totally rely. Some are likely to be party members sitting in Parliament, while others may be party loyalists who belong to the business or academic community. There have been occasions when it has appeared that the Prime Minister's advisers were having a greater influence on policy than their Cabinet colleagues.

The ideological background of the Prime Minister and the composition of the government may give some indication of the direction of government policy. Organizations should study the composition of the government to try to predict future policy on issues such as government spending and personal taxation.

Ministers of State

The government of the country is divided between a number of different departments of state (see Figure 2.3). Each is headed by a Minister or Secretary of State who is a political appointee, usually a member of the House of Commons. They are assisted in their tasks by junior ministers. The portfolio of responsibilities of a department frequently changes when a new government comes into being. Ministers are often given delegated authority by Parliament, as where an Act may allow charges to be made for certain health services, but the minister has the delegated power to decide the actual level of the charges.

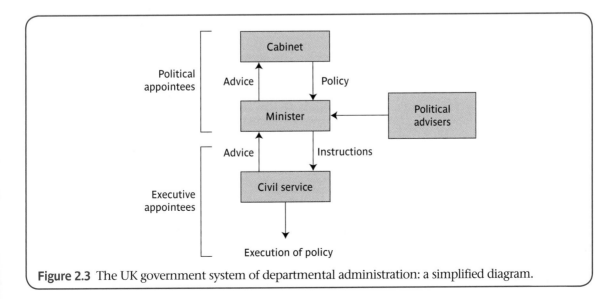

Figure 2.3 The UK government system of departmental administration: a simplified diagram.

2.6.3 The civil service

The **civil service** is the secretariat responsible for implementing government policy. In the UK, civil servants are paid officials who do not change when the government changes, adding a degree of continuity to government (although in some countries, such as the USA, it is customary for senior officials to be political appointees and therefore replaced following a change of government). Although, legally, civil servants are servants of the Crown, they are technically employed by a separate government department and are responsible to a minister. Each department is generally headed by a Permanent Secretary, responsible to the Public Accounts Committee of Parliament. The Permanent Secretary is a professional administrator who gives advice to his or her minister, a political appointee who generally lacks expertise in the work of the department.

The fact that civil servants are relatively expert in their areas and generally remain in their posts for much longer than their minister gives them great power. A delicate relationship develops between the Permanent Secretary and the minister, based on sometimes conflicting goals. The minister may view an issue in terms of broader political opportunities while the civil servant may be more concerned about his or her status and career prospects resulting from a change affecting his or her department.

The nature of the career civil servant is changing with the emergence of non-departmental public bodies (NDPBs – often referred to as 'quangos') to take over many of the activities of civil service departments (see below). In theory, these new executive agencies should be much freer of ministerial control, meeting longer-term performance standards with less day-to-day ministerial intervention as to how this should be achieved.

Organizations seeking to influence government policy must recognize the power that civil servants have in advising their minister, especially on the details of proposed legislation. Civil servants are usually involved in consultation exercises – for example, on the details of proposed food regulations. In some countries, business may seek to influence the policy-making process at this stage through overt or covert bribery. This is not a feature of most mature democracies such as Britain, and business seeks to exert influence in a more mutually cooperative manner. Civil servants require information on the background to policy and need to understand its possible implications. A close dialogue between the business community and civil servants can increase the chances of civil servants' policy recommendations being based on a sound understanding of business needs, rather than ignorance.

2.6.4 The judiciary

Democratic systems of government provide a number of checks and balances against the abuse of executive power. The **judiciary** is independent of government, and judges in the UK are answerable to the Crown and not to politicians. Through the court system, citizens can have some redress against a legislature, executive or civil service that acts beyond its authority. If complainants believe that they have suffered because a government minister did not follow statutory consultation procedures, they may apply to the courts for a **judicial review** of the case. A court may order that ministers reconsider the matter by following statutory procedures.

Business organizations have become increasingly willing to use the courts to challenge allegedly incorrect government procedures that have put them at a disadvantage. The proliferation of industry-sector regulators in the UK has created many opportunities for aggrieved business organizations to challenge the processes of the regulator. As an example, the UK National Lottery regulator Oflot was challenged in the High Court during 2000 by Camelot – the existing Lottery franchise holder – when it alleged that it had been procedurally incorrect in the way that it granted a new franchise to the rival People's Lottery. The Court instructed the regulator to reconsider its decision.

↻ Thinking around the subject

Minister for Spin?

Britain's system of government has often been held out as an example of good governance. Politicians decided policy and if the electorate didn't like their policies, they could be thrown out of office at the next election. Civil servants were the loyal servants of politicians who got on and implemented their masters' policies. Because the electorate could not throw out a civil servant directly, ministers took responsibility for the actions of their civil servants. Carefully honed sets of procedures and codes of conduct were developed, which made the UK civil service an example to the world of professionalism.

What, then, are we to make of recent developments that would appear to blur the distinction between elected politicians and an appointed civil service? Within government, there has been a growing number of policy advisers who report to the Prime Minister or other senior ministers, but who are still technically civil servants. These special advisers are overtly chosen by ministers on the basis of their political views, breaking the tradition of neutrality within the civil service. They have often been given the label of 'spin doctor' for the way in which they represent the views of their minister. Do these advisers debase the whole principle of a politically neutral civil service? Are they one step towards the development of a presidential style of government on the American model? Are 'spin doctors' merely providing a substitute for substantive actions by the politicians? Against this, isn't good government all about strong leadership? Could these special advisers be beneficial in the way that they cut through the delaying tactics of the civil service machinery in their efforts to see the politically accountable executive's wishes implemented?

The blurred distinction between functions doesn't end with special policy advisers. Governments have been increasingly enthusiastic about the use of **'task forces'** and so-called policy 'czars' to implement policy in such areas as crime, education, housing and environmental protection. These may draw on individuals' special skills, or draw membership from a wide range of interests, but they are invariably political appointments and not democratically accountable in the way that a civil servant is accountable to their minister. Are the possible benefits for good government worth the possible price of less accountability to the electorate?

2.7   Regional and national government

Although many European countries, such as Germany and France, have historically had some degree of **regional government**, this has been largely absent in the UK. The end of the 1990s saw a potentially fundamental change in the structure of government in the UK with the emergence of regional elected government. However, this is only a partial system of regional government covering some parts of the UK, and the constitution and powers of each are very different.

2.7.1 Scotland

Scotland was granted devolution by the passing of the Scotland Act in 1998, which means that Scotland has a parliament with 'devolved' powers within the UK. Any powers that remain with the UK Parliament at Westminster are 'reserved', and set out in Schedule 5 of the Scotland Act. Essentially the powers of the Scottish Parliament are defined by what it does not have legislative competence in, rather than by what it can do. Devolved powers include matters such as education, health and prisons. Reserved powers comprise all other areas of decision making, such as defence and foreign policy which have a UK-wide or an international impact.

The Scottish Parliament is made up of 129 members (MSPs), one of whom is elected by the Parliament to serve as the Presiding Officer. Like the UK Parliament, the Scottish Parliament passes laws. It also scrutinizes the work and policies of the Scottish Executive. The Scottish Parliament is staffed by civil servants who serve the Parliament and, like the Presiding Officer, they must remain neutral.

The Scottish Executive is the government in Scotland for all devolved matters. It is formed from the party or parties holding a majority of seats in the Parliament. The Executive is led by the First Minister, who appoints other ministers and is supported by six administrative departments staffed by civil servants.

The Scottish Assembly has powers to vary income tax by plus or minus up to 3p in the pound to spend as it wishes. This, combined with the Scottish Parliament's ability to alter Scots law, increasingly leads to disparities with the rest of the UK, for example with respect to university tuition fees and charges for the care of elderly people.

The UK government continues to appoint a Secretary of State for Scotland, who remains a member of the UK Cabinet and is responsible for reserved items of government within Scotland.

2.7.2 Wales

In Wales, the National Assembly for Wales consists of 60 members elected throughout Wales. The Welsh Assembly is responsible for developing and implementing policies and programmes for all issues that have been devolved to Wales, which include agriculture, ancient monuments and historic buildings, culture, economic development, education and training, the environment, health services, highways, housing, industry, local government, social services, sport and leisure, tourism, town and country planning, transport and roads, and the Welsh language. The First Minister leads the Assembly and chairs a Cabinet of eight other ministers. All ministers are accountable to the Assembly and its committees for their actions. Unlike the Scottish Parliament, the Welsh Assembly has no tax-raising powers, although a referendum held in 2011 voted to seek more powers for the Welsh assembly.

2.7.3 Northern Ireland

In Northern Ireland, an Assembly was established as part of the Belfast (or 'Good Friday') Agreement. Northern Ireland had previously had a high level of devolved administration through the UK government's Northern Ireland Office, and the Good Friday Agreement sought to re-establish a form of Parliament that had previously been suspended during two decades of the 'Troubles'. The newly established Northern Ireland Assembly consists of 108 elected members – six from each of the 18 Westminster constituencies. Its role is primarily to scrutinize and make decisions on the issues dealt with by government departments, and to consider and make legislation. A First Minister and a Deputy First Minister are elected to lead the Executive Committee of Ministers. Due to the history of divisions within Northern Ireland society, there is a complicated system whereby the First Minister and Deputy First Minister must stand for election jointly and, to be elected, they must have cross-community support. Decisions in the Assembly are taken by a 'parallel consent formula', which means that a majority of both the members who have designated themselves Nationalists and those who have designated themselves Unionists, and a majority of the whole Assembly, must vote in favour. After a troubled start, the restored Northern Ireland Assembly has assumed responsibility for government functions previously handled by the UK government's Northern Ireland Office, and is allocated its block allocation of government expenditure.

2.7.4 London

In London, a referendum established the Greater London Authority. This provides for a directly elected Mayor (Ken Livingstone was the first Mayor, elected in 2000, and re-elected until 2008, when he was succeeded by Boris Johnson), who has the role of a policy leader and 'Champion for London'. The Mayor's office is the executive of London's government – managing a budget of over £8 billion and having revenue-raising powers (e.g. the London Congestion Charge is determined by the Mayor). The London Assembly – an elected body – scrutinizes the Mayor's policies, decisions and budget.

The Greater London Authority is made up of the Mayor, the London Assembly and a team of over 600 staff supporting their work to develop and implement London-wide policies in respect of transport, policing, fire and emergency services, economic development, planning, culture and the environment. The Mayor works closely with, and sets budgets for, Transport for London (TfL), the London Development Agency (LDA), the Metropolitan Police Authority (MPA), and the London Fire and Emergency Planning Authority (LFEPA). The Mayor also works closely with London's borough councils, which are responsible for providing many local services. The Mayor works with the boroughs to ensure that local and London-wide policies work together for maximum effect.

2.7.5 Other regional assemblies

Outside of Scotland, Wales, Northern Ireland and London, UK government policy on regional government has been ambivalent. In principle, governments have generally been in favour of more devolution to the regions, but some policies, such as the abolition of Regional Development Agencies in 2010, have appeared to go against this policy.

Advocates of regional government argue that it will allow legislation and economic policy to be developed that is better suited to the needs of their area. Critics would argue that regional government creates more bureaucracy, which will cost businesses time and money. Instead of devolving powers down from central government, a Local Government Association study in 2004 suggested that regional assemblies would actually lead to the transfer of authority upwards from local authorities to the new regional government bodies. Some saw evidence of the effect of this in the Welsh Assembly Government budget for 2008, which critics claimed increased spending by the Assembly but cut the funding allocated to local councils. There has been a muted response to proposals for further regional assemblies. In 2005, a referendum on a proposal to establish a regional assembly in north-east England was overwhelmingly rejected.

Delays in implementing policies may occur where the aims of national and regional governments differ, but cooperation between the two is essential if a regional policy is to be implemented successfully. Legal challenges by the London Assembly against the Department of Transport, Environment and Regions over privatization of the London Underground demonstrated that interdependencies between regional and national governments are likely to remain strong.

The likely effects of regional governments on business organizations are ambiguous. On the one hand, it can be argued that increasing amounts of UK legislation are merely enactments of EU directives, which would need to be enacted regardless of whether it is the UK Parliament or a regional assembly that assumes the responsibility. On the other hand, there are many areas of discretion, which can lead to differences between regions. Where it has tax-raising powers, regional assembly funds can be directed towards what are considered to be regionally important social goals. As an example of the differences that can emerge, the Scottish Parliament has funded long-term care for elderly people, something that was not available in England, and thereby opening up business opportunities in Scotland that were not available in England.

2.8 Local government

Local authorities in the UK are responsible for a wide range of services, from social services and education to refuse collection and street cleaning. The structure of **local government** that was implemented in 1974 divided the largely rural areas of England into counties ('shire counties'), each with a county council. The chief responsibilities of these county councils included education, social services, emergency services, highways and refuse disposal. Shire counties were further subdivided into district councils (sometimes designated as borough or city councils), which had responsibilities for housing, leisure services and refuse collection. Districts in rural areas were usually further divided into parishes with a parish council (sometimes designated as a town council) responsible for local matters such as the maintenance of playing fields.

In the larger conurbations, metropolitan district councils had greater functions than their shire county counterparts – for example, they were additionally responsible for education and social services. Following the abolition of metropolitan county councils in 1986, responsibility for conurbation-wide services (such as public transport and emergency services) passed to a series of joint boards governed by the district councils. In London, the pattern of government has been broadly similar to that of metropolitan areas, although there is now an assembly for the capital (see above). In Scotland, the structure of local government has been based on a two-tier system of regional and district councils.

From the mid-1990s, the basic structure of local government set up by the Local Goverment Act 1974 has been changed further by the appointment of commissions to study the needs of local government in individual areas. This has led to the emergence of 'unitary' authorities that combine the functions of district and county councils. Many large urban areas, such as Leicester, Nottingham and Bristol, have gained their own unitary authorities, in the hope that previous duplication of facilities provided by district and council councils can be avoided. As an example, the 'unitary' authority for Leicester combines previous city council functions of housing, refuse collection and car parking (among others) with responsibilities transferred from Leicestershire County Council for education, social services and highways.

Arguments for large county councils based on economies of scale and centralized provision have given way to a philosophy based on small, locally responsive units acting as enablers for services provided by subcontracted suppliers. Even a small, re-created county such as Rutland, it is argued, can provide many services previously considered too complex for such a small unit, by buying them in from outside suppliers, or by acting in partnership with other local authorities.

2.8.1 The relationship between central and local government

It has been argued that local government in Britain is losing its independence from central government, despite claims by successive governments that they support a philosophy of less government and a decentralization of powers. There is a great deal of evidence of this erosion of local autonomy.

- Over half of local government income now comes in the form of grants from central government.

- Local authorities have had the ability to set rates on business premises taken away from them altogether and these are now determined by central government.
- Furthermore, central government has the power to set a maximum permitted total expenditure for a local authority and to set a maximum amount for its council tax due from householders.

In addition, legislation setting performance standards in education and social services (among others) has limited the independence of local government to set locally determined standards. Local authorities now have less local discretion in determining what is an acceptable standard for services in their area and in deciding between competing priorities.

Local authorities have had increasing numbers of functions removed from their responsibility and placed with non-departmental public bodies (NDPBs) which are no longer answerable to the local authority (for example, colleges of further education now have their own governing bodies).

2.9 The European Union

The **European Union (EU)**, formerly known as the European Community (EC), was founded by the Treaty of Rome, signed in 1957 by France, West Germany, Italy, Belgium, the Netherlands and Luxembourg. Britain joined the EC in 1972, together with Ireland and Denmark, to be joined by Greece in 1981, Spain and Portugal in 1986, and Austria, Finland and Sweden in 1995. A more significant expansion to the EU occurred in May 2004 when ten countries of central and eastern Europe joined: Cyprus, the Czech Republic, Estonia, Hungary, Latvia, Lithuania, Malta, Poland, Slovakia and Slovenia. Romania and Bulgaria joined the EU in 2007 and these additions brought the EU's population to over 450 million people in 27 countries. Turkey has begun accession talks, but membership still seems far from certain. Further expansion of the EU appears now to be less of a priority, as the EU grapples with the task of integrating countries at different stages of economic and social development. When some of the weaker EU countries (Portugal, Ireland and Greece) needed support from the EU in 2010/11, many politicians in the 'old' and stronger members of the EU, principally Germany and France, questioned the wisdom of further expansion. Norway and Switzerland have always declined to join the EU, but enjoy a similar freedom of movement of capital, goods, people and services, as part of the wider **European Economic Area (EEA)**.

2.9.1 Aims of the EU

An important aim of the Treaty of Rome was the creation of a common market in which trade could take place between member-states as if they were one country. The implication of a common market is the free movement of trade, labour and capital between member-states. Agriculture was the first sector in which a genuinely common market was created, with a system of common pricing and support payments between all countries and free movement of produce between member-states. Further development of a common market has been impeded by a range of non-tariff trade barriers, such as national legislation specifying design standards, the cost and risk of currency exchange and the underlying desire of public authorities to back their own national industries. The creation of the single European market in January 1993 removed many of these barriers, but many practical barriers to trade remain, of which differences in language and cultural traditions are probably the most intractable.

There is considerable debate about the form that future development of the EU should take and, in particular, the extent to which there should be political as well as economic union. Recent debate has focused on the following issues.

- The creation of a common unit of currency has been seen by many as crucial to the development of a single European market, avoiding the cost and uncertainty for business and travellers of having to change currencies for cross-border transactions. A strong single currency would also be able to act as a true international currency comparable to the US dollar, in a way that few individual national currencies could hope to achieve on their own. The launch of the euro (now adopted by 17 of the 27 EU countries) has reduced transaction costs for trade between member-states and has allowed member-states' central banks to reduce their holdings of foreign currency. Within the UK, opposition to monetary union has been based on economic and political arguments. Economically, a common currency would deny to countries the opportunity to revalue or devalue their currency to suit the needs of their domestic economy.

- The lack of political and economic harmonization within the EU Eurozone countries has led to crises within those countries where governments had borrowed heavily in euros, but could not devalue their currency to reduce their indebtedness, something that had been a classic solution to previous financial crises. This lack of flexibility implies a political sacrifice, as control of currency is central to government management of the economy (although it should be noted that the UK government has handed over control of monetary policy to the Bank of England in an attempt to de-politicize financial policy). During 2010, four European countries – Greece, Ireland, Portugal and Spain – faced severe economic problems and many commentators suggested that a common European currency was unsustainable where national economies had not converged. The suggestion has been made that the stronger countries of Europe – notably Germany and France – would benefit from a separate currency to those poorer EU member-states that had weaker economies and poorer management of their governments' budgets.

- Argument continues about the amount of influence the EU should have in nation-states' social and economic policy. For example, previous UK governments have shown reluctance to agree to EU proposals that would harmonize personal taxation and social welfare benefits. The UK government has supported the idea of 'subsidiarity', whereby decisions are taken at the most localized level of government that is compatible with achieving EU objectives. Cynics have, however, pointed out that the UK government has not always been willing to practise this principle at home, as witnessed by the gradual erosion of the powers of local authorities in favour of central government.

- There is concern that enlargement of the EU to include the less developed economies of central and eastern Europe, and possibly Turkey, could put strains on EU budgets. Many have argued that enlargement should allow the EU to become a loose federation of states, rather than a centralizing bureaucracy, which many critics claim it has become.

- The principle of free movement of people across borders remains controversial in view of the possibility of large numbers of refugees or economic migrants being admitted by one state and then being automatically allowed to migrate to other member-states. Following the entry of a number of former communist countries to the EU in 2004, an estimated 600,000 people made their way from these relatively poor countries to find work in the UK during the first year of accession. This sudden influx made planning for public services such as schools and hospitals very difficult.

- Member-states still have difficulty in formulating a coherent foreign policy for the EU as a whole, as was seen in the fragmented approach taken towards the 2004 invasion of Iraq.

- There remains widespread concern about the lack of democratic accountability of EU institutions, not helped by allegations of excessive bureaucracy and corruption.

- In order to meet the challenges posed by growth in the EU, attempts have been made to formalize the rights and responsibilities of member-states through some form of constitution. Inevitably, member-states have widely differing experiences of written constitutions, and there has, not surprisingly, been a lot of debate about what such a constitution should cover (see below).

between countries can be resolved through negotiation rather than force. In the field of international trade, the UN has sought to encourage freedom of trade through the United Nations Conference on Trade and Development (UNCTAD). In matters of national security, the UK is a member of the North Atlantic Treaty Organization (NATO), whose role is changing following the end of the 'Cold War'.

Because the importance to the UK of international treaties and organizations lies to such a great extent in their benefits for international trade, they are considered in more detail in Chapter 14.

⟳ Thinking around the subject

Can banks be too big for governments?

Throughout the twentieth century, financial markets in most countries became increasingly deregulated. Even in the former communist countries of eastern Europe, state-owned banks, which once controlled investment decisions throughout the whole economy, were gradually sold off to the private sector and decisions about lending left to market forces rather than government diktat.

In the post-Second World War recovery period, government control of banks had been seen as vital to a coordinated and sustained industrial recovery. By the 1980s, many countries had begun to see government control of banks as a hindrance to further economic development. Banks were therefore increasingly able to determine their lending criteria on the basis of their own corporate objectives, rather than the needs of the country as a whole. To free market economists, there should be no contradiction between the needs of banks and the needs of the country, because it was presumed that profit-seeking banks would simply respond to the needs of lenders and borrowers, and if they did not win favour with customers they would not make profits and would not continue in business.

In 2008, politicians' faith in deregulated financial services sectors was rudely shaken with the collapse of many banks around the world, culminating in the collapse of the mighty Lehman Brothers in September 2008. Even in the USA, noted for its favour of free markets, the Federal government bailed out failed banks with billions of dollars of support. The UK government followed suit, and used public funds effectively to nationalize Northern Rock, Royal Bank of Scotland and the Lloyds banking group.

It seemed that the banks had become too big for governments to allow them to fail, in the way that free-market purists would have allowed. The failure of the big banks would have severely limited the amount of liquidity in the economy, with firms unable to borrow money to invest in productive capacity, slowing down the rate of job creation, reducing corporate profits, increasing unemployment and cutting consumer spending. In short, the failure of the banks could have led to an economic 'meltdown'.

From 2008, governments throughout the world became much more involved in the banking sector. As well as bailing out failed banks, regulation of the financial services sector was tightened – for example, by requiring banks to have a higher level of capital relative to their lending. Free-market, deregulated banking had taken national economies to the brink of economic collapse, and governments were determined that the failure of big banks should never again be allowed to destabilize their national economies. It seemed that – as in many aspects of the political environment – the pendulum had swung again from having a lot of government control, to much less, and now it had increased again.

2.11   Improving the standards of government administration

There have been a number of government initiatives to improve the standards of public-sector services that are provided in an environment where there is no market discipline. These generally use a combination of carrot and stick approaches, offering rewards to those public bodies that are performing well, while taking funds away from those that are failing.

In this section, we will consider a number of recent UK government initiatives: performance measures, 'best value indicators' and the sometimes elusive aim of bringing about 'joined-up government'.

2.11.1 Government performance targets

Government organizations have been set increasingly detailed performance targets – for example, the average waiting time for a hospital appointment, the percentage of household waste that is recycled, and the time taken to process a passport application. Managers are often paid a bonus based on their achievement of targets. Of course, such micromanagement by government through targets can lead to dysfunctional outcomes. It was famously noted that when the centralized Russian government set output targets for state-owned nail factories by weight, the factories simply produced very large nails, which few people wanted. To overcome this problem, targets need to be specified in more detail, resulting in a greater data collection burden for managers, and the possibility of further dysfunctional consequences occurring as individual managers seek to maximize their own performance targets, regardless of their effects on other people's targets.

An alternative approach is to encourage public-sector organizations to achieve more general status labels based on their performance. The **Charter Mark** is a UK government award scheme that aims to recognize and encourage excellence in public service. A wide range of government organizations have been successful in applying for a Charter Mark, including branches of the Benefits Agency, NHS Trusts, the Courts Service, and local HGV testing stations. In local government, the **Beacon Council** scheme was set up to facilitate the sharing of excellent practice among local authorities by holding out such authorities as exemplars to be followed by others As an example, Bexley Council was chosen in 2004 as a Beacon Council for its success in cutting anti-social behaviour and crime.

The Local Government Act 1999 introduced the concept of 'best value' in specified local authorities. The Act places on authorities a duty to seek continuous improvement in the way they exercise their functions. At the heart of best value is a statutory performance management framework, which provides for a set of national performance indicators and standards set by central government.

2.11.2 Joined-up government

Central, regional and local government can at times seem an amorphous mass of departments, each not appearing to know what the others are doing. There have been many documented cases where different government departments have taken completely opposing policy directions, thereby cancelling each other out (see 'Thinking around the subject' on p. 69). In recent times, it has been noted, for example, that while the UK's Department for Business, Innovation and Skills has been actively encouraging more overseas students to come to UK universities, the Home Office has been simultaneously made it more difficult by making student visas more expensive and difficult to obtain. In any large organization, the existence of internal 'silos' of people who do not speak to each other is common, so it is probably not surprising that this happens within government. To overcome the problem, central government has conducted a number of reviews that have tried to see service delivery from the perspective of actual users, rather than members of individual departments. The appointment of 'czars' and 'task forces', mentioned above, has been one way of initiating this process. One exercise of integrated-service teams simulated members of the public experiencing one of a number of major life events, such as leaving school, becoming unemployed, changing address, having a baby or retiring. Team members contacted the relevant departments and agencies direct, and this provided insights into the problems resulting from the way services are organized, and what might be done to improve things. Typical points that may be picked up, for example, are the way that people had to give the same information more than once to different – or even the same – organizations – for example, housing benefit and income support forms both ask for very similar information.

Creating 'joined-up' thinking is never easy, even within profit-orientated private-sector organizations. In seeking to achieve integration within government, the administration must balance the need to share responsibilities with the need to hold manageable-sized units accountable for their actions.

Thinking around the subject

How good is the National Health Service?

One of the recurring problems of public-sector services is monitoring their performance in an environment where market mechanisms alone will not reward the good performers and punish the bad. The UK has prided itself on a centralized National Health Service (NHS), which is free to consumers and paid for largely out of government taxation. But how do you measure the performance of doctors, either individually or in teams? The NHS has focused its efforts on quality-of-service issues. It routinely monitors, for example, the waiting time to see a consultant or to have elective surgery undertaken. But even such apparently simple indicators can mask a lot of problems. What does it mean when one consultant is shown to keep their patients waiting for longer than another consultant? To many people, a long waiting list may be a sign of a top-rated consultant who is very popular with patients, rather than a failing professional who cannot keep up with the demands placed on them. And then, of course, figures for waiting times can often be manipulated, scrupulously or unscrupulously. For example, Accident & Emergency departments use triage nurses to assess new patients upon arrival, thereby keeping within their Patients' Charter target for the time taken to initially see a new patient; however, the hospital may be slower to provide actual treatment. Some ambulance services have been reprimanded for trying to make their response times appear better than they actually are, by measuring the response time from when an ambulance sets out, rather than when a call for help is received.

Attempts to measure doctors' medical performance are much less developed, with debate about the most appropriate methodologies for assessing the efficacy of an operation or clinical diagnosis. Many medical outcomes cannot be assessed simply on the basis of success/failure, but require more subjective quality-of-life assessments to be taken into account. However, even the routine monitoring of patients' recovery rates could have unexpected dysfunctional consequences for patients. Some critics have argued that, in order to keep their performance indicators up, consultants may refuse to treat patients who have complications and a high risk of failure, and instead concentrate on easier cases with more predictable outcomes.

Some doctors have expressed a concern that merely publishing performance indicators pushes up users' expectations of service delivery, so that in the end they may become more dissatisfied even though actual performance has improved. Is there a case for treating doctors as professionals whose professional ethics leads them to do their very best for their patients? Or is this inward-looking approach to professional standards becoming increasingly untenable in an era of well-informed consumers who know their rights and have high expectations?

2.12   Impacts of government on business operations

We will now return to impacts of the political environment on business organizations and discuss three levels of effect:

1 the transformation of many government departments into 'quangos' (or non-departmental government bodies), so that they act more like a business organization rather than a government department

2 the **outsourcing** of many government functions, and collaboration with the private sector through public–private partnerships (PPPs)

3 the effects of government legislation on business operations.

2.12.1 Quangos (non-departmental public bodies)

It is too simplistic to divide organizations into those belonging to the public sector and those belonging to the private sector. '**Quangos**' (quasi-autonomous non-governmental organizations) or, more correctly, **non-departmental public bodies (NDPBs)**, are a form of organization that shares characteristics of both. In Britain, quasi-governmental bodies exist because direct involvement by a government department in an activity is considered to be inefficient or undesirable, while leaving the activity to the private sector may be inappropriate where issues of public policy are concerned. The quasi-government body therefore represents a compromise between the constitutional needs of government control and the organizational needs of independence and flexibility associated with private-sector organizations.

There is nothing new in arm's length organizations being created by governments – for example, the Arts Council has existed since before the Second World War. As the size of the state increased in the early post-Second World War period, there was concern that government departments were becoming overloaded. Their existence has at times owed a lot to political dogma, with incoming governments often keen to make a statement by handing over some central government activities to arm's length bodies in the interests of 'efficiency', or on the other hand abolishing them, often also using arguments about improving efficiency and effectiveness. Government policies have sometimes appeared ambiguous on the role of quangos – for example, the incoming coalition government of 2010 sought to achieve popularity by announcing the abolition of many apparently unpopular and bureaucratic quangos, but had to reverse this when it realized that their work still had to be carried out by someone and the quango was the most efficient type of organization for doing this.

These are some examples of quangos in the UK:

- Ofcom, which regulates the communications industries
- Ofwat, which regulates private-sector water supply companies
- the Driver and Vehicle Licensing Agency (DVLA).

Quangos enjoy considerable autonomy from their parent department and the sponsoring minister has no direct control over the activities of the body, other than making the appointment of the chairman. The minister therefore ceases to be answerable to Parliament for the day-to-day activities of the body, unlike the responsibility that a minister has in respect of a government department. The responsibilities of quangos vary from being purely advisory to making important policy decisions and allocating large amounts of expenditure. Their income can come from a combination of government grant, precepts from local authorities and charges to users.

The main advantage of delegation to quangos is that action can generally be taken much more quickly than may have been the case with a government department, where it would probably have been necessary to receive ministerial approval before action was taken. Ministers may have less time to devote to the details of policy application with which many quangos are often involved, and may also be constrained to a much greater extent by broader considerations of political policy. Being relatively free of day-to-day political interference, quangos are in a better position to maintain a long-term plan free of short-term diversions, which may be the result of direct control by a minister who is subject to the need for short-term political popularity.

Against the advantages, quangos have a number of potential disadvantages. It is often argued that quangos are not sufficiently accountable to elected representatives for their actions. This can become an important issue where a quangos is responsible for developing policy or is a monopoly provider of an essential service. The actual independence of quangos from government has also been questioned, as many are still dependent on government funding for block grants. Quangos can easily become unpopular with the public, especially where senior managers are seen paying themselves high salaries as they take 'business-like' decisions to cut back on the services that they provide to the public. For this reason, politicians may seek popularity by promising to abolish unpopular quangos, but finding an alternative organizational form may be more difficult.

A major objective of delegation to quangos has been to ensure that services are provided more in line with users' requirements rather than political or operational expediency. High-level appointments to quangos have been made from the private sector with a view to bringing about a cultural change that develops a customer-focused ethos. For the marketing services industry, the development of quangos has resulted in many opportunities as they increasingly use the services of market research firms, advertising agencies and public relations consultants.

⟳ Thinking around the subject

Does the left hand know what the right hand is doing?

The government of a large modern economy necessarily involves dividing responsibilities between departments, each of which is given increasingly clear aims and objectives, as well as what are usually vague objectives 'to coordinate their activities with other departments'. But despite talk about 'joined-up government', evidence of disjointed government is often all too clear to see. Consider the following cases.

Farming in Britain and the EU has traditionally relied on high levels of government intervention and farmers have often spotted inconsistencies in government policy. For a period during the 1990s, the Department of Agriculture was paying farmers to drain wetlands to turn into farmland, while at the same time the Department of Environment was paying landowners to create ponds and marshland from farmland in order to foster wildlife.

The Department of Education has promoted the recruitment of students from overseas, which is good for the national economy and the longer-term cultural benefits of having students study in the UK. However, the Home Office has sharply increased its fees for issuing visas to overseas students. Were the government and the country any better off as a result of these apparently conflicting actions?

In 2004, the problem of 'binge drinking' late at night in town centres became a priority area for the Home Office. It was particularly concerned by pubs' practice of offering a 'happy hour' in which drinks were sold at a reduced price, leading to problems of drunkenness. The Home Office urged pubs to drop their happy hours. In one Essex town, pub landlords met under the auspices of their local Licensed Victuallers Association and agreed with the Home Office that the happy hour should be abolished. The pub landlords realized that it would be pointless for just one pub to abolish it, because customers would simply go to those pubs that retained cheap drinks. They therefore agreed collectively to abolish the happy hour for all pubs in the town. But this upset another government agency, the Office of Fair Trading, which claimed that the pub landlords were in danger of prosecution for breaching competition law, which made any agreement between suppliers to fix prices illegal.

Some businesses have exploited gaps in government thinking to their own advantage – for example, in the example above, unscrupulous farmers may have sought government grants for both draining their land and creating wetland out of other land. However, to many businesses, such as the well-meaning pub landlords, the appearance that the left hand of government doesn't know what the right hand is doing can be very frustrating. But how in practice can such a large institution as a national government be made to be entirely consistent in the diverse objectives its departments set?

2.12.2 Public–private partnerships (PPPs)

Throughout Europe, collaborative partnerships between the public and private sectors have become increasingly popular. In the UK, **public–private partnerships (PPPs)** is the umbrella name given to a range of initiatives that involve the private sector in the operation of public services. The **Private Finance Initiative (PFI)** is the most common initiative but PPPs could also extend to other forms of partnership – for example, joint ventures. The key difference between the PFI and conventional ways of providing public services is that the public sector does not own the assets. The authority makes an annual payment to the private company, which provides the building and associated services.

Traditionally, government has procured facilities and services that the private sector has supplied under contract to the public sector. For example, under the traditional route, a private-sector contractor would build a new school to a Local Education Authority's (LEA) specification, with associated maintenance and services then being provided by a range of private companies and the LEA itself. With PPPs, one contractor provides the school and then operates a range of specific services such as maintenance, heating and school meals on behalf of the LEA through a long-term contract. This new way of working allows the private sector to contribute its expertise to the process, so as to find innovative solutions and secure better value for money. A typical PFI project will be owned by a company set up especially to run the scheme. These companies are usually consortia including a building firm, a bank and a facilities management company. While PFI projects can be structured in different ways, there are usually four key elements: design, finance, build and operations. In the case of new hospitals funded by PFI schemes, the clinical, medical and nursing services continue to be provided by the NHS, while the private sector finances the building of the new hospital and runs the non-clinical services in it such as maintenance, cleaning, portering and security.

The most significant benefits to government of PPP come through transferring risk to the private sector. This means that, should a project under the PPP overrun its budget, the government and taxpayers should not be left to pick up the bill. Contrast this with a major project taken forward under direct contract to the public sector, such as Transport for London's Jubilee Line Extension. This overran its planned budget by around £1.4 billion and opened nearly two years late, forcing the government to use taxpayers' money and grant additional funds to get the project completed.

In principle, a PPP should result in a lower level of government borrowing and should also achieve best value. A public-sector comparator is developed in order to establish whether the PPP represents better value than government providing the service by itself. It will show the overall cost of raising the finance and actually doing the work under a wholly public-sector arrangement.

Critics of PPPs argue that the price of involvement by the private sector inevitably includes a high premium to cover the risk of a budget overrun, which could come about for a variety of extraneous reasons. Although the government is saved the initial capital expenditure, over the longer term it has to pay rental charges for the use of facilities, which could work out more expensive than undertaking the whole task itself. The private sector borrows at higher rates of interest than the public sector, and this cost has to be passed on to the purchasing government department. Audit Scotland has calculated these costs as adding £0.2–£0.3 million each year for every £10 million invested. PFI projects can also have high set-up costs due to lengthy negotiations involving lawyers and consultants employed by both sides. It has been reported that the first 15 NHS trust hospital PFIs spent £45 million on advisers, an average of 4 per cent of the capital value (Clark and Simpkins 2006).

There is growing evidence that PFI projects escalate both in scale and cost, reflecting not just inflation but the very nature of PFI itself. In many cases, the PFI agreement places some responsibility for cost overruns with the government rather than the private sector, especially where specifications have changed during the duration of the contract. The higher costs can lead to an affordability gap for the procuring authority that is met by reductions in services and capacity. As with outsourcing contracts in general, there is a need for flexibility to be built in to PPP agreements in order to accommodate the environmental and internal changes that can occur over the lifetime of a contract (Ketter 2008).

There have been casualties among PFI providers. In 2007, Metronet – a company set up to operate some of London's underground railway lines in a PPP with the government body Transport for London – was placed into administration. The companies behind the Metronet consortium – Bombardier, Balfour-Beatty and WS Atkins – came to the conclusion that they could not bear any further cost overruns, which had been disputed with the public-sector partner. They therefore left Transport for London to pick up responsibility for maintaining and renewing the underground lines concerned.

2.12.3 Impacts of government legislation on business operations

Very few governments, whether free market or interventionist, would claim to have made life more difficult for businesses to operate. Yet a frequent complaint of many businesses, especially

Thinking around the subject

Political vision helps win Olympic Games for London

When London was chosen to host the 2012 Olympic Games, the initial cheers rather overlooked the enormous amount of collaborative work that lay behind London's successful bid, and the even more extensive network of relationships that would be necessary to deliver a successful Olympic Games. It has been claimed that having an elected Mayor and Assembly greatly assisted London in its successful bid to host the Games. At a time when much of the country was ambivalent about bidding for the Games, the Mayor provided a focal point for championing the interests of London. The Games would bring more than 28 days of sporting activities, and provide a lasting legacy in terms of economic growth and social regeneration. Thousands of individual service providers stood to benefit from the Games, ranging from small restaurants catering for construction workers and visitors to the Games through to large infrastructure providers. As well as stimulating the development of world-class sporting facilities, including swimming pools, a velodrome and hockey facilities, it was hoped that the Games would inspire a new generation to greater sporting activity and achievement.

© Pete Tripp

The Mayor agreed with the government a funding package of up to £2.375 billion to help meet the costs of staging the Olympics. The first £2.050 billion would be met, with up to £1.5 billion from the Lottery and up to £550 million from London council tax, which would cost the average London household £20 a year, or 38p a week. At the centre of the collaborative relationships was the Olympic Delivery Authority (ODA). The ODA has statutory backing through the London

Olympic Games and Paralympic Games Act 2006, and has to use a combination of power and persuasion to coordinate the efforts of multiple service providers, who will collectively make up the total Olympic experience for those who visit the Games in person, or who watch on television. The ODA must work closely with key partners such as the London Organising Committee of the Olympic Games, Transport for London (which is responsible for developing transport infrastructure to serve the Games), the London Development Agency and other regional development agencies such as the London Thames Gateway Development Corporation, in order to ensure not only that the Games are successful, but also that the infrastructure achieves long-term planning goals.

The ODA is responsible for making arrangements for building works, which it has done through a series of partnerships and subcontractor arrangements. At the same time as managing relationships with numerous suppliers, the ODA has to work closely with the International Olympic Committee (IOC) to ensure that standards are met. The ODA has responsibilities for protecting the Olympic logo and rights to use it by sponsors and other commercial users, and this requires the ODA to manage a large network of sponsors who contribute to the cost of holding the Games.

small business owners, is that government expects them to do too much administration on behalf of the government. Despite frequent high-profile government campaigns against 'red tape', the volume of **regulation** continues to have a major impact on the costs of business organizations. While large organizations may be able to afford specialists to handle administrative matters and can spread the cost over large volumes of output, government regulation can hit small businesses very hard. Consider some of the following examples of regulations that have added to the costs of business organizations in recent years.

- Value added tax (VAT) effectively makes most business organizations tax collectors on behalf of government, and small business owners must become familiar with complex sets of regulations.
- Legislation to give additional rights to employees bears down particularly heavily on small businesses. The granting of maternity rights to new mothers may easily be absorbed by large organizations, but a small business may experience great difficulties when one person who represents a large and critical part of the workforce decides to exercise their rights.
- The mounting volume of consumer protection and health and safety legislation has a particularly big impact on small businesses, which do not generally have the expertise to readily assimilate the provisions of new regulations.

A number of attempts have been made to quantify the costs to business organizations of government regulation. The British Chamber of Commerce's 'Burdens Barometer' is independently compiled by the London and Manchester Business Schools. Its Barometer for 2008 estimated that the cost of 46 major regulations introduced by the UK government since 1998 resulted in annual costs to business of over £65 billion. Table 2.2 shows a sample of these 46 regulations and the estimated resulting financial burden on business (BCC 2008).

Even the internet, which was supposed to simplify many administrative tasks, has led to new government-imposed burdens on businesses. Worried at the prospect of organized crime using the internet, the government passed the controversial Regulation of Investigatory Powers (RIP) Act 2000. This was bitterly contested by business for its provisions enabling the interception of emails and electronic correspondence.

Incoming governments have a tendency to make high-profile initiatives to simplify life for business – for example, by exempting small businesses from certain obligations. However, further regulation has a tendency to creep back into government policy.

2.13 Influences on government policy formation

Political parties were described earlier as organizations that people belong to in order to influence government policy, generally over a range of issues. Political parties aim to work within the political system – for example, by having members elected as MPs or local councillors. A distinction can be drawn between political parties and pressure groups or interest groups. These latter groups seek to change policy in accordance with members' interests, generally advancing a relatively narrow cause. Unlike members of political parties, members of pressure

Table 2.2   Estimated costs to UK businesses of compliance with selected regulations.

Regulation	Year of first implementation	Estimated annual recurring cost to UK business (£m)	Cumulative cost to UK businesses from date of introduction to July 2008 (£m)
The Working Time Regulations 1999	1999	1,795	16,005
Employment Act 2002	2002	219	1,302
Flexible Working (Procedural Arrangements) 2002	2003	296	1,588
The Maternity and Parental Leave (Amendment) Regulations 2001	2001	5	95
The Money Laundering Regulations 2003	2004	106	472
The Consumer Credit Regulations 2004	2005	102	681
The Tax Credit Acts 1999 and accompanying regulations	2000	100	865
The Part-time Workers (Prevention of Less Favourable Treatment) Regulations 2000	2000	27	218
The Stakeholder Pensions Schemes Regulations 2000 and 2005	2001	78	660
The Disability Discrimination (Providers of Services) (Adjustments to Premises) Regulations 2001	2004	189	1,721
The Animal By-products Regulations 2003	2003	100	540
The Electricity and Gas (Energy Efficiency Obligations) Order 2004	2005	467	1,401
Total for all government regulations on business			65,993

Source: adapted from the British Chambers of Commerce *Burdens Barometer* (BCC 2008).

groups generally work from outside the political system and do not become part of the political establishment.

2.13.1 Pressure groups

Pressure groups can be divided into a number of categories. In the first place there is a division between those that are permanently fighting for a general cause, and those that are set up to achieve a specific objective and are dissolved when this objective is met – or there no longer seems any prospect of changing the situation. Pressure groups set up to fight specific new road-building proposals fit into the latter category.

Pressure groups can also be classified according to their functions. Sectional groups exist to promote the common interests of their members over a wide range of issues. Trades unions and employers' associations fall into this category. They represent their members' views to government on diverse issues such as proposed employment legislation, import controls and vocational training. This type of pressure group frequently offers other benefits to members, such as legal representation for individual members and the dissemination of information to members. Promotional groups, on the other hand, are established to fight for specific causes, such as animal welfare, which is represented by, say, the League Against Cruel Sports.

Businesses themselves also frequently join pressure groups as a means of influencing government legislative proposals that will affect their industry sector. An example of a powerful commercial pressure group is the British Road Federation, which represents companies with interests in road construction and lobbies government to increase expenditure on new road building.

Pressure groups can influence government policy using three main approaches.

1 The first, propaganda, can be used to create awareness of the group and its cause. This can be aimed directly at policy formers, or indirectly by appealing to the constituents of policy formers to apply direct pressure themselves. This is essentially an impersonal form of mass communication.

2 A second option is to try to represent the views of the group directly to policy formers on a one-to-one basis. Policy formers frequently welcome representations that they may see as preventing bigger problems or confrontations arising in the future. Links between pressure groups and government often become institutionalized, such as where the Department for Transport routinely seeks the views of the RAC Foundation on proposals to change road traffic legislation. Where no regular contacts exist, pressure groups can be represented by giving evidence before a government-appointed inquiry, by approaching sympathetic MPs or by hiring the services of a professional lobbyist.

3 A third approach used by pressure groups is to carry out research and to supply information. This has the effect of increasing public awareness of the organization and usually has a valuable propaganda function. The British Road Federation frequently supplies MPs with comparative road statistics purporting to show reasons why the government should be spending more money on road building.

Pressure groups are most effective where they apply pressure in a low-key manner – for example, where they are routinely consulted for their views. The lobbying of MPs – which combines elements of all three methods described above – has become increasingly important in recent years.

Sometimes pressure groups, or sectional interests within them, recognize that they are unlikely to achieve their aims by using the channels described above. Recent years have seen an increase in 'direct action' by pressure groups, or breakaway sections of mainstream groups, against their target. Campaigners for animal rights, or those opposed to the use of genetically modified (GM) crops, have on occasion given up on trying to change the law and have instead sought to disrupt the activities of those organizations giving rise to their concerns. Organizations targeted in this way may initially put a brave face on such activities by dismissing them as inconsequential, but often the result has been to change the organization's behaviour, especially where the prospect of large profits is uncertain. Action by animal rights protestors contributed to the near collapse of Huntingdon Life Sciences (an animal testing laboratory), and many farmers were discouraged from taking part in GM crop trials by the prospect of direct action against their farms.

It is not only national governments to which pressure groups apply their attention – local authorities are frequently the target of pressure groups over issues of planning policy or the provision of welfare services. Increasingly, pressure is also being applied at EU level. Again, the European Commission regularly consults some groups, while other groups apply direct pressure to members of the Commission.

Business organizations have achieved numerous reported triumphs in attempting to influence the political environment in which they operate. The pressure group representing the tobacco industry – the Tobacco Advisory Council – had a significant effect in countering the pressure applied by the anti-tobacco lobby, represented by Action on Smoking Health. Legislation to ban cigarette advertising was delayed, and the pressure group has lobbied against a proposed ban on smoking in public places.

Pressure groups themselves are increasingly crossing national boundaries to reflect the influence of international governmental institutions such as the EU and the increasing influence of multinational business organizations. Both industrial and consumer pressure groups have been formed at a multinational level to counter these influences – a good example of the latter is Greenpeace.

2.13.2 The role of the media

The media – press, radio, television and increasingly the internet – not only spread awareness of political issues but also influence policy and decision making by setting the political agenda and influencing public opinion. The broadcast media in the UK must by law show balance in their coverage of political events, but the press is often more openly partisan. Campaigns undertaken by the press frequently reflect the background of their owners – the *Daily Telegraph* is more likely to support the causes of deregulation in an industry, while the *Guardian* will be more likely to put forward the case for government spending on essential public services. It is often said that *The Times* and the BBC Radio 4 *Today* programme set the political agenda for the day ahead.

⟳ Thinking around the subject

Political apathy becomes militant online

A casual glance at the politics pages in many newspapers in western Europe may lead to the conclusion that most people don't really care about politics. Most countries have seen a succession of broadly moderate political parties, with very few parties proclaiming extreme views that capture the support of large numbers of people. This has been matched by growing levels of apathy about the political process, evidenced in many countries by a declining number of people voting in elections. In the elections for the EU held in the UK in 2004, it was noted that more people voted in television's *Big Brother* contest than voted for European MEPs. But are we right to dismiss such disengagement from politics as evidence of individuals' lack of concern for political issues? While voting in elections may be declining, there is no sign of people staying silent when their cherished views are challenged. Some countries, such as France, have a tradition of popular protest on the streets. In Britain, a more consensual approach has been more traditional. But, even here, there are signs that frustration with the political process can spill over into the streets, witnessed by the nearly half a million people who marched in London in 2002 under the guise of the Countryside Alliance, to protest about government policy on the countryside, and the thousands of students who descended on London in 2010 to protest against proposed increases in university tuition fees.

New technology has opened up new opportunities for people to express their political views without going to the ballot box. One example is the facility for any individual to initiate an online petition to 10 Downing Street. In May 2010, the government announced that those e-petitions that receive 100,000 signatures or more would be eligible for debate in Parliament. One an example of an e-petition is that launched in 2007 by Peter Roberts and a small group who were opposed to the idea of charging for the use of roads; it attracted 1.8 million signatures. Is this the true democratization of politics? For businesses, rather than looking at politicians to try to judge future policy, would it be just as good an idea to look at what really brings people on to the streets, or to an online petition, in order to understand the pressures that politicians will probably eventually respond to?

Case study:
Should government be running the railways?

© Linda Steward

Throughout the world, there have been strong social and economic arguments for state ownership of railways. Railways are often seen as a vital part of the public infrastructure, which allows spatially dispersed economies to function. Some remote areas rely on railways as a vital lifeline, and many of our large conurbations would be unimaginably congested if rail commuters suddenly switched to their cars. The sheer costs and risks involved in building and operating a railway have deterred private investors, mindful of the many bankruptcies that have occurred during earlier 'railway booms'.

To the Conservative government of the 1990s, Britain's railways were suffering from a lack of entrepreneurship, which could be overcome by replacing public-sector employees and finance with new ideas and new capital brought in from the private sector. Britain led the way in privatizing its railways during the 1990s, and many other governments have followed by loosening their countries' railway links with government. the UK government embarked on a radical plan to deliver train services through a franchising system, which in principle copied the approach of a fast-food franchise. But implementing a franchising system was much more difficult and threw up many new problems. Britain's railways have been treated as a political football, and questions have been raised about the relative merits of state ownership and privatization. Along the way, there have been many opportunities, and headaches, for private-sector organizations that have been attracted to the sector.

The principle of rail franchising is simple. The government defined individual routes or groups of routes, and specified a minimum standard of service that it required. It then invited private companies to bid for the right to run the franchise for a specified number of years. For highly profitable routes, the successful bidder would pay the government an annual fee in return for rights to run the service. As with a fast-food franchise, the franchisee could increase its profits by generating more revenue from customers and/or by operating its service more efficiently. In the case of highly profitable routes such as the East Coast Main Line, a bidding war resulted in high payments being made by the franchisee to the government, but in other cases, such as the Valleys Lines of South Wales, it was recognized that these services would never be profitable, and the successful franchisee was the company that could provide the required level of service for the minimum level of government subsidy. In 2009, the UK government paid £3.9 billion in subsidies to rail operators.

So far, the comparison with a fast-food franchise may be fairly sound, but the implementation then raises some very tricky additional issues. First, railways serve a vital function in life, and many people, such as commuters into central London, are effectively captive, something that cannot really be said of McDonald's customers. As a result, franchise agreements include a long list of requirements set by the government to safeguard the interests of passengers and society generally – for example, a requirement for inter-availability of tickets on the services of competing rail operators. In recent years, there has been a tendency for the government to 'micro-manage' franchisees with ever increasing detail, leading many to question the purpose of having private-sector entrepreneurs involved when they are so constrained in using their entrepreneurial skills.

A further problem has occurred where franchise rail operators have made inaccurate assumptions about future costs and revenues, and have been forced to renegotiate or hand back their franchise, leaving the government to take over operations. In 2009, the operator of the East Coast Main Line franchise, National Express, found the £1.4 billion franchise fee that it was committed to paying the government over the life of the franchise

3.2   The cultural environment

The *Oxford English Dictionary* defines **culture** as a 'trained and refined state of understanding, manners and tastes'. Central to culture is the concept of the learning and passing down of values from one generation to the next. A culture's values are expressed in a complex set of beliefs, customs and symbols, which help to identify individuals as members of one particular culture rather than another. The following are typical manifestations of cultural identity.

- Shared attitudes – for example, towards the role of women or children in society.
- Abstract symbols and rituals, which can be seen in historic cultures by such events as religious practices, harvest festivals and maypole dancing, and in more modern times by support for local football teams.
- Material manifestations – for example, the literature and art of a culture, or the style of decoration used in private houses.

It is common to distinguish between 'core' and 'secondary' cultural values.

- Core cultural values tend to be very enduring over time. In Britain, for example, the acceptance of monogamy represents a core belief and one that very few people would disagree with.
- Secondary cultural values are more susceptible to change over time. While there may be a core belief in the family, this does not prevent changes in attitudes towards the form that families should take, as is evident from the growing incidence of divorce and the increasing number of single-parent families. It is shifts in these secondary cultural values that it is particularly important for business organizations to monitor.

3.2.1 Effects of culture on business organizations

It is crucial for business organizations to appreciate fully the cultural values of a society, especially where an organization is seeking to do business in a country that is quite different from its own. The possible consequences of failing to do this can be illustrated by the following examples.

- When McDonald's entered the UK market, it initially found hostility from the British, who did not appreciate the brash, scripted, 'Have a nice day' mentality of its staff. The company subsequently adapted its style of business to cater for British preferences.
- The UK retailer Sainsbury's failed in its attempt to replicate supermarkets on the British model in Egypt, a country that had no tradition of supermarket shopping. Worse still, at the height of a Palestinian uprising, a story went round that Sainsbury's had Jewish connections, a rumour encouraged by local shopkeepers. After just two years, and losses of over £100 million, Sainsbury's pulled out of Egypt.
- Many UK businesses have set up operations overseas and gone about business in an open and above-board manner, only to find that corruption and the use of bribes is endemic in the local culture and essential for business success.

Cultural sensitivity affects many aspects of business planning and operations.

- Understanding processes of buyer behaviour (for example, the role of men in buying routine household goods varies between countries, leading sellers to adjust their product specification and promotional efforts to meet the needs of the most influential members of the buying unit).
- Some products may be unacceptable in a culture and must be adapted to be culturally acceptable (e.g. the original formulation for the McDonald's 'Big Mac' is unacceptable in Muslim cultures).

- Symbols associated with products, such as the design and colour of packaging, may be unacceptable in some cultures (e.g. the colour white is associated with purity in most western European cultures, but in other cultures it is associated with bereavement).

- Distribution channel decisions are partly a reflection of cultural attitudes, and not just economics and land use. Retailers and wholesalers may be seen as a vital part of a culture's social infrastructure and individuals may feel a sense of loyalty to their suppliers. Although it may appear economically rational for shoppers to buy in bulk, small local shops opening for long hours may be seen by consumers as an extension of their pantry.

- Advertising messages do not always translate easily between different cultures, reflecting culturally influenced standards of what is considered decent and appropriate.

- Methods of procuring resources can vary between cultures. In some Far Eastern countries, it is essential to establish a trusting relationship with a buyer before the buyer will even consider placing an order. Sometimes, it is essential to know personally the key decision maker or to offer a bribe, which is considered routine business practice in some cultures.

- Obtaining good-quality staff can be influenced by cultural factors. The notion of punctual timekeeping and commitment to the employer is often an unfamiliar set of values in cultures where commitment to the family comes very strongly first and timekeeping has little meaning.

Even in home markets, business organizations should understand the processes of gradual cultural change and be prepared to satisfy the changing needs of consumers. The following are examples of contemporary cultural change in western Europe and the possible business responses.

- Women are increasingly being seen as equal to men in terms of employment expectations and household responsibilities. According to the ONS, the proportion of women in employment has grown steadily. In 1971, 56 per cent of UK women were in employment, compared with 70 per cent in 2009 (ONS 2010). This compares with a similar-sized decrease in the employment rate for men over the same period, with the male employment rate falling from 92 per cent to 78 per cent. The growth in the number of career-orientated and financially independent women has presented opportunities for new goods and services – for example, childcare facilities and ready-prepared meals, which save time for busy working women who need to juggle work, family and social roles.

- Greater life expectancy is leading to an ageing of the population and a shift to an increasingly 'elderly' culture. This is apparent in product design, which reflects durability rather than fashionability.

- Leisure is becoming an increasingly important part of many people's lives, and businesses have responded with a wide range of leisure-related goods and services.

- Increasing concern for the environment is reflected in a variety of 'green' consumer products.

3.2.2 Cultural convergence

There has been much recent discussion about the concept of **cultural convergence**, referring to an apparent decline in differences between cultures. It has been argued that basic human needs are universal in nature and, in principle, capable of satisfaction with universally similar solutions. Companies have been keen to pursue this possibility in order to achieve economies of scale in producing homogeneous products for global markets. There is some evidence of firms achieving this – for example, the worldwide success of Coca-Cola and McDonald's. In the case of fast food, many western chains have capitalized on the deep-seated habits in some Far Eastern countries of eating from small hawkers' facilities by offering the same basic facility in a clean and hygienic environment.

The desire of a **subculture** in one country to imitate the values of those in another has also contributed to cultural convergence. This is nothing new. During the Second World War, many individuals in western Europe sought to follow the American lifestyle, and nylon stockings from the USA became highly sought-after cultural icons by some groups. The same process is at work today in many developing countries, where some groups seek to identify with western cultural values through the purchases they make. Today, however, improved media communications allow messages about cultural values to be disseminated much more rapidly. The development of satellite television and the internet hastens the process of creating shared worldwide values.

It can be argued that business organizations are not only responding to cultural convergence, they are also significant contributors to that convergence. The development of global brands backed up by global advertising campaigns has contributed to an increasing uniformity in goods and services offered throughout the world. Many commentators have described an 'MTV' generation that views global satellite television channels, and who converge in their attitudes to consumption. The internet, cheap telecommunications and air travel have contributed to this process of apparent global homogenization.

🔁 Thinking around the subject

New magazines for new men?

Until a few years ago, the shelves of most newsagents would have been loaded with many general interest women's magazines (e.g. *Woman's Own*, *Woman's Weekly*, *Cosmopolitan*), but very few general interest magazines aimed at men. Why? Some cynics might have argued that women were more likely to have spare time at home and could sit around reading, while 'busy' men were out at work, in the pub or watching sport, and did not have time to read magazines There may just have been a bit of truth in this, but the main reason has been that women's magazines have been popular with advertisers, who generally provide a high proportion of total income for a magazine publisher. In the traditional household, it has been women who have made decisions on a wide range of consumer goods purchases. Advertising the benefits of toothpaste, yoghurt or jam would have been lost on most men, who had little interest in which brand was put in front of them and may have played a very minor role in the buying process.

Take a look at the news-stand now and it will carry a wide range of men's general interest magazines, such as *FHM*, *Maxim*, *Nuts* and *Zoo*. Why have they suddenly mushroomed in number and in readership? Again, the answer lies in their attractiveness to advertisers. Talk of a male identity crisis may have spurred some sales. More importantly, it is evident that men are now involved in a much wider range of purchasing decisions than ever before, and therefore likely to be of much greater interest to advertisers. While some 'new men' may be taking a more active interest in the household shopping, many more are marrying later and indulging themselves in personal luxuries, an option that is less readily available to their married counterparts. With support from advertisers, the leading men's magazine in the UK, *FHM*, had a circulation of 192,596 copies per issue in 2010 (Audit Bureau of Circulation). Sales of all magazines – men's and women's – have suffered in recent years as more people seek out content online, but in the late 1990s, *FHM* magazine had even overtaken the leading women's monthly magazine, *Cosmopolitan*.

Critics of the trend towards cultural convergence have noted individuals' growing need for *identity* in a world that is becoming increasingly homogenized. Support for regional breakaway governments (e.g. by the Kurdish and Basque people) may provide some evidence of this. During the Iraq war in 2003, many consumers in Arab countries used purchases of Muslim products to identify themselves with an anti-American cause. Many western service brands have become despised by some groups as symbols of an alien identity. Banks in many Muslim countries have reported increased interest in sharia-based banking services, and many UK banks have developed bank accounts targeted specifically at Muslims.

In some countries, cultural convergence has been seen as a threat to the sense of local identity that culture represents. Governments have therefore taken measures in an attempt to slow down this process of cultural homogenization. This has achieved significance in France where legislation requires the use of the French language – an important means of creating identity for any culture – in packaging and advertising for products.

3.2.3 Multicultural, multi-ethnic societies

The UK, like many western countries, is increasingly becoming a culturally and ethnically diverse society (see Table 3.1). By ethnicity, we are talking about groups based on their common racial, national, tribal, religious, linguistic or cultural origin. An important reason for increasing ethnic diversity in most western countries is the growing numbers of immigrant people from overseas cultures, attracted by, among other things, economic prosperity in the host country, and motivated to leave their native country by the relative lack of opportunities available. Immigrants can bring with them a distinctive set of cultural and religious values, and adapting to the values of the host country can be a difficult task. In some countries, church and state may be closely linked, leading to an expectation that religious principles should be the basis for governance. For some religious groups, the power of a religious leader transcends any government institution. A lack of understanding from members of the host country may cause

Figure 3.2 How can Coca-Cola be sure that its brand name and product offer will be the object of aspiration for the dominant groups in a country, rather than a hated symbol of an alien system of capitalism? Coca-Cola is often at the top of league tables of global brands, and most people in the world have access to the company's beverages. But Coca-Cola has been challenged by numerous functionally similar cola drinks, which seek to appeal to consumers' need for cultural identity. By rejecting Coca-Cola in favour of Mecca Cola (shown here), individuals have made a statement about their sense of cultural identity. Mecca Cola has donated 10 per cent of its profits to fund humanitarian projects in Palestine, and a further 10 per cent to charities in the countries in which the drink is sold – mainly Arab countries, and European countries with significant Arab communities. An activist stance has been reflected in the company's slogan, which has appeared on all its products: 'Shake your Conscience', and in the company's pledge to support 'associations who work towards peace in the world and especially for peace in the conflict between Palestinians and fascist Zionist apartheid'.

Table 3.1 Population of Great Britain by religion, 2001.

Religion	Number (000)	% of total population	% of non-Christian religious population
Christian	41,015	71.8	
Muslim	1,589	2.8	51.9
Hindu	558	1.0	18.3
Sikh	336	0.6	11.0
Jewish	267	0.5	8.7
Buddhist	149	0.3	4.9
Others	159	0.3	5.2
All non-Christian religions			100.00
No religion	8,596	15.1	
Not stated	4,434	7.8	
Total	**57,103**	**100.00**	

Source: based on Census of Population (2001).

some immigrants to be seen as arrogant, lazy or lacking in humour by the standards of the host culture, but they may nevertheless be perfectly normal by the standards of their home culture. Where members of ethnic minorities are concentrated into distinct areas (within the UK this occurs in certain suburbs of London, Leicester and Bradford), their traditional cultural values may be strengthened and prolonged by mutual support and the presence of an infrastructure (such as places of worship and specialized shops) to support the values of the culture.

The presence of concentrations of ethnic subcultures in a town presents opportunities for businesses that cater for distinctive cultural preferences. In many towns catering for people of Asian origin, these include halal butchers, bureaux for arranged marriages, and travel agents specializing in travel to India and Pakistan. In some cases, completely new markets have emerged specifically for minority ethnic groups, such as the market for black sticking plasters. It has sometimes proved difficult for established businesses to gain access to immigrant segments. Many established companies have not adequately researched the attitudes and buying processes of these groups, with the result that, in markets as diverse as vegetables, clothing and travel, **ethnic minorities** have supported businesses run by fellow members of their minority group.

A report published in 2010 by the Institute of Practitioners in Advertising (IPA) identified a number of challenges in addressing the needs of ethnic minorities. It has been noted that consumers from these groups are typically younger, more likely to own a business than others, tend to live in large urban centres – creating opportunities for cost-effective marketing – and are close-knit, making word-of-mouth recommendation a powerful force. However, they tend to be very fragmented, with intergenerational differences, requiring that businesses commission professional research to gain in-depth understanding of their target markets.

As producers, members of ethnic minorities have contributed to the diversity of goods and services available to consumers in the host country. The large number of Indian restaurants in Britain, for example, can be attributed to the entrepreneurial skills of immigrants, while many food products (such as kebabs and Chinese food) have followed the example of immigrants.

Immigrants have tended to be of working age and have filled a vital role in providing labour for the economy. In 2004, the labour market in many parts of Britain was overheating, with labour shortages and a lack of people prepared to work in jobs involving unpleasant working conditions or anti-social hours. The opening of the UK labour market to migrants from the new EU member-states of eastern and central Europe helped to alleviate these shortages with a supply of hard-working and flexible workers. Some ethnic groups have brought vital entrepreneurial skills to the economy, often at a high cost economically and socially to the less developed countries they have left.

It must be recognized that there are great differences between ethnic subgroups. Entrepreneurship is much greater among the Chinese group, where 21 per cent were classified as self-employed by the ONS in the Annual Population Survey 2004, compared to 15 per cent for white Irish, 12 per cent for white British, but less than 10 per cent for mixed or black groups. The age structure of minority ethnic groups gives rise to differences in the proportion that are dependent. Within the Bangladeshi group, for example, 42 per cent are under 16 (compared to a figure of 20 per cent for whites), while only 20 per cent are in the economically most active group of 35–64 (compared with 37 per cent for whites). These figures are reversed for the Chinese community, where only 17 per cent are under 16 and 38 per cent are between 35 and 64.

3.2.4 Social class

In most societies, divisions exist between groups of people in terms of their access to privileges and status within that society. In some social systems, such as the Hindu caste system, the group that an individual belongs to exerts influence from birth and it is very difficult for the individual to change between groups. Western societies have class systems in which individuals are divided into one of a number of classes. Although the possibilities for individuals to move between **social classes** in western countries are generally greater than the possibilities of movement open to a member of a caste system, class values tend to be passed down through families. The very fact that it is seen as possible to move classes may encourage people to see the world in a different way from that which has been induced in them during their years of socialization.

While some may have visions of a 'classless' society that is devoid of divisions in terms of status and privileges, the reality is that divisions exist in most societies, and are likely to persist in some form. It is common in western societies to attribute individuals with belonging to groups that have been given labels such as 'working class' or 'middle class'. This emotional language of class is not particularly helpful to businesses that need a more measurable basis for describing differences within society, and later in this chapter we will look at some of the ways class is measured.

Why do business organizations need to know about the social grouping to which an individual belongs? The basic idea of a classification system is to identify groups that share common attitudes and behaviour patterns, and access to resources. This can translate into similar spending patterns. There are, for example, many goods and services that are most heavily bought by people who can be described as 'working class', such as the *Daily Star* newspaper and betting services, while others are more often associated with 'upper-class' purchasers, such as Jaguar cars, the *Financial Times* and investment management services.

Businesses need to take note of the changing class structure of society. As the size of each class changes, so market segments, which are made up of people who are similar in some important respects, also change. In the UK during the 1960s and 1970s it has been observed that more people were moving into the 'middle classes'. The effects of taxation, the welfare state and access to education had flattened the class structure of society. For car manufacturers, this translated into a very large demand for mainstream middle-of-the-road cars. However, during the 1980s and 1990s, both the upper and lower classes tended to grow in what had become a more polarized society. In terms of car sales, there was a growing demand for luxury cars such as Jaguars and BMWs at one end of the market and cheaper cars such as Kias at the other.

↻ Thinking around the subject

How far can halal food go?

One consequence of the increasing cultural diversity in the UK is the emergence of a market in halal fresh meat and processed foods. Worldwide, a report published in 2010 by the consultancy firm AT Kearney estimated the value of the halal market to be £2 trillion a year. Halal means 'lawful and permitted', and, in food terms, products are not halal if they contain alcohol, any part of a pig, carnivorous animal meat or blood. Foods are also not halal if meat has not been slaughtered according to Islamic law.

The UK market for halal meat was estimated to have a value of £460 in a report by Mintel (Mintel 2002). The main market for halal food in the UK is the estimated 1.9 million Muslims who account for about 3.2 per cent of the population. However, Muslims have a varied ethnic background and in Britain are mainly drawn from Pakistan, Bangladesh, India and the Middle East, each with their own food preferences. Those from the Indian subcontinent are known to prefer hot, spicy food, while those from the Middle East have blander tastes, similar to those of native British people.

For butchers, who have had a hard time following a series of food scares and an increase in the number of vegetarian consumers, the emergence of the halal market offers a welcome opportunity. Mintel estimated that halal fresh meat accounted for 11 per cent of the value of all meat sales in the UK, but it appeared that just 3.2 per cent of the population was accounting for a disproportionate volume of halal meat sales.

Small independent butchers' shops have dominated halal meat sales. There have been problems in verifying the authenticity of halal meat, so trust is an important element of fresh meat supply, and it is likely that independent butchers' shops are used regularly as consumers have learned to trust the meat that they buy there. This is particularly true of older and more traditional Asian shoppers, who are much less likely to use supermarkets. Mintel observed that a large proportion of Muslim women play the traditional role of home-maker, which means that they have more time available for shopping in independent outlets – particularly those where their native language is spoken – and for preparing meals from scratch. However, it is unlikely that third-generation Muslims onwards will be satisfied with such a lifestyle. Third-generation Muslim women are more likely to have careers, and their busy lifestyles are likely to lead them to seek the convenience of one-stop shopping at supermarkets and online rather than using specialist small suppliers. They are also more likely to seek the convenience of ready-prepared meals, rather than cooking from raw ingredients as their parents did.

Already, halal brands have emerged, including Tahira (frozen, chilled, ambient foods) and Maggi (sauces and seasonings). Could other convenience food retailers further develop this market? Fast-food chains such as McDonald's are already experienced in catering for Muslim consumers in countries such as Malaysia – would there be a market for a halal burger in the UK?

Another intriguing question is whether the cultural traditions of Muslims may spread to the population generally. After all, Indian and Chinese restaurants now appeal to the UK population at large, rather than the narrow groups they initially served. Could halal food become mainstream rather than a niche market? One opportunity arises among the 3.4 million vegetarians in the UK, to whom meat-free halal foods are ideally placed to appeal.

⟳ Thinking around the subject

Equality is good for society, especially if you are on top

It is often claimed that one of the big trends in most western developed societies over the past few decades has been increased fairness, by reducing inequalities in life opportunities that result from differences in gender, age and ethnic background (among other things). However, a report published in 2010 by the UK's Equality and Human Rights Commission (EHRC) questioned the reality of equality in Britain today (EHRC 2010). The chairman of the EHRC, Trevor Phillips, noted that while British attitudes towards issues of race, gender and sexuality were now 'light years' ahead of previous generations, the reality on the ground had yet to fully catch up. Consequently, there were deep divisions in Britain's classrooms, different experiences of the criminal justice system, and a large pay gap between men and women. In full-time work, women in 2010 were still paid 16.4 per cent less than men, and in some sectors this was significantly worse (for example, the difference was 55 per cent in the finance sector).

The report noted that issues of inequality were often complex and interconnected, observing that 'Inequality and disadvantage don't come neatly packaged in parcels marked age, or disability, or gender, or race. They emerge often as a subset of a strand – not as a disability issue, but as a mental health issue; not as a generalised ethnic penalty, but as a result of being Pakistani; not a pay gap for working women, but a pay gap for working mothers.'

More worryingly, the report indicated that it appeared to have become increasingly difficult for children to escape from the social background into which they were born. Children born in to disadvantaged families faced a much greater struggle to succeed than those born into a more comfortable background. One example of this was seen in the way that young people from deprived backgrounds appear to be frozen out of top jobs because they are not well enough connected, or rich enough, to accept unpaid internships.

Societies function where people believe that, by working harder, they can improve their life chances. What are the implications for the business environment of a society where people feel increasingly trapped in their background? Is this exacerbated in a multimedia environment where the disadvantaged groups in society can easily become envious of other groups that they aspire to join, but see no realistic route to get there?

3.3   The family

The family represents a further layer in the socialization process. It is important that business organizations understand changes in family structures and values because change in this area can impact on them in a number of ways. Consider the following impacts of families on business organizations.

- Many household goods and services are typically bought by family units – for example, food and package holidays. When family structures and values change, consumption patterns may change significantly.
- The family is crucial in giving individuals a distinctive personality. Many of the differences in attitude and behaviour between individuals can be attributed to the values that were instilled in them by their family during childhood. These differences may persist well into adult life.
- The family has a central role as a transmitter of cultural values and norms, and can exercise a strong influence on an individual's buying behaviour.

3.3.1 Family composition

Many people still live with the idea that the typical family comprises two parents and an average of 2.4 children. In many western European countries this is increasingly becoming a myth, with single-person and single-parent households increasingly common. The following factors have contributed to changes in family composition:

- an increasing divorce rate, with about one-third of all marriages in the UK now ending in divorce
- marriage and parenthood are being put off until later; the average age of first marriage has increased by around five years since 1961, to 30 for men and 28 for women (based on UK 2001 Census)
- the gap between people leaving school, settling down to get married and starting a family has grown steadily, and young people are now enjoying freedom from parental responsibility for longer than ever before
- more people are living on their own outside a family unit, either out of choice or through circumstances (e.g. divorce, widowhood)
- family role expectations have changed, with an increasing number of career-orientated wives.

Changes in family composition have led firms to develop new goods and services that meet the changing needs of families, such as crèche facilities for working mothers and holidays for single parents. Advertising has increasingly moved away from portraying the traditional family group, which many individuals may have difficulty in identifying with. Examples that portray the new reality include an advertisement for McDonald's in which a boy takes his separated father to one of the company's restaurants, and one for Volkswagen in which a career-minded woman puts her car before her husband.

3.3.2 Family roles

As well as changing in composition, there is evidence of change in the way that families operate as a unit. Many household products have traditionally been dominated by either the male or female partner, but these distinctions are becoming increasingly blurred as **family roles** change.

A report by the Future Foundation showed that, in the UK, the proportion of couples in which the man has the final say in big financial decisions has fallen from 25 per cent in 1993 to 20 per cent in 2003 (Future Foundation 2004). This reflects an increase in the number of couples who claim that they have an equal say from 65 per cent to 69 per cent. The data also show that the number of couples where the female partner has the final say has risen from 10 per cent to 12 per cent. Men still make the major financial decisions in 40 per cent of couples aged over 65. Conversely, in couples under the age of 35, the woman is more likely to control major financial decisions. However, women still have the main responsibility for shopping in 47 per cent of couples, compared with 11 per cent of couples where men do it.

The scope for individual freedom of expenditure has increased significantly, and increasing affluence has widened the scope for discretionary spending in general. There are a number of markets, such as clothing, that benefit from this independent spending, although this finding is not consistent across the different age groups. Among couples aged over 65, a majority of men said their partner has at least an equal influence in the clothes they wear. This is lower in couples aged under 45, with only 19 per cent of men claiming that their partner mainly chooses their clothes for them. On the other hand, none of the women surveyed by Future Foundation said that their partner always chooses their clothes and a very small number indicated any significant influence.

The Future Foundation also highlighted a number of other changes in **roles** within family units.

- Cooking is still dominated by women, although men are increasingly sharing the task of preparing the main evening meal.

- Although men may say they believe household tasks should be shared, only 1 per cent say they always do the washing and ironing. Household cleaning is carried out mainly by women in nearly two-thirds of households, and this proportion has been falling gradually over the last two decades.

- The view that a man's task is to earn money, while a wife's job is to look after the family and home, has fallen consistently over the last decade.

- More women are stating that work and careers are more important than home and children.

There has been much debate about the fragmentation of families into **cellular households** in which family members essentially do their own activities independently of other members. This is reflected in individually consumed meals rather than family meals, and leisure interests that are increasingly with a family member's peer groups rather than other family members. Businesses have responded to the needs of the cellular household with products such as microwave ovens and portable televisions, which allow family units to function in this way. It can also be argued, however, that new product developments, combined with increasing wealth, are actually responsible for the fragmentation of family activities. The microwave oven and portable television may have lessened the need for families to operate as a collective unit, although these possible consequences were not immediately obvious when they were launched. The family unit can expect to come under further pressures as new products, such as online entertainment and information services, allow individual members to consume in accordance with their own preferences rather than the collective preferences of the family.

⟳ Thinking around the subject

Pocket-money pester power packs a punch

What role do children play in the purchase of the goods and services that they ultimately consume? In the UK, children aged just 7 to 14 years old receive an estimated £1.5 billion in pocket money and financial handouts, according to a report by Mintel (Mintel 2004). There has been considerable debate about the extent of 'pester power', where parents give in to the demands of children. Increasingly, advertisers are aiming their promotional messages over the heads of adults and straight at children. The ethics of doing this have been questioned by many, and some countries have imposed restrictions on television advertising of children's products. However, even with advertising restrictions, companies have managed to get through to children in more subtle ways – for example, by sponsoring educational materials used in schools and paying celebrities to endorse their products. When it comes to items such as confectionery and toys, just what influence do children exert on the purchase decision? And when football clubs deliberately change their strip every season, is it unethical for the clubs to expect fanatical children to pester their parents to buy a new one so that they can keep up with their peer group? Does the role of children in influencing purchase decisions say a lot about the structure of a society? In some cultures, children should be 'seen but not heard', but in others children may be treated as responsible adults from a much earlier age.

3.4   Reference groups

The family is not the only influence on an individual as they develop a view of the world. Just as individuals learn from and mimic the values of parents and close relations, so too they also learn from and mimic other people outside their immediate family. Groups that influence individuals in this way are often referred to as **reference groups**. These can be one of two types.

1 Primary reference groups exist where an individual has direct face-to-face contact with members of the group.

2 Secondary reference groups describe the influence of groups where there is no direct relationship, but an individual is nevertheless influenced by the group's values.

3.4.1 Primary reference groups

These comprise people with whom an individual has direct two-way contact, including those with whom an individual works, plays football and goes to church. In effect, the group acts as a frame of reference for the individual. Small groups of trusted colleagues have great power in passing on recommendations about goods and services, especially those where a buyer has very little other evidence on which to base a decision. For many personal services, such as hairdressing, word-of-mouth recommendation from a member of a peer group may be a vital method by which a company gains new business. If an individual needs to hire a builder, the first thing they are likely to do is ask friends if they can recommend a good one on the basis of their previous experience. For many items of conspicuous consumption, individuals often select specific brands in accordance with which brand carries most prestige with its primary reference group.

    The development of social network media such as Facebook has brought new energy to the role of primary reference groups, as individuals post and read comments about what should be accepted as social norms among their circle of friends.

3.4.2 Secondary reference groups

These are groups with which an individual has no direct contact, but that can nevertheless influence a person's attitudes, values, opinions and behaviour. Sometimes, the individual may be a member of the group and this will have a direct influence on their behaviour patterns, with the group serving as a frame of reference for the individual member. Individuals typically belong to several groups that can influence attitudes and behaviour in this way – for example, university groups, trades unions and religious organizations. A member of a trades union may have little active involvement with the organization, but may nevertheless adopt the values of the union, such as solidarity.

    At other times, an individual may not actually be a member of a group, but may aspire to be a member of it. Aspirational groups can be general descriptions of the characteristics of groups of people who share attitudes and behaviour. They range from teenage 'wannabes' who idolize pop stars through to businessmen who want to surround themselves with the trappings of their successful business heroes. Commentators have talked about a 'celebrity culture' in which individuals can be guided in their lives by the actions of celebrities in much the same way as followers of a religion are influenced by the icons and creeds associated with that religion. It can be difficult to identify just which aspirational groups are highly sought after at any one time. Middle-aged marketers marketing youth products may find it difficult to keep up with which pop stars and fashion models are currently in favour with teenagers.

The influence of secondary groups on purchases tends to vary between products and brands. In the case of products that are consumed or used in public, group influence is likely to affect not only the choice of product but also the choice of brand. (For example, training shoes are often sold using a 'brand spokesperson' to create an image for the shoe. There are some people who are so influenced by the images developed by famous athletes wearing a particular brand that they would not want to be seen wearing anything else.) For mass-market goods that are consumed less publicly (e.g. many grocery items), the effects of reference groups are usually less.

3.5   Values, attitudes and lifestyles

Many organizations have recognized that traditional indicators of social class are poor predictors of buyer behaviour. An analysis of changing attitudes, values and lifestyles is considered to be more useful.

3.5.1 Values

Values represent an individual's core beliefs, and tend to be deep-seated and relatively enduring. They tend to be learned at an early age and passed on through generations. They form an underlying framework that guides an individual's construction of the world and their response to events in it. Typical underlying value systems may include the belief that it is wrong to get into debt; a belief that family is more important than work; and that it is important to be the winner in any competitive event.

The term *values* should be distinguished from *value*. Economists describe value as the ratio of the benefit arising from a product relative to its cost. The distinction between values and value is that an individual's value system influences the value they place on any particular object. A person with a value system that rates security and reliability highly may place a high value on a car that is solidly built but not particularly attractive. Another person whose value system ranks recognition by others as being more important may place a higher value on a car that is not necessarily reliable, but has 'street cred'.

Although value systems tend to be deeply ingrained, they have a tendency to change through an individual's life cycle. So it follows that the value system of a teenager is likely to be different from that of a young adult parent, and different again from that of an elderly retired person.

3.5.2 Attitudes

Compared to values, **attitudes** are relatively transient sets of beliefs. Attitudes should be distinguished from the behaviour that may be manifested in a particular lifestyle. An individual may have an attitude about a subject, but keep their thoughts to themselves, possibly in fear of the consequences if these do not conform to generally accepted norms. A man may believe that it should be acceptable for men to use facial cosmetics, but be unwilling to be the first to actually change behaviour by using them.

It is important for businesses to study changes in social attitudes, because these will most likely eventually be translated into changes in buying behaviour. The change may begin with a small group of social pioneers, followed by more traditional groups who may be slow to change their attitudes and more reluctant to change their behaviour. They may be prepared to change only when something has become the norm in their society.

Businesses have monitored a number of significant changes in individuals' attitudes in western Europe – for example:

- healthy living is considered to be increasingly important
- consumers have a tendency to want instant results, rather than having to wait for things
- attitudes are increasingly based on secular rather than religious values.

Business organizations have been able to respond to these attitude changes creatively – for example:

- demand for healthy foods and gymnasium services has increased significantly; at first, it was only a small group of people whose attitude towards health led them to buy specialist products – now it is a mainstream purchase
- the desire for instant gratification has been translated into strategies to make stock always available, next-day delivery for mail-order purchases, instant credit approval and instant lottery tickets
- supermarkets in England have capitalized on the secularization of Sunday by opening stores and doing increasing levels of business on Sundays.

3.5.3 Lifestyles

Lifestyles are the manifestation of underlying value systems and attitudes. Lifestyle analysis seeks to identify groups within the population based on distinctive patterns of behaviour. It is possible for two people from the same social class carrying out an identical occupation to have very different lifestyles, which would not be apparent if businesses segmented markets solely on the basis of easily identifiable criteria such as occupation. Consequently, product development and marketing communications have often been designed to appeal to specific lifestyle groups. This type of analysis can be very subjective and quantification of numbers in each category within a population at best can only be achieved through a small sample survey.

Studies have indicated a number of trends in lifestyles, which have impacts on business organizations.

Figure 3.3 There can be a big difference between what people actually do, what they say they do, and what they would like to do. For businesses planning to offer new goods or services, it may be easy for a respondent to a survey to say that they would buy it, but when they have to get their money out, they may have other ideas. This gulf between attitudes and behaviour can be particularly great in the case of some health-related goods and services. Many people make 'new year's resolutions' to change their lifestyle, often after a Christmas of overindulgence, but their best intentions are not always matched by their actions. Many people believe that they should be fitter, perhaps based on reports about the effects of overeating and sedentary lifestyles. Many of these will simply rationalize away reasons for doing nothing to make themselves fitter ('I don't have time'; 'I get enough exercise anyway'; 'I don't want to risk the possibility of an injury while exercising'). Some will take positive action – for example, by joining a local gym; indeed, membership registrations rise sharply in January. However, industry research suggests that a high proportion of these people stop going to the gym after six months. Marketers face

a dilemma, because what people actually do is the best guide to what they spend their money on, but businesses are also continually trying to understand latent needs that have not yet been expressed in the form of actual purchases. How can a researcher tell whether a consumer's wish will be transformed into an actual purchase? (Photo reproduced with permission of Fitness First).

- A growing number of individuals are becoming money rich, but time poor. Such individuals quite commonly seek additional convenience from their purchases, even if this means paying a premium price. Businesses have responded with products such as gourmet ready-prepared meals.

- As individuals become financially more secure, their motivation to buy products typically changes from a need for necessities to a desire for the unusual and challenging. Businesses have responded with ranges of designer clothes, adventure holidays and personalized interior design services.

- With the increase in the number of single-person households, the symbolic meaning of the home has changed for many people. Businesses have responded with a range of home-related products such as widescreen home cinema systems and gas-fired barbecues.

Gaining knowledge of the current composition and geographical distribution of lifestyle segments is much more difficult than monitoring occupation-based segments, for which data are regularly collected by government and private-sector organizations. This is discussed again later in this chapter.

Thinking around the subject

A penny for your thoughts?

Businesses have become increasingly interested in individuals' deep-seated unconscious emotions, on the basis that these offer a much better guide to how they will actually behave than their considered responses to questions about their attitudes and beliefs. Enter the brave new world of 'neuro-marketing', which seeks to go straight to individuals' brains, rather than understanding them through what they say. One American organization, the Bright House Institute for Science, has used magnetic resonance imaging (MRI) to try to learn more about how marketing cues activate different parts of the brain.

The idea of trying to understand how people's brains function is not new, and has occupied scientists and criminologists, among others, for some time. The debate about the relative power of nature (a hard-wiring of the brain) versus nurture (the effects of socialization processes on our behaviour) is a long-running one. Marketers have already found some limited role for experimental methods of understanding deep-seated processing – for example, research into advertising effectiveness has used tachistoscopes to record individuals' unconscious eye movements.

Should neuro-marketing be regarded as a great hope for the future? Or is it overhyped? Critics have been quick to argue that it is one thing being able to identify a pattern of brain activity, but quite another to be able to infer causative links between brain patterns and buying behaviour. Some have dismissed neuro-marketing as a management fad, and a device used by research companies to get their foot in the door of the client, then selling more conventional research.

Is neuro-marketing ethical? To many people, neuro-marketing sounds like an Orwellian nightmare, which could play straight into the hands of the 'thought police'. Could an understanding of people's deep-seated thought processes potentially allow companies to wrongly exploit emotions that are against a consumer's best interest? Could food companies exploit an emotional need for high-calorie 'comfort' food at the expense of a more considered need for healthy food? At a broader level, what are the implications for democracy if politicians can understand and manipulate individuals' deep-seated attitudes?

3.6 Identifying and measuring social groups

So far we have discussed the changing composition of society in general terms, but now we need to turn our attention to possible methods by which organizations can identify specific groups within society. This is important if business organizations are to be able to target differentiated goods and services at groups that have quite distinctive sets of attitudes and lifestyles.

The aim of any system of social classification is to provide a measure that encapsulates differences between individuals in terms of their type of occupation, income level, educational background and attitudes to life, among other factors. There are three theoretical approaches to measuring social groupings.

1 *By self-measurement*: researchers could ask an individual which of a number of possible groups they belong to. This approach has a number of theoretical advantages for organizations, because how an individual actually sees him or herself is often a more important determinant of behaviour than an objective measure. If people see themselves as working class, they are probably proud of the fact, and will choose products and brands that accord with their own self-image. The danger of this approach is that many people tend to self-select themselves for 'middle-of-the-road' categories. In one self-assessment study, over two-thirds of the sample described themselves as 'middle class'.

2 *By objective approaches*: these involve the use of measurable indicators about a person, such as their occupation, education and spending habits, as a basis for class determination A number of these are discussed below.

3 *By asking third parties*: this combines the objective approach of indicators described above with a subjective assessment of an individual's behaviour and attitudes.

⟳ Thinking around the subject

Complicated lifestyles

Some indication of the minutiae of changing lifestyles, and their implications for marketing, was revealed in the report *Complicated Lives II – The Price of Complexity*, commissioned by Abbey National bank from the Future Foundation. The report brought together quantitative and qualitative research with extensive analysis of a range of trends affecting families and their finances. The findings show that, between 1961 and 2001:

- the average time women spent in a week doing cleaning and laundry fell from 12 hours and 40 minutes to 6 hours and 18 minutes
- the average time that parents spent helping their children with homework had increased from 1 minute a day to 15 minutes
- time spent caring for children increased from 30 minutes a day to 75 minutes
- the average amount of time spent entertaining went up from 25 minutes to 55 minutes per day
- time spent cooking has decreased for women, down from more than 1 hour and 40 minutes to just over an hour (73 minutes) per day; at the same time, men marginally increased their time in the kitchen from 26 to 27 minutes per day.

The growing number of money-rich, time-poor households presents new opportunities for businesses to provide convenient solutions to this group at a premium price. Sainsbury's was an early retailer to identify this opportunity and has developed a home delivery service that delivers customers' shopping to their home or place of work. The service has proved particularly popular with families who have difficulties in finding childminders, thereby avoiding the need to drag children round a supermarket. Some people have predicted the end of high-street shops as we know them, noting that internet-based distribution can be more efficient for a wide range of goods and services. However this overlooks the social needs that can be satisfied by a visit to a 'real' shopping centre – for example, a group of girls out shopping for clothes on a Saturday afternoon would probably consider online shopping to be a poor substitute, not only because of the technical limitations of the internet to convey properly the experiential values of clothes, but also because shopping with friends can be a social experience.

Social scientists have traditionally used the second of these approaches as a basis for defining social groupings, largely on account of its objectivity and relative ease of measurement. However, organizations must also recognize that an individual's attitudes can be crucial in determining buying behaviour, and have therefore been keen to introduce more subjective and self-assessed bases for classification. In the following sections we will review some bases commonly used by businesses for identifying social groups.

3.6.1 IPA classification system

One of the most long-standing and still widely used bases for social classification is the system adopted by the Institute of Practitioners in Advertising (IPA). It uses an individual's occupation as a basis for classification, on the basis that occupation is closely associated with many aspects of a person's attitudes and behaviour. The classes defined range from A to E, and Table 3.2 indicates the allocation of selected occupations to groups.

Thinking around the subject

Sandwich statement

What does an individual's choice of sandwich say about them? The retailer Tesco undertook research that showed how complex the market for ready-made sandwiches had become, with clear segments emerging of people who sought quite different types of sandwich. In an attempt to define and target its lunch customers more precisely, the company found that well-paid executives invariably insisted on 'designer' sandwiches made from ciabatta and focaccia with sun-dried tomatoes and costing about £2.50. Salespeople and middle-ranking executives were more inclined to opt for meaty triple-deckers. Upwardly mobile women aged 25–40 chose low-calorie sandwiches costing around £1.49. Busy manual workers tended to grab a sandwich that looked affordable, simple and quick to eat, such as a ploughman's sandwich that Tesco sold for £1.15. Tesco's research claimed that sandwiches have become an important statement made by individuals, and need to be targeted appropriately. What do your snack meals say about you?

3.7 Demography

Demography is the study of populations in terms of their size and characteristics. Among the topics of interest to demographers are the age structure of a country, the geographic distribution of its population, the balance between males and females, and the likely future size of the population and its characteristics.

3.7.1 The importance of demographic analysis to business organizations

A number of reasons can be identified why business organizations should study demographic trends.

- First, on the demand side, demography helps to predict the size of the market that a product is likely to face. For example, demographers can predict an increase in the number of elderly people living in the UK and the numbers living in the south-west region of the country. Businesses can use this information as a basis for predicting, for example, the size of the market for retirement homes in the south-west.

- Demographic trends have supply-side implications. An important aim of business organizations is to match the opportunities facing an organization with the resource strengths that it possesses. In many businesses, labour is a key resource and a study of demographics will indicate the human resources that an organization can expect to have available to it in future years. Thus a business that has relied on relatively low-wage, young labour, such as retailing, would need to have regard to the availability of this type of worker when developing its product strategy. A retailer might decide to invest in more automated methods of processing transactions and handling customer enquiries rather than relying on a traditional but diminishing source of relatively low-cost labour.

- The study of demographics also has implications for public-sector services, which are themselves becoming more marketing orientated. Changing population structures influence the community facilities that need to be provided by the government. For example, fluctuations in the number of children have affected the number of schools and teachers required, while the increasing number of elderly people will require the provision of more specialized housing and hospital facilities suitable for this group.

- In an even wider sense, demographic change can influence the nature of family life and communities, and ultimately affects the social and economic system in which organizations operate. The imbalance that is developing between a growing dependent elderly population and a diminishing population of working age is already beginning to affect government fiscal policy and the way in which we care for the elderly, with major implications for business organizations.

Although the study of demographics has assumed great importance in western Europe in recent years, study of the consequences of population change dates back a considerable time. T.R. Malthus studied the effects of population change in a paper published in 1798. He predicted that the population would continue to grow exponentially, while world food resources would grow at a slower linear rate. Population growth would be held back only by 'war, pestilence and famine' until an equilibrium point was again reached at which population was just equal to the food resources available.

Malthus's model of population growth failed to predict the future accurately and this only serves to highlight the difficulty of predicting population levels when the underlying assumptions on which predictions are based are themselves changing. Malthus failed to predict, on the one hand, the tremendous improvement in agricultural efficiency that would allow a larger population to be sustained and, on the other hand, changes in social and cultural attitudes that were to limit family size.

3.7.2 Global population changes

Globally, population has been expanding at an increasing rate. The world population level at AD 1000 has been estimated at about 300 million. Over the next 750 years, it rose at a steady rate to 728 million in 1750. Thereafter, the rate of increase became progressively more rapid, doubling in the following 150 years to 1550 million in 1900, and almost doubling again to 3000 million in the 62 years to 1962. The UN estimated total world population in 2007 to be 6.6 billion, and predicted that this would rise to 9.1 billion by 2050 (UNFPA 2009). The growth of world population has not been uniform, with recent growth being focused on the world's poorer countries, especially Korea and China, as well as South America. Within the EU countries, the total population in recent times has increased at a natural rate of about 1 per 1000 population (that is, for every 1000 deaths, there are 1001 births). However, this hides a range of rates of increase with, at each extreme, Ireland having a particularly high birth rate and Germany a particularly low one. This has major implications for future age structures and consumption patterns (see below). Much faster population growth is expected to occur in Africa and Latin America.

An indication of the variation in population growth rates is given in Figure 3.6. It should, however, be noted that there is still considerable debate about future world population levels, with many predictions being revised downwards.

A growth in the population of a country does not necessarily mean a growth in business opportunities, for the countries with the highest population growth rates also tend to be those with the lowest gross domestic product (GDP) per head. Indeed, in many countries of Africa, total GDP is not keeping up with the growth in population levels, resulting in a lower GDP per head. On the other hand, the growth in population results in a large and low-cost labour force, which can help to explain the tendency for many European-based organizations to base their design capacity in Europe but relatively labour-intensive assembly operations in the Far East.

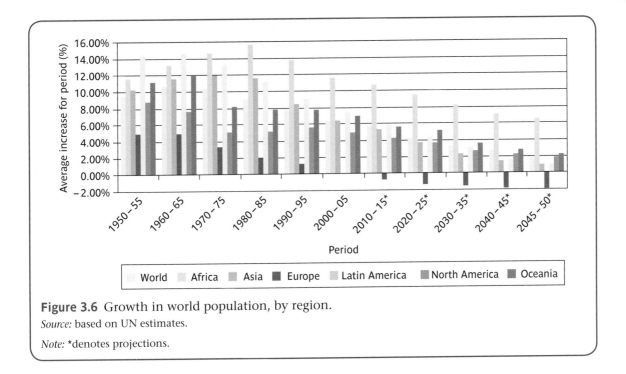

Figure 3.6 Growth in world population, by region.

Source: based on UN estimates.

Note: *denotes projections.

3.7.3 Changes in UK population level

The first British Census was carried out in 1801 and the subsequent ten-yearly Census provides the basis for studying changes in the size of the British population. A summary of British population growth is shown in Table 3.4.

The fluctuation in the rate of population growth can be attributed to three main factors: the birth rate, the death rate, and the difference between inward and outward migration. The fluctuation in these rates is illustrated in Figure 3.7. These three components of population change are described below.

3.7.4 The birth rate

The **birth rate** is usually expressed in terms of the number of live births per 1000 population. Since the Second World War, the birth rate of the UK has shown a number of distinct cyclical tendencies. The immediate post-war years are associated with a 'baby boom', followed by a steady decrease in the number of births until 1956. Following this, the rate rose again until the mid-1960s during a second, but lesser, baby boom. The birth rate then fell until the mid-1970s, rising again in recent years. Worldwide, the UN has estimated that the average birth rate per female has fallen from 5 in 1953 to 2.56 in 2007 (UNFPA 2009). Of the 44 countries in the developed world, all except Albania were reported to have birth rates below the natural replacement rate of 2.1 per female (the level needed to maintain a stable population level).

In order to explain these trends, it is necessary to examine two key factors:

1 the number of women in the population who are of childbearing age
2 the proportion of these women who actually give birth (this is referred to as the fertility rate).

Table 3.4   Population growth, England, Wales and Scotland, 1801–2031.

Year	Population of England, Wales and Scotland (000)	Average increase per decade (%)
1801	10,501	13.9
1871	26,072	9.4
1911	40,891	4.5
1941	46,605	5.8
1971	54,369	0.8
1981	54,814	2.4
1991	55,831	2.8
2001	57,424	2.3
2011	58,794	1.7 (projected)
2031	58,970	0.5 (projected)

Source: based on *Annual Abstract of Statistics*, Government Actuary's Department and population censuses.

The peak in the birth rate of the early 1960s could be partly explained by the 'baby boom' children of the immediate post-war period working through to childbearing age. Similarly, the children of this group have themselves reached childbearing age, accounting for some of the recent increase in the birth rate. Greater doubt hangs over reasons for changes in the fertility rate, usually expressed in terms of the number of births per 1000 women aged between 16 and 44. This has varied from a peak of 115 at the beginning of the twentieth century to a low point of 56.8 in 1983 (see Table 3.5).

There are many possible explanations for changes in fertility rates and it is our difficulty in understanding the precise nature of these changes that makes population forecasting a difficult task. Some of the more frequently suggested causes of the declining fertility rate are described below.

- A large family is no longer seen as an insurance policy for future parental security. The extended family has declined in importance and state institutions have taken over many of the welfare functions towards elderly members of the family that were previously expected of children. Furthermore, infant and child mortality has declined, and consequently the need for large numbers of births has declined. Alongside this falling need for large numbers of children has come a greater ability to control the number of births.

- Children use household resources that could otherwise be used for consumption. The cost of bringing up children has been increasing as a result of increased expectations of children and the raising of the school leaving age. Although in many western countries this is partly offset by financial incentives for having children, the cost of child rearing has increased relative to consumer purchases in general. According to a survey carried out by the UK's largest friendly society, LV, parents typically spend £9610 a year to feed, clothe and educate each of their children. The total cost of raising a child to the age of 21 was estimated to be £201,809, excluding private school fees (Smithers 2010).

- With the number of younger people declining as a proportion of the workforce, employers are increasingly looking to older people to fill their vacancies.

- The growing proportion of older people in the population may change the values of a youth-orientated culture. For example, the emphasis on fashion and short-life products

⟳ Thinking around the subject

How to defuse a demographic time bomb

The term demographic time bomb is often used to describe the effects of the increasing average age of populations in the EU. What will the effects of this 'time bomb' be on the business environment?

In 2005, the European Commission published a Green Paper on demographic change, which claimed that, from 2005 until 2030, the EU would lose 20.8 million (6.8 per cent) people of working age. By 2030, Europe would have 18 million fewer children and young people than in 2005. By 2030, the number of 'older workers' (aged 55 to 64) would have risen by 24 million as the baby boomer generation become senior citizens, and the EU would have 34.7 million citizens aged over 80 (compared to 18.8 million in 2005). Average life expectancy has also risen by five years since 1960 for women and nearly four years for men. The number of people aged 80+ is expected to grow 180 per cent by 2050. At the same time, the EU's fertility rate fell to 1.48 in 2003, below the level needed to replace the population (2.1 children per woman). As a result of these demographic changes, the proportion of dependent young and old people in the population will increase from 49 per cent in 2005 to 66 per cent in 2030.

For many people, the most pressing consequence of an ageing population focuses on pensions provision, but according to the European Employment and Social Affairs Commissioner, Vladimir Spidla, the looming crisis raises issues that are much broader. 'This development will affect almost every aspect of our lives – for example, the way businesses operate and work is organized, our urban planning, the design of houses, public transport, voting behaviour and the infrastructure of shopping possibilities in our cities,' he said.

The EU report noted that modern Europe has never experienced economic growth without rising birth rates, and suggested that 'ever larger migrant flows may be needed to meet the need for labour and to safeguard Europe's prosperity'.

How can Europe increase the size of its working population to serve the growing proportion of the population that is dependent? One strategy is to ensure that all people who are of working age and able to work actually do so. This would entail eliminating unemployment through retraining and changes to government social payments. Another strategy to increase long-term employment levels is to promote a higher birth rate. But there is an apparent contradiction here, because there is evidence that pressure on families to work harder has been having the effect of reducing the birth rate. The EU report found that Europe's low birth rate is largely the result of constraints on families' choices – late access to employment, job instability, expensive housing and lack of family-focused incentives (such as parental leave and childcare). Incentives of this kind can have a positive impact on the birth rate and increase employment, especially female employment.

A further way of expanding the workforce is to rely on immigration, but this raises a number of issues. First, there is the emotive issue to many people of diluting a national culture. More significantly, from a demographic perspective, what happens when these immigrant workers themselves get old and become dependent? They will need yet more immigrants to look after them. There is also a moral issue associated with immigration, because a common source of immigrants is the developing world. Given that many immigrants are the better-educated members of the society that they come from, is it morally right for the prosperous West to deprive developing countries of trained staff, such as doctors and nurses?

In presenting the EU report, Commissioner Spidla noted that 'Politics alone cannot solve the problem . . . they have to go hand in hand with a picture in society that does not stamp women who re-enter the labour market after maternity leave as "bad mothers" and men that take care of children as "softies".' Why do some cultures find this challenge insurmountable, whereas others readily accept working mothers as a valuable addition to the workforce? Is this the best way to defuse the 'demographic time bomb'?

may give way to an emphasis on quality and durability as the growing numbers in the older age groups increasingly dominate cultural values.

3.7.8 Household structure

Reference was made earlier in this chapter to the changing role and functions of family units, and this is reflected in an analysis of **household structure** statistics. A number of important trends can be noted.

- First, it was noted above that there has been a trend for women to have fewer children. From a high point in the 1870s, the average number of children for each woman born in 1930 was 2.35, 2.2 for those born in 1945, and it is projected to be 1.97 for those born in 1965. There has also been a tendency for women to have children later in life. In the UK, the average age at which women have their first child moved from 24 years in 1961 to 28 in 2001. There has also been an increase in the number of women having no children. According to the Office of Population Census and Surveys, more than one-fifth of women born in 1967 are expected to be childless when they reach the age of 40, compared with 13 per cent of those born in 1947.

- Alongside a declining number of children has been a decline in the average household size. The total number of dwellings in the UK is estimated to have risen by 9 per cent between 1992 and 2002, significantly outstripping population growth, which was 2.3 per cent for the same period. The result is a reduction in the number of people per household, falling continuously from an average of 3.1 people in 1961 to 2.4 in 2001 (Mintel 2003). There has been a particular fall in the number of very large households with six or more people (down from 7 per cent of all households in 1961 to under 2 per cent in 2001) and a significant increase in the number of one-person households (up from 14 per cent to 30 per cent over the same period). A number of factors have contributed to the increase in one-person households, including the increase in solitary survivors, later marriage and an increased divorce rate. The business implications of the growth of this group are numerous, ranging from an increased demand for smaller units of housing to the types and size of groceries purchased. A single-person household buying for him or herself is likely to use different types of retail outlet compared to the household buying as a unit – the single person may be more likely to use a niche retailer than the (typically) housewife buying for the whole family, whose needs may be better met by a department store. Mintel showed a number of ways in which the spending patterns of single-person households deviate from the average. For example, compared to the British average, a person living in a single-person household spends 49 per cent more on tobacco, 26 per cent more on household services and 23 per cent less on meat (Mintel 2003).

- There has been an increase in other non-traditional forms of household. Households comprising lone parents with children have increased, and in 2001, 20 per cent of all households in England and Wales with dependent children comprised only one adult. Further variation is provided by house sharers, who live independent lives within a household, pragmatically sharing the cost of many household items, while retaining the

⟳ Thinking around the subject

More elderly people, so why are homes for the elderly closing?

Ageing of the population is a major opportunity for many organizations. However, the link between growth in size of the elderly population and demand for a company's products can be complex. Nursing homes may expect a boom in demand as the population ages. However, during the period 1995–2004, the number of elderly people in residential care in the UK fell, and many care homes and their operators went out of business, despite a growth in the number of elderly people during this period. Trying to forecast future demand for care homes is complicated by uncertainty over the future health needs of elderly people – will the elderly people of the future be healthier and able to look after themselves for longer? Will they make greater efforts to live in their own homes, rather than in a residential care home? Some care homes, such as this one, have spotted this trend and now offer an outreach service to care for people in their own homes. Costs of operating residential care homes are likely to increase, fuelled

by increasing government regulations, and wages rising in real terms, reflecting a scarcity of people of working age relative to the number of elderly people. How much will elderly people and their relatives be able or willing to pay for residential care home accommodation? How much will the government be prepared to pay towards care? The Scottish Parliament announced in 2003 that it would provide financial support for elderly people in residential care homes, making the sector more attractive to operators in Scotland compared with the rest of the UK.

independence of mind more typical of a single-person household. The number of shared households has increased as young people find themselves priced out of the property market, and shared ownership (or shared rental) offers lifestyle opportunities that may otherwise be closed to a single person. In some cases, two families have shared the cost of a house, living as separate units within it.

- Very significant differences occur throughout the EU in home ownership patterns, with implications for demand for a wide range of home-related services. The proportion of households living in owned accommodation ranges from 57 per cent in Germany to 74 per cent in the UK and Belgium (Eurostat 2007).

3.7.9 Geographical distribution of population

The population density of the UK of 231 people per square kilometre is one of the highest in the world. However, this figure hides the fact that the population is dispersed very unevenly between regions, and between urban and rural areas. The distribution of population is not static.

Regional distribution

The major feature of the regional distribution of the UK population is the dominance of the south-east of England, with 30 per cent of the population. By contrast, the populations of Scotland, Wales and Northern Ireland account in total for only 17 per cent of the UK population.

Movement between the regions tends to be a very gradual process. In an average year, about 10 per cent of the population will change address, but only about one-eighth of these will move to another region. Nevertheless, there have been a number of noticeable trends. First, throughout the twentieth century there had been a general drift of population from the north to the Midlands and south. More recently, there has been a trend for population to move away from the relatively congested south-east to East Anglia, the south-west and the Home Counties. This can be partly explained by the increased cost of industrial and residential location in the south-east, the greater locational flexibility of modern industry and the desire of people for a pleasanter environment in which to live. The inter-regional movement of population is illustrated in Figure 3.9.

Urban concentration

Another trend has been a shift in the proportion of the population living in urban areas. Throughout most of western Europe, the nineteenth and twentieth centuries have been associated with a drift from rural areas to towns. In the UK, this has resulted in the urban areas of Greater London, Greater Manchester, Merseyside, Greater Glasgow, the West Midlands, West Yorkshire and Tyneside having just one-thirtieth of the UK's surface area, but nearly one-third of the total population. From the 1960s, the trend towards urbanization was partly reversed, with many of the larger conurbations experiencing a decline in population, combined with a deterioration in many inner-city areas. Those moving out have tended to be the most economically active, leaving behind a relatively elderly and poor population. Much of the movement from the conurbations has been towards the rural areas just beyond the urban fringe. For example, London has lost population to the Home Counties of Berkshire, Buckinghamshire, Hertfordshire and Essex. The increasingly large dormitory population of these areas remains dependent on the neighbouring conurbation. Movement from urban to rural areas has brought about a change in lifestyle, which has implications for businesses. Higher car ownership in rural areas has led more households to make fewer shopping trips for household goods, to travel

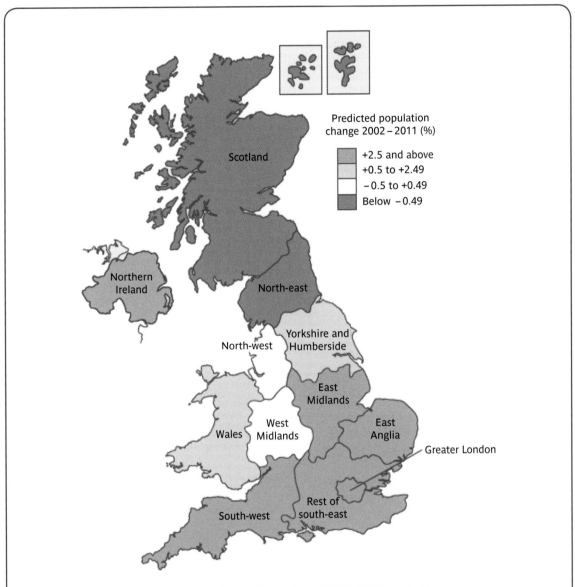

Figure 3.9 Percentage population change by region, 2002–2011 projections.

Source: based on information published by the Office of Population Censuses and Surveys, General Register Office (Scotland) and General Register Office (Northern Ireland).

further to the shop that best suits their lifestyle and to spend more on each trip. In this changed shopping pattern, the decision-making unit may comprise more members of the household than in an urban area where the (typically) wife may have made more frequent trips to the local supermarket by herself.

More recently, there has been a trend for young professional people to move back into town centres. For this group, having the facilities of a town centre close at hand without the need for increasingly expensive and time-consuming commuting has proved attractive. Town centres, which were once deserted in the evening, have often been brought back to life, helped by this group's patronage of wine bars, restaurants and all-night convenience stores.

The geographical distribution of the population differs between EU member-states. For example, EU statistics show that the proportion of the population living within metropolitan areas varies from 13 per cent in Italy to 44 per cent in France. The resulting differences in lifestyles can have implications for goods and services as diverse as car repairs, entertainment and retailing.

Case study:
A journey through Liverpool – European Capital of Culture 2008

By Damian Gallagher, University of Ulster

Photo reproduced with permission of Liverpool City Council.

To many people, Liverpool's culture is characterized by the 'Scouser', an individual with a jovial, happy-go-lucky sense of humour, a strong, distinct accent and sense of community spirit. The Scouser's love of music and entertainment is epitomized by Liverpool being the birthplace of the Beatles, and home to one of the world's greatest football teams. But scratch beneath the surface of Scouser culture and you will find a number of subcultures. It has always been that way, and a historical excursion through the city's culture demonstrates how the evolution of Scouser culture has influenced the business environment of Liverpool.

In 1660, the population of Liverpool was a modest 1200, but over the course of the next three centuries this was to change dramatically in the face of unrelenting urban and commercial growth. By 1775 the culture of Liverpool was dominated by commerce and the population had increased to 35,000; by 1801 this had doubled to more than 82,295 as more people were drawn to its ever developing port facilities and transport links, and it grew to become one of the most important ports in the world, trading in almost everything, including sugar, tobacco, grain, cotton and even people.

As well as growing in size, the population had grown in its cultural diversity. Between 1830 and 1930 Liverpool became a centre for transcontinental migration as almost 9 million people used its port as a gateway to a new life. Many sought escape from the events of their own countries of origin, such as the Irish famine and social unrest in eastern Europe, via emigration to Canada, the USA, Australia, New Zealand, South Africa and South America. Many immigrant seafarers settled in the area and others moved from neighbouring agricultural areas attracted by the work available. Between 1845 and 1849, 1.25 million Irish people used Liverpool in this way, but many had to stay, as they could not afford to go any further. By 1851, 25 per cent of Liverpool's population was Irish.

By the mid-nineteenth century, Liverpool had become a city of social extremes. There was a distinctly unequal distribution of wealth, headed by the wealthy elite of merchant traders, bankers and shipping agents who benefited from Liverpool's prospering port and invested heavily in the city's architecture, but very little in the education, housing or healthcare of its workers. This allowed ghetto-like segregation to develop in the city, with lots of poverty and deprivation. As the population increased, the city's boundaries expanded, but its infrastructure struggled to cope with the sheer number of people, and many poor Irish, Caribbean, Chinese, Dutch, German, Jewish, Welsh, Filipino and African working-class slum areas developed around the Scotland Road and Sebastapol Dock areas. Houses built to accommodate 19 were often found to contain over 90 people, where typhus, dysentery, cholera and lack of adequate sanitation saw average life expectancy at only 38 for women and 37 for men compared to the national averages of 42 and 40 respectively.

In the years prior to the Second World War, Liverpool's population peaked at 867,000. However, the twentieth century saw massive changes in the world's economic order, with many political and commercial changes having a negative impact upon Liverpool. As the century drew to a close, the last of the working docks had closed and the once thriving port was a shadow of its former self. The population fell to 439,473, with many having chosen to leave the city in the face of rising unemployment.

High unemployment has often played a major role in the life of Liverpool. Manufacturing, which had boomed in the early post-war years, declined in the 1970s and 1980s. The docks were also shrinking rapidly and many of the inner-city docks closed, with the once strong workforce being replaced by machinery and new technologies. This led to much social and political unrest as answers and solutions were sought by the 22 per cent of the male population who were unemployed (compared to the national average of 10 per cent). In some areas of Liverpool, unemployment was as high as 90 per cent. In 1981, social unrest exploded into the notorious Toxteth riots. While racial tensions between the police and black youths provided the spark, it is now widely accepted that this was not a 'race riot'. Many underlying social issues lay at the heart of the problems in the form of chronic unemployment, bad housing and poor education. Many white youths from neighbouring areas saw the riots as an excuse to vent their frustrations and joined in the fierce battles that raged for most of that summer, causing millions of pounds' worth of damage and leading to over 500 arrests.

Many people in these areas also blamed the recently elected Thatcher Conservative government for making their problems worse, seeing no role for the working classes in its policies of free-market enterprise and the reduced role of trades unions. This gave birth in the mid-1980s to a radical militant local government in the city. Based on the Far Left of the Labour Party, it was seen by many as a revolt against Thatcherism as it embarked upon largely confrontational policies that were detached from the central Conservative government. In challenging the Conservative government's house-building policies, among others, the socialist government of Liverpool appeared to be riding on a wave of popular support from the disadvantaged Scousers who had lost out in the economic and social reforms of the Thatcher government.

This militancy was seen by many as a hangover from the working-class labour organizations of the docks that were opposed to the aims of the Conservative government. Negative media images of a city with many social and economic problems did little to attract inward investment to the city or alleviate the sense of decline felt by its inhabitants.

By the 1990s, while the extremes of wealth and poverty still existed in Liverpool, though perhaps not as pronounced as in earlier years, a substantial middle-class population had also emerged. A new generation of young affluent and well-educated professionals with ambition and drive for success helped to fuel the social and economic regeneration of the city – some even point out with irony that these were the products of the Thatcherism that was once so reviled by the traditional Scouser. The smart coffee bars that this group gravitates to today are in another world compared with the rough pubs and ale houses of their predecessors.

An aerial view of Liverpool today reveals a city that is symbolized by its two cathedrals, one Catholic and one Anglican, standing at opposite ends of Hope Street. However, this hides the underlying multicultural make-up of the city, which remains from its days as a successful trading port. The Irish influence on the city remains strong, with many Scousers being fourth- and fifth-generation Irish, and the city often being referred to as the 'capital of Ireland'! Muslims, Jews, Hindus, Sikhs, Buddhists and Taoists of Europe's second-largest Chinese community still play a substantial role in the city. From 2004 onwards, many Poles headed for Liverpool, following the expansion of the EU to eastern Europe. Many businesses specifically target these ethnic and cultural groups, whose cultures are celebrated in events such as the annual Chinese New Year celebrations, the Irish Festival, the Caribbean Carnival and the Liverpool Welsh Choral Union, as well as the recent gay, lesbian, bisexual and transsexual Homotopia festivals.

In 2008, the city of Liverpool was named European Capital of Culture. It was looking to its Capital of Culture celebrations as a key driver for economic and social regeneration in the same way as previous hosts had experienced (e.g. Glasgow in 1990). With unemployment at its lowest rate for 30 years as a good starting point, the city saw many benefits to be obtained before, during and after 2008; The docks area that temporarily lay derelict has been subject to regeneration and redevelopment, and is now home to many expensive luxury apartments and trendy bars, shops, restaurants and cafes, art galleries and museums. In 2004, Liverpool's Pier Head was even designated a UNESCO World Heritage site.

A monitoring study undertaken by the University of Liverpool reported in 2010 that there had been 9.7 million additional visits specifically influenced by the Capital of Culture celebrations generating direct expenditure of £753.8 million across the north-west in 2008 alone. Researchers also found, for the first time in decades, positive stories about the city's cultural assets dominated over the traditional, negative emphasis on social issues. By the end of 2008, 85 per cent of Liverpool residents agreed that the city was a better place to live than before the European Capital of Culture award. The researchers also found that 99 per cent of visitors to the city liked the 'atmosphere' and 'welcoming' feel of the city, well above the response in other UK popular tourist destinations and previous years' findings for Liverpool.

Will such an influx bring about further change in the composition of Liverpool's cultural groups? And will the traditional working-class solidarity derived from the days of the docks survive in an era of consumerism and competitive service industry employment?

Sources: Liverpool Capital of Culture website, **www.liverpool08.com/**; University of Liverpool, IMPACTS 08 - European Capital of Culture Research Programme, at www.liv.ac.uk/impacts08/.

QUESTIONS

1 Summarize the changes in the cultural composition of Liverpool that have occurred during the last two centuries, and explain why business organizations should be interested in understanding these changes.

2 The case describes periods of social unrest in Liverpool that resulted from rising levels of unemployment following the decline of many traditional industries. Should business organizations seek to address issues of social exclusion such as that which occurred in Liverpool in the 1980s? If so, how could they help?

3 Identify the possible effects on businesses in Liverpool resulting from being European Capital of Culture 2008.

Summary

Societies are not homogeneous and this chapter has explored the processes by which individuals develop distinct social and cultural values. The concepts of social class, lifestyles, reference groups, family structure and culture are important reference points for businesses, and change in these must be monitored and addressed. Population totals and structures change, and this chapter has reviewed the impact of demographic change on the marketing of goods and services. A changing population structure also has implications for the availability of employees.

There is a close link between this chapter and **Chapter 5**, where we look at the social responsibility of businesses. As attitudes change, there has been a trend for the public to expect business organizations to act in a socially more acceptable manner. There are close links between the social environment and the political environment (**Chapter 2**), with the latter reflecting changes in the former. It has also been noted that technology can have a two-way effect with the social environment, and understanding the complexity of society's changing needs calls for an information system that is comprehensive and speedy (**Chapter 4**). When a company enters an overseas market, it is likely to face a quite different set of cultural values (**Chapter 14**).

Key Terms

Age structure (111)

Attitude (89)

Birth rate (109)

Cellular household (96)

Ethnic minorities (91)

Family roles (95)

Geodemographic analysis (104)

Household structure (116)

Life stage (105)

Lifestyle (99)

Census of population (103)

Cultural convergence (88)

Culture (87)

Demography (108)

Migration (112)

Reference group (97)

Role (95)

Social class (92)

Subculture (89)

Values (98)

Online Learning Centre

To help you grasp the key concepts of this chapter, explore the extra resources posted on the Online Learning Centre at **www.mcgraw-hill.co.uk/palmer**. Among other helpful resources there are chapter-by-chapter test questions, revision notes and web links.

Chapter review questions

1 Examine the ways in which the different culture of a less developed country may affect the marketing of confectionery that has previously been marketed successfully in the UK.

2 In what ways are the buying habits of a household with two adults and two children likely to change when the children leave home?

3 Critically assess some of the implications of an increasingly aged population on the demand for hotel accommodation in the UK.

Activities

1 Postcodes can reveal a lot about the social and economic composition of an area. If you live in the UK, go to the *Up My Street* website (www.upmystreet.com) and enter a selection of postcodes that you are familiar with. You will be given a range of information about each area – for example, house prices, nearby schools and crime levels. Click on the demographics button and you will be presented with a description of the area based on its ACORN code classification. How well do the ACORN classifications match the characteristics of inhabitants that you are familiar with?

2 If you live in a multi-ethnic area, examine advertising material for businesses catering for distinctive ethnic groups. What, if any, differences can you spot in how these businesses have differentiated their product, compared to similar goods and services offered by other companies to the indigenous population? To what extent do you see evidence of common underlying needs, but distinct cultural manifestations?

3 Consider a recent case when you went out with a group of friends to a restaurant, a bar or cinema. Critically examine the processes involved in deciding between the alternatives available. Explore the effects of the attitudes, values and lifestyles of the individuals concerned. What was the effect of social pressure on the final decision?

Further reading

Social classification has been discussed widely and the following texts are useful in a marketing context.

Devine, F., Savage, M., Scott, J. and Crompton, R. (2004) *Rethinking Class: Cultures, Identities and Lifestyles*, Basingstoke, Palgrave Macmillan.
Mihić, C. and Ćulina, G. (2006) 'Buying behavior consumption: social class versus income', *Management*, Vol. 11, No. 2, pp. 77–92.

For further discussion of market segmentation methods, the following texts show practical application of methods to identify groups within society that have similar consumption patterns.

Dibb, S. and Simkin, L. (2007) *Market Segmentation Success: Making it Happen!*, New York, Haworth Press.
McDonald, M. and Dunbar, I. (2010) *Market Segmentation: How to Do It, How to Profit from It*, Oxford, Butterworth-Heinemann.
Yankelovich, D. and Meer, D. (2006) 'Rediscovering market segmentation', *Harvard Business Review*, February, pp. 1–10.

For statistics on the changing structure of UK society and its habits, the following regularly updated publications of the Office for National Statistics (ONS) provide good coverage.

Family Expenditure Survey: a sample survey of consumer spending habits, providing a snapshot of household spending, published annually.
Population Trends: statistics on population, including population change, births and deaths, life expectancy and migration.
Regional Trends: a comprehensive source of statistics about the regions of the UK, allowing regional comparisons.
Social Trends: statistics combined with text, tables and charts, which present a narrative of life and lifestyles in the UK, published annually.

References

Census of Population (2001), UK Office for National Statistics.
Economist, The (2001) 'The new demographics', *The Economist*, Vol. 361, No. 8246, 11 March, Special Section, pp. 5–8.
EHRC (2010), *How Fair is Britain?* London, Equality and Human Rights Commission.
Eurostat (2007) *Eurostat Yearbook 2006–07*, Luxembourg, Statistical Office of the European Communities.
Future Foundation (2004) *Changing Lives*, London, Future Foundation.
IPA (2010) *The Marketing Opportunities for Advertisers and Agencies in Multi-cultural Britain*, London, Institute of Practitioners in Advertising.
Mintel (2002) *Halal Foods – UK*, London, Mintel.

Mintel (2003) *British Lifestyles*, London, Mintel.

Mintel (2004) *Pocket Money – Food and Drink in the UK 2004*, London, Mintel.

ONS (2010) Annual Survey of Hours and Earnings, London, Office for National Statistics.

Smithers, R. (2010) 'Cost of raising child breaks £200,000', *Guardian*, 23 February.

UNFPA (2009) *State of World Population Report 2009*, New York, United Nations Population Fund.

Chapter 4

The Technological and Information Environment

You probably take for granted that you can book a cheap airline flight at 2 o'clock in the morning from the comfort of your home, and pay no more than the cost of a pair of jeans to fly away to somewhere exciting. Just 20 or 30 years ago, this might have seemed an impossible dream, but the dream has become a reality, and advances in technology have been a major contributor to this. New fuel-efficient aircraft, using many new lightweight materials, and information technology to make booking a seat more efficient have had a big impact on the market. But airlines still need to be thinking about what the next generation of customers will want to buy in 10 or 20 years' time. What about trips into outer space? A dream today, but like previous dreams of cheap transatlantic travel, could this dream become an everyday affordable reality? Or will issues of climate change and the depletion of natural resources make travel an unaffordable luxury, fuelling further innovation to make 'virtual' tourism an acceptable and enjoyable treat for all? Companies cannot afford to stand still, but the future is invariably uncertain. It is easy to look back at successful innovations, but much more difficult to predict the future. This chapter will explore not only the technological uncertainties about the future, but also the interaction between the technological environment and the social, economic and political environment.

✓ Learning Objectives

This chapter will explain:

- ✓ The diversity of technological impacts on business.
- ✓ The increasing speed of technological development.
- ✓ Innovation as a source of companies' and countries' competitive advantage.
- ✓ The effects of the social environment on technology acceptance.
- ✓ The impact of the internet on communication between organizations and their environment.

4.1

What is technology?

The word 'technology' can easily be misunderstood as simply being about computers and high-tech industries such as aerospace. In fact, technology has a much broader meaning and influences our everyday lives. It impacts on the frying pan (Teflon-coated for non-stick), the programmable central heating timer, cavity wall insulation, the television, DVD player, washing machine, car – in fact, just about everything in the home. The impact at work can be even greater, as technology changes the nature of people's jobs, creating new jobs and making others redundant. It influences the way we shop, our entertainment, leisure, the way we work, how we communicate, and the treatment we receive in hospital. The aim of this chapter is to explore the many ways in which technology impacts on business, and will focus on:

- the development of new or better products
- reduction in the cost of making existing products
- improvements in the distribution of goods and services
- new methods of communicating with customers and suppliers.

Technology is defined in the *Longman Modern English Dictionary* as 'the science of technical processes in wide, though related, fields of knowledge'. Technology therefore embraces mechanics, electrics, electronics, physics, chemistry and biology, and all the derivatives and combinations of them. The **technological fusion** and interaction of these sciences is what drives the frontiers of achievement forward. It is the continuing development, combination and application of these disciplines that give rise to new processes, materials, manufacturing systems, products and ways of storing, processing and communicating data. The fusion and interaction of knowledge and experience from different sciences is what sustains the 'technological revolution' (see Figure 4.1).

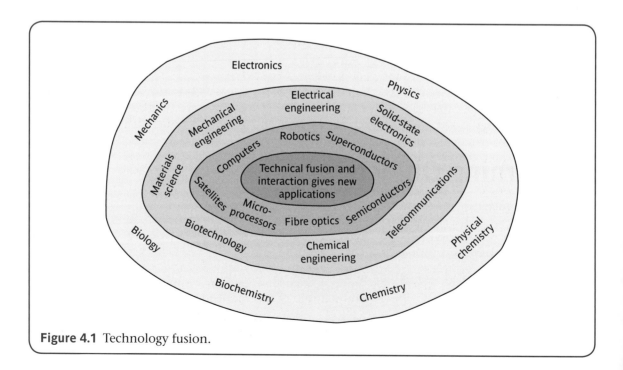

Figure 4.1 Technology fusion.

The term **demand-technology life cycle** is used to help explain the relevance to businesses of technological advances. Products are produced and marketed to meet some basic underlying need of individuals. An individual product or group of products may be only one way of meeting this need, however, and indeed is likely to be only a temporary means of meeting this need. The way in which the need is met at any period is dependent on the level of technology prevailing at that time. Kotler (1997) cited the need of the human race for calculating power. The need has grown over the centuries with the growth of trade and the increasing complexity of life. This is depicted by the 'demand life cycle' in Figure 4.2, which runs through the stages of emergence (E), accelerating growth (G_1), decelerating growth (G_2), maturity (M) and decline (D).

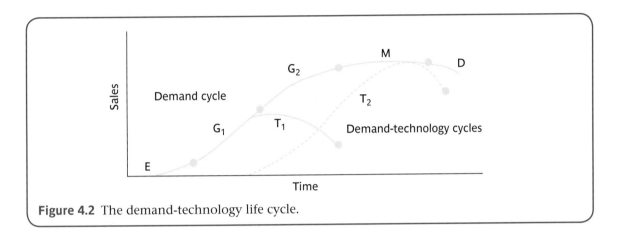

Figure 4.2 The demand-technology life cycle.

Over the centuries, the need for calculating power has been met by finger-counting, abacuses, ready-reckoners, slide rules, mechanical adding machines (as big as an office desk), electrical adding machines (half the size of an office desk), electric calculators (half the size of a typewriter), battery-powered hand calculators and now palm-sized computers. Kotler suggests that 'each new technology normally satisfies the need in a superior way'. Each technology has its own 'demand-technology life cycle', shown in Figure 4.2 as T_1 and T_2, which serves the demand cycle for a period of time. Each demand-technology life cycle will have a history of emergence, rapid growth, slower growth, maturity and decline, but over a shorter period than the more sustainable longer-term demand cycle.

Business organizations should watch closely not only their immediate competitors but also emerging technologies. Should the demand technology on which their product is based be undermined by a new demand technology, the consequences may be dire. If the emerging demand technology is not recognized until the new and superior products are on the market, there may be insufficient time and money available for the firm to develop its own products using the competing technology. Companies making mechanical typewriters, slide rules, gas lights and radio valves all had to adjust rapidly or go out of business. One way executives can scan the technological environment in order to spot changes and future trends is to study technology transfer.

The term **technology transfer** can be used in a number of contexts. It is used to refer to the transfer of technology from research establishments and universities to commercial applications. It may also be used in the context of transfers from one country to another, usually from advanced to less advanced economies. Transfers also occur from one industry to another; technology then permeates through the international economy from research into commercial applications in industries that can sustain the initially high development and production costs. As the costs of the new technology fall, new applications become possible. Applications of technology first developed for the US space programme, for example, may now be found in many domestic and industrial situations. NASA (the National Aeronautics and

Space Administration) established nine application centres in the USA to help in transferring the technology that was developed for space exploration to other applications.

4.2   Impacts of technology on business operations

From the previous discussion, it should be clear that technology has widespread impacts on business organizations. In extreme cases, technological development could be the reason for companies coming into existence in the first place (think of start-up companies created in the field of biotechnology), or the reason for a company's death (e.g. UK-based car manufacturers who, among other things, were slower than their Japanese competitors in adopting low-cost, high-quality manufacturing systems). In this chapter, we will explore a number of ways in which technological development has had impacts on the way organizations do business:

- product design and development
- manufacturing and processing
- supply chain management
- point of sale, order and payment processing
- communicating with customers
- managing customer relationships
- performance measurement
- the ecological environment.

Of course, many of these themes overlap – for example, performance measurement is an important aspect of most companies' efforts at managing relationships with customers – databases allow the company to identify who are the most profitable customers. In the following sections we will introduce general principles for assessing technology. In a later section, we will look specifically at the impact of the internet.

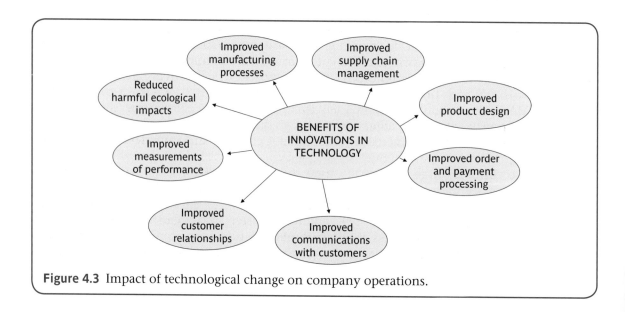

Figure 4.3 Impact of technological change on company operations.

4.3 Technology and society

At a broader level, business organizations are affected by the rate at which technology permeates the business world generally. Product life cycles are typically becoming shorter. Expertise in a particular technology may no longer be a barrier preventing competitors from entering an industry. New entrants into an industry may benefit from the falling costs of technology or may be able to bypass the traditional technology by using some new and alternative technology.

Businesses managers should be interested in the degree to which technology influences their business. Consider some historical antecedents: Bic produces a disposable plastic razor to challenge Wilkinson and Gillette; the fountain pen is challenged by the ballpoint, and in turn the ballpoint is challenged by the fibre-tip. Failure to identify changes in technology soon enough may cause severe and sometimes terminal problems for companies. Although there can be sudden changes in technology that impact on an industry, it is the gradual changes that creep through the industry that may be harder to detect. Companies that anticipate, identify and successfully invest in emerging technologies should be able to develop a strategic advantage over the competition. As the demand-technology life cycle goes through the stage of rapid growth, they will grow with it. As growth slows and the cycle matures, competitors will find it increasingly hard to gain a foothold in the new and by now dominant technology.

Our lives are affected by the interaction between technological changes and the social, economic and political systems within which we live and work. Over the last half-century the life of a mother has changed dramatically. With washing machines, tumble dryers, dishwashers, fridge-freezers and microwave ovens, modern textiles that are easier to wash and iron, convenience foods, and possibly the use of a car, the time devoted to household chores is much reduced. Partly as a result of these innovations, women are better educated and more likely to be in paid employment, and thus contributing to an increased disposable income. Also flowing from these developments, shopping patterns change from daily shopping in small local shops, limited to what can be carried and with transport via the bus, to weekly shopping (perhaps even on a Sunday or in the middle of the night) using the car or online grocery shopping with home delivery. The lives of schoolchildren also change, with even the youngest being introduced to the computer. Business people now have a truly mobile office with a laptop computer, PDA and mobile phone, which have merged into integrated 'smartphones'. They may be working from the car, from home, or even from a client's office. We are experiencing the casualization of communications, with people using personal phones, faxes, email and SMS text messages and expecting immediate responses but of a less formal nature. Within the family, life can become more dysfunctional as individual members pursue their own lives and activities. With more TV channels and choice, there is a greater need for additional TVs, at least one of which is likely to be linked to a games console. Space will also need to be found for at least one computer.

The impacts of technological development can differ between countries. In some newly industrializing countries people may view the rush in western economies to automated self-service as perplexing. In India and other Asian countries, where labour is relatively cheap and plentiful, the rising incomes of the middle classes would be used to employ more domestic help rather than to buy a washing machine or vacuum cleaner, for example. Consumers in different parts of the world will have different priorities according to wealth and circumstances. In China, where the opportunity to buy your own home or car is more limited than in the UK, consumers with rising incomes are more likely to spend on TVs and mobile phones.

4.4 Forecasting new technologies

It can be very difficult to forecast the development and take-up of new technologies. Those nations and companies that are first to develop a technological lead will grow, as the technology is embedded in new industries and products. Early developments in biotechnology in the USA and UK, for example, in the mid-1980s have developed into a billion-dollar global industry impacting on agriculture, pharmaceuticals, health and chemicals. Developments in the software industry transformed Silicon Valley, California, in the 1980s and 1990s, just as the car industry transformed Detroit, USA, in the 1950s. The interaction between a favourable political and social climate, higher education and research, and entrepreneurial individuals, may transform a whole economy and have a global impact.

There is a complex relationship between customers' demand for new technology and the ability of private and governmental organizations to supply it. There are many well-documented examples of new technologies that emerged through 'blue sky' research, in which technological advancement arose from scientific curiosity rather than a clearly identified customer demand. In recent years, the development of Post-it notes and music cassette players did not arise because of a careful analysis of customer demand, but nevertheless they went on to become great commercial successes.

Many new technologies experience initial scepticism from consumers, sometimes referred to as a **'hype cycle'**. At first, many thought that bank ATM machines would never become popular with customers, who would prefer to deal with bank staff face to face. Of course, ATMs have now become the routine method of withdrawing cash from a bank account. Similar voices of scepticism were raised with internet banking. So how does a company try to predict the take-up of new technologies by consumers?

Models of technology adoption have their origins in the disciplines of psychology, information systems and sociology. The Technology Acceptance Model (TAM) (Davis, Bagozzi and Warshaw 1989), based on the Theory of Reasoned Action (Ajzen and Fishbein 1980; Fishbein and Ajzen 1975), has become well established as a model for predicting acceptance of new IT-based services. The model (Figure 4.4) introduces two specific beliefs that are relevant for technology usage, namely perceived usefulness (U) and perceived ease of use (E). Actual behaviour is determined by behavioural intention (BI); however, behavioural intention is jointly determined by the individual's attitude towards a technology (A) and perceived usefulness (U). Finally, perceived ease of use (E) is a direct determinant of attitude (A) and perceived usefulness (U). In the case of older bank customers, where there is often nothing to be gained by switching to computer-mediated banking because other banking methods are available, it is likely that perceived ease of use would have a stronger influence on behavioural intentions than would perceived usefulness. However, in a business banking context, perceived usefulness is likely to be a stronger predictor of behavioural intention than attitude. There is considerable evidence that young people have been more ready to adopt new technologies than older people (O'Cass and Fenech 2003).

Sometimes, consumers are faced with the simultaneous emergence of two new competing technologies, and it can be difficult at the outset to predict which one will win out. In the 1970s, video recording became a mass-market possibility, but although the Betamax format was claimed to offer higher quality, it was the VHS format that eventually became dominant. Once a new technology passes a tipping point, with backing from key stakeholders, it can acquire an unstoppable momentum. The battle of technology formats came to a head again in 2008 in the struggle between two alternative versions of high-definition DVD recorders. Walt Disney, 20th Century Fox and Metro Goldwyn Mayer had lined up behind Blu-ray while Universal supported the competing HD-DVD format. The costlier Blu-ray accounted for an estimated three-quarters of world-wide sales in 2007, but how long could this last? The film-makers were desperate for a new format to emerge in order to revive sales of DVDs, which had begun to slow down. However,

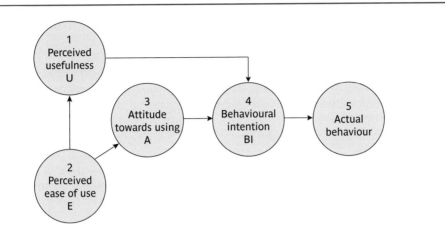

Figure 4.4 Companies often encourage their customers to adopt new self-service technologies, thereby reducing their costs, especially staffing costs. They may also promote the fact that service users can obtain additional benefits by using an automated form of service delivery. However, many service users may remain deeply sceptical, failing to see the benefits to themselves, and influenced by horror stories in the media of how the new technology has previously let customers down (for example, many people remain cautious about giving their credit card details over the internet, although, rationally, this is safer than giving details over the telephone). When planning the expansion of self-service facilities, companies need to be able to estimate the take-up rate, so that queues do not form or capacity remain unused. This model has been developed to explain the influences of perceived usefulness and attitude on consumers' intention to use, and actual use of new technology.

Source: based on Davis, Bogazzi and Warshaw (1989, p. 985).

they were concerned that consumers' confusion could lead to deferred purchases, and eventually high-definition DVD technology could lose out to digital downloads or video-on-demand. In this war of the formats, the winner would be the format with support from the majority of film studios and equipment manufacturers. The losing format would probably become increasingly marginalized and eventually go the way of Betamax.

Demand forecasting for new technologies often begins by trying to predict general changes in the macro-marketing environment. This in itself can be very difficult; for example, economists frequently disagree in their forecasts of economic growth during the year ahead. When it comes to predicting macroenvironmental change, larger companies often retain expert consultants, such as the Future Foundation (www.futurefoundation.net) and Trendspotting (www.trendspotting.com), which employs economists, sociologists and psychologists, among others, to try to build a picture of the world as it will evolve. Such macro-level forecasts can inform more detailed forecasts about market size, growth rates, market share, and so on.

The UK government's 'Foresight Programme', which brings together industry, academia and government to consider how the UK can take advantage of opportunities to promote wealth creation through innovation. Foresight, and its associated 'horizon scanning centre', aims to provide challenging visions of the future, and to develop effective strategies for meeting them. It does this by providing a core of skills in science-based future projects and access to leaders in government, business and science. Foresight operates through a rolling programme that looks at three or four areas at any one time. The starting point for a project area is either a key issue where science holds the promise of solutions, or an area of cutting-edge science where the potential applications and technologies have yet to be considered and articulated. In 2009, active projects included land use futures, global food and farming futures, global environmental migration and international dimensions of climate change (Foresight 2009).

When it comes to forecasting demand for completely new technologies, simply asking potential buyers whether they would buy the product can be fraught with difficulties. And simply asking somebody what they would use a new product for is likely to be limited to the scope of respondents' imagination. In the context of developing a low-cost car, Henry Ford once famously commented that if he had asked people what they wanted, they would have simply replied 'faster horses', rather than being able to imagine ever owning a car. For intangible services, the problem of consumers' limited vision can be even greater, requiring more sophisticated research methods that seek to understand deep-seated needs and motivators. Where possible, companies have sought to experiment with new products targeted at trial groups, before committing themselves to large-scale provision. This may be a valid approach where capital commitments are high and the market is relatively stable, but in fast-moving markets, too much time spent trying to understand consumer behaviour may allow competitors to gain a lead in an emerging new service sector. In the early days of the internet, many new online services were developed with very little research; indeed, in those days, the problem of Henry Ford's horses was ever more present, with most consumers having little idea of how they might use the internet. So, in order to be first to market and have 'first mover' advantage, the process of understanding customers and forecasting demand was often based more on intuition and judgement than on a rigorous analysis.

⟳ Thinking around the subject

Too many chips in the kitchen?

How does a company developing high-technology consumer products predict whether a new product is going to be a hit with consumers or a miserable failure? One very simple, but naive, solution would be to ask target consumers whether they would purchase the proposed new product. But, for radically new technologies, consumers may have very little idea of what the product involves and how it would fit in to their lives. They would probably have difficulty articulating their thoughts about the product to a researcher. Is it any wonder then that an estimated 80 per cent of new products fail?

One method used by companies to try to predict better the likely take-up of new products is based on ethnographic research. This involves supplying participating households with prototype versions of the product and watching how they actually use and interact with the product. In return for an incentive, a family may be filmed and a diary recorded of their activities, typically over a two- or three-week period.

Researchers have been curious to understand how automation, and the internet, can be brought into the domestic kitchen. The Korean firm LG developed an 'intelligent fridge' that used bar code readers to record items put into the fridge, and then taken from it and used up. This was linked to a simple stock-control programme, which drew up a shopping list for the household, which in turn could be sent through the internet to the household's preferred online grocer. In principle, the household need not worry about shopping or running out of any of its favourite grocery items. But the developers of the intelligent fridge didn't take account of the loss of a sense of control felt by the household. Ethnographic researchers pointed out that what appeared to be a technologically neat solution did not meet the lifestyle requirements of households.

The electronics companies Electrolux and Ericsson joined forces for another study involving human guinea pigs and their use of domestic refrigerators. They wanted to test the concept of a 'screen fridge', which allowed the user to download recipe ideas from the internet, store shopping lists and had a built-in video camera to record messages. Among the questions that they sought answers to were: To what extent are households adventurous in their use of recipes? What is the typical number of recipes that a household relies on when cooking family meals? Who would show most interest in the technology – male members of the household who like gizmos, or the women who do most of the cooking?

The idea of being watched by television cameras throughout the house might seem very Orwellian. However, a rash of reality television shows such as Big Brother have made many people more open to the idea of being watched. However, the question is often asked – as it has been for the Big Brother series – whether what is being seen is reality or the actions of a self-selecting idiosyncratic group who like to be watched? There is apparently no shortage of individuals and households who are willing to be filmed, and stories abound of semi-professional people who make a decent part-time living through such research. But is this really research that represents the population as a whole?

Source: based on Jones (2004).

Figure 4.5 Would you ever want to travel into outer space? Would you invest millions in developing space tourism? In 2001, the world's first space tourist, Dennis Tito, paid a reported $20 million for a visit to the International Space Station. Already a number of companies are looking at the possibilities for mass-market space tourism. Although the price of travelling into space may still appear prohibitive, analogies have been drawn with the early days of transatlantic air travel. In 1939, it cost the equivalent of £79,000 in today's inflation-adjusted money to make a return flight from Britain to the USA, something which can be routinely done today for around £400. Sir Richard Branson's Virgin Galactic plans to begin commercial passenger flights into space, departing from Spaceport America in New Mexico. The flights will allow the public to experience the thrill of weightlessness outside the Earth's atmosphere, gain their astronaut wings and witness spectacular views of the planet at a cost of £120,000 per ticket. Virgin Galactic has already taken several hundred reservations and tens of millions of dollars in deposits, but will space tourism

© *Getty Images*

go the same way as transatlantic air travel by eventually becoming mass-market? What would be the price at which space tourism really begins to grow? Who will be the innovators, and just how many people in the later adopter groups really want to have the space experience? Of greater uncertainty in planning for the future is the effect of aircraft emissions on global warming. Could these lead to prohibitively high taxes on operations, or a feeling of guilt by potential passengers about the effects of their travel into space on climate change?

Source: www.virgingalactic.com.

4.5 Expenditure on research and development

Technological advancement derives from investment in research and development. **Research and development (R&D)** expenditure is often classified into three major types: basic, applied and experimental.

1 Basic or fundamental research is work undertaken primarily for the advancement of scientific knowledge without a specific application in view.

2 Applied research is work undertaken with either a general or specific application in mind.

3 Experimental development is the development of fundamental or applied research with a view to introduction of new, or the improvement of existing, materials, processes, products, devices and systems.

Classification is also often carried out on a sectoral basis, e.g. public or private, and by type of industry. The International Standard Industrial Classification Code (ISIC) is often used.

International comparisons of R&D expenditure should be used with caution. Difficulties in comparing statistics stem from:

■ differences in the basic definitions of R&D and the boundaries between R&D and education, training, related scientific expenditure and administration costs

■ differences in counting numbers employed in R&D; e.g. definitions of full-time/part-time, directly or indirectly employed, qualifications and occupation

■ discrepancies in the sources and destination of funds; e.g. private and commercial organizations receive some public funds, but public bodies also receive some funding from private sources; this makes it difficult to calculate the proportion of R&D expenditure financed by governments as compared to that financed by the private sector; university expenditure is typically a mix of the two, for instance

■ difficulties in distinguishing the R&D element of large-scale defence programmes

■ difficulties in assessing R&D funds flowing between countries, particularly between the components of multinational firms (Young 1993); the consolidated accounts of a multinational may show R&D expenditure, but in which country was it spent?

■ R&D expenditure undertaken by small firms is not usually recorded by government agencies (Lopez-Bassols 1998).

In order to overcome these difficulties, economists at the Organization for Economic Co-operation and Development (OECD) issue guidelines in the form of the *Frascati Manual* for use by government statisticians. This helps to ensure that statistics are collected by each country on a similar basis, thereby aiding international comparison. The manual is also updated regularly to take account of new issues, such as software R&D expenditure, for example. However, caution still needs to be exercised when using international comparative statistics. Variations in exchange rates, purchasing power of the currency in the domestic market, and the reliability and comparability of the statistics all give grounds for caution.

R&D expenditure across all OECD countries averaged 2.28 per cent of GDP in 2007, which is higher than the average for the EU countries (1.77 per cent) (OECD 2010a). Finland, Japan, Korea and Sweden were the only OECD countries in which the R&D-to-GDP ratio exceeded 3 per cent, well above the OECD average. Since the mid-1990s, R&D expenditure in real terms has been growing faster in turkey and Portugal, both with average annual growth rates above 10 per cent.

Some emerging countries have robust and growing budgets for R&D – for example, according to the OECD, China increased its R&D intensity from 0.9 per cent in 2000 to 1.44 per cent in 2007, and its growth in real R&D spending since 2000 has exceeded 20 per cent per year.

An alternative approach to comparing countries' R&D activities is to measure the number of people employed in R&D activities. Researchers are individuals engaged in the conception and creation of new knowledge, products, processes, methods and systems, as well as those who are directly involved in the management of projects. They include researchers working in both civil and military research in government, universities and research institutes, as well as in the business sector. In the OECD area, around 4 million people were employed in R&D in 2006. Approximately two-thirds of these were engaged in the business sector. In 2006, there were about 7.6 researchers per 1000 of employed people in the OECD area, compared with 5.9 per thousand employed in 1995. This indicator has increased steadily over the last two decades. Among the major OECD areas, Japan has the highest number of researchers relative to total employment, followed by the USA and the EU (OECD 2010).

The UK's R&D figures do not make happy reading for the country's industrialists and politicians, with expenditure in manufacturing being particularly bad, and declining R&D expenditure in almost every sector. In real terms the UK's R&D expenditure has declined in recent years in mechanical engineering, electronics, electrical engineering, motor vehicles and aerospace. Increases in expenditure have occurred in chemicals, other manufactured products and non-manufactured products. The UK is well down the international league table on expenditure. Add to this the controversy surrounding cuts in science research budgets affecting UK universities and the picture looks even worse. Research and development is the seedcorn for the new technologies, processes, materials and products of the future. Failure in this area is likely to mean that UK companies are less competitive in the future.

According to the OECD, the UK's expenditure on R&D between 1981 and 2007 declined from 2.4 per cent of gross domestic product (GDP) to 1.82 per cent (EU average 1.77 per cent) (OECD 2010). The UK's ranking against other major industrial nations (Group of Seven, or G7, nations), except Italy, has slipped (see Figure 4.6).

Spending on R&D is not the only indicator of technological innovation. The number of patents registered in a country is also a reflection of a healthy R&D culture and advanced economy. As might be expected, the USA and Japan lead the way in patent registrations, but Europe is also a significant contributor via the European Patent Office. However, with multinationals conducting

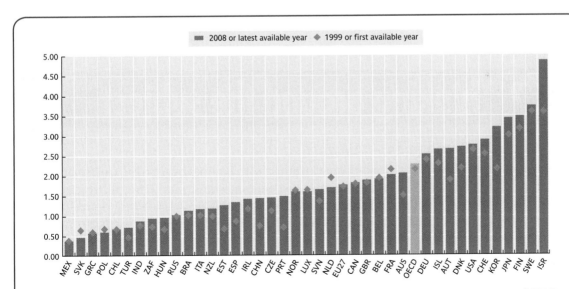

Figure 4.6 Gross domestic expenditure on research and development as a percentage of GDP for OECD countries, 2008.

Source: based on OECD (2010a).

research in many countries and with multiple international registrations, it is becoming more difficult to track expenditure and patents by country.

Having taken the broad macro view of technology, the rest of this chapter looks more specifically at how technology impacts on a business and where it may be applied to improve business operations. The following areas of technology application will be discussed: product design, manufacturing and processing systems, storage and distribution, order and payment processing, materials handling, document handling, computerized information and communications, and office automation (see Figure 4.7).

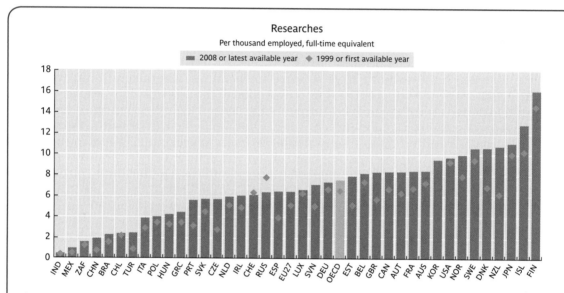

Figure 4.7 Researchers per thousand employed, full-time equivalent, for selected OECD countries.

Source: based on OECD Factbook (2010b).

⟳ Thinking around the subject

Soap powder companies – All washed up?

The soap powder companies are popularly attributed with having invented modern marketing and have continuously been at the forefront of new sales and marketing techniques. But could their progress be undone by recent developments in technology? A South Korean firm, Kyungwon Enterprise Company, is reported to have developed a washing machine that does not use detergent to clean clothes.

According to the company, a device inserted into a washing machine is able to transform water into electrically charged liquid that cleans with the same results as a conventional synthetic detergent. Water is transformed inside the machine by forcing it through layers of special catalysts planted between electrodes. The system utilizes the natural tendency of water to return to a stable state and harnesses it for laundering, deodorizing and killing viruses. The system also promises to cut water consumption and reduce the growing problem of water pollution by detergents. The developers of the system have applied for patents in over 60 countries. How are existing washing machine and detergent manufacturers likely to react? The washing machine manufacturer Hotpoint is reported to have been monitoring developments closely and would doubtless seek a licence to use the technology, or develop an alternative technology not covered by patent.

But what about the detergent manufacturers? Their market is unlikely to disappear overnight. The new system has still to be proven and, even if it is shown to be effective, important segments for detergent could remain out of inertia or simply because the new technology does not cope with all tasks as well as traditional methods. The detergent companies may also embrace the new technology by developing ranges of complementary products, such as fragrant conditioners. Another possibility is that the detergent companies might seek to buy the patents to the new process and then not use them. The inventor of the technology would receive a payout and the detergent companies would continue to sell detergent, but what would be the effects on consumers?

4.6   Product design and development

It is often argued that the life expectancy of products has tended to shorten as technology has advanced. It took radio 30 years, from 1922 to 1952, to reach 50 million users. Television required 13 years to do the same thing. Cable television became available in 1974 and achieved this level of worldwide take-up in ten years. It took the internet approximately five years to reach an estimated 100 million users (*Harris Interactive*: www.harrisinteractive.com). The increasingly rapid pace of technological change means that nearly all companies must have a strategy for developing new products, to replace those that become redundant. Typewriter manufacturers who did not embrace the move towards electronic word processing eventually saw their sales decline sharply. Central to companies' understanding of change in their technological environment is the concept of the **product life cycle** (PLC). This is a means of plotting sales and profits of a product over time (see Figure 4.8) in such a way that different stages in the life cycle can be identified and appropriate marketing strategies applied.

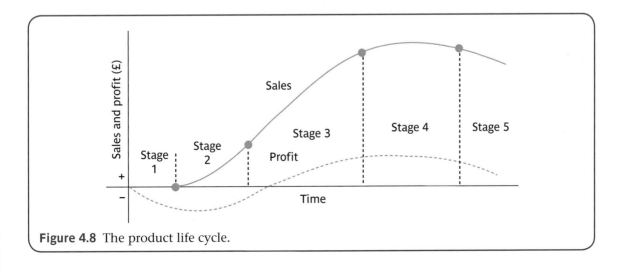

Figure 4.8 The product life cycle.

Five stages in the product life cycle can be identified.

1 *Product development prior to launch:* at this point, sales are zero, and development and investment costs are rising. The new technology may as yet be unproven, so this can be a very risky stage.

2 *Introduction of the product into the market:* this means expensive launch costs and promotion. Profitable sales may take some time to develop.

3 *Growth stage:* this is when the product is fully accepted into the market and healthy profits begin to materialize on the strength of increasing sales.

4 *Maturity:* this refers to the period over which sales growth begins to slow and eventually stop. Profits may begin to decline as increasing competition puts pressure on prices and forces up promotional expenses to defend the market share. New technologies are now mature, and easy for competitors to copy. Patents may have expired.

5 *Decline:* at this point sales begin to fall off and profits decline due to a lower volume of production. New technologies are likely to have appeared that take sales away from the product.

⟳ Thinking around the subject

Do patents encourage or stifle innovation in business?

Patents grant their owner a limited monopoly on the 'idea' defined by the patent. Such monopoly rights restrict competition for the length of the patent, which some may argue is socially harmful (the example of drugs companies pricing AIDS-related drugs out of the reach of most people in developing countries is often mentioned). On the other hand, a patent helps the owner to achieve a return on the research expenditures that went into the discovery of the patented idea. This makes large expenditures for easily copied products, such as pharmaceuticals, easier to justify, arguably increasing research and development activity throughout an industry.

But could granting of patents slow down, rather than encourage, technological development? And are there cases where it may be considered immoral to grant patents for knowledge that should be freely available to all?

One of the biggest public concerns voiced in recent times against the patent system is in relation to the granting of patents by the United States Patent Office (USPTO) for inventions in biotechnology, especially those based on genetic information. The Human Genome Project has sought to identify the structure of DNA, sometimes referred to as the building blocks of life. An understanding of human genes offers the prospect of new medical treatments. But can and should gene sequences be patented? It is reported that, by 2005, four leading private companies had already patented about 750 human genes between them and had applications for a further 20,000 pending. If all of these pending patents were awarded (which is unlikely), those four private companies could own half of the human genome.

There have been conflicting results in studies of the impact on research of gene patents. Is there a risk that a lack of reasonable access to the genetic codes will stifle further basic research? Will it slow down the development of commercial products? In one study, it is reported that

⟶

25 per cent of US university and commercial laboratories were refraining from providing genetic tests or continuing with some of their research for fear of breaching patents or because they lacked the funds to pay licence fees or royalties. Patents appeared to be challenging the traditional academic approach to a shared community of knowledge (Press and Washburn 2003).

On the other hand, turning genetic research into marketable treatments implies a long-term investment, for which there is no certainty of success. In a report on genetics patents, the OECD suggested that patents have the effect of making 'knowledge a tradable commodity which both encourages the circulation of new information and promotes a division of labour'. It found little evidence that growth in the number and complexity of biotechnology patents had caused a breakdown in the patent system or prevented access to inventions by researchers and health service providers. In fact patents and licences for genetic inventions appeared to have stimulated research, knowledge flows and the entry of new technology into markets (OECD 2002).

A distinction can be made between product category (say computers), product forms (e.g. networked, desktop PC, laptop, notebook and PDA) and brands (individual product brands offered by particular manufacturers such as Dell, Toshiba and Apple). Product categories tend to have the longest life cycles and stay in the mature stage for very long periods. They may begin to decline only with significant and fundamental changes in technology (as when typewriters come to be replaced by personal computers) or major shifts in consumer preferences. Product forms tend to show a more classical PLC, with each subsequent form showing a similar history to the previous one. For example, manual typewriters moved through the stages of introduction, growth and maturity, and entered decline as electronic typewriters were introduced. These then followed a similar history until they began to decline as personal computers were introduced. The old product category entered a decline stage as the new product category of personal computers went through a growth stage, and indeed has since gone into maturity. Individual brands follow the shortest life cycle, as companies are constantly attempting to update their products to keep abreast of changes in technology, fashion, customer preferences and competitors' offerings. Rapid advances in technology may mean shortening product life cycles in some industries. In consumer electronics, for example, advances in technology have allowed manufacturers to add more and more product features, and to reduce prices as costs have fallen. Consumer electronic products may have a life expectancy of only 18 months before they are withdrawn and replaced.

Managing the development of new products is a complex and risky business. While many textbooks will identify a linear process, usually comprising about five stages, the reality involves a complex interaction between a number of forces. These external forces comprise technological developments, market demand, competitor activity and possibly government influence. The internal organizational factors include management culture, research and development capabilities, engineering skills, production experience, management competence, access to finance, and marketing ability.

The linear model of the **new-product development (NPD) process** can be seen in Figure 4.9.

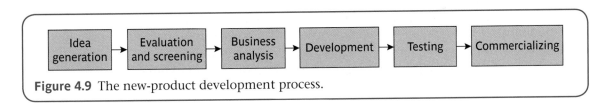

Figure 4.9 The new-product development process.

The process starts with idea generation, which involves the search for new ideas. The next step is evaluation and screening, during which the ideas are assessed for potential. If the company has a short-term planning horizon and a conservative culture, then revolutionary and innovative ideas may be dropped at this stage. As the company focuses on the short term and operates in its comfort zone it may reduce risks but it may also be producing 'me too' products. In doing so it may also miss innovative developments and technological shifts and, as a result, jeopardize its long-term competitive position or even its survival. The purpose of this stage is to reduce the number of ideas and to focus on the further development of those with potential. Before engaging in expensive research and development an initial business analysis should be undertaken to assess the market potential of new ideas. For products involving minor innovation, and aimed at an existing well-defined market, estimating total market potential should be relatively straightforward. But what will be the share taken by a completely new product, especially if it is aimed at a new group of buyers? How will consumers take to the new product? Will distributors like the product? How will competitors react? Will competitors launch a similar product? What price should be charged and how will this affect demand? Is the new product likely to cost more, the same or less than the existing product to make? These are all questions that need to be considered when calculating potential sales and profit.

For those products remaining, the next stage is development. This is where the expenses, mainly associated with research and development and/or engineering, are heaviest. Can the idea and new technology be developed into a workable product that can be produced in volume, at a reasonable cost, and that is practicable for the consumer? The testing stage may involve a number of activities. Testing the functional capabilities of the product may include technical tests, reliability tests and performance tests. Market testing involves testing consumers' and dealers' attitudes to the product. The final decision as to whether to launch the product is made at this stage.

Commercializing is the last stage, and can involve the highest expenditure as the product is prepared for manufacture and launch into the market. Decisions on expected sales, what volume to manufacture, what to contract out and what to manufacture in-house can all be critical. Product decisions, such as the final form of the product, the number of variants to offer, features, size, colours, branding and packaging, all have to be made, as have decisions on pricing and dealer margins. Promotional strategies have to be finalized, and the timing and logistics of the launch planned.

These stages are often presented as sequential linear activities with one stage being completed before the next commences. In reality not all of the new product ideas come together and start the process at the same time. Ideas are generated at odd times and come from a wide variety of sources. The company needs to capture and evaluate these as and when they arise. From here on the company will have a number of products at different stages in the process at any one time. The development of some may be speeded up or slowed down as priorities are reassessed. Neither is the process completed in separate and distinct stages as described above. Some new ideas may come from the company's blue-sky (speculative) research, so a certain amount of 'development' will have been done before the 'evaluation and screening' stage. 'Testing' is likely to begin before the 'development' stage is finished, and planning for 'commercialization' will commence before 'testing' is finished. The important point to note is that there should be formal reviews and reappraisal at regular intervals. Transition periods between the stages identified in the NPD process are appropriate times for such reviews.

There are of course internal barriers to the adoption of new technology-based products. Individuals may be resistant to change in the organizational setting. They may have a fear of new technology itself, or for their job, or the disruption that change may bring. Change may disturb existing management structures, departmental power bases, individual authority and working relationships.

Products should be designed with a view to keeping material, manufacturing, handling and storage costs to a minimum. These issues should be considered at the outset of the design brief and not as an afterthought. Reducing product costs by 5 or 10 per cent can mean huge savings over the life of a product. In many industries **computer-aided design (CAD)** gives more flexibility and a speedier response to customer needs. As production methods may now give greater flexibility, it is possible to produce a wider variety of styles, colours and features based on a basic product. These planned variations should be designed in at the initial design stages, even though they may not be offered for sale until much later.

The new product development process can be extremely complex, with many examples of cost overruns and delayed results (Kim and Wilemon 2003). A key to more effective new-product development activity is close working relationships between marketing and operational functions. Even simple administrative matters such as rapid communication following the results of one stage can help to speed up the process. The complexity of the new-product development process has often led to companies outsourcing the whole process to specialist companies that have developed an expertise in product development and market testing (Howley 2002). The use of an outside consultancy can also be useful where a company's ethos is production orientated and it seeks to bring on board broader marketing skills. It has been noted that brilliant inventors do not necessarily make good marketers of a new product (Little 2002).

4.7 Manufacturing and processing

Technology impacts on manufacturing and processing systems, particularly in computerized numerical control (CNC) machine tools, **computer-aided manufacturing (CAM)**, integrated manufacturing systems (IMS) and **just-in-time (JIT) systems**. With CNC, a machine tool is directly linked to a computer so that the instructions can be stored and repeated. This gives greater reliability and quicker changeover times. CAM involves linking computers to a number of machine tools and assembly robots that are interfaced with computer-controlled material handling systems. Sections of the manufacturing process are thus integrated into the same production control system. CAD/CAM (computer-aided design/computer-aided manufacturing) is where parts designed on a computer can be programmed directly into the machine tool via the same computer system. These systems can save many hours over previous methods involving the separate activities of design, building models and prototypes, and then programming separate machines for production.

Integrated manufacturing systems (IMS) enable a number of CAM sub-systems to be integrated together within a larger computer-controlled system. A number of manufacturers are attempting to integrate the total manufacturing process. This, however, is very difficult to do in practice, as plant and equipment are often of different ages, were designed by different companies and use different control systems. While it is possible to design a total IMS from scratch, the investment costs are likely to be prohibitive for most companies.

JIT systems are designed to limit stockholding and handling costs. A supplier is often expected to deliver components to the right delivery bay, on a specific day and at a specific time. There may be heavy penalties for failing to deliver on time. Components can then be moved directly on to the production floor ready for use on the line. This requires close cooperation between the manufacturer and supplier, and usually is made possible only by the use of computerized information systems and data links.

These developments in technology impact on small companies and large, and on traditional industries such as textiles and shoes, as well as on new ones. Generally speaking, modern manufacturing systems allow production lines to be run with greater flexibility and higher quality, making it easier to produce product variations and allowing a speedier changeover between products, thus minimizing downtime.

Developments in production technology present companies with a number of opportunities for gaining a competitive advantage. First, developments in these areas are likely to contribute to a reduction in costs. Aiming to be a low-cost manufacturer should help in achieving a higher return on investment by allowing a higher margin and/or a higher volume of sales at lower prices. Second, modern manufacturing techniques allow for greater flexibility in production; thus, a wider variety of product variations may be produced without incurring onerous cost penalties. Recent advances in integrated manufacturing systems using computer-controlled industrial robots have meant that carmarkers, for example, can produce totally different models on the same production line. Third, lead times between orders and delivery can be improved. Finally, it is possible to ensure that the quality of the products is more consistent and of a higher standard.

4.8 Supply chain management

The storage and distribution of goods has also benefited from advances in technology. In particular, the increased capacity and reliability of computerized data processing and storage combined with improved data transmission and computer-controlled physical handling systems have led to reductions in costs and improvements in service. It is now possible to hold less stock at all stages in the distribution chain for a given product variety. From a retailer's perspective the amount of stock kept on the sales floor and in the back room can be greatly reduced.

As companies come to rely very heavily on IT systems, any problems in the system can have an adverse effect on logistical and financial operations. During 2001, the children's goods retailer Mothercare opened a new UK distribution centre at Daventry. The aim was to increase the efficiency and effectiveness of deliveries to the company's nationwide store network. In reality, poor implementation of IT systems caused stock to be lost within its system. Instead of getting 'hot' products quickly to the shelves where customers were eager to buy them, they arrived at the shop only after market preferences had changed and the goods had to be sold at discounted 'clearance' prices. As a direct result of its distribution problems, the company was forced to issue a series of profit warnings and its share price slumped, threatening the continued independent existence of the company (Keers 2002).

Retail groups acquiring competitor companies now face a much more difficult task in integrating the newly acquired stores. Previously the takeover focused on re-branding with the new company's logo and house style, selling off old stock and replacement with new, and refurbishment of some stores. Now all tills and local computer systems are likely to need replacing, the newly acquired stores must be networked into the group computer, information and communication systems, and staff need to be trained in the new systems (see Figure 4.10).

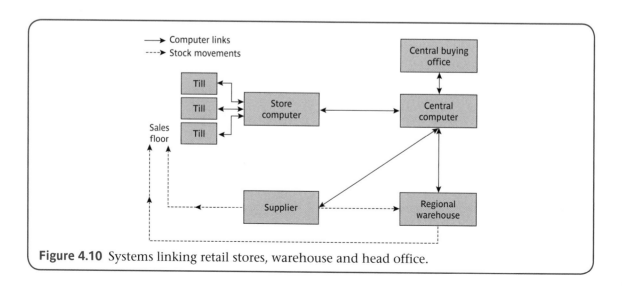

Figure 4.10 Systems linking retail stores, warehouse and head office.

experiential values of virtual reality systems be improved so that users get a greater sense of actually being there? Will virtual tourism become an aspirational first choice, or will it only ever become the second choice when real travel becomes too difficult and expensive? Will the availability of virtual tours whet people's appetites, so that in fact instead of being a substitute for travel, it will encourage even more travel to explore real destinations? If you were managing a museum or gallery in a tourist town, how could you adapt to the needs of virtual tourists?

In this evolving role for the internet, some see a greater need for government control, or at least influence in the development of the internet. The OECD Sacher Report identified three priority areas for governments. The first is for governments actively to support the development of electronic commerce by encouraging the development of the infrastructure. Governments have traditionally controlled telecommunications and television industries by either direct ownership or licensing. Technologies in computing, telecommunications, data networks and television are now converging rapidly. The report recommends that governments should encourage this by modifying regulatory regimes where necessary and by working to commonly agreed international protocols.

organizations. The development of peer-to-peer sites such as youtube and Facebook have challenged many assumptions about the role of traditional advertising, for example. Customer review sites are increasingly becoming an important source of evaluation in the buying decision process, but such sites are much more difficult to control than conventional paid-for advertising. There is also some evidence of websites being used to 'educate' a customer prior to a face-to-face encounter with an organization. For example, one study of medical practitioners showed how patients engaged in virtual, parallel service encounters through the internet, changing the nature of their appointment with the doctor and presenting challenges to medical professionals both in terms of doctor–patient relationships and their professional judgement (Hogg, Laing and Winkelman 2003).

The second recommendation was that all governments should 'raise the visibility of electronic commerce and promote new partnerships with the private sector in order to coordinate technical, economic and political choices'. It is suggested that governments may seek to appoint a Chief Information Officer to coordinate these activities.

The third recommendation was that governments themselves should acquire the skills to participate in the electronic information age. Regulatory issues need to be dealt with urgently and as they arise. Legal issues surrounding the 'definitions, practices and structures' of electronic commerce are now being addressed. International protocols need to be further developed for dealing with consumer protection, fraud, crime prevention, the protection of intellectual property, electronic identity, definitions of residence, liability, auditing, and the control, unauthorized use and protection of databases. The issue of taxation is also of concern, particularly for taxes based on sales. Sales taxes are often refunded to exporters at despatch but re-applied on receipt in the country of importation. These issues have not been fully resolved for internet transactions.

The Economist Intelligence Unit (EIU), working in collaboration with IBM, publishes annual 'e-readiness' ratings for countrie (Economist Intelligence Unit 2010). It defines 'e-readiness' as a measure of the quality of a country's information and communications technology (ICT) infrastructure, and the ability of its customers, businesses and governments to use ICT to their benefit. When a country uses ICT to conduct more of its activities, the economy can become more transparent and efficient. E-readiness takes into account a wide range of factors, which include connectivity and technology infrastructure (20 per cent), business environment (15 per cent), social and cultural environment (15 per cent), legal environment (10 per cent), government policy and vision (15 per cent), and consumer and business adoption (25 per cent) (Economist Intelligence Unit 2010). Denmark reclaimed the world's e-readiness leadership in the EIU's 2009 rankings, a position it had relinquished to the USA in the previous year. According to the 2009 e-readiness rankings, Scandinavian countries have, among other attributes, high levels of ICT usage – following Denmark's first ranking were Sweden (second), Norway (fourth) and Finland (tenth). The UK was in 13th position (Table 4.1).

Table 4.1   E-readiness of top ten ranked countries, 2009.

Country	Rank
Denmark	1
Sweden	2
Netherlands	3
Norway	4
USA	5
Australia	6
Singapore	7
Hong Kong	=8
Canada	=8
Finland	10

Source: based on Economist Intelligence Unit: e-readiness rankings 2009, the usage imperative, http://graphics.eiu.com/pdf/E-readiness%20rankings.pdf

4.14.2 Governments and the development of a knowledge-based economy

Although no single individual organization can own or control the internet, there have been calls for governments to become involved in promoting, managing and regulating the internet environment. Some countries with a tradition of government media censorship, such as China, Iran and North Korea, have no qualms about regulating use of the internet by their citizens. There have, for example, been many documented cases of the Chinese government seeking to block access to search engines such as Google. In western countries with a democratic tradition, the issue of government involvement in the internet can be much more complex. In the early days of the internet, many western governments were reluctant to interfere with the free-market nature of the internet, besides which the borderless nature of the internet made it very difficult for individual countries to regulate it. As an example, gambling is restricted in many American states, and the US government has found it very difficult to prevent American citizens getting access to gambling websites, most of which are located in foreign countries and made available to US citizens through the internet. The US Constitution and operational difficulties have made it almost unthinkable that the US government would try to block access to gambling sites, therefore it has resorted to trying to control them through indirect means – for example, by making it illegal for American banks to use credit cards to pay for online gambling services, or prosecuting the owners of offshore gambling sites when they set foot in American territory.

Nevertheless, there are many measures that governments can take to encourage the development of e-business. A report by the UK research and consultancy group Gartner identified a number of pressing challenges for the EU in its attempts to create an e-commerce friendly environment.

- Anti-trust authorities will have to resolve, more rapidly than at present, complex competition issues raised by mergers in the media and telecoms sectors, electronic marketplaces, wireless portals and public service providers.

- Enterprises will need more flexible employment schemes and laws to cope with skills shortages in the information technology sector. Employers need the ability to import and outsource skills as required, and a clearer legislative framework for teleworking.

- Tax regulations need to be brought up to date, to recognize the presence of internet transactions. The Gartner study predicted that the difference between European and US internet tax schemes would become a major source of friction in international trade.

- In order to boost consumers' trust in e-commerce and reduce legal uncertainty for enterprises, governments need to develop privacy laws that are relevant to the internet.

The report painted a picture of national governments throwing money at the microenvironment of **electronic commerce (e-commerce)**, such as grants for computer training, often displacing money that could readily be provided by the private sector. Developing the macroenvironment for e-commerce throughout the EU is a much bigger challenge. The question remains as to just what it is possible for governments to do to create an e-commerce-friendly environment. Is responsibility for achieving it best left to the EU rather than national governments? Or is even the EU too small a unit for making decisions, when the internet is progressively breaking down national boundaries?

⟳ Thinking around the subject

The internet and the law of unintended consequences

'The world will never be the same again.' This was the bold message being proclaimed by many pundits at the dawn of the internet age. In one sense, they were quite right, because the internet has had significant effects on how individuals have gone about their lives. Business processes have been transformed, often resulting in great cost savings and improvements in service to customers. But, in many respects, the nature of the change that has resulted from the development of the internet has not quite been what was expected. The complex interaction between the technological, social and economic environments has produced some unexpected consequences of technological development.

Consider the following predictions, which were made in 2000 when 'dotcom' mania was at its height.

- Predictions were made that there would be less commuting as people would work from home, using the internet to communicate with their work colleagues. Traffic congestion would disappear and commuter rail services would lose customers. In fact, technology has allowed many people to choose a pleasant residential environment and to live much further away from their work, because they now have to travel to the office on only a couple of days each week rather than every day. Overall, the travelling distances of many people in this situation have actually increased, resulting in more rather than less total commuting.

- Conferences were predicted to disappear in favour of videoconferencing. Why bother travelling to a meeting or conference when you could meet 'virtually' from the comfort of your own desk or armchair, and at lower cost? However, face-to-face conferences have

⟳

continued to prosper. The technology that causes many people to work in isolation may have indirectly contributed to a desire to counter this with more face-to-face meetings with a greater social content.

■ High-street shops were being written off in 2000 when, quite extraordinarily, the pure internet company lastminute.com had a market capitalization value far in excess of the 110-outlet Debenhams store. The convenience of shopping in the high street or at out-of-town shopping centres, and the problems of arranging the home deliveries of internet suppliers were underestimated by advocates of internet-based shopping.

■ Pre-dating all of these predictions has been the expectation that we will need to work fewer hours, as we live in a world of leisure where machines do the work, leaving consumers with more leisure time. In reality, average working hours have tended to increase in recent years, not fall.

We seem to have an inherent tendency to overstate the short-term effects of technological change, but to understate the long-term effects on our behaviour. With the development of new technologies enabling high-speed mobile internet services, further predictions were being made in 2008. Would we really want to download full-length feature films to watch on our mobile phones? Would we really want to surf the net while travelling on a train? Would there be unforeseen 'killer applications' such as SMS text messaging, which was almost left out of the specification of first-generation mobile phones because no useful role for it was foreseen? Perhaps the long-term effects of the internet may be more subtle by contributing to individuals' sense of connectedness with narrowly selected commercial and social groups, no matter where they may be located, while the sense of community with diverse groups of people forced to live together in close proximity may be reduced.

The unforeseen consequences of the internet emphasize how difficult it can be for organizations to understand the consequences of new technologies. These examples demonstrate the importance of understanding the linkages between different elements of the business environment, so developments in the technological environment can be sensibly understood only in conjunction with changes in the social environment.

4.14.3 E-retailing

At the height of the dotcom boom in 2000, the hype cycle in relation to e-retailing had reached its peak. At that time, predictions were being made that conventional shops would soon be eclipsed by online shopping. Why would a retailer want to incur the costs of running a network of shops in expensive retail locations? And why would customers struggle through traffic jams and crowded car parks to buy something that they could order from the comfort of their own home? The appeal of e-retailing might have seemed irresistible to some, and indeed there has been remarkable growth in the value of retail sales through the internet, although there is now some sign that the rate of increase is slowing down (Table 4.2). Some retailers have closed a number of branches or reduced their salesforce, and instead offer customers access to their product range via a website. Several UK suppliers of books, music, computer games and flowers have the logistical support to develop their businesses on the internet.

While e-retailing can offer cost savings to the seller and added convenience to the buyer, a number of challenges remain:

■ small orders
■ high transport costs

Table 4.2 Value of online retail sales for selected countries for 2009 and 2010.

	Online sales 2009 (bn)	Online sales 2010 (bn)	% increase 2009 vs 2010	Online sales per customer per year	Average number of items purchased per year	Online share of retail trade 2009
UK	£38.0	£42.7	12.4%	£1,101	37	9.5%
Germany	£29.7	£34.8	17.2%	£680	22	6.9%
France	£22.0	£28.9	31.4%	£884	20	4.9%
Benelux	£7.4	£9.0	22.8%	£630	16	3.5%
Italy	£7.3	£8.8	20.5%	£830	17	0.8%
Spain	£5.6	£7.0	25.0%	£692	12	1%
Denmark	£3.5	£4.1	17.9%	£1,078	24	6.1%
Sweden	£3.4	£4.0	18.0%	£712	20	4.8%
Switzerland	£3.4	£4.0	21.0%	£771	19	4.8%
Norway	£2.9	£3.5	20.7%	£979	13	6.3%
Finland	£2.3	£2.8	23.0%	£867	18	4.9%
Poland	£2.2	£3.0	36.4%	£321	10	2%
Total/Avg	£127.7	£152.8	19.6%	£774	20	4.7

Source: adapted from A.C. Nielson Global Trends in Online Shopping (June 2010).

- goods not compatible with the letter/mail box
- difficulty in offering a timed delivery window
- most economical delivery times for companies are 9 am to 5 pm, Monday to Friday, when the customer is most likely to be out
- difficulty of returning goods.

The delivery of goods to the final consumer has not shown the productivity gains that internet-based ordering has achieved (see Yrjölä 2001). This is probably not surprising when it is remembered that home delivery remains a labour-intensive activity in which two of the main costs – labour and transport – are likely to continue to increase in real terms. We should not forget that, in the UK, the milkman has almost disappeared because efficiency of delivery could not be improved relative to the cost of consumers collecting milk from large, efficient supermarkets. The problem of buyers being at home to accept goods is also one that has been slow to resolve. Retailers have experimented with 24-hour collection points at local convenience stores, and delivery companies have experimented with evening and weekend deliveries. In the UK, the Royal Mail announced in October 2010 that it was to experiment with evening deliveries of mail to cater for busy professionals who are out at work all day and unable to receive deliveries at the time when retailers and delivery companies have traditionally made their deliveries.

There are also many high-involvement goods where buyers feel more comfortable being able to see and feel the goods before they commit to a purchase. When buying clothes, many buyers would prefer to try the items on and to feel the texture of the clothes. Some retailers have introduced 'virtual reality' systems to help simulate the shop buying experience – for example, some retailers allow customers to develop their personal avatar, which they can then use to judge how an item of clothing would look on them. Despite a lot of hype about the potential of virtual reality systems, and hope that these could be used in a peer-to-peer environment, progress appears to have been slow. Uptake of the virtual reality social network website 'Second Life' is reported to be lower than original expectations predicted.

Retailing often fulfils a social function – for example, a group of friends may 'have a day out shopping', which might include stopping for coffee, having a meal and sharing experiences of new purchases. Many have doubted the ability of the internet to replace this social function, even with further development of virtual reality peer-to-peer networks.

As e-retailing has developed, customers' expectations have risen. When ordering online, they expect to have prices and stock confirmed, as well as a delivery date and preferably the time. Customers also expect to be told of any delays, particularly when they are waiting in for the delivery.

Although many companies have set up internet retail sites in an attempt to cut out intermediaries, routes to market for e-retailers have become increasingly complex. E-retailing can be extremely competitive, with customers being just a click away from a competitor – they don't even have to make the effort of walking into a competitor's shop. Getting a customer into your site increasingly involves the use of online intermediaries, including search engines, affiliate sites and price comparison sites. These would usually seek a percentage of the sales revenue, or a payment per 'click-through' in return for providing the link to the retailer's site.

4.15 Data security and privacy

Technology has undoubtedly allowed businesses to do things that were previously unimaginable – for example, in the way that data are handled and analysed. While much of this development has been beneficial to companies and their customers, some commentators have pointed to more harmful consequences for personal privacy and security.

Data protection has become a very big issue, as it is not just companies that can easily collect and manipulate information – so too can criminals. There is also concern on the part of some consumers that their personal data may be misused, if not in a criminal way certainly in a way that they would consider unethical. These concerns have grown with developments in technology. When personal records were entirely paper based, it was difficult to appropriate data for improper uses. If paper records were lost, they were probably only likely to turn up in a rubbish skip or a place that only a small number of people have access to. The bank customer could be reasonably confident that their personal information would not get out of their local branch, and it would be difficult for anybody else to get hold of their records. Today, their personal information is likely to be held on servers that are accessible remotely by a range of authorized employees.

Unfortunately, unauthorized people may be able to access personal information held on databases. Instead of having to break in laboriously to several bank branches to obtain large volumes of customer data, there have been many reported cases (and probably many more unreported) of skilled hackers being able to get into a bank's database and view the records of thousands or even millions of customers. Where customer information is held on transportable discs, huge amounts of data can accidentally or deliberately end up in the wrong hands. In November 2007, many people in the UK were concerned to hear that the government had 'lost' two CDs containing personal information on 25 million recipients of government benefits. There was concern that this information could be used by criminals wrongly to impersonate another person and obtain credit or benefits to which they were not entitled.

Within the EU, the 1981 European Convention for Individuals with regard to Automatic Processing of Personal Data, implemented through Directive 95/46/EC provides a framework for data privacy and security. This has been implemented in the UK in the 1988 Data Protection Act, and policed by the Data Protection Commissioner. The Act covers electronically stored data, which can be used to identify a living person, including names, birthday and anniversary dates, addresses, telephone numbers, fax numbers, email addresses, etc. A number of principles guide companies' use of data, and require, among other things, that personal data shall be processed fairly and lawfully, and shall not be used for any purpose that is not compatible with the original purpose. There is a requirement for companies to keep accurate records that are not unnecessarily excessive in detail, and data shall not be kept for longer than is necessary for the purpose of collecting them. Appropriate technical and organizational measures must be taken against unauthorized or unlawful processing of personal data and against its accidental loss or destruction. The Data Protection Act 1988 and the Freedom of Information Act 2000 give some rights of access to data.

The internet has created problems for consumers in verifying who they are actually dealing with. There have been many cases of sham online companies that have set up in business with enticing offers, but have rapidly disappeared without trace. Some have been set up to obtain customers' personal information, which has then been used fraudulently, after the company has disappeared. But it is not just customers who should be wary of rogue companies, companies also need to be wary of rogue customers. In a real-life environment, a company can see who is coming into its site and remove visibly disruptive elements, such as drunks disturbing the atmosphere of a restaurant. In the case of online service processes, it can be much more difficult to judge whether visitors to a company's website are benign or malicious. Malicious visitors may disrupt a company's service processes by planting viruses, bombing it with mass emails or disrupting the codes of its operating system. The reasons for this action may be a grudge against the company, or simply the challenge for a computer hacker of beating a system. Where a company is dependent on online transactions for the bulk of its revenue, the effects of such malicious intrusions can be devastating, not only resulting in a short-term loss of revenue, but long-term harm to its brand reputation where customers' details are obtained or used in an unauthorized way. In designing the online environment, companies must strike a balance between making a site easily accessible to all, and difficult for those with malicious intentions.

Case study:
Will the bank of the future be 'mobile'?

By Nicole Koenig-Lewis, Swansea University, and Alexander Moll, Visual Identity AG

© David Clark

Internet banking is now taken for granted by many people, who may be relieved at not having to visit a bank branch or use a telephone call centre to undertake many banking transactions. Mobile banking ('m-banking') is probably ten years behind internet banking in its development. In ten years' time, will we be taking mobile banking similarly for granted?

Whenever any new banking technology comes along, there are sceptics who doubt that the new technology will catch on with the public. When ATM machines first appeared, many people thought they would never be popular because people liked to go in to a branch and deal with a human being. In the late 1990s, when the internet was only beginning to catch the public's imagination, doubters expressed major concerns about privacy, security, download speeds and access to the internet. When Egg bank launched its then revolutionary online banking service in 1998, even Egg itself turned out to have been unduly cautious as prospective customers appeared in unexpectedly high numbers, crashing its servers and swamping its telephone lines.

Mobile phones have become an essential part of our lives. We have adopted the phone as a personal organizer, as a camera and music player to consume and share music, pictures, games, ringtones, etc. A report by Juniper, for example, highlighted that many young people would not leave home without their mobile phone (Wilcox 2009b). But what is happening with mobile banking?

More recently, high hopes have been held for m-banking, following the more general development of mobile commerce, which in turn has been helped by the appearance of sophisticated, easy-to-use smartphones such as the iPhone. M-banking enables customers to access their bank accounts through mobile devices to check their balance or to conduct financial transactions. The range of services that can be undertaken while mobile is likely to increase, and many have suggested that mobile phones are likely to evolve as ubiquitous payment devices, allowing a mobile phone to be used in a similar way to a credit card (Wilcox 2009a). But will the growth of m-banking be as swift as the previous growth of online banking? Some critics have argued that banks have less to gain from promoting m-banking than they had from promoting the first generation of internet banking. It has been claimed that m-banking does not provide significant cost saving benefits for banks in comparison to those that can be achieved by migrating customers from traditional banking methods to online banking (Laukkanen *et al.* 2007). If consumers do not see advantages in m-banking, will banks significantly increase the allocation of resources to support it?

Although phones have now achieved very high levels of ownership in most developed countries (with more mobile phones than people in the UK), doubters have pointed out that most users of smartphones (and not-so-smart phones) rarely use them to their full capacity, and the majority of phones that are capable of internet browsing are never actually connected to the internet (ICT Statistics 2009).

Forecasting the likely uptake of new technologies is vital for the rapidly changing communication sector, where new applications/services appear daily. However, these forecasts are very difficult to make and there are many cases of inaccurate forecasting. For example, in the 1980s many experts failed to predict the rapid adoption of mobile phones. Also the uptake of texting was completely unexpected. On the other hand, picture phones and video calling have largely failed to take off, while Bluetooth adoption has been much slower than predicted.

In the short life of m-commerce, forecasters appear to have had only limited success in accurately predicting take-up of m-banking, which reportedly still does not meet industry expectations (Kim *et al.* 2009). Forrester Research reported in 2009 that only 4 per cent of the nearly 25 million Bank of America online customers were active users of m-banking (Khan 2008). A recent study by the Mobile Marketing Association revealed that, while m-banking is gaining popularity, it is still far away from becoming mainstream, as only 14 per cent of UK adult consumers, and 9 per cent of French and German consumers, use mobile phones for banking, with SMS being the most popular medium for viewing account balances (Mobile Marketing Association and Lightspeed Research 2010). However, these figures are higher for young consumers aged between 18 and 34, with 24 per cent of UK young people and 20 per cent of German young people already engaging in m-banking (Mobile Marketing Association and Lightspeed Research 2010). It seems that young people are more predisposed to adopt m-commerce services in general than other internet users because these services are usually low-cost entertainment services (e.g. ringtones, songs), which fit with their lifestyle (Bigne *et al.* 2005).

Many predictions of the likely take-up of m-banking have been made. For example, Juniper Research in 2007 suggested that, worldwide, the number of consumers using m-banking would reach 816 million by 2011, which would be a tenfold increase on the number using these services in 2007 (Goode 2008). In addition, it has been predicted that by the end of 2011 more than 150 million subscribers worldwide would have used their mobile phone not only for banking information services but also for transactional m-banking services (Wilcox 2009b). In making predictions, analysts have tried to draw comparisons with previous adoption patterns for new technology, which have typically got off to a slow start as they target relatively high-income, innovative segments and eventually become affordable to all. In an attempt to improve forecasts, models of consumer adoption have been applied, most notably the Technology Acceptance Model (TAM) and Innovation Diffusion Theory (IDT). These models are not without their problems – for example, it has been pointed out that the

TAM typically explains only about 40 per cent of variance in purchase intention (Venkatesh and Davis 2000).

In western countries, m-banking adoption has been moving slowly and it might therefore at first sight seem surprising that the West lags far behind some developing countries such as Kenya and South Africa. In Kenya, about 7 million people use the M-Pesa service, which was launched by Safaricom in partnership with Vodafone in 2007 and allows customers to use their mobile phone to pay bills, deposit cash and send cash to other mobile phone users. The adoption of the M-Pesa service has been speedy, with 11,000 new registrations per day during 2009. Even though the average transaction per person is very small, $1.9 billion have been moved in person-to-person transactions since the launch of the service (Mwangi 2009).

This rapid adoption of the M-Pesa service in Kenya can be largely explained by the lack of a landline telephone network and a poorly developed banking infrastructure. The Financial Access Survey 2009 shows that only 23 per cent of the Kenyan adult population have a bank account but 48 per cent own a mobile phone, with the rate of ownership rising to 72.8 per cent in urban areas and 80.4 per cent in Nairobi (FSD Kenya and Central Bank of Kenya 2009). Furthermore, Africans with bank accounts have to pay high charges for moving cash around. M-Pesa provides a service that allows the safe transfer of cash without facing high costs. Setting up an account is straightforward. Similar successful m-banking examples exist in other non-western countries – for example, Globe Telecom's GCash service is available in the Philippines, which transforms the mobile phone into a virtual wallet for secure, quick and convenient money transactions.

In Europe the situation is different with fewer incentives to use m-banking services as there are a range of digitized payment methods already accessible for bank customers. Thus there is a trend for banks to offer services that are unique to m-banking customers. NatWest, for example, launched a mobile banking service that allows Polish workers in the UK to send money home (Montia 2008). According to one survey, other m-banking services of interest to customers are geo-location, which leads customers to their nearest ATM or bank branch, and the use of the mobile phone to make in-store payments, and to receive deposit and withdrawal notices (Mobile Marketing Association and Lightspeed Research 2010).

The mobile phone is the one piece of technology that most people worldwide own. Technology providers and financial institutions believe that m-banking will one day reach a critical tipping point, after which it will become mainstream. But what will it take to reach this tipping point? Will it be the availability of even more sophisticated, useful phones? Will it occur when consumers overcome their fears about the security of mobile banking and recognize a new generation of phones as really easy to use? Will widespread adoption occur only when mobile phones become widely used as easy payment devices, making it easy for a customer to use their phone to pay for a bus ticket or a drink in a bar? Or will the tipping point occur only when banks put serious resources into the further development of m-banking?

QUESTIONS

1 Discuss the causes of uncertainty in forecasts of levels of consumer adoption of new technology-based services such as m-banking.

2 Identify methods by which a bank could seek to improve the accuracy of its forecasts of take-up of m-banking.

3 Discuss the concept of a 'tipping point' in the adoption of new technology-based services. What factors do you consider would contribute to a tipping point for m-banking? How are these likely to differ between western and non-western countries?

Summary

This chapter has considered technological change from the macro perspective and examined the impact of technology on different aspects of business at the micro level. In both instances the relevance of technological change to business success has been stressed. At the macro level of technological change, the key points to remember concern the demand-technology life cycle. This will be influenced by the level of R&D expenditure, not only in a particular industry but also in related and sometimes unrelated industries. The fusion and interaction of different technologies results in new applications and processes which eventually may give rise to whole new industries. Technology permeates through from academic and research institutions into industry, from one industry to another, and from one economy to another.

At the micro level, this chapter has considered the impact of technology on a company's products and operations: product design and development, manufacturing and processing; storage and distribution; order and payment processing; and information and communication systems via electronic business. Managers should seek to improve the efficiency of business operations and also to ensure that the benefits are passed on to the customer. These customer benefits may include better pre-order services, such as product availability and specification, information, faster quotations, quicker design customization and shorter delivery times.

The technological environment is a constantly changing one. In many industries during the 2000s and beyond, change will be the norm rather than the exception. Companies that focus on customer needs, competitor activity and technological developments, rather than simply aiming to sell what the factory makes, are more likely to succeed.

There is a close link between this chapter and **Chapter 8**, which looks at networks and relationships between companies. The use of technology to improve supply chain efficiency is often a key element of business-to-business relationships. The interrelationship between technology and society is stressed in **Chapter 3** and this chapter has explored not only technology's response to changes in society, but also the effects of changing technology on social values.

Technology has opened up many opportunities for businesses to enter global markets, and these are discussed in more detail in **Chapter 14**.

Finally, issues of privacy and security surrounding new technologies have attracted the attention of the law (**Chapter 6**) and raised ethical concerns (**Chapter 5**).

Key Terms

Article numbering (145)

Computer-aided design (CAD) (143)

Computer-aided manufacturing (CAM) (143)

Demand-technology life cycle (129)

Electronic commerce (e-commerce) (159)

Electronic data interchange (EDI) (155)

Electronic point of sale (EPOS) (146)

Hype cycle (132)

Internet (155)

Just-in-time (JIT) system (143)

New product development (NPD) process (141)

Product life cycle (139)

Research and development (R&D) (136)

Technological fusion (128)

Technology transfer (129)

Online Learning Centre

To help you grasp the key concepts of this chapter, explore the extra resources posted on the Online Learning Centre at *www.mcgraw-hill.co.uk/palmer*. Among other helpful resources there are chapter-by-chapter test questions, revision notes and web links.

Chapter review questions

1 Discuss the extent to which marketing managers should be involved in the R&D process. What should their role be?

2 Critically discuss the role of governments in fostering an R&D culture and in encouraging technological development?

3 Using examples, discuss ways in which new technologies have altered social relationships.

Activities

1 Assume you are working for a multinational manufacturer of electrical goods. Your main retailer in the UK has had a number of your vacuum cleaners returned recently with a serious malfunction. It appears to be a problem with the on/off switch. The product is assembled at the company's plant in Spain, but the on/off switch is manufactured in China. However, the miniature circuit board in the vacuum could have been made in Japan or Korea (two suppliers). It may be just one batch of switches or circuit boards that was faulty. To recall all the products sold in the UK in recent months would be extremely expensive. Also it is not known as yet if the vacuums sold in other countries are affected, or if other products (such as hair-dryers) use the same switch or other switch designs with the same circuit board.

   How would you trace the identity of the batch of vacuums and other products affected before enacting a product recall?

2 In the pub one Friday evening two men were overheard discussing electronic shopping. Both men worked in the computer industry, had lots of 'kit' at home, and had been connected to the World Wide Web for some time. They were exchanging views about the latest developments on the internet, and getting quite excited about the possibilities of buying their weekly groceries over the net and having them delivered. This would take the drudgery out of supermarket shopping, they agreed. Both men worked long hours and when asked the last time they had seen the inside of a supermarket, neither could remember. Both were married. One wife, although quite capable of holding a good job, did not work at all, had no need to work, and was quite happy to look after the family (two children) and do the supermarket shopping. The other was in a very similar position, although she had taken up part-time work, as the children were a little older. Neither woman was much taken with computers and thought that being tied to a computer all day and half the evening would be a life of drudgery.

   Discuss the advantages and limitations of online grocery shopping in the social context described above.

3 Now revisit the case of online shopping and identify the technological innovations that have made this method of shopping a sustainable business model. Think carefully about technology innovation at all points in the supply chain.

Further Reading

The following provide contemporary insights into the role of innovation in organizations and the relationship between business and R&D.

Crawford, C.M. and Di Benedetto, A. (2011) *New Product Management*, 10th edn, Boston, MA, McGraw-Hill Higher Education.

Dodgson, M. Gann, D. and Salter, A. (2008), *Management of Technological Innovation: Strategy and Practice*, Oxford, Oxford University Press.

Javi, R. Triandis, H.C. and Weick, C.W. (2010) *Managing Research, Development and Innovation: Managing the Unmanageable*, 3rd edn, New Jersey, John Wiley & Sons.

McGourty, J. Tarshis, L.A. and Dominick, P. (2009) Managing innovation: lessons from world class organizations', *International Journal of Technology Management*, Vol. 11, No. 3/4, pp. 354–368.

Trott, P. (2008) *Innovation Management and New Product Development*, 4th edn, London, FT Prentice Hall.

There are now lots of books about e-business, ranging from textbooks to quick 'how to' books.

Introduction

'The customer is king' is a traditional business maxim and, according to this, everything that a company does should be geared towards satisfying the needs of its customers. But should commercial organizations also have responsibilities to the public at large? The question is becoming increasingly important, as commercial organizations have never before been subjected to such critical assessment from those who are quick to identify the harmful side effects of their activities. There have been many recent cases of large organizations, such as Enron, WorldCom and Parmalat, that failed to govern themselves in a responsible manner – for example, by exaggerating the value of their assets in a way that misleads investors and may ultimately leave suppliers with unpaid bills, customers with undelivered goods and services, employees without a job and government without tax revenues due. Many more have been accused of harming the environment through noxious emissions.

It is often suggested that business organizations should act in a responsible manner, not only to members of their immediate microenvironment, but also to society at large. There are philosophical and pragmatic reasons for this.

Philosophically, models of a responsible society would have companies doing their bit to contribute towards a just and fair society, alongside the contributions of other institutions such as the family and the Church. More pragmatically, commercial organizations need to take account of society's values because, if they do not, they may end up isolated from the values of the customers, employees and investors that they seek to attract.

Any discussion of corporate social responsibility should recognize that organizations typically produce a wide range of external costs. These represent resources (such as clean water or fresh air) that are used in the organization's production processes, but the costs of which are borne not by the company, but by somebody else. A simple example would be a factory emitting noxious fumes from its chimney. It could save on production costs by not cleaning its emissions, but in this case it has simply passed on some form of cost to its neighbours, who must now suffer an unpleasant environment. The precise costs may be very difficult to quantify, but could include short- and long-term health problems, and damage to buildings.

The opposite of external costs produced by organizations are external benefits. These are benefits that the organization produces, but for which it does not get any direct income benefit. A very simple example would be a company that puts a large clock on the outside of its building for the convenience of passers-by. This is an external benefit, in the sense that the company cannot charge users for the benefits of being able to tell the time.

As societies develop economically and socially, there are rising expectations about the level of external benefits that organizations should provide to society. At the same time, societies have become increasingly critical of organizations' external costs. Social pressure, combined with legislation, has had the effect of making organizations bear a higher proportion of their external costs, so that they become conventional internal costs. We will see below how, in the case of external costs caused by greenhouse gas emissions, a system of carbon trading has attempted to internalize the cost of emissions.

Rising consumer incomes have resulted in the external benefits provided by consumer purchases becoming a larger element of the total product offering, which consumers use to judge competing products in increasingly competitive markets. Consumers' changing evaluation of a company's external costs and benefits can be illustrated using the framework of Maslow's hierarchy of needs. This framework holds that individuals are motivated by their lowest level of unsatisfied need. According to Maslow, when individuals' basic physiological and social needs are satisfied, higher-order needs become motivators that influence their buying behaviour. Fifty years ago, a packet of washing powder would have largely satisfied a need to produce tangible cleanliness. With most of the population being able to afford cleaning powders that could produce this effect, emphasis moved to promoting washing powder on the basis of satisfying social needs. So one brand was differentiated from another by signifying greater care for the family, or was seen to produce results that were visibly valued by peer groups. Today, manufacturers of washing powder recognize that a significant segment seeks to buy more than the packet of washing powder – they seek also to buy a chance to change the world by reducing ecological damage caused by washing powders containing high levels of harmful phosphates. Although Maslow's framework has been extensively criticized, especially on account of its preoccupation with western value systems, it reminds us that our views on what is considered socially responsible can change over time.

Criticisms of the concept of corporate responsibility take two forms: philosophical and pragmatic.

At a *philosophical* level, it has been argued by the followers of Milton Friedman that firms should concentrate on doing what they are best at: making profits for their owners. The idea of social responsibility by firms has been criticized as it would allow business organizations to become too dominant in society. By this argument, any attempt by firms to contribute to social causes is a form of taxation on the customers of their businesses. It would be better for firms to leave such money in the hands of their customers, so that customers themselves can decide what worthy causes they wish to support. Alternatively, donations to social causes should be handled by government, which is democratically accountable, unlike business firms. There is particular strength in this argument where benefits are provided by private-sector organizations that have considerable monopoly power, such as utility companies. It may be too simplistic to say that customers voluntarily buy a company's products and therefore consent to the payment of social contributions. In reality, many markets are uncompetitive and customers may have very little choice.

At a *pragmatic* level, critics see corporate responsibility as being essentially about short-term and cynical manipulation by a company of its principal stakeholders. There is no such thing as altruism, and firms go out of their way to act responsibly, not for the benefit of society, but to improve corporate performance. As examples, litter bins sponsored by a fast-food restaurant, the provision of recycling points by supermarkets and donations to animal charities are not altruism but simply a new way of buying awareness of a company and liking of it, using values that are currently fashionable. It has been suggested that organizations may be quite keen to support good causes that are popular with the public in general, or the particular groups of customers that they target. Many consumer goods companies, for example, have supported child and animal welfare charities, knowing that this will be popular with their target audiences.

However, there may be other groups, such as refugees or the mentally ill, that represent even more deserving causes for an organization's activities, but in general these groups have been shunned by the corporate sector.

Governments have recently sought to pass on responsibility for many aspects of social provision (e.g. sponsorship of the arts). Is there a danger in expecting commercial organizations to undertake such a role? They tend to be very selective in terms of which sections of society they support.

Collectively, consumers represent roughly the same group as the electorate. Electors have always expected government to act in the best public interest, otherwise – in the extreme – the government will not be re-elected. Many consumers are developing similar expectations towards the suppliers of private-sector goods. If they do not feel the company is acting in the public interest, their goods will not be purchased. In taking on this role, some have suggested that private-sector companies are becoming more important than governments in setting the agenda for ecological reform. There are examples of where this has happened, such as the development of organically grown vegetables and the replacement of CFCs in aerosols. These initiatives originated primarily with the private sector rather than the government. However, there is a danger that corporate responsibility initiatives may follow short-term popular trends, rather than being based on a more rigorous scientific analysis.

This chapter begins by discussing challenges to the simple notion that markets are unquestionably the best means of allocating resources within society. Challenges to this are discussed, particularly the apparent failure of market-based mechanisms to address concerns about ecological harm caused by consumers, pursuit of goods and services, and firms' pursuit of profits. This chapter will conclude by identifying the key stakeholder groups that business organizations should have responsibilities towards, and discusses issues of governance and ethics for regulating the relationships between these stakeholders.

5.2 Challenges to the market-led business environment

The dominant assumption in western societies has been that a market-orientated business environment is better than one that involves government dominating decisions about the allocation of resources. Through what Adam Smith called the 'invisible hand' of market forces, resources would be allocated according to the preferences of consumers. Government alone could not second-guess consumers' preferences; instead, a market-based environment for allocating resources allows millions of people making everyday transactions to decide through their spending power how resources are allocated. We will explore in Chapter 11 the principles of market forces and how this 'invisible hand' worked to bring about an apparently efficient allocation of resources.

Market-based allocation of resources has come under increasing critical scrutiny in recent years, and it must not be assumed that a market-based approach is necessarily the best approach to making all goods and services available. Markets are motivated by the self-interest of individuals and companies. Without this self-interest, there will be little motivation for firms to provide better goods and services, workers to work harder and consumers to aspire to a higher level of consumption. But some moral philosophers have drawn a fine line between self-interest that helps markets work more effectively for the benefit of all, and a self-interest that becomes greed and a divisive force that undermines communities and is eventually self-destructive. Furthermore, there are many goods and services that money used in market-based transactions cannot – or should not – be able to buy.

The moral philosopher Michael Sandel has described a process by which markets triumphed during the three decades from the 1980s, but, in doing so, undermined many vital public interests such as civic security, national defence, and health and welfare, which increasingly became outsourced, and delivered or created through market-based mechanisms. Markets may lead individuals to commodify public services and undermine a sense of shared pride and moral righteousness in services provided for the community (Sandel 2009).

In this section, we will consider a number of areas of goods and service provision where the debate about the role of marketing is greatest: 'essential' public services; the provision of services by not-for-profit organizations; and the debate about the environmental impacts of market-based competition.

5.2.1 Essential public services

What is considered marketable varies between cultures and has changed over time. In the UK, some goods and services that were previously considered suited only to distribution through centrally planned methods are now routinely distributed using market-based mechanisms. Electricity supply, for example, was for a long time centrally planned with no semblance of a market. Today, several electricity-generating companies, specialist energy retailers and even supermarkets vie with one another to sell gas and electricity to consumers. Some countries would consider this approach to be wasteful or harmful to planning for long-term energy needs, and have retained more of a planned rather than a market-based approach to electricity and gas distribution.

The provision of road facilities in the UK may have been considered until recently to be totally unmarketable, for the reasons described above. More recently, however, marketing principles have been introduced, with users of roads in central London now charged a 'congestion charge' for the use of scarce peak-time road capacity. Similarly, users of the M6 motorway in the West Midlands now have a choice of roads, and some road users prefer to pay a fee to use an alternative, relatively uncongested toll motorway.

Some have argued that vital public services should not be left to decisions made by profit-seeking companies whose individual objectives may be contrary to the greater public interest. In theory, markets would punish companies that did not serve the public interest, because they would lose customers and eventually go out of business. Unfortunately, the reality is that markets may not be efficient, or sufficiently rapid, in punishing companies that do not satisfy the wider public good. Consider the following cases that have been cited as evidence of market-based distribution of services.

- The financial services sectors of many western countries were deregulated from the 1980s, with lending and investment decisions made by banks increasingly free of regulation by government regarding the volume and type of transactions that they should undertake. One consequence was a goal-driven culture that saw a lot of high-risk investments made by and between banks, and that began to unwind during the 'credit crunch' of 2008. Some would argue that as a result of short-term greed by market-orientated banks, the banking system as a whole came close to collapse, with financial institutions reacting harshly by drastically reducing the amount of credit made available for investment by companies in the economy generally.

- The railway sector in the UK has been privatized and deregulated, arguably leaving a lot more discretion to managers than was the case when the railways were state owned. Although the decisions of railway operators are constrained by government regulations, they are often tempted to put their own corporate interests before the national interest. Consider the case of bad snowfall, which has the potential to disrupt train services. Many train operators may choose to avoid the costs of maintaining a service during the bad weather, but this may cost businesses and consumers much more when shops, offices and factories have to close because workers cannot get to work as the trains are not running.

Following the 'credit crunch' of 2008, many commentators argued that some public services were simply too important for the rest of the economy to be left to market forces. Advocates of a centrally planned approach to the provision of essential public services pointed to countries such as France and Germany, which had retained a much higher level of central control of essential public services, and their economies appeared to be less badly affected by the disruptive effects that occurred when bad, market-based decisions taken earlier by private-sector companies harmed the rest of the economy. In particular, some argued that banking was an essential public service and the relatively unregulated actions of banks in the UK and USA had precipitated the credit crunch. More regulated financial services sectors in other countries did not suffer such a fall-out. The importance of the financial services sector to the rest of the economy was reflected in the decisions by many governments to nationalize failing banks or to provide substantial support for them. In the UK, the government effectively nationalized Lloyds TSB Bank and Royal Bank of Scotland, realizing that if these banks were to become bankrupt, there would be very serious implications for investment and financial transactions in all sectors of the economy.

In practice, a business sector cannot be described simply as being either market based or centrally planned. In between these extremes, a variety of operating environments exist. Many apparently private-sector, market-based service providers, such as telephone, electricity and railway providers, nevertheless are subject to extensive government regulation, which may determine, among other things, the markets they serve, the services they offer, the prices they can charge and the investments they must make. Some cynics have argued that railway managers in the UK actually had more freedom to serve their customers under state ownership than under their current private, but heavily regulated, ownership.

5.2.2 Voluntary and not-for-profit sector marketing

The principles of marketing have increasingly been applied to services that have traditionally been provided by voluntary or not-for-profit organizations, and for which many people might be dubious about the value of marketing. Why should you need marketing to promote a school that should be judged by the quality of its teaching, or to encourage donations to a charity whose cause people should recognize as a socially useful one in its own right?

A feature of many services activities in recent years has been for marketing to become involved where, previously, provision was determined by community interests and involvement. Instead of a church-based group providing childminding facilities according to local need and the church's mission, parents have increasingly looked to the services of market-based kindergartens. Instead of extended families and community groups looking after elderly or disabled people, a market in retirement homes and disabled living support has emerged. Services that were once undertaken informally between friends and family or within a community have been increasingly 'marketized'. This implies putting a price on everything that goes into a transaction, which is more likely to be formal rather than informal. In response to competition from commercially provided services, which have often led to heightened expectations by consumers, many voluntary and not-for-profit organizations have tried to counter this by adopting many of the principles of marketing themselves. Schools, for example, increasingly use the services of advertising and public relations agencies to attract students.

This creeping marketization of traditional community-based services has attracted strong criticism from those who see market forces 'crowding out' the efforts of the voluntary sector. One well-documented example of this is the case of blood donation services, which in many countries are operated as community-based voluntary activities, whereas in others, blood donation is based on the market principles of paying money to individual donors in return for a valuable product. Richard Titmus showed how monetary compensation for donating blood could crowd out the supply of blood donors. Blood had been reduced to a commodity to be bought and sold, and this market-based calculation had crowded out individuals' evaluation based on moral rightness and benefit to the community (Titmus 1970). In short, there seemed to be evidence that introducing the market disciplines might actually have a perverse effect on service provision.

⟳ Thinking around the subject

Marketing without markets?

Can you have marketing in a situation where there is no market? The link between marketing and markets has been extensively discussed, with some confusion about the role of marketing. Many public-sector organizations have employed people with titles such as 'marketing officer', often with responsibilities that include services for which consumers may have little or no choice. Even many police forces have appointed marketing officers. Although there may be some instances where such a person would genuinely need to apply the principles of marketing (for example, where police forces compete against one another to provide cover at regional football matches), most of their work is likely to be involved with promotion and possibly learning more about public opinion. For most services provided by police forces, there is no market, and indeed soliciting payment from some groups may sound like corruption. When one police force accepted sponsorship of its cars from the security company Chubb, it was widely accused of leaving itself open to accusations of favouritism if the sponsor were ever considered to be involved in an offence. Many of the tools of marketing – such as pricing and market segmentation are clearly not available to the police service. It can also be difficult to identify who the customer is - it may be members of society more generally, who benefit from a safer community, but with whom there is no exchange relationship.

So can we have marketing without markets? Karl Marx once questioned whether you could have capitalism without capital. Perhaps marketing without a market is a similar oxymoron?

5.3   The stakeholders of organizations

We now broaden our discussion of corporate responsibility by identifying groups of people and organizations who are affected by the actions of an organization, and that are collectively referred to as 'stakeholders'. Stakeholders may not necessarily have any direct dealings with a company, but they are nevertheless affected by its actions. There is an argument that an organization has responsibility to these stakeholders that goes beyond the basic legal relationship that it has with customers, suppliers and employees, etc. In turn, a company can be significantly affected by the actions of *its* stakeholders.

The following section identifies the principal stakeholders in business organizations. Some of these are primary, with direct impacts of the organization on the stakeholder, and vice versa. Others can be considered secondary in that their impacts are more indirect. Very often, stakeholders have different agendas and may disagree over what constitutes good behaviour by an organization. As stakeholders in local industry, local community groups may have quite different reactions to the prospect of a company planning to create a new distribution centre in their area. Some may welcome the increase in job opportunities the new facility presents, while others may be against the proposal because of the additional traffic congestion that it will be likely to generate. Although Figure 5.1 presents a simple model of stakeholders, we should always bear in mind that some stakeholders are more influential than others, and this importance is likely to vary from one situation to another. Moreover, each group is not homogeneous and may present a variety of views about how an organization should behave.

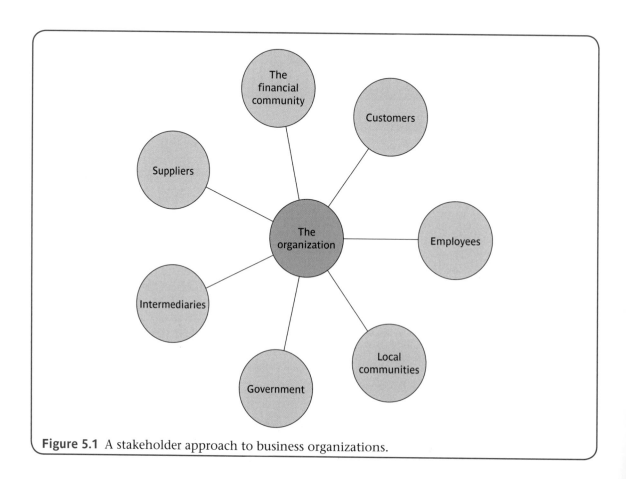

Figure 5.1 A stakeholder approach to business organizations.

5.3.1 Customers

In increasingly discriminating markets, buyers may opt for the more socially responsible company. Acting in an anti-social way may have a long-term cost for a company and ultimately not serve the needs of those customers who prefer to deal with a socially acceptable company. Anti-social behaviour by companies may also attract the attention of regulatory bodies, which often have the power to add to a company's production costs, or to make it impossible to satisfy customer demand in the first place.

There is an argument that the customer is *not* always right in the goods and services they choose to buy from a company. Customers may sometimes not be aware of their true needs or may have these needs manipulated by exploitative companies. Taking a long-term and broad perspective, companies should have a duty to provide goods and services that satisfy these longer-term and broader needs rather than customers' immediately felt needs. There have been many examples where the long-term interests of customers have been ignored by companies. Increasingly, legislation is saying that the customer is *not* always right and organizations have a duty to consider the long-term interests of customers as stakeholders. In the UK, this has been illustrated in a series of 'mis-selling' scandals, in which regulatory authorities have fined companies for selling goods and services to people, which were not in the customers' best interests. The Financial Services Authority, for example, has fined insurance companies for inappropriately selling insurance to people that was intended to provide some financial cover if they became unemployed. However, the terms and conditions effectively meant that many buyers of the insurance would never be able to benefit from the cover – for example, there may have been no cover for people who were self-employed. Regulators in such situations have held that the seller has a duty not to sell a product where it knows that it would be of no benefit to the buyer. Financial services are based on trust and this could be undermined if financial services companies abuse the trust placed in them by customers.

There are many more examples of situations where customers are probably *not* right and their long-term interests have been neglected by companies, including:

- tobacco companies that have failed to impress upon customers the long-term harmful effects of buying and consuming their cigarettes
- fast-food restaurants that promote unhealthy food to obese people
- car manufacturers that add expensive stereo equipment to cars as standard equipment but relegate vital safety equipment to the status of optional extra.

In each of these cases, most people might agree that, objectively, buyers are being persuaded to make a choice against their own long-term self-interest. But on what moral grounds can society say that consumers' choices in these situations are wrong? According to some individuals' sense of priorities, an expensive music system may indeed be considered to offer a higher level of personal benefit than an airbag.

As well as being unable to evaluate the consequences of a purchase on them personally, customers often also fail to evaluate the external costs that they cause other consumers collectively to incur. **External costs** can be defined as the cost of consuming a product that is not borne directly by the consumer, and can take many forms, such as:

- congestion, which one car driver causes to other drivers
- the pollution suffered by residents living near waste tips, caused by the disposal of fast-food packaging
- noise nuisance suffered by people living near a noisy nightclub.

In each case, market mechanisms have failed to make buyers of a good or service pay for the external costs that they have forced on others. Organizations that think strategically would recognize that socially unacceptable levels of external costs might bring pressure for legislation that results in higher costs, or prohibition of an activity completely. For the organization, this will have the effect of raising selling prices to customers or making impossible the provision of goods and services demanded by customers.

It is also sometimes argued that companies have a duty to provide goods and services to groups of customers who may not be commercially viable to serve, but whom the company should have a moral duty to supply. There are many examples of types of consumers that companies may prefer not to serve, because they are considered likely to be difficult to process. Here are some examples.

- Banks may unreasonably decline applications from poorer groups of the population, thereby forcing them into a financial ghetto where they cannot benefit from the good deals that are available to richer groups.

- Disabled consumers often cost more to process than able-bodied consumers, because of the requirement to redesign buildings and vehicles, etc. and it may take legislation to induce some organizations to serve these groups.

- Schools and universities have been accused of being reluctant to take academically weak students because of the extra remedial support they may require. Weak students may also disrupt student-to-student interaction in class.

In each of these cases, companies must recognize wider social pressures to provide access to disadvantaged groups. What may be seen initially as anti-social behaviour by a company is likely, sooner or later, to be translated into government legislation requiring service providers to address these wider social concerns. In short, if the market does not provide access to disadvantaged groups, legislation is likely to intervene to provide it. So, throughout the EU, governments have developed policies to ensure that children or students from disadvantaged socioeconomic groups are not denied access to schools or universities. Denying a bank account to an individual also denies that individual the opportunity of benefiting from online services that are available only to individuals with a bank account. In the UK, the government has put pressure on banks to offer a basic bank account to individuals who would not normally qualify for full banking facilities. In the case of access to disabled groups, the UK Disability Discrimination Act 1985 (based on an EU directive) has progressively required companies to make reasonable adaptations to their service processes in order to accommodate disabled customers. Case law is being developed as to what are reasonable measures that a company should take in order to provide access. As the Act is implemented, specific requirements on companies are increasing – for example, all new buses must be capable of access by wheelchairs.

Some companies have taken an early cue from social pressures, and learned how to handle disadvantaged groups of customers ahead of legislation. This experience has sometimes put them at a competitive advantage when the sector as a whole has been required to adopt wider access policies. Those universities that had developed outreach projects to disadvantaged communities found government pressure for wider access relatively easy to manage, compared with those universities that had been set in their traditional ways. However, in markets where cost leadership is crucial to gaining competitive advantage, government pressure, and indeed legislation, may be tested to the limit, and companies may continue to avoid their obligations as far as possible. The airline Ryanair, which has built a successful business model based on ruthlessly controlling costs, has faced legal challenge in respect of its provision for disabled customers. It has, for example, argued that disabled customers should pay for the use of wheelchairs, in much the same way as its able-bodied customers pay for additional services such as baggage and in-flight food. Is the airline's low-cost model and charging for use of wheelchairs compatible with the Disability Discrimination Act?

5.3.2 Employees

It used to be thought that customers were not concerned about how their goods were made, just so long as the final product lived up to their expectations. This may just have been true for some manufactured goods, but probably never was for services, where production processes are highly visible. Today, increasingly large segments of the population take into account the ethics of a firm's employment practices when evaluating alternative products. If all other things are equal, a firm that has a reputation for ruthlessly exploiting its employees, or not recognizing the legitimate rights of trades unions, may be denigrated in the minds of many buyers. For this reason, some companies, such as Nike and Marks & Spencer, have gone to great lengths to challenge allegations made about the employment practices of their overseas suppliers.

Firms often go way beyond satisfying the basic legal requirements of employees. For some businesses, getting an adequate supply of competent workers is the main constraint on growth and it would be in their interest to promote good employment practices. This is true of many high-tech industries. In order to encourage staff retention, in particular of women returning to work after having children, companies have offered attractive packages of benefits, such as working hours that fit around school holidays and sponsoring events that promote a caring image.

Can going beyond legal requirements for employees ever be considered altruistic rather than just good business? Quaker companies such as Cadbury had a historic tradition of paternalism towards their staff. But could such altruism essentially be seen as an investment by an organization, which will have a payback in terms of better motivated staff?

5.3.3 Local communities

Market-led companies often try to be seen as a 'good neighbour' in their local community. Such companies can enhance their image through the use of charitable contributions, sponsorship of local events and being seen to support the local environment. Again, this may be interpreted either as part of a firm's genuine concern for its local community, or as a more cynical and pragmatic attempt to buy favour where its own interests are at stake. If a metal manufacturer installs improved noise reduction equipment, is it doing so in order to genuinely improve the lives of local residents, or merely attempting to forestall prohibition action taken by the local authority?

⟳ Thinking around the subject

Welcome to the bank – if you are rich

'Sorry, you are too poor to come into this bank branch' was the message many people read into the actions of HSBC Bank when, in April 2007, it converted its branch at Canford Cliffs near Poole, Dorset, into a centre for 'premier banking' customers. To qualify, premier customers were required to have savings of at least £50,000, or a mortgage of £200,000, or a salary of £75,000 a year. Customers who did not meet these criteria had to travel a mile to the nearest HSBC bank where full service facilities were available to them.

Local community groups expressed dismay at the bank's action, with the local Member of Parliament describing the bank as moving towards social exclusion, rather than financial inclusion, which was high on the government's policy agenda. The local Citizens Advice Bureau described the bank as providing second-class access for people on moderate incomes. The elderly and those on low incomes would be disadvantaged most by the need to travel to a bank. Despite great developments in online access to banking facilities, these groups are the least likely to have internet access.

Was the bank being socially irresponsible by denying access to the branch to all except financially well-heeled customers? Are the bank's actions compatible with its stated agenda for **corporate social responsibility?** Or is its decision based on sound principles of segmentation and targeting? With Canford Cliffs having among the highest household incomes and property prices in the UK, isn't it just good business sense that the bank provides enhanced facilities for high net worth customers? Other banks have opened offices specifically for such customers, but did HSBC inflame the social exclusion debate by restricting a branch that was previously accessible to all, rather than building a completely new facility?

5.3.4 Government

The demands of government agencies often take precedence over the needs of a company's customers. Government has a number of roles to play as stakeholder in commercial organizations.

- Commercial organizations provide governments with taxation revenue, so a healthy business sector is in the interests of government.
- Government is increasingly expecting business organizations to take over many responsibilities from the public sector – for example, with regard to the payment of sickness and maternity benefits to employees.
- It is through business organizations that governments achieve many of their economic and social objectives – for example, with respect to regional economic development and skills training.

As regulators impact on many aspects of business activity, companies often go to great lengths in seeking favourable responses from such agencies. In the case of many UK private-sector utility providers, promotional efforts are often aimed more at regulatory bodies than final consumers. In the case of the water industry, promoting greater use of water to final consumers is unlikely to have any significant impact on a water utility company, but influencing the disposition of the Office of Water Regulation, which sets price limits and required service standards, can have a major impact.

5.3.5 Intermediaries

Companies must not ignore the wholesalers, retailers and agents that may be crucial interfaces between themselves and their final consumers. These intermediaries may share many of the same concerns as customers and need reassurance about the company's capabilities as a supplier that is capable of working with intermediaries to supply goods and services in an ethical manner. Many companies have suffered because they failed to take adequate account of the needs of their intermediaries (for example, Body Shop and McDonald's have previously faced protests from their franchisees where they felt threatened by a business strategy that was perceived as being against their own interests).

5.3.6 Suppliers

Suppliers can sometimes be critical to business success. This often occurs where vital inputs are in scarce supply or it is critical that supplies are delivered to a company on time and in good condition. The way in which an organization places orders for its inputs can have a significant effect on suppliers. Does a company favour domestic companies rather than possibly lower-priced overseas producers? (Marks & Spencer has traditionally prided itself on buying the vast majority of its merchandise from UK producers, so concerns were raised when it announced in

- Both supporters and opponents of proposals to build bypasses around towns use environmental arguments to support their arguments. Opponents argue that a new road in itself will create more road traffic, which is environmentally harmful, while supporters argue that environmental impacts will be lessened by moving traffic out of town to where it causes less harm.

- Refer back to the case study in Chapter 1, and you will recall that the airline Ryanair claimed that it was a friend of the ecological environment by using more efficient aircraft than its competitors.

Another issue is the presumed benefits for the ecological environment of new, efficient, low-energy products. If we save ecological resources in one form of activity, will that simply leave us with more money to use more resources in other forms of activity? Consider the example of cars. It is certainly true that, for any class of car, the typical fuel consumption has dropped over the past decade or so. A family-sized car such as the Volkswagen Golf, which 20 years ago might have achieved 34 miles per gallon, today may achieve nearer to 40. Unfortunately, the falling costs of running a car that are associated with greater fuel efficiency mean that customers can now afford a bigger and better car, which will doubtless use more fuel. So, over the past decade or so, the fastest growth in car sales to private consumers has been larger sports utility vehicles and multi-people vehicles. It is as if individuals have a set proportion of their income that they allocate to transport. If the cost per mile of running their vehicle comes down, they may trade up to the larger 'luxury' vehicle. This effect has been seen in a number of other sectors. The ecological benefits of increasingly fuel-efficient aircraft have been partly offset by the resulting lower prices of air transport, leading to more people taking short-break holidays. The Boeing 737–800 series aircraft uses much less fuel than the original Boeing 737 of 20 years ago, and has also allowed budget airlines to develop a whole new market of low-cost air travel. It has been estimated by Friends of the Earth that half a billion tonnes of carbon dioxide were emitted by aircraft into the atmosphere in 2002, up on previous years, despite the development of more efficient aircraft engines. The advent of budget airlines may also have brought tourists flocking to previously underdeveloped areas, causing ecological damage in the process.

Most members of the public are not experts on the technical aspects of **ecological impacts** of business activities. They may therefore be easily persuaded by the most compellingly promoted argument, regardless of the technical merit of the case. Very often, a firm may have a technically sound case, but fail to win the hearts and minds of consumers who seem intent on believing the opposite argument, which is in accordance with their own prejudices. This has been seen in the debate on biofuels, referred to above.

5.6.2 Opportunities for business arising from ecological concerns

The ecological environment can present opportunities as well as challenges for services businesses. Proactive companies have capitalized on ecological issues by reducing their costs and/or improving their organizational image, as the following examples demonstrate.

- Many markets are characterized by segments that are prepared to pay a premium price for a product that has been produced in an ecologically sound manner. Some retailers, such as Body Shop, have developed valuable niches on this basis. What starts off as a 'deep green' niche soon expands into a larger 'pale green' segment of customers who prefer ecologically sound products but are unwilling to pay such a high price premium. However, many companies may make token concessions to ecological responsibility without making any significant contribution to the ecological environment. Such 'greenwash' (or 'green tosh', as it is sometimes called) is likely to be found out sooner or later, and the dishonesty of a company's claims may ultimately harm its reputation. On the other hand, many consumers are quite happy to go along with the crowd and to be seen 'doing something

Figure 5.2 This chapter has discussed some of the consequences of firms' depletion of natural resources and emission of pollutants into the atmosphere. Although the emphasis has been on the need for regulation to protect the environment against firms' activities, firms themselves need to be on their guard against environmental change. At least some of this change may be attributable to manufacturing activity, as in the case of climate change, which has been linked to manufacturing industries' production of 'greenhouse gases'. There has been much debate about greenhouse gas emissions, and their effects on weather patterns and sea levels. While there is still some debate about the causes and extent of such changes, it is evident that more businesses are likely to find themselves threatened by extreme weather conditions. This advertisement by the Environment Agency is designed to alert businesses to the dangers of flooding. Although firms may by themselves be unable to do much to reduce flooding in their area, they can nevertheless take actions that reduce the consequences for their operations, including the preparation of a flood plan. (Picture reproduced with permission of the Environment Agency.)

green' even if their actions have a negligible, or even harmful, effect. Somebody driving to a recycling centre to drop off an unwanted television may feel good about doing their bit for the environment, but they may actually cause more harmful consequences by driving their car. They may also fail to ask themselves why they didn't repair the television, thereby saving even more resources.

- Being 'green' may actually save a company money. Often, changing existing environmentally harmful practices primarily involves overcoming traditional mindsets about how things should be done (e.g. fast-food chains using recycled packaging materials and overcoming a one-way logistics mindset by returning their waste materials for recycling).

- In western developed economies, legislation to enforce environmentally sensitive methods of production is increasing. A company that adopts environmentally sensitive service processes ahead of compulsion can gain a competitive advantage.

- The challenges of using resources in a more efficient and less polluting way has spurred R&D, and some companies have developed valuable niches. Wind turbines, solar panels, heat pumps and carbon capture technology have presented tremendous opportunities for companies to improve the efficiency of a product and their marketing to business and consumers. For the future, there are many more new products awaiting further development – for example, lightweight, long-life batteries for electric cars.

⟳ Thinking around the subject

Too much heat in the garden?

In an age that is preoccupied with issues of global warming, how politically correct is it to own a patio heater? These gas-powered devices, which provide heat in a garden, have become very popular. Following a period of strong economic growth throughout western Europe, and falling real energy prices, ownership of patio heaters grew sharply. For private consumers, a patio became a 'must have' accessory, which allowed them to make use of their garden during cool evenings and in the spring and autumn. Patio heaters became popular with pubs, especially following bans on smoking in many countries. Pubs can still keep the trade of smokers, who can sit and smoke outside under a warm patio heater. According to the UK's Energy Saving Trust, there were 1.2 million patio heaters in the UK in 2007, and it predicted that, within three years, this figure would almost double to 2.3 million.

Against this background, it may seem surprising that the DIY chain B&Q announced in January 2008 that it would stop selling patio heaters. Was it simply seeking favourable publicity, especially at a time when gas-powered patio heaters were drawing the wrath of environmentalists, who pointed out that each patio heater could emit as much carbon dioxide in a year as 1.5 cars? Was it being altruistic in its concern for the environment? Or could there have been a pragmatic business benefit of discontinuing patio heaters? Patio heaters were no longer a new product commanding high margins, as new sources of supply pushed down prices and margins. After a decade of falling energy prices, prices started to increase sharply from 2007 – would patio heaters fall out of favour as they became more costly to operate? Was B&Q simply getting out while the going was still good? Did it foresee further government restrictions on the sale and use of such heaters, so if it got out now, it could gain the credit for leading, rather than being pushed if it waited until later? The EU Commission had already started to talk about the possibility of a ban on patio heaters. Some cynics argued that B&Q had built up large stocks of patio heaters, and only committed itself to stop selling them when stocks ran out. Could the publicity have actually helped B&Q sell even more patio heaters than it would otherwise have done?

Case study:
'Bikes for all' may be a big plus for the environment, but a big challenge for all stakeholders

By Rod McColl and Irena Descubes, ESC Rennes International School of Business

© *mario loiselle*

It may be many people's idea of an ecological dream – make bikes easily accessible, and people will be tempted to make short journeys across town by pedal power rather than drive a car, use scarce fossil fuels and emit pollutants to the atmosphere. Cycling has become increasingly popular in recent years, spurred on by many factors, including increasing concern for personal fitness, the rising costs of running a car, gridlocked city streets, an increasing number of segregated cycle lanes, and the social acceptability of bike use – once seen as a poor person's means of transport, but now a sign of the fit and ecologically friendly citizen.

Many towns have in the past experimented with shared bicycle schemes, by which people can pick up a bike at one place, use it for a short journey, then deposit it for the next person to use. But actually getting such a scheme to work can be a nightmare involving reconciling the interests of lots of different stakeholder groups. Typical problems that have either prevented the launch of new schemes, or have led to the abandonment of established schemes include the following.

- Who is going to pay for the scheme? Most public urban bicycle rental schemes need to be subsidized, so how much can be justified by way of subsidy? Which public authorities should pay?
- How will the scheme be made sufficiently attractive for genuine users, but not too attractive that it attracts thieves and fraudsters?
- How would you reconcile grand ideas of satisfying a public need, and possible conflict with stakeholder groups – for example, traders who may not want a bicycle rack outside their shop, or private-sector bike rental businesses who find their business undercut by the publicly subsidized scheme?
- As a public service, should it be provided by government directly, or outsourced through a private-sector organization?
- Who is going to be responsible for maintaining the bikes, and who will be legally liable if a bike causes injury?

The city of Rennes in western France has pioneered the development of an urban cycle rental scheme, and learned how to tackle some of these problems. The first bike rental scheme was established in Rennes in 1998, and the current scheme, called Vélo STAR, has been operated since 2009 by the leading French transport operator Keolis SA. The company receives a €17 million subsidy from the municipality for an eight-year contract period, in return for meeting specified performance targets. Keolis promised the city that it would introduce a geographically dispersed cycle rental scheme consisting of 82 bike rental stations with 900 bikes in the first phase. Later, it would incorporate outlying villages, growing the system to 117 stations and 1285 bikes. Keolis proposed a maximum distance of 330 metres between each of the 82 city stations. Bike rental stations varied in size depending on the forecast demand, coping with either 16, 30 or 50 bike parking spaces. Keolis had grand ambitions for making a bike easily accessible to all, with a much higher level of accessibility than had been provided by the previous operator of the cycle scheme – Clear Channel – which provided only 25 stations with 12 cycle stands in each, and limited the number of registered users of the scheme to 5000 at any one time.

The first issue in making bikes accessible was to develop a system for registration and payment by users. One approach could have been to install a coin slot at each bike station by which users paid each time that they wanted to rent a bike. This would have been inconvenient for users, and costly for the operator to set up and maintain. The previous system had required individuals to obtain an access card from a central office, which was free but the user had to pay a refundable deposit, and their card was deactivated if they did not use it for three months. The system was not very user friendly and may have been one factor contributing to the bike scheme 'running out of steam', with just 280 rentals per day citywide in 2008. Keolis made access to a bike easier by allowing renters to use their annual bus/metro pass as a bike access card. Alternatively, users could purchase an access card using a credit card at one of the ten main rental stations at a cost of €1 for 24 hours or €5 for a seven-day access.

So far, so good – it was now in principle easier for a user to get access to the bike rental system, but Keolis now had to make sure that bikes were available at the places that users wanted to rent them. It had learned a lot from experience of usage patterns during the previous ten years. Users tended to be relatively young, with 40 per cent aged under 25 years; 55 per cent of the total system usage was concentrated between the seven city-centre stations. Keolis developed a model to predict patterns of usage, and from its analysis, priority areas for development of new bike rental stations were identified – near to places used by young adults, especially the city's universities. More stations were established at other key points, such as bus and train interchanges and suburban employment and shopping centres. The company used a modular system of cycle station, so the capacity of a station could be reduced or enlarged in response to changes in demand, or to correct an error in forecasts of demand.

Having a bike rental station is one thing, but actually having bikes available can be another. In principle, there should be a constant flow of bikes in and out of each station, but unfortunately stations had a tendency to accumulate bikes or to run out completely. Students travelling to lectures would deplete bikes at the stations near to residential accommodation at the start of the day, and they would pile up at campus stations. Another quirky imbalance that needed to be addressed was the tendency for more bikes to be rented to make short downhill journeys rather than making the return journey uphill. To resolve the problem of imbalances in flow, the operator uses cycle transporters to move bikes around the system. It has a central control room that collates information about the status of each bike station and can take action in response to this. At first, it was mainly reactive, moving bikes from stations with a surplus to stations with a shortage. With more experience of operation, it has developed a predictive model to better understand when shortages will occur, so that it can move bikes in anticipation. It has found, for example, that Monday and Thursday mornings are particularly busy times for a number of stations used by students.

To avoid the inconvenience of a user trying to rent a bike from an empty bike rack, Keolis has developed a website showing the real-time availability of bikes at each rental station (www.levelostar.fr/fr/les-stations/liste-des-stations.html). It has experimented with a format that is easily available through mobile devices for potential renters who are already on the move – for example, a passenger arriving on a train can check before they arrive on the availability of bikes at the station bike rack, and if none is available there, they will be informed about the nearest alternative availability.

Keolis has had to strike a fine balance between making bikes easily accessible to genuine users, and too easily available to thieves. In the past, some towns have operated voluntary bike rental schemes which allow anybody to borrow a bike without prior registration, and they are then trusted to return it. This invariably turned out to be an unsustainable model, as users 'borrowed' bikes without returning them. In Rennes, more than half of the 900 bikes in the system were stolen from the racks between September and November 2009. A defective hook connecting the bike to the console made it relatively easy for bikes to be stolen. Since then the design has been improved, to the point where very few bikes now go missing.

The Rennes bike rental scheme is not intended to be a profit-making venture, and the local municipality subsidizes the scheme for environmental benefits. In fact, only 2 per cent of users use their bike beyond the first 30-minute period which is free of charge to registered users. In commercial markets, money tends to follow individuals' preferences for availability of a service, but in this case, there is only a very weak market signal to guide service access decisions. Instead, accessibility decisions made by Keolis are governed by a variety of key performance indicators (KPIs) specified by the municipality in return for the annual subsidy. This has resulted in some apparently odd behaviour – for example, users frequently return their bike to a rack just before the end of the 30-minute free period and then immediately rent the bike again. There is no limit to how often a user can do this. Keolis doesn't mind, because this action boosts the number of recorded bike rentals – one of its KPIs. The existence of KPIs may have inhibited some possible marketing initiatives – for example, there is a surplus of bikes at the weekend when there could be a great demand for leisure use of bikes for longer periods,

but the price mechanism is too inflexible to encourage this, and the company's KPIs wouldn't benefit from such an initiative.

Making a bike more accessible to users has been a key part of the marketing strategy of the Rennes bike rental scheme. It is undoubtedly one factor that has resulted in an increase in usage from just 280 rentals per day in 2008 to 2650 in February 2010.

QUESTIONS

1 Identify the principal stakeholders in this scheme and discuss how you would go about evaluating the benefits of the scheme to each of them.

2 Evaluate the role of technology in its widest sense in making bikes available to users.

3 How should Keolis balance the need for easy access to bikes by genuine users with the need to prevent theft and abuse?

Summary

In a mature business environment, organizations must think beyond their own customers to society as a whole. There are good philosophical and pragmatic reasons why firms should act in a socially responsible manner. At a time of increasing competition in many markets, good social credentials can act as a differentiator in the eyes of increasingly sophisticated buyers. Although social responsibility by firms can achieve long-term paybacks, there can still be doubt about what is the most responsible course of action. But, as we have seen in this chapter, discussion about ecological issues and ethics is often muddied by lack of agreement on what is right and wrong.

The following key linkages to other chapters should be noted: ethics is founded upon what a society considers right and wrong, and social values are constantly changing (**Chapter 3**), reflected in legislation by governments (**Chapters 2** and **6**). Fierce competition within a market and a high degree of price sensitivity by buyers can encourage firms to engage in unethical practices (**Chapters 11** and **12**). New technologies are continually posing new challenges and opportunities for organizations in their efforts to act responsibly (**Chapter 4**). Expectations of responsibility by firms can differ markedly between countries (**Chapter 14**). Internally, ethical practice is closely linked to human resource management practices (**Chapter 10**).

🔑 Key Terms

Corporate governance (183)   External cost (179)

Corporate social responsibility (182)   Financial community (183)

Ecological impact (191)   Supplier (182)

Ethics (186)

Online
Learning Centre

To help you grasp the key concepts of this chapter, explore the extra resources posted on the Online Learning Centre at *www.mcgraw-hill.co.uk/palmer*. Among other helpful resources there are chapter-by-chapter test questions, revision notes and web links.

Chapter review questions

1 Is it possible to define an ethical code of conduct that is applicable in all countries? How should a multinational company attempt to define a global ethical code of conduct?

2 What is meant by good corporate governance, and why has the topic become an important issue in many countries?

3 What should be the response of businesses to pressure groups' claims that their activities are causing ecological damage?

Activities

1 You are employed by a phone company as a commission-based sales assistant. The more people you get to sign up and switch from other phone companies, the more commission you will be paid. However, you know in your heart that most of the people you are selling to could get a much better deal with another company. Moreover, you realize that hidden in the small print of the contract are clauses that will result in additional charges to the customer that are not mentioned in the glossy, colourful brochure that you send out.

   As a salesperson, would you consider yourself to be acting ethically by selling something when you know that buyers could get better elsewhere? Is it ethical not to alert buyers to the potentially disadvantageous terms contained in the small print, and just lure them to sign on the dotted line with the bait of free gifts and a glossy brochure? What would you do?

2 Select two or three campaigns by pressure groups with which you are familiar – for example, Greenpeace, Friends of the Earth or the Countryside Alliance. Review their websites and recent press releases to assess the effect that their campaigning is likely to have on a

manufacturer of consumer goods. How widely do you consider the opinions expressed by these groups represent the population as a whole? If you were a manufacturer, how would you address the issues raised?

3 If you are studying at a university or college, identify the key stakeholders in your institution. To what extent do you think the institution should be held responsible to these stakeholders? What conflicts may occur as it tries to reconcile conflicting demands from different groups of stakeholders?

Further reading

The following provides an overview of general issues of corporate social responsibility.

Blowfield, M.E. and Murray, A. (2008) *Corporate Responsibility: A Critical Introduction*, Oxford, Oxford University Press.

For a general review of the policy implications of ecological issues, the following provide a useful overview.

Freeman, R.E., Pierce, J. and Dodd, R. (2005) *Environmentalism and the New Logic of Business*, Oxford, Oxford University Press.

Hepburn, C. (2010) 'Environmental policy, government, and the market', *Oxford Review of Economic Policy*, Vol. 26, No. 2, pp. 117–136.

Leonidou, C.N. and Leonidou, L.C. (2011) 'Research into environmental marketing/management: a bibliographic analysis', *European Journal of Marketing*, Vol. 45, No. 1/2, pp. 68–103.

Issues of socially responsible and ecologically sound marketing are explored in the following.

Chamorro, A., Rubio, S. and Miranda, F.J. (2009) 'Characteristics of research on green marketing', *Business Strategy and the Environment*, Vol. 18, No. 4, pp. 223–239.

Hitchcock, D. and Willard, M. (2006) *The Business Guide to Sustainability: Practical Strategies and Tools for Organizations*, Oxford, Earthscan.

Peatie, K. and Peattie, S. (2009) 'Social marketing: a pathway to consumption reduction?', *Journal of Business Research*, Vol. 62, No. 2, pp. 260–268.

Webb, D.J., Mohr, L.A. and Harris, K.E. (2008) 'A re-examination of socially responsible consumption and its measurement', *Journal of Business Research*, Vol. 61, No. 2, pp. 91–98

For a discussion of business ethics the following texts are useful.

Bibb, S. (2010) *The Right Thing: An Everyday Guide to Ethics in Business*, Chichester, John Wiley.

Carrington, M.J., Neville, B.A. and Whitwell, G.J. (2010) 'Why ethical consumers don't walk their talk: towards a framework for understanding the gap between the ethical purchase intentions and actual buying behaviour of ethically minded consumers', *Journal of Business Ethics*, Vol. 97, No. 1, pp. 139–158

Crane, A. and Matten, D. (2010) *Business Ethics: Managing Corporate Citizenship and Sustainability in the Age of Globalization*, 3rd edn, Oxford, Oxford University Press.

Stanwick, P. and Stanwick, S. (2008) *Understanding Business Ethics*, Oxford Prentice Hall.

The following texts provide insights into issues of corporate governance.

Malin, C. (2010) *Corporate Governance,* 3rd edn, Oxford, Oxford University Press.

Monks, R.A.G. and Minow, N. (eds) (2007) *Corporate Governance*, 4th edn, Oxford, Blackwell Publishing.

References

DEFRA (2005) *Comparative Life-cycle Assessment of Food Commodities Procured for UK Consumption Through a Diversity of Supply Chains*. London, Department for Environment, Food and Rural Affairs.

Environmental Change Institute (2006) *Predict and Decide: Aviation, Climate Change and UK Policy*, Oxford, Oxford University.

Laroche, M., Bergeron, J. and Goutaland, C. (2001) 'Targeting customers who are willing to pay more for environmentally friendly products', *Journal of Consumer Marketing*, Vol. 18, No. 6, pp. 503–520.

Murray, S. (2001) 'Green products: consumers count cost over ecology', *Financial Times*, 5 November, p. 4.

Sandel, M.J. (2009), *Justice: What's the Right Thing to Do?* New York, Allen Lane.

Titmus, R. (1970) *The Gift Relationship: From Human Blood to Social Policy*, London, Allen and Unwin.

Chapter 6

The Legal Environment

Some 30 or 40 years ago, a shopkeeper in Britain could afford to be fairly laid back in his attitude to the law. He might have restricted customers' rights to complain if goods were faulty, and might have been 'economical with the truth' in the claims that he made for his goods. He might have enjoyed a cigarette with his workers at the back of a shop that had lots of steps, which made access for disabled people difficult. He might have had a quiet word with other local shopkeepers about agreeing not to undercut one anothers' prices. And he might have had a preference for employing people based on their gender, ethnicity and age. Today, that same shop owner might need a lawyer to make sure he didn't fall foul of the minefield of legislation that faces even small businesses. False claims about goods can result in criminal prosecution and civil claims from consumers. Health and safety regulations have become more onerous, and a raft of employment legislation now affects how he recruits, manages and fires staff. Even a friendly chat with other local shopkeepers could bring action from the regulatory authority if it suspects collusion. The legal environment is one aspect of most organizations' environments that has become increasingly complex in recent years; it and is explored in this chapter.

✓ Learning Objectives

This chapter will explain:

- ✓ The key legal challenges and opportunities facing business organizations, in respect of their relationships with customers, suppliers, employees and intermediaries.
- ✓ Sources of law – common law and statute law.
- ✓ The basic principles of law – contract and tort.
- ✓ Legal proccesses.
- ✓ Quasi-law based on voluntary codes of conduct.
- ✓ Legal protection of intellectual property.

6.1 Introduction

It was noted in the first chapter that all societies need some form of rules that govern the relationship between individuals, organizations and government bodies. In the absence of rules, chaos is likely to ensue, in which the strongest people will survive at the expense of the weakest. Businesses do not like to operate in environments in which there are no accepted rules of behaviour, because there is no guarantee that their investments will be protected from unauthorized seizure. This may partly explain why some countries of central Africa, which have been regarded as lawless areas without proper government, have failed to attract significant inward investment by businesses.

However, a system of rules does not necessarily imply a formal legal system. Many less developed economies manage with moral codes of governance that exert pressure on individuals and organizations to conform to an agreed code of conduct. In such countries, the shame inflicted on the family of a trader who defrauds a customer may be sufficient to ensure that traders abide by a moral code of governance.

In complex, pluralistic societies, moral governance alone may be insufficient to ensure compliance from business organizations. The tendency therefore has been for legal frameworks to expand as economies develop. One observer has pointed out that the Ten Commandments – a biblical code for governing society – ran to about 300 words. The American Bill of Rights of 1791 ran to about 700 words. Today, as an example of the detailed legislation that affects our conduct, the Eggs (Marketing Standards) Regulations 1995 run to several pages. The law essentially represents a codification of the rules and governance values of a society, expressed in a way that allows aggrieved parties to use an essentially bureaucratic system to gain what the society regards as justice. The legal environment of western developed economies is very much influenced by the political environment, which in turn is influenced by the social environment. In this sense, the law does not exist in a vacuum. Developments in the business environment have led to changes in the law affecting businesses, and the law in turn has affected the activities of business organizations.

In previous chapters we have considered the relationship between elements of an organization's micro- and macroenvironments at a fairly abstract level. In reality, these relationships are governed by a legal framework that presents opportunities and constraints for the manner in which these relationships can be developed.

We can identify a number of important areas in which the legal environment impinges on the activities of business organizations.

- The nature of the relationship between the organization and its customers, suppliers and intermediaries is influenced by the prevailing law. Over time, there has been a tendency for the law to give additional rights to buyers of goods and additional duties to the seller, especially in the case of transactions between businesses and private individuals. Whereas the nineteenth-century entrepreneur in Britain would have had almost complete freedom to dictate the terms of the relationship with its customers, developments in statute law now require, for example, the supplier to ensure that the goods are of satisfactory quality and that no misleading description of them is made. Furthermore, the expectations of an organization's customers have changed over time. Previous generations may have resigned themselves to suffering injustice in their dealings with a business, but today the expectation is increasingly for perfection every time. Greater awareness of the law on the part of consumers has produced an increasingly litigious society.

- In addition to the direct relationship that a company has with its customers, the law also influences the relationship that it has with other members of the general public. The law may, for example, prevent a firm having business relationships with certain sectors of the market, as where children are prohibited by law from buying cigarettes or drinking in public houses. Also, the messages that a company sends out in its advertising are likely to be picked up by members of the general public, and the law has intervened to protect the public interest where these messages could cause offence (adverts that are racially prejudicial, for example).

- Employment relationships are covered by increasingly complex legislation, which recognizes that employees have a proprietary interest in their job. Legislation seeks to make up for inequalities in the power between employers and employee.

- The legal environment influences the relationship between business enterprises themselves, not only in terms of contracts for transactions between them, but also in the way they relate to one another in a competitive environment. The law has increasingly prevented companies from joining together in anti-competitive practices, whether covertly or overtly.

- Companies need to develop new products, yet the rewards of undertaking new product development are influenced by the law. The laws of copyright and patent protect a firm's investment in fruitful research.

- The legal environment influences the production possibilities of an enterprise and hence the products that can be offered to consumers. These can have a direct effect – as in the case of regulations stipulating car safety design requirements – or a more indirect effect – as where legislation to reduce pollution increases the manufacturing costs of a product, or prevents its manufacture completely.

The legal environment is very closely related to the political environment. In the UK, law derives from two sources: common law and statute law.

1 The **common law** develops on the basis of judgments in the courts – a case may set a precedent for all subsequent cases to follow. The judiciary is independent of government and the general direction of precedents tends gradually to reflect changing attitudes in society.

2 **Statute law**, on the other hand, is passed by Parliament and can reflect the prevailing political ideology of the government.

We can draw a distinction between *civil* law and *criminal* law. Civil law provides a means by which one party can bring an action for a loss it has suffered as the direct result of actions by another party. A party who is injured by a defective vehicle, or has suffered loss because a promised order for goods has not been delivered, can use the civil law to claim some kind of recompense against the other party. By contrast, criminal law is invoked when a party causes harm to society more generally. In this case, it is the government that brings a claim against a wrongdoer and punishment generally takes the form of a fine or a prison sentence. Most of the subjects covered in this chapter are concerned with the civil law – that is, relationships between an organization and other individuals and organizations in their business environment. However, business organizations are increasingly being prosecuted for breaches of criminal law. Cases discussed in this chapter include breaches of food safety law, breaches of health and safety law, and providing misleading price information.

The law is a very complex area of the business environment. Most businesses would call upon expert members of the legal profession to interpret and act upon some of the more complex elements of the law. The purpose of this chapter is not to give definitive answers on aspects of the law as it affects business organizations – this would be impossible and dangerous in such a short space. Instead, the aim is to raise awareness of legal issues in order to recognize in general terms the opportunities and restrictions that the law poses, and the areas in which business organizations may need to seek the specialized advice of a legal professional.

This chapter will begin by looking at some general principles of law: the law of contract, the law relating to negligence and the processes of the legal system in England. Although the detail will describe the legal system of England, many of the principles apply in other judicial systems. The chapter will then consider the following specific areas of applications of the law, which are of particular relevance to businesses:

- dealings between organizations and their customers for the supply of goods and services
- contracts of employment
- protection of **intellectual property rights**
- legislation relating to production processes
- legislation to prevent anti-competitive practices.

6.2   The law of contract

A **contract** is an agreement between two parties where one party agrees to do something (e.g. supply goods, provide a service, offer employment) in return for which the other party provides some form of payment (in money or some other form of value). A typical organization would have contracts with a wide range of other parties, including customers, suppliers, employees and intermediaries.

There can be no direct legal relationship between a company and any of these groups unless it can be proved that a contract exists. An advertisement on its own only very rarely creates a legal relationship. The elements of a contract comprise offer, acceptance, intention to create legal relations, consideration, capacity, and terms and representations. We will consider these in turn.

- *Offer:* an 'offeror' indicates that they intend to be legally bound on the terms stated in the offer, if it is accepted by the person to whom the offer is made (the 'offeree'). An offer must be distinguished from an invitation to treat, which can be defined as an invitation to make offers. Normally, advertisements are regarded as invitations to treat, rather than an offer. Similarly, priced goods on display in shops are invitations to treat. Therefore, if a leather jacket is priced at £20 (through error) in the shop widow, it is not possible to demand the garment at that price. As the display is an invitation to treat, it is the consumer who is making the offer, which the shopkeeper may accept or reject as he wishes.

- *Acceptance:* this may be made only by the person(s) to whom the offer was made, and it must be absolute and unqualified (i.e. it must not add any new terms or conditions, for to do so would have the effect of revoking the original offer). Acceptance must be communicated to the offeror unless it can be implied by conduct. An offer may be revoked at any time prior to acceptance

- *Intention to create legal relations:* generally, in all commercial agreements it is accepted that both parties intend to make a legally binding contract and therefore it is unnecessary to include terms to this effect. In some circumstances, however, there may be no intention on the part of one or both parties to create legal relations, as occurs where a donor casually gives money to a charity organization. In the absence of such intention, a contract cannot exist.

- *Consideration:* consideration is generally essential in any contract and has been defined as some right, interest, profit or benefit accruing to one party, or some forbearance, detriment, loss or responsibility given, suffered or undertaken by the other (i.e. some benefit accruing to one party or a detriment suffered by the other). In commercial contracts generally, the consideration takes the form of a cash payment. However, in contracts of barter, which are common in some countries, goods are often exchanged for goods.

- *Capacity:* capacity refers to the ability of a company or individual to enter into a contract. Generally, any person or organization may enter into an agreement, which may be enforced against them. Exceptions include minors, drunks and mental patients; for this reason, companies usually exclude people under 18 from offers of goods to be supplied on credit. Limited companies must have the capacity to make a contract identified in their Objects clause within their Articles and Memorandum of Association (see Chapter 7).

■ *Terms and representations:* a distinction can be made between the terms of a contract and representations, which were made prior to forming the contract. Generally, it is assumed that statements that are made at the formation of a contract are terms of that contract, but many statements made during the course of negotiations are mere representations. If the statement is a term, the injured party may sue for breach of contract and will normally obtain damages that are deemed to put him or her in the position they would have been in had the statement been true. If the statement is a mere representation, it may be possible to avoid the contract by obtaining an order – known as rescission – which puts the parties back in the position they were in prior to the formation of the contract.

Thinking around the subject

Is a business relationship a contract?

One of the trends in the business environment that we discussed in Chapter 1 is towards closer relationships between companies in a supply chain. So, instead of buying 'job lots' of components and raw materials from the cheapest buyer whenever they are needed, a buyer and seller will come to an arrangement for their supply over the longer term. The parties may not be able to specify the precise products or volumes that they will need to buy, but just by understanding each other's processes and likely future requirements, the supply chain can be made more efficient and effective.

Many of these business relationships are based on 'gentlemen's agreements' with little formal specification in writing. So is this a contract? Can either party unilaterally end a gentleman's agreement?

The question was tested in 2002 in the case of *Baird Textile Holdings Ltd v Marks & Spencer plc* (M&S). Baird had been making lingerie, women's coats and men's clothes for M&S for over 30 years, and had largely built its business round the retail chain's requirements. However, the parties had resisted formalizing the arrangement in order to maintain maximum flexibility in their relationship. But increased competition in the high street led M&S to look for cheaper sources of manufacturing overseas, and Baird was told that with immediate effect its goods were no longer required by M&S.

Baird argued that although there was no written contract governing their relationship, there was an implied term that either party would give reasonable notice of any change to the relationship. The supplier claimed for damages of £53.6 million, which included a £33 million charge to cover redundancy payments, and further amounts in respect of asset write-downs, including IT equipment it used to help fulfil its M&S clothing orders. The claim was intended to put Baird back into the position it would have been in had M&S given it three years' notice, rather than suddenly terminating its agreement. But did the agreement between the two constitute a contract?

The Court of Appeal held that the long-term arrangements between Baird and M&S did not constitute a contract. It stated that there was a clear mutual intent not to enter into a legal agreement and this view was supported by the absence of any precise terms. Both parties clearly wished to preserve flexibility in their dealings with each other. A contract existed only in respect of individual orders when they were placed, but there was no contract governing the continuity of orders.

6.3 Non-contractual liability

Consider now the situation where a consumer discovers that goods are defective in some way but is unable to sue the retailer from which they were supplied because the consumer is not a party to the contract (which may occur where the goods were bought as a gift by a friend). The product may also injure a completely unconnected third party. The only possible course of action here has been to sue the manufacturer. This situation was illustrated in 1932 in the case of *Donaghue v Stevenson,* where a man bought a bottle of ginger beer manufactured by the defendant. The man gave the bottle to his female companion, who became ill from drinking the contents, as the bottle (which was opaque) contained the decomposing remains of a snail. The consumer sued the manufacturer and won. The House of Lords held that on the facts outlined there was remedy in the **tort** of negligence.

To prove **negligence**, there are three elements that must be shown:

1 that the defendant was under a duty of care to the plaintiff

2 that there had been a breach of that duty

3 that there is damage to the plaintiff as a result of the breach, which is not too remote a consequence.

In the case, Lord Atkin defined a **duty of care** by stating that:

You must take reasonable care to avoid acts or omissions which you can reasonably foresee would be likely to injure your neighbour. Who then is my neighbour? The answer seems to be persons who are so closely and directly affected by my act that I ought reasonably to have them in contemplation as being so affected when I am directing my mind to the acts or omissions which are called in question.

The law of negligence is founded almost entirely on decided cases, and the approach adopted by the courts is one that affords flexibility in response to the changing patterns of practical problems. Unfortunately, it is unavoidable that with flexibility comes an element of uncertainty. Whether or not liability will arise in a particular set of circumstances appears to be heavily governed by public policy, and it is not clear exactly when a duty of care will arise. At present, the principles, or alternatively the questions to be asked in attempting to determine whether a duty exists, are:

■ is there foreseeability of harm and, if so …

■ is there proximity – a close and direct relationship – and, if so …

■ is it fair and reasonable for there to be a duty in these circumstances?

Having established that a duty of care exists, defendants will be in breach of that duty if they have not acted reasonably. The question is 'What standard of care does the law require?' The standard of care required is that of an ordinary prudent man in the circumstances pertaining to the case. For example, in one case it was held that an employee owed a higher standard of care to a one-eyed motor mechanic and was therefore obliged to provide protective goggles – not because the likelihood of damage was greater, but because the consequences of an eye injury were more serious (*Paris v Stepney BC,* 1951). Similarly, a higher standard of care would be expected from a drug manufacturer than from a greetings cards manufacturer because the consequences of defective products would be far more serious in the former case.

Where a person is regarded as a professional (i.e. where people set themselves up as possessing a particular skill, such as a plumber, solicitor or surgeon) then they must display the type of skill required in carrying out that particular profession or trade.

With a liability based on fault, the defendant can be liable only for damages caused by him or her. The test adopted is whether the damage is of a type or kind that ought reasonably to have been foreseen even though the extent need not have been envisaged. The main duty is that of manufacturers, but cases have shown that almost any party that is responsible for the supply of goods may be held liable. The onus of proving negligence is on the plaintiff. Of importance in this area is s. 2(1) of the Unfair Contract Terms Act 1977, which states: 'a person cannot by reference to any contract term or notice exclude or restrict his liability for death or personal injury resulting from negligence'. Also s. 2(2): 'in the case of other loss or damage, a person cannot so exclude or restrict his liability for negligence except in so far as the contract term or notice satisfies the test of reasonableness'. Thus, all clauses that purport to exclude liability in respect of negligence resulting in death or personal injuries are void, and other clauses (e.g. 'goods accepted at owner's risk') must satisfy the test of reasonableness.

6.4   Legal processes

It is not only changes in the law itself that should be of concern to businesses, but also the ease of access to legal processes. If legal processes are excessively expensive or time-consuming, the law may come to be seen as irrelevant if parties have no realistic means of enforcing the law. In general, developed economies have seen access to the law widened, so that it is not exclusively at the service of rich individuals or companies. As well as individuals and companies having the right to protect their own legal interests, a number of government agencies facilitate enforcement of the law.

In England, a number of courts of law operate with distinct functional and hierarchical roles.

- The Magistrates' Court deals primarily with criminal matters, where it handles approximately 97 per cent of the workload. It is responsible for handling prosecutions of companies for breaches of legislation under the Trade Descriptions and the Consumer Protection Acts. More serious criminal matters are 'committed' up to the Crown Court for trial.

- The Crown Court handles the more serious cases that have been committed to it for trial on 'indictment'. In addition, it also hears defendants' appeals as to sentence or conviction from the Magistrates' Court.

- The High Court is responsible for hearing appeals by way of 'case stated' from the Magistrates' Court or occasionally the Crown Court. The lower court, whose decision is being challenged, prepares papers (the case) and seeks the opinion of the High Court.

- The Court of Appeal deals primarily with appeals from trials on indictment in the Crown Court. It may review either sentence or conviction.

- County Courts are for almost all purposes the courts of first instance in civil matters (contract and tort). Generally, where the amount claimed is less than £25,000, this court will have jurisdiction in the first instance, but between £25,000 and £50,000, the case may be heard here, or be directed to the High Court, depending on its complexity.

- When larger amounts are being litigated, the High Court will have jurisdiction in the first instance. There is a commercial court within the structure that is designed to be a quicker and generally more suitable court for commercial matters; bankruptcy appeals from the County Court are heard here.

- Cases worth less than £5000 are referred by the County Court to its 'Small Claims' division, where the case will be heard informally under arbitration, and costs normally limited to the value of the issue of the summons.

- The Court of Appeals' Civil Division hears civil appeals from the County Court and the High Court.

- The Supreme Court is the ultimate appeal court for both criminal and domestic matters, having been created in 2009 to take over the role previously carried out by the House of Lords.

■ However, where there is a European issue, the European Court of Justice will give a ruling on the point at issue, after which the case is referred back to the UK court.

In addition to the court structure (see Figure 6.1), there are numerous quasi-judicial tribunals that exist to reconcile disagreeing parties. Examples include Rent Tribunals (for agreeing property rents), Valuation Tribunals (for agreeing property values) and Employment Tribunals (for bringing claims covered by employment legislation).

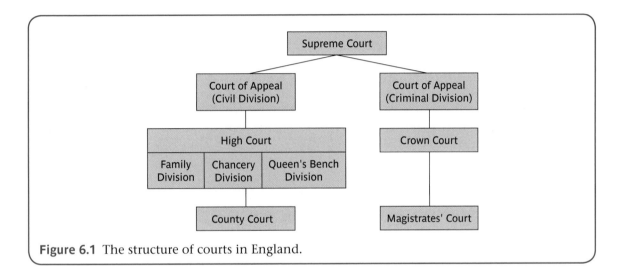

Figure 6.1 The structure of courts in England.

Despite the existence of legal rights, the cost to an individual or a firm of enforcing its rights can be prohibitive, especially where there is no certainty that a party taking action will be able to recover its legal costs. For a typical inter-company dispute over a debt of £50,000, the party suing the debtor can easily incur legal expenses of several thousand pounds, not counting the cost of its employees' time. Where a case goes to the Court of Appeal, a company could be involved in inestimable costs. The legal process can also be very slow. In the case of an intercompany debt claim, a case may take up to ten years between the first issue of a writ and compensation finally being received.

Numerous attempts have been made to make the legal system more widely accessible, such as the small claims section of the County Court, which handles claims of up to £5000 in a less formal and costly manner than a normal County Court claim. There have also been attempts to reduce the risks to individuals by allowing, in certain circumstances, solicitors to charge their clients depending upon results obtained in court (often referred to as a 'no win, no fee' system). Many people feel that the costs of running the courts system could be cut by reducing many bureaucratic and restrictive practices within the legal profession.

Despite moves to make legal remedies more widely available, access to the law remains unequal. Among commercial organizations, a small under-resourced firm may be unable to put the money upfront to pursue a case against a larger company that could defend itself with an army of retained lawyers. Similarly, private consumers are unequal in their access to the law. It has often been suggested that easy access to the law is afforded to the very rich (who can afford it) and the very poor (who may be eligible to receive legal aid). An apparent paradox of attempts to make the law more accessible is that these attempts may themselves overwhelm courts with cases with which they are unable to cope. As an example, the Small Claims Court is reported to have been overwhelmed in 2007 by thousands of bank customers suing their banks for a refund of 'unreasonable' charges levied by the banks. The flood of litigants was assisted by the availability online of template letters promoted by consumer group sites and the ability of aggrieved customers to submit small claims online (www.moneyclaim.gov.uk).

Central and local government is increasingly being given power to act as a consumer champion and to bring cases before the courts that are in the interest of consumers in general. Bodies that pursue actions in this way include the following.

- Trading Standards Departments, which are operated by local authorities, have powers to investigate complaints about false or misleading descriptions of prices, inaccurate weights and measures, consumer credit and the safety of consumer legislation. Consumers' knowledge of their rights has often stretched the resources of Trading Standards Departments so that, at best, they can take action against bad practice only selectively.

- The Environmental Health Departments of local authorities deal with health matters such as unfit food and dirty shops and restaurants. A consumer who suspects that they have suffered food poisoning as a result of eating unfit food at a restaurant may lodge a complaint with the local Environmental Health Department, which may collate similar complaints and use this evidence to prosecute the offending restaurant or take steps to have it closed down.

- Utility regulators have powers to bring action against companies that are in breach of their licence conditions.

6.5 Legislation affecting the supply of goods and services

Prior to 1968, there was very little statutory intervention in the contractual relationship between business organizations and their customers, with a few exceptions such as those that came within the scope of the Food and Drugs Act 1955. Since the 1960s there has been an increasing amount of legislation designed to protect the interests of private consumers, who legislators have seen as unequal parties to a contract. In recent years EU directives have been incorporated into UK legislation to provide additional duties for suppliers of goods and services. It should be noted that much of the legislation applies only to business-to-consumer contracts and not business-to-business contracts. In the latter case, legislation has often presumed that parties have equal bargaining power and therefore do not need additional legislative protection.

⟳ Thinking around the subject

Who benefits from a 'compensation culture'?

Are we becoming a litigious society, dominated by a 'compensation culture'? Newspapers are continually reporting claims made by individuals that at first may seem quite trivial and not warranting legal intervention. Recent reported claims, which some would argue typify a compensation culture, include a teacher who won £55,000 after slipping on a chip, and the parents of a Girl Guide who sued after she was burned by fat spitting from a sausage. Aggrieved parties may have been spurred on by the rise of 'personal injury advisers' who offer to take on a claim at no risk to the claimant. They have sometimes been referred to as 'ambulance chasers' for the way they pursue injured parties, making them aware of the possibility of claiming for a loss or injury, which they may otherwise have written off in their minds as just bad luck. If their claim is rejected by the court, the claimant will pay nothing. If it succeeds, they pay the company handling the claim a percentage of the damages awarded. Such companies have been accused of unrealistically raising clients' expectations of damages, and looking for confrontation where alternative methods of reconciliation may be more effective. The business practices of some companies have been criticized, and one company, the Accident Group, went out of business in 2004 after accumulating large debts and failing to deliver promised benefits to many of its customers.

Is the compensation culture necessarily a bad thing for society? Defending cases costs companies time and money, which will inevitably be passed on in the form of higher prices charged to consumers. Claims against companies sometimes even lead to goods or services no longer being made available to consumers because of an open-ended risk of being sued if there is a problem with the product.

But shouldn't consumers expect businesses to deliver their promises in a responsible manner? Is a compensation culture essentially about redressing the balance between relatively weak consumers and more powerful organizations? If those organizations did their job properly, would there be no case for even talking about a compensation culture? If the cost of obtaining justice made it difficult for aggrieved customers to bring a claim against a company, would the company simply carry on acting irresponsibly because it realized it was beyond reproach? In the case of very dubious claims, such as a customer who sued a restaurant because their cup of coffee was 'too hot', could the company attract sympathy from the majority of its customers, who might regard such a claim as frivolous?

In this section, we consider the following important pieces of statute law that have an impact on the relationship between an organization and its customers:

- the Trade Descriptions Act 1968
- the Sale of Goods Act 1979
- the Misrepresentation Act 1967
- the Consumer Protection Act 1987
- the Consumer Credit Act 1974.

This chapter can provide only a brief summary of a small number of laws that affect business – consumer relationships. Businesses frequently complain about the vast number of regulations that cover their particular sector.

In addition, this section reviews a number of quasi-legal codes of conduct operated by industry bodies.

6.5.1 Trade Descriptions Act 1968

The Trade Descriptions Act 1968 makes it an offence for a person to make a false or misleading trade description and creates three principal offences, as described below.

A false trade description to goods

Under s. 1, this states that 'a person who, in the course of business, applies false trade descriptions to goods or suppliers or offers to supply goods to which a false description has been applied is guilty of an offence'. Section 2 defines a false trade description as including 'any indication of any physical characteristics such as quantity, size, method of manufacture, composition and fitness for purpose'. A description is regarded as false when it is false or, by s. 3(2), misleading to a material degree. In some cases consumers are misled by advertisements that are economical with the truth. A car was advertised as having one previous 'owner'. Strictly this was true, but it had been owned by a leasing company, which had leased it to five different users. The divisional court held this was misleading by s. 3(2) (*R. v London Borough of Wandsworth, The Times*, 20 January 1983).

A false statement of price

Section 11 makes a false statement as to the price an offence. If a trader claims that its prices are reduced, it is guilty of an offence unless it can show that the goods have been on sale at the higher price during the preceding six months for a consecutive period of 28 days (more specific requirements concerning pricing are contained in the Price Marking Order 2004).

A false trade description of services

Section 14 states that it is an offence to make false or misleading statements about services. An example of this is illustrated in the case of a store that advertised 'folding doors and folding door gear – carriage free'. This statement was intended to convey to the consumer that only the folding door gear would be sent carriage-free on purchase of the folding doors. It was held that the advert was misleading and that it was irrelevant that it was not intended to be misleading (*MFI Warehouses Ltd v Nattrass* [1973] 1 All ER 762).

Traders can use a number of defences under the Act, set out in s. 24(i):

(a) that the commission of the offence was due to a mistake or to reliance on information supplied to the company or to the act or default of another person, an accident or some other cause beyond its control, and

(b) that the company took all reasonable precautions and exercised all due diligence to avoid the commission of such an offence by itself or any person under its control.

For the defence to succeed, it is necessary to show that both sub-sections apply. In a case concerning a leading supermarket, washing powder was incorrectly advertised as being 5p less than the price actually charged in the store. The defendants said that it was the fault of the store manager who had failed to go through the system laid down for checking shelves. The court held that the defence applied; the store manager was 'another person' (s. 24(i)(a)) and the store had taken reasonable precautions to prevent commission of the offence (*Tesco Supermarkets Ltd v Nattrass* [1971] 2 All ER 127).

6.5.2 Sale of Goods Act 1979

What rights has the consumer if he or she discovers that the goods purchased are faulty or different from those ordered? The Sale of Goods Act (SOGA) 1979 contains terms specifically to protect the consumer. The term 'consumer' is defined by s. 20(6) of the Consumer Protection Act 1987, and essentially covers situations where a purchase is made for private consumption, rather than for use in the course of a business.

Section 13 of the Sale of Goods Act 1979 states that, 'Where there is a contract for the sale of goods by description there is an implied condition that the goods will correspond with the description.' Goods must be as described on the package. If a customer purchases a blue long-sleeved shirt and on opening the box discovers that it is a red short-sleeved shirt, then he is entitled to a return of the price for breach of an implied condition of the contract.

Section 14(2), as amended by the Sale and Supply of Goods Act 1994, states that where a seller sells goods in the course of a business, there is an implied term that the goods supplied under the contract are of satisfactory quality. For the purposes of this Act goods are of satisfactory quality if they meet the standard that a reasonable person would regard as satisfactory, taking account of any description of the goods, fitness for all the purposes for which goods of the kind in question are commonly supplied, appearance and finish, safety, durability, freedom from minor defects, the price (if relevant) and all other relevant circumstances.

However, s.14(2C) states and which the standard of satisfactory quality need not apply in respect of faults which should be reasonably apparent to a buyer before purchase and which are specifically drawn to the buyer's attention before the contract is made.

The implied term of satisfactory quality applies to sale goods and second-hand goods, but clearly the consumer would not have such high expectations of second-hand goods. For example, a clutch fault in a new car would make it unsatisfactory, but not so if the car were second-hand. In a second-hand car – again, depending on all the circumstances – a fault would have to be major to render the car unsatisfactory. Thus, the question to be asked is, 'Are the goods satisfactory in the light of the contract description and all the circumstances of the case?'

It is often asked for how long the goods should remain satisfactory. It is implicit that the goods remain satisfactory for a length of time reasonable in the circumstances of the case and the nature of the goods. If a good becomes defective within a very short time, this is evidence that there was possibly a latent defect at the time of the sale.

Under s. 14(3), there is an implied condition that goods are fit for a particular purpose where the seller sells goods in the course of a business and the buyer, expressly or by implication, makes known to the seller any particular purpose for which the goods are being bought. Thus, if a seller, on request, confirms suitability for a particular purpose and the product proves unsuitable, there would be a breach of s. 14(3); if the product is also unsuitable for its normal purposes, then s. 14(2) would be breached too. If the seller disclaims any knowledge of the product's suitability for the particular purpose and the consumer takes a chance and purchases it, then if it proves unsuitable for its particular purpose there is no breach of s. 14(3). The only circumstance in which a breach may occur is, again, if it were unsuitable for its normal purposes under s. 14(2).

In business contracts, implied terms in ss. 13–15 of the Sale of Goods Act 1979 can be excluded. Such exclusion clauses, purporting, for example, to exclude a term for reasonable fitness for goods (s. 14), are valid subject to the test of reasonableness provided that the term is incorporated into the contract. However, for consumer contracts, such clauses that purport to limit or exclude liability are void under s. 6(2) of the Unfair Contract Terms Act 1977.

The Supply of Goods and Services Act 1982 (SGSA) offers almost identical protection where goods and services are provided. Section 3 corresponds to s. 13 of SOGA and s. 4 corresponds to s. 14 of SOGA. Section 13 of SGSA provides that, where the supplier of a service under a contract is acting in the course of a business, there is an implied term that the supplier will carry out the service with reasonable care and skill. Reasonable care and skill may be defined as 'the ordinary skill of an ordinary competent man exercising that particular act'. Much will depend on the circumstances of the case and the nature of the trade or profession.

6.5.3 Misrepresentation Act 1967

The Misrepresentation Act 1967 provides remedies for victims of misrepresentation. For the purpose of the Act, an actionable misrepresentation may be defined as 'a false statement of existing or past fact made by one party to the other before or at the time of making the contract, which is intended to, and does, induce the other party to enter into the contract'.

Since the 1967 Act, it has been necessary to maintain a clear distinction between fraudulent misrepresentation, negligent misrepresentation and wholly innocent misrepresentation (s. 2(1)). Rescission of a contract is a remedy for all three types of misrepresentation. In addition to rescission for fraudulent misrepresentation, damages may be awarded under the tort of fraud, and in respect of negligent misrepresentation damages may be awarded under s. 2(1) of the

1967 Act. Under s. 2(2) damages may also be awarded at the discretion of the court, but, if so, these are in lieu of rescission.

6.5.4 The Consumer Protection Act 1987

The Consumer Protection Act 1987 implements an EU directive, and provides a remedy in damages for anyone who suffers personal injury or damage to property as a result of a defective product. The effect is to impose a strict (i.e. whereby it is unnecessary to prove negligence) tortious liability on producers of defective goods. The Act supplements the existing law; thus, a consumer may well have a remedy in contract, in the tort of negligence or under the Act if he or she has suffered loss caused by a defective product.

The producer will be liable if the consumer can establish that the product is defective and that it caused a loss. There is a defect if the safety of the goods does not conform to general expectations with reference to the risk of damage to property or risk of death or personal injury. The general expectations will differ depending on the particular circumstances, but points to be taken into account include the product's instructions, warnings and the time elapsed since supply, the latter point to determine the possibility of the defect being due to wear and tear.

The onus is on the plaintiff to prove that loss was caused by the defect. A claim may be made by anyone, whether death, personal injury or damage to property has occurred. However, where damage to property is concerned, the damage is confined to property ordinarily intended for private use, thus excluding commercial goods and property. It is not possible to exclude liability under the Consumer Protection Act.

The Act is intended to place liability on the producer of defective goods. In some cases the company may not manufacture the goods, but may still be liable, as outlined below.

- Anyone carrying out 'industrial or other process' to goods that have been manufactured by someone else will be treated as the producer where 'essential characteristics' (e.g. modifications to a product) are attributable to that process.
- If a company puts its own brand name on goods that have been manufactured on its behalf, thus holding itself out to be the producer, that company will be liable for any defects in the goods.
- Any importer who imports goods from outside EU countries will be liable for defects in the imported goods.

The Act is also instrumental in providing a remedy against suppliers who are unable to identify the importee or the previous supplier to them. If the supplier fails or cannot identify the manufacturer's importee or previous supplier, then the supplier is liable.

6.5.5 Consumer Credit Act 1974

This is a consumer protection measure to protect the public from, among other things, extortionate credit agreements and high-pressure selling off trade premises. The Act became fully operational in 1985, and much of the protection afforded to hire purchase transactions is extended to those obtaining goods and services through consumer credit transactions. It is important to note that contract law governs the formation of agreements coming within the scope of the Consumer Credit Act. Section 8(2) defines a consumer credit agreement as personal credit providing the debtor with credit not exceeding £25,000. Section 9 defines credit as a cash loan and any form of financial accommodation.

There are two types of credit. The first is a running account credit (s. 10(a)), whereby the debtor is enabled to receive from time to time, from the creditor or a third party, cash, goods and services to an amount or value such that, taking into account payments made by or to the credit of the debtor, the credit limit (if any) is not at any time exceeded. An example of this is a credit card facility, e.g. Visa or MasterCard. The second type is fixed-sum credit, defined in s. 10(b) as any other facility under a personal credit agreement whereby the debtor is enabled to receive credit. An example here would be a bank loan.

The Act covers hire purchase agreements (s. 189), which are agreements under which goods are hired in return for periodical payments by the person to whom they are hired and where the property in the goods will pass to that person if the terms of the agreement are complied with – for example, the exercise of an option to purchase by that person. In addition to hire purchase agreements, also within the scope of the Act are conditional sale agreements for the sale of goods or land, in respect of which the price is payable by instalments and the property (i.e. ownership) remains with the seller until any conditions set out in the contract are fulfilled, and credit sale agreements, where the property (ownership) passes to the buyer when the sale is effected.

Debtor–creditor supplier agreements relate to the situation where there is a business connection between creditor and supplier (i.e. a pre-existing arrangement) or where the creditor and the supplier are the same person. Section 55 and ss. 60–65 deal with formalities of the contract between debtor and creditor, their aim being that the debtor be made fully aware of the nature and the cost of the transaction, and his or her rights and liabilities under it. The Act requires that certain information must be disclosed to the debtor before the contract is made. This includes total charge for credit, and the annual rate of the total charge for credit that the debtor will have to pay expressed in an approved format. All regulated agreements must comply with the formality procedures and must contain, among other things, the debtor's right to cancel and to pay off the debt early.

If a consumer credit agreement is drawn up off business premises, the agreement is cancellable, and debtor is entitled to a 'cooling-off' period during which the contract can be set aside without penalty. This is designed to counteract high-pressure doorstep selling.

6.5.6 Codes of practice

Codes of practice do not in themselves have the force of law. They can, however, be of great importance to businesses. In the first place, they can help to raise the standards of an industry by imposing a discipline on signatories to a code not to indulge in dubious marketing practices, which – although legal – act against the long-term interests of the industry and its customers. Second, voluntary codes of practice can offer a cheaper and quicker means of resolving grievances between the two parties compared with more formal legal channels. For example, the holiday industry has its own arbitration facilities, which avoid the cost of taking many cases through to the courts. Third, business organizations are often happy to accept restrictions imposed by codes of practice as these are seen as preferable to restrictions being imposed by laws. The tobacco industry in the UK for a long time avoided statutory controls on cigarette advertising because of the existence of its voluntary code, which imposed restrictions on tobacco advertising.

The Director General of the Office of Fair Trading is instrumental in encouraging trade associations to adopt codes of practice. An example of a voluntary code is provided by the Vehicle Builders and Repair Association, which, among other items, requires members to: give clear estimates of prices; inform customers as soon as possible if additional costs are likely to be incurred; complete work in a timely manner. In the event of a dispute between a customer and a member of the Association, a conciliation service is available that reduces the need to resort to legal remedies. However, in April 2005, the National Consumer Council accused the motor industry of failing to regulate itself adequately, by providing 'shoddy services and rip-off charges'. The Council pledged to submit a 'super complaint' to the Office of Fair Trading (OFT), which would force the OFT to investigate its allegations, unless the industry took prompt remedial action. This raised the possibility of a licensing system for car repairers, something the industry had resisted so far and realized would be more onerous than a voluntary code of conduct.

Useful leaflets published by the OFT giving information regarding codes of practice can be obtained from local Consumer Advice Bureaux.

6.5.7 Controls on advertising

There are a number of laws that influence the content of advertisements in Britain. For example, the Trade Descriptions Act 1968 makes false statements in an advertisement an offence, while the Consumer Credit Act 1974 lays down quite precise rules about the way in which credit can be advertised. However, the content of advertisements is also influenced by voluntary codes. In the UK, the codes for advertising are the responsibility of the advertising industry through two Committees of Advertising Practice: CAP (Broadcast) and CAP (Non-broadcast). CAP (Broadcast) is responsible for the TV and radio advertising codes, and CAP (Non-broadcast) is responsible for non-broadcast advertisements, sales promotions and direct marketing. Both are administered by the Advertising Standards Authority (ASA). The Office of Communications (Ofcom) is the statutory regulator for broadcast advertising in the UK and has delegated its powers to the ASA, which deals with all complaints about such advertising.

The ASA codes are subscribed to by most organizations involved in advertising, including the Advertising Association, the Institute of Practitioners in Advertising, and the associations representing publishers of newspapers and magazines, the outdoor advertising industry and direct marketing.

The Code of Advertising Practice (Non-broadcast) requires that all advertisements appearing in members' publications should be legal, decent, honest and truthful. Two adjudications illustrate how the ASA interprets this. In one case, a national press advert for the retailer Lidl featured a Landmann Lava Rock Gas Barbecue and the message '£10 cheaper compared to B&Q'. It was held that the comparison was misleading, because the precise model sold by B&Q was not accurately specified, therefore the fact of '£10 cheaper' could not be established. In another case from 2008, an advert in the *Daily Mail* for Ryanair under the headline 'Hottest back to school fares . . . one-way fares £10' featured a picture of a teenage girl or woman standing in a classroom and wearing a version of a school uniform consisting of a short tartan skirt, a cropped short sleeved shirt and tie, and long white socks. The ASA considered the model's clothing, together with the setting of the ad in a classroom strongly suggested she was a schoolgirl and considered that her appearance and pose, in conjunction with the heading 'Hottest', appeared to link teenage girls with sexually provocative behaviour. It considered the advert was likely to cause serious or widespread offence, and was in breach of the Code's sections governing social responsibility and decency.

Although the main role of the ASA is advisory, it does have a number of sanctions available against individual advertisers that break the code, ultimately leading to the ASA requesting its media members to refuse to publish the advertisements of an offending company. More often, the ASA relies on publicizing its rulings to shame advertisers into responding (although some critics would say that press coverage of companies breaching the code simply provides free awareness-grabbing publicity for the company).

The advertising codes are continually evolving to meet the changing attitudes and expectations of the public. Thus, restrictions on alcohol advertising have been tightened up – for example, by insisting that young actors are not portrayed in advertisements and by not showing them on television when children are likely to be watching. On the other hand, advertising restrictions for some products have been relaxed in response to changing public attitudes. Television adverts for condoms have moved from being completely banned to being allowed, but only in very abstract form, to the present situation where the product itself can be mentioned using actors in life-like situations.

Numerous other forms of voluntary control exist. As mentioned previously, many trade associations have codes that impose restrictions on how they can advertise. Solicitors, for example, were previously not allowed to advertise at all, but now can do so within limits defined by the Law Society.

The Control of Misleading Advertisements Regulations 1988 (as amended) provides the legislative back-up to the self-regulatory system in respect of advertisements that mislead. The Regulations require the OFT to investigate complaints, and empower the OFT to seek, if necessary, an injunction from the courts against publication of an advertisement. More usually it would initially seek assurances from an advertiser to modify or not repeat an offending advertisement. Before investigating, the OFT can require that other means of dealing with a complaint, such as the ASA system mentioned above, have been fully explored. Action by the OFT therefore usually results only from a referral from the Advertising Standards Authority where the self-regulatory system has not had the required impact.

In general, the system of voluntary regulation of advertising has worked well in the UK. For advertisers, voluntary codes can allow more flexibility and opportunities to have an input to the code. For the public, a code can be updated in a less bureaucratic manner than may be necessary with new legislation or statutory regulations. However, the question remains as to how much responsibility for the social and cultural content of advertising should be given to industry-led voluntary bodies rather than being decided by government. Do voluntary codes unduly reflect the narrow financial interests of advertisers rather than the broader interests of the public at large? Doubtless, advertisers realize that if they do not develop a code that is socially acceptable, the task will be taken away from them and carried out by government in a process where they will have less influence.

6.6 Statutory legislation on employment

Employment law is essentially based on the principles of law previously discussed. The relationship between an employer and its employees is governed by the law of contract, while the employer owes a duty of care to its employees and can be sued for negligence where this duty of care is broken. Employers are vicariously liable for the actions of their employees, so if an employee is negligent and harms a member of the public during the course of their employment, the injured party has a claim against the employer as well as the employee who was the immediate cause of the injury.

The common law principles of contract and negligence have for a long time been supplemented with statutory intervention. Society has recognized that a contract of employment is quite different from a contract to buy consumer goods, because the personal investment of the employee in their job can be very considerable. Losing a job without good cause can have a much more profound effect than suffering loss as a result of losing money on the purchase of goods. Governments have recognized that individuals should have a proprietary interest in their jobs and have therefore passed legislation to protect employees against the actions of unscrupulous employers who abuse their dominant power over employees. Legislation has also recognized that employment practices can have a much wider effect on society through organizations' recruitment policies.

In this section we consider some of the areas in which statutory intervention has affected the environment in which organizations recruit, reward and dismiss employees. The information here cannot hope to go into any depth on particular legislative requirements, as legislation is complex, detailed and continually changing. There is also considerable difference between countries in terms of legislation that affects employment. The following brief summary can only aim to identify the main issues of concern covered by legislation, in England specifically. This chapter should also be read in conjunction with Chapter 10, on the internal environment. In that chapter we look in general terms at issues such as the need for flexibility in the workforce. This chapter identifies particular legal opportunities and constraints, which help to define an organization's internal environment.

6.6.1 When does an employment contract occur?

It is not always obvious whether a contract of employment exists between an organization and individuals providing services for it. Many individuals working for organizations in fact provide their services as self-employed subcontractors, rather than as employees. The distinction between the two is important, because a self-employed contractor does not benefit from the legislation, which only protects employees. There can be many advantages in classifying an individual as self-employed rather than as an employee. For the self-employed, tax advantages result from being able to claim as legitimate business expense items that in many circumstances are denied to the employee. The method of assessing National Insurance and income tax liability in arrears can favour a self-employed subcontractor. For the employer, designation as self-employed could relieve the employer of some duties that are imposed in respect of employees but not subcontractors, such as entitlement to sick pay, notice periods and maternity leave.

There was a great move towards self-employment during the 1990s, encouraged by the trend towards outsourcing of many non-core functions by businesses (see Chapter 8). Not surprisingly, the UK government has sought to recoup potentially lost tax revenue and to protect unwitting self-employed individuals, by examining closely the terms on which an individual is engaged. The courts have decided the matter on the basis of, among other things, the degree of control that the organization buying a person's services has over the person providing them, the level of integration between the individual and the organization, and who bears the business risk. If the organization is able to specify the manner in which a task is to be carried out, then an employment relationship generally exists. If, however, the required end result is specified but the manner in which it is achieved is left up to the individual, then a contract for services will exist – in other words, self-employment. There is still ambiguity in the distinction between employment and self-employment, which has, for example, resulted in numerous appeals by individuals against classification decisions made by HMRC.

6.6.2 Flexibility of contract

Organizations are increasingly seeking a more flexible workforce to help them respond more rapidly to changes in their external environment. In Chapter 10 we see some of the benefits to an organization of developing flexible employment practices.

Short-term employment contracts are becoming increasingly significant in a number of European countries, partly due to the existence of labour market regulations that make it difficult for employers to recruit and dismiss permanent staff. Within Europe, there has been a tendency for national legislation to reflect EU directives by imposing additional burdens on employers of full-time, permanent employees. This can affect the ease with which staff can be laid off or dismissed should demand fall – for example, in Germany, the Dismissals Protection Law (*Kundigungsschutzgesetz*) has given considerable protection to salaried staff who have been in their job for more than six months, allowing dismissal only for a 'socially justified' reason.

The move towards short-term contracts is a Europe-wide phenomenon. In 2005, about 34 per cent of the Spanish workforce was employed with contracts of limited duration compared to less than 16 per cent 20 years previously, while in France the proportion of employees with contracts of limited duration climbed from 6.7 per cent in 1985 to about 13 per cent by 2005 (Eurostat 2006–07). The spread of short-term contracts is most apparent among young workers employed in insecure and highly mobile areas of the labour market, such as the retail, distribution, communication and information technology sectors.

The EU and most member-state governments have been keen to ensure that workers on short-term contracts enjoy similar legal rights as those in full-time, permanent employment. In the UK, the Employment Relations Act 1999 requires the appropriate secretary of state to make regulations to ensure that part-time workers are treated no less favourably than full-time workers. These regulations include provisions to implement the EU-level social partners' agreement and subsequent Council Directive on part-time work (97/81/EC).

Despite imposing additional burdens, many European governments have encouraged the greater use of short-term contracts as a way of improving the flexibility of their national economies – for example, through changes in welfare benefits that do not penalize short-term working.

QUESTIONS

1 What factors could explain the increasing amount of legislation that now faces tour operators?

2 Summarize the main consequences of the EU Directive referred to above on the marketing of package holidays in the UK.

3 Is there still a role for voluntary codes of conduct in preference to legislation as a means of regulating the relationship between a tour operator and its customers?

Summary

This chapter has noted the increasing effects that legislation is having on businesses. The principal sources of law have been identified. Statute law is becoming increasingly important, with more influence being felt from the EU. Legal processes and the remedies available to a firm's customers have been discussed.

Voluntary codes of conduct are often seen as an alternative to law, and offer firms lower cost and greater flexibility.

The discussion of business ethics in **Chapter 5** relates closely to the legal environment. To many people, law is essentially a formalization of ethics, with statute law enacted by government **(Chapter 2)**. The competition environment **(Chapter 11)** is increasingly influenced by legislation governing anti-competitive practices. We saw in **Chapter 4** that legal protection for innovative new technologies is vital if expenditure on research and development is to be sustained. In addition to the aspects of law discussed in this chapter, legislation affects the status of organizations **(Chapter 7)** – for example, in the protection that is given to limited liability companies.

Key Terms

Code of practice (213)

Common law (202)

Contract (203)

Discrimination (219)

Dismissal (220)

Duty of care (205)

Intellectual property rights (203)

Misrepresentation (211)

Negligence (205)

Patent (222)

Statute law (202)

Tort (205)

Trademark (222)

 Online Learning Centre

To help you grasp the key concepts of this chapter, explore the extra resources posted on the Online Learning Centre at *www.mcgraw-hill.co.uk/palmer*. Among other helpful resources there are chapter-by-chapter test questions, revision notes and web links.

Chapter review questions

1 Discuss the main ways in which the legal environment impacts on the activities of the sales and marketing functions of business organizations.

2 Giving examples, evaluate the criticism that government legislation impacts primarily on those firms that can least afford to pay for it, mainly the small and the competitively vulnerable.

3 Using an appropriate example, evaluate the virtues and drawbacks of using voluntary codes of practice to regulate business activity.

Activities

1 Think back to a time when you had a problem with a good or service that didn't meet the agreed specification (e.g. a DVD you ordered didn't have as many tracks as advertised; the seats you ended up with at a rock concert were not as good as the ones you had ordered). Identify the methods of conflict resolution available to you, short of taking legal action. Did the supplier make it easy to resolve the problem? What more could it have done? Is there a voluntary code of conduct or arbitration service that you could have used? Is it easy to use? What factors would encourage or discourage you from taking legal action?

2 Philip, shopping at a large department store, sees a colourful spinning top, which he buys for his grandson Harry. While purchasing the toy, he sees a prominent notice in the store, which states: 'This store will not be held responsible for any defects in the toys sold.' The box containing the spinning top carries the description 'Ideal for children over 12 months, safe and non-toxic' (Harry is 15 months old). Within four weeks the spinning top has split into two parts, each with a jagged edge, and Harry has suffered an illness as a result of sucking the paint. Philip has complained vociferously to the store, which merely pointed to the prominent notice disclaiming liability. Philip has now informed the store that he intends to take legal action against it.

Draft a report to the managing director setting out the legal liability of the store.

3 Zak runs his own painting and decorating business, and has been engaged to decorate Rebecca's lounge. While burning off layers of paint from the door with his blowtorch, Zak's attention is diverted by the barking of neighbour Camilla's Yorkshire terrier and, as he turns round, the flame catches a cushion on the sofa. Within seconds the room is filled with acrid smoke. Both the carpet and sofa are damaged beyond repair, and the dog, terrified, rushes into the road, where it is run over by a car. Consider Zak's legal liability.

Further reading

The following texts provide a general overview of law as it affects commercial organizations.

Adams, A. (2010) *Law for Business Students*, 6th edn, London, Longman.
Clayton, P. (2009) *Essential Law for Your Business: A Practical Guide to all Legal and Financial Requirements*, 13th edn, London, Kogan Page.
Riches, S. and Allen, V. (2009) *Business Law*, 5th edn, Harlow, Pearson.

This chapter has discussed the basics of the law of contract and the following texts provide useful further reading.

Elliott, C. and Quinn, F. (2010) *Contract Law*, 7th edn, London, Longman.

Poole, J. (2010) *Textbook on Contract Law*, 10th edn, Oxford, Oxford University Press.
Trademarks and patent laws are discussed in the following text.

Hart, T., Fazzani, L. and Clark, S. (2009) *Intellectual Property Law*, 5th edn, Basingstoke, Palgrave Macmillan.

A valuable overview of employment law is provided in the following.

Lewis, D. and Sargeant, M. (2009) *Essentials of Employment Law*, 10th edn, London, Chartered Institute of Personnel and Development.

References

Berthoud, R. (2005) *Incomes of Ethnic Minorities*, York, Joseph Rowntree Foundation.
Eurostat (2006–07) *Eurostat Yearbook 2006–07*, Luxembourg, Statistical Office of the European Communities.

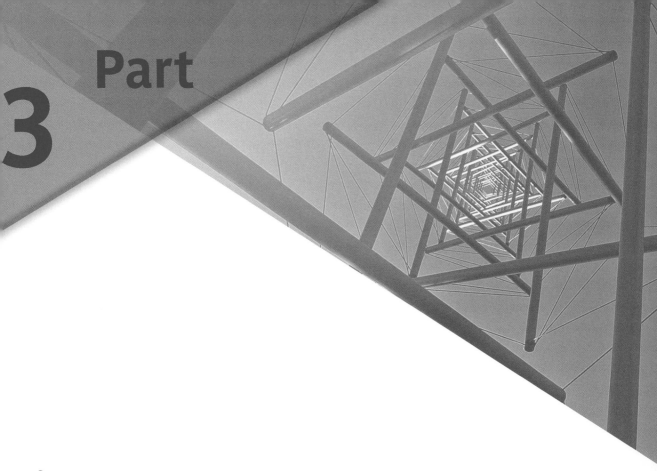

3 Part

Firms

Part contents

Chapter 7

Types of Business Organization

Walk through the business district of most towns and you will find small insurance brokers competing with national giants such as AXA and Aviva; privately run banks such as Barclays competing with state-owned banks such as RBS and Lloyds, and with various forms of cooperatively or mutually owned banks such as the Co-operative Bank and the building societies that can be found on most British high streets. Similar diversity can be found in many other sectors — for example, small specialist electronics retailers compete with national chains such as PC World, and in the restaurant sector, countless small family-run restaurants co-exist with national chains. The diversity of business organizations reflects their ability to adapt to their environment, so there is a role in the business environment for both the small specialist retailer and the national chain store. The nature of diversity within business organizations is explored in this chapter.

 Learning Objectives

This chapter will explain:
- ✓ The diversity of organizational types.
- ✓ The advantages and disadvantages of sole traders, partnerships and limited companies.
- ✓ The role of public-sector organizations and non-departmental public bodies.
- ✓ The effects of organizational form and size on responsiveness to environmental change.

7.1   Introduction: organizations and their environment

Previous chapters have focused on the external environment that affects business organizations. In this chapter we begin to turn our focus inward, to look at the nature of business organizations. We need to understand the factors that facilitate or inhibit an internal response to external environmental change.

But first, we need to ask a basic question: 'Why do organizations exist?' The main reason is that some forms of value creation can be carried out much more efficiently within organizations than by individuals acting alone. Imagine individuals trying to build an aircraft and you can appreciate that they will achieve their objective much more effectively if they come together in some form of organization. However, if a group of individuals want to go into business as household decorators, they might find that the costs of managing the organization put them at a competitive disadvantage compared to individuals acting on their own. Business organizations are extremely diverse in their forms and functions, even within a single business sector. It is therefore difficult to define an 'ideal' organization. Instead, all organizational forms have advantages and disadvantages relative to the environment in which they operate, and successful organizations capitalize on their advantages while recognizing their disadvantages. In a single business sector, there can be a role for both the one-person owner-managed business and the multinational organization. Both can adapt and find a role.

Analogies can be drawn between business organizations and their environment and the animal kingdom. In a natural habitat, the largest and most powerful animals can co-exist with much smaller species. The smaller species can avoid becoming prey for the larger ones by being more agile, or developing defences such as safe habitats that are inaccessible to their larger predators. Sometimes, a symbiotic relationship can develop between the two. In a bid to survive, animals soon learn which sources of food are easily obtainable and abandon those that are either inedible or cause them to face competition from more powerful animals. In Darwinian terms, the 'fittest' survive, and an ecosystem allows for co-existence of living organisms that have adapted in their own way to the challenges of their environment. As in the business environment, macroenvironmental change can affect the relationships between species – as, for example, has occurred with deforestation and the use of intensive farming methods.

Just as any study of the animal world may begin by examining the characteristics of the participants, so an analysis of the business environment could begin by looking at the characteristics of the organizations that make it up. Businesses need to understand the diversity of organizational types for a number of reasons.

- Different types of organization will be able to address their customers, suppliers and employees in different ways. Lack of resources could, for example, inhibit the development of expensive new products by a small business. Sometimes, the objectives of an organization – either formal or informal – will influence what it is able to offer the public.

- As a seller of materials to companies involved in further manufacture, a company should understand how the buying behaviour of different kinds of organization varies. A small business is likely to buy equipment in a different way to a large public-sector organization.

- We should be interested in the structure of business units at the macroeconomic level. Many economists have argued that a thriving small business sector is essential for an expanding economy, and that the effect of domination by large organizations may be to reduce competition and innovation. We should therefore be interested in the rate of new business creation and trends in the composition of business units.

7.1.1 Classification of business organizations

There are many approaches to classifying organizations that would satisfy the interests identified above. Organizations are commonly classified according to their:

- size (e.g. turnover, assets, employees, geographical coverage)
- ownership (e.g. public, private, cooperative)
- legal form (e.g. sole trader, limited company)
- industry sector.

A good starting point for classifying business organizations is to look at their legal form. A business's legal form is often closely related to its size, objectives, and the level of resources it has available for marketing and for new product development (the issues of organizational size and objectives are considered in more detail in the next chapter).

This chapter will first consider private-sector organizations, which range from the small owner-managed sole trader to the very large public limited company. It will then review the diverse range of publicly owned organizations that operate as businesses. A third, and growing, group of organizations cannot be neatly categorized into private or public sector and includes 'quangos' (quasi-autonomous non-governmental organizations) and charities. To put the diversity of organizations into context, Figure 7.1 illustrates the types of organization that will be described in this chapter.

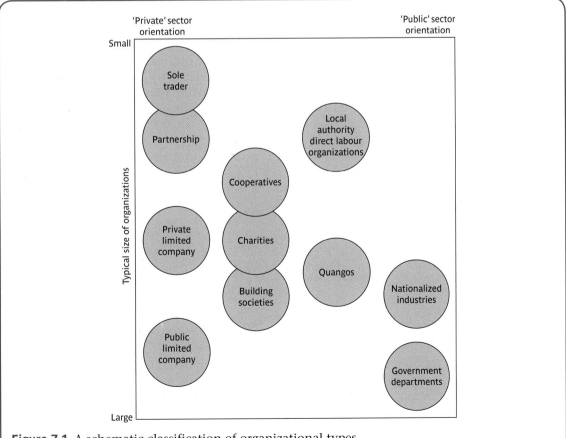

Figure 7.1 A schematic classification of organizational types.

7.2   The sole trader

The most basic level of business organization is provided by the **sole trader**. In fact, the concept of a separate legal form does not apply to this type of organization, for the business and the individual are considered to be legally indistinguishable. The individual carries on business in his or her own name, with the result that the individual assumes all the rights and duties of the business. It follows that if the business is sued for breach of contract, this amounts to suing the individual. If the business does not have the resources to meet any claim, the claim must be met out of the private resources of the individual.

Becoming a sole trader requires the minimum of formality and for this reason it can be difficult to tell how many are being created or are in existence at any one time. The most commonly used indication is provided by VAT registrations, although this does not give a complete picture as businesses with a turnover of less than £70,000 (2010/11) do not need to register. Maintaining a business as a sole trader also requires a minimum of formality – for example, there is no obligation to file annual accounts, other than for the assessment of the individual's personal tax liability.

It has been estimated that about 80 per cent of all businesses in the UK are sole traders, although they account for only a small proportion of gross domestic product (GDP). In some sectors of the economy they are a very popular business form, and dominate sectors such as newsagents, window cleaners and hairdressers. Sole traders can grow by taking on additional employees. There is no legal limit on the number of employees that a sole trader may have and there are many examples of sole traders employing over 100 people. At the other extreme, it is sometimes difficult to describe just when a sole trader business unit comes into existence, with many sole traders operating on a part-time basis – some 'moonlighting' without the knowledge of the tax authorities. Estimates of the annual value of this so-called 'black economy' are as high as £200 million per annum.

We should recognize a number of important characteristics of sole traders. First, they tend to have limited capital resources. Risk capital is generally provided only by the sole proprietor or close personal backers, and additional loan capital is often made available only against security of the individual's assets. In the field of new product development, this type of business has very often made discoveries, but has been unable to see new products through to production and launch on account of a lack of funds. If a new product does make it into a competitive market, this type of business may face competition in price, promotional effort or product offering from larger and better-resourced firms. The larger firm is likely to have greater resources to mount a campaign to see off a newer competitor.

The small sole trader could find that it is too small to justify having its own expertise in many areas. Many do not have specialists to look after the accounting or advertising functions, for example. Furthermore, the goals and policies of the business can become totally dominated by the owner of the business. Although goals can be pursued determinedly and single-mindedly, the sole trader presents a narrower view than may be offered by a larger board of directors. The goals of a sole trader may appear very irrational to an outsider; for instance, many individuals may be happy to continue uneconomic ventures on emotional grounds alone. Many very small caterers, for example, may be financially better off drawing unemployment benefit, but being a sole trader may satisfy wider goals of status or the pursuit of a leisure interest.

Many sole traders fail after only a short time, often because of the lack of management skills of an individual who may well be an expert in his or her own field of specialization. Others continue until they reach a point where lack of expertise and financial resources impose a constraint on growth. At this point, many sole traders consider going into partnership with another individual, or setting up a company with limited liability.

7.2.1 Sole trader or employee?

It can sometimes be difficult to decide whether a person is a self-employed sole trader or an employee of another organization. The distinction is an important one, because a trend in recent years has been for large organizations to outsource many of their operations, often buying in services from apparently self-employed individuals. There can be many advantages in classifying an individual as self-employed rather than an employee. For the self-employed person, tax advantages could result from being able to claim as legitimate some business expense items that are denied to the employee. The method of assessing income tax liability in arrears can favour an expanding small business. For the employer, designation as self-employed could save on National Insurance payments. It also relieves the employer of many duties that are imposed in respect of employees but not subcontractors, such as entitlement to sick pay, notice periods and maternity leave.

The problem of distinction is particularly great in the construction sector and for service sectors (such as market research), which employ large numbers of part-time workers. The courts would decide the matter, among other things, on the basis of the degree of control that the employer has over the employee and their level of integration within the organization. If the employer is able to specify the manner in which a task is to be carried out, and assumes most of the risk in a transaction, then an employment relationship generally exists. If, however, the required end result is specified but the manner in which it is achieved is left up to the individual, who also bears the cost of any budget overrun, then it is most likely that a contract for services will exist – in other words, self-employment.

Thinking around the subject

A mountain of paperwork

One of the biggest complaints from sole traders is the amount of paperwork that they are required by government to complete. Most small business owners have a vision of what they want to do: open a hairdressing salon, install kitchens, run a convenience store or exploit a new invention. But the reality is that they are likely to become bogged down in completing paperwork, some of which they may never have envisaged. According to a NatWest survey, conducted on a quarterly basis by the Open University Business School, the average small firm spent 26.7 hours a month in 2006 completing government paperwork. The burden of red tape fell hardest on small sole traders. Businesses with more than 25 staff spend 1.5 hours per employee on forms, whereas those with more than 50 staff spent 0.6 hours per employee. More than half the firms surveyed said the cost of employee regulation and paperwork had meant they employed fewer staff than they would like. More than a third said they would avoid employing more people, while 18 per cent said that growing levels of regulation had led them to reduce their workforce. After employment paperwork, main gripes concerned the paperwork associated with VAT, and the form-filling associated with health and safety assessments. The Small Business Council has been campaigning to keep paperwork simple and to reduce the time it takes to fill out forms. It has pointed out that, for every hour a sole trader spends filling out forms, they are not able to use the time to sell more products or develop new ones. While large companies may be able to employ specialists to cope with paperwork, for the small business, productivity suffers.

Governments continually say that they wish to reduce the paperwork burden on small businesses, but how can this be achieved in practice?

7.3 Partnerships

Two or more persons in partnership can combine their resources and expertise to form what could be a more efficient business unit. The Partnership Act 1890 defines a **partnership** as 'the relation which subsists between persons carrying on a business with a view to profit'. Partnerships can range from two builders joining together to a very large accountancy or solicitors' practice with hundreds of partners.

Partnerships are generally formed by contract between the parties, although, where this is not done, the Partnership Act 1890 governs relationships between the partners. Among the main items in a Partnership Agreement will be terms specifying:

- the amount of capital subscribed by each partner
- the basis on which profits will be determined and allocated between partners, and the management responsibilities of each partner – some partners may join as 'sleeping partners' and take no active part in the management of the business
- the basis for allocating salaries to each partner and for drawing personal advances against entitlement to profits
- procedures for dissolving the partnership and distributing the assets of the business between members.

Despite this internal agreement between partners, partnerships in England and Wales have not had their own legal personality. As a consequence, the partners incur unlimited personal liability for the debts of the business. Furthermore, each partner is jointly liable for the debts incurred by all partners in the course of business. An added complication of a partnership is that the withdrawal of any one partner, either voluntarily or upon death or bankruptcy, causes the automatic termination of the partnership. A new partnership will come into being, as it would if an additional partner were admitted to the partnership.

Because of the lack of protection afforded to partners, this form of organization tends to be relatively uncommon, except for some groups of professional people, where business risks are low and for whom professional codes of practice may prevent the formation of limited companies. To overcome the problem of limited liability, the Limited Liability Partnerships Act 2000 created a new form of partnership with limited liability. The Act extends limited liability to partnerships in specified circumstances, and is most popular with professional partnerships of accountants, solicitors, dentists and opticians.

7.4 Limited companies

It was recognized in the nineteenth century that industrial development would be impeded if investors in business always ran the risk of losing their personal assets to cover the debts of a business over which very often they had no day-to-day control. At the same time, the size of business units had become larger, causing the idea of a partnership to become strained. The need for a trading company to have a separate legal personality from that of its owners was recognized from the Middle Ages, when companies were incorporated by Royal Charter. From the seventeenth century, organizations could additionally be incorporated by Act of Parliament. Both methods of incorporating a company were expensive and cumbersome, and a simpler method was required to cope with the rapid expansion of business enterprises that were fuelling the Industrial Revolution. The response to this need was the Joint Stock Companies Act 1844, which enabled a company to be incorporated as a separate legal identity by the registration of a Memorandum of Association and payment of certain fees. The present law governing the registration of companies is contained in the Companies Act 1985. Today, the vast majority of trading within the UK is undertaken by **limited companies**. The legislation of most countries allows for organizations to be created that have a separate legal personality from their owners. In this way, separate legal identity is signified in the USA by the title 'Incorporated' after a company's name, by 'Société Anonyme' (SA) in France, 'Gmbh' in Germany and 'Sdn. Bhd.' in Malaysia.

When a limited company is created under UK legislation, it is required to produce a Memorandum and Articles of Association. The Memorandum includes a statement as to whether the liability of its members is limited, and if so what the limit of liability will be in the event of the company being wound up with unpaid debts. The majority of companies are limited by shares – members' liability to contribute to the assets of the company is limited to the amount (if any) that is unpaid on their shares. Another important element of the Memorandum is the objects clause, which specifies the scope within which the company can exercise its separate legal personality. Any act that the company performs beyond its powers is deemed to be *ultra vires* and therefore void.

While the Memorandum regulates the relationships of the company with the outside world, the Articles of Association regulate the internal administration of the company, the relations between the company and its members, and between the members themselves. The Articles cover such matters as the issue and transfer of shares, the rights of shareholders, meetings of members, the appointment of directors, and procedures for producing and auditing accounts.

Most limited companies are registered as private limited companies, indicated in company names by the designation 'Limited'. However, a larger company may choose to register as a public limited company (plc) and will thus face tougher regulatory requirements. These are described later in this chapter.

7.4.1 Company administration

A company acts through its directors, who are persons chosen by shareholders to conduct and manage the company's affairs. The number of directors and their powers are detailed in the Articles of Association and, so long as they do not exceed these powers, shareholders cannot normally interfere in their conduct of the company's business. The Articles will normally give one director additional powers to act as managing director, enabling him or her to make decisions without reference to the full board of directors.

Every company must have a secretary on whom Companies Acts have placed a number of duties and responsibilities, such as filing reports and accounts with the Registrar of Companies. The secretary is the chief administrative officer of the company, usually chosen by the directors.

7.4.2 Shareholders

The **shareholders** own the company, and in theory exercise control over it. A number of factors limit the actual control that shareholders exercise over their companies. The Articles of a company might discriminate between groups of shareholders by giving differential voting rights. Even where shareholders have full voting rights, the vast majority of shareholders typically are either unable or insufficiently interested to attend company meetings, and are happy to leave company management to the directors, so long as the dividend paid to them is satisfactory. In the case of pension funds and other institutional holders of shares in a company, their concern may be mainly with the stability of the financial returns from the business. In most large organizations, private investors are in a distinct minority in terms of the value of shares owned. There has been a tendency in recent years for individual shareholders to use their privileged position to raise issues of social concern at companies' annual shareholders' meetings. For example, in 2007, Ben Birnberg, a retired solicitor and small shareholder in Tesco, amassed enough support to force the issue of ethical trading on to the agenda at Tesco's annual shareholders' meeting. Mr Birnberg, who was also the company secretary of the charity War on Want, won the support of more than 100 shareholders – enough to force Tesco to include a resolution to be put to shareholders requiring the supermarket to adopt higher standards in its dealings with suppliers and farmers in low-wage countries.

7.4.3 Company reports and accounts

A company provides information about itself when it is set up, through its Memorandum and Articles of Association. To provide further protection for investors and people with whom the company may deal, companies are required to provide subsequent information.

An important document that must be produced annually is the annual report. Every company having a **share capital** must make a return in the prescribed form to the Registrar of Companies, stating what has happened to its capital during the previous year – for example, by describing the number of shares allotted and the cash received for them. The return must be accompanied by a copy of the audited balance sheet in the prescribed form, supported by a profit and loss account that gives a true and fair representation of the year's transactions. Like the Memorandum and Articles of Association, these documents are available for public inspection, with the exception of unlimited companies, which do not have to file annual accounts. Also, most small companies need only file an abridged balance sheet and do not need to submit a profit and loss account.

As well as providing the annual report and accounts, the directors of a company are under a duty to keep proper books of account and details of assets and liabilities.

7.4.4 Liquidation and receivership

Most limited companies are created with a view to continuous operation into the foreseeable future (although, sometimes, companies are set up with an expectation that they should cease to exist once their principal objective has been achieved). The process of breaking up a business is referred to as **liquidation**. Voluntary liquidation may be initiated by members (for example, where the main shareholder wishes to retire and liquidation is financially more attractive than selling the business as a going concern). Alternatively, a limited company may be liquidated (or wound up) by a court under s.122 of the Insolvency Act 1986. Involuntary liquidation involves the appointment of a receiver, who has authority that overrides the directors of the company. An individual or company that has an unmet claim against a company can apply to a court for it to be placed in **receivership**. Most receivers initially seek to turn round a failing business by consolidating its strengths and cutting out activities that brought about failure in the first place, allowing the company to be sold as a going concern. The proceeds of such a sale are used towards repaying the company's creditors and, if there is a sufficient surplus, the shareholders of the company. However, many directors who have lost their businesses claim that receivers are too eager to liquidate assets, and unwilling to take any risks that may eventually allow both creditors and shareholders to be paid off. The Insolvency Act 1986 allows a period of 'administration' during which a company can seek to put its finances into order with its creditors, without immediate resort to receivership. Section 5.8 of the Act defines the circumstances in which an administration order may be made by a court.

In 2008, the UK retailer Woolworths was placed into administration. Like many administrative orders, this one followed poor trading (in this case, lower than expected levels of Christmas sales), which left the company short of cash. The lack of available credit, exacerbated by the 'credit crunch' fuelled Woolworths' problem. Deloitte was appointed as administrator, and its first task was to control unnecessary expenditure, resulting in redundancies of staff who were not essential to the continued operation of the chain. The administrator then set about selling the chain as a going concern. Despite expressions of interest from several companies, both trade buyers and venture capital firms, no offers for the whole chain were

Table 7.1 (*Continued*)

Leyland Bus Company	1987	Trade sale
British Steel	1988	Public sale of shares
Rover Group	1988	Trade sale
Regional water companies	1989	Public sale of shares
Regional electricity companies	1990	Public sale of shares
Powergen/National Power	1991	Public sale of shares
Scottish electricity companies	1991	Public sale of shares
British Coal	1994	Trade sale
British Rail	1994–97	Public sale of shares/trade sales
National Air Traffic Services	2001	Sale of 51% of shares to airline consortium in public–private partnership
London Underground	2001	Franchise-type agreement with private-sector Metronet and Tube lines to operate and develop infrastructure
Qinetiq	2001	Sale to private equity company

Note: This is not a complete list. In some cases, the sale of shares was phased over a number of periods.

of private-sector consortia, which receive bonus-related payments in return for work undertaken.

Prior to their privatization, many state-owned organizations have been restructured to make them more attractive to potential buyers. This has typically involved writing off large amounts of debt and offering generous redundancy payments to workers who would not therefore become a liability to a new owner. In doing this, Conservative governments have been accused of providing subsidies for private buyers, although, very often, such action has been essential to provide a buyer with a competitive business proposition.

While governments may be ideologically committed to reducing the role of state-owned industries, it has proved difficult to sell many of them, for a variety of practical and ideological reasons. In the case of the Post Office, ideological objections have been raised at the prospect of the Royal Mail letter delivery monopoly being owned by a private-sector company. This has not, however, prevented the Post Office from being reorganized along business lines, with private limited companies being formed for the main business units, one of which – Girobank – was sold off to the Alliance & Leicester Building Society, while another – the parcel delivery service – was restructured to act more like one of the private parcel companies with which it is having to compete in an increasingly competitive market. The letter business was opened to competition in 2005, following EU measures to deregulate postal services.

It is also possible that attitudes towards privatization may be turning, and it is now possible to see the problems as well as the benefits. Very few people would advocate turning back the clock in sectors such as telecommunications, where privatization and deregulation have been associated with rapidly falling prices and improving service standards. However, it is more doubtful whether privatization of the bus or water supply industries has been entirely beneficial. Customers of newly privatized train companies have pointed out that punctuality fell sharply in the years immediately after privatization, while public subsidies more than doubled. The complex relationships between companies in the rail industry have led many people to suggest that gaps in safety coverage exist, and that the centralized 'command and control' approach of the former state-owned British Rail offered a safer railway at a lower cost.

The importance of a customer orientation within public corporations has been influenced by the nature of the market in which they operate. Following the nationalizations of the late 1940s, marketing was seen in many of the nationalized industries as being very secondary to production. The relative unimportance of marketing was often associated with some degree of monopoly power granted to the industry. In these circumstances, public corporations could afford to ignore marketing. However, as production of the basic industries caught up with demand and the economy became more deregulated during the 1980s, consumers increasingly had a choice between the suppliers offered to them. For example, the deregulation of the coach industry in 1981 and the growth in private car ownership placed increasing competitive pressure on British Rail, and hence an increasing importance for the organization to become customer-orientated. British Rail was increasingly set profit objectives rather than poorly specified social objectives.

What could be seen as either a strength or a weakness for the state-owned industries has been finance for investment and new product development. Investment comes from government – either directly or through guarantees on loans from the private sector. Profits earned have not necessarily been ploughed back into the business. The public sector has, since the 1930s, been seen as one instrument for regulating the economy, cutting back or increasing investment to suit the needs of the national economy rather than the needs of the particular market that the corporation is addressing. As well as limiting the amount of investment funds available, government involvement has also been accused of delay caused by the time it has taken to scrutinize and approve a proposal. By the time approval had been granted, the investment could be too late to meet changed market conditions.

State-owned industries are perceived as an instrument of government and although, theoretically, they may have an independent constitution, government is frequently accused of exercising covert pressure in order to achieve political favour. Electricity prices, rail fares and telephone charges have all at some time been subject to these allegations, which makes life more difficult for managers in nationalized industries because of confused objectives.

Britain is widely credited with having taken the lead in privatizing state-owned industries, and many countries have followed. The EU has taken action to reduce the anti-competitive consequences of having large subsidized public-sector organizations distorting markets. This has been particularly true in the case of airlines, where some European countries have continued to support loss-making state-owned carriers. In 2005, the EU Transport Commissioner investigated a proposal by the Italian government to rescue the near-bankrupt state-owned airline Alitalia with public money. By EU rules, such funding had to be justified as part of a restructuring process with the objective of returning the airline to profitable private-sector ownership, and could not be allowed as a straightforward operating subsidy.

7.5.2 Local authority enterprise

In addition to providing basic services such as roads, education, housing and social services, local authorities have a number of roles in providing marketable goods and services in competitive markets. For a long time, local authorities have operated bus services and leisure facilities, among others. Initially they were set up for a variety of reasons – sometimes to have introduced stricter controls over their activities in order to reduce abuses of their status – for example, private schools have previously qualified as 'charities', benefiting parents who are arguably among the better-off members of society). Where a charity has substantial trading activities, it is usual for these to be undertaken by a separately registered limited company, which then hands over its profits to the charity.

Thinking around the subject

People power at John Lewis

Capitalism has always had critics who dislike the idea of private companies exploiting employees and customers in order to provide maximum profits for shareholders. But public-sector ownership is not without its critics, who point to public-sector monopolies that provide poor service and little choice to their captive customers. Problems associated with extreme public- and private-sector-type organizations have led to the development of a variety of hybrid organizations that incorporate the public interest, but not necessarily through government ownership.

Many countries, such as France and Spain, have a long tradition of cooperative-type organizations, which are owned by their employees, often with financial support from banks or government. Some have argued that, today, novel forms of organization provide a solution that neither pure public- nor private-sector organizations can provide.

During the credit crunch of 2008, many private-sector retailers went bankrupt or faced severe financial difficulties because of over-borrowing. But one retailer – John Lewis – stood out from the crowd and appeared to prosper where others were failing. Many attributed its success to its relatively unusual ownership model.

John Lewis is a partnership-based organization, which owns 32 John Lewis shops across the UK, 241 Waitrose supermarkets (www.waitrose.com), an online and catalogue business, johnlewis.com (www.johnlewis.com), a production unit and a farm, with a turnover of nearly £7.4 billion in 2010. All 70,000 permanent staff are 'Partners' and share in the benefits and profits of the business.

When the founder, John Spedan Lewis, set up the partnership in 1928, he was careful to create a governance system, set out in its constitution, that would be both commercial – allowing it to move quickly in a competitive environment – and also democratic, by giving every Partner a voice in the business they co-own. Achieving this involves a careful balancing act.

The Chairman, the Partnership Board, the Divisional Management Boards and the Group Executive form the management of the company. The Partnership Council, which elects five partnership board directors, the divisional and branch-level democracy, make up the democratic bodies that give Partners a voice and hold the management to account. High standards of corporate governance are at the heart of the partnership – the structure is claimed to give managers the freedom to be entrepreneurial and competitive in the way they run the business for long-term success, while giving the company's owners, the Partners, the rights and responsibilities of ownership through active involvement in the business.

Was John Spedan Lewis ahead of his time with his combination of commercial acumen and corporate conscience? Was the ownership structure the main reason for the retailer's continuing success following the credit crunch of 2008, at a time when many of its competitors failed? If the model is such a success, why haven't many other businesses adopted it?

Source: Adapted from www.johnlewis.com.

In some respects, charities have become more like conventional trading organizations – for example, in their increasingly sophisticated use of direct marketing techniques. However, in other respects they can act very differently from private- and public-sector organizations. Customers may show a loyalty to the charity's cause, which goes beyond any rational economic explanation. Employees often work for no monetary reward, providing a dedicated and low-cost workforce, which can help the organization achieve its objectives.

Thinking around the subject

The National Health Service goes to market

The National Health Service (NHS) is Britain's largest employer and has traditionally operated with a command and control structure. Money was allocated by government and distributed between regions, then between hospitals, and then allocated between wards. There was a sense of security in this centralized planning, and hospitals – even wards – could reasonably expect that their budget in the following year would not be drastically different to that in the current year. Hospitals developed specialisms and tended to take on a steady workload of patients referred through an established network of consultants and primary care trusts. The development of 'Foundation'-status hospital trusts from 2003, and the introduction of a market for hospital services, were intended to improve the effectiveness and efficiency with which trusts operated. From 2004, the government introduced privately operated 'treatment centres' to provide a wide range of elective treatment, such as eye cataract operations and MRI scans. These effectively took 'business' away from NHS hospitals, which would in future have to compete for these patients. In the new NHS market, money followed the patients, and patients were given more choice, while family doctors were increasingly being encouraged to take control of their budgets.

But were managers of the traditionally bureaucratic command-and-control NHS ready for the uncertainty of a market economy? More worryingly, what would happen if a hospital with Foundation Trust status ran out of money? Could it 'go bust'? Foundation Trust hospitals are free-standing businesses that depend on government for their cash flow. Doubts were raised when Bradford Teaching Hospital, one of the first Foundation Trusts, went from a projected surplus of £1 million in 2005 to a potential deficit of £11 million in a matter of months of it coming into existence. At the same time, a number of other Foundation Trusts faced lesser financial difficulties.

The government claimed to have in place procedures for dealing with a failing Foundation Trust hospital. The first resort would be to put in new management. If the failing was more serious, it could be taken over by another Foundation Trust. Ultimately, the Trust could be returned to the Secretary of State's ownership. The government would doubtless be mindful of the political consequences of allowing a hospital trust to close down, or concentrating services in one centralized facility.

In many parts of the country, hospitals provide overlapping services, with very complex sets of relationships with Primary Care Trusts (to be replaced with groups of commissioning GPs), purchasing hospital services. In the new NHS market, the financial skills of boards were called for if a chaotic and unstable environment was to be avoided. It was almost unheard of for a British hospital to go out of business but, as the government pursues a market discipline for the NHS, is going out of business a logical consequence that should be shared with the private sector?

7.8.3 Building societies

Building societies are governed by the Building Societies Acts, which have evolved over time to reflect their changing role. They were for some time seen as almost monopoly providers of money for house purchases, with strict regulations on the powers of societies in terms of their sources of funds and the uses for which loans could be advanced. With the liberalization of the home mortgage market, building societies now have wider powers of lending and borrowing, and face much greater competition. As a result of this, societies have had to embrace marketing activities more fully. The Building Societies Act 1986 further allowed building societies the possibility of converting to plc status, eliminating the remaining controls imposed by the Building Society Acts (Figure 7.2). However, with greater freedom came greater danger, and in 2008 many building societies that had been market led in their lending found themselves unable to raise sufficient capital from the commercial money markets on which they had become dependent. Many smaller building societies, such as the Dunfermline and Cheshire Building Societies, were rescued by larger rivals that had better access to wholesale finance.

Figure 7.2 Public limited companies have grown in number in recent years and added a number of former building societies whose members voted for conversion. Although plc status does give numerous benefits over mutual status, there are also many benefits of remaining mutual. The Coventry Building Society has stressed the benefits of remaining mutual, arguing that it is achieving high levels of customer satisfaction and a financial performance that matches that of plcs and returns the benefits to members. During the 'credit crunch' of 2008, distrust in banks – which many blamed for the financial crisis in world money markets – spread rapidly. Building societies played on this distrust by stressing that they were owned by their members and didn't give big bonuses to greedy bankers. However building societies themselves faced problems and weaker ones, including the Cheshire and Scarborough societies had to be rescued by bigger societies. Coventry Building Society sought greater strength through a merger with the Stroud and Swindon society. However, their fate was not as bad as that which faced those building societies which had chosen to become plcs by replacing their membership structures with shareholders. Of these, Northern Rock and Bradford and Bingley went bankrupt and had to be rescued by government, with members who became shareholders losing the value of their shareholding. (Picture reproduced with permission of Coventry Building Society.)

Case study:
Cooking by yourself or with company?

© Kelly Cline

The restaurant sector in Britain is dominated by thousands of small owner-managed businesses, which compete and co-exist with much larger managed enterprises. Many people dream about setting up their own restaurant, and a BBC television show in 2007 even saw the celebrity chef Raymond Blanc 'rewarding' the winner of a competition with their own restaurant. For somebody who loves food, the prospect of giving up a 9–5 office job and spending all their working life developing new menus may seem irresistible. Sadly, although thousands of people have ventured down the route to becoming a restaurateur, their success rate is low. Estimates vary, but it is generally reckoned that about three-quarters of all new restaurants are not a success and close within three years of opening (see Parsa *et al.* 2005). Large corporate restaurant chains generally do better, but it is the sole trader that is particularly likely to face problems. Instead of experimenting with new recipes for beef bourguignon or duck à l'orange, the small restaurant owner is likely to spend much of their time on more mundane matters: filling out the VAT return, recruiting staff, calculating their income tax and paying their National Insurance contributions, keeping abreast of new legislation concerning minimum wage levels, maternity leave and disability discrimination are all distractions from the kitchen. Then there is the never-ending task of promoting the restaurant. Many restaurateurs think that customers will beat a path to their door, but diners can be fickle and as soon as a new restaurant opens in town, they may be off to try it out. With so much to do in simply running the business, it is not surprising that many small restaurateurs become disillusioned and move on. Some fail simply because they have not developed a realistic business plan.

There are clearly many advantages to a restaurant that can operate on a larger scale and spread many of these burdensome administrative tasks over a larger volume of business. However, it can be very difficult for a small restaurant owner to establish a chain of outlets. With so much attention to detail needed, a potential chain could be harmed if the standard of service at one restaurant is not the same as the standards elsewhere. For example, a customer eating at a branch of Gordon Ramsay's restaurant may expect the celebrity chef's attention to detail to be present in all places at all times, but ensuring this actually happens demands a high level of management effort and a willingness to delegate.

Nevertheless, large chains of restaurants have prospered, and many have achieved international success. But how can this be done? One approach is a 'command and control' type of management, in which each restaurant is run by a manager who is paid a salary by the company. The successful manager will have earned a bonus and probably promotion within the organization. However, this type of approach can become very bureaucratic and may fail to inspire individuals in an industry where attention to detail can be vital.

One approach adopted by many restaurant chains is to incorporate small businesses within the umbrella of a large franchise organization. We will look in more detail at **franchising** in the next chapter, but essentially this allows the small entrepreneur to run their own business, while at the same time relying on the franchisor for promotional and administrative support, for which they pay a proportion of their turnover. Within the restaurant sector, franchising has been relatively slow to take hold at the gourmet end of the market, where the owner's individuality and style can add to the appeal of a restaurant. But in the convenience food sector, franchising has really taken hold and allows dedicated individuals to build a secure and profitable business.

The pizza chain Domino's has grown rapidly throughout the world by franchising out its operations to smaller businesses. In some cases, franchisees are sole traders, but can also take the form of large limited companies that operate many outlets. The company has used the energy of talented and hard-working individuals to deliver good financial rewards to its franchisees and quality pizzas to its customers.

In 2004, Domino's reported that ten of its 100-plus UK and Ireland franchisees owned businesses that were worth more than £1,000,000 each. These figures are based on a standard calculation of twice annual turnover. With a typical start-up cost of £250,000 per store this is a significant return on franchisees' initial investment. Only two years previously, one in ten of Domino's stores had a turnover of £10,000 a week; by 2004 this figure was one in three. In 2002, Domino's franchisees earned around £120,000 a year on average (although some considerably more), which was more than three times the average income of a typical business manager (£38,107). Furthermore, no Domino's franchise failed during the year, compared with over 22,000 business failures elsewhere in the UK economy.

Founded in 1960, Domino's makes and delivers nearly 6 million pizzas a week in more than 60 countries around the world. By 2006, it had 8190 stores serving a total of over 1 million pizzas a week. From humble beginnings in 1960, franchising has been a key element of the company's mission to bring pizza to the world. By 2006, 85 per cent of its outlets were owned by franchisees. The UK was an early target for Domino's expansion, and it established a subsidiary company, Domino's Pizza Group Limited, which holds the exclusive master franchise to own, operate and franchise Domino's Pizza stores in the UK and Ireland. In 2010, it operated 665 stores with a total sales turnover of £485 million and a profit before tax of £18.7 million.

Domino's research into the skills set and characteristics of the most successful franchisees, both in the UK and internationally, has uncovered the fact that the majority of franchisees believe the traditional corporate management career path failed to offer either the scope to succeed or the financial rewards within the timescale they want. Typical of the hard-working individuals attracted to a Domino's franchise was James Swift. As a 16-year-old delivery driver for Domino's Pizza, Swift spotted the potential to run his own business at an early age. He soon secured a position as the manager of Domino's branch in Swindon and learned everything there was to know about running a store. This operational experience was critical for learning everything from how to make a pizza to how to manage a team. It was about three years later that he got the chance to buy a share in the franchise. By the age of 24, he had become co-franchisee of three Domino's outlets in Swindon, Newbury and Bath. He put his success down to sheer hard work and determination, with the backing of a renowned brand and the commitment that only the owner of a business can give.

Maybe one day, James Swift would match the success of Richard P. Mueller Jr, Domino's Pizza's most successful global franchisee. Mueller joined Domino's in 1967 as a delivery driver and became a franchisee in 1970. By 2003 he owned 158 stores in the USA and employed over 3000 team members. His company sold over 10 million pizzas a year, as many as the entire UK Domino's business. That equated to 5 million pounds of dough, 5 million pounds of cheese and enough pizza sauce to fill a large swimming pool. In the process of growing his business, Mueller had become a millionaire.

Given the stressful, tedious conditions of most fast-food operations, it is vital that staff are motivated to succeed. While many part-time staff, such as students and parents of young school children, are happy to just do a few hours of work in return for a bit of extra cash, the business needs to be able to accommodate the ambitions of people who could make good leaders of people. A bureaucratic 'jobsworth' culture will not allow a pizza company to compete effectively with more agile and committed competitors.

Although franchising has figured prominently in Domino's growth, the company retains a proportion of directly managed outlets. As well as providing an internal benchmark against which franchisees can be judged, these outlets are useful for developing new product ideas that may be too risky for individual franchisees to undertake on their own. Recent examples of innovation have included the introduction of an iPhone app for ordering, which accounted for over £1 million of sales in the three months after its UK launch in September 2010. The company has also involved its franchisees in the social media arena. Would such developments be possible without the support of a strong, centrally managed franchise?

Source: based on material provided on the Domino's (www.dominos.com) and British Franchise Association's (www.britishfranchise.org) websites.

QUESTIONS

1 Summarize the relative advantages and disadvantages of the small sole trader, and the large limited company chain within the restaurant sector.

2 What problems does a franchise such as Domino's face in trying to reconcile the individualism of entrepreneurial franchisees with the need for brand consistency?

3 Why do you think that 15 per cent of Domino's outlets are managed directly by the company, rather than by franchisees?

Summary

There are numerous ways of classifying business organizations. Classification based on legal status is useful because this is often related to other factors such as size, the ability to raise fresh capital and the level of constraints imposed on managers. Private-sector organizations range from the informality of the sole trader to the formality of the plc. In between is a diverse range of organizations, each of which has its role in the business environment. Some of these differences will become apparent in **Chapter 11**, which reviews competition within markets. While small sole traders may be associated with perfectly competitive markets, the reality of most markets is domination by a small number of plcs. This chapter has explored the reasons behind the recent resurgence in small business units. The ability to keep in touch with customers and to react to changes in the marketing environment were noted as important advantages. There is also diversity within public-sector organizations, although this group as a whole has tended to diminish in relative importance in most western countries. **Chapter 2** discussed organizational structures within the public sector by focusing on government bodies that are policy making rather than operational. **Chapter 8** will discuss how organizations grow, and this chapter has laid the groundwork by suggesting that there are differences in organizations' inherent ability to grow.

🔑 Key Terms

Building society (255)

Charity (252)

Cooperative society (251)

Franchising (256)

Limited company (241)

Liquidation (242)

Multinational company (243)

Nationalized industry (244)

Partnership (240)

Privatization (245)

Public limited company (243)

Receivership (242)

Share capital (242)

Shareholder (241)

Sole trader (238)

**Online
Learning Centre**

To help you grasp the key concepts of this chapter, explore the extra resources posted on the Online Learning Centre at *www.mcgraw-hill.co.uk/palmer*. Among other helpful resources there are chapter-by-chapter test questions, revision notes and web links.

Chapter review questions

1 For what reasons might a manufacturer of fitted kitchens seek plc status? What are the advantages and disadvantages of this course of action?

2 Why have governments found it difficult to privatize state-owned postal services? Suggest methods by which private-sector marketing principles can be applied to state-owned postal services.

3 Critically assess the benefits to the public of turning branches of the National Health Service into self-governing trusts.

Activities

1 Identify three quangos operating in the following areas: education, housing and transport. Critically evaluate the suitability of quango status. Do you think these organizations' service to the public would be improved if they were either purely private-sector or purely public-sector organizations?

2 Choose one of the following business sectors: hotels, fashion retailers, restaurants. Identify a sample of small sole traders and larger limited companies within each sector, and critically examine the ways that their marketing efforts differ.

3 Examine the charges made by a public-sector hospital. These may typically include charges for car parking, telephones and catering. To what extent do you think the organization is business orientated in relation to these? How successfully has it managed to combine its social objectives with its business objectives?

Further reading

A useful starting point for further reading is one of a number of books discussing the nature of different types of organization.

Carnall, C. (2007) *Managing Change in Organizations*, 5th edn, London, FT Prentice Hall.

Clegg, S., Pitsis, T. and Kornverger, M. (2008) *Managing Organizations: An Introduction to Theory and Practice*, 2nd edn, London, Sage.

Down, S. (2010) *Enterprise, Entrepreneurship and Small Business*, London, Sage.

For a review of current statistics on the composition of business units, the following sources are useful.

Department of Trade and Industry, *SME Statistics*, London, The Stationery Office.

Office for National Statistics, *Annual Abstract of Statistics*, London, The Stationery Office.

The nature of public-sector organizations has changed considerably in recent years and the following provides an overview of this change.

Schedler K. Proeller, I. and Siegelm, J.P. (2011) *Strategic Management in the Public Sector*, London, Routledge.

Charities are becoming increasingly involved in business activities and their distinctive characteristics are discussed in the following text.

Sargeant, A. (2009) *Marketing Management for Non-profit Organizations*, 3rd edn, Oxford, Oxford University Press.

Reference

Parsa, H.G., Self, J.T., Njite, D. and King, T. (2005) 'Why restaurants fail', *Cornell Hotel and Restaurant Administration Quarterly*, Vol. 46, No. 3, pp. 304–322.

Chapter 8

Business Relationships and Networks

You are thrilled with the new Hewlett-Packard notebook computer that you have just bought, but pause to think about how much of that notebook is actually attributable to Hewlett-Packard. Sure, the badge on the front says Hewlett-Packard, but you look inside and find that the battery is made by Sony, the processor is made by Intel, and the hard disc drive is made by Seagate. Then you realize that the manufacturer of the disc drive would have bought in components for its drives from other manufacturers, who in turn would probably have bought in raw materials. You also start to reflect on how you bought your new laptop – not direct from Hewlett-Packard but from an online retailer to which you were attracted by a price comparison site. Then there was the DHL delivery service that delivered your laptop, the banking system that somehow transferred your money to Hewlett-Packard through all of the intermediaries involved. The reality is that even simple products can involve a complex network of business relationships to bring the final product to you, and the nature and complexity of these relationships is explored in this chapter.

 ## Learning Objectives

This chapter will explain:

☑ The nature of relationships between business organizations.

☑ Theories underlying the development of relationships between businesses.

☑ Methods used by firms to turn casual business transactions into ongoing relationships.

8.1 Introduction

The activities of just about every business organization are likely to involve a complex network of relationships with members of its environmental set. Some links in the network will become particularly important, and characterized by long-term cooperative relationships, rather than short-term bargaining over a series of one-off transactions. For example, computer manufacturers have relied on a network of component manufacturers to create value-added products that are worth more than the sum total of the component inputs. They also often rely on independent intermediaries to make their computers available to buyers. As far as consumers are concerned, such **networks** of relationships may remain, by and large, hidden, so somebody who buys a Dell laptop may not be aware – or may not even care – that the battery has been made by Sony, or the disc drive by Seagate. On the other hand, customers of services companies may actually come into contact with many of the suppliers in a company's network – for example, outsourced security staff at a sporting venue.

Central to an understanding of business-to-business relationships is the concept of a value chain. Value chains were introduced in Chapter 1, and you will recall that this describes the way in which a succession of organizations add value to a basic raw material, so that when it reaches the final consumer, it has higher value in the eyes of a consumer. Raw coffee beans may have a value of just a few pennies on the farm of an African grower, but a cup of coffee can sell for over £3 in a branch of Starbucks. In between these two ends of the value chain, a variety of wholesalers, agents and processors would have been involved in adding value to the coffee beans – for example, by sorting, grading, processing, transporting and storing them.

To be sustainable in a competitive business environment, a value chain must add more value relative to costs than competing value chains. How quickly do the beans get from the grower to the Starbucks customer? How efficient is the process of adding value throughout the chain? Are there any bottlenecks in the chain? Could different parts of the value-adding process be simplified so that the value chain becomes more efficient, allowing a given level of value to be added for a lower level of cost? Does the value chain ensure continuity of supply, so that Starbucks does not run out of coffee and the processing factory does not run out of raw beans to process?

It is often not just the efficiency of individual stages of a value chain that create value, but the way in which transitions from one stage to the next are handled. Value can be destroyed, for example, if a food processor has to keep high levels of inventory because it cannot rely on continuity of supplies from a raw materials supplier, or if it distrusts the supplier's quality standards so much that it has to check all supplies again very thoroughly and undertake remedial work. It follows that value chains often work more efficiently and effectively where members of the chain work closely together, rather than treating each purchase or sale as a series of isolated, individually bartered incidents.

In this chapter, we will explore the great variety of relationships that exist between organizations in the process of creating value.

8.2 Types of business relationship

An idea of the complexity of networks of business relationships that may impact on consumers can be provided by the following example of an Air France flight from Birmingham, UK, to Paris, France, in March 2010. Consider the following network of relationships that are connected with the flight.

- A customer would probably begin their encounter with one of the many intermediaries (online and offline) that Air France deals with. Travel agents themselves are likely to be linked into one of the major global distribution networks (such as Amadeus).

- Some customers may have bought their ticket with an Air France credit card, which is actually provided by American Express.

- The airport at Birmingham is not owned by Air France, which must rely on service-level agreements in order to ensure that facilities available (access facilities, availability of information, general maintenance, etc.) are consistent with the total service offer of Air France.

- At Birmingham, check-in and baggage handling for Air France is carried out on its behalf by Servisair. This supplier of ground services operates on behalf of a number of airlines flying into Birmingham and, for most people, is the first face-to-face contact they have with a representative of Air France.

- Some passengers would be travelling with a ticket issued by another airline. The service from Birmingham to Paris is a 'code-share' flight with Alitalia, so Air France must seek to make a seamless journey for Alitalia customers who are travelling to Italian destinations via Paris. Likewise, many Air France customers from Birmingham may be travelling onwards from Paris using an Air France code-share flight that was actually operated by another airline.

- Air France is a member of the 'SkyTeam' alliance of leading airlines, including Delta, Continental, Alitalia, Aero Mexico, Czech Airlines and Korean Air. Passengers on the flight from Birmingham to Paris who were members of the alliance's frequent-flyer programme would earn points that could be redeemed with any of the alliance members.

- After checking in, a customer must then pass through immigration and security controls. At many airports, airlines have been frustrated by their relationship with these services, over which they have little control.

- The flight itself is not actually operated by Air France, but on its behalf by the Irish-based airline City Jet. Air France has calculated that it is more cost-effective to subcontract operation of its more peripheral routes.

- On arrival in Paris, a new set of network relationships are present, although in this case, because Paris is an important base for Air France, many of the services that were subcontracted in Birmingham (such as check-in) are provided directly by the company itself.

In addition to these visible relationships, which a consumer directly encounters, there is a very large network of invisible relationships whose performance is crucial to the successful operation of a flight. These include relationships to maintain aircraft, provide technology support for the airline's computer systems, catering supplies, etc.

We will come back to the example of the Air France flight to illustrate some of the principal classifications of networks and relationships. The following headings do not provide an exhaustive and mutually exclusive analysis, but a useful summary of the literature on crucial aspects of networks and relationships.

8.2.1 Outsourcing

A company may undertake many different activities in the process of creating value. However, some of these activities will be less central to its process of value creation, and it may be less efficient at these activities than a specialist company. It may therefore choose to *outsource* these activities to another organization. Outsourcing has been defined as 'the strategic use of outside resources to perform activities traditionally handled by internal staff and resources' (Cain 2009). For manufacturing companies, outsourcing the manufacture of component parts has been a long-term trend, so, for example, car manufacturers have tended to make a smaller proportion of components themselves, and instead outsource the manufacture of the majority to other companies. More recently, the process of outsourcing has become very popular with services-based companies. Outsourced contracts range from a small factory replacing kitchen assistants with a contract caterer, through to the Greater London Authority's outsourcing of the collection of the London Congestion Charge to Capita plc. Many companies that have traditionally employed their own cleaning, catering and security staff now subcontract or outsource these to specialist suppliers through a process sometimes referred to as business process outsourcing. Sometimes, employees of the organization are transferred to the new supplier and hence become employees of the specialist contractor. This contractor then provides an agreed level of service to the organization for a specified contract period. At the end of this period the organization is able to evaluate competing suppliers before placing the next contract. The specialist supplier assumes profit and loss responsibility for the delivery of the service, as well as taking on the employment rights of the employees. From the Air France example above, you should be able to identify many examples of outsourcing. It would be quite uneconomic for Air France to produce many specialized services itself, such as computer support and catering, so these are outsourced to specialists who have the capability to provide a better standard of service at a lower cost.

Outsourcing offers many advantages to a company seeking to reduce its own inputs to the value chain, including:

- allowing the business to focus its activities on its core activities
- giving access to cutting-edge skills that it would be difficult for the company to acquire and learn on its own; the company does not have to worry about continually introducing new technologies
- sharing risks of service provision, especially in the case of activities that are new to the company
- outsourcing can improve service quality where a contract provides rewards for good performance
- a company's scarce human resources can be freed up and redeployed in higher-value-adding activities
- outsourcing can free up cash flow, allowing it to be reinvested in core business activities (e.g. an airline outsourcing its maintenance operations can use cash that was previously invested in its maintenance facilities to invest in better aircraft)
- it can make the business more flexible to changes in the external environment.

However, outsourcing also has disadvantages.

- Major disruptions can occur if the outsourced service provider ceases to trade (e.g. through bankruptcy).
- Employees may react badly to outsourcing, especially where it is associated with a pay cut, and it is possible that their quality of work may subsequently suffer. There may be bad feeling among those employees who remain working for the company.
- Outsourcing may involve redundancy costs.
- There may be a career progression problem with the loss of talent generated internally.
- Other companies may also be using the service provider, resulting in a possible conflict of interest by the outsourced service provider.
- The company may lose direct contact with its customers.

Some have argued that outsourcing undermines a coherent internal focus on meeting customers' needs. The outsourced supplier may be so focused on meeting its own narrowly defined performance targets that it overlooks the more qualitative aspects of delivering value to customers. The UK's National Health Service has used outsourcing extensively for the cleaning of hospital wards. There may have been significant cost savings from this move, but the cleaners who come in and do the work have been accused of not having the same team spirit as those cleaners who are employed by the hospital and directly answerable to the matron. Over time, and through an acculturalization process, a ward-based cleaner may learn to be the eyes and ears of nurses – for example, identifying symptoms of medical problems that doctors and nurses may have missed. Now they may just 'tick the box' and do no more than the cleaning specified in their service agreement.

Outsourcing is now being undertaken on a global scale. Although manufacturers have traditionally outsourced the manufacture of component goods to countries with low costs, the inseparability of services has until now generally reduced opportunities for the global outsourcing of services. However, improved telecommunications have provided new opportunities – for example, the call centres and internet support operations that many western companies have 'offshored' to relatively low-cost countries such as India. We will return to this subject in Chapter 14.

8.2.2 Franchising

Franchising refers to trading relationships between companies in which a franchisor grants the right to a franchisee to operate a business using the franchisor's business format (see Figures 8.1 and 8.2). Franchising has been a rapidly growing type of business relationship. According to the annual NatWest/British Franchise Association survey, the total number of franchise systems in the UK in 2009 was 842. These were linked to a total of 34,800 franchisees, with an annual turnover of £11.8 billion, and employed an estimated 465,000 people (British Franchise Association 2010). Franchising offers a ready-made business opportunity for the entrepreneur who has capital but does not want the risk associated with setting up a completely new business afresh. A good franchise operation will have a proven business format and would already be well established in its market. The franchisee would be required to pay an initial capital sum for the right to use the name of the franchisor. The NatWest/British Franchise Association survey found that in 2009 the average initial cost of starting a franchise was £46,700 (including franchise fee, working capital, equipment and fittings, stock and materials) (British Franchise Association 2010). Franchisees typically pay between 5 per cent and 10 per cent of their sales in recurring fees to their franchisors. This may sometimes seem high, but represents a relatively less risky investment than starting a completely new business. It has been estimated that, whereas up to 90 per cent of all new businesses fail within three years of starting up, 90 per cent of all franchisees survive beyond this period (British Franchise Association 2010). Although franchisees are typically small sole traders, in fact they are often large public limited companies. It is quite common for a large company to have a franchise to operate, for example, a number of fast-food restaurants on behalf of the franchise owner.

As well as the initial capital sum, a franchise agreement will usually include provisions for the franchisee to purchase stock from the franchisor and to pass on a percentage of turnover or profit. The franchisor undertakes to provide general marketing and administrative back-up for the franchisees.

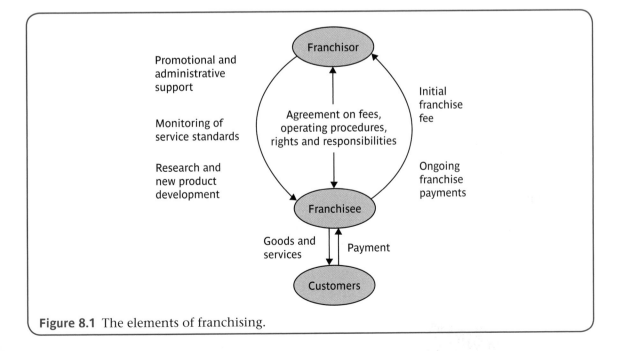

Figure 8.1 The elements of franchising.

⟳ Thinking around the subject

Powering up computers through outsourcing

Seeboard, a West Sussex-based energy company that supplies gas and electricity to approximately 2 million customers in the UK, identified its core competence as being the distribution of energy at lower prices and with higher customer service levels than its competitors. Of course, low prices and top-quality services can easily lead to a loss, so the company has had to keep a very close eye on its costs, as well as ensuring that the best people deliver its services.

Outsourcing has played an important role for the company. Seeboard began its first outsourcing contract with Accenture in 1993, subsequently adding Siemens to its outsourced suppliers. Since 2001, the company has outsourced the management of its desktop computers and network servers to the specialist IT services company Computacenter.

IT has become increasingly important to Seeboard. Like many companies, Seeboard has web-enabled many of its business processes, with examples including an online service for customers to submit their own meter readings. The company also realized that expansion of its IT needs would rapidly outgrow the resources of its in-house team.

Computacenter was brought in to manage Seeboard's computers in a contract that covered 3000 desktops, 400 laptops and 200 servers at various sites across London and the south-east. Computacenter was given responsibility for developing standard desktop builds, configuring servers, rolling out new software and hardware, day-to-day support and the disposal of redundant equipment.

By working with Computacenter, Seeboard was able to access a much wider pool of technical knowledge and benefited from Computacenter's experience gained through other IT projects and outsourcing contracts. As a result Seeboard benefited from worldwide best practice, requiring fewer staff than if it had carried out the work itself in-house, and claimed to have cut its total IT operating costs. Just by implementing a standard desktop configuration, it saw a decrease in support calls and, as a result, support overheads.

It must not be forgotten, however, that Seeboard's aim was not just to cut costs, but also to improve customer service – a vital source of competitive differentiation. A cheap outsourced operation that leaves the company's websites down for lengthy periods would not be good for customers and profitability. Seeboard used a balanced scorecard system with internal and external users to assess the service-level standards, responsiveness, customer satisfaction and project performance, and claimed to be happy with the results.

How far can a company such as Seeboard go in its outsourcing? Like many utility services it saw advantages in supplementing outsourcing with 'offshoring' – moving many of its service processes overseas to lower-cost providers. Some electricity companies have transferred call centres and bill processing functions to India, where a high-quality workforce can usually undertake the job at lower cost. But if it went down this route, would it still be able to maintain high levels of customer service? Would customers be as happy speaking to a call centre worker in Bangalore as a Seeboard worker in Brighton?

Public services are increasingly being delivered by franchised organizations in order to capitalize on the motivation of smaller-scale franchisees. Public-sector franchises can take a number of forms as described below.

- The right to operate a vital public service can be sold to a franchisee, which in turn has the right to charge users of the facility. The franchisee will normally be required to maintain the facility to a required standard and to obtain government approval of prices to be charged. In the UK, the government has offered private organizations franchises to operate vital road links, including the Dartford river crossing, the Severn Bridge and the M6 West Midlands Toll Motorway. In the case of the latter, the Australian-based Macquarie Investment Group acquired the right to collect tolls from motorway users, and in return agreed to construct and maintain the road.

- Government can sell the exclusive right for private organizations to operate a private service that is of public importance. Many governments sell the right to operate mobile phone services to private-sector companies who pay a fee for the right to provide services within a specified area for a specified time and subject to terms specified in a licence agreement.

- Where a socially necessary but economically unviable service is provided in a market-mediated environment, government can subsidize provision of the service by means of a franchise. An example of this can be seen in the way subsidies are paid by government to privatized train companies in order to support train services.

- In the UK, possibly the longest-established public-sector franchise is seen in the Post Office. In addition to government-owned 'Crown' post offices, 'sub' post offices have traditionally been operated on a franchise basis in smaller towns. Franchises have been taken up by a variety of small shops and newsagents, and generally offer a more limited range of postal services compared to Crown offices.

Figure 8.2 Franchising has firmly taken root in the market for fast printing services, with names such as Prontaprint, Kwik-Print and Kenkos being familiar, well-developed franchise systems. The development of low-cost offset litho and photocopying machines lowered the entry barriers to printing, which had previously confined it to craft-trained individuals. Prontaprint is typical in selling a franchise to people that can demonstrate commitment to high standards and profitable growth. For a small investor looking for a business of their own, a Prontaprint franchise offers the security of a brand name that customers have come to trust. Like most fast printing companies, Prontaprint's franchisees offer essentially simple, straightforward printing services that can easily be described in a business blueprint. More complex and variable printing services, such as carton printing, tickets and high-volume magazine printing, are less likely to be franchised out.

8.2.3 Horizontal collaborative relationships

There are many situations where two or more organizations providing an essentially similar product, at the same point in a supply chain, can create greater value for customers by working together. In some cases, these collaborative networks may span an entire industry. There are two principal benefits from such collaboration.

1 Customers may benefit where potentially competing suppliers agree on common technical standards. The growth of the mobile phone sector in Europe has been greatly facilitated by agreement among the main operators on the common GSM standard. Some have argued that mobile phones developed more slowly in the USA because of a lack of agreement among operators on shared standards. Referring to the Air France case (see p. 262), the airline sector has benefited from many agreements on technical standards brokered through the International Air Transport Association (IATA). Even a simple agreement, such as common bar codes used to identify bags as they travel through airports throughout the world, has the potential to reduce costs and to improve customer satisfaction by reducing the number of mislaid bags.

2 A second, and sometimes related, form of collaboration occurs where an organization recognizes that its product offer may be too small in scope or range to have an impact on customers, but if it collaborates with its potential competitors, it can offer more choice and achieve a critical mass that has an impact on customer value. Banks in Britain cooperate through the Link network to make their cash machines available to their competitors' customers, and they collaborate at a global level through Maestro to create further benefits to customers, who can use their credit cards at cash machines throughout the world. Bank customers in many countries take the benefits of such collaboration for granted, in contrast to those countries where customers of a bank are allowed to use only the ATMs operated by that bank. Airlines frequently cooperate to provide 'seamless' travel between potentially competing airlines. The code-share flights referred to above (p. 263) allowed Alitalia customers to travel seamlessly on an Air France flight, as if the flight was actually provided by Alitalia. Alitalia was able to reduce the cost of its route network, while offering a more extensive network to its customers than would have been the case had it simply not provided a connection to Birmingham. Global alliances between airlines (for example, SkyTeam and Oneworld) offer further opportunities for customers to seamlessly acquire and use frequent-flyer benefits.

Strategic alliances are becoming increasingly important within the manufacturing and service sectors. They take a number of forms, but are essentially agreements between two or more organizations where each partner seeks to add to its competencies by combining its resources with those of a partner. These competencies can take many forms, including access to customers, capital, licences or key staff. Strategic alliances are frequently used to allow individual companies to build upon the relationship they have developed with their clients by allowing them to sell on goods and services that they do not produce themselves, but are produced by another member of the alliance. This arrangement is reciprocated between members of the alliance. A strategic alliance generally involves cooperation between partners rather than joint ownership of a subsidiary set up for a specific purpose, although it may include agreement for collaborators to purchase shares in the businesses of other members of the alliance.

Strategic alliances often operate at an international level, where they can bring together a company that has a particular strength in technology or finance with an overseas company that has knowledge and access to its local market. Together, the first company can expand its technology to new markets, while the second can capitalize on its local knowledge and reputation.

A particular form of collaboration that has become common in many countries is the **public–private partnership** (PPP). These were discussed in more detail in Chapter 2, and you may recall that the underlying logic of PPPs is essentially similar to that for strategic alliances generally. Through a PPP, partners hope that they can create more value by working together, rather then separately. Typically, a government department would see the private sector as a valuable partner for introducing new ideas, finance and management techniques in order for government policy objectives to be met more cost effectively. For the private-sector collaborators, partnership with government potentially provides a stable source of income and access to public-sector work that it would otherwise be denied.

Against the benefits to customers and suppliers resulting from collaboration, competition authorities throughout the world are becoming increasingly concerned about business practices that directly or indirectly have the effect of restricting competition within a market. To refer back to the examples given above, the UK Office of Fair Trading (OFT) conducted an investigation into an agreement between the main UK banks to charge customers to use ATM cards in machines operated by other members of the Link network. Their report showed that, although the banks' sharing of ATMs brought benefits to customers, the banks' collective monopoly supply of ATMs in the UK led to excessive prices charged to customers, and the banks were subsequently ordered to reduce some charges (OFT 2003). In the case of airlines, the European Commission has taken a growing interest in global alliances and their possible anti-competitive implications. In 2006, it launched an inquiry into alleged price fixing between SkyTeam alliance members (which included Air France, KLM, Delta and Alitalia) for airfreight rates (*Financial Times* 2006). Karl Marx observed that capitalists were more concerned with *avoiding* risks rather than *taking* risks. The development of networks of horizontal collaborative relationships between companies may be seen as a means of reducing entrepreneurs' exposure to risk, thereby reducing some of the presumed benefits of a competitive market environment.

8.2.4 Virtual relationships

In the early days of the internet, it was widely predicted that relationships between organizations and their suppliers and customers would become simpler, as new technology offered the prospect of dealing directly with thousands or even millions of suppliers and customers, thereby reducing the need for intermediary relationships. The growth of direct-selling intermediaries such as Direct Line Insurance appeared to confirm the ability to cut out intermediaries, who were often portrayed as parasitic and delaying middlemen. The inelegant term 'disintermediation' has been used to describe the process of removing intermediaries from a distribution channel and developing direct communications.

There is some evidence that companies have used the internet strategically to make their distribution activities more efficient. For example, some manufacturers of specialized products deal directly with customers through their website rather than involving intermediaries. Some retailers have closed branches or reduced their sales force and instead offer customers access to their product range via a website. Many manufacturing companies have used online auctions to sell stock or to procure raw materials.

On the other hand, the internet has had an observed tendency to make some relationships more complex. In the new era of internet-based distribution, a lot of thought has to go into how to get access to potential buyers most cost-effectively. The models for achieving cost-effective online 'routes to market' seem to grow in number each year. A new generation of 'informediaries' have emerged, which seek to simplify buyers' choice by offering variety in one location. Many companies have also developed networks of 'affiliates', whereby a site that refers an individual to the company's site through a web page link receives an agreed level of commission. As a further refinement of this model, some websites, such as 'Topcashback.com', pass part of this commission back to the end customer. Another type of affiliate relationship is the use of comparison websites, which allow a visitor to enter their specific service needs and the site then lists alternatives available to them, based on price, rating or some other criteria. Comparison sites exist for most search-based services provided in a competitive market – for example, gas and electricity (www.uswitch.com), loans and savings accounts (www.moneysupermarket.com), and car insurance (www.confused.com). The price comparison site generally receives a payment for each visitor to its site who clicks

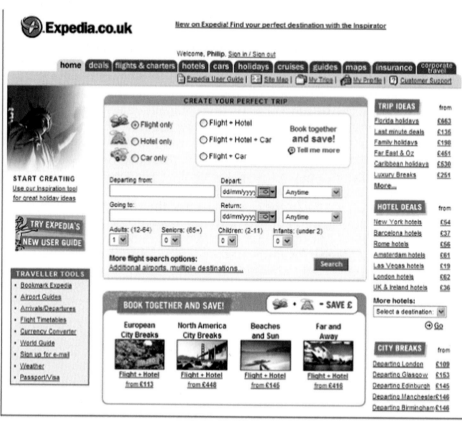

Figure 8.3 Many people thought that the internet would fundamentally change the pattern of distribution for goods and services, by allowing companies to distribute their products efficiently and effectively without the use of intermediaries. In the travel sector, budget airlines have been notable for the way in which they have managed to use their websites to cut out intermediaries and thereby pass on cost savings to customers (easyJet, for example, claims that over 95 per cent of its customers book through its website). However, customers looking for choice may prefer to use the website of one of the many web-based travel intermediaries, that have emerged, and whose diversity has continued to grow. Some web-based travel intermediaries, such as Skyscanner simply provide a listing of availability on a particular route, but provide no booking facility or customer support. Other intermediaries provide a full service similar to that provided by traditional high-street travel agencies. Expedia.co.uk is a leading online travel agency and is particularly valuable to consumers where guidance is needed on the options available. Airlines and hotels selling online direct to the public generally provide no choice of service providers, therefore the use of an online agency such as Expedia can simplify the search process, especially for more complex long-haul journeys, which are not well served by budget airlines' relatively simple websites. Expedia can provide customers with valuable help and reassurance in the booking process, especially where customers are buying multiple services from different service providers (e.g. an airline ticket, hotel and car hire). Where a customer books two or more such elements of a travel with a company such as Expedia, the law provides additional protection to buyers. 'ATOL' protection applies and the agency has a greater responsibility to relocate or support the customer if there are any problems with their booking. The use of an online agency such as Expedia can help to overcome the nightmare stories that have been told by travellers who have booked their airline ticket and hotel separately with different providers, then encountered difficulties when one of the bookings changes. For example, an airline might reschedule the flight times of a booking already made, which means that the hotel booking is no longer usable. However, if the hotel was booked separately, the hotel operator may have no obligation to amend or refund the booking. (Picture reproduced with permission of Expedia.co.uk.)

through and or subsequently makes a purchase. Companies also offer a range of coupons and voucher codes to segment their markets and, again, a number of intermediaries, such as myvouchercodes.com and discountvouchers.com, have appeared to facilitate the process of bringing buyer and seller together. Increasingly, companies are bidding with search engines such as Google for key search terms to be listed at the top of the visitors' search results, and this can sometimes result in a manufacturer competing against the intermediaries that are selling its products.

8.3 Theories and explanations underpinning networks and relationships

Some business relationships prove to be extremely enduring – for example, many businesses have worked with the same accountants or advertising agency for decades. On the other hand, some relationships can end in bitterness and recrimination. Why do some succeed and others fail? What is the value of ongoing relationships between businesses when many transactions are undertaken with no intention of an ongoing relationship? To address these questions, we need to explore the underlying theoretical reasons for business-based relationships being developed in the first place.

Several researchers have identified an organization's ability to develop and manage a network of relationships as a source of its competitive advantage (e.g. Araujo and Easton 1986) The types of network relationship that were described earlier have been analysed and a number of attempts made to develop theoretical frameworks to explain them. A number of overlapping streams of literature are particularly relevant here: contracting theory, transaction cost economics and resource dependence theory. In addition, models of consumer choice help to explain why consumers seek relationships with suppliers. This is not an exhaustive list of the theoretical roots of commercial relationships, but the overlapping ideas contained in these theories have made significant contributions to the subject.

Contract theory, given prominence by McNeil (1980), discusses the bases of contracts that combine, on the one hand, freedom for both parties to adapt to changing circumstances, but that, on the other hand, must reduce the temptation for one party to exploit the other. In general, details about the whole range of rights and obligations cannot be defined in advance for complex transactions, and it must be recognized that a formal contract is just a part of the process of governing relations between parties. Overlying this is a shared understanding that arises when parties develop longer-term relationships with each other, rather than making a series of one-off transactions with different parties. Developing on this, Williamson, in his book *Markets and Hierarchies,* addressed the question 'Why do organizations exist?' He argued that organizations are created in order to reduce uncertainty and opportunism in the marketplace (Williamson 1975). By extension, networks of cooperating organizations reduce the costs and uncertainty associated with acting alone as isolated business units through series of one-off transactions.

Transaction cost economics, given prominence by Williamson (1975), is based on the notion that there are costs of doing business that are in addition to readily identifiable resource costs. These costs can cover administrative costs, and the cost of insuring against risk and contingencies when dealing with unknown customers and suppliers (Williamson 1985). According to Williamson, firms exist as a means of reducing the risk (and hence transaction costs) of dealing with the uncertainties of a market, thereby reducing transaction costs. On the other hand, market forces can stimulate competition, and hence bring down production costs. Firms seek to reduce their total costs and, in reality, 'hybrid' types of organization emerge. Networks of buyer–seller relationships represent a hybrid type of organization that reduces the uncertainty of pure market-mediated exchanges, while overcoming the inefficiencies of internal (hierarchical) systems of exchange. Cooperation between firms, which creates value through lowering transaction costs and/or increasing benefits to each party, may result in one or both parties giving preferential treatment to the other. Within a transaction cost framework, this could come about as a result of growing levels of trust, which reduces the need for contingencies against risk and uncertainty in transactions. It can also arise where scale benefits encourage preference being given to one partner who is capable of delivering increasing levels of benefits relative to costs.

Resource dependency theory approaches commercial relationships by conceptualizing them as a strategic response by firms to conditions of uncertainty (Pfeffer and Salanick 1978). Firms have been conceptualized as bundles of competencies, such as tacit knowledge, skills, etc., and this framework has been extended to the study of inter-organizational relationships. Through cooperation, partners can exchange core competencies and thereby avoid the risk of tackling novel products or markets alone. In the discussion on strategic relationships between organizations, the ability of member organizations to exchange their technical and marketing competencies has been noted (Hamel, Doz and Prahalad 1989). As an example, many alliances between airlines and hotels are formed where individual companies calculate that there will be benefits in sharing access to each other's customers who are mutually exclusive in terms of their geographical representation and/or product requirements. Networks of relationships have been shown to be particularly valuable where 'strategic holes' exist in the connectivity between members, and the network can create social capital by bringing together disparate individuals and organizations (Baker 1994; Burt 1992).

A further school of thought based on models of buyer behaviour sees business relationships as being essentially about a process of *choice reduction* (Sheth and Parvatiyar 2002). From the buyer's perspective, having excessive choice involves spending time and effort evaluating the competing alternatives. Models of buyer behaviour have been developed to show how buyers reduce the total available set of products to a more manageable 'choice set', which typically may involve just five or six products that are evaluated in greater detail. A relationship is one way of managing this process of choice reduction – in other words, a buyer will initially confine their search to those suppliers with whom they have already established a satisfactory relationship.

Finally, sociologists have noted the effect of culture on individuals' approaches to business relationships. It has been observed that the pattern of doing business in many countries may be based on a tightly knit network of relationships between buyers, sellers, suppliers and distributors, typified by Japan's manufacturing and distribution *keiretsus* (Cutts 1992; Ohmae 1989). In many Asian countries, the idea of a relationship based on tightly specified contracts may be viewed as an insult, and a relationship would develop only over time, through mutual trust. US culture, by contrast, may view a detailed contract as essential for the development of a relationship.

8.4 'Just-in-time' relationships

Close business-to-business relationships are often developed in order to exploit the benefits of just-in-time (JIT) management. This is based on the view that inventory is waste and that large inventories merely hide problems such as inaccurate forecasts, unreliable suppliers, quality issues and production bottlenecks. The JIT concept aims to eliminate the need for safety stock, with parts for manufacture (or goods for reselling) arriving just as they are needed. As a result, small shipments must be made more frequently. Order requirements can specify the exact unloading point and time of day, with suppliers having to respond accordingly. This level of planning occurs, for example, with retailers such as Sainsbury's, who stipulate 'windows' for each delivery, so that these can be moved directly to the sales floor, without the need to hold them first in expansive warehouse space. Specialist distribution companies, such as DHL and TNT, often manage the logistics of supply-chain management on behalf of the principal partners in the supply chain.

Table 8.1 The effects on organizational behaviour of the transition to a 'just-in-time' logistics system.

	Traditional 'just-in-case' supply chain management	With the development of a 'just-in-time' approach to supply chain management
Inventory levels	Large inventories resulting from manufacturing economies of scale and safety stock provision	Low inventories resulting from reliable, 'continuous flow' delivery
Flexibility	Minimal flexibility with long lead times	Short lead times and customer service drive flexibility
Relationships between logistics channel members	Tough, adversarial negotiations	Joint venture partnerships
Number of logistics channel members	Many, to avoid sole dependency	Fewer, but in long-term relationships
Communications	Minimal and with many secrets	Open communication and sharing of information to enable joint problem solving

Successful implementation of JIT systems relies on high levels of cooperation and information exchange between members of a value chain. These closer relations can exist both upstream and downstream from the producer/manufacturer. This can affect the whole culture of an organization and the way that it goes about business. Table 8.1 summarizes the changes in a supply chain that occur as it moves from a 'just in case' mentality to one of 'just in time'.

The JIT concept is not without its problems, with claims that it is unnecessarily expensive to implement. It has been claimed that, during the 1980s, suppliers tolerated the system because it strengthened the relationship between them and their customers. Once manufacturers had become used to a steady flow of materials from one company, they were unlikely to go elsewhere. However, in recent years, the costs of frequent small deliveries have sometimes become insupportable, with reports that some manufacturers have been demanding three deliveries a day, where previously one would have been sufficient.

8.5 Power in business networks

All partners to a business relationship, or members of a network of relationships, are unlikely to possess equal power. Invariably, some will have power over others, meaning that they are able to exert greatest influence over the agenda of the relationship and how it undertakes its activities. It is quite likely that power changes over time. In recent years, power in UK distribution channels has tended to pass to a small number of dominant retailers and away from manufacturers. The growing strength of grocery retailers has put them at the focal point of a value chain. By building up their own strong brands, large retailers are increasingly able to exert pressure on manufacturers in terms of product specification, price and the level of promotional support to be given to the retailer. According to market research group TNS Worldpanel, the UK's 'big four' grocery retailers – Tesco, Asda, Sainsbury's and Morrisons – now account for more than three-quarters of the grocery market. However, while many manufacturers may be dependent on the big four for further sales, this dependency is not reciprocated, with very few retailers relying on one single supplier for more than 1 per cent of their supplies.

Most countries have legislation that prevents one company having dominant power in a market, unless there are public interest benefits. Some evidence of the power of grocery retailers was provided in a 2008 report on supermarkets by the UK Competition Commission (**Competition Commission 2008**). It found evidence of the large supermarkets using their dominant position retrospectively to demand discounts from suppliers, who felt obliged to grant them, for fear of losing a large contract. It also highlighted how supermarkets had used their power to charge the cost of shoplifting to manufacturers, when the manufacturers' products were stolen while in the supermarket. The Competition Commission argued that the large supermarket chains were using their power to transfer excessive risk to suppliers, and proposed a new ombudsman, dubbed 'Offshop', to investigate grievances by suppliers at the hands of supermarkets. The new regulator would be able to hear and investigate complaints from farmers and any other company or traders in the grocery supply chain, including abattoirs, dairies, processors, the food service industry, wholesalers and manufacturers.

In Chapter 11 we will review market structure and the lengths that regulatory authorities go to in order to prevent distortion of markets caused by anti-competitive business relationships and power imbalances within relationships.

8.6 Developing close relationships with customers

So far, we have concentrated on relationships between business organizations themselves. Now we turn our attention to the relationships developed by companies that sell goods and services to the final consumer, as distinct from other business buyers in a value chain.

Today, firms are very keen to turn one-off, casual transactions with their customers into ongoing relationships. There is nothing new in firms seeking to do this. In simple economies, where production of goods and services took place on a small scale, it was possible for the owners of businesses to know each customer personally and to come to understand their individual needs and characteristics. They could therefore adapt goods and services to the needs of individuals on the basis of knowledge gained during previous transactions, and could suggest appropriate new product offers. They would also be able to form an opinion about customers' creditworthiness. Some advocates have claimed that relationship marketing, represents a paradigm shift in marketing, while some sceptics have argued that it is really all about well-established business practices dressed up as something new. Table 8.2 illustrates the principal differences between traditional transaction-based marketing and relationship marketing in consumer markets.

Table 8.2   The components of transactional and relational exchange compared.

Traditional transaction-orientated marketing	Relationship marketing
Focus on a single sale	Focus on customer retention
Short-term orientation	Long-term orientation
Sales to anonymous buyers	Tracking of named buyers
Salesperson is the main interface between buyer and seller	Multiple levels of relationship between buyer and seller
Limited customer commitment	High customer commitment
Quality is the responsibility of production department	Quality is the responsibility of all

Recent resurgence of interest in developing close relationships with customers has occurred for a number of reasons.

- In many markets, relationships have become a new source of product differentiation. In increasingly competitive markets, good products alone are insufficient to differentiate an organization's products from those of its competitors. For example, in the car sector, manufacturers traditionally differentiated their cars on the basis of superior design features such as styling, speed and reliability. Once most companies had reached a common standard of design, attention switched to differentiation through superior added service facilities, such as warranties and finance. Once these service standards became the norm for the sector, many car manufacturers sought to differentiate their cars on the basis of superior relationships. So most major car manufacturers now offer customers complete packages that keep a car financed, insured, maintained and renewed after a specified period. Instead of a three-yearly one-off purchase of a new car, many customers enter an ongoing relationship with a car manufacturer and its dealers, which gives the customer the support she or he needs to keep their car on the road and to have it renewed when this falls due (Figure 8.4).

Figure 8.4 One of the great marketing successes of the car industry in recent years has been to transform the sale of a car into what is effectively an ongoing relationship with the car manufacturer. For many private buyers, the traditional way of buying a car has been to pay a sum of money for the car (either by cash or through a loan), keep the car for probably three or four years, then trade it in for a new one and make a fresh payment for the new car. Today, a wide variety of relationship-based service arrangements are available to private buyers, which give them the use of a car for a defined period of time and, just as importantly, service benefits that allow them to make the greatest use of their car. A relationship-based approach to car sales typically includes a loan that is repaid over two or three years, an extended warranty and a breakdown support service, some of which have been increasingly sophisticated in the benefits they offer car buyers to keep them mobile (for example, many support packages include the provision of a temporary replacement car, and overnight accommodation if necessary). Many agreements give the car buyer the option of returning their car at the end of a specified period and exchanging it for a newer model. Instead of spending £15,000 every three years for a tangible object, the car buyer now typically pays £200–£300 a month for a service-based relationship with a car company and its dealers.

- A second major reason why firms pursue ongoing relationships is because it is generally more profitable to retain existing customers than continually seek to recruit new customers to replaced lapsed ones. A 'leaky bucket' has often been used as an analogy to illustrate the effects of high levels of customer 'churn' (Figure 8.5). A bucket that has holes in its sides and bottom will leak water, so if a stable level is required, this can be achieved only by topping up the bucket with fresh water. This may be an expensive process, so it would make more sense to prevent water escaping in the first place, perhaps by investing in a better-quality bucket that does not leak. So too for businesses that 'lose' customers. There have been many exercises to calculate the effects on a company's profits of even a modest improvement in the rate at which customers defect to competitors (e.g. Reichheld 1993; Reichheld and Sasser 1990). Fewer defections mean less expenditure on recruiting new customers to replace lost ones, although some studies have questioned assumptions about the strength of the link between loyalty and profitability (e.g. Helgesen 2006).

■ Of course, customers are not all equally profitable, and there may be some categories of customer who a company would rather lose than pursue a relationship with. Being able to identify these segments is therefore also an important part of a **relationship marketing** strategy. Many companies use past records to develop a profile of the most promising groups to target and do less to encourage those inherently disloyal groups who are likely to leave the company as quickly as they were attracted to it. Sometimes, companies go through their customer list and actively seek to terminate their relationship with groups that are unprofitable. Many UK banks have attracted media criticism when they have closed the accounts of customers who kept only minimal account balances and did not buy any other services offered. Like many banks and financial services companies, they had recognized that relationship marketing needs to focus on profitable customers and that an exit strategy may be needed for unprofitable ones. Naturally, one bank's target customers for relationship development may be the same as its competitors' targets, so intense competition can occur for key types of customer. This competition can create a dynamic tension in which customers' loyalty is continually challenged by the efforts of competitors to undermine it.

■ Developments in information technology have had dramatic effects on firms' abilities to develop close relationships with customers. The development of powerful user-friendly databases has allowed organizations to re-create in a computer what the individual small business owner knew in his or her head. Large businesses are now able to tell very quickly the status of a particular customer – for example, their previous ordering pattern, product preferences and profitability. Developments in information technology have also allowed

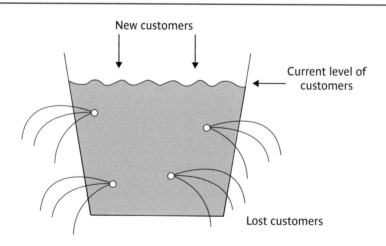

Figure 8.5 The 'leaky bucket' model of customer retention and defection. A leaky bucket is costly to maintain because, in order to maintain a constant level of water, new water must be acquired in order to replace that which has been lost through wastage. Similarly, if a company seeks to maintain a constant number of customers, it is generally easier to avoid wastage of existing customers, so that it does not have expensively to recruit new ones.

⟳ Thinking around the subject

A lifetime of eating?

What is the lifetime value of a restaurant customer? A first-time customer may be spending only £20 on this occasion, but if they like what they get, how much are they likely to spend in the future? A typical diner eating out just once a month could be worth £1200 in just five years. If they are happy, they are likely to tell their friends. If they're not, they are likely to tell even more of their friends. It follows that customers should be seen as investments, to be nurtured carefully over time. When things go wrong (for example, through overbooking) it would probably be to the restaurant's advantage to spend heavily on putting things right for the customer (e.g. by offering money off a future meal). Judged on the basis of the current transaction, the restaurant may make a loss, but it has protected its investment in a future income stream. Like all investments, some customers are worth more than others. Some attempts have been made to develop predictive models to calculate the likely lifetime value of a customer (e.g. Reinartz and Kumar 2003), but these have often proved difficult to operationalize. How should a company decide which customers are priority relationships to invest in? And what level of investment can be justified in terms of the expected future profitability from the relationship?

companies to enter individual dialogues with their customers through direct mail and email (although managing databases effectively can present many problems for organizations). Increased production flexibility based on improved technology allows many manufacturers and service organizations to design unique products that meet the needs of individual customers, rather than broad segments of customers.

However, although many companies may claim to be developing close relationships with their customers, the reality of relationships may be perceived quite differently by the customers themselves. In the service sector, many organizations are simplifying and 'industrializing' their processes, usually in an attempt to improve their operational efficiency and consistency of performance. Such companies may talk about relationship development with customers, based on a dialogue that is driven by information technology. But such relationships can be qualitatively quite different from those based on social bonds and trust. While UK banks have become vigorous in their development of customer databases and named personal banking advisers, many customers would feel that the relationship with their bank is qualitatively worse than when a branch manager was able to enter into a more holistic dialogue with customers.

8.7 Relationships between connected customers

Finally, we must not overlook the networks that can exist between the customers of a company. *Anthropological and sociological approaches* have contributed an understanding of individuals' desire to identify with groups and the goods and services that they consume (e.g. Sierra and McQuitty 2005). Relationships satisfy individuals' affiliation and attachment needs, and there is some evidence that commercial relationships have replaced church, family and work-based relationships as a means of satisfying these needs (Palmer and Gallagher 2007). The term **tribal marketing** has been used to explain how marketers can take advantage of individuals' desire to belong to a group (Cova and Cova 2002).

M
Merton Dene Hotel

JOIN OUR MAILING LIST!

Keep up to date with our latest special offers by adding your name to our mailing list. Please complete the information below. :

Name _____

Address_____ Postcode _____

e-mail: _____

Was your stay with us: Business _____
                                   Leisure _____
                                   Business and leisure _____

How many times a year do you take short breaks at hotels in the UK? _____

Which age group do you belong to?   18 – 35 _____
                                       36 – 45 _____
                                       46 – 55 _____
                                       56 – 65 _____
                                       66+ _____

Simply hand this form into reception and you could be the winner in our monthly prize draw – see promotional material for details and terms and conditions.

Figure 8.6 In an age when marketing communication is increasingly becoming one-to-one, companies often use every opportunity to build up a database of their customers. A customer database should help to provide a good idea about what a customer is likely to want to buy next, and therefore what kinds of communication messages they will be most likely to act upon. This hotel uses a basic card to invite customers to stay in touch, either through conventional printed mail messages, or through e-mail. Although this request for information is very brief, the information sought - age group, location and frequency of using hotels - can be crucial in understanding the most promising propositions to put to a customer. Over time, a company with an effective database will add additional information about customers based on each time they make a purchase, and also this may be supplemented with bought-in information.

The ability of customers to be connected with one another is not new, but today, the development of various Web 2.0 social networking technologies has extended the possibilities for such connectedness. A distinguishing feature of social network sites is the apparent willingness and ability of individuals to communicate their thoughts to others, including people they do not know. Many strong service brands, such as Skype, have been built with very little paid-for advertising and have instead relied on referral through online communities.

Online communities present a number of opportunities for companies to get close to their markets, including observing and collecting information, hosting or sponsoring communities, providing content to communities (such as music, information or entertainment), and participating as members of online communities (Miller, Fabian and Lin 2009). Companies would generally love their product to be at the heart of a community, and there have been many examples of companies that have developed social networking media to put them there. Starbucks, for example, has a Facebook site that claimed to have 1,727,314 'fans' in 2009; it is present on Twitter, has its own YouTube channel and its own online community web pages (MyStarbucksIdeas, Starbucks V2V and StarbucksRed).

A company's involvement in social networking sites can result in a wide range of strategic and operational benefits. By inviting feedback, or simply observing conversations, a company can learn about customers' needs and inform its new product development policy (Constantinides and Fountain 2008).

Online communities can pose a threat as well as an opportunity to companies as they can rapidly spread the views of dissatisfied, angry customers. As an example, the HSBC bank announced in 2007 that it intended to end interest-free overdrafts for students after they had graduated, but was subsequently forced to do a U-turn and restore the facility. Many commentators attributed this change of heart to the strength of feeling expressed through Facebook circles of friends. Another example is provided by two employees from Domino's pizza in North Carolina, who posted a video of disgusting food preparation on YouTube (Vogt 2009).

Case study:
Contaminated food spreads through the value chain from the fields of India to the supermarkets of Sheffield

© *Evgenij Mymrin*

Our ancestors may have grown much of their own food, or at least may have bought food that was grown locally. Today, with the industrialization of farming processes, and consumers becoming increasingly sophisticated in their tastes and their preferences for prepared food available 24/7, value chains for food have become much more complex. Even a simple bag of potato crisps can involve very complex networks of ingredients processors and distributors The growing complexity of value chains can become apparent during a food safety scare, of which the UK has seen several in recent years – salmonella in chickens, BSE in cows, chemicals in 'pure' bottled water, to name but a few.

In 2005 newspapers found themselves reporting another food scare, this time of contaminated chilli powder, which had made its way into hundreds of manufactured foods. An analysis of this incident reveals a lot about the nature of value chains, inter-organizational relationships and risk.

Events began in India, where the chillies were grown, harvested and dried. Thousands of small-scale farmers were involved in growing the chillies, which were sold to spice mills where they were ground and an illegal red dye, called Sudan 1, was added. This dye adds colour to chilli powder, and is normally used to colour wax and floor polish. Laboratory experiments involving rats had shown the presence of cancer-causing toxins in Sudan 1. There was argument about just how real the risk was to humans when taken in very small doses, but

nevertheless the Food Standards Agency had banned the dye from all food products sold in the UK.

The adulterated chilli powder was purchased by an unknown trader. At this stage, it was a commodity product, worth a few pennies per kilogram. The consignment was then purchased by Clacton-on-Sea-based East Anglia Food Ingredients, a wholesaler of basic raw materials for the food industry. It then sold the consignment to Unbar Rothon, an Essex-based food processor that adds value to raw materials by providing graded ingredients to the food manufacturing industry.

The contaminated chilli powder was then sold to Premier Foods, a major manufacturer of foods to the consumer and food-processing sector. One of the products it used the chilli powder in was its Crosse & Blackwell Worcestershire sauce. Some of these bottles of Worcestershire sauce went to supermarkets and were purchased by consumers. Further catering packs were sold to wholesalers, which subsequently sold them to manufacturers of a wide range of value-added food products. The list of products included Pot Noodle, Walkers Worcestershire sauce crisps, Sainsbury's 'Taste the Difference' sausages, and a chicken and vegetable casserole ready meal made by Unilever but sold with the Tesco brand name. From a basic raw material costing a few pence, the chilli powder had become a value-added component of a wide range of food products, with mass distribution across the UK (see Figure 8.7).

A widespread product recall followed the discovery of the contaminated batch of chilli powder, covering more than 420 individual food items. Would such a recall have been possible just two or three decades earlier?

The business environment of food producers has changed considerably. Traceability of food was very limited 20 or 30 years ago, but now, detailed records allowed each transaction in the value chain to be identified. The prospect of identifying specific batches of over 420 final consumer products that might have been contaminated would previously have been very difficult.

Consumers' perceptions of risk had also changed. The actual risk to a human of consuming

9.1 Introduction

Most organisms have a tendency to grow, whether they are human, animal or organizational. Growth can take a number of forms; in the case of human growth, this can be reflected in terms of accumulation of assets, networks of family and friends or esteem. In the case of an organization, growth may bring prestige to the people who own it and work in it, and size may give it greater security in the environment in which it operates. Of course, not all organizations pursue a strategy of growth, either explicitly or implicitly. Many small business owners, for example, are quite happy to remain small. But where organizations seek to expand, finance is likely to be central to their strategic thinking. Without finance, it can be difficult to invest in new equipment or an expanding volume of work in progress. When sources of finance become difficult to obtain, it may be difficult for organizations to grow, or even to survive.

In this chapter, we will explore the links between growth and the financial environment. We will begin by examining the objectives of organizations. It can be an oversimplification to state that all organizations exist to make as much profit as possible, and we will explore the diversity of objectives that exist. In most cases, the availability of finance will be critical to achieving growth, whether this is growth in profits or, in the case of many public-sector services, growth in the volume of service provided to users. The chapter will then review sources of finance for organizations.

9.2 The objectives of organizations

All organizations exist to pursue objectives of one description or another. It is important to understand the nature of organizational goals as these will affect – among other things – the way the organization makes purchases, sets prices or pursues a market share strategy. Whether somebody is selling to or competing with another organization, a study of the organization's objectives will help to understand how it is likely to respond to changes in its environment. Think of the difference between the small entrepreneurs who set up internet businesses as soon as the technology appeared and the established business that they often competed against. The small entrepreneurs may have been more focused on short-term profits but many did not have the financial resources to see their project through to major growth. The larger, established businesses, by contrast, were more likely to focus on maximizing medium- to long-term growth for their shareholders and had sufficient financial resources to cushion them from the effects of new start-ups. Their objectives could often be met by waiting until the market for internet services had developed, sometimes acquiring their smaller competitors who had run out of money.

The link between **organizational objectives** and organizational structure, discussed in Chapter 8, should never be forgotten. As the example of the dotcom entrepreneur indicates, the history and structure of an organization can profoundly affect its objectives. Just compare the effects that ownership and objectives have had on the patterns of growth shown by charities, public limited companies and state-owned enterprises.

Very broadly, organizational goals can be classified into a number of categories:

- those that aim to make a profit for their owners
- those that aim to maximize benefit to society
- those that aim to maximize benefit to their members.

Of course, many organizations combine these objectives, as in the case of the trading activities of charities that aim to make maximum profits, which can in turn benefit disadvantaged groups in society.

9.2.1 Profit maximization

It is often assumed that business organizations will always try to maximize their profits, through a combination of maximizing revenue and minimizing costs. It is usually thought that the pursuit of **profit maximization** is the unifying characteristic of all private-sector business organizations and, indeed, economic theory is very much based on the notion of the profit-maximizing firm.

However, simple models of profit maximization are open to question, even if it is recognized for the moment that profit may be of only marginal relevance to organizations that exist largely for their members' or society's benefit. The following are some of the more important limitations on the assumption that profit maximization is a principal aim of commercial organizations.

- The profit-maximizing objective must be qualified by a time dimension. A firm pursuing a short-term profit-maximizing objective may act very differently to one that seeks to maximize long-term profit. This may be reflected in a differing emphasis on research and development, new product development and market development strategies. Whether an organization is able to pursue long-term profit-maximizing objectives will be influenced by the nature of the environment in which it operates. It has frequently been suggested that the financial environment of the UK and the emphasis on short-term results has caused UK organizations to pursue much more short-term profit goals than organizations in, for example, Japan, where the nature of organizational funding has allowed a longer time for projects to achieve profits. Similarly, an organization operating in a relatively regulated environment – such as patented medicines – will be in a stronger position to plan for long-term profit maximization than one that is operating in a relatively unpredictable and competitive market.

- A second major criticism of profit maximization as a dominant business objective is that maximization is often not observed to occur in practice. In most organizations, there is a separation of ownership from management, where the managers of the company have little or no stake in the ownership of the company. Managers may be inclined to pursue policies more in line with their own self-interest, so long as they make *sufficient* profit to keep their shareholders happy. Instead of pursuing maximum profits, the managers of the company may pursue a policy of maximizing sales turnover, subject to achieving a satisfactory level of profits.

- In practice, it can be very difficult to quantify the relationship between production costs, selling prices, sales volumes and profit. Managers may have inadequate knowledge about these linkages with which to pursue profit maximization effectively.

9.2.2 Market share maximization

Market share maximization may coincide with profit maximization in cases where there is a close correlation between market share and return on investment. It has been suggested that this occurs in many sectors, such as UK grocery retailing. There are other instances, however, where there is a less straightforward relationship between market share and profitability. For example, in the UK retail travel agency sector, both the market leader and small specialist retailers have achieved reasonable returns on investment, but many medium-sized firms have faced below-average returns.

There are circumstances and reasons why a firm may pursue a policy of maximizing market share independently of a short-term profit-maximizing objective. Domination of a particular market may give stability and security to the organization. This might be regarded as a more attractive option for the management than maximizing profits. Building market share may itself be seen as a short-term strategy to achieve longer-term profits, given that there may be a relationship between the two.

Pursuing a market share growth objective may influence a number of aspects of a firm's business activities – for example, it may cut prices and increase promotional expenditure, accepting short-term losses in order to drive its main rivals out of business, leaving it relatively free to exploit its market in the longer term.

9.2.3 Corporate growth

As an organization grows, so too does the power and responsibility of individual managers. In terms of salaries and career development, a growth strategy may appear very attractive to these people, not only for their own self-advancement but also as an aid to attracting and retaining a high calibre of staff, attracted by the prospects of career development. However, such enthusiasm for growth could lead the owners of the business to pursue diversification into possibly unknown and unprofitable areas. As an example, the fashion retailer Next, which is now very successful, earlier came very close to bankruptcy when it expanded too rapidly into relatively unknown activities such as the operation of convenience stores and travel agencies. Shareholders are often happy to back the management and take risks when times are good but may benefit in the longer term by being more cautious and critical of the management's recommendations.

9.2.4 Satisficing

Very often, the managers of a business will not get any direct financial benefit if their company makes maximum profits. The argument has been advanced that managers aim to make *satisfactory* rather than *maximum* possible profits. Provided that sufficient profit is made to keep shareholders happy, managers may pursue activities that satisfy their own individual needs, such as better company cars for themselves, or may pursue business activities that give them a relatively easy life or massage their ego. To achieve these diverse individual objectives, part of the organization's profit that could be paid out to shareholders is diverted and used to pay for managerial satisfaction. The extent to which **satisficing** represents an important business objective can be debated. It can be argued that, in relatively competitive markets, competitive pressures do not allow companies to add the costs of these management diversions to their selling prices. If they did, they would eventually go out of business in favour of companies whose shareholders exercised greater control over the costs of their managers. Only in stable and less competitive markets can these implied additional costs be borne by adding to prices.

There has been a growing tendency for the owners of a business to give senior managers of the business contracts of employment that are related to profit performance. While this may lessen the extent of the apparent conflict of objectives for management, a trade-off may still have to be made where, for example, a decision has to be made on whether to spend more money on better pension arrangements for managers. Should they spend the money and get all the benefit for themselves, or save costs in order to increase profits, of which they will receive only a share?

Satisficing behaviour can have a number of implications for a company's operations. Buying behaviour in any organization is likely to be complex, but companies that are satisficing are likely to attach greater importance to the intangible decision factors such as ease of ordering, familiarity with a sales representative and the level of status attached to a particular purchase, rather than the more objective factors such as price and quality. There may be a tendency to recruit staff on a more informal basis, with the implication that recruitment is driven by a desire to be surrounded by like-minded people, rather than the type of employee who is most effective at maximizing income from customers.

9.2.5 Survival

For many organizations, the objective of maximizing profit is a luxury for management and shareholders alike – the overriding problem is simply to stay in business. Many businesses have had to close not because of poor profitability – their long-term profit potential may have been very good – but because they ran out of short-term cash. Without a source of finance to pay for current expenses, a longer-term profit-maximizing objective cannot be achieved. **Cash flow** problems could come about for a number of reasons, such as unexpected increases in costs, a fall in revenue resulting from unexpected competitive pressure or a seasonal pattern of activity that is different to that which was predicted.

Survival as a business objective can influence business decisions in a number of ways. Pricing decisions may reflect the need to liquidate stock regardless of the mark-up or contribution to profit. This was evident during the 'credit crunch' of 2008 when many retailers found borrowing from banks to finance working capital had become very difficult. In a desperate bid to raise cash to pay for wages and other demands that became due, many retailers held 'stock liquidation' sales to turn stock into cash, sometimes almost regardless of how much it had cost the retailer to purchase the stock in the first place. For many retailers, such actions kept them in business. Other retailers that had longer-term loans that needed renewing faced more difficult challenges, and the reluctance of banks to provide loan capital led to some otherwise reasonably strong retailers, such as the general retailer Woolworths and the shoe retailer Stylo, going into bankruptcy. The need to survive can also affect an organization's promotional activities. An advertising campaign to build up long-term brand loyalty may be sacrificed to a cheaper sales promotion campaign that has a shorter payback period. In order to survive, a firm may impose a 'freeze' on new staff recruitment and capital investment. The company may hope that this will be sufficient to overcome the short-term problem, but it may be creating longer-term problems by weakening the ability of the company to meet customers' needs effectively and profitably.

9.2.6 Loss-making

A company may be part of a group that needs a loss-maker to set off against other companies in the group that are making profits that are heavily taxed by the Inland Revenue. Situations can arise where a subsidiary company makes a component that is used by another member of the group and although that subsidiary may make a loss, it may be more tax efficient for the company as a whole to continue making a loss rather than buying in the product at a cheaper price from an outside organization.

9.2.7 Personal objectives

Many businesses, especially smaller ones, appear to be pursuing objectives that have no economic rationality. They do not pursue maximum profits, and indeed may be quite happy making no profits at all. They may have no desire to grow and may be in no immediate danger of failure. Many small businesses are created to satisfy a variety of personal objectives. This was illustrated by the results of a survey undertaken by RBS/NatWest Bank into the reasons why individuals set up their own business. Top of the list is the desire to gain more control over their lives and avoid being told what to do, which was cited by 17 per cent of respondents. The desire to make critical business decisions as the boss outweighed the aspiration to make money by almost three to one. In second place, 16 per cent report that they set up their own business because they had spotted a market opportunity that they were ready to exploit. Many new business owners also sought to combine a business with a hobby activity, a desire to remain active and the opportunity for friendly encounters with customers. The survey also showed that although growth is high on the agenda of nearly half the respondents, one-fifth were happy to remain at their current size (RBS/NatWest 2010).

Many small businesses are set up by individuals using a capital lump sum that they have received (such as an inheritance or a redundancy payment). Many people in such circumstances have used their lump sum to invest in what are perceived as relatively pleasant and enjoyable businesses, such as antique shops, tea rooms and restaurants. Many fail in a competitive environment where personal objectives cannot be achieved without undue economic sacrifice (e.g. it has been estimated that around three-quarters of all new restaurants fail within two years of opening). However, many others continue to provide goods and services for an acceptable sacrifice from the owners in a marketplace where profit-motivated companies would be unable to meet their objectives. This may partly explain the domination of UK antique shops by small owner-managers and the absence of large chains of profit-motivated businesses.

9.2.8 Social objectives of commercial organizations

Occasionally, commercial organizations have overt **social objectives** of one form or another, usually alongside a financial objective – for example, a requirement that the organization must at least break even. The trading activities of charities such as Oxfam, while having clear objectives in maximizing their revenue, also state their objectives in terms of which groups they seek to benefit. Their social objectives may result in buying supplies from disadvantaged groups, even though this may not be the most commercially profitable option.

Historically, many owners of commercial companies have adopted social objectives. For example, Quakers such as Cadbury and Rowntree sought to maximize the moral welfare of their workforce. In modern times, Body Shop has had an objective of not supporting experiments on animals, which pervades many aspects of the company's business activities, including new product development and promotion. Even organizations that, for the most part, are pursuing profit objectives may pursue social objectives in some small areas of activity, as where an organization runs a sports or social club for its employees at a loss. The social responsibility of organizations, and the views of critics who are cynical about firms' social objectives, are discussed further in Chapter 5.

9.2.9 Maximizing benefits to consumers

An overriding objective of a marketing-orientated organization is to maximize consumer satisfaction. However, this has to be qualified by a second objective that requires the organization to meet its financial objectives. In the case of consumer **cooperatives**, maximizing the benefits to their customers has had significance beyond the normal marketing concept of maximizing consumer satisfaction. The cooperative movement was originally conceived to eliminate the role of the outside shareholder, allowing profits to be passed back to customers through a dividend that is related to a customer's spending rather than their shareholding. Any action that maximized the returns to the business by definition maximized the benefits to consumers.

The importance of consumer cooperatives has declined since the 1950s for a number of reasons. Consumer cooperatives could appear very attractive to consumers at a time when firms were essentially production orientated and when the demand for goods exceeded their supply. With the reversal of this situation, other retailers with greater organizational flexibility and a more overt marketing orientation have attracted custom by offering additional services to customers, often at lower prices.

Building societies should in principle have an aim of maximizing benefits to consumers, given that they are owned by members of the society. Many building societies have been keen to promote the fact that they do not have to satisfy the needs of shareholders and can therefore pass on savings directly to members. Following the crisis of the banking sector in 2008, many building societies capitalized on the public's perception of bankers employed by the big commercial banks as being greedy, bonus-driven individuals who had done harm to the national economy, and instead presented themselves as the more socially responsible alternative. However, in the turmoil of the money markets, which occurred from 2008, many building societies found themselves in trouble. Many had used liberalization of the regulations governing building societies to act in a more market-orientated manner, copying many of the practices of private-sector banks. This included borrowing money on wholesale money markets and targeting specialized sectors of a market – for example, buy-to-let mortgages. When wholesale money markets dried up, and the specialist sectors of the market became unattractive, many building societies found themselves with severe liquidity problems, and many, including the Dunfermline, Scarborough and Cheshire Building societies, had to be rescued by larger organizations.

Thinking around the subject

Cooperatives on a mission for shoppers

The cooperative movement in the UK was founded by the 'Rochdale Pioneers' in 1844. From the very beginning, the objectives of the cooperative retail movement have been dominated by a focus on satisfying consumers' needs in an ethical manner. In the 1840s, this would have led the organization not to put copper dye in its tinned vegetables in order to make them look green. Adding dye may have been consistent with the objectives of profit-motivated retailers, but it went against the principles of the cooperative movement to protect the interests of the customers that owned it. Today, the cooperative movement is represented by a number of societies that all share a focus on acting ethically, and can afford to think long term, without the need to satisfy the short-term interests of shareholders. As an example, the Midcounties Co-op states that its purpose is 'to be a successful consumer co-operative, working towards creating a better, fairer world, and to enhance the lives of our colleagues, members, customers and the communities we serve'. The society returns surplus profits to its members through a dividend, based on members' spending during the previous year. To improve governance of the Co-op, rewards are given to members who attend meetings of the society.

9.2.10 Maximizing public benefits

In many government and charity organizations, it is difficult to talk about the concept of profit or revenue maximization. Instead, the organization is given an objective of maximizing specified aspects of public benefit, or **externalities**, subject to keeping within a resource constraint. Public-sector hospitals are increasingly embracing the philosophy of marketing, but it is recognized that it would be inappropriate for them to be given a strictly financial set of objectives. Instead, they might be given the objective of maximizing the number of operations of a particular kind within a resource constraint. Similarly, a charity campaigning for improved road safety may set an objective of maximizing awareness of its cause among important opinion formers.

There is frequently a gap between the publicly stated objectives of a public-sector organization and the interpretation and implementation of these objectives by the staff concerned. As in a private-sector organization, management in the public sector could promote secondary objectives that add to their own individual status and security, rather than maximizing the public benefit. A manager of a hospital may pursue an objective of maximizing the use of high technology because this may be perceived as enhancing his or her career, even though the public benefit could be maximized more efficiently with simpler technology. Charities have sometimes been accused of becoming self-perpetuating bureaucracies, anxious to protect their organization, rather than being driven primarily by a passion for the cause that they promote.

In recent years, more pressure has been placed on public services such as education and defence to operate according to business criteria. As suppliers of services, public-sector organizations are increasingly being set quantified objectives that reflect the needs of their clients. These are often expressed as service standards: to reduce waiting times for hospital appointments or the turnaround of applications for passports or driving licences, for example. Improved research methods to find out more about client needs and more effective communication of their offering to clients have been part of this process towards a greater business orientation. Many public services have themselves become major consumers of services as peripheral activities such as cleaning and catering have been outsourced. This has resulted in the growth of a market-orientated service sector. Sometimes, the management and staff previously providing an ancillary service within a public-sector organization have bought out the operation from their employer and now have to sell the service back to the authority. Their objectives have changed from a vague notion of maximizing public benefit to one of maximizing their own profit.

9.2.11 Complexity of objectives

A number of possible objectives for organizations have been suggested above. In practice, an organization is likely to be pursuing multiple objectives at any one time. Furthermore, objectives are likely to change through time. Trying to identify the objectives that are influencing the behaviour of an organization can present a number of practical problems.

The first place to look for a statement of an organization's objectives might be its Memorandum and Articles of Association. In the UK, this statement is required by the **Companies Acts** for all limited companies, and includes an objects clause. In practice, companies frequently draw up their objects clause in a way that is so wide that the company can do almost anything.

A more up-to-date statement of objectives may be found in the annual report and accounts that UK companies must produce annually and submit to Companies House where they are available for public inspection. Larger companies must include a directors' report, which may give an indication of the goals that the company is working towards. Many companies publish a **mission statement**, which gives a broad statement of the anticipated future direction that its business will take. We will return to the subject of mission statements in the following chapter.

Beyond this, the true objectives may be difficult for an outsider to determine. Indeed, clearly stating objectives in too much detail may put a firm at a commercial disadvantage when competitors adapt their behaviour accordingly. Even insiders may have difficulty identifying objectives.

What is the right size for an organization?

A quick look at many business sectors will see very large organizations co-existing alongside the very smallest. In fact, the business sector is dominated by small-scale organizations, at least when measured by the number of business units. Think about the last time you had your hair cut, travelled in a taxi or consulted a solicitor, and the chances are that you would have been dealing with a small business. At the same time, many small businesses have to co-exist with larger organizations that also operate in their sector – so, for example, a large number of small solicitors compete with bigger groups such as Eversheds.

This chapter now turns to the issue of organizational size, and explores the reasons for the co-existence of small and large organizations, and the reasons why many business organizations have a tendency to grow. Some would argue that growth is a natural human state, and enterprising business owners continually seek to grow their business, in terms of scope, sales and profitability. However, many small businesses remain that way – single-outlet providers with small, local and loyal customers. The owner may not have the inclination or ability to grow their business beyond this small local scale, and may even see their business more as a lifestyle activity rather than a profit-orientated enterprise.

Many small businesses have successfully made the transition to become multi-outlet organizations, often employing several thousand staff, with customers around the world. Many of the large businesses that we are familiar with today, such as McDonald's restaurants, Starbucks coffee shops and Google, started life as small businesses. The following sections explore the challenges and opportunities facing the growing business. But we will start by looking at the nature of small businesses, the reasons for their continued existence alongside multinational organizations, and the factors that motivate them to grow.

9.3.1 Small and medium-sized enterprises (SMEs)

By far the majority of business organizations in most countries are small. The term 'small business' (or SME, standing for small and medium-sized enterprise) is difficult to define. In an industry such as car manufacture, a firm with 100 employees would be considered very small, whereas among solicitors, a practice of that size would be considered quite large. The term small business is therefore a relative one, based typically on some measure of numbers of employees or capital employed. Within the EU, the Eurostat definition of small business is often used:

- small organizations – up to 50 employees
- medium-sized organizations – 50–250 employees
- large organizations – 250+ employees.

In addition, many statistical analyses define a category of 'micro' or 'size class zero' businesses, which do not have any employees. It should be noted that even apparently objective statistics that record the size of business units involve some judgements – for example, the EU definition records a 'headcount' rather than the number of people who can strictly be defined as an employee.

In the UK, the Department for Business, Innovation and Skills Small and Medium Size Enterprise statistics highlight a number of features of the small business sector.

- There were an estimated 4.8 million private-sector enterprises in the UK at the start of 2009, an increase of 51,000 (1.1 per cent) since the start of 2008.

- Almost all of these enterprises (99.3 per cent) were small (0 to 49 employees). Only 27,000 (0.6 per cent) were medium-sized (50 to 249 employees) and 6000 (0.1 per cent) were large (250 or more employees).

- At the start of 2009, there were 3.6 million enterprises with no employees, which is equivalent to 74.8 per cent of all private-sector enterprises, and represents an increase of 68,000 (1.9 per cent) since the start of 2008.

- Small and medium-sized enterprises (SMEs) together accounted for more than half of employment (59.8 per cent) and turnover (49.0 per cent) in the UK.

- Small enterprises alone (0 to 49 employees) accounted for 48.2 per cent of employment and 35.7 per cent of turnover

- The proportion of businesses employing fewer than 50 people varies between sectors. In agriculture, fishing and forestry, 92.6 per cent of employment was in small enterprises, but in financial intermediation this figure was only 18 per cent.

Advocates of small businesses argue that they are important to the economy for a number of reasons. Most large firms started off as very small businesses, so it is important to the health of the economy that there is a continuing supply of growing companies to replace those larger firms that die. According to a study carried out by the Globalisation and Economic Policy Centre at the University of Nottingham, firms employing fewer than 100 workers accounted for 65 per cent of new jobs in the UK in the period from 1997 to 2008. On the other hand, they accounted for only 45 per cent of those destroyed (Wright 2010).

It is suggested that many of Britain's competitors, such as Far Eastern economies, have attributed their growth to a strong small business sector. During recent years, developed economies have seen a significant increase in the number of small businesses, especially in the expanding services sector.

The change in the structure and organization of industry and commerce, the growing emphasis on specialized services and the application of new technology have tended to encourage small business. Technology is increasingly enabling businesses to function at a much lower level of throughput than previously. An example is in printing services, where new production processes have allowed entrepreneurs to undertake small print runs on relatively inexpensive machinery. Small, local printing services now provide a design and printing service that would previously have been undertaken by larger centralized printers. The success of the small printer has been further encouraged by the proliferation of small business users of printed material requiring small print runs and a rapid turnaround of work.

The tendency for large companies to outsource functions such as cleaning and catering in order to concentrate on their core business has also given new opportunities to the small business sector. Many catering businesses, for example, have been started when a company's catering staff bought out the operations of their former employer, and now provide their services on a subcontract basis.

Many small businesses are created to satisfy a variety of personal objectives. It was noted above that an RBS/NatWest Bank survey showed how many new business owners also sought to combine a business with a hobby activity, a desire to remain active and the opportunity for friendly encounters with customers. The survey also showed that although moderate growth was the aim of most companies, a majority of the smallest firms aimed to remain at their present size or had 'no growth' targets (RBS/NatWest 2010).

While small businesses have seen a resurgence in recent years, it should also be recognized that they have a very high failure rate. Conclusive evidence of the failure rate of small businesses is difficult to obtain, especially in view of the problem of identifying new businesses that do not need to register in the first place. However, one indication of failure rates comes from an analysis of VAT (value added tax) registrations, which show that, during the 1990s, only about one-third of businesses set up ten years previously were still registered. Further evidence of the high failure rate is provided by RBS/NatWest, which noted that in 2007 almost half a million firms closed their doors and this rate of failure had not been seen since the 1992 recession. In another study, Barclays Bank estimated that over half of all new firms fail in the first three years. Businesses started by 50-to 55-year-olds were found to be more likely to survive compared with those launched by people in their twenties (Barclays 2004).

9.3.2 Marketing advantages of small businesses

It may at first sight seem remarkable that small firms can exist in sectors that appear to be dominated by large national or multinational organizations. Small businesses survive and prosper where they are able to exploit the marketing advantages of being small. The following are often cited as key competitive advantages.

Small businesses generally offer much greater adaptability than larger firms. With less bureaucracy and fewer channels of communication, decisions can be taken rapidly. A larger organization may be burdened with constraints that tend to slow the decision-making process, such as the need to negotiate new working practices with trades union representatives or the need to obtain the Board of Director's approval for major decisions. As organizations grow, there is an inherent tendency for them to become more risk averse by building in systems of control that make them slower to adapt to changes in their business environment. In some cases, large organizations with inflexible internal processes have created new small subsidiaries (or acquired existing small businesses) to act as an example to the mainstream business. In the UK bus industry, many large, highly unionized companies acquired or created small coach operators, in order that they could have the operational flexibility that was necessary to enter some markets. They additionally may have expected the culture of flexibility in the smaller business to filter back into the main business.

It is also argued that small businesses tend to be good innovators. This comes about through greater adaptability, especially where large amounts of capital are not required. The internet opened many opportunities for small entrepreneurs to establish novel business formats, and this effect can be seen in the travel agency sector, where it was small businesses that innovated with web-based sales facilities, while the larger travel agency chains took some time to set up their own internet facilities. Small firms can be good innovators where they operate in markets dominated by a small number of larger companies and the only way in which a small business can gain entry to the market is to develop an innovatory service aimed at a small niche.

Politically, small business owners can be a vociferous group, which governments seek to appease with concessions. The presence of large numbers of small businesses in a market is also useful for increasing the competitiveness of markets, thereby achieving government objectives of a more flexible economy and lower inflation. Concessions made by the UK government to small businesses exempt small firms with a turnover of less than £70,000 (2009/10) from the need to charge VAT. This reduces the administrative costs of small businesses, and can give a price advantage in price-sensitive markets where larger competitors must add VAT to their prices. Small businesses have often been exempted from statutory duties that apply to larger companies, including some relating to employment rights. They have also frequently been targeted with government incentives for investment and training.

Customers often associate small businesses with a bundle of positive attributes such as friendliness, flexibility, originality and individuality, whereas 'big' may be associated with negative connotations such as impersonal, inflexible, standardized and lacking a human dimension. The term 'small is beautiful' is commonly attributed to Schumacher who challenged conventional economic thinking for failing to consider the most appropriate scale for an activity (Schumacher 1999). Although his original work challenged the notions that 'bigger is better' in the context of developing economies, the concept of an appropriate scale has attracted continuing debate in western developed economies. While considerable research has been undertaken to investigate links between size of production units and indices of efficiency, effectiveness and profitability (e.g. Hill 2001), there has been relatively little research into the consequences of size on consumers' evaluations of service outcomes and processes. Among the limited research into consumers' perceptions of small businesses, Uusitalo (2001) found in a study of Finnish grocery shoppers that respondents particularly appreciated personal contacts with staff, which were stronger in smaller stores than larger stores. Small business owner-managers tend to be 'generalists' and it would be wrong to suggest that they should become 'marketing specialists'. This observation seems quite consistent with recent thinking that all individuals within an organization – large or small – should be boundary-spanners and perform the role of 'part-time marketers' (Gummesson 2008).

Another issue is that small businesses can survive and prosper not by using their own brand, but by linking it to the brand of a franchise or a voluntary consortium. The principles of franchising were discussed in Chapter 8, where it was noted that franchising allowed a franchisor to expand rapidly using the enthusiasm and capital of franchisees, who are often (but certainly not always) small businesses. This is an attractive route for an entrepreneur seeking to set up in business, because the failure rate for franchisees is much lower than for small businesses in general.

⟳ Thinking around the subject

Big or small, the market accommodates then all

In many sectors, the public perception of large, dominant organizations is contrasted by the reality of domination by a large number of small businesses. This is true of the hospitality and accommodation sector, where for every large Hilton or Holiday Inn chain there are hundreds of small-guest-house owners, bed and breakfast businesses, and operators of self-catering accommodation. Small businesses, such as the guest house pictured, manage to hold their own against the larger hotel chains for a number of reasons. They generally offer a much more personal and friendly welcome than large hotel chains, especially to guests who tire of the same format of the branded chain hotels. Guest houses have lower overheads, because the owners often would not employ any staff and this saving can be passed on as lower prices. Many owners of guest houses would probably not see themselves as being business people at all, but simply earning additional income by taking people into what is, after all, their home. Nevertheless, guest houses cannot

afford to be complacent. The growth of low-cost 'budget' hotel chains, such as Premier Inn, has attracted many guests who would otherwise have chosen the guest house on the basis of price. Guest-house owners must also be alert to the changing expectations of customers – for example, in terms of the range of in-room entertainment equipment provided.

9.3.3 Organizational scale

There is continuing debate about whether there is an 'ideal' size for business organizations. In fact, there are advantages and disadvantages of large firms and they can be found co-existing with much smaller firms in most sectors. This section reviews recent debate about the benefits of large organizations against small business units.

9.3.4 Economies of scale

In some industries there are significant **economies of scale** in production processes. This is particularly true of industries where fixed costs of production are a high proportion of total costs. Therefore sectors such as car manufacture and banking allow large organizations to spread the high cost of capital equipment over a greater number of units of output, thereby pursuing what Porter (1980) described as a cost leadership strategy. In sectors that use high technology, or that require highly trained labour skills, a learning curve effect may be apparent (also called a cost experience curve). By operating on a larger scale than its competitors, a firm can benefit more from the learning curve and thereby achieve lower unit costs. While this may be true of some industries, others face only a very low critical output at which significant economies of scale occur – plumbing and hairdressing, for example. For organizations in these sectors, cost leadership would be a difficult strategy as many rival firms would also be able to achieve maximum cost efficiency.

As well as being more efficient at turning inputs into outputs, larger firms may be able to acquire their inputs on more advantageous terms in the first place. One reason for the success of large-scale retailers is the much greater bargaining power they have over suppliers, compared to smaller retailers. Often, smaller organizations have joined together in voluntary buying chains in order to increase their bargaining power with suppliers. Many farmers' cooperatives realize that a group of farmers can collectively achieve lower prices from suppliers than one farmer negotiating alone. As well as being able to bring greater bargaining power to negotiations with suppliers, buying on a large scale can give savings in the logistical costs of transferring goods from supplier to buyer.

Large-scale production can allow for 'economies of scope', by allowing a wider range of goods and services to be offered. This can take the form of additional design features that could not be included if production was on a small scale (e.g. small manufacturers of food products may not be able to afford to spend as much as their larger competitors on designing eye-catching packaging) or additional services that a firm is able to offer (large building societies may, for example, be able to offer a much more comprehensive range of investment services than their smaller competitors).

A company's promotion effort can be much more efficient where it is aimed at a large-volume national (or even international) market, rather than a purely local one. National television and press advertising may be an efficient medium for a large-scale national company, which gives it a promotional advantage over smaller-scale local producers that must rely on various local and regional media.

Investors generally prefer companies that have a proven track record of stability. By being able to diversify into a number of different products and market segments, companies are able to offer this stability, resulting in 'blue chip' companies being able to obtain equity and loan capital at a lower cost than smaller companies.

With relationship marketing becoming an important part of many organizations' strategy, the ability to cross-sell related goods and services becomes crucial. By operating on a larger scale with a broad portfolio of products, cross-selling can be facilitated.

9.3.5 Diseconomies of scale

Most organizations pursue growth to a greater or lesser degree. However, there are limits to how far and how fast a company can grow. Growth by acquisition is commonly associated with high borrowings, resulting in a high level of gearing. The use of relatively cheap debt capital may be attractive while the company is profitable, but can leave it dangerously exposed when conditions deteriorate. Faced with a fixed charge for interest, the organization may be forced to liquidate some of its assets by disposing of subsidiaries, to raise cash to meet its interest payments. Many internet companies that grew rapidly during the late 1990s found themselves unable to service debt repayments when the sector faced severe problems from 2000. Organizations that grew organically at a slower rate without reliance on such a high level of borrowed capital rode the subsequent recession better.

The ability of the management structure of a company to respond to growth sets a further limit to growth. Many companies have benefited by having a dynamic personality leading during a period of rapid growth, only to find that a large organization needs a much broader management base once it passes a critical size. Organizations such as Next and Amstrad are reported to have had difficult periods in the past where their management structure has not grown to meet the needs of a very different type of organization. If a company does not restructure itself as it grows, **diseconomies of scale** may set in.

Legislative constraints are increasingly limiting the ability of firms to grow. In industry sectors where there are significant economies of scale in production, and competition takes place at a global level, there is often a great logic behind the motivation to merge and grow. However, the need to compete from a position of strength needs to be balanced against regulators' increasing concern that the competitiveness of markets should be maintained. It can be difficult for regulators to define this balance, with government policy objectives often pulling in different directions. Most countries have laws to prevent one firm dominating a market or having undue influence over it, and the EU is playing an increasingly important role in this respect. We will return to the subject of legislation governing anti-competitive situations in Chapter 12.

9.3.6 Globalization and multinational organizations

Increasingly, organizations are finding that, in order to achieve economies of scale, they can no longer confine their sales to their domestic market – they must enlarge their market by going overseas. Many industry sectors have witnessed a series of mergers as companies grow in order to achieve economies of scale. In the case of volume car manufacturers, this has resulted in a shrinking number of firms, but those that remain now incorporate a number of brands. General Motors, for example, acquired Daewoo and Saab, to add to Vauxhall Opel, Chevrolet and other brands that it owns. There are major economies of scale open to car manufacturers. Companies operating on a large scale are able to maintain a cost-effective position at the leading edge of design through investment in research and development, whose cost can be spread over a large volume of output. The Volkswagen group, for example, is able to spread the enormous development costs of a new car 'platform' over three quite distinct brands: Volkswagen, Audi and Skoda. If each of these brands had to undertake its own development work, its cars would lose competitive advantage to a company that was able to spread development costs over larger volume.

A company may find itself forced to expand into overseas markets because of saturation of its domestic market. Saturation can come about where a product reaches the maturity stage of its life cycle in the domestic market, while being at a much earlier stage of the cycle in less developed foreign markets. The market for cigarettes may be mature in most western markets, but China represents a new growth opportunity for western companies.

By expanding overseas, a company that has developed a strong brand can stretch the coverage of that brand. By developing in a foreign market, the company will start with the advantage that some visitors from its domestic market will already understand what the brand stands for. Similarly, for residents of the new market, many may already have become familiar with the brand during visits to the manufacturer's home market. In short, there are economies of scale in promoting a brand in multiple markets simultaneously.

International markets are becoming increasingly homogenized. The car industry serves as a good example of one where distinctive national preferences have diminished, and companies are able to manufacture one product, with only minor adaptations to make it suitable for the whole world. Instead of talking about market segments defined by national boundaries, companies operating on a global scale increasingly talk about cross-national segments of socioeconomic and lifestyle groups. Against this assumption of cultural convergence, many commentators have noted the need for individuals to retain a distinct cultural identity, and this has been seen in the preference of some Muslim consumers for Mecca Cola, as a cultural statement in preference to the global brand values of Coca-Cola.

Multinational companies have been at the forefront of efforts to exploit comparative cost advantage differences between countries. There has been a tendency for multinational organizations to focus manufacture of one product line (e.g. a car model) in just one or a small number of factories, to serve the whole world. Such factories typically also benefit by being located in a country where production costs (e.g. wage rates or taxation) are comparatively low. Companies in fiercely competitive markets often calculate that it is cheaper to manufacture a product in a low-cost country such as China and to ship the finished product to the country where there is demand for it. Most British clothes companies now manufacture the bulk of their clothing in less developed countries, where wages paid to staff can be a fraction of those that would be paid to UK staff.

Some authors have noted a subculture in many societies, which holds a negative attitude to big businesses, which are associated with a range of problems, including increasing world inequality, favouring of the interests of capital over the interests of labour, lack of democratic accountability and a cultural uniformity of output (Klein 2001; Notes From Nowhere Collective 2003; Wall 2005). By implication, small businesses are seen to be less tainted.

🔄 Thinking around the subject

Big plane, big risks

Developing a new commercial aircraft requires an investment in development costs that is beyond the resources of most individual companies. Furthermore, as projects get bigger and more expensive, the risk to a company can become unacceptable. Even the mighty Rolls-Royce was brought down by an overrun in the cost of developing its RB211 jet engine in the 1980s. The European civil aviation sector has traditionally been fragmented, with a manufacturer based in each of the main western European countries. Such a fragmented industry provided little opportunity to compete effectively with the American Boeing company, whose access to a large domestic market had propelled it to the position of world leader in the manufacture of large passenger aircraft. In an attempt to challenge this dominance, a number of European manufacturers – initially France's Aerospatiale and Germany's Daimler-Benz Aerospace (later joined by British Aerospace, now BAE Systems, and Spain's Casa) – joined forces to create Airbus, realizing that no single European manufacturer had the resources to overcome the US giants. Each of the joint venture partners has specialized in different components of the Airbus – for example, BAE

Systems produces wing structures and Aerospatiale manufactures fuselages. The results of such technical specialization and cooperation have been to improve the design quality of Airbus aircraft and, through economies of scale, to lower the manufacturing cost per aircraft. By 2004, worldwide sales of Airbus aircraft had exceeded those of Boeing, something that would have seemed difficult to imagine a couple of decades earlier. Inspired by its success, the Airbus consortium embarked on its greatest joint-venture project to date: the A380 'super jumbo'. This was seen as too much of a risk even for the combined resources of the partners that owned Airbus, and the project proceeded only after government intervention to guarantee part of the project. The risks became apparent when problems attributed to the 530 km (330 miles) of wiring in each aircraft resulted in a two-year delay in delivery of the first aircraft, and an increase in total development costs from €8.8 billion to €11 billion in 2007 when the first aircraft was delivered.

News of delays in 2006 knocked 26 per cent off the value of shares in EADS, the parent company of Airbus, and led to the resignation of its chief executive. Another consequence of delays was cancellation of orders from some airlines, and deferment of a freighter version until at least 2014, which lost further Airbus orders from both Federal Express and UPS, and raised its expected earnings shortfall up to 2010 to €4.8 billion ($6.8 billion). Would the Airbus A380 eventually become the standard large aircraft used by the world's airlines, and steal the glory and profits from Boeing's tried and trusted 747? Or would the A380 go down in history as another unjustifiable risk, on a scale similar to that earlier example of Anglo-French cooperation, Concorde?

9.4   Patterns of growth

A small business (or indeed any business) may be tempted to grow for a number of reasons.

- The markets in which the organization operates may be growing, making growth in output relatively easy to achieve. In addition, in a rapidly growing market, if an organization were to maintain a constant output, its market share would be falling. Growth may be considered not so much of a luxury as a necessity if it is to maintain its position in the marketplace. This could be particularly important for industries where there are significant economies of scale.

- A critical mass may exist for the size of firms in a market, below which they are at a competitive disadvantage. For example, a retail grocery chain that is aiming for a broad market segment will need to achieve a sufficiently large size in order to obtain bulk discounts from suppliers, which can in turn be passed on in lower prices to customers. Size could also give economies of scale in many other activities, such as advertising, distribution and administration. Many new businesses may include in their business plan an objective to achieve a specified critical mass within a given time period.

- An overt policy of growth is often pursued by organizations in an attempt to stimulate staff morale. A growing organization is likely to be in a strong position to recruit and retain a high calibre of staff.

- In addition to the formal goals of growth, management may in practice pursue objectives that result in growth. Higher rates of growth can bring greater status and promotion prospects to managers of an organization, even if a more appropriate long-term strategy may indicate a slower rate of growth.

- Some organizations may grow by acquiring competitors in order to limit the amount of competition in a market where this is considered to be wasteful competition. Many local bus operators in the UK have acquired routes from their competitors for this purpose, although the Competition Commission may impose conditions on such takeovers where there is a serious threat to the public interest. We will return to this subject in Chapter 12.

Given that many organizations have a tendency to grow, we should be able to identify patterns of such growth. In this section, we will explore growth patterns with respect to:

- expansion of products/markets served
- growth in order to achieve a balanced portfolio of products
- growth driven by the need for more integrated, efficient operations
- patterns of growth that can be explained by the position of the company in its organizational life cycle.

9.4.1 Product/market expansion

An organization's growth can conceptually be analysed in terms of two key development dimensions: markets and products. This conceptualization forms the basis of the product/market expansion grid (or 'growth matrix') proposed by Ansoff (1957). Products and markets are each analysed in terms of their degree of novelty to an organization, and growth strategies identified in terms of these two dimensions. In this way, four types of growth strategy can be identified. The four growth options are associated with differing sets of problems and opportunities for organizations. These relate to the level of resources required to implement a particular strategy and the level of risk associated with each. It follows, therefore, that what might be a feasible growth strategy for one organization may not be for another. The characteristics of the four strategies are described below.

1 *Market-penetration strategy*: this type of strategy focuses growth on the existing product range by encouraging higher levels of take-up among the existing target markets. In this way a specialist tour operator in a growing sector of the holiday market could – all other things being equal – grow naturally, simply by maintaining its current business strategy. If it wanted to accelerate this growth, it could do this, first, by seeking to sell more holidays to its existing customer base and, second, by attracting customers from its direct competitors. If the market was in fact in decline, the company could grow only by attracting customers from its competitors through more aggressive marketing policies and/or cost reduction programmes. A market penetration strategy offers the least level of risk to an organization – it is familiar with both its products and its customers.

2 *Market-development strategy*: this type of strategy builds on the existing product range that an organization has established, but seeks to find new groups of customers for them. In this way a specialist regional ski-tour operator that has saturated its current market might seek to expand its sales to new geographical regions or aim its marketing effort at attracting custom from groups beyond its current age/income groups. While the organization may be familiar with the operational aspects of the product that it is providing, it faces risks resulting from possibly poor knowledge of different buyer behaviour patterns in the markets it seeks to enter. As an example of the potential problems associated with this strategy, many UK retailers have sought to offer their UK shop formats in overseas markets only to find that those features that attracted customers in the UK failed to do so overseas.

3 *Product-development strategy*: as an alternative to selling existing products into new markets, an organization may choose to develop new products for its existing customers. For example, a ski-tour operator may have built up a good understanding of the holiday needs of a particular market segment, such as the 18- to 35-year-old affluent aspiring segment, and then seek to offer a wider range of services to them than simply skiing holidays. It might offer summer activity holidays in addition, say. While the company minimizes the

risk associated with the uncertainty of new markets, it faces risk resulting from lack of knowledge about its new product area. Often a feature of this growth strategy is collaboration with a product specialist that helps the organization produce the service, leaving it free to market it effectively to its customers. A department store wishing to add a coffee shop to its service offering may not have the skills and resources within its organization to run such a facility effectively, but may outsource to a catering specialist, leaving it free to determine the overall policy that should be adopted.

4 *Diversification strategy*: here, an organization expands by developing new products for new markets. **Diversification** can take a number of forms. The company could stay within the same general product/market area, but diversify into a new point of the distribution chain. For example, an airline that sets up its own travel agency moves into a type of service provision that is new to the organization, as well as dealing directly with a segment of the market with which it had previously probably had few sales transactions. Alternatively, the airline might diversify into completely unrelated service areas aimed at completely different groups of customers – by purchasing a golf course or car dealership, for example. Because the company is moving into both unknown markets and unknown product areas, this form of growth carries the greatest level of risk. Diversification may, however, help to manage the long-term risk of the organization by reducing dependency on a narrow product/market area.

An illustration of this framework, with reference to the specific options open to a seaside holiday hotel, is shown in Figure 9.1.

In practice, most growth that occurs is a combination of product development and market development. In very competitive markets, organizations would probably have to adapt their products slightly if they are to become attractive to a new market segment. For the leisure hotel seeking to capture new business customers, it may not be enough to simply promote existing facilities; in order to meet business people's needs, it might have to offer refurbished facilities to make them more acceptable to business customers and offer new facilities (e.g. the facility for visitors to pay by account).

It has been argued that most successful growth initiatives take place in markets that are adjacent to a company's existing business (Zook 2004). Problems are likely to arise when companies take two or three steps at once – for example, offering new customers a new product

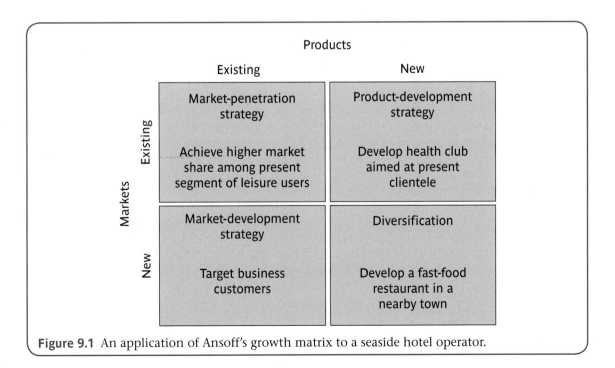

Figure 9.1 An application of Ansoff's growth matrix to a seaside hotel operator.

through a new channel. But even growth into adjacent markets can end in trouble, and a common pitfall occurs where management attention is drawn away from the core business. For example, in the 1990s, the Ford car company expanded into automotive services such as finance and insurance, but it neglected to develop world-class models for its core car business.

Thinking around the subject

Diversify if you dare

Should a company 'stick to its knitting' and do what it is good at, or search continually for new products and new markets? Countless companies have reported disastrous results after growing into areas they knew very little about. Many UK clearing banks diversified into estate agency but regretted the move later. WHSmith went through bad years in the mid-1990s when the newsagent's diversification into DIY retailing and television, among other things, failed to work. Boots the Chemists bought the Halfords car parts and repair garages, but sold them in 2002 when it realized that Halfords had a poor fit with the rest of the Boots businesses and failed to gain a strong competitive advantage.

But isn't growth into new markets essential for companies, especially those facing static or declining markets? One of the UK's leading grocery retailers, Asda (now a subsidiary of Wal-Mart), would not be where it is today had not the Associated Dairy company taken a risk and set up a retailing operation. The security services company Securicor knew that it was taking a risk when it invested in a joint venture with British Telecom to create the successful Cellnet mobile phone network (now called O_2). And a small manufacturing company called WPP (standing for Wire Plastic Products) took huge risks on its way to becoming the owner of one of the world's leading advertising agencies, J Walter Thompson.

It is fine with hindsight to criticize a firm's decisions about which direction its corporate growth should take. But in an uncertain world, risks have to be taken. A sound analysis of a company's strengths and weaknesses and of its external environment certainly helps, but successful growth also depends on an element of luck.

9.4.2 Portfolio planning

Another way of approaching the subject of growth is to consider the idea of the portfolio of products that a company should offer. Over-reliance on one product, aimed at one segment, can make the survival of the organization dependent upon the fortunes of this one product/segment and its liking for its product. In any event, the fact that most markets change to some extent over time, and products generally go through some form of life cycle, would imply that a company would eventually go into decline.

Risk spreading is an important element of portfolio management, which goes beyond marketing planning. Some companies deliberately provide a range of services that – quite apart from their potential for cross-selling – act in contrasting manners during the business cycle. For this reason, accountancy firms have become potentially more stable units as they have amalgamated, by allowing pro-cyclical activities such as management buy-out expertise and venture capital investment to be counterbalanced by contra-cyclical activities such as insolvency work. Service organizations often take on a base load of relatively unattractive but predictable work to counterbalance highly cyclical

reason for a merger is to allow greater cross-selling opportunities between the two companies' sets of customers and to allow for more efficient sharing of resources. The benefits of a merger can be particularly great where two merging companies have complementary resources. In the case of the British Airways–Iberia merger, BA had a strong network of routes to the Far East, which Iberia lacked, while BA lacked the coverage in South America Iberia had.

As with takeovers, proposed mergers often fail because of cultural differences between the companies involved. One reason cited for the failure of the merger between the German car manufacturer Mercedes-Benz and the American company Chrysler was the difference in culture that existed within the two organizations.

Mergers, like takeovers, also run the risk of being blocked by regulatory authorities on the grounds that they may restrict the extent of competition in a market. This is considered further in Chapter 12.

9.6.4 Joint ventures

Diversification into new business areas can be risky, even for a cash-rich business. It may lack the management skills necessary in the market that it seeks to enter, while the barriers to entry may present an unacceptably high level of risk to the company. One way forward is to set up a **joint venture**, where companies with complementary skills and financial resources join together. A new limited company is usually formed, with shares allocated between the member companies and agreement reached on where the financial and human resources are to come from. There are many examples of joint ventures to be found in new high-technology, high-capital sectors such as telecommunications and broadcasting. Within the mobile phone sector, the Symbian joint venture was established between Psion, Siemens, Nokia, Motorola, Matsushita and Ericsson to reduce the cost of developing new operating systems, and to provide an advanced, open, standard operating system for data-enabled mobile phones that would benefit all members of the joint venture. Joint ventures are a common feature in the aerospace sector, where development costs can be high.

A joint venture is commonly used where a company seeking international expansion joins forces with a local or regional company that has a well-developed technology base. This was a foundation for the relationship between America's General Motors and China's Shanghai Automotive Industry (SAIC). Shanghai General Motors Co. Ltd is a 50–50 joint venture between the two companies, formed in 1997 to bring GM's technology to the growing Chinese car market through partnership with a locally based manufacturer.

Where joint ventures are a success, the partners often seek to liquidate their investment by 'floating' the joint venture as a public limited company in its own right. (The mobile phone operator O_2, previously called Cellnet, first became an independent venture when its two joint venture collaborators – British Telecom and Securicor – floated their joint venture as a public limited company.) Of course, many joint ventures end in failure, often because of unrealistic expectations of the partners involved. This later happened to O_2, which invested over £1.5 billion in a joint venture with Dutch Railways to create a new Dutch-based phone operator, Telfort. However, Telfort failed to achieve higher than fifth ranking in the Dutch market and, in April 2003, O_2 admitted defeat and sold its interest in Telfort for just £16 million.

9.6.5 Management buy-outs

A **management buy-out** is an autonomous company that is created by the management and/ or employees of an organization buying part or all of the business of their former employers. Funding a buy-out often leaves the company highly 'geared', with the management putting in relatively little of their own equity capital relative to the loan capital provided by a merchant bank. Such buy-outs often involve very complex financing, with the merchant bank seeking a route by which its minority shareholding can be liquidated by **flotation** very quickly afterwards, or assets of the newly formed business sold off to repay the loans. This method of financing growth can be very attractive at times when there is an expanding economy and relatively low interest rates. Management use a relatively small amount of their own capital and a relatively high proportion of borrowed capital, but benefit disproportionately from a subsequent increase in the market value of the company. For example, the train-leasing company Porterbrook was bought by its managers from British Rail in 1997, with senior managers investing about £100,000 of their own funds. This was doubtless a big risk to the individuals concerned, who may have had to offer their homes as security for money that they personally borrowed. Further finance for the purchase came from banks using loans that were secured against the assets of the company. Two years after the buy-out, the company was sold to Stagecoach plc, which acquired all the managers' shares and assumed responsibility for the bank loans. Individual managers' initial investments of £100,000 were now worth over £5 million each.

Of course, not all management buy-outs are as successful for the managers as in the Porterbrook case. A high level of gearing has spelt difficulty for many new buy-outs when the state of the economy turned out to be below expectation and interest rates rose above the level that had been budgeted for. Companies could not defer payment of interest on loans in the way that they could defer paying a dividend to the risk-taking shareholders. In 2004, managers of the Birmingham-based airline Maersk bought out the British operations of the Danish parent company and relaunched the airline with a new name – Duo. The company had underestimated the strength of competition from 'budget' airlines and failed to achieve a high enough number of passengers paying a high enough level of fares to ensure profitability and adequate cash flow. The banks that had supported the management buy-out became concerned at the poor performance of the airline and within three months of launch they withdrew their loan facilities and the airline was grounded. Managers who had invested in the buy-out had lost their entire equity investment.

A management 'buy-in' is a transaction in which an external management team is backed by an investor to acquire a business. In most cases the management buy-in team joins with some of the incumbent management to ensure continuity, so the deal also has an element of a management buy-out.

9.6.6 De-mergers

Most organizations pursue growth to a greater or lesser degree. However, there are limits to how far and how fast a company can grow. Growth by acquisition is commonly associated with high borrowings resulting in a high level of gearing. The use of relatively cheap debt capital may be attractive while the company is profitable, but can leave it dangerously exposed when conditions deteriorate. Faced with a fixed charge for interest, the organization may be forced to liquidate some of its assets by disposing of subsidiaries, to raise cash to meet its interest payments. Many companies that grew rapidly during the boom years of the 2000s found themselves unable to service debt repayments when the sector faced severe problems from 2008. Organizations that grew organically at a slower rate without reliance on such a high level of borrowed capital rode the subsequent recession better.

Conglomerates sometimes reach a size and diversity that produce more problems than opportunities for the group as a whole. A number of conglomerates have therefore split themselves up in a reversal of the process of merging, sometimes referred to as de-merging. The initial cause of a de-merger is often the recognition that shareholders' total share value would increase if they had shares in two or more separate businesses rather than the one conglomerate holding company. Stock markets often have difficulty placing a value on the shares of highly diversified companies, and many de-mergers have seen the combined value of the de-merged companies' shares very quickly exceed the previous price of the shares of the former holding company. In an important paper published in 1995, Berger and Ofek found that the US stock market undervalued diversified companies by between 13 and 15 per cent, compared to the value of their component parts. Evidence for a similar but smaller 'diversification discount' was found in the UK and Japan. It has been suggested that this anomaly might arise because managers find it easier to build empires that satisfy their personal goals, rather than maximizing shareholder value. Diversification reduces the transparency of corporate financial reporting.

Some recent examples of de-mergers have included the following.

- Chrysler and Daimler-Benz: although the logic of combining these two car companies seemed sound at the time, Daimler-Benz soon regretted taking on a large-volume car maker, with which few synergies were developed and with which there was a large cultural gap. The two companies eventually de-merged in 2007.

- The Kingfisher retail group found little fit between its predominantly large, out-of-town B&Q and Comet business units, and the more town-centre, low-value focused chains of Woolworths and Superdrug. The latter were de-merged from Kingfisher (now known as KESA) in 2001.

- The Six Continents company (previously called Bass) found itself with a portfolio of hotels and pubs with few synergies between them, and a pessimistic stock market valuation of the whole. The hotels were de-merged to become InterContinental Hotels, and the pub chain became Mitchells & Butlers.

De-merging of activities sometimes follows an investigation by the Competition Commission, and may be a condition of a merger between two companies proceeding (for example, following a Competition Commission inquiry, the Airport operator BAA was forced to sell off its Gatwick Airport to another organization in 2010).

Case study:
Can Tesco become too big?

© Liz Leyden

Tesco is widely recognized as a very successful organization, having expanded both geographically and in terms of the services it provides. In 2008, it was estimated by Verdict Research that Tesco accounted for £1 in every £7 of all consumers' retail spending in the UK, derived not just from its core supermarkets, but also through sales of insurance, personal finance, telephone and energy services. Part of the explanation for the company's continued successful growth has been the development of a strong, trusted brand, an ability to apply this to emerging service sectors, and secure sources of funding. However, as the company has grown, it has had to overcome a change of attitude among many members of the public, who once saw Tesco as a pioneering consumer champion, but were now quite likely to see it as a bullying, market-dominating organization.

Nowadays, it seems that when a company becomes market leader, it not only has to worry about being resented because of its size – it also stands a good chance of being targeted by anti-globalization protesters, the green lobby, labour activists and government regulators, among others. It may also catch the attention of the competition authorities, which are becoming increasingly circumspect about companies with dominant market positions. Sam Walton, founder of the world's biggest retailer, Wal-Mart, may have been regarded as a pioneer in the company's early days by bringing low prices to the American masses. But, today, the company has become a target for protesters, who have alleged, among other things, that Wal-Mart has underpaid and exploited its US workforce, and employed sweatshop labour overseas, while inflating the US trade deficit by importing most of its goods. It has also been accused of being simply too powerful, squeezing suppliers and driving other retailers out of business. For years, Wal-Mart refused to engage in a discussion about these allegations, sensing that most Americans still shared a pride in the success of the company and the benefits it had brought to ordinary people. But, from 2005, it began a campaign to get its message across with the launch of a website called Wal-Martfacts.com to defend its records on employment, outsourcing and the other allegations that had been made against it.

Could Britain's Tesco suffer the same fate as Wal-Mart? In 2006 Wal-Mart had 8 per cent of all retail sales in the USA, but even the mighty Wal-Mart seemed insignificant in its market share compared to Tesco's share of the UK market of almost 12 per cent.

Like most large and successful organizations, Tesco started small, being founded shortly after the First World War when Jack Cohen left the Flying Corps with just £30 of capital available to him. He invested most of this in the bulk purchase of tins of surplus war rations, which he then sold from a barrow in the street markets of London.

The Tesco brand name became particularly important to Cohen when he expanded beyond his single market barrow. He initially acted as a wholesaler to other traders, then opened his first shop in Tooting, London, before going on to open further shops. In December 1947, Tesco became a public company, and the money provided by the sale of shares was used to develop larger stores, in particular the new style of self-service store, which was modelled on the American example and proved increasingly successful for Tesco. In the 1950s, the power of a retailer to influence the decision of customers was being reduced with the development of mass media, particularly following the introduction of commercial television. Retailers became dispensers of manufacturers' branded goods, and buyers came to rely on the manufacturers' advertising, rather than the retailers' persuasion, when making purchase decisions.

However, the abolition of Resale Price Maintenance in 1964 was to be extremely beneficial to

Tesco's business strategy in which low prices were a key element of its marketing. It was only from the 1980s that the power of UK retailer brands really came to match the power of manufacturers, with the emergence of five very large retailers in the grocery sector. It became more important to manufacturers that they should have access to Tesco's shelf space, than for Tesco to have access to particular manufacturers' branded products. Throughout the 1990s, Tesco had carefully nurtured its brand, increasingly identifying with a number of good causes – for example, lead-free petrol and educational charities. The company also had a comprehensive corporate social responsibility agenda, and went out of its way to present itself as a good citizen.

By 1997, Tesco plc had overtaken Sainsbury's for the distinction of being the largest grocery retailer in the UK and, by the year ending February 2010, operated 4811 stores worldwide, with total profits of £2.3 billion. It seemed that the Tesco brand had become an unstoppable juggernaut, as the company developed new store formats with separate sub brands – Tesco Extra for very large out-of-town stores selling a wide range of non-food items, and Tesco Metro stores for convenience shopping in town centres. Tesco Online was launched in 2001, and soon became the biggest online retail operation in Britain. Tesco realized that the customers who trust its brand for their weekly shopping are also likely to trust it with a wide range of other services. It has therefore capitalized on this by developing a range of banking, insurance, telephone and energy services. When faced with a confusing range of service providers, loyal Tesco customers would look first to those organizations that they know and trust. To facilitate the task of encouraging customers to spend more of their total expenditure with the company, Tesco has developed various communication vehicles that allow it better to understand individual customers' needs, and for customers to receive well-targeted offers that are of immediate relevance. The company was a trailblazer with its 'Clubcard' loyalty programme, which gives customers rewards proportionate to their expenditure but, more importantly, gives Tesco valuable information about individual customers' demographics and spending patterns. It has also developed narrowly targeted services aimed at particular groups – for example, a mother and baby club for young mothers, and an online dietary advice service.

The company has realized that although having 12 per cent of overall consumer expenditure in the UK is impressive, there are clearly limits to growth at home. It has therefore been active in extending its brand to overseas countries, through a combination of new start-up businesses, joint ventures and acquisitions. By February 2010, the company had operations in 13 overseas markets, including the USA, six countries in Europe, five in Asia and a franchise agreement in India, where Tesco planned to open its first cash and carry store by December 2010. Inevitably, the Tesco brand has often had to start from scratch in these markets, and brand values that have worked in Britain have not always been as relevant in overseas markets.

Could Tesco become too powerful and the brand suffer because of the negative connotations that market dominators often attract? When Tesco announced strong profits for the year 2009, the company talked down its profit prospects for the year ahead and seemed to go out of its way to avoid antagonizing the apparently growing number of people who resented the 'Tescoization' of Britain. The company had already had skirmishes with farmers' groups over the low price that Tesco was accused of paying them for their milk and the large mark-up that Tesco applied when it resold that same milk to customers. Environmental campaigners had protested that the company's trucks unnecessarily transported goods around the country, so that potatoes grown by a farmer just a few miles away from a Tesco store could travel hundreds of miles between distribution centres before they ended up in that store. There were suspicions that Tesco was trying to distort competition by holding large 'land banks', which prevented new store developments by competitors. The company had upset small shopkeepers, who felt threatened by Tesco's move into the convenience store sector, following its acquisition of the One Stop chain and the development of its Tesco Express format. Even government agencies seemed apparently resigned to being 'bullied' by Tesco. It was reported that in one town in northern

England, the company built a new store that was larger than it had been given planning permission for, but the local authority baulked at the prospect of spending large amounts of local taxpayers' money fighting the best lawyers that Tesco could afford. At the same time, the authority apparently felt no such qualms about coming down heavily on a small retailer that had installed shutters on the front of its store without permission.

Senior managers who have spent their working lives learning how to manage and grow their business are increasingly required to become politicians – a role requiring a different set of skills and for which they may be ill suited. Faced with the 'curse of growth', companies can throw money at the problem by hiring armies of PR people, reputation management consultancies who may try to defuse criticism and protect the brand through a corporate social responsibility agenda. But, better still, they could avoid such problems in the first place by acting as 'good citizens' in the eyes of key stakeholder groups.

It seemed that Tesco was not going to suffer the fate of Wal-Mart. There was none of the triumphalism to antagonize its detractors, conveniently fitting in with a British sense of reserve. The company also had a comprehensive corporate social responsibility agenda, and went out of its way to be seen as a good citizen through sponsorship of good causes. It has carefully monitored emerging areas of social concern, and responded. For example, as climate change became a mainstream concern, the company emphasized its eagerness to address the issue – for example, by transporting imported wine from Liverpool to Manchester by canal barge, rather than by road. Was this just a PR gimmick? Would there be any actual effect on the environment? Or was this kind of action symptomatic of the changing mindset of managers in the organization?

QUESTIONS

1 Critically assess the factors that explain the successful development of the Tesco brand.

2 Is it in the public interest that successful companies should be able to grow to a point where they dominate a market?

3 If large, dominant companies such as Tesco really are seen as bullying, manipulative operators, how do you explain their continuing popularity with customers in a fiercely competitive market environment? Is it in the public interest that successful companies should be able to grow to a point where they dominate a market?

Summary

Organizations pursue diverse objectives, some formal and others informally held by managers. Most organizations have a tendency to grow, thereby satisfying the needs of a wide range of internal and external interests. It has been noted that certain types of organization, such as public limited companies, have the ability to grow faster than others where availability of external finance imposes a constraint on growth (**Chapter 7**). This chapter has discussed various growth strategies, noting that growth that is too rapid or too dependent on loan capital can be highly risky. For most organizations, the sustainability of growth is highly dependent on the state of the national or international economic environment (see **Chapter 13**).

A large organization is able to achieve numerous advantages over a smaller one, including the ability to invest in new technologies (**Chapter 4**) and the exploitation of overseas markets (**Chapter 14**). In principle, large organizations should be better able to invest in comprehensive information systems (**Chapter 4**), although it must be remembered that size in itself can create barriers between customers and decision makers. Increasing concern about the possible harmful effects for consumers of market domination by large organizations is discussed further in **Chapter 12**.

🔑 Key Terms

Acquisition (311)	Joint venture (313)
Cash flow (290)	Management buy-out (313)
Companies Acts (293)	Merger (312)
Consolidation (311)	Mission statement (293)
Cooperative (291)	Organic growth (310)
Debenture (310)	Organizational life cycle (307)
Director (309)	Organizational objective (287)
Diseconomy of scale (299)	Profit maximization (288)
Diversification (303)	Prospectus (308)
Economy of scale (298)	Rights issue (309)
Equity capital (308)	Satisficing (289)
Externality (293)	Social objective (291)
Factoring (310)	Stock Exchange (312)
Flotation (313)	Takeover (312)
Globalization (316)	Vertical integration (306)
Horizontal integration (306)	

Online
Learning Centre

To help you grasp the key concepts of this chapter, explore the extra resources posted on the Online Learning Centre at *www.mcgraw-hill.co.uk/palmer*. Among other helpful resources there are chapter-by-chapter test questions, revision notes and web links.

Chapter review questions

1 Discuss the reasons why businesses of different sizes exist. Is there any relationship between the size of the business and the market in which it operates?

2 What problems for the management of a furniture manufacturer might arise from rapid growth?

3 Critically assess the problems and opportunities for marketing management arising from a policy of growth through diversification.

Activities

1 Get hold of a copy of your local *Yellow Pages* directory. Examine companies advertising under the following business classifications: road haulage services; garden centres; restaurants. What can you tell about the types of organization that operate in each sector? How can you explain why large and small organizations co-exist within the sector?

2 Go to the 'corporate information' pages of websites for: a large, established public limited company; a small, rapidly expanding, ethically driven business; a cooperative society; a charitable organization. Critically examine their stated objectives and identify how these are reflected in their business practices.

3 Consider the case of a large, diversified, multi-product company with which you are familiar Analyse its portfolio of products in terms of the BCG growth-share matrix shown in Figure 9.2.

Further reading

Numerous authors have sought to prescribe strategies for successful, profitable growth. The following are classic contributions to the field.

Ansoff, H.I. (1957) 'Strategies for diversification', *Harvard Business Review*, Vol. 25, No. 5, September–October, pp. 113–124.

Levitt, T. (1960) 'Marketing myopia', *Harvard Business Review*, Vol. 38, No. 4, July–August, pp. 45–56.

Porter, M. (1980) *Competitive Strategy: Techniques for Analyzing Industries and Competitors*, New York, Free Press.

More recent contributions to the debate are found in the following.

Graham, K. (2009) *Diversification Strategy: How to Grow a Business by Diversifying Successfully*, London, Kogan Page Ltd.

Johnston, K. (2009) 'Extending the marketing myopia concept to promote strategic agility', *Journal of Strategic Marketing*, Vol. 17, No. 2, pp. 139–148.

Mergers and acquisitions often generate a lot of press coverage when they are contested, and a lot can be learned by following coverage in the *Financial Times*. For a general review of the subject, the following texts are useful.

DePamphilis, D. (2010) *Mergers and Acquisitions Basics*, Burlington, Academic Press.

Gaughan, P.A. (2010) *Mergers, Acquisitions, and Corporate Restructurings*, New York, John Wiley.

Vachon, D. (2007) *Mergers and Acquisitions*, New York, Hutchinson.

Finance for organizational growth can be a complex topic, but the following texts provide a useful insight.

Atrill, P. and McLaney, E.J. (2011) *Accounting and Finance for Non-specialists*, 7th edn, London, FT Prentice Hall.

McLaney, E. (2011) *Business Finance: Theory and Practice*, 9th edn, London, FT Prentice Hall.

The following provide a useful set of readings on multinational businesses.

Collinson, S. and Morgan, G. (2009) *The Multinational Firm*, London, Wiley-Blackwell.

Stonehouse, G., Hamill, J. and Campbell, D. (2010) *Global and Transnational Business: Strategy and Management*, 3rd edn, Chichester, John Wiley & Sons.

For a review of the role of small businesses and the reasons for their recent resurgence, the following texts are useful.

Burns, P. (2010) *Entrepreneurship and Small Business*, 3rd edn, Basingstoke, Palgrave Macmillan.
Williams, S. (2011) *Business Start Up,* London, Financial Times Guides.

Regularly updated statistics on the UK SME sector can be obtained from the following.

Department for Business, Innovation and Skills (2010) *Small and Medium-sized Enterprise (SME) Statistics for the UK 2010*, London, DBERR.

References

Ansoff, H.I. (1957) 'Strategies for diversification', *Harvard Business Review*, Vol. 25, No. 5, September–October, pp. 113–124.
Barclays (2004) *Start-ups and Closures*, London, Barclays Bank SME Market Research Team.
Berger, P.G. and Ofek, E. (1995) 'Diversification's effect on firm value', *Journal of Financial Economics*, Vol. 37, No. 1, pp. 39–65.
Cyert, R.M. and March, J.G. (1963) *A Behavioural Theory of the Firm*, Englewood Cliffs, NJ, Prentice Hall.
Ennew, C., Wong, P. and Wright, M. (1992) 'Organizational structures and the boundaries of the firm: acquisitions and divestments in financial services', *Services Industries Journal*, Vol. 12, No. 4, pp. 478–497.
Grenier, L.E. (1972) 'Evolution and revolution', *Harvard Business Review*, July–August, pp. 37–46.
Gummesson, E. (2008) *Total Relationship Marketing: Marketing Management, Relationship Strategy and CRM Approaches for the Network Economy*, 3rd edn, Oxford, Butterworth-Heinemann.
Hill, J. (2001) 'A multidimensional study of the key determinants of effective SME marketing activity: part 1', *International Journal of Entrepreneurial Behaviour & Research*, Vol. 7, No. 5, pp. 171–204.
Hudson, M. (1995) *Managing Without Profit: The Art of Managing Third Sector Organizations*, London, Penguin Books.
Klein, N. (2001) *No Logo*, London, Flamingo.
Krabuanrat, K. and Phelps, R. (1998) 'Heuristics and rationality in strategic decision making: an exploratory study', *Journal of Business Research*, Vol. 41, No. 1, January, pp. 83–93.
Notes from Nowhere Collective (2003) *We Are Everywhere: The Irresistible Rise of Global Anticapitalism*, London, Verso.
Porter, M. (1980) *Competitive Strategy: Techniques for Analyzing Industries and Competitors*, New York, Free Press.
RBS/NatWest (2010) *Small Business Monitor 2010*, on line at www.rbs.com/media/news/press-releases/.
Sasser, W.E., Olsen, R.P. and Wyckoff, D.D. (1978) *Management of Service Operations: Texts, Cases, Readings*, Boston, MA, Allyn & Bacon.
Schumacher, E.F. (1999) *Small is Beautiful: Economics as if People Mattered: 25 Years Later … With Commentaries*, Vancouver Hartley & Marks Publisher.
Uusitalo, O. (2001) 'Consumer perceptions of grocery retail formats and brands', *International Journal of Retail & Distribution Management*, Vol. 29, No. 5, pp. 214–225.
Wall, D. (2005) *Babylon and Beyond: The Economics of Anti-Capitalist, Anti-Globalist and Radical Green Movements*, London, Pluto Press.

Wright, P. (2010) 'Small firms driving UK job creation', Globalisation and Economic Policy Centre University of Nottingham, online at http://bulletinacademic.co.uk/243_small-firms-driving-uk-job-creation/ (accessed 2 November 2010).

Zook, C. (2004) *Beyond the Core: Expand Your Market Without Abandoning Your Roots*, Boston, MA, Harvard Business School Press.

Chapter 10

People in Organizations

You are just about to complain to Royal Mail about a parcel that has been delayed because of a strike at the local depot. It seems that nothing much has changed over the years at this state-owned organization, which has an effective monopoly on some mail delivery services. Then you receive a parcel delivered by the private company Yodl, delivered in the evening at a time that you specified and when most Royal Mail employees would probably prefer to be back home themselves. You think that there may be a link between the external and internal environment. The parcel delivery sector in the UK has been deregulated for a number of years and companies have experimented with new types of service, which in turn have required new patterns of working by their employees. On the other hand, the letter market is still protected from competition, and maybe the management and employees have little incentive to change the way they work. Then you hear that deregulation of the letter market is imminent and wonder how Royal Mail might adapt to possible new competition. This chapter explores the link between the external and internal environments.

Learning Objectives

This chapter will explain:
- ✓ The link between an organization's external and internal environments.
- ✓ How organizations organize their structures and processes in order to respond to external demands.
- ✓ How organizations manage their human resources, so that they have a highly motivated workforce that has the flexibility to respond to environmental change.

10.1 The link between internal and external environments

Much of this book has been concerned with the way external environmental forces impact on an organization's activities. But we must also recognize that the ability of the organization to respond to challenges and opportunities in its external environment is often very dependent on its internal environment. A new development in technology, for example, may present an organization with a major opportunity, but if it has a poorly motivated staff, or if its management structures and processes are ineffective, the opportunity may pass it by. There have been countless examples of companies that have understood their external environment and the change that has been going on in it, but have nevertheless been unable to adapt to the change. The organization's structures and processes may have been so bureaucratic that by the time it had responded to external change, more nimble competitors had already gained a competitive advantage; the slow and bureaucratic organization was left to wither and die. This has been particularly true of public-sector organizations, which have faced newly deregulated markets. The state-owned Italian airline Alitalia was driven to the point of bankruptcy in 2009 after its management and trades unions failed to react to the challenges posed by 'low-cost' airlines such as Ryanair in the newly deregulated domestic air travel market.

But it is not just public-sector organizations that can fail to adapt to a changed environment. Many companies have grown large and complacent, and acquired procedures and structures that have weighed them down when they have needed to change. The retailer Marks & Spencer and the computer maker IBM have in the past been accused of losing their market leadership position because of internal complacency.

The concept of a value chain was introduced in Chapter 1, where the chain was seen as something linking organizations. However, the value chain model can be extended to incorporate the internal value-adding activities that occur before a product leaves a company and enters the external value chain.

In this chapter, we will look at how organizations organize themselves in terms of their internal structures. Related to this are the internal processes that can help or hinder the task of responding to environmental change – for example, if all employees share a sense of trust in management and a shared vision for the future, adaptation to external environmental change should be facilitated. In order to achieve this trust and shared vision, we need to gain a better understanding of the **human resource management (HRM)** practices that can facilitate or inhibit this. But, first, we go back to the model of a value chain that was introduced in Chapter 1, by extending and applying the framework to the internal environment.

10.1.1 Internal value chains

A value chain describes the process of transforming simple, commodity-type products into goods and services that buyers are prepared to pay a high price for. Think back to Chapter 1 – and the further discussion in Chapter 8 – and you will recall that a variety of suppliers, assemblers, manufacturers and distributors are likely to be involved in turning a basic product into a sought consumer item.

What about the idea of an internal value chain? The principles are similar to those involved in an external value chain. But here we are talking about groups of employees moving a product through a value-creating process, so that basic, low-value items that enter a firm's production process are progressively transformed into high-value products that customers want to buy. Internal value chains can be very short, involving only one or two stages. This is typical of companies that focus on a single, very specialized process. Alternatively, the company may have multiple parallel processes that bring together a variety of basic inputs and combine them to create a complex output. Think of the difference between the internal value chain of a specialist tyre-fitting business and a car manufacturer.

Every organization can be considered to be a marketplace consisting of a diverse group of employees who engage in exchanges between one another to create value. In order for them to be able to create value, employees are often dependent upon internal services provided by other departments or individuals within their organization. These internal exchanges include relationships between front-line staff and back-room staff, managers and the front-line staff, managers and back-room staff and, for large organizations, between the head office and each branch.

This idea of a value chain and internal trading of goods and services is closely related to the idea of 'next operation as customer' (NOAC) (Denton 1990). NOAC is based on the idea that each group within an organization should treat the recipients of their output as an internal customer and strive to provide high-quality outputs for them (e.g. Lukas and Maignan 1996). Through this approach, quality will be built into the product delivered to the final customer (Figure 10.1).

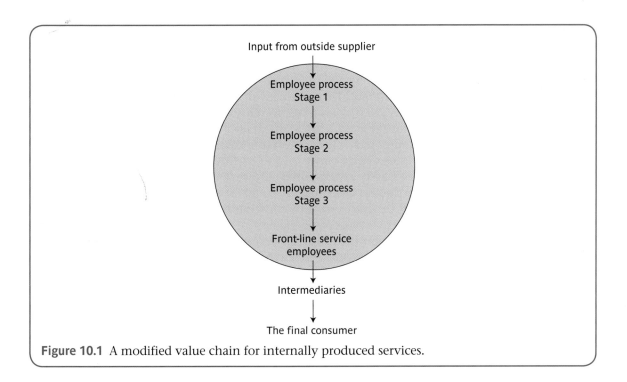

Figure 10.1 A modified value chain for internally produced services.

There is a widely held view that if employees are not happy with their jobs, external customers will never be uppermost in their minds. Researchers have tended to agree that satisfied internal 'customers' are a critical prerequisite to the satisfaction of external customers. Nevertheless, many have recognized the three-way fight between the firm, the employees and the customer. Delivering goods and services is thus a 'compromise between partially conflicting parties' (Bateson 1989). To give an example, it may sound like a good idea to give employees longer rest breaks because this satisfies their needs as internal 'customers'. But longer rest breaks may result in greater waiting time for external customers, as fewer staff are now available to serve them. A fine balance has to be drawn and there is no conclusive proof that in all situations happier employees necessarily result in happier external customers and a more profitable business.

Increasingly, organizations are requiring internal service departments, such as information technology, human resources, accounting and media services, to be more accountable. This has resulted in employees effectively trading services with other employees within their organization. In a growing number of instances, organizations have outsourced the services traditionally provided by such internal departments, resulting in extended 'network' or 'virtual' organizations. With the development of outsourcing and virtual business relationships, the distinction between internal and external value chains is becoming increasingly blurred.

10.2   Defining the organizational strategy

Before we begin a detailed discussion of an organization's structures and processes, we need to note that these structures and processes derive from the strategic position that the organization has adopted. Just consider the differences that exist between two airlines that compete with each other: British Airways and Ryanair. British Airways has a strategy of being a full-service airline, offering customers a comprehensive network of routes with high-quality service at relatively high prices. Ryanair, by contrast, offers a relatively simple series of point-to-point services, a 'no frills' approach to quality, and emphasizes low prices. British Airways has traditionally moved more slowly than its newer competitors. This is partly due to the size and history of the airline, the extensive network of alliances that it operates with other airlines, which cannot always be changed easily, and the expectations of its customers that it will not chop and change its schedules at short notice. Ryanair, by contrast, is adept at moving into new routes, trying them out and quickly withdrawing them if a better opportunity comes along. It is not surprising that many aspects of the two airlines' employment practices should reportedly differ. For example, while British Airways employs many staff who have been loyal to the company for many years, Ryanair has spotted opportunities for recruiting staff on short-term contracts from low-wage countries. When the company launched domestic services in Italy in 2005, it was reported that the inaugural flight was staffed by a Czech crew.

From an organization's strategy, an organizational culture develops, and it is this culture that contributes to structures and processes. Of course, it could be argued that there is a reciprocal process here, with structures and processes in turn contributing to the organizational culture. We return to this later.

For now, we will focus on an organization's mission statement, which can be seen as an overarching statement of the strategic position that an organization seeks for itself. A corporate mission statement is a means of reminding everybody within the organization of its essential purpose. Drucker (1973) identified a number of basic questions that management should ask when it perceives itself drifting along with no clear purpose, and that form the basis of a corporate mission statement.

- What is our business?
- Who is the customer?
- What is value to the customer?
- What will our business be?
- What should our business be?

By forcing management to focus on the essential nature of the business that they are in and the nature of the customer needs that they seek to satisfy, the problem of 'marketing myopia' advanced by Levitt (1960) can be avoided. Levitt argued that in order to avoid a narrow, shortsighted view of business, managers should define their business in terms of the needs that they fulfil rather than the products they produce. In the classic example, railway operators had lost their way because they defined their service output in terms of the technology of tracked vehicles, rather than in terms of the core benefit of movement that they provided. Accountants learnt the lesson of this myopic example by redefining their central purpose away from a narrow preoccupation with providing 'accounting services' to a much broader mission statement that spoke about providing 'business solutions'. More recently, many freight transport companies have defined their mission in terms of managing customers' complete logistical needs.

In the services sector, where the interface between the consumer and production personnel is often critical, communication of the values contained within the mission statement can be very important for ensuring consistency between internal and external audiences (see Figure 10.2). The statement is frequently repeated by organizations in staff newsletters and in notices at their place of work.

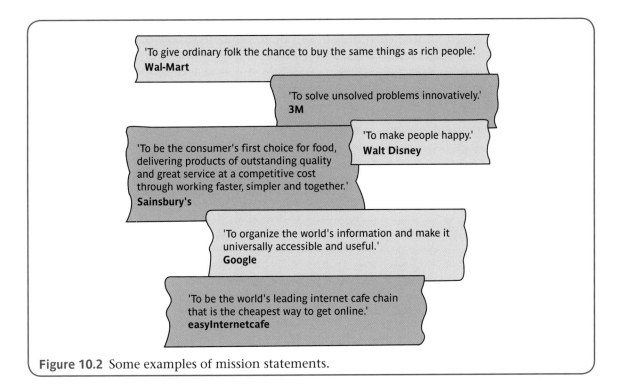

'To give ordinary folk the chance to buy the same things as rich people.'
Wal-Mart

'To solve unsolved problems innovatively.'
3M

'To make people happy.'
Walt Disney

'To be the consumer's first choice for food, delivering products of outstanding quality and great service at a competitive cost through working faster, simpler and together.'
Sainsbury's

'To organize the world's information and make it universally accessible and useful.'
Google

'To be the world's leading internet cafe chain that is the cheapest way to get online.'
easyInternetcafe

Figure 10.2 Some examples of mission statements.

The nature of an organization's mission statement is a reflection of a number of factors:

- the organization's ownership, which can lead to marked contrasts in the mission statements of public-sector, private-sector and charity organizations
- the previous history of the organization, in particular any distinct competencies it has acquired or images it has created in the eyes of potential customers
- environmental factors, in particular the major opportunities and threats that are likely to face the organization in the foreseeable future
- resources available – without resources available for its accomplishment, a mission statement has little meaning.

Missions define in general terms the direction in which an organization seeks to move. They contain no quantifiable information that allows them to be operationalized: for this to happen, objectives need to be set.

10.2.1 Organizational culture

Organizational culture concerns the social and behavioural manifestation of a whole set of values that are shared by members of the organization and can be defined as 'the specific collection of values and norms that are shared by people and groups in an organization and that control the way they interact with each other and with stakeholders outside the organization' (Hill and Jones 2001).

Cultural values can be shared in a number of ways, including:

- the way work is organized and experienced
- how authority is exercised and delegated
- how people are rewarded, organized and controlled
- the values and work orientation of staff
- the degree of formalization, standardization and control within the organization
- the value placed on structured processes of planning, analysis and control, rather than instinct and gut feeling, etc.
- how much initiative, risk-taking, scope for individuality and expression is given
- rules and expectations about such things as informality in interpersonal relations, dress, personal eccentricity, etc.
- status accorded to senior members of the organization, or particular functions
- expectations for team working or success on the basis of individual efforts.

There are often many visible manifestations of these deep-seated cultural values, including the type of buildings occupied by the organization and the image projected in its publicity and public relations.

An organization's culture may be quite imperceptible; indeed, people who have belonged to it for a long time may not be aware of any alternative way of doing things. Elements of the culture may be questioned where individual or group expectations do not correspond to the behaviours associated with the prevailing values of those who uphold 'the culture'. Central command and control cultures within an organization may become increasingly questioned at a time when other social institutions are embracing more democratic cultures.

There have been many attempts to develop typologies of organization culture types. A widely cited typology, developed by Handy, identifies four types of organizational culture (Handy 1989).

1 The *power culture* is found mainly in smaller organizations where power and influence stem from a single central source, through which all decisions, communication and control are channelled. Because there is no rigid structure within the organization, it is theoretically capable of adapting to change very rapidly, although its actual success in adapting is dependent on the abilities of the central power source.

2 The *role culture* is characterized by a formal, **functional organization** structure in which there is relatively little freedom and creativity in decision making. Such organizations are more likely to be production orientated and can have difficulty responding to new market opportunities.

3 The *task culture* is concerned primarily with getting a given task done. Importance is therefore attached to those individuals who have the skill or knowledge to accomplish a particular task. Organizations with a task-orientated culture are potentially very flexible, changing constantly as new tasks arise. Innovation and creativity are highly prized for their own sake.

4 The *person culture* is characterized by organizations that are centred on serving the interests of the individuals within them. It is a relatively rare form of culture in any market-mediated environment, but can characterize campaigning pressure groups.

As individual organizations develop, it is essential that the dominant culture adapts. While a small business may quite successfully embrace a centralized power culture, continued growth may cause this culture to become a liability. It can be difficult to change cultural attitudes when the nature of an organization's business environment has significantly changed – as an example, the privatization of public utilities has called for a transformation from a bureaucratic role culture to more of a task-orientated culture.

An alternative approach, by Cooke, uses an 'Organizational Culture Inventory' to measure 12 aspects of behaviour within organizations, from which three general types of organizational cluster are identified:

1 *Constructive Cultures*, where employees are encouraged to interact with others and approach tasks in ways that facilitate meeting their higher-order satisfaction needs
2 *Passive/Defensive Cultures*, where employees believe they must interact with others in ways that will not threaten their own security
3 *Aggressive/Defensive Cultures*, where employees are expected to approach tasks in an aggressive manner to protect their status and security (Cooke and Szumal 1991).

10.2.2 Leadership

Many of the most successful commercial organizations, including Virgin Group, Federal Express and McDonald's, attribute their success in part to the quality of **leadership** within their organizations. The results of poor leadership are evident in many failing organizations.

What is good leadership for one organization need not necessarily be so for another. Organizations operating in relatively stable environments may be best suited to a leadership style that places a lot of power in a hierarchical chain of command. In the UK, many banks until recently had leadership styles that had been drawn from models developed in the armed forces, evidenced by some managers having titles such as superintendent and inspector. Such rigid, hierarchical patterns of leadership may be less effective where the business environment is changing rapidly and a flexible response is called for (as has happened in the banking sector). The literature has developed two typologies of leadership – transactional

⟳ Thinking around the subject

A public-sector vs private-sector culture gap?

The gap between the public and private sectors has been narrowing over time, and Chapter 2 noted that many public-sector services have been transformed into agencies modelled more on a private-sector organization than the traditional civil service. However, to many observers, people who work in the public and private sectors could come from different planets. Even their language can differ sharply, as private-sector employees talk about 'customers' while public-sector workers talk about 'users'.

In the UK, public-sector culture has traditionally been characterized by an emphasis on procedure rather than outcome. In a large government bureaucracy, it is necessary to have clearly specified rules and procedures in order to prevent inequitable outcomes. Customers' rights and expectations are often specified in the form of government-inspired standards, so staff have little incentive for innovating and delivering better service to users. Staff promotion within the civil service has often been on the basis of seniority, rather than the ability of an individual better to satisfy the needs of external users. And there has been a belief that public-sector workers are well paid, with generous holidays, and an even more generous final-salary pension scheme. Until a few years ago, it would have been almost unheard of for public-sector employees to lose their jobs through redundancy.

Private-sector employees have been presumed to work harder and to have to think on their feet much more than is the case in the public sector. If the external environment turns against them, they will have to adapt or face the risk of losing their job. In this environment, a concern with outcomes must take priority over internal procedures.

The degree of discretion given to a public-sector manager is usually less than that given to a counterpart in the private sector. Statutorily determined standards generally affect public-sector organizations to a greater extent than the private sector – for example, the provision of educational facilities is constrained by the need to adhere to the National Curriculum. Even where a local authority has a significant area of discretion, the checks and balances imposed on many public-sector managers reflect the fact that the public sector is accountable to a wider constituency of interests than the typical private-sector organization.

Is the apparent cultural gap between private and public sectors narrowing? Many public-sector services, such as museums, are increasingly being given clearly defined business objectives that make it much more difficult for officers to continue doing what they like doing rather than what the public they serve wants. Many civil servants now work in agencies modelled on the private sector. Even many of the cherished working practices of public-sector workers have come under scrutiny, including government-funded final salary pensions.

The cultural gap appears to have been reduced most in the case of public-sector services that provide marketable goods and services, such as swimming pools and municipal bus services, but is it possible to close the gap where the service is a monopoly provider of a statutory service, such as fire and police services?

and transformational – which broadly correspond with control and empowerment strategies respectively.

What makes a good leader of people? Are leaders born, or can individuals acquire the skills of leadership? On the latter point there is little doubt that development is possible, and successful companies have invested heavily in leadership development programmes. As for what makes a successful leader of organizations, there have been many suggestions of desirable characteristics, including:

- setting clear expectations of staff
- recognizing excellence appropriately and facilitating staff in overcoming their weaknesses
- leading by example
- being able to empathize with employees
- showing adaptability to changing circumstances.

In too many companies, bad leadership is characterized by:

- 'management by confusion' in which expectations of staff are ambiguously stated and management actions are guided by a secretive 'hidden agenda'
- reward systems that are not based on performance and are perceived as being unfair
- the deliberate or inadvertent creation of an 'us and them' attitude
- failing to understand the aspirations of employees
- failing to take the initiative where environmental change calls for adaptation.

⟳ Thinking around the subject

Shop managers lead by example

Beginning with a small shop in Dundalk in 1960, the Irish grocery retailer SuperQuinn has grown to a successful chain, in 2010 owning 23 stores throughout Ireland and employing over 3000 people. A large part of this success has been attributed to the leadership style of the company's founder, Feargal Quinn, and the emphasis on linking employees' activities to excellence in service quality. But what makes such a leadership style distinctive?

An important principle is that managers should lead by example and never lose contact with the most important person in the organization – the customer. It is the task of a leader to set the tone for customer-focused excellence. To prevent managers losing sight of customers' needs, Quinn uses every opportunity to move them closer to customers, including locating their offices not in a comfortable room upstairs, but in the middle of the sales floor. Managers regularly take part in customer panels where customers talk about their expectations and perceptions of SuperQuinn. Subcontracting this task entirely to a market research agency is seen as alien to the leadership culture of the company. The company requires its managers to spend periods doing routine front-line jobs (such as packing customers' bags), a practice that has become commonplace in many successful service organizations. This keeps managers close to the company and improves their ability to empathize with junior employees.

Does this leadership style work? Given the company's level of growth, profits and rate of repeat business, it must be doing something right, contradicting much of scientific management theory that management is a specialist task that can be separated from routine dealings with customers and employees.

10.3 Creating engagement by employees

It can be difficult for an organization to respond to environmental change if it doesn't have the support of its employees, for whom change may be viewed with suspicion. While it is probably unrealistic to say that a happy workforce necessarily results in an organization that is more effective at embracing change, there are many things that an organization can do to secure the active participation of its employees in change. We will now review some key factors that underlie employees' sense of **engagement** with their organization.

Historically, there have been numerous approaches by which management has engaged with employees. The *scientific management* approach sought to make work as efficient as possible by allocating duties to individuals, as though they were machines. What Taylor (1985), the leading advocate of scientific management, did not expect was the hostility of employees to what is often described as the process of de-skilling. It is necessary to balance the benefits of specialization and improved efficiency against employees' sense of alienation from their job, which can occur where they are involved in only a very small part of a production process.

An alternative approach – *paternalism* – is often associated with Quaker employers such as Cadbury and Rowntree, who attempted to show that they were interested in their workforce at home as well as at work. By providing a range of welfare benefits for employees, an attempt was made to encourage employee identification with the company.

In contrast to the economically based consent strategies of scientific management, the *human relations* approach looks at man as a social animal. Mayo, in his study of General Electric in the USA (1933), argued that productivity was unrelated to work organization and economic rewards as suggested by scientific management. Mayo emphasized the importance of atmosphere and social attitudes, group feelings and the sense of identification that employees had. Mayo's work is similar in focus to that of Herzberg (1966) and Maslow. Maslow (1943) suggested that humans have psychological as well as economic needs. Only when the psychological needs have been catered for do the economic needs come into play.

10.3.1 Motivating employees

Motivation is essentially concerned with individuals' desire to satisfy various levels of need. Maslow (1943) noted that these can range from basic needs such as hunger, through to higher-order social and self-esteem needs. Individuals can be motivated by a range of tangible rewards – for example, money – or intangible (e.g. commendations or awards that add to status or self-esteem). An organization has to bring about congruence between its own goals and those of its employees. Within the UK tourist attractions sector, a comparison can be made between many commercial operations (e.g. Alton Towers and Warwick Castle), where financial **incentives** are an important motivator, and the National Trust, which attracts many unpaid volunteers, motivated by a desire to share in the preservation of historic buildings. Employees' attitudes and opinions about their employers, their colleagues and the work environment may make all the difference between workers merely doing a good job and providing exceptional performance (Arnett, Laverie and McLane 2002).

10.3.2 Communication

Internal communication between management and employees is usually most notable when it is absent. Rumours about revised working arrangements, reductions in the workforce and changes to the terms of employment often circulate around companies, breeding a feeling of distrust by employees in their management. Some managers may take a conscious decision to give employees as little information as possible, perhaps on the basis that knowledge is power. There are sometimes good strategic reasons for not disseminating information to employees (for example, business strategy may be a closely guarded secret in order to keep competitors guessing). However, in too many organizations information is withheld unnecessarily from employees, creating a feeling of an underclass in terms of access to information. Such practices do not help to generate consent and involvement by employees.

In good-practice organizations, information can be communicated through a number of channels. The staff newsletter is a well-tried medium, but in many instances these are seen as being too little, too late, and with inadequate discussion of the issues involved. Many organizations use team briefings to cascade information down through an organization and to permit communication back upwards again. The internet has offered new possibilities for communicating information to a company's employees and allows much greater personalization to the specific needs of individual employees. Management communication is often seen as boring, and more effect may be obtained where the communication style appeals to staff. Staff at a call centre may delete endless boring email messages from managers about new corporate strategy, but the message might just sink in if the company could afford to hire a celebrity to talk to staff during an office party. External advertising should regard the internal labour force as a secondary target market. The appearance of advertisements on television can have

be more general and relate to the whole organization, whereas quality circles relate to the specific work activity of a particular group of employees. Any general points of satisfaction or dissatisfaction can be aired in briefings and then taken up in specific quality circles.

■ Quality circles (QCs) are small groups of employees that meet with a supervisor or group leader in an attempt to discuss their work in terms of production quality and service delivery. To be successful, the QC leader has to be willing to listen to and act upon issues raised by QC members. Circle members must feel their participation is real and effective, therefore the communication process within the QC must be two-way. If QCs appear to become only a routinized listening session, members may consider them to be just another form of managerial control.

■ The pattern of ownership of an organization can influence the level of consent and participation. Where the workforce owns a significant share of a business, there should in principle be less cause for 'us and them' attitudes to develop between management and the workforce. For this reason, many labour-intensive service organizations have significant worker shareholders and there is some evidence that such companies can outperform more conventionally owned organizations.

Figure 10.5 How does this chain of coffee shops put a smile on her face, even when she is feeling down and facing disappointed customers? A number of issues are explored in this chapter, including making her feel a valued part of a team and matching the rewards on offer – financial and non-financial – to her needs and expectations. There is some research evidence that people earning a minimum wage level can be happier than those on high salaries, suggesting that the design of the job can result in marketing benefits by having happy, motivated staff facing customers. And there can be a virtuous circle, with happy staff leading to happy customers, which can itself lead to a pleasant working environment which adds to the happiness of staff. It is not just in day-to-day encounters with customers that happy, engaged staff can be of great value to an organization. During times of turbulence in the external environment, highly engaged staff are likely to be more amenable to change, rather than being suspicious of management's attempts to respond to change. As an example, if a new coffee shop with extended hours opened close to this employee's shop, would she join with her management in rising to the challenge

© Nuno Silva

of the new shop, or would she become demotivated when her manager requires her to work new shifts which she doesn't like?

10.4   Training and development

Training refers to the acquisition of specific knowledge and skills that enable employees to perform their job effectively. The focus of staff training is the job. In contrast to this, **staff development** concerns activities that are directed to the future needs of the employee, which may themselves be derived from the future needs of the organization. As an example, workers may need to become familiar with computer programs that as yet are not elements within their own specific job requirements.

Training is essential if any process of change is to be actively consented to by the workforce. Initially this may be merely an awareness-training programme whereby the process of change is communicated to the workforce as a precursor to the actual changes. It may involve making employees aware of the competitive market pressures the organization faces and how the organization proposes to address them. This initial process may also involve giving employees the opportunity to make their views known and to air any concerns they might have. This can help to generate involvement in the process of change and could itself be the precursor to an effective participation forum.

A practical problem facing many organizations that allocate large budgets to staff training is that many other organizations in their sector may spend very little, relying on staff being poached from the company doing the training. This occurs, for example, within the UK banking sector where many building societies have set up banking operations using the skills of staff attracted from the 'big four' UK banks. The problem also occurs in many construction-related industries and in the car repair business. While the ease with which an organization can lose trained staff may be one reason to explain UK companies' generally low level of spending on training and development, a number of policies can be adopted to maximize the benefits of such expenditure to the organization. Training and development should be linked to the generation of loyalty by employees. Where such efforts to increase engagement are insufficient to retain trained staff, an organization may seek to tie an individual to it by seeking reimbursement of any expenditure if the employee leaves the organization within a specified time period. Reimbursement is most likely to be sought in the case of expenditure aimed at developing the general abilities of an individual as opposed to their ability to perform a functional and organization-specific task.

Another mechanism that can assist an organization in its goals of recruiting and retaining staff is a clearly defined career progression pathway. Career progression refers to a mechanism that enables employees to visualize how their working life might develop within an organization. There should be clearly defined expectations of what an individual employee should be able to achieve within an organization, and clear statements of promotion criteria. An organization can introduce vertical job ladders, or age- or tenure-based remuneration and promotion programmes to assist in the retention of core employees.

During periods of scarcity among the skilled labour force, offers of defined career paths may become essential if the right calibre of staff are to be recruited and retained. Conversely, during a period of recession it can become very difficult for employers to maintain their promises, with a consequent demotivating effect on staff.

It has been claimed that career development opportunities have also been affected by the tendency, described in Chapter 8, for many companies to outsource some of their business processes. Legendary stories of staff who started working for a bank as a cleaner or driver, and rose through a combination of career development and good luck to become a senior executive, are now harder to achieve where the bank's cleaning and driving requirements are outsourced to a completely different company with its own career paths.

⟳ Thinking around the subject

No staff, no service

In many prosperous parts of Britain, it is quite common to find shops and restaurants advertising for staff – sometimes, it seems, putting as much effort into this as they put into advertising for customers. The British Chamber of Commerce's autumn 2010 quarterly survey showed that, despite the recessionary conditions at the time, 68 per cent of manufacturing companies that were recruiting staff reported having difficulties finding suitable employees. For services companies, the number of recruiters reporting difficulties was 47 per cent, lower than at the depth of the recession, but still a source of concern for many businesses.

Service businesses operating on very tight profit margins cannot afford to pay premium wage rates and still remain competitive in attracting price-sensitive customers. But many services sectors require staff to work long, anti-social hours, and many jobs themselves are not particularly pleasant. It is not surprising, therefore, that many businesses find their growth constrained by the availability of staff, rather than the availability of customers. Service organizations around the world have benefited from immigrants filling the jobs that cannot be filled with local people. The wave of immigrants from eastern Europe to the UK, which occurred following the removal of immigration restrictions in May 2004, saw an estimated 600,000 eastern Europeans finding employment in the UK in the following year, predominantly in the services sector, driving buses, serving in restaurants, and working in a range of labour-intensive care services for the young and elderly.

But it is not just unfilled low-wage jobs that have held back the development of services organizations. Many sectors have faced acute specific skills shortages. Companies involved in computer maintenance, for example, have developed innovative schemes to recruit and retain staff, with some companies having 'talent retention programmes'. Companies have been known to give bonuses to existing employees who recommend friends who are subsequently recruited as employees.

Nor is it just in the prosperous countries of the western developed world where staff shortages occur. Many people associate China with being a country of labour surplus, and having an economy that has grown rapidly on the basis of the availability of cheap labour. Nevertheless, many service organizations in China have reported skills shortages holding back their development. In 2007, HSBC Bank claimed that a lack of skilled staff, trained in the financial services sector, was holding back its growth in China. Gradual liberalization of the financial services sector in China, and the appearance of international banks in China, had squeezed the pool of available staff, making it harder for companies to hire and retain qualified staff. To give some indication of the size of the problem, the *Financial Times* reported that, in 2007, HSBC sought to hire 1000 additional people, in addition to its existing 3000 staff. Citigroup planned a similar increase, and Standard Chartered increased its number of employees from 1200 to 2200 in the previous year (*Financial Times* 2007).

Would paying staff a higher wage solve a company's recruitment problems and allow it to grow, or would that growth simply be unprofitable if customers were not prepared to pay more than the going price for its services? Would greater investment by a company in staff training help, or would newly trained staff simply complete their training, then leave to find a better wage elsewhere? Although many labour-intensive service industries have relied on immigrant sources of labour, could there be a danger of cheap labour sources undermining attempts to develop technology-based solutions? Also, for the host economy as a whole, could an increased number of immigrant workers then create even more demand as immigrant workers themselves become consumers of labour-starved industries? And would their home countries – usually poorer developing countries – suffer as a result of losing skilled workers?

10.5   Rewarding staff

The process of staff recruitment and the retention of staff is directly influenced by the quality of reward on offer. The central purpose of a reward system is to improve the standard of staff performance by giving employees something they consider to be of value in return for good performance. What employees consider to be a good reward is influenced by the nature of the motivators that drive each individual. For this reason, one standardized reward system is unlikely to achieve maximum motivation among a large and diverse workforce.

Reward systems have been seen by many (e.g. Milkovich and Newman 2002) as an essential tool to link corporate goals, such as customer orientation, with individual and organizational performance. While some studies have demonstrated the positive effects of incorporating non-financial measures into employees' reward schemes (e.g. Widmier 2002), many companies have encountered problems in linking pay to customer satisfaction. Reasons for this can be attributed to the problem of measuring customer satisfaction, as well as to the missing link between customer satisfaction and customer retention.

Rewards to employees can be divided into two categories: non-monetary and monetary. Non-monetary rewards cover a wide range of benefits, some of which will be a formal part of the reward system – for example, subsidized housing or sports facilities and public recognition for work achievement (as where staff are given diplomas signifying their level of achievement). At other times, non-monetary rewards could be informal and represent something of a hidden agenda for management. In this way, a loyal, long-standing restaurant waiter may be rewarded by being given a relatively easy schedule of work, allowing unpopular Saturday nights to be removed from their duty rota.

Monetary rewards are a more direct method of improving the performance of employees and a more formal element of HRM policy. In the absence of more informal and unquantifiable benefits, monetary rewards can form the principal motivator for employees. A number of methods are commonly used by organizations to reward employees financially.

- Basic hourly wages are used to reward large numbers of secondary, or non-core, employees. These reflect inputs rather than outputs.
- A fixed salary is more commonly paid to the core workers of an organization. Sometimes the fixed salary is related to length of service – for example, many public-sector service workers in the UK receive automatic annual increments not related to performance. As well as being administratively simple, a fixed salary avoids the problems of trying to assess individuals' eligibility for bonuses, which can be especially difficult where employees work in teams. A fixed salary can be useful to a firm where long-term development of relationships with customers is important and staff are evaluated qualitatively for their ability in this respect

rather than quantitatively on the basis of short-term sales achievements. Many financial services companies have adopted fixed salaries to avoid possible unethical conduct by employees who may be tempted to sell commission-based services to customers whose needs have not been properly assessed.

- A fixed annual salary plus a variable commission is commonly paid to personnel who are actively involved in selling, as a direct reward for their efforts.

- Performance-related pay (PRP) has become increasingly important within organizations. PRP systems seek to link some percentage of an employee's pay directly to their work performance. In some ways PRP represents a movement towards the individualization of pay. A key element in any PRP system is the appraisal of individual employees' performance. For some workers, outputs can be quantified relatively easily – for example, the level of new accounts opened forms part of most bank managers' performance-related pay. More qualitative aspects of job performance are much more difficult to appraise – for example, the quality of advice given by doctors or dentists. Qualitative assessment raises problems about which dimensions of job performance are to be considered important in the exercise and who is to undertake the appraisal. If appraisal is not handled sensitively, it could be viewed by employees with suspicion as a means of rewarding some individuals according to a hidden agenda. However, some form of performance-related pay is generally of great use to organizations. It can allow greater management control and enable management to quickly identify good or bad performers. If handled appropriately, it can also assist in the generation of consent and moral involvement, because employees will have a direct interest in their own performance.

- Profit-sharing schemes can operate as a supplement to the basic wage or salary, and can assist in the generation of employee loyalty through greater commitment. Employees can be made members of a trust fund set up by their employer where a percentage of profits are held in trust on behalf of employees, subject to agreed eligibility criteria. Profit-sharing schemes have the advantage of encouraging staff engagement in their organization. Such schemes do, however, have a major disadvantage where, despite employees' most committed efforts, profits fall due to some external factor such as an economic recession. There is also debate about whether profit sharing really does act as a motivator to better performance in large companies, or merely becomes part of basic pay expectations.

- In many service organizations, an important element of the financial reward comes directly from customers in the form of tipping. The acknowledgement of tipping by employers puts greater pressure on front-line service staff to perform well and, in principle, puts the burden of appraisal directly on the consumer of a service. It also reduces the level of basic wage expected by employees. While customers from some countries – such as the USA – readily accept the principle of tipping, others – including the British – are more ambivalent. In the public sector, attempts at tipping are often viewed as a form of bribery.

⟳ Thinking around the subject

Bonuses may be good news for employees, but are they bad news for everybody else?

One aftermath of the 'credit crunch' of 2008 was the vilification of employees who earned large bonuses, especially senior employees working in the banking sector. For many years, bonuses had been presented as a means of improving the performance of employees, who through a process of Pavlovian operant conditioning, responded to the promise of a bonus by working harder and smarter. It seemed that the bonus was now the cause of so many problems, and not their solution.

During 2009 a report published in the UK by the House of Commons Treasury Select Committee said that the banking crisis had 'exposed serious flaws and shortcomings' in remuneration policies. The report specifically criticized bonus schemes for encouraging risk-taking at the expense of shareholders' interests and the long-term health of the banks themselves. The report highlighted practices such as cash bonuses paid immediately regardless of the long-term impact of a deal or transaction. Bonuses might have been earned for hitting targets for new lending, but this may have resulted in staff making loans to individuals and companies who were quite probably not going to be able to pay back the loan. For the bank employee, one more loan might have resulted in a bigger bonus, and meant that the bank could report higher levels of lending, to the delight of shareholders – at least in the short term. But many of these loans would come back to haunt the banks, when customers could not repay their loans. Further criticism of the bonus culture came from the Financial Services Authority's Turner Report, which found a 'strong prima facie' case that inappropriate bonus policies had contributed to the financial crisis of the credit crunch. Bonuses seemed to be out of control, and MPs on the Treasury Select Committee found evidence that 'remuneration consultants' had the effect of ratcheting up bonuses paid throughout the sector by recommending the payment of increasing levels of bonuses.

But can you realistically run a complex business without the use of bonuses? Ater all, they had been introduced to avoid staff becoming complacent in their jobs. Without bonuses, would staff be motivated to go that extra mile to generate new business or provide a higher level of customer service? And what about junior banking staff, who may be motivated to work even harder to improve the quality of service they provide? A junior bank manager may be far removed from the bonus culture of high finance in the City, but isn't it reasonable to expect that they would smile harder at their customers, or put more effort into making sure their ATMs were not out of order, if they thought that a bonus would come their way for providing better service? Even the MPs 'wholeheartedly' supported continued bonus payouts for RBS staff on modest salaries, who they said should 'not be penalized for failures at the top of the organization'.

Debate about the bonus culture initially focused on bankers, whose greed was blamed in the eyes of many people for the problems of the credit crunch. But it seemed that a bonus culture was raising issues in many other service sectors, where critics accused a bonus mentality of leading employees to put their own interests before those of customers, the company or the economy generally. In the education sector, it emerged that many head teachers were being paid large performance bonuses. In 2009, the Association of Teachers and Lecturers said that a banking-style 'bonus culture' was creeping in to state schools. It claimed that heads running chains of schools could earn £200,000 a year, and some senior staff in schools were earning bonuses of more than £50,000 on top of their regular salary. The union claimed that, while the vast majority of school leaders in England and Wales still saw education as a public service, a few had been seduced into seeing it as a chance to make money. The debate in the education sector seemed to be similar to the debate in baking – could bonuses actually hinder the process of providing services that met the needs of users and society in general in the long term?

All these departments should 'think customer' and work together to satisfy customers' needs and expectations. There is argument as to what authority the traditional marketing department should have in bringing about this customer orientation. In a truly mature marketing-orientated company, marketing is an implicit part of everybody's job. In such a scenario, marketing becomes responsible for a narrow range of specialist functions such as advertising and marketing research. Responsibility for the relationship between the organization and its customers is spread more diffusely throughout the organization. Gummesson (2008) uses the term 'part-time marketer' to describe staff working in service organizations who may not have any direct line-management responsibility for marketing, but whose activities may indirectly impinge on the quality of service received by customers.

It has even been argued that the introduction of a marketing department as the principal interface between an organization and its competitive environment can bring problems as well as benefits. In a survey of 219 executives representing public- and private-sector service organizations in Sweden, Grönroos (1982) tested the idea that a separate marketing department may widen the gap between marketing and operations staff. This idea was put to a sample drawn from marketing as well as other functional positions, and the results indicated that respondents in a wide range of service organizations considered there to be dangers in the creation of a marketing department – an average of 66 per cent agreed with the notion, with higher than average agreement being found among non-marketing executives, and those working in the hotel, restaurant, professional services and insurance sectors.

In the following discussion of organizational structures, we will focus on examples from the private sector, but similar principles apply with public-sector organizations, especially where they operate in a market-based environment. Of course, some functions of public-sector organizations, such as sales management, have relatively little place in a public-sector body that takes its clients as given and, instead of maximizing sales, aims to meet government-specified performance targets.

10.9 Bases for organizing a commercial organization

Four basic approaches to allocating management responsibilities within an organization can be identified although, in practice, most organizations use a combination of approaches. The four approaches that will be discussed below are:

1 management by functions performed
2 management by geographical area covered
3 management of products or groups of products
4 management by groups of customers served.

10.9.1 Organization based on functional responsibilities

A common basis for allocating responsibilities within an organization is functions performed. In most commercial organizations, a number of core functions can be identified, the most typical being operations, marketing, personnel and finance. The exact title of these functions may vary between organizations, so, for example, personnel is often referred to as the human resources function. In larger organizations, these functions are further subdivided into areas of specialist responsibility – for example, the marketing function would typically be divided into functions covering advertising, sales, marketing research and customer services. The nature of an organization's environment will influence the relative size and importance of each of its functional areas of management. Buying and merchandising are likely to be an important feature in a retailing organization, while research and development will be an important function for technology-based companies.

The main advantage of allocating responsibilities by function is that it allows individuals and groups of individuals to develop expertise in their functional area. Personnel managers can become expert in the latest employment legislation, or be familiar with the latest thinking on recruitment policies. This expertise may not be developed if personnel management responsibilities are dispersed throughout the organization. A further advantage of functional approaches to management lies in their administrative simplicity. Clearly defined hierarchical structures can allow for rapid identification of lines of authority and responsibility.

Against these advantages, division of responsibilities solely on the basis of functions can have disadvantages. Most seriously, there can be a tendency for corporate goals to become secondary to functional managers' much narrower functional goals. Functions should be seen as a means to an end (in private-sector organizations, this is usually defined in terms of corporate profitability) and should not come to be seen as ends in their own right. It is not uncommon to find destructive rivalry between functional specialists for their share of budgets.

10.9.2 Management by product type

Multi-output organizations frequently appoint a product manager to manage a particular product or group of products. This form of organization does not replace the functional organization, but provides an additional layer of management that coordinates the functions' activities. The product manager's role includes a number of key tasks:

- developing a long-range and competitive strategy for a product or group of products, and preparing a budgeted annual plan
- working with internal and external functional specialists to develop and implement programmes – for example, in relation to advertising and sales promotion
- monitoring the product's performance and changes occurring in its business environment
- identifying new opportunities and initiating product improvements to meet changing market needs.

A product management organization structure offers a number of advantages.

- The product benefits from an integrated cost-effective approach to planning. This particularly benefits minor products that might otherwise be neglected.
- The product manager can, in theory, react more quickly to changes in the product's business environment than would be the case if no one had specific responsibility for the product. Within a bank, a mortgage manager is able to devote a lot of time and expertise to monitoring trends in the mortgage market, and can become a focal point for initiating and seeing through change when this is required because of environmental change.
- Control within this type of organization can be exercised by linking product managers' salaries to performance.

Against this, product management structures are associated with a number of problems.

- The most serious problem occurs in the common situation where a product manager is given a lot of responsibility for ensuring that objectives are met, but relatively little control over the resource inputs they have at their disposal. Product managers must typically rely on persuasion to get the cooperation of marketing, operations and other functional specialist departments. Sometimes this can result in conflict – for example, where a product manager seeks to position a service in one direction, while the advertising manager seeks to position it in another in order to meet broader promotional objectives.
- Confusion can arise in the minds of staff within an organization as to whom they are accountable for their day-to-day actions. Staff involved in selling insurance policies in a

branch bank, for example, may become confused at possibly conflicting messages from an operations manager and a product manager.

- Product management structures can lead to larger numbers of people being employed, resulting in a higher cost structure that may put the organization at a competitive disadvantage in price-sensitive markets.

- Research has suggested that the existence of the optimal product management form is rare and that it is typically associated with an unwillingness of senior management to delegate authority to product managers. While the product management form may be appropriate for a diversified conglomerate, it may be inappropriate for complex multi-output organizations where many functions and products are closely interdependent, allowing very little freedom of action for individual product managers.

10.9.3 Market management organization

Many organizations provide goods and services to a diverse range of customers who have widely varying needs. As an example, a cross-channel ferry operator provides a basically similar service of transport for private car drivers, coach operators and freight operators, among others. However, the specific needs of each group of users vary significantly. A coach operator is likely to attach different importance compared with a road haulier to service attributes such as flexibility, ease of reservations and the type of accommodation provided. In such situations, market managers can be appointed to oversee the development of particular markets, in much the same way as a product manager oversees particular products. Instead of being given specific financial targets for their products, market managers are usually given growth or market share targets. The main advantage of this form of organization is that it allows management efforts to be focused on meeting the needs of distinct and identified groups of customers – something that should be at the heart of all truly marketing-orientated organizations. Market managers can keep a close eye on their market sector and should be in a strong position to respond to environmental change. It is also likely that innovative goods and services are more likely to emerge within this structure than where an organization's response is confined within traditional product management boundaries. Market management structures are also arguably more conducive to the important task of developing relationships with customers, especially for business-to-business services. Where an organization has a number of very important customers, it is common to find the appointment of key account managers to handle relationships with those clients in order to exploit marketing opportunities that are of mutual benefit to both.

Many of the disadvantages of the product management organization are also shared by market-based structures. There can again be a conflict between responsibility and authority, and this form of structure can also become expensive to operate.

⟳ Thinking around the subject

Chinese walls put barriers between staff

The idea of an integrated internal work environment may be fine in theory, and may reassure customers that 'the left hand really does know what the right hand is doing'. But in practice, there are many instances where professional codes of conduct require that staff within an organization do *not* talk to one another. This often happens in financial services institutions where one group of employees may have 'inside information' about the shares, activities or financial condition of a company, which, if made public, would be likely to have an effect on the price of that company's shares. As an example, information about a proposed takeover bid for a company may be price-sensitive in relation to other companies in the same sector. This leads many institutions to create 'Chinese walls', which are barriers to the passing of information. They are designed to manage confidential information and prevent the inadvertent spread and misuse of information. Many banks have set up global Chinese wall policies. Those areas that routinely have access to inside information (e.g. corporate finance) and are considered 'inside areas', must be physically separated from those areas that deal in or advise on financial instruments (e.g. bonds and shares), which are considered 'public areas'.

Chinese walls are also used by solicitors in cases where they are dealing with clients who may be in dispute with each other. But even a Chinese wall may be insufficient to overcome the conflict of interest that may arise. This was seen in the Court of Appeal's ruling about the solicitor Freshfields Bruckhaus Deringer's role in the 2004 £9 billion takeover bid for Marks & Spencer by Philip Green. The court ruled that Freshfields must not act for the Philip Green consortium in its bid for Marks & Spencer. It held that a potential conflict of interest was likely given that Freshfields had acted for Marks & Spencer in the past in relation to its Per Una clothing line. Despite pledges by Freshfields to increase confidentiality within the firm, this was considered insufficient to prevent a conflict of interest arising.

Other service industries can be identified where similar ethical problems can be lessened by the adoption of a product management structure – accountants selling both auditing services and management consultancy services to a company may be tempted to gain business in the latter area at the expense of integrity in the former. How do large diversified firms convince their customers that information given in confidence to one section of the organization will not be used against them in another?

10.9.4 Organization based on geographical responsibilities

Organizations providing goods and services to national or international markets frequently organize many of their functions on a geographical basis. This particularly applies to the sales function, although it could also include geographically designated responsibilities for new product development (e.g. a retailer with regional management structures responsible for new store opening) and some local responsibility for promotion.

In most organizations with some form of regional structure, a delicate balance has to be maintained between the responsibilities of headquarters and the branches. Some delegation of responsibilities to regional branch managers can be vital to secure speedy and effective responses to purely local issues. This is especially true of delegated responsibility in overseas markets where headquarters management may have little idea of the cultural factors that affect the dynamics of a distant overseas market. On the other hand, too much delegation can result in inconsistencies in the way that a global brand is developed and promoted.

10.9.5 Integrated approaches

Overall, the management structure of an organization must allow for a flexible and adaptable response to customers' needs within a changing environment, while aiming to reduce the level of confusion, ambiguity and cost inherent in some structures. The differences in organizational structures described above, and their typical application to a car-ferry operator, are illustrated in Figure 10.6. The great diversity of organizational structures highlights the fact that there is not one unique structure that is appropriate to all firms, even within the same industry sector.

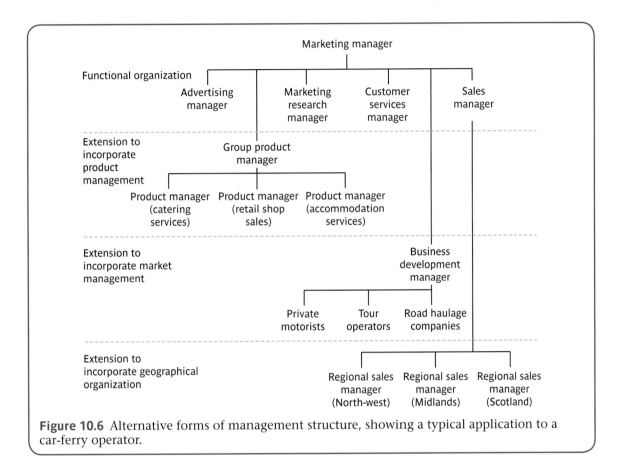

Figure 10.6 Alternative forms of management structure, showing a typical application to a car-ferry operator.

Indeed, most organizational structures exhibit characteristics of all four basic approaches discussed above.

The problem of how to bring people together in an organization to act collectively, while also being able to place responsibility on an individual is one that continues to generate considerable discussion. We will now consider two ideas that seek to integrate these approaches. The first – the matrix approach to management – is essentially about creating a flexible organization based on a combination of the design characteristics discussed above. The second approach – often referred to as business process re-engineering – starts the process of organizational design with a clean sheet of paper, and develops structures and processes that are most appropriate for the environment in which an organization operates.

10.9.6 Matrix approach to management

Organizations that produce many different products for many different markets may experience difficulties if they adopt a purely product- or market-based structure. If a product management structure is adopted, product managers would require detailed knowledge of very diverse markets. Likewise, in a market management structure, market managers would require detailed knowledge of possibly very diverse product ranges. The essence of a **matrix organization structure** is to allow individuals to concentrate on a functional, product, market or geographical specialization, and to bring them together in task-force teams to solve problems, taking an organizational view rather than their own narrow specialist view (Figure 10.7). Product managers can concentrate on excellence in production, while market managers focus on meeting consumer needs without any preference for a particular product. An example of matrix structures can be found in many vehicle distributors, where market managers can be appointed to identify and formulate a market strategy in respect of the distinct needs of private customers and contract hire customers etc., as well as being appointed to manage key customers. Market managers work alongside product managers who can develop specialized activities such as servicing, bodywork repairs and vehicle hire, which are made available to final customers through the market managers.

The most important advantages of matrix structures are that they can allow organizations to respond rapidly to environmental change. Short-term project teams can be assembled and disbanded at short notice to meet changed needs. Project teams can bring together a wide variety of disciplines, and can be used to evaluate new services before full-scale development is undertaken. A bank exploring the possibility of developing a banking system linked to customers' mobile phones might establish a team drawn from staff involved in marketing to personal customers and staff responsible for technology-based research and development. The former may include market researchers and the latter computer development engineers.

The flexibility of matrix structures can be increased by bringing temporary workers into the structure on a contract basis as and when needed. As well as cutting fixed costs, such 'modular' or 'virtual' organizations have the potential to respond very rapidly to environmental change.

Where matrix structures exist, great motivation can be present in effectively managed teams. Against this, matrix-type structures can be associated with problems – most serious are the confused lines of authority that may result. Staff may not be clear about which superior they are responsible to for a particular aspect of their duties, resulting in possible stress and demotivation. Where a matrix structure is introduced into an organization with a history and culture of functional specialization, it can be very difficult to implement effectively. Staff may be reluctant to act outside a role that they have traditionally defined narrowly and guarded jealously. Finally, matrix structures invariably result in more managers being employed within an organization. At best this can result in a costly addition to the salary bill. At worst, the existence of additional managers can also slow down decision-making processes where the managers show a reluctance to act outside a narrow functional role.

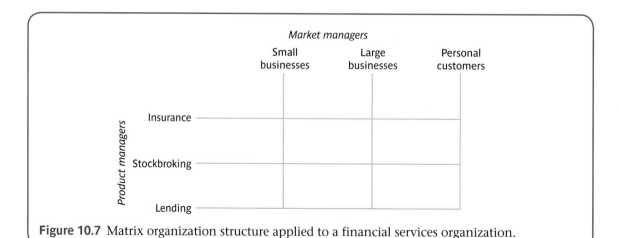

Figure 10.7 Matrix organization structure applied to a financial services organization.

10.9.7 Business process re-engineering

Most management change within organizations occurs incrementally. The result of this is often a compromised organization structure that is unduly influenced by historic factors that are of no continuing relevance. Vested interests within an organization frequently result in an organization that is production rather than customer focused.

The underlying principle of business process re-engineering is to design an organization around key value-adding activities. Essentially, re-engineering is about *radically* redesigning the *processes* by which an organization does business in order that it can achieve major savings in cost or improvements in output, or both. Seen as a model, the organization that is most effective is the one that adds most value (as defined by customers) for the least cost.

Business process re-engineering focuses on operational aspects of a business, rather than its strategy, and starts the design of processes and structures with a clean sheet of paper. This is in contrast to most organizational change, which starts with an analysis of the existing structure and attempts to tinker with it. Re-engineering starts by asking 'If we were a new company, how would we organize ourselves?' It follows that re-engineering can stand for a total sudden change, inevitably challenging the vested interests of people who are comfortably established within their own departmental boundaries.

To be effective, re-engineering needs to be led by strong individuals who have authority to oversee implementation from beginning to end. They will need a lot of clout because fear, resistance and cynicism will inevitably slow the task down. At first sight, though, this approach to reorganization would appear to be in conflict with the principles of participative schemes that stress **employee involvement** in change. Successful companies therefore seek to involve their employees in the detail of implementation, even if the radical nature of the agenda is not negotiable.

⟳ Thinking around the subject

Who's in charge around here?

Many books and articles have described models for managing employees within the context of organization structures. Typically, management will be based on a hierarchy of authority and the division into functional areas. The diagram presented in Figure 10.6 is typical of a prescriptive model for an organizational structure. But who is really in control in a professional service organizations where the front-line staff have unique and valuable skills? How can managers control such people when they themselves may not share the specialist skills of those employees who they are responsible for managing? Is empowering specialist staff to do what they think is best a professional necessity, or something that goes against the principles of consumer sovereignty and the idea that the 'customer is always right'? Many organizations are grappling with the challenge of how to reconcile a management/market logic with a professional service-based logic.

Health services present an interesting case study. The UK's National Health Service (NHS) has seen an increase in the number of managers who have no clinical background. Increasingly, marketing managers are being appointed by Health Service Trusts, mindful that, in an increasingly market-driven health sector, understanding and responding to patients' needs becomes increasingly important. Indeed, the language of some hospital managers now refers to 'customers' rather than 'patients'.

⟲

Although the chief executive of a National Health Service Trust in principle has ultimate authority over all employees, many people would recognize that it is the medical consultants who have the real power in a hospital. If they do not like a change that is proposed by the chief executive, they can point to their professional codes of conduct and years of training that have given them knowledge-based power. Consultants may argue that they have patients' long-term interests at heart, because they have invested heavily in their specialized training and will be around for many years to pick up the consequences of their actions. By contrast, managers are perceived as having relatively simple training, and move on to another job with no professional responsibility to see through the consequences of their actions. Managers with a non-clinical background may become too focused on relatively superficial quality-of-service issues, such as car parking and food, while consultants could argue that only they can judge the true quality of the core service of a hospital, namely the outcome of medical and surgical procedures. They point out that a typical patient is incapable of assessing clinical performance, owing to their limited knowledge and the fact that the outcomes of many clinical procedures will not fully present themselves for many months, or even years, into the future.

For a chief executive, the professional knowledge-based power of consultants may be seen as a source of frustration that is difficult to control. As an example, it has been claimed that many NHS hospitals' operating theatres are under-utilized on Friday afternoons. For a chief executive, one method of increasing the number of patient admissions would be to use these very expensive facilities on Friday afternoons, rather than leave them idle. Consultants would argue that it is bad professional practice to commence operations just before the weekend, when there is only limited cover available in a hospital to rectify any clinical complications. Cynics may argue that consultants are using professional arguments as a smokescreen for giving themselves a long weekend and the chance to get away early to play golf. Some have pointed out that consultants may nevertheless use Friday afternoons to undertake profitable private surgery elsewhere. How can a chief executive with a non-clinical background argue with the knowledge and professional responsibilities of a consultant? Should consultants be empowered to use their skills in the way that they consider best? After all, non-technical management may have practical difficulties in controlling such specialists. Or is health too important to be left to a group of people who, although they have specialist skills, may treat empowerment as an opportunity to put their own interests first?

10.10   The flexible organization

We have seen how management structures can help or hinder the task of responding to change at a strategic level. We will now consider how organizations can be made more flexible to environmental change at a more short-term or operational level. To use the analogy of a central heating system and its environment, we will now move from looking at how the system adapts to long-term climatic change, to how it copes with day-to-day changes in weather.

For many organizations, employees are the biggest item of cost, and potentially the biggest cause of bottlenecks in responding rapidly to environmental change. Having the right staff in the right place at the right time can demand a lot of flexibility on the part of employees. Too often, customers are delayed because, although staff are available, they are not trained to perform the task that currently needs performing urgently. At other times, employees may go about a back-room task oblivious of the fact that delays are occurring elsewhere. Worse still, employees could have a negative attitude towards their job, see a customer's problem as nothing to do with them and take no interest in finding staff who may be able to help. Many service industries have been notorious in the past for rigid demarcation between jobs that were organization-focused rather than customer-focused. In Britain, train drivers and guards for a long while existed as two separate groups that were not able to stand in for one another. With privatization and increased competition for rail franchises, this mindset has been changed, so that employees who are trained in one area can substitute in the other, if required and suitably trained.

To improve their flexibility, many organizations have sought to develop multiple skills among their employees so that they can be switched between tasks at short notice. Within the hotel sector, for example, it is quite usual to find staff multi-skilled in reception duties, food and beverage service, and room service. If staff shortages occur within one area, staff can be rapidly transferred from less urgent tasks where there may be sufficient staff coverage anyway. An effective multi-tasking strategy must be backed up by adequate training so that employees can effectively perform all the functions that are expected of them.

Flexibility in working also applies to the rostering of employees' duties. Where patterns of demand are unpredictable, it is useful to have a pool of suitably trained staff who can be called up at short notice. Many service providers therefore operate 'standby' or 'call-out' rotas, where staff are expected to be available to go into work at short notice.

Flexibility within an organization can be achieved by segmenting the workforce into core and peripheral components. Core workers have greater job security and have defined career opportunities within an internal labour market. In return for this job security, core workers may have to accept what Atkinson (1984) termed 'functional flexibility', whereby they become responsible for a variety of job tasks. The work output of this group is intensified, but in order for this to be successful, employees require effective training and motivation, which in turn has to be sustained by effective participation methods.

Peripheral employees, on the other hand, have lesser job security and limited career opportunities. In terms of Atkinson's prescription, they are 'numerically flexible', while financial flexibility is brought about through the process of 'distancing'. In this situation a firm may utilize the services and skills of specialist labour but acquire it through an external commercial contract as distinct from an employment contract. The principal characteristics of the flexible firm are illustrated in Figure 10.8.

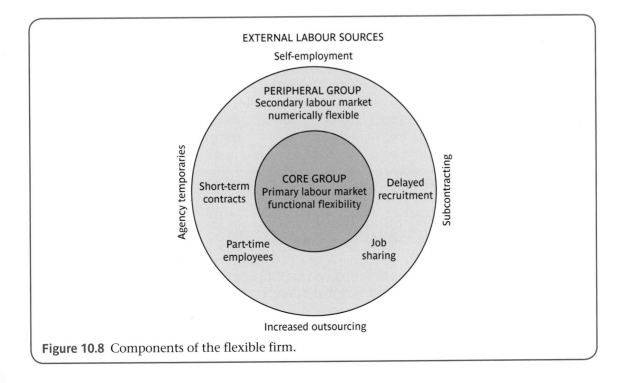

Figure 10.8 Components of the flexible firm.

A **flexible workforce** sounds attractive in principle, but there are some drawbacks. Training in multiple skills would appear to be against the principles of scientific management, wherein employees specialize in one task and perform this as efficiently as possible. Multiple-skill training represents an investment for firms, and in industry sectors with high turnover, such as the hospitality sector, the benefits of this training may be short-lived. Recruiting staff may become more expensive, with staff capable of performing numerous tasks able to command higher salaries than somebody whose background allows them to perform only a narrower range of tasks. Finally, there is also the problem that requiring staff to work flexible hours may make their working conditions less attractive than a job where they had certainty over the days and times that they will be working. Expecting excessive flexibility may be contrary to the principles of **internal marketing** (discussed later in this chapter), exacerbating problems where there is a shortage of skilled staff. If staff are required to be excessively flexible, this could cause stress, and ultimately a high level of staff turnover. Companies may also be liable to compensate employees who have suffered excessive stress at work (see case study). Companies have to compete with other employers for the best staff and, if a job is perceived as offering too much stress and uncertainty, staff may prefer to work elsewhere where working conditions are more predictable.

As a strategic tool, the model of the flexible firm has important implications for organizations that operate in an unstable environment. However, critics of the concept have suggested that the strategic role attributed to the flexibility model is often illusory, with many organizations introducing 'flexibility' in very much an opportunistic manner. It has been noted that the opportunities for introducing this model of flexibility are greater in Britain than in most other EU countries, where stricter rules on staff layoffs apply.

Thinking around the subject

A flexible workforce or opportunistic cost cutting?

One sign of the increased need for flexibility sought by employers is a growing number of people who work part-time rather than full-time at a job. This was particularly evident in the recession from 2008, when many companies chose to reduce the hours of existing workers, rather than lay people off completely. Reporting 'a marked shift to shorter working hours', a study published in 2010 by the Chartered Institute of Personnel and Development (CIPD) showed that the recession had resulted in both a fall in total employment and a shift to part-time work. Total employment was down 580,000 over the two years to spring 2010, while part-time employment had increased by 330,000. During this period, employment fell only 3 per cent, while the economy shrank by 6 per cent. One implication was that companies would be unlikely to hire additional staff when the economy picked up - they still had plenty of slack in their own workforces. A further study by the Institute for Public Policy Research (IPPR) showed that the number of people working part-time because they could not find full-time employment had reached record levels, fuelling fears that the phenomenon of 'midworking' would see a generation of people in a job but employed for only just enough hours to cover their essential spending.

The IPPR report noted that the recession had hit the poorest groups hardest. Employment for people with fewer than five GCSEs had fallen by more than 8 per cent since the recession began – higher than other groups. The report also noted that more than one in five involuntary part-time workers were aged between 16 and 24: Similarities with the USA were noted, where there is a much higher level of 'underemployment' among less educated, lower-skilled and lower-income households, contributing to a growing inequality in incomes.

Businesses often talk about the need for flexibility in their workforce, and the recession may have encouraged some previously reluctant managers and unionized workers to think that flexibly reducing employees' hours was better than them having no job at all. But what are the long-term consequences for society and the economy as a whole of having a growing number of people whose spending power is greatly reduced and who do not feature in the regularly published unemployment statistics? Will the slack implied by an underemployed workforce allow companies to expand rapidly when the economic recovery comes, rather than suffering as they have in the past when it has been difficult to recruit skilled staff in a rising economy?

10.11 Reducing dependence on human resources

Employees are an expensive and difficult resource to manage, and therefore many organizations have actively sought to reduce the human element of their production process. The aim of employee replacement schemes can be to improve outcomes by reducing variability, to reduce costs, or both. Cost cutting could be important where an organization is pursuing a cost leadership strategy, allowing it to gain a competitive advantage.

A number of strategies to reduce dependency on the organization's employees can be identified.

- At one extreme, the human element in a service production and delivery process can be completely replaced by automatic machinery. Examples include bank ATM machines, vending machines and automatic car washes. Constraints on employee replacement come from the limitations of technology (for example, completely automatic car washes can seldom achieve such high standards of cleanliness as those where an operator is present to perform some operations inaccessible to machinery), the cost of replacement equipment (it is only within the past few years that the cost of servers and access to the internet has fallen to a point where retailers can move from labour-intensive telephone sales to automated online sales), and the attitudes of consumers towards automated service delivery (some segments of the population are still reluctant to use internet banking services, preferring instead the reassurance provided by human contact).

- Equipment can be used alongside employees to assist them in their task. This often has the effect of de-skilling their task by reducing the scope they have for exercising discretion, thereby reducing the variability in quality perceived by customers. In this way computerized accounting systems in hotels reduce the risk of front-of-house staff adding up a client's bill incorrectly. Similarly, the computer systems used by many airline reservation staff include prompts that guide their interaction with clients.

- Companies often introduce self-service production by customers, which not only reduces the need to employ as many staff, but cost savings can be passed on to customers as low prices. In this way, most petrol service stations expect customers to fill their own cars with fuel, rather than have this task undertaken by the station's own staff. Many supermarket chains have introduced customer-operated scanners, which reduces the need to employ checkout staff.

Case study:
A 24/7 society may be good for customers, but can employees cope with the stress?

© Daniel Deitschel

What happens when a company's customers want access to its goods and services 24 hours a day, and they want immediate access, not a promise of delivery tomorrow or sometime in the future? The sad fact is that one consequence is often stress at work for those who are charged with responding to a company's promises, which it must make if it is to stay alive in a competitive business environment.

The 24/7 culture has had a big impact on employees' lifestyles, with many individuals having to adjust to varying and often unsocial shift patterns. Employees often have to accept that Saturdays and Sundays are part of their normal working week, and this trend looks set to continue. Research undertaken by the Future Foundation (2004) predicted that, by 2020, over 13 million people in the UK will be operating in an out-of-hours economy (outside the traditional Monday–Friday hours of 9 am–6 pm), compared to the 7 million who did so in 2003.

While flexibility serves the interests of those who can afford to exploit the 24/7 society, the supporting workforce may see little reward for the unsociable hours they put in. Managers and supervisors, under pressure to meet targets and boost sales, are also hard-hit, often working extended hours as unpaid overtime.

It is not just in the highly visible retail sector where staff are expected to be flexible – many backroom jobs in other sectors have become more stressful. The entertainment sector, for example, increasingly employs casual contract workers to meet its needs. The BBC has struggled to compete against satellite and cable television services, all intent on meeting viewers' demand for entertainment 24/7. It now employs a large number of freelancers who give it greater flexibility at lower cost.

Evidence is mounting of the cost to UK business of stress in the workplace.

- The government's Labour Force Survey estimated that 420,000 individuals working in the UK in 2007/08 believed that they were experiencing work-related stress at a level that was making them ill. The survey also suggested that work-related stress, depression or anxiety accounted for an estimated 13.5 million lost working days during the year.

- The Health & Safety Executive reported that the 2007 Psychosocial Working Conditions (PWC) survey showed that around 13.6 per cent of all working individuals thought their job was very or extremely stressful.

- The Chartered Institute of Personnel Development (CIPD) estimated that, in 2008, the direct cost of sickness absence was £635 per person per year.

- Estimates of the total cost to society of work-related stress vary widely. In 2009, the International Stress Management Association UK put the national cost of stress and chronic ill health in the workplace at £100 billion per year.

- The Industrial Society showed that juggling home and work demands was a major source of stress for 70 per cent of respondents, while half cited unrealistic deadlines and constant time pressures as an additional factor (Industrial Society 2001).

Employers are increasingly having to recognize the sometimes hidden costs to their business of having high levels of stress in their workforce. Moreover, the law is now requiring them to take some responsibility for employees' stress at work. As an example, Birmingham City Hospital was forced in

Chapter review questions

1 Discuss the ways in which improvements in the internal environment of organizations can lead to more effective responsiveness to changes in the external environment.

2 Do you agree with the notion that a marketing department can actually be a barrier to the successful development of a marketing orientation? Give examples.

3 Discuss the ways in which a fast-food restaurant can increase the level of engagement among its staff.

Activities

1 Consult the jobs section of your local newspaper and examine jobs advertised by local private- and public-sector services organizations. To what extent is the organizations' communication through their job advertisements consistent with their communication to customers? Does the business environment of an organization influence the way it seeks new staff – for example, is there a difference between private-sector, public-sector and not-for-profit-sector organizations?

2 Go to the 'Corporate Information' page of the website for a number of companies for whom you are a customer. Try to find the company's mission statement, or a statement that is similar in nature. Then critically assess the usefulness of this statement. Do you think it has guided the actions of the company's employees? What effect would such a statement have on you if you were employed by the company?

3 Review a selection of television or newspaper advertisements by consumer goods or services companies. Critically discuss the extent to which the advertisements are aimed at the companies' employees. If you were an employee seeing the advert, how would you react?

Further reading

This chapter has discussed very briefly some of the basic principles of HRM as they apply to service organizations. For a fuller discussion of these principles, the following texts are recommended.

Gilmore, S. and Williams, S. (2009) *Human Resource Management*, Oxford, Oxford University Press.

Torrington, D., Taylor, S. Hall, L. and Atkinson, C. (2010) *Human Resource Management*, Harlow, Pearson.

The issue of organizational culture is covered well in the following texts.

Hofstede, G. and Hofstede, G.J. (2004) *Cultures and Organizations: Software for the Mind*, Maidenhead, McGraw-Hill.

Zheng, W., Yang, B. and McClean, G.M. (2010) 'Linking organizational culture, structure, strategy, and organizational effectiveness', *Journal of Business Research*, Vol. 63, No 7, pp. 763–771.

The following text provides further insight into the importance of leadership styles within organizations.

Schein, E. (2010) *Organizational Culture and Leadership*, 4th edn, San Fransisco Jossey Bass.

Empowerment of employees is discussed in the following case study.

Lashley, C. (2000) 'Empowerment through involvement: a case study of TGI Friday's restaurants', *Personnel Review*, Vol. 29, No. 6, pp. 791–815.

References

Ahmed, P. and Rafiq, M. (2003) 'Internal marketing issues and challenges', *European Journal of Marketing*, Vol. 37, No. 9, pp. 1177–1186.

Arnett, D.B., Laverie, D.A. and McLane, C. (2002) 'Using job satisfaction and pride as internal marketing tools', *Cornell Hotel and Restaurant Administration Quarterly*, Vol. 43, No. 2, pp. 87–96.

Atkinson, J. (1984) 'Manpower strategies for flexible organizations', *Personnel Management*, August.

Bateson, J.E.G. (1989) *Managing Services Marketing – Text and Readings*, 2nd edn, Forth Worth, TX, Dryden Press.

Berry, L.L. (1995) 'Relationship marketing of services – growing interest, emerging perspectives', *Journal of the Academy of Marketing Science*, Vol. 23, No. 4, pp. 236–245.

Bowen, D.E. and Lawler, E.E. III (1992) 'The empowerment of service workers: what, why, when, and how', *Sloan Management Review*, Spring, pp. 31–39.

Cooke, R. and Szumal, J. (1991) 'The reliability and validity of the organizational culture inventory', *Psychological Reports*, Vol. 72, pp. 1299–1330.

Denton, D.K. (1990) 'Customer focused management', *HR Magazine*, August, Lexington, MA, pp. 62–67.

Drucker, P.F. (1973) *Management: Tasks, Responsibilities and Practices*, New York, Harper & Row.

Financial Times (2007) 'HSBC highlights China staffing woes', London, 3 April, p. 15.

Future Foundation (2004) *Life in the 24/7? The Shape of Things to Come*, London, Future Foundation.

Grönroos, C. (1982) *Strategic Management and Marketing in the Service Sector*, Helsingfors, Finland, Swedish School of Economics and Business Administration.

Gummesson, E. (2008) *Total Relationship Marketing: Marketing Management, Relationship Strategy and CRM Approaches for the Network Economy*, 3rd edn, London, Butterworth-Heinemann.

Handy, C.B. (1989) *The Age of Unreason*, Boston, MA, Harvard Business School Press.

Hartline, M.D. and Ferrell, O.C. (1996) 'The management of customer contact service employees: an empirical investigation', *Journal of Marketing*, Vol. 60, October, pp. 52–70.

Herzberg, F. (1966) *Work and the Nature of Man*, Cleveland, World Publishing Co.

Hill, C.W.L. and Jones, G.R. (2001) *Strategic Management*, Littlehampton Houghton Mifflin.

Industrial Society (2001) *Managing Best Practice No. 83: Occupational Stress*, London.

Levitt, T. (1960) 'Marketing myopia', *Harvard Business Review*, July–August, pp. 45–56.

Lukas, B.A. and Maignan, I. (1996) 'Striving for quality: the key role of internal and external customers', *Journal of Market Focused Management*, Vol. 1, pp. 175–197.

Martins, L.P. and Grahl, J. (2010) 'Customer relations and HRM restructuring: theory and some new evidence', *Human Resource Management Journal*, Vol. 20(1), pp. 1–12.

Maslow, A. (1943) 'A theory of human motivation', *Psychological Review*, Vol. 50, No. 4, pp. 370–396.

Mayo, E. (1933) *The Human Problems of Industrial Civilization*, New York, Macmillan.

McGregor, D. (1960) *The Human Side of Enterprise*, New York, McGraw-Hill.

Milkovich, G.T. and Newman, J.M. (2002) *Compensation*, 7th edn, New York, McGraw-Hill.

Taylor, F.W. (1985) *Principles of Scientific Management*, Easton, Hive (originally published 1911).

Widmier, S. (2002) 'The effects of incentives and personality on salespersons' customer orientation', *Industrial Marketing Management*, Vol. 31, No. 7, pp. 609–615.

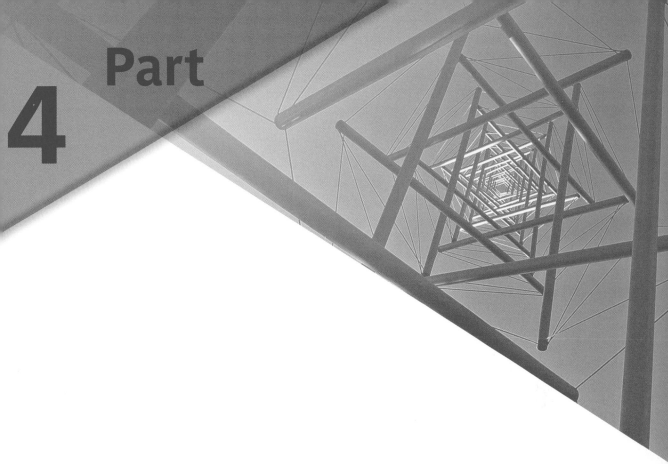

Part
4

Markets

Part contents

Chapter 11

The Principles of Market Forces

Millions have been captivated by the BBC television series *The Apprentice*, in which millionaire businessman Lord Sugar gives apprentices a series of tasks to prove their potential as a chief executive of the future. Lord Sugar now controls a complex business organization with many subsidiaries and a range of products sold into vastly differing market conditions. But he never forgets the basics of business, which he learned from trading very simple products in the fiercely competitive local markets of east London. So before the apprentices get anywhere near a boardroom position, Lord Sugar gives the hopefuls quite basic tasks that go back to the primitive roots of marketing. Getting tourists to buy T-shirts, caterers to buy a new line of sausages or shops to stock a new ice cream goes to the heart of marketing. The apprentices must survive in a fiercely competitive market in which competitors are just waiting for them to make a mistake, or they simply try to undercut their price by a few pennies. This chapter explores the basics of the fiercely competitive markets in which these TV apprentices had to survive. It describes the basic building blocks of competitive forces – we will look at how the apprentices might try to overcome competitive market forces by trying to create a market niche for themselves.

 ## Learning Objectives

This chapter will explain:

☑ The concept of market structure and the range of structures from atomistic competition to pure monopoly.

☑ The principles of atomistic competition as basic building blocks for understanding a firm's pricing and output decisions.

☑ The interaction of demand and supply leading to price determination.

☑ Elasticity of demand and supply.

11.1 Introduction

'Market forces' is a widely used term that implies some kind of external pressure on an organization, acting as a constraint (and an opportunity) for the goods and services that it buys and sells. A company may have to accept a lower price for the goods it sells because 'market forces' don't allow it to sell its goods at the higher price that it seeks. Similarly, a company may have to pay higher wages to its employees because market forces in the labour market have put upward pressure on wage rates, and if the company is going to be able to employ the staff that it seeks, it will have to pay market rates of pay.

Market forces are a crucial fact of life to most organizations operating in a commercial environment. They occur where companies seek to attract customers from rival companies by offering better products and/or lower prices. Market forces also have an effect in the acquisition of resources, and where these are scarce relative to the demand for them, rival buyers will bid up their price. However, competition in customer and resource markets can be complex and a full understanding of each market is needed if the effects of market forces on an organization are to be fully appreciated. This chapter begins by reviewing the fundamental building blocks on which markets are based. However, all **markets** are not equally aggressive in the way in which 'market forces' operate, and in many cases, an observer would be forgiven for doubting the existence of a market. So before we begin our microeconomic investigation of how markets operate in practice, we will review different types of market structure, to illustrate the very limited circumstances in which market forces are fully effective. In Chapter 12, we will explore the nature of imperfections to markets, which limit the effects of market forces that are described in this chapter.

11.1.1 Market structure

The market conditions facing suppliers of goods and services vary considerably. Customers of water supply companies may feel they are being exploited with high prices and poor service levels by companies that know that their customers have little choice of supplier. On the other hand, customers are constantly wooed by numerous insurance companies that are all trying to sell basically similar products in a market that provides consumers with a lot of choice. Differences in the characteristics and composition of buyers and sellers define the structure of a market.

The term **market structure** is used to describe:

- the number of buyers and sellers operating in a market
- the extent to which the market is concentrated in the hands of a small number of buyers and/or sellers
- the degree of collusion or competition between buyers and/or sellers.

An understanding of market structure is important to businesses, not only to understand the consequences of their own actions but also the behaviour of other firms operating in a market.

Market structures range from the theoretical extremes of perfect competition to pure monopoly. In practice, examples of the extremes are rare and most analysis therefore focuses on levels of market imperfection between the two extremes (Figure 11.1).

It is easy to take a static view of market structure but, in reality, markets are often in transition. This has been most apparent in the economies of the former Soviet bloc countries, which until the late 1980s allocated resources according to their governments' central planning processes. Officially, market forces had little role to play, although they often existed informally, especially in the more liberal Soviet bloc countries such as Hungary. The collapse of communism brought about a major change in the way that resources were allocated in the national economy, with the interaction of supply and demand leading to the price mechanism being used as a means of allocating scarce resources, rather than government bureaucrats. In many countries that have emerged from communism, the transition to market forces has not been an easy one (see 'Thinking around the subject' on p. 366).

given number of consumers demanding cheese being prepared to pay a higher price). There are a number of possible causes of the shift of the demand curve from D1 to D2.

- Consumers could have become wealthier, leading them to demand more of all goods, including cheese.
- The price of substitutes for Cheddar cheese (e.g. meat or other types of cheese) could have increased, thereby increasing demand for cheese.
- Demand for complementary goods (such as savoury biscuits) may increase, thereby leading to an increase in demand for Cheddar cheese.
- Consumer preferences may change. This may occur, for example, if Cheddar cheese is found to have health-promoting benefits.
- An advertising campaign for Cheddar cheese may increase demand for cheese at any given price.

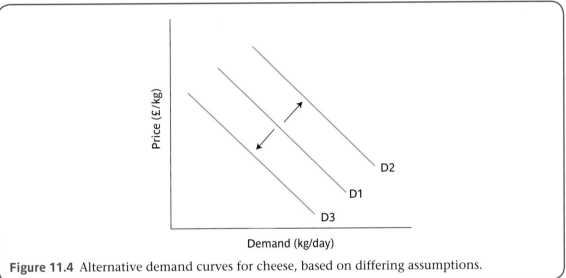

Figure 11.4 Alternative demand curves for cheese, based on differing assumptions.

Similarly, a number of possible reasons can be put forward to explain the shift from demand curve D1 to D3, where, for any given price level, less is demanded.

- Consumers could have become poorer, leading them to demand fewer of all goods, including cheese.
- The price of substitutes for Cheddar cheese (e.g. meat or other types of cheese) could have decreased, thereby making the substitutes appear more attractive and reducing demand for Cheddar cheese.
- Demand for complementary products may fall.
- Cheddar cheese may become associated with health hazards, leading to less demand at any given price.
- An advertising campaign for substitute products may shift demand away from Cheddar cheese.

The demand curves shown in Figures 11.3 and 11.4 have both been straight, but this is a simplification of reality. In fact, demand curves would usually be curved, indicating that the relationship between price and volume is not constant for all price points. There may additionally be significant discontinuities at certain price points, as where buyers in a market have psychological price barriers, above or below which their behaviour changes. In many markets, the difference between £10.00 and £9.99 may be crucial in overcoming buyers' attitudes that predispose them to regard anything over £10 as being unaffordable and anything below it as a bargain.

Actually collecting information with which to plot a demand curve poses theoretical and practical problems. The main problem relates to the cross-sectional nature of a demand curve – that is, it purports to measure the volume of demand across the ranges of price possibilities. However, this kind of information can often only be built up by a longitudinal study of the relationship between prices and volume over time. There is always the possibility that, over time, the assumptions on which demand is based have changed, in which case it is difficult to distinguish between a movement along a demand curve and a shift to a new demand curve. It is, however, sometimes possible for firms to conduct controlled cross-sectional experiments where a different price is charged in different regions and the effects on volume recorded. To be sure that this is accurately measuring the demand curve, there must be no extraneous factors in regions (such as differences in household incomes) that could partly explain differences in price/volume relationships.

The demand curves shown in Figures 11.3 and 11.4 slope downwards, indicating the intuitive fact that, as price rises, demand falls, and vice versa. While this is intuitively plausible, it is not always the case. Sometimes, the demand curve slopes upwards, indicating that, as the price of a product goes up, buyers are able and willing to buy more of the product. Classic examples of this phenomenon occur where a product becomes increasingly desirable as more people consume it. A telephone network that has only one subscriber will be of little use to the first customer, who will be unable to use a telephone to call anyone else. However, as more customers are connected, the value of the telephone network becomes greater to each individual, who is correspondingly willing to pay a higher price. This phenomenon helps to explain why large international airports can charge more than smaller regional airports for aircraft to land. As the number of possible aircraft connections increases, airlines' willingness to pay high prices for landing slots increases.

Upward-sloping demand curves can also be observed for some products sold for their 'snob' value. Examples include some designer-label clothes where high price alone can add to a product's social status. Upward-sloping demand curves can be observed over short time periods where a 'bandwagon' effect can be created by rapidly rising or falling prices. For example, in stock markets, the very fact that share prices are rising may lead many people to invest in shares.

11.2.2 Supply

Supply is defined as the amount of a product that producers are willing and able to make available to the market at a given price over a particular period of time. Like demand, it is important to note that at different prices there will be different levels of supply, reflecting the willingness and/or ability of producers to supply a product as prices change.

A simple supply curve for medium-fat Cheddar cheese is shown in Figure 11.5. The supply curve slopes upwards from left to right, indicating the intuitively plausible fact that, as market prices rise, more suppliers will be attracted to supply to the market. Conversely, as prices fall, marginal producers (such as those who operate relatively inefficiently) will drop out of the market, reducing the daily supply available.

It is again important to distinguish movements along a supply curve from shifts to a new supply curve. The supply curve S1 is based on a number of assumptions about the relationship between price and volume supplied. If these assumptions are broken, a new supply curve based

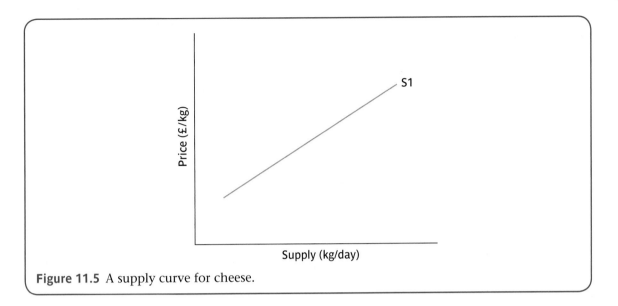

Figure 11.5 A supply curve for cheese.

on the new set of assumptions needs to be drawn. In Figure 11.6, two new supply curves, S2 and S3, are shown. S2 indicates a situation where, for any given price level, total supply to the market is reduced. This could come about for a number of reasons, including the following.

- Production methods could become more expensive – for example, because of more stringent health and safety regulations. Therefore, for any given price level, fewer firms will be willing to supply to the market as they will no longer be able to cover their costs.
- Extraneous factors (such as abnormally bad weather) could result in producers having difficulty in getting their produce to market.
- Governments may impose additional taxes on suppliers (e.g. extending the scope of property taxes to cover agricultural property).

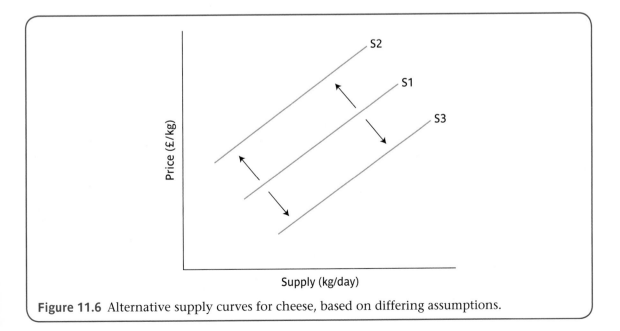

Figure 11.6 Alternative supply curves for cheese, based on differing assumptions.

The new supply curve S3 indicates a situation where, for any given price level, total supply to the market is increased. This could come about for a number of reasons, including the following.

- Changes in production technology that result in Cheddar cheese being produced more efficiently and therefore suppliers being prepared to supply more cheese at any given price (or, for any given volume supplied, suppliers are prepared to accept a lower price).
- Extraneous factors (such as favourable weather conditions) could result in a glut of produce that must be sold, and the market is therefore flooded with additional supply.
- Governments may give a subsidy for each kilogram of cheese produced by suppliers, thereby increasing their willingness to supply to the market.

11.2.3 Price determination

An examination of the demand and supply graphs indicates that they share common axes. In both cases the vertical axis refers to the price at which the product might change hands, while the horizontal axis refers to the quantity changing hands.

It is possible to redraw the original demand and supply lines (D1 and S1) on a single graph (Figure 11.7). The supply curve indicates that, the lower the price, the less cheese will be supplied to the market. Yet at these lower prices, customers are willing and able to buy a lot of cheese – more than the suppliers collectively are willing or able to supply. By following the supply curve upwards, it can be observed that suppliers are happy to supply more cheese, but at these high prices, there are few willing buyers. Therefore, at these high prices supply and demand are again out of balance.

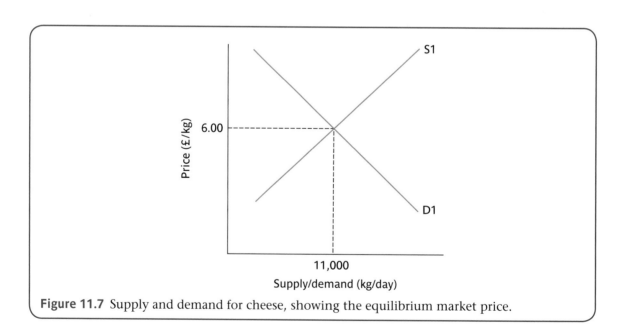

Figure 11.7 Supply and demand for cheese, showing the equilibrium market price.

Between the two extremes there will be a price where the interest of the two groups will coincide. This balancing of supply and demand is the foundation of the theory of market price, which holds that in any free market there is an 'equilibrium price' that matches the quantity that consumers are willing and able to buy (i.e. demand) with the quantity that producers are willing and able to produce (i.e. supply). Working out what this equilibrium price is, is called **price determination**.

In perfectly competitive markets, the process of achieving equilibrium happens automatically without any external regulatory intervention. Perfectly competitive markets do not need any complicated and centralized system for bringing demand and supply into balance, something that is difficult to achieve in a centrally planned economy, such as those that used to predominate in eastern Europe.

In Figure 11.7, supply and demand are brought precisely into balance at a price of £6.00. This is the equilibrium price and, at this price, 11,000 kg of cheese per day will be bought and sold in the market. If a company wants to sell its cheese in the market, it can only do so at this price. In theory, if it charged a penny more, it would get no business because everybody else in the market is cheaper. If it sells at a penny less, it will be swamped with demand, probably selling at a price that is below its production costs.

It is important to remember that in a perfectly competitive market, individual firms are price takers. The market alone determines the 'going rate' for their product. Changes in the equilibrium market price come about for two principal reasons:

1 assumptions about suppliers' ability or willingness to supply change, resulting in a shift to a new supply curve

2 assumptions about buyers' ability or willingness to buy change, resulting in a shift to a new demand curve.

The effects of shifts in supply are illustrated in Figure 11.8. From an equilibrium price of £6.00 and volume of 11,000 kg, the supply curve has shifted to S2 (perhaps in response to the imposition of a new tax on production). Assuming that demand conditions remain unchanged, the new point of intersection between the demand and supply lines occurs at a price of £6.50 and a volume of 10,500 kg. This is the new equilibrium price. A similar analysis can be carried out on the effects of a shift in the demand curve, but where the supply curve remains constant.

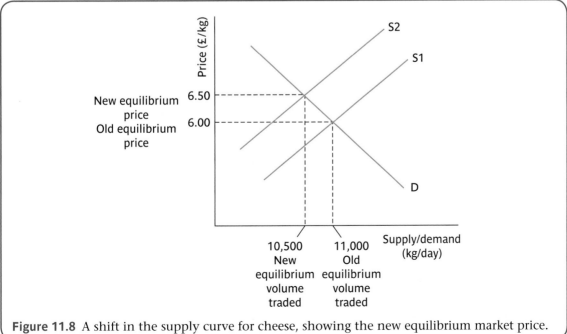

Figure 11.8 A shift in the supply curve for cheese, showing the new equilibrium market price.

New equilibrium prices and trade volumes can be found at the intersection of the supply and demand curves. In practice, both the supply and demand curves may be changing at the same time.

The speed with which a new equilibrium price is established is dependent upon how efficiently a market is working. In pure commodity markets, where products are instantly perishable, rapid adjustments in price are possible. Where speculators are allowed to store goods, or large buyers and sellers are able to unduly influence a market, adjustment may be slower. The extent of

Thinking around the subject

Effects of increased government regulation

Many industry sectors have complained of the burden of increased government regulation. But how are the effects reflected in demand/supply analysis? Consider the following recent examples.

- *EU Directive on Traditional Herbal Medicinal Products*: the directive requires traditional, over-the-counter herbal remedies to be made to assured standards of safety and quality. Some small-scale producers have not been able to justify the elaborate testing that the directive would require, and have therefore withdrawn from the market – their cost curve had effectively shifted upwards.

- *Financial Services and Markets Act 2000*: required all businesses selling insurance to be registered with the Financial Services Authority and to meet its criteria from January 2005. Some small travel agents, who previously sold travel insurance as an ancillary part of a holiday, decided that the cost of compliance was too great and withdrew from selling insurance.

- *Housing Act 1996*: introduced a discretionary local authority licensing scheme for houses in multiple occupation. To obtain a licence, landlords would need to satisfy a number of standards – for example, in relation to fire exits. Some landlords decided that the cost of improvements to their property could not be justified by the likely returns on their investment.

- *Disability Discrimination Act 1995 Part III – Access to Goods and Services*: from 2004, companies have been required to take 'reasonable measures' to ensure equality of access to a company's goods and services for disabled people. Some organizations are reported to have closed facilities to the public rather than spend money in upgrading them.

The effects of these regulations can be assessed using supply–demand analysis. Each of these regulations may have the effect of increasing producers' costs – some producers more than others. This can be shown as an upward shift in the supply curve. How much of the increase in cost will be passed on to customers? This will depend on the elasticity of demand for the product in question. A highly elastic demand curve may result in customers buying substitute products instead – for example, buying mainstream medicines rather than herbal medicines. If the regulation applies to the whole sector, firms are likely to differ in their ability to absorb additional costs, and the least efficient producers may be forced out of the market because the market price for their product is now below their cost of production.

Try showing the effects of each of the regulations described above on a supply–demand graph, and observe what is likely to happen to the equilibrium price.

changes in price and volume traded is also dependent on the elasticities of demand and supply, which are considered in the following sections.

11.3 Bartering and auctions

Bartering and auctions are traditional methods of determining prices based on interaction between buyer and seller. The practice of bartering is familiar to buyers in Eastern bazaars in which the seller opens with a high offer price and, through a process of negotiation, eventually finds out the maximum price that a buyer is prepared to pay.

The principles of bartering and auctions have attracted renewed interest with the emergence of online auction sites such as eBay. Many more companies have developed auction sites to sell off spare goods or surplus capacity to the highest bidder. If a company is short of cash and desperate to sell its surplus, it might be more willing to accept the best available price that the market is prepared to pay.

As well as consumer sales, internet auctions have found a valuable role for business-to-business procurement (Timmins 2003). A company can put out a tender and invite suppliers to bid, following which it would choose the lowest-price bidder that meets its specifications.

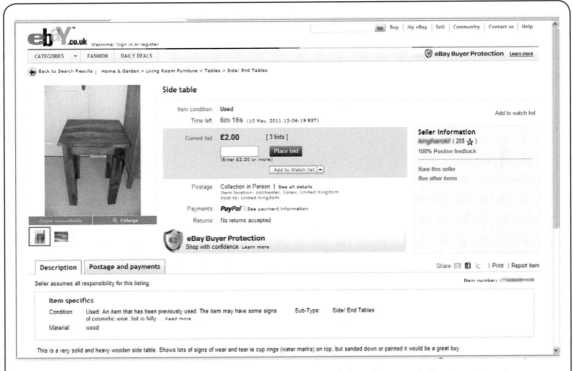

Figure 11.9 The online auction site eBay shows many of the characteristics of a fiercely competitive market. It typically has many small-scale sellers and buyers, with no domination of the market by any individual. There is a good level of information about the organizations in the market, including ratings for sellers' previous performance. Goods and services offered for sale are classified so that a prospective buyer can immediately see what is available for any particular product category and assess whether it meets their requirements. Like any market, eBay requires rules to govern the conduct of buyers and sellers, and the company has taken measures to ensure that the market works efficiently – for example, by reducing the possibilities for fraudulent trading.

11.4   Going rate pricing

The principles of market forces are often seen in markets where competing businesses set their prices according to the 'going rate'. Here, demand may be so sensitive to price that a firm would risk losing most of its business if it charged just a small amount more than its competitors. On the other hand, charging any lower would result in immediate retaliation from competitors. Where cost levels are difficult to establish, charging a going rate can avoid the problems of trying to calculate costs. As an example, it may be difficult to calculate the cost of renting out a video film, as the figure will be very dependent upon assumptions made about the number of uses over which the initial purchase cost can be spread. It is much easier to take price decisions on the basis of the going rate among nearby competitors.

Figure 11.10 In many town centres, clusters of restaurants offer a 'dish of the day' at roughly the same price. The meal is likely to be quite generic (such as fish and chips or chicken tikka masala) and prices for one restaurant will be established by reference to what other restaurants are charging. Restaurants may take a 'going price' from the market and design their meal offering around this price. Just what can they offer for the going rate of £6.00? Although the price of standard set menus may be very strongly determined by competitors' prices, each restaurant may nevertheless offer more specialized meals for which it faces less direct competition and therefore has greater discretion in setting its prices. Differentiation as a means of avoiding direct price competition is discussed later in this chapter.

⟳ Thinking around the subject

Marketing or markets?

Is marketing a natural ally of free markets, or is it really an enemy? To advocates of marketing, marketing is all about bringing together customers who want to buy with sellers who want to sell. By carefully studying what buyers want to buy, marketers contribute towards the efficient operation of a market. Advocates of marketing would contrast the benefits of having marketers controlled by market disciplines with the inefficiency of having a central bureaucracy making resource allocation decisions.

However, marketers are not always so benign in their thoughts about markets. While most marketers would publicly endorse the power of free markets, many of their activities, consciously or unconsciously, undermine the spirit of free markets. Consider three of the defining characteristics of competitive markets that were discussed above: a homogeneous product; freely available information; and freedom of entry to and exit from the market. Now consider some common marketing strategies.

The idea of all companies selling a homogeneous product is anathema to one of the basic philosophies of marketing, which is to add value to products through differentiation. The following chapter will discuss ways in which companies use branding to try to differentiate their products from those of the competitors. Faced with shelves of slightly differentiated bottled water carrying different brand names, can this be said to be a market in a homogeneous product? Is there any meaningful difference between many of the brands? How can buyers tell?

Information available in a market is often difficult to assimilate, and some people have accused marketers of making their information even more difficult to understand. Try comparing mobile phone calling plans, or the different tariffs offered by gas and electricity companies, and you could come to the conclusion that the companies' information may be freely available to all, but actually understood by very few. Some would accuse marketers of engaging in 'confusion marketing' to try to make informed comparisons more difficult.

Marketers often do their best to reduce the ease of entry to or exit from a market. One consequence of the recent trend towards 'relationship marketing' has been to try to tie customers to the company through a long-term contract. Customers of mobile phone companies cannot easily leave their existing supplier if they are committed to a 12-month contract. Many manufacturers have sought exclusivity contracts with retailers, which makes it difficult for new competitors to enter the market.

Karl Marx once observed that capitalism was essentially all about *reducing* risk rather than *taking* risk. Could marketing be more about trying to undermine the value of markets rather than trying to make them work more efficiently?

Case study:
Can market mechanisms reduce global climate change?

© *Michael Graham*

To anti-capitalism protestors, the cause of global climate change can be attributed to market forces. Market forces imply that individuals focus on buying goods and services for the lowest price, and producers focus on producing those goods and services for the lowest cost. Both buyers and sellers are quite likely to concentrate their evaluation on the costs they directly incur, rather than the 'external' costs – those costs that are incurred by other people. For many shoppers, the price of a pair of shoes is the most important basis for choosing between competing shoes, and market forces have helped to drive down the price of shoes, so that we can now regard shoes almost as a disposable fashion item, regardless of the impact of short-life shoes filling up landfill sites and using scarce natural resources. Similarly, shoe manufacturers have used market forces to cut ruthlessly their production costs, even if this means moving shoes and their component materials long distances round the world, adding to greenhouse gas emissions in the process. So, market forces may indirectly have contributed to current problems of global warming, but can those same market forces also be used to try to redress the problem? Backers of carbon trading hope so.

Greenhouse gases are blamed for causing climate change because they absorb infrared radiation and prevent it from being dispersed into space, thereby having the effect of warming the Earth. This not only increases global average temperatures, but is also claimed to lead to increasingly unpredictable weather. Probable results of climate change include more frequent and fiercer storms, droughts and

floods. If warming causes enough of the world's ice to melt, rises in sea levels could occur, leading to flooding in coastal areas. It is also claimed that melting ice from the Arctic could disrupt the flow and direction of the Gulfstream, having the effect of cooling parts of Europe.

Very few businesses can claim not to be affected by climate change. Bad weather (such as hurricanes, floods and gale-force winds, which have been attributed to climate change) affects companies when they come to renew their insurance policies. The storms that hit the UK in autumn 2000 are estimated to have cost UK insurers more than £1 billion, and these costs were ultimately passed on to businesses and consumers in the form of higher premiums. Damage caused to property by storms can close down a company's factories and disrupt the supply of its raw materials. If the weather becomes more unpredictable, risk will increasingly have to be factored into business planning.

As well as being affected by climate change, companies are increasingly being called upon to take some of the responsibility for slowing the rate of greenhouse gas emissions. An important focus for these efforts was the Kyoto Treaty, drawn up in 1997. This required signatory countries to reduce their dependence on fossil fuels, which produce the greenhouse gases blamed for causing climate change.

One outcome of the Kyoto Treaty was the introduction in 2005 of the EU's Emissions Trading Scheme (ETS), which essentially sought to reduce carbon emissions through a system of quotas traded through market mechanisms. The scheme capped the amount of carbon dioxide that could be emitted from large installations, such as power generation and carbon-intensive factories, and covered almost half the EU's total CO_2 emissions. All businesses in the UK covered by the scheme were allocated a share of the 756 million tonnes of carbon dioxide that the UK was allowed to produce. If they emitted above their individually allocated amount, they would have to buy carbon permits in the specialist carbon trading market that emerged. On the other hand, if they did not need all their quota, they could sell surplus through these same markets. In principle, companies had a strong incentive to reduce their carbon emissions, as market forces would reward them with income from the sale of unused carbon permits.

However, market forces were not as straightforward as first appeared. The ETS commenced with excessive permits for emissions being issued, many would argue in response to political pressure to reduce the immediate effect on high-emissions sectors. There had been many loopholes and incentives for industries to exaggerate their emissions in order to increase the number of permits they were allocated. One consequence of the over-issue of quotas was that most firms had little difficulty in achieving emission levels below their cap, and were therefore able to sell their surplus quota on the open carbon market. Of course, with a generous allocation of quota, there were more sellers of carbon permits than buyers, with the result that the price of carbon permits fell by 60 per cent within the first year of operation of the scheme. The incentive for companies to reduce their emissions was, accordingly, much less than it could have been. Perversely, one estimate claimed that the UK's biggest polluters had earned a 'windfall' profit of nearly £1 billion as a result of over-generous allocation of carbon quotas, which they were able to sell.

The use of market mechanisms to solve the problem of global warming is an innovative way of trying to internalize companies' external costs. Rather than imposing a bureaucratic solution, a market-based system was seen by many as an attractive means by which businesses could overcome an ecological problem by doing what they are good at – trading. However, some argued that markets were inherently incapable of solving the pressing problems of climate change and more drastic action based on strict limits on emissions would bring about more rapid change. There was also the issue that without world agreement on permitted carbon emissions, manufacturers would simply shift production to countries with fewer restrictions on emissions. Another perverse consequence of the ETS could be to shift production from relatively clean and modern European factories to relatively heavy-polluting factories in developing countries. Moreover, additional emissions may have been generated in the process of transporting raw materials and finished goods to take advantage of the favourable emissions regime. It follows therefore that the market-based ETS could actually have led to an increase in total carbon emissions.

A major weakness of the original emissions trading scheme was that the world's biggest economy – the USA – refused to join it, claiming that it would adversely affect the competitive position of its manufacturers. However, with the election of President Obama in 2009, it appeared that the USA was becoming increasingly amenable to taking action. Some in the USA argued that restrictions on fossil fuels could help American industry, and pointed to the strong competitive position and market opportunities for its wind turbine industry.

Meanwhile, some argued that, ultimately, market forces would provide a solution to greenhouse gas emissions because of growing shortages of raw materials and fossil fuels. In 2008, the price of oil and many raw materials rose sharply. At the time, many people blamed this on speculators driving up the market, but price rises continued two years later, even though much of the western world was in the midst of a recession, which would normally have led to reduced demand. It seemed that the insatiable appetite from the increasingly wealthy populations of China, India, Brazil and Russia was pushing up prices. With oil prices reaching new heights during 2010, many companies renewed their efforts to cut down their use of oil and scarce natural resources. Would Adam Smith's 'invisible hand' come to the rescue of the ecological environment by pricing out the use of polluting materials?

QUESTIONS

1 Critically assess the opportunities and challenges for energy-intensive businesses, such as a metal manufacturer, resulting from the introduction of carbon trading.

2 Show, using supply/demand analysis, the effects of the over-issuing of carbon quotas described in the case study.

3 Discuss the extent to which the carbon market represents a perfectly competitive market. What would be the most likely causes of market distortion?

Summary

This chapter has reviewed the variety of market structures that exist, and the effect market structure has on a firm's pricing and product decisions. Perfectly competitive markets are presumed to favour consumers, but can limit the revenues of profit-seeking firms. In its purest extreme, this market structure is unusual; however, the basic building blocks of demand, supply and price determination provide a foundation for understanding more complex market structures. We will return to these market structures in **Chapter 12**. The trend towards globalization of business (**Chapter 14**) is having the effect of making markets more competitive. This chapter has taken a microeconomic perspective on pricing and competition. Pricing is also affected by macroeconomic factors, and these are discussed in **Chapter 13**.

Key Terms

Demand (368)	Markets (364)
Elasticity of demand (377)	Perfect competition (365)
Elasticity of supply (381)	Price determination (373)
Market structure (364)	Supply (370)

Online Learning Centre

To help you grasp the key concepts of this chapter, explore the extra resources posted on the Online Learning Centre at **www.mcgraw-hill.co.uk/palmer**. Among other helpful resources there are chapter-by-chapter test questions, revision notes and web links.

Chapter review questions

1 In the context of market structure analysis, what are the options available to firms in a highly competitive market to improve profitability? Select one of the options and discuss it, making clear how lasting the profit improvement is likely to be in the long run. (*Based on a CIM Marketing Environment Examination question.*)

2 'Elasticity of demand is a fine theoretical concept of economists, but difficult for marketers to use in practice.' Critically assess this statement.

3 Show, using diagrams, what would happen to the price of whisky if a new technological development suddenly allowed it to be produced at a much lower cost than previously.

Activities

1 Collect information on prices charged for the following products: a top ten DVD film to buy; car insurance quotes; mobile phone charges. What do the prices tell you about the competitiveness of these markets? Identify strategies that companies in these markets have pursued in order to reduce the effects of direct competition.

2 Try to construct a demand curve for an item of consumer technology whose price is falling – for example, a mobile phone with a GPS system. Try to construct a demand curve on the basis of your friends' statements about their likelihood of buying the product at specified price levels. What limitations are there in this approach to determining the demand curve for the product?

3 Identify the impact and discuss the likely marketing response to the following environmental changes affecting a major oil refining and distributing company:

- the introduction of a carbon tax
- a breakthrough in cost-effective solar power stations
- a well-financed new entrant entering its main market
- teleconferencing and telecommunications growing rapidly.

(*Based on a CIM Marketing Environment Examination question.*)

Further reading

This chapter has provided only a very brief overview of the principles of economics as they affect pricing. For a fuller discussion, one of the following texts would be useful.

Begg, D. (2009) *Foundations of Economics*, 2nd edn, Maidenhead, McGraw-Hill.
Begg, D. and Ward, D. (2009) *Economics for Business*, Maidenhead, McGraw-Hill.
Lipsey, R.G. and Chrystal, K.A. (2011) *Economics*, 12th edn, Oxford, Oxford University Press.

References

Timmins, N. (2003) 'A bid to save money for the government: online auctions', *Financial Times*, 29 January, p. 12.

Chapter 12

Distortions to Market Forces

You drive along a short stretch of road, passing a number of petrol filling stations, and notice that the price charged by each of them is identical. Is this a good example of the power of competition driving down prices to the lowest possible level, or is it evidence of collusion between the petrol station operators to keep prices high? The owners of the petrol stations might have realized that cut-throat competition is bad for their profit margins and, for a commodity product such as petrol, if one of them lowered its price, every other station would have to lower its price or lose business. Maybe a 'gentleman's agreement' not to compete on price might be in their best interests, but it almost certainly would not be in petrol buyers' best interest if prices charged were held artificially high. But how can you tell if the identical prices of petrol are a result of fierce competition or collusion? This chapter explores some of the ways in which competitive markets may become distorted by collusion among suppliers, or the dominance of a big supplier.

✓ Learning Objectives

This chapter will explain:

✓ The dynamics of competition and how it impacts on an organization's activities.

✓ Methods used by firms to avoid head-on competition.

✓ The role of brands in providing product differentiation.

✓ Market imperfections and the steps taken by government agencies to counter abuse of monopoly power.

12.1 Introduction

Perfectly competitive markets may be ideal for consumers because they have a tendency to minimize prices paid for any given goods and services. However, lower prices are not attractive to suppliers because, for any given level of output, lower prices mean lower revenue and therefore lower profit. It is not surprising therefore that firms seek to limit the workings of market forces. This chapter looks at **imperfect competition**. It could be argued that most firms would like to be in the position of a monopolist and able to control the price level and output of their market. This is an unrealistic aim for most firms, but, in practice, firms can create imperfections in markets that give them limited monopoly power over their customers.

One of the assumptions of perfect competition is that products offered in a particular market are identical. An entrepreneur can seek to avoid head-on competition with its competitors by trying to sell something that is just a little bit different compared to the offerings of its competitors. Therefore, in a market for fresh vegetables, a vegetable trader may try to get away from the fiercely competitive market for generic fresh vegetables, for which the price is determined by the market, by slightly differentiating its product. The following are some possible differentiation strategies in respect of the sale of potatoes that it could pursue.

- The trader might concentrate on selling specially selected potatoes – for example, ones that are particularly suited to baking.
- A delivery service might be provided for customers.
- The potatoes could be packed in materials that prevent them being bruised.
- The trader might offer a no-quibble money-back guarantee for people who buy potatoes that turn out to be bad.
- The potatoes could be baked and offered with a range of fillings.
- The potatoes might be processed into tinned or dried potatoes.
- As a result of any of the above actions, the trader could develop a distinct brand identity for the potatoes, so that buyers do not ask just for potatoes but for 'Brand X' potatoes by name.

In this simple example, the trader has taken steps to turn a basic commodity product into something that is quite distinctive, so it has immediately cut down the number of direct competitors that it faces. In fact, if its product really is unique, it will have no direct competition; in other words, it will be a monopoly supplier of a unique product. However, it must not be forgotten that although the way the trader has presented the potatoes may be unique, they are still broadly similar to the potatoes that everybody else is selling. The trader therefore still faces indirect competition, including competition from other foods such as rice and pasta, which provide a substitute for potatoes.

If a trader has successfully differentiated its product, it is no longer strictly a price taker from the market. It may be able to charge 10p a kilo more than the going rate for its selected and packaged potatoes if customers think that the higher price is good value for a better product. It will be able to experiment to see just how much more buyers are prepared to pay for its differentiated product.

12.1.1 The development of brands

The process of branding is at the heart of organizations' efforts to remove themselves from fierce competition between generic products. Many have seen brand building as the only way for a firm to build a stable, long-term demand at profitable margins (see Figure 12.1). Through adding value that will attract customers, firms are able to provide a base for expansion and product development, and to protect themselves against the strength of intermediaries and competitors. There has been much evidence linking high levels of advertising expenditure to support strong brands with high returns on capital and high market share. As organizations grow, the brands they own may become their greatest asset. Many takeover bids for companies have been based on the value of the brands owned by a target company.

© Tamara Murray

Figure 12.1 Toblerone has removed itself from the fierce competition for chocolate by developing a distinctive brand; by developing a unique identity and maintaining high quality standards, the brand commands a premium price among those chocolate buyers who value its distinctive attributes.

Brands are important in guiding buyers when choosing between otherwise seemingly similar competing goods and services. Consider the following cases.

- Buyers of pension plans are typically not very knowledgeable about pensions, yet several tens of thousands of British people have entrusted their pension provision to Virgin Group, largely on the strength of its brand reputation for honesty and openness, and despite the company being a relative newcomer to the pensions industry, with no proven track record. The Virgin brand name has added to customers' perceptions of value, so that they are no longer buying a generic pension policy, but a differentiated Virgin policy.

- When booking an overseas hotel, many travellers would choose from a shortlist of hotel brand names with which they are familiar, despite the existence of locally run hotels that would probably offer better quality at a lower price.

- Buyers of package holidays in the UK are often prepared to pay a premium for the Thomson brand name, in preference to less well-known competitor brands that offer lower prices for an apparently identical holiday.

There have been many conceptualizations of the unique attributes of a brand and how these affect buying esses. These usually distinguish between elements that can be objectively measured (such as the reported reliability of an airline) and the subjective values that can only be defined in the minds of consumers (such as the perceived personality of the Virgin airline brand). Gardner and Levy (1955) distinguished between the 'functional' dimensions of a brand and its 'personality', while other dimensions have been identified as utilitarianism versus value expressive (Munson and Spivey 1981), need satisfaction versus impression management (Solomon 1983), and functional versus representational (De Chernatony, McDonald and Wallace 2010). The functional dimensions of a brand serve to reassure buyers that important

to provide additional, and possibly completely unrelated, products. Corporate reputation can be very important in simplifying the choice for buyers, who may have little knowledge about a complex product that is new to them, and may be unwilling to trust a relatively unknown company. There are many examples of companies that have used a strong corporate reputation to extend their brand into completely new product areas. Virgin Group has used its brand to expand from music to airlines, financial services and mobile phones. The Boots company (now part of Alliance Boots plc) has used the Boots corporate brand to expand into opticians and dentistry services. To be successful, the single corporate branding strategy adopted by companies such as Virgin and Boots demands a relentless maintenance of the organization's reputation. Unethical business practices, or poor reliability in one aspect of the organization's service provision, could undermine general trust in the company, and affect sales of goods and services that may have had no operational connection with the product that gave rise to problems. In the case of Virgin Group, does the frequently reported unreliability of its UK train services (or at least perceptions of unreliability) undermine consumers' perceptions of the reliability of its financial services?

12.2 Oligopoly

One step on from imperfect competition is a market structure often referred to as **oligopoly**. It lies somewhere between imperfect competition and pure monopoly. An oligopoly market is one that is dominated by a small number of sellers that provide a large share of the total market output. The crucial point about oligopoly markets is that all suppliers in the market are interdependent. One company cannot take price or output decisions without considering the specific possible responses of other companies.

An oligopoly is a particularly important market structure in industries where economies of scale are significant. It is typical of oil refining and distribution, pharmaceuticals, car manufacturing and detergents. Customers of oligopoly organizations may not immediately appreciate that the products they are buying come from an oligopolist, as such firms often operate with a variety of brand names (the detergent manufacturers Unilever and Procter & Gamble between them have over 50 apparently competing detergent products on sale in the UK).

Oligopolists generally understand their relationship to one another and there is often a reluctance to 'rock the boat' by upsetting the established order. One firm is often acknowledged as the price leader and firms wait for its actions before adjusting their own prices. In the UK car market, it has often been suggested that other manufacturers wait for Ford to adjust its prices before making their own price decisions. It has been suggested that firms may not match upward price movements, in the hope of gaining extra sales, but they would match downward price changes for fear of losing market share. Price wars between oligopolists can be very expensive to participants, so there is a tendency to find alternative ways to compete for customers, such as free gifts, coupons, added-value offers and sponsorship activities.

Oligopolists have often been accused of collusion and creating barriers to entry for newcomers (such as signing exclusive distribution rights with key retailers). It has therefore been suggested that an oligopoly market structure is against the public interest. Against this argument, the public interest may benefit from economies of scale, which allows products to be made at a lower unit cost than would be achievable by smaller-scale companies. Furthermore, while oligopolists may have a cosy market in their home country, they may face severe competition as an outsider in overseas markets. The benefits of scale in their domestic market can give them the resources and low unit costs with which to tackle an overseas market, thereby helping a country's balance of trade and creating additional employment.

At a local level, it has frequently been suspected that groups of building contractors, school bus contractors, solicitors and estate agents covertly agree not to 'rock the boat' by agreeing to conform to guidelines for pricing and tendering. The existence of trade and professional associations may provide legitimate cover for such relationships and understandings to develop. In societies where business life is closely intermingled with social standing, the temptation to conform may be strengthened, and studies of Eastern trading systems have highlighted this influence (Fock and Woo 1998; Tsang 1998). Some evidence of this can be seen in the extensive network of cooperative *keiretsus* and relationships among Japanese distributors, which have led selling prices to consumers to be higher than in comparable overseas markets.

12.3   Analysing competitive forces within a market

The competition environment of most organizations is dynamic and interdependent, with new organizations and technologies emerging to challenge a company's position. A widely used framework for analysing the dynamism of the competitive environment is Porter's **Five Forces model** (Porter 1985). This model helps to identify the factors that affect the intensity of competition within a particular industry, and illustrates the relationship between different players and potential players in the industry. The five forces requiring evaluation are: the power of suppliers; the power of buyers; the threat of new entrants; the threat of substitute products; the intensity of rivalry between competing firms (see Figure 12.4).

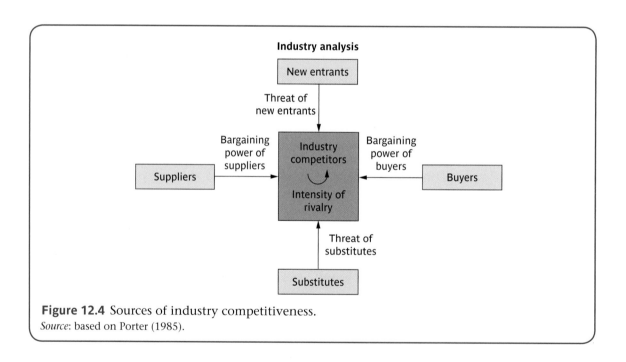

Figure 12.4 Sources of industry competitiveness.
Source: based on Porter (1985).

The power of suppliers

The power of suppliers is likely to be high if the number of suppliers are few and/or the materials, components and services are in short supply. The suppliers of microprocessor silicon chips have in the past held a powerful market position due to their dominance of technology and high demand for their products relative to available supply.

The power of buyers

Buyer power is likely to be high if there are relatively few buyers, if there are alternative sources of supply and if the buyer has low switching costs. During the past couple of decades, Britain's grocery retailing sector has become increasingly dominated by five very large organizations. According to market research group Kentar Worldpanel, the UK's 'big four' grocery retailers – Tesco, Asda, Sainsbury's and Morrisons – accounted for more than three-quarters (76.1 per cent) of the grocery market value in 2010. Since the 1970s the power in the marketplace has steadily shifted away from the manufacturers of grocery products to the grocery retailers.

The threat of new entrants

The threat of new entrants will be higher if there are low barriers to entry. New entrants may already be in the industry in another country but decide to move into your geographic market. A number of South Korean car manufacturers, including Hyundai and Kia, moved into the UK and other European markets during the 1990s. Some Indian motorcycle and car manufacturers (who have a very strong home market and low costs of production) are beginning to show interest in European markets. Alternatively, new entrants may arrive from outside the industry. Bic, whose technology base was plastic moulding, made disposable ballpoint pens; some years ago it was able to successfully diversify into the wet shave razor market with plastic disposable razors, thus challenging established market leaders such as Gillette and Wilkinson in their core business.

The threat of substitute products

Substitute products are likely to emerge from alternative technologies, particularly as the economics of production change. Initially the new technology may have high costs associated with it. However, as the technology and experience develops, the level of investment rises and production volumes increase, then costs of production will fall with economies of scale. Manufacturers will then look for more and more applications. Artificial sweeteners for sugar, lighters for matches, plastic containers for glass, polyester for cotton, and personal computers for typewriters are obvious examples. These substitutes may change the whole economics of an industry and threaten the survival of the traditional product providers.

Intensity of rivalry between competing firms

The intensity of rivalry may be high if two or more firms are fighting for dominance in a fast-growing market. For example, this occurred in the UK's mobile phone market during the mid-1990s. There may also be a fight to establish the dominant technology in a sector, something that occurred in 2007–8 in the fight between the Blu-ray and HD-DVD formats for high-definition DVD players. The need is to become established as the dominant technology or brand before the industry matures. Companies are likely to engage heavily in promotional activity involving advertising and promotional incentives to buy. In a mature industry, particularly if it is characterized by high fixed costs and excess capacity, the intensity of competitive rivalry may be very high. This is because manufacturers or service providers need to operate at near maximum capacity to cover overhead costs. As the industry matures, at times of cyclical downturn or when a number of companies have invested in new capacity, firms fight to maintain their maximum level of sales. Price cuts and discounting may become commonplace and profits will be eroded. Low-cost producers with high brand loyalty have the best chance of survival.

12.4 Monopolistic markets

At the opposite end of the scale to perfect competition lies pure **monopoly**. In its purest extreme, monopoly in a market occurs where there is only one supplier to the market, perhaps because of the regulatory, technical or economic barriers to entry that potential competing suppliers would face. Literally speaking, a monopoly means that one person or organization has complete control over the resources of a market. However, this rarely occurs in practice. Even in the former centrally planned economies of eastern Europe, there have often been active 'shadow' markets that have existed alongside official monopoly suppliers. Sometimes, monopoly control over supply comes about through a group of suppliers acting in collusion to form a 'cartel'. As with the pure monopoly, companies would join a cartel in order to try to protect themselves from the harsh consequences (for suppliers) of competition. Probably the best example of a cartel is OPEC (the Organization of Petroleum Exporting Countries), which during the 1970s and 1980s had significant monopoly power over world oil price and output decisions.

Government definition of a monopoly is less rigorous than pure economic definitions. In the UK, two types of monopoly can occur:

1 a scale monopoly occurs where one firm controls 25 per cent of the value of a market

2 a complex monopoly occurs where a number of firms in a market together account for over 25 per cent of the value of the market, and their actions have the effect of limiting competition.

It can, however, be difficult to define just what is meant by 'the market'. While in Britain there may be just a few companies that between them have a near monopoly in the supply of bananas, when looked at in the context of the fruit market more generally, monopoly power diminishes. Also, is it most appropriate to confine attention to the UK market or to include overseas markets in a definition of monopoly? A firm may have a dominant market position at home, but may face severe competition in its overseas markets. In fact, the EU now takes a Europe-wide perspective for assessing monopoly power for many products that can only sensibly be marketed Europe-wide. Therefore, although BAE Systems (formerly British Aerospace) has a dominant position in a number of its UK markets, when seen in a European context, it does in fact face severe competitive pressure.

12.4.1 Effects on prices and output of monopoly

A monopolist can determine the market price for its product and can be described as a 'price maker' rather than a 'price taker'. Where there are few substitutes for a product and where demand is inelastic, a monopolist may be able to get away with continually increasing prices in order to increase its profits.

In a pure monopoly market, consumers would face prices that are higher than would have occurred in a perfectly competitive market. Furthermore, because prices are higher, a downward-sloping demand curve would indicate that output would be lower than in a competitive market. It is therefore commonly held that monopolies are against the public interest by leading to higher prices and lower output. Although there are occasionally circumstances where monopoly yields greater public benefit than free competition (discussed later in this chapter), the general policy of governments towards monopolies has been to restrict their power.

12.4.2 Implications of monopoly power for a firm's marketing activities

In a pure monopoly, a firm's output decisions would be influenced by the elasticity of demand for its products. So long as demand is inelastic, it could continue raising prices and thereby its total revenue. While a firm may have monopoly power over some of its users, it may face competition if it wishes to attract new segments of users. It may therefore resort to differential pricing when targeting the two groups. As an example, train operating companies have considerable monopoly power over commuters that need to use their trains to arrive at work in central London by 9 am on weekdays. For such commuters, the alternatives of travelling to work by bus or car are very unattractive. However, leisure travellers wishing to go shopping in London at off-peak times may be much more price sensitive. Their journey is optional to begin with and their flexibility with respect to their time of travel is greater. For them, the car or bus provides a realistic alternative. As a result, train operators offer a range of price incentives aimed at off-peak leisure markets, while charging full fare for their peak-period commuters.

Organizations that think strategically will be reluctant to exploit fully their monopoly power. By charging high prices in the short term, a monopolist could give signals to companies in related product fields to develop substitutes that would eventually provide effective competition. Blatant abuse of monopoly power could also result in a referral to the regulatory authorities (see below).

12.5　Competition policy

The vision of competitive markets that bring maximum benefit to consumers is often not achieved. The imperfections described above can be summarized as resulting from:

- the presence of large firms that are able to exert undue influence over participants in a market – for example, through scale economies
- collusion between sellers (and sometimes buyers), which has the effect of restricting price competition and the availability of products
- barriers to market entry and restraints on trade, which may prevent a company moving into a market (e.g. a manufacturer may prevent a retailer from selling competing manufacturers' products)
- rigidity in resource input markets, which prevents supply moving to markets of strong demand (e.g. labour inflexibility may prevent a company from exploiting markets that have high levels of profitability).

Because of the presumed superiority of competitive markets, the law of most developed countries has been used to try to remove market imperfections where these are deemed to be against the public interest. This section initially considers the common law of England as a method by which anti-competitive practices have been curbed. More significantly, a growing body of legislation based on statute law is now available to governments and organizations seeking to curb anti-competitive practices.

12.5.1 Common law approaches to improving market competitiveness

Common law evolves over time on the basis of case judgments, which set a precedent for subsequent cases (see Chapter 5). In the UK, there is case law which holds that agreements between parties that have the effect of restraining free trade are unlawful. Sometimes, it may appear to be sensible for a business person to make a contract with another company by which he or she agrees to limit the parties with whom they can trade in the future. In return for an exclusivity clause, the business person may receive preferential treatment from the other party. Such agreements have frequently been used, for example, in contracts between oil companies and petrol station owners. An agreement would typically contain a tying covenant by which the station owner agrees, in return for a rebate on the price, to sell only the supplier's brand of petrol, a compulsory trading covenant that obliges the garage owner to keep the garage open at reasonable hours, and a continuity covenant that requires him or her, if the business is sold, to obtain acceptance of the agreement by the purchaser. In one important case, a garage owner had two garages and a solus agreement in respect of each, one for 4½ years and the other for 21 years. The garage owner felt that the actions of the oil company were threatening its profits and sought to obtain its petrol from a cheaper source, in defiance of his agreement. The case came before the House of Lords, which held that the essence of the agreements was to restrict unreasonably the garage proprietor's freedom of trading.

It is important to note the word 'reasonable'. In deciding whether the agreement between the oil company and petrol station owner was reasonable and therefore valid, the Law Lords stressed the importance of taking into account the public interest and held the 4½-year agreement reasonable but the 21-year agreement too long, and therefore unreasonable and invalid. The petrol-station owner was therefore free to buy his fuel from another source, regardless of the agreement. The 'public interest' is important in deciding whether a restrictive agreement is reasonable or not. The courts may feel that by tying a company to a supplier for 21 years, effective competition in a market is reduced, thereby resulting in higher prices for everybody.

The case of the petrol station dated from the 1960s, but provides a precedent for more recent common law challenges. In the UK, tenants of pubs owned by breweries and pub companies often sign agreements that prevent them buying much of their beer or soft drinks from third parties, in return for which the landlord may provide support for the tenant. A number of tenants have approached the courts to have clauses restricting their rights to make third-party purchases of beer set aside, on the grounds that they have the effect of unreasonably restricting trade. To independent brewers seeking new outlets for their beer, it is important that such restraints on trade are removed to allow them access to the market.

A claim of restraint of trade can also be made against a company buying a business that restricts the future business activity of the person from whom they have bought the business. An individual who has set up a successful estate-agency business may often be tempted by a takeover bid from another company. The acquiring company may be keen to grow so that it can achieve economies of scale, or it may simply want access to the target company's customers. Whatever the reason for the takeover, the acquiring company will often seek a clause restricting the seller of the business from going straight back into the marketplace and setting up another business that is in competition with the one that it has just sold. The owners of such businesses are usually required to agree to a clause that limits their rights to set up another estate-agency business in competition with that of the acquiring company. Again, any clause has to be 'reasonable'. A clause prohibiting the seller of an estate-agency business from setting up a new estate agency within a 25-mile radius of its base for a period of three years from the date of sale would almost certainly be considered reasonable. A clause prohibiting the seller from entering into any form of business anywhere in the country within ten years would almost certainly be deemed to be unreasonable. If a clause in an agreement is deemed by a court to be unreasonable, it may remove it from the contract. It can, however, be difficult to know what a court will consider to be 'reasonable' in the circumstances of a particular case.

12.5.2 Statutory intervention to create competitive markets

Common law has proved inadequate on its own to preserve the competitiveness of complex, well-developed markets. It has therefore been supplemented by statutory legislation – that is, laws passed by government as an act of policy. One outcome of statutory intervention has been the creation of a regulatory infrastructure, which in the UK includes the Office of Fair Trading (OFT), the **Competition Commission** and regulatory bodies to control specific industries. However, much of the current regulatory framework in the UK is based on the requirements of Articles 85 and 86 of the Treaty of Rome.

12.5.3 Articles 85 and 86 of the Treaty of Rome

Article 85 of the Treaty of Rome prohibits agreements between organizations and arrangements between organizations that affect trade between member-states of the EU, and in general prohibits **anti-competitive practices**, such as price-fixing, market-sharing and limitations on production. However, Article 85(3) provides for exemptions where restrictions on competition may be deemed to be in the public interest.

Article 86 prohibits the abuse of a dominant market position within the EU in so far as it may affect trade between member-states; the fact that a business has a monopoly position is not in itself prohibited.

The European Commission – which oversees the implementation of Articles 85 and 86 – can prohibit mergers where the combined turnover exceeds €200 million or where the company will have over 25 per cent of a national market and the merger will have an adverse effect on competition.

The European Commission is playing an increasingly important role in the policing of competition and has taken on very large multinational companies, such as Microsoft, which might have been too much of a challenge for individual member-states acting alone (see 'Thinking around the subject').

⟳ Thinking around the subject

Is Microsoft too powerful?

Switch on your computer and it is quite likely that you will hear the familiar notes to accompany the launch of a Microsoft operating system. In fact, it has been estimated that about 95 per cent of desktop and laptop computers run worldwide use a Windows operating system, while about four out of five corporate servers use some form of Windows system. Is this because windows is simply so good, or does it represent a successful effort by Microsoft to corner the market and keep out rivals?

The EU Commission has long taken interest in the competition implications of Microsoft's dominance. Its first investigation, concluded in 2004, focused on the way the company controlled access to its Windows operating system. The Commission fined the company €497 million and ordered that Microsoft must 'unbundle' its Media Player from its operating system so that it would be easier for rival applications to be used to listen to music or watch videos online. The Commission also demanded that the company give rival software producers more information about the code used in its programs, to help developers create their own programs.

The Commission became frustrated at Microsoft's slow progress in implementing the 2004 ruling, and in 2006 it imposed a daily fine on the company that added up to a further €280.5 million. While Microsoft has unbundled its software, it then proceeded to charge a royalty for the information needed by developers of rival server software. The Commission decided that these charges were unreasonable.

By 2008, the EU had imposed fines on Microsoft for anti-competitive behaviour, totalling €1.68 billion over the previous four years. But it still continued its own enquiries – for example, by investigating whether the company illegally refused to give rivals access to interoperability information from its suite of Office and .NET products, following a complaint from the Norwegian Software developer Opera.

Where do you draw the line between being successful and having unfair domination of a market? Would users be happy if Microsoft products were less well developed than their rivals? Or do they simply never get the chance to try out alternatives because of the domination by Microsoft of distribution channels?

The requirement contained in Articles 85 and 86 of the Treaty of Rome that competition shall not be distorted implies the existence in the market of *workable competition*. This can be interpreted as the degree of competition necessary to ensure the observance of the basic requirements and attainment of the objectives of the Treaty, in particular the creation of a single market achieving conditions similar to those of a domestic market. *Workable* competition reflects an economic pragmatism. *Perfect* competition, where producers respond instantly and inevitably to consumer demand and where the efficient allocation of resources is ensured, is in practice an illusion. Workable competition is concerned to achieve the most efficient resource allocation available given the constraints of a modern economy where consumer choice cannot be perfectly expressed.

The EU often has difficulty in reconciling the need for a firm to operate globally at a large scale, and the resultant domination of the EU market by that firm. Mergers between European airlines (e.g. the merger between Air France and the Dutch airline KLM) have raised the issue of whether it was justifiable to sacrifice competition on a small number of domestic routes in order to give an enlarged, efficient carrier a chance of taking on American carriers that were already operating on a large scale.

12.5.4 UK competition legislation

Domestic legislation is used to control anti-competitive practices where their effects are confined within national boundaries. In the UK, the 1998 Competition Act reformed and strengthened competition law by prohibiting anti-competitive behaviour. The Act introduced two basic prohibitions: a prohibition of anti-competitive agreements, based closely on Article 85 of the EC Treaty; and a prohibition of abuse of a dominant position in a market, based closely on Article 86 of the EC Treaty. The Act prohibits agreements that have the aim or effect of preventing, restricting or distorting competition in the UK. Since anti-competitive behaviour between companies may occur without a clearly delineated agreement, the prohibition covers not only agreements by associations of companies, but also covert practices. The Enterprise Act 2002 strengthened the Competition Act by including provision for a new Competition Appeal Tribunal (CAT) and its supporting body the Competition Service. The Act introduced criminal sanctions with a maximum penalty of five years in prison for companies that operate agreements to fix prices, share markets, limit production and rig bids. The voice of consumers was strengthened with designated consumer bodies able to make 'super-complaints' to the Office of Fair Trading.

In addition, a number of organizations are active in either using legislation to protect the competitiveness of markets (such as public utility regulators), or by drawing attention to abuses in monopoly power. At a local level, Trading Standards Departments have powers to prosecute companies using misleading prices, among other things. Consumer champions that can draw attention to anti-competitive practices include Citizens Advice Bureaux, Ombudsmen and the media (discussed in more detail in Chapter 5).

The Competition Commission has no power to initiate its own investigations but investigates alleged anti-competitive pricing practices referred to it by a number of designated bodies, including the Secretary of State for Business, Enterprise and Regulatory Reform, the OFT and industry regulatory bodies.

12.5.5 Evaluating claims of anti-competitive practice

A fine balance often exists between the cooperation among firms that leads to lower prices/better products for consumers, and cooperation that leads to collusion and a reduction in consumers' choice. There is diversity in interpretation of the notion of the 'public interest', which may be explained partly by cultural/political factors, and developments in our understanding of the consequences of market imperfection. It is evident, for example, that contemporary interpretations of anti-competitive practices differ significantly between Japanese and European systems of government regulation.

An investigation by the Competition Commission is normally completed within three months. The Commission has power only to make recommendations to the referring body. It is up to the latter whether the recommendations should be implemented. In the case of existing or potential monopolistic situations, the Commission can recommend divestment of assets or other action to reduce the undesirable elements of monopoly power.

Regulatory bodies are increasingly recognizing that cooperative relationships between companies can become anti-competitive. The following examples give an indication of recent thinking in the UK.

- In 2009, a Competition Commission inquiry concluded that the airports operator BAA had significant monopoly power, especially in the London area, and it was ordered to sell both Gatwick and Stansted airports, and also either Glasgow or Edinburgh. However, BAA issued an initially successful challenge through the Competition Appeal Tribunal, accusing the Competition Commission decision of 'apparent bias'.

- In 2007, the OFT fined British Airways £121.5 million for colluding with Virgin Atlantic over the imposition of fuel surcharges. Investigation of the alleged cartel focused on the movement of fuel price surcharges, with BA and Virgin appearing to move in step from when they were first introduced in May 2004. BA introduced a £2.50 surcharge on 13 May and Virgin did the same thing six days later. By April 2006, both airlines were charging £35 extra on a long-haul flight. In addition to the fine, British Airways was faced with a potential compensation bill of £80 million from customers who had been overcharged. Virgin escaped a fine from the regulator, because it had 'blown the whistle' on the price-fixing arrangement and provided evidence for the OFT.

- In 2006, the OFT found that an agreement between 50 of the UK's fee-paying independent schools to exchange detailed fee information was in breach of the Competition Act, and imposed penalties totalling just under £500,000 on the schools. The schools concerned had exchanged confidential information relating to their intended fee levels for boarding and day pupils through a survey known as the 'Sevenoaks Survey'.

- The Competition Commission doesn't just involve itself with national organizations – it also investigates local abuse of monopoly power. Since the deregulation of the UK bus industry, the Commission has investigated several alleged anti-competitive practices by bus companies. In the Lancashire town of Preston, for example, the bus operator Stagecoach acquired Preston Bus in 2009, prompting an investigation by the Competition Commission, which found evidence of a monopoly situation that was against the public interest, and therefore ordered the Scottish-based Stagecoach to sell its recent acquisition.

⟳ Thinking around the subject

Consumers smell a rat rather than perfume

A typical bottle of perfume may cost only pennies to make, but can end up selling for £30–£50 in UK stores. Inevitably, consumer groups have cried foul, accusing perfume companies of fixing prices. The companies' critics have pointed to the low prices charged for identical products in overseas markets where buyers are more price sensitive and the companies cannot sustain high prices. They also point to the refusal of the companies to supply perfumes to discount stores such as Tesco and Asda, which pledge to lower the prices charged to consumers. This all sounds like a very anti-competitive situation that the OFT should seek

⟩

to eradicate. But, in fact, the OFT investigated the perfume sector in 1997 and amazed some of its critics by giving the perfume companies a clean bill of health. Restricting sales to discount chains could be justified because such shops do not have trained staff to give advice about the companies' products. More importantly, the OFT recognized that price often adds to the perceived value of a perfume. If a perfume became known for being low in price, the cachet associated with wearing it would be lost. People like to flaunt the fact that they have an expensive perfume.

Undaunted, discount retailers sought to obtain supplies of perfumes from the 'grey' (unofficial distribution channels) market in countries overseas where price levels are generally lower. Who is right? Should we be able to buy low-price designer fragrances from the retailer that is prepared to obtain the best price? Or will the low price in the long run destroy the value of the item that we seek?

12.5.6 Control on price representations

One of the assumptions of a perfectly competitive market is that participants in it have complete information about competing goods and services. In reality, buyers may find it very difficult to judge between competing suppliers because prices are disclosed in a deceptive or non-comparable manner. Legislation, such as the Consumer Protection Act 1987, makes it illegal for a company to give misleading statements about the price of goods or services. This not only helps to protect consumers from exploitation, but also helps to preserve the competitiveness of a market. Consumer protection legislation is considered in more detail in Chapter 5.

12.5.7 Regulation of public utilities

During the 1980s, the privatization of many UK public-sector utilities resulted in the creation of new private-sector monopoly companies, including those providing gas, water, telephones and electricity. The UK led the way in privatizing public utilities and many other countries have now followed its example.

To protect the users of these services from exploitation, the government's response has been twofold.

1 First, government has sought to increase competition, in the hope that the invisible forces of competition will bring about lower prices and greater consumer choice. In this way, the electricity-generating industry was divided into a number of competing private suppliers, while conditions were made easier for new generators and distributors to enter the market. The problem here is that there may be real barriers to entry in markets where the capital cost of getting started can be very high. For many of the newly privatized monopolies, effective competition proved to be an unrealistic possibility. It has not been possible, for example, to develop a competitive market for domestic water supply.

2 Where competition alone has not been sufficient to protect consumers' interests, government has created a series of regulatory bodies that can determine the level and structure of charges made by these utilities. The regulatory bodies can determine the pattern of competition within a sector by influencing relationships between competitors and easing barriers to entry. These are some of the more significant regulatory bodies in the UK:

- Ofcom, regulates the telecommunications and broadcasting sectors
- Ofgem, regulates the gas and electricity sectors
- Ofwat, regulates the water supply sector.

In general, private-sector companies operating in monopoly utility markets require a licence from their regulator to do so. The regulator takes a view as to what constitutes the public interest when reviewing operators' licences to trade. Prices charged, standards of service and speed of service are all factors that the regulator can insist the companies implement if they are to carry on trading. Unresolved issues can be referred from a regulator to the Competition Commission.

In utility markets where competition is absent, regulators have to balance what is desirable from the public's point of view with the companies' need to make profits, which will in turn provide new capital for investment in improvements. Over the long term, favouring consumers with short-term price constraints may result in lower investment in a sector, leading to supply shortages. Regulators are trying to combine market forces with a degree of centralized planning and there have been concerns about the difficulties of achieving this.

Even within the apparently more competitive telecommunications sector, the regulator has frequently intervened with instructions to operators to reduce specific categories of prices; for example, the EU Commission has acted to cut the charges imposed by mobile phone companies on customers who use their phones abroad (see case study).

12.5.8 Control of government monopolies

Although the UK government has gone a long way in privatizing and deregulating markets that were previously the preserve of state organizations, there are still many services that cannot be sensibly privatized or deregulated. It is difficult, for example, to privatize roads or to expose consumers to serious competition for road space. It would be almost impossible to deregulate social services or the police force. It used to be thought that because the government actually provided the service, the public interest was thereby automatically protected. Government and the public were considered one and the same thing. However, with an increasingly consumerist society, it has become clear that what government thinks is good for the public is not necessarily what the public actually wants. Therefore, where it is impractical to privatize publicly provided services, government has introduced a number of measures to try to protect consumers from exploitation. The following are some of the methods that have been used.

Arm's length organizations

It was noted in Chapter 2 that agencies that operate at 'arm's length' from government have grown in number in recent years. With these types of organization, managers are given defined targets that are intended to reflect the interests of the users of the service, rather than just the narrower interests of government. The separation of operational issues from policy issues allows such agencies to focus more single-mindedly on meeting policy objectives, even if this means making politically unpopular decisions in the process.

Market testing

Sometimes, local and central government test the market to see whether part of the work of a department can be subcontracted to an outside organization, or whether internal production represents 'best value'. It is sometimes argued that a clear producer–buyer division makes it much easier for the body providing money for a service to exercise control over standards of performance and to create a market at the point of production, even if not at the point of consumption. For example, a local authority producing its own refuse collection services has to balance the needs of consumers with its need for good industrial relations. By contracting out the service, the authority can concentrate single-mindedly on ensuring that the contractor is performing to the agreed standard.

Customers' 'charters'

These have become popular as a method of providing consumers of public services with standards of service that government organizations are expected to meet. They have been introduced to protect

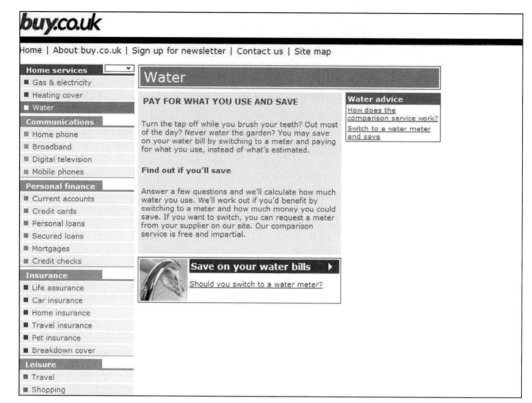

Figure 12.5 Better information about prices may help to improve the competitiveness of markets. In the UK, gas and electricity were for a long time supplied by government organizations, which had a monopoly position. From the 1980s, these markets were deregulated and opened to price competition, yet the UK government has been concerned that relatively few private customers have switched their supplier, possibly because of confusion about the true cost of competing companies' supplies. Some companies give introductory discounts, some give high-user or low-user discounts, and many give discounts for payment by direct debit. The energy regulator Ofgem has encouraged comparison websites such as this one, operated by www.uswitch.com. Ofgem has approved its comparison methodology, which guides consumers through all the gas and electricity choices available, and identifies which supplier and price plan is best for them. It is claimed that an average family that switches suppliers on buy.co.uk or uSwitch.com saves £140 on their annual energy bills. (Reproduced with permission of uswitch.com).

health service patients and parents of schoolchildren, among others, against poor service provided by a public-sector monopoly organization. Cynics have dismissed them as government hype, which conceals underlying expenditure cuts and unnecessarily raises consumers' expectations. However, by setting out standards of performance, a charter gives a clear message to the management and employees of a state organization about the standards that users expect of it.

Figure 12.6 Governments are usually monopoly providers of roads, and users generally have no choice of service provider. Furthermore, roads are usually paid for out of general taxation, with no direct link between the price of using a road and the decision whether or not to use road space. This has arisen largely because of the impracticality of road pricing and issues of equity between users. However, with improved technology and growing realization of the social and economic costs of traffic congestion, there has been a move towards pricing the use of roads using some of the principles of market forces. The London Congestion Charge, introduced in 2003, provides evidence that pricing a public service can change consumers' behaviour, with traffic volumes in 2006 reported to have fallen by 26 per cent compared with their levels immediately before the introduction of the charge. Around 50–60 per cent of this reduction was attributed to transfers to public transport, 20–30 per cent to vehicle journeys avoiding the charging zone, and the remainder to car-sharing, reduced number of journeys, more travelling outside the hours of operation, and increased use of motorbikes and cycles.

Case study:
Competitive market for mobile phones still needs regulation

© drflet

If you have bought a mobile phone recently, you would have doubtless been aware of a seemingly bewildering array of offers and price plans. Does the proliferation of price and service plans simply indicate the lengths that phone companies have gone to in addressing the needs of specific market segments? Or do the phone companies have a more sinister aim of trying to confuse buyers with low headline prices, but then make up their margins with hidden charges and specialist services such as music downloads and international roaming?

Only a couple of decades ago, a mobile phone would have been unaffordable for most people, and a ten-minute landline phone call from Britain to America an expensive luxury to be used only for special occasions or when absolutely necessary. Today, the price of both of these is unexceptional, and rapidly falling prices (and improved facilities) have been brought about by a combination of technological development and increased competitiveness within the telecommunications sector.

Some indication of the importance of market structure in contributing to the downward trend in telecommunication prices was indicated by the Organization for Economic Co-operation and Development (OECD), which in a report published in 2004 examined the effects of market structure on prices charged to users of mobile phones in OECD member-states. Its statistics revealed a strong link between competition and prices. Countries with the cheapest phone services tended to have a larger number of operators. Those at the

expensive end of the table had just two or three operators. The cheapest country in which to own a mobile phone was Denmark, where a typical total annual cost was £130. The most expensive was Poland, at £520, with Britain at £310, sitting at number 22 in a league table of 29 countries. It appeared to be no coincidence that Denmark had a fiercely competitive market, with a number of 'virtual' networks competing for custom, while Poland still had a very regulated market, which was dominated by the previous government telephone monopoly.

Within Britain, the appearance of new entrants to the mobile phone market has often been accompanied by intense competitive pressures. When the Hong Kong-based company Hutchison Whampoa launched its '3' network in 2003, it precipitated ferocious price-cutting as it sought to build market share from a customer base of zero. A decade earlier, the launch of Orange and One-to-One (now T-mobile) had brought price pressure on the then duopoly of BT Cellnet (now O_2) and Vodafone. To add to the competitive pressure, a number of companies that had no connection with the phone industry, such as retailers Tesco and Sainsbury's, moved into the market. Through agreements with network operators, these firms were hoping to use their buying power with the network operators, and the trust they had earned from their shoppers, to develop a profitable segment of the market.

For UK consumers, buying phone services had become much more complex than it had been a couple of decades or so earlier. Then, British Telecom had a monopoly and offered a very limited range of tariffs. Prices were transparent, with a very limited range of options. Today, consumers are overloaded with choice, as companies refine their segmentation techniques with product offers aimed at ever more specific groups of phone users. An occasional mobile phone user? A heavy text user? A frequent caller to overseas numbers? Need mobile internet access? Phone companies have developed service offers and price plans to meet each of these specific needs. But in this proliferation of service offers, has the basic idea of a perfectly competitive market been lost? Recall from the previous chapter that the defining characteristics of a perfectly competitive market included a product offer that was undifferentiated between competitors, perfect information about competing offers, and no barriers to entry.

Clearly, the idea of a generic, undifferentiated product does not hold true in the modern mobile phone market. The proliferation of plans noted above has produced a bewildering array of choice. Many buyers of mobile phone services have been overwhelmed at the choices available to them – in the UK the final purchase decision has to be made from a permutation of five basic network operators (plus many other 'virtual networks'), dozens of different tariffs for each network, hundreds of different handsets and thousands of retail outlets. To many people, the tariff plans offered by the phone companies seem unbelievably complex, with an array of peak/off-peak price plans, 'free' inclusive minutes and discounts for loyalty. Comparing a few 'headline' prices may be difficult enough, but the task becomes even harder when account is taken of the extras that are often hidden in the small print – for example, the charges made for itemized billing and multimedia messages, or for using a phone abroad. One professor of mathematics calculated that it would take a UK buyer over a year to evaluate the costs and benefits of all permutations of networks, tariffs and handsets.

The term 'confusion marketing' has been used by commentators to describe the practices of some phone service providers. Even staff working for phone companies have been heard to use the term, off the record. In an ideal world, we would all be able to evaluate the options open to us and make a rational choice from the available options. Classical economic theory is based on an assumption of informed decision making. But how do you go about the task of evaluation when there is enormous choice, and service providers appear to go out of their way to confuse buyers with excessive, missing or inappropriate information?

With apparently fierce competition between phone companies, it might be presumed that there would be no need for government regulation of the sector. However, as noted above, the UK mobile phone market falls far short of meeting the criteria for a perfectly competitive market, therefore the government's regulator Ofcom intervenes to address market failures. The competition regulator is always aware that, with only five network operators and significant barriers to entry, the phone

companies could come to understandings among themselves to limit competition in the market. Some have accused established network operators of being reluctant to let new entrants share their network capacity. For example, in the fixed-line sector, deregulation meant that, in theory, new entrants could require the incumbent operator, British Telecom (BT), to make its final link from the exchange to the user's home available for other companies to use. However, one company that sought to use this right, Carphone Warehouse, complained in 2007 that BT was abusing its dominant position by making access slow and difficult.

Regulation is also needed because information is not available as freely and openly as required for a perfectly competitive market. Phone companies have a habit of highlighting a few key prices, but hiding additional charges in the small print where consumers are less likely to comprehend them. As an example, most mobile phone buyers concentrate their evaluation on how much it would cost them to make a call from their phone, rather than how much it will cost other people to call them from a fixed landline. Competition was fierce in respect of outgoing prices, but not in respect of incoming prices. So, in June 2004, Ofcom ordered mobile phone operators to reduce the price of incoming calls to mobiles. Similarly, most buyers of mobile phones do not rigorously evaluate the price of making or receiving calls while they are out of the country, which until a few years ago could have typically cost the UK phone user £1 per minute to make a call back to the UK from France. As a result, phone operators had allowed these seemingly hidden charges to rise. The EU Telecoms Commissioner has therefore become increasingly involved in limiting the prices that phone companies can charge. The first move was to limit the cost of receiving and making calls between countries, so that instead of being typically over £1 per minute, from July 2010, the limit was set at 32p per minute for outgoing calls and 12.5p for incoming calls. However the EU Commission's action has resulted in what some people have described as a 'waterbed' effect: as they force down the prices of some categories of charges, the phone companies simply make up for this by pushing up other charges. So they allowed data roaming charges to rise, until the Commission imposed the mandatory cut-off of €50 on customers' accounts unless they had specifically authorized larger roaming bills to be incurred.

The phone companies challenged the legality of this 'micro-management' of prices by the Commission, but in 2010 the European Court of Justice rejected a legal challenge against such EU Commission interference, stating that the Commission was right to 'protect consumers against excessive prices ... even if it might have negative economic consequences for certain operators'.

Is the apparently confusing pricing of mobile phone services an inevitable consequence of deregulation in an increasingly competitive market? Or are the phone companies continually trying to outsmart the workings of the market through their complex service offers?

QUESTIONS

1 In the context of this case, critically discuss the view that there is a tendency in competitive markets inevitably to provide less transparent information on which competing products can be compared.

2 Justify the case for continued government regulation of the mobile phone market.

3 What are likely to be the reasons for retailers such as Tesco or Sainsbury's entering the mobile phone market? Discuss the key challenges and opportunities they face.

Summary

Although perfect competition may be fine in theory, it is rarely found in practice. This chapter has explored some of the distortions to the competitiveness found in markets. Branding represents an attempt to create a monopoly for a unique product, which is nevertheless substitutable with close alternatives. The most limiting form of competition is provided where a monopoly supplier controls a market in which there are few realistic substitutes available. Regulatory authorities generally presume in favour of competitive markets, and this chapter has reviewed some of the procedures and criteria by which such agencies assess anti-competitive practices.

Product differentiation is a means by which a firm can avoid head-on competition and can be strengthened with the application of new technologies to develop new products (**Chapter 4**). The trend towards globalization of business (**Chapter 14**) is having the effect of making markets more competitive. This chapter has taken a microeconomic perspective on pricing and competition. Pricing is also affected by macroeconomic factors and these are discussed in **Chapter 13**. Public policy usually seeks control of anti-competitive practices and the legal framework for controlling such practices is discussed further in **Chapter 6**.

🔑 Key Terms

Anti-competitive practice (400)

Competition Commission (400)

Five Forces model (396)

Imperfect competition (389)

Monopoly (397)

Oligopoly (395)

Online
Learning Centre

To help you grasp the key concepts of this chapter, explore the extra resources posted on the Online Learning Centre at *www.mcgraw-hill.co.uk/palmer*. Among other helpful resources there are chapter-by-chapter test questions, revision notes and web links.

Chapter review questions

1 Identify strategies that companies have pursued in order to reduce the effects of direct competition.

2 In a medium-sized English town, one bus company recently agreed to buy the operations of another operator, giving the acquiring company over 80 per cent of the local market for scheduled bus services. In view of a possible referral of the takeover by the OFT to the Competition Commission, assess the advantages and disadvantages to the public of the existence of a local monopoly.

3 Summarize the problems facing governments in their attempts to control the price of public water supply.

Activities

1 Consider one of the following markets, which are characterized by a variety of cheap generic products, manufacturers' branded products and retailers' own branded products: casual shirts; disposable batteries; cheese; carbonated drinks. Collect price information for a selection of products in your chosen category. What is the connection between the apparent brand strategy and the price charged? Critically discuss the features and benefits associated with the most expensive branded product, which allow it to command a higher price than others.

2 Look through a Sunday newspaper magazine supplement and examine a selection of adverts. What brand message is communicated by these adverts? Identify the functional and emotional elements of the firms' branding strategy.

3 Examine prices for train services on a route where there is service provision by at least two companies. What evidence is there of competition between the two operators? Is it desirable that there should be extensive competition, rather than a coordinated approach?

Further reading

The following texts provide an introduction to the principles of branding.

De Chernatony, L. McDonald, M. and Wallace, E. (2010) *Creating Powerful Brands*, 4th edn, Oxford, Butterworth-Heinemann.

Keller, K., Aperia, T. and Georgson, M. (2011) *Strategic Brand Management: A European Perspective*, Harlow, Pearson.

Olins, W. (2008) *The Brand Handbook*, London, Thames & Hudson.

For further discussion of the application of general branding principles to not-for-profit organizations, refer to the following text.

Stride, H. and Lee, S. (2007) 'No logo? No way: branding in the not-for-profit sector', *Journal of Marketing Management*, Vol. 23, No. 1/2, pp. 107–122.

For a general discussion of competitive strategy, the following texts provide a useful overview.
Hooley, G., Saunders, J. and Piercy, N.F. (2011) *Marketing Strategy and Competitive Positioning*, 5th edn, London, FT Prentice Hall.
Porter, M.E. (2004) *Competitive Advantage*, New York, Free Press.

Competition policy and law is reviewed in the following texts.

Motta, M. (2004) *Competition Policy: Theory and Practice*, Cambridge, Cambridge University Press.
Rodger, B. and MacCulloc, A. (2009) *Competition Law and Policy in the EC and UK*, 4th edn, Oxford, Routledge.

References

Cova, B. (1997) 'Community and consumption – towards a definition of the 'linking value' of products or services', *European Journal of Marketing*, Vol. 31, No. 3/4, pp. 297–316.
Croft, M. (2008) 'Consumers in control', *Marketing Week*, Vol. 31, No.14, pp. 29–30.
De Chernatony, L, McDonald, M. and Wallace, E. (2010) *Creating Powerful Brands*, 4th edn, Oxford, Butterworth-Heinemann.
Fock, H. and Woo, K. (1998) 'The China market: strategic implications of Quanxi', *Business Strategy Review*, Vol. 7, No. 4, pp. 33–43.
Gardner, B.B. and Levy, S.J. (1955) 'The product and the brand', *Harvard Business Review*, Vol. 33, No. 2, pp. 33–39.
Hitwise (2008) 'The impact of social networking in the UK', online at: http://www.i-marketing-net.com/wp-content/uploads/2008/02/hitwise-social-networking-report-2008.pdf (accessed 2 August 2011).
Microsoft Digital Advertising Solutions (2007) 'Word of the web guidelines for advertisers: understanding trends and monetising social networks', online at: http://advertising.microsoft.com/uk/WWDocs/User/en-uk/Advertise/Partner%20Properties/Piczo/Word%20of%20the%20Web%20Social%20Networking%20Report%20Ad5.pdf (accessed 10 February 2009).
Miller, G. (2009) 'Biggest brand movers on the Virtue social media index for January 2009', *Virtue*, online at: http://vitrue.com/blog/2009/02/10/biggest-brand-movers-on-the-vitrue-social-media-index-for-january-2009/ (accessed 20 May 2009).
Munson, J.M. and Spivey, W. (1981) 'Product and brand-user stereotypes among social classes', *Journal of Advertising Research*, Vol. 21, No. 4, pp. 37–46.
OECD (2004) *Mobile Baskets*, April.
Porter, M.E. (1985) *Competitive Advantage: Creating and Sustaining Superior Performance*, New York, Free Press.
Sherry, J.F. (1998) 'The soul of the company store: Nike Town Chicago and the emplaced brandscape', *Servicescapes: The Concept of Place in Contemporary Markets*, Lincolnwood, IL, NTC Business Books.
Solomon, M. (1983) 'The role of products in social stimuli: a symbolic interactionism perspective', *Journal of Consumer Research*, Vol. 10, No. 3, pp. 319–329.
Tsang, W.K. (1998) 'Can Quanxi be a source of sustained competitive advantage for doing business in China?', *The Academy of Management Executive*, Vol. 12, No. 2, pp. 64–74.
Universal McCann International (2008) 'Power to the people – social media tracker wave 3', online at: www.slideshare.net/mickstravellin/universal-mccann-international-social-media-research-wave-3 (accessed 20 May 2009).

Chapter 13

The National Economic and Financial Environment

The workers at the local car components company have been put on reduced-hours working, so their income goes down. Because they work for only three days and not five days a week, they have less money in their pockets, so they don't go as often to the local corner shop to buy their cigarettes, bottles of Coke and bars of chocolate. The corner shop owner sees his income go down, so he postpones his order for replacement windows. Lots of businesses are doing the same, so the window supplier cuts its staff, so households in the area have even less money to spend in the shops. So they lay off more people, or even go out of business completely. All the time, the economy is shrinking and governments suffer as taxation revenue drops. But in order to try to get the economy moving again, governments may feel compelled to borrow money to pump in to the system so that consumers now have money to spend, which results in new jobs being created by firms whose employees spend more money in the shops, and helps to increase the government's tax revenues. These are the basic ideas underlying linkages within national economies that are explored in this chapter. And, with an increasingly globalized business environment, these economic and financial linkages cross national boundaries.

 ## Learning Objectives

This chapter will explain:

✓ The structure of national economies, distinguishing between consumer, producer and government sectors.

✓ Methods of measuring activity within the economy.

✓ Financial linkages and interdependencies between sectors.

✓ The business cycle – causes and consequences for business organizations.

✓ Government economic policy objectives.

✓ Methods used by governments and central banks to manage the national economy.

13.1   Macroeconomic analysis

In the previous chapter, microeconomic analysis of a firm's competitive environment made a number of assumptions about the broader economic environment in which the firm operates. In the analysis of supply and demand in any given market, changes in household incomes or government taxation were treated as an uncontrollable external factor to which a market responded. For most businesses, a sound understanding of this broader economic environment is just as important as understanding short-term and narrow relationships between the price of a firm's products and demand for them.

An analysis of companies' financial results has often indicated that business people attribute their current success or failure to the state of the economy. For example, a retail store that has just reported record profit levels may put this down to a very high level of consumer confidence, while a factory that has just laid off workers may blame a continuing economic recession for its low level of activity. Few business people can afford to ignore the state of the economy because it affects the willingness and ability of customers to buy their products. It can also affect the price and availability of its inputs. The shop that reported record profits may have read economic indicators correctly and prepared for an upturn in consumer spending by buying in more stocks or taking on more sales assistants.

This chapter is concerned with what is often described as **macroeconomic analysis**. Although the workings of the economy at a national level are the focus of this chapter, it must be remembered that even national economies form part of a larger international economic environment.

The chapter begins by analysing the structure of the national economy and the interdependence of the elements within this structure. The national economy is a complex system whose functioning is influenced by a range of planned and unplanned forces. While unplanned forces (such as turbulence in the world economic system) can have significant impacts on the national economic system, organizations are particularly keen to understand the planned interventions of governments that seek to influence the economy for a variety of social and political reasons. Money is a factor that brings together the different elements of the macroenvironment, with money linking buyers and sellers, firms and households; individuals who have surplus savings with individuals who want to borrow; and flows of money link public and private sectors. In the increasingly globalized business environment, flows of money link strong countries that generate cash with those weaker and growing economies that need to borrow it.

13.2   The structure of national economies

Analyses of national economies have traditionally divided the productive sectors into three categories.

1 The *primary sector*, which is concerned with the extraction and production of basic raw materials from agriculture, mining, oil exploration, etc.

2 The *secondary sector*, which transforms the output of the primary sector into products that consumers can use (e.g. manufacturing, construction, raw material processing).

3 The *services sector*, which comprises intangible products such as hairdressing, and business services such as accounting.

Comparisons can be drawn between the three sectors described above and value chains (described in Chapter 1). In general, these three sectors add progressively higher levels of value to a product. In practice, most organizations are involved in two or more of these production categories; for example, the Ford car company manufactures cars, but it also produces a wide range of services, including financial services, extended warranties and insurance.

A further division in the economy occurs between the production sector and the consumption sector. The production sector creates wealth (e.g. making cars, providing meals in a restaurant), while the consumption sector essentially destroys wealth (using the car until it is worn out, eating the restaurant meal so that there is nothing left to show for it). Distinction is often made between government and private sectors of the economy. Government becomes involved in the economy as both a producer (e.g. educational services) and as a consumer on behalf of the public (e.g. through the purchase of equipment for schools).

The relationship between producers and consumers is the basis for models of the circular flow of income, discussed later in this chapter.

13.2.1 Measures of economic structure

The relative importance of the three productive sectors described above has been changing. Evidence of this change is usually recorded by reference to three key statistics:

1 the share of gross domestic product (GDP) that each sector accounts for
2 the proportion of the labour force employed in the sector
3 the contribution of the sector to a nation's balance of payments.

A key trend in Britain, as in most developed economies, has been the gradual decline in importance of the primary and manufacturing sectors and the growth in the services sector. The extent of the change in the UK **economic structure**, when measured by shifts in GDP and employment, is indicated in Table 13.1.

While the statistics in Table 13.1 appear to show a number of clear trends, the figures need to be treated with a little caution for a number of reasons.

- Fluctuations in the value of GDP for the primary sector often have little to do with changes in activity levels, but instead reflect changes in world commodity levels. Oil represents a major part of the UK's primary sector output, but the value of oil produced has fluctuated

Table 13.1 Composition of the UK productive sector.

	1969	1979	1989	1995	2000	2007
Primary						
GDP (%)	4.3	6.7	4.2	4.4	4.1	3.7
Workforce (%)	3.6	3.0	2.1	1.4	1.5	1.3
Secondary						
GDP (%)	42.0	36.7	34.5	29.4	25.5	24.5
Workforce (%)	46.8	38.5	28.9	18.3	20.8	19.2
Services						
GDP (%)	53.0	56.5	61.3	66.2	70.4	75.0
Workforce (%)	49.3	58.5	69.0	76.5	77.7	79.5

Source: compiled from 'Economic trends', *Employment Gazette.*

from the very high levels of the early 1980s to the very low levels of the 1990s, largely reflecting changes in oil prices.

■ The level of accuracy with which statistics have been recorded has been questioned, especially for the services sector. The system of Standard Industrial Classifications (SICs) for a long while did not disaggregate the service sector in the same level of detail as the other two sectors.

■ Part of the apparent growth in the services sector may reflect the method by which statistics are collected, rather than indicating an increase in overall service level activity. Output and employment is recorded according to the dominant business of an organization. Within many primary- and secondary-sector organizations, many people are employed in service-type activities, such as cleaning, catering, transport and distribution. Where a cook is employed by a manufacturing company, output and employment is attributed to the manufacturing sector. However, during recent years, many manufacturing firms have contracted out some of these service activities to external contractors. Where such contracts are performed by contract catering, office cleaning or transport companies, the output becomes attributable to the service sector, making the service sector look larger, even though no additional services have actually been produced – they have merely been switched from internally produced to externally produced.

Nevertheless, the figures clearly indicate a number of significant trends in the economy.

■ The primary sector in the UK, as in most developed economies, has been contracting in relative importance. There are supply- and demand-side explanations for this trend. On the supply side, many basic agricultural and extractive processes have been mechanized, resulting in them using fewer employees and thereby consuming a lower proportion of GDP. Many primary industries have declined as suppliers have been unable to compete with low-cost producers in countries that are able to exploit poor working conditions. On the demand side, rising levels of affluence have led consumers to demand increasingly refined products. In this way, consumers have moved from buying raw potatoes (essentially a product of the primary sector) to buying processed potatoes (e.g. prepared ready meals), which involve greater inputs from the secondary sector. With further affluence, potatoes have been sold with the added involvement of the service sector (e.g. eating cooked potatoes in a restaurant).

■ The output of the secondary sector in the UK fell from 42 per cent of GDP in 1969 to 25.5 per cent in 2008, reflecting the poor performance of the manufacturing industry (the comparable figure for the 25 EU countries was 25.8 per cent). This can again partly be explained by efficiency gains by the sector, requiring fewer resources to be used, but more worryingly by competition from overseas. The emergence of newly industrialized nations with a good manufacturing infrastructure and low employment costs, rigidities in the UK labour market, declining research and development budgets relative to overseas competitors, and the effects of exchange rate policy have all contributed to this decline.

■ In respect of its share of GDP, the services sector saw almost continuous growth during the period 1969–99, with banking, finance, insurance, business services, leasing and communications being particularly prominent. In 2006, the services sector accounted for 75 per cent of UK GDP, up from 53 per cent in 1969.

13.2.2 Towards a service economy?

There is little doubt that the services sector has become a dominant force in many national economies. According to Eurostat, services accounted for 71.6 per cent of GDP in the 25 EU countries in 2005 (Eurostat 2006). Between 1970 and 1997, it is reported that about 1.5 million new jobs per year were created in the services sectors within the EU – twice the average for the rest of the economy (Eurostat 1998).

The UK, like many developed economies, has traditionally run a balance of trade deficit in manufactured goods (i.e. imports exceed exports), but has made up for this with a surplus in 'invisible' service 'exports'. In 2009, there was a trade surplus in services of £49.9 billion (or £55.4 billion in 2008), but this was more than offset by a deficit of £81.9 billion in manufactured goods (or £93.1 billion in 2008) (ONS 2010).

During periods of **recession** in the manufacturing sector, the service sector has been seen by many as the saviour of the economy. Many politicians have been keen to promote the service sector as a source of new employment to make up for the diminishing level of employment within the primary and secondary sectors. A common argument has been that the UK no longer has a **competitive cost advantage** in the production of many types of goods, and therefore these sectors of the economy should be allowed to decline and greater attention paid to those service sectors that showed greater competitive advantage. The logic of this argument can be pushed too far, as outlined below.

- A large part of the growth in the service sector during the 1980s and 1990s reflected the buoyancy of the primary and secondary sectors during that period. As manufacturing industry increases its level of activity, the demand for many business-to-business services, such as accountancy, legal services and business travel, increases. During periods of recession in the manufacturing sectors, the decline in manufacturing output has had an impact on the services sector, as evidenced, for example, through lower demand for business loans and export credits.

- The assumption that the UK has a competitive cost advantage in the production of services needs to be examined closely. In the same way that many sectors of UK manufacturing industry lost their competitive advantage to developing nations during the 1960s and 1970s, there is some evidence that the once unquestioned supremacy in certain service sectors is being challenged. High levels of training in some of Britain's competitor nations have allowed those countries to, first, develop their own indigenous services and then to develop them for export. Banking services that were once a net import of Japan are now exported throughout the world.

- Over-reliance on the service sector could pose strategic problems for the UK. A diverse economic base allows a national economy to be more resilient to changes in world trading conditions.

13.2.3 International comparisons

There appears to be a high level of correlation between the level of economic development in an economy (as expressed by its GDP per capita) and the strength of its services sector. Within the EU there is variation around the mean share of value added from services of 71.6 per cent, with more developed member-states being above this figure (e.g. UK 75 per cent, France 76 per cent), and less developed member-states below (e.g. Lithuania 55 per cent, Slovakia 63 per cent) (Eurostat 2006). According to the International Labour Organization, 71.5 per cent of the total workers from developed economies are employed in the services sector. Lower figures are found in many of the developing economies of Asia – for example, East Asia (34.7 per cent), Southeast Asia and the Pacific (37 per cent), South Asia (30.3 per cent). The lowest level of services employment is found in the least developed countries for example, those in Sub-Saharan Africa (25.7 per cent) (ILO 2008).

It is debatable whether a strong services sector leads to economic growth or is a result of that economic growth. The debate can partly be resolved by dividing services into those 'consumer services' that are used up in final consumption and 'business to business' services that provide inputs to further business processes (see below).

13.2.4 Consumer, producer and government sectors

Consumer goods and services are provided for individuals who use up those goods and services for their own enjoyment or benefit. No further economic benefit results from the consumption of the product. In this way, the services of a hairdresser can be defined as consumer services. On the other hand, producer goods and services are those that are provided to other businesses in order that those businesses can produce something else of economic benefit. In this way, a road haulage company sells services to its industrial customers in order that they can add value to the goods that they produce, by allowing their goods to be made available at the point of demand.

The essential difference between production and final consumption sectors is that the former creates wealth while the latter consumes it. Traditionally, economic analysis has labelled these as 'firms' and 'households' respectively. The discussion later in this chapter will indicate the problems that may arise where an apparently prosperous household sector is not backed by an equally active production sector.

There has been continuing debate about the role of government in the national economy, which has led to shifts in the proportion of GDP accounted for by the public sector. During the 1980s, the UK government regarded the public sector as a burden on the country and set about dismantling much of the state's involvement in the economy. Privatization of public corporations and the encouragement of private pensions were just two manifestations of this. By the mid-1990s, the proportion of UK government expenditure as a proportion of total GDP appeared to have stabilized in the range 38–42 per cent, with increasing social security spending offsetting much of the reduction in expenditure accounted for by state-owned industries. Figure 13.1 illustrates the cyclical nature of public spending and taxation as a proportion of UK GDP.

Governments do not always take such a 'hands-off' approach. The economies of eastern Europe have in the past been dominated by central planning in which the government determined the bulk of income and expenditure in the economy. Even in Britain shortly after the Second World

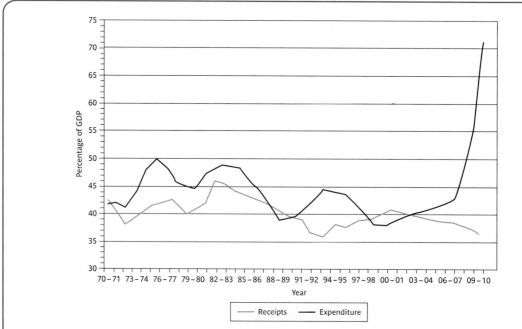

Figure 13.1 Trends in UK government taxation and spending as a proportion of GDP, 1970–2010.

Source: based on HM Treasury Financial Statement and Budget Report, March 2010.

War, the government assumed a very major role in the economy, with the nationalization of many essential industries. Even today, there are variations within western Europe in the proportion of GDP accounted for by the government sector. Many Scandinavian countries, for example, have higher proportions than the UK, reflecting, among other things, a general acceptance by their populations that taxation revenues will be wisely spent on socially necessary expenditure.

Organizations need to keep their eyes on political developments that shift the balance of resources between public and private sectors. A company that is involved in the marketing of health service products, for example, will be very interested in the government's view about the respective roles to be played by the private sector and the National Health Service.

⟳ Thinking around the subject

Service dominant logic?

To some people, the services sector may be seen as economically quite inferior to the manufacturing sector, conjuring up images of fast food, restaurants and hairdressers. But services have in recent years been seen by many as the driving force of the economy rather than simply an 'add on' to traditional manufacturing sectors. The emerging theory of 'service dominant logic' holds that raw materials and manufactured goods have no value without services that create 'value in use' (Vargo and Lusch 2008). Think about trees that have just been felled in the forest to provide timber. Without transport services to move them to customers, intermediaries to handle and process them, and possibly banks to finance stock, the timber would have no value. In many markets, suppliers begin with designing the service level, then developing the physical product offer comes second. Within the manufacturing sector, many companies now compete on service – for example, office equipment is often sold with the benefit of financing schemes, delivery, installation, maintenance contracts and warranties. These may be an important point of differentiation in markets where product design features are fairly standard. Inevitably, when a new idea such as 'service dominant logic' comes along, there are critics who argue about the validity of the new idea. Services can certainly be seen to be driving many sales of manufactured goods, but if the product itself is not well designed, would the service offer make up for this? The photocopying machine may come with a very good maintenance and breakdown repair service, but wouldn't it be better to design a machine that didn't break down in the first place?

13.3   The circular flow of income

Households, firms and government are highly interdependent and the level of wealth created in an economy is influenced by the interaction between these elements. Money is a mediating device which flows between the different elopements. To understand the workings of a national economy, it is useful to begin by developing a simple model of a closed economy comprising just two sectors – firms and households – which circulate money between each other.

The simplest model of a **circular flow of income** involves a number of assumptions.

- Households earn all their income from supplying their labour to firms.
- Firms earn all their income from supplying goods and services to households.
- There is no external trade.
- All income earned is spent (i.e. households and firms do not retain savings).

In this simple model, the income of households is exactly equal to the expenditure of firms, and vice versa. It follows that any change in income from employment is directly related to changes in expenditure by consumers. Similarly, any change in sales of goods and services by firms is dependent upon employment. In this simplified economy, income, output, spending and employment are all interrelated (Figure 13.2). Of course, this simplified model of the economy is almost impossible to achieve in practice, because most economies are affected by factors that upset this stable equilibrium pattern of income and expenditure.

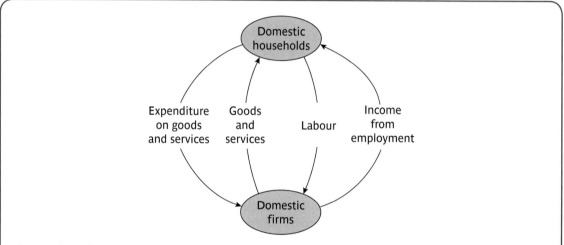

Figure 13.2 The circular flow of income, based on a simplified model of a national economy.

Instability in this static model can come about for two principal reasons: additional money can be injected into the circular flow, while money currently circulating can be withdrawn. Injections have the effect of increasing the volume and speed of circulation of money within this flow, while withdrawals have the opposite effects.

Withdrawals can take a number of forms:

■ savings by households that occur when income is received by them, but not returned to firms

■ government taxation, which removes income received by households and prevents them from returning it to firms in the form of expenditure on goods and services; taxation of businesses diverts part of their expenditure from being returned to households

■ spending on imported goods and services by households means that this money is not received by firms, which cannot subsequently return it to households in the form of wages.

The opposite of withdrawals are **injections** and these go some way to counterbalancing the effects described above, in the following ways.

■ Firms may earn income by selling goods to overseas buyers. This represents an additional source of income that is passed on to households.

■ Purchases by firms of capital equipment, which represents investment as opposed to current expenditure.

■ Instead of reducing the flow of income in an economy through taxation, governments can add to it by spending on goods and services.

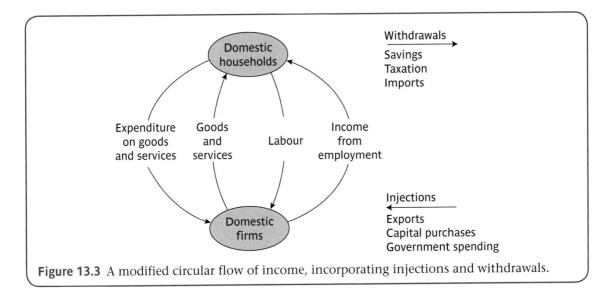

Figure 13.3 A modified circular flow of income, incorporating injections and withdrawals.

A revised model of the circular flow of income, incorporating these modifications, is shown in Figure 13.3.

This modified model of the economy still involves a number of fairly unrealistic assumptions (e.g. that consumers do not borrow money). In addition, it is unrealistic to assume that households earn income only from employment activity; they also receive it from returns on investments, property rentals and self-employment. However, it serves to stress the interdependence of the different sectors of the economy and the fact that, through this interdependence, changes in behaviour by one group can result in significant changes in economic performance as a whole. Of particular interest to government policy makers and businesses alike is the effect on total economic activity of changing just one element in the circular flow.

Another issue that is not fully reflected in this simple model is the role of the banking sector in circulating funds between and within the household and firm sectors. If firms rely on their own capital for growth, their growth would probably be very slow; therefore expanding economies have been associated with high levels of borrowing by firms. In the case of developing economies, this borrowing usually comes from overseas, representing a major injection to their national economies. If firms and banks do not feel confident about lending to each other (or do not feel confident about borrowing money), the circular flow of income will slow down. This was clearly seen in late 2007 when the so-called 'credit crunch' led to a liquidity crisis as banks became reluctant to lend money, both to firms and to private consumers. This led to a sharp downturn in consumer expenditure.

13.3.1 The multiplier effect

The **multiplier effect** can be compared to the effects of throwing a stone into a pool of water. The impact of the stone with the water will cause an initial wave to be formed, but beyond this will be waves of ever decreasing strength. The strength of these ripples will lessen with increasing distance from the site of original impact and with the passage of time. Similarly, injecting money into the circular flow of income will have an initial impact on households and businesses directly affected by the injection, but will also be indirectly felt by households and firms throughout the economy.

The multiplier effect can be illustrated by considering the effects of a major capital investment by private-sector firms or by government. The firm making the initial investment spends money buying in supplies from outside (including labour) and these outside suppliers in turn purchase more inputs. The multiplier effect of this initial expenditure can result in the total increase in household incomes being much greater than the original expenditure. A good example of the multiplier effect at work in the UK is provided by the Millennium Dome project at Greenwich, opened in 2000 (now known as the O_2). An important reason for the government supporting this project was the desire to regenerate an economically depressed part of London. Government expenditure initially created expenditure during the construction of the Dome and from employment within the Dome itself. This expenditure then rippled out to other business sectors, such as hotels and transport. The level of activity generated additional demand for local manufacturing industry – for example, visitors require food that may be produced locally, the producers of which may in turn require additional building materials and services to increase production facilities. On an even larger scale, the Mayor of London, supported by central government, successfully bid to host the 2012 Olympic Games, largely on the basis of the multiplier benefits that would result.

The extent of the multiplier effects of initial expenditure is influenced by a number of factors. Crucial is the extent to which recipients of this initial investment recirculate it back into the national economy. If large parts of it are saved by households or used to buy imported goods (whether by firms or by households), the multiplier effects to an economy will be reduced. In general, income that is received by individuals that have a high propensity to spend each additional pound on basic necessities is likely to generate greater multiplier benefits than the same money received by higher-income households that have a greater propensity to save it or to spend it on imported luxuries. The implications of this for government macroeconomic policy will be considered later.

The multiplier effect can be used to analyse the effects of withdrawals from the circular flow as well as injections. Therefore, if firms spend less on wages, household income will fall as a direct result, leading indirectly to lower spending by households with other domestic firms. These firms will in turn pay less to households in wages, leading to a further reduction in spending with firms, and so on.

Multiplier effects can be studied at a local as well as a national level. Government capital expenditure is often used with a view to stimulating areas of severe unemployment (as in the case of the Millennium Dome and grants given by Regional Development Agencies to support private-sector investment in Tyneside). The presence of a university in a town usually generates strong multiplier benefits – for example, one study in Wales estimated that the university in Newport, with a turnover of around £30 million per annum, and employing between 800 and 900 people, generated multiplier benefits to the local economy of around £80 million per annum in 2000. However, whether the local economy is helped will depend upon how much subsequent expenditure is retained within the area. In a study of the regional multiplier effects of siting a call centre for British Airways in a deprived part of Tyneside, it was found that a high proportion of the staff employed commuted in from other, more prosperous areas, thereby limiting the multiplier benefits to the deprived area.

As well as examining the general macroeconomic effects of spending by firms on household income, and vice versa, multiplier analysis can also be used to assess the impact of economic activity in one business sector upon other business sectors. Many economies suffer because vital economic infrastructure remains undeveloped, preventing productivity gains in other sectors. The availability of transport and distribution services has often had the effect of stimulating economic development at local and national levels – for example, following the improvement of rail or road services. The absence of these basic services can have a crippling effect on the development of the primary and manufacturing sectors – for instance, one reason for Russian agriculture not having been fully exploited has been the ineffective distribution system available to food producers.

One approach to understanding the contribution of one business sector to other sectors of the economy is to analyse input–output tables of production, and data on labour and capital inputs. In one study (Wood 1987), these were used to estimate the effects that productivity improvements in all the direct and indirect supply sectors had on the productivity levels of all other sectors. Thus, some apparently high-productivity sectors (such as chemicals) were shown to be held back by the low productivity of some of their inputs. On the other hand, efficiency improvements in some services, such as transport and distribution, were shown to have had widespread beneficial effects on the productivity contribution of other sectors. This is reflected in the common complaint among manufacturing businesses in the UK that their productivity is severely reduced by traffic congestion, which adds to their delivery costs and the costs of their supplies.

13.3.2 The accelerator effect

Changes in the demand for consumer goods can lead, through an **accelerator effect**, to a more pronounced change in the demand for capital goods. This accelerator effect occurs when, for instance, a small increase in consumer demand leads to a sudden large increase in demand for plant and machinery with which to satisfy that demand. When consumer demand falls by a small amount, demand for plant and machinery falls by a correspondingly larger amount.

The accelerator effect is best illustrated by reference to an example (Figure 13.4) based on consumers' demand for air travel and airlines' demands for new aircraft. In this simplified example, an airline operates a fleet of 100 aircraft and, during periods of stable passenger demand, buys ten new aircraft each year and retires ten older aircraft, retaining a stable fleet size of 100 aircraft. Then, some extraneous factor (e.g. a decline in the world economy) may cause the airline's passenger demand to fall by 3 per cent per annum. The airline responds to this by reducing its capacity by 3 per cent to 97 aircraft (we will assume, perhaps unrealistically, that it can reschedule its aircraft so that it is able to accommodate all its remaining passengers). The easiest way to achieve this is by reducing its annual order for aircraft from ten to seven. If it continued to retire its ten oldest aircraft, this would have the effect of reducing its fleet size to 97, in line with the new level of customer demand. What is of importance here is that while consumer demand has gone down by just 3 per cent, the demand facing the aircraft manufacturer has gone down by 30 per cent (from ten aircraft a year to seven). If passenger demand settles down at its new level, the airline will have no need to cut its fleet any further, so will revert to buying ten new aircraft a year and selling ten old ones. If passenger demand

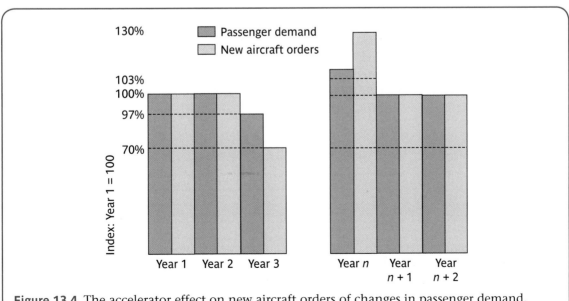

Figure 13.4 The accelerator effect on new aircraft orders of changes in passenger demand.

picks up once more, the airline may seek to increase its capacity by ordering not ten aircraft but, say, 13.

13.3.3 Inflation

It should be apparent that multiplier effects are associated with injections to the circular flow of income, causing more money to chase a fixed volume of goods and services available for consumption. This leads to the classic case of demand-pull **inflation**, when excessive demand for goods and services relative to their supply results in an increase in their market price level. Demand-pull inflation can result from an increase in the availability of credit, excessive spending by government, and tax cuts that increase consumers' disposable incomes, so allowing them to buy more goods and services.

An alternative cause of inflation is referred to as cost-push inflation. On the supply side, increases in production costs (such as higher wage costs, rising raw material costs, higher overheads and additional costs of health and safety legislation) may push up the price at which companies are prepared to supply their goods to the market, unless they are offset by increases in productivity.

An inflationary spiral can be created where higher wages in an economy result in greater spending power, leading to demand-pull inflation. The resulting higher cost of consumer goods leads workers to seek wage increases to keep them ahead of inflation, but these increases in wage costs add a further twist to cost-push inflation, and so on. Because markets are seldom perfectly competitive and therefore unable to correct for inflation, governments are keen to intervene to prevent inflationary processes building up in an economy (see below). The opposite of inflation – deflation – can occur where money is taken out of the circular flow, and a cycle can be created of falling prices for goods and services leading to lower income for households, resulting in turn to lower demand for goods and services, which causes their price to fall further.

13.3.4 Complex models of the economy

The simple **model** of the economy presented above is based on many assumptions, which need to be better understood if model making is to make a useful contribution to policy making. It is important for governments to have a reasonably accurate model of how the economy works so that predictions can be made about the effects of government policy. A model should be able to answer such questions as the following.

- What will happen to unemployment if government capital expenditure is increased by 10 per cent?
- What will happen to inflation if income tax is cut by 2p in the pound?
- What will be the net effect on government revenue if it grants tax concessions to firms investing in new capital equipment?

Companies supplying goods and services also take a keen interest in models of the economy, typically seeking to answer questions such as the following.

- What effect will a cut in income tax have on demand for new car purchases by private consumers?
- How will company buyers of office equipment respond to reductions in taxation on company profits?
- Will the annual budget create a feeling of confidence on the part of consumers, which is sufficiently strong for them to make major household purchases?

Developing a model of the economy is very different from developing a model in the natural sciences. In the latter case, it is often possible to develop closed models where all factors that can affect a system of interrelated elements are identifiable and can be measured. Predicting behaviour for any component of the model is therefore possible, based on knowledge about all other components. In the case of economic models, the system of interrelated components is open rather than closed. This means that not only is it difficult to measure components, but it can also be difficult to identify what elements to include as being of significance to a national economy. For example, few models accurately predicted that a sudden rise in oil prices by OPEC producers would have a major effect on national economies throughout the world. Furthermore, it is very difficult to develop relationships between variables that remain constant through time. Whereas the relationship between molecules in a chemistry model may be universally true, given a set of environmental conditions, such universal truths are seldom found in economic modelling. This has a lot to do with the importance of the attitudes of firms and consumers, which change through time for reasons that may not become clear until after the event. For example, a 2 per cent cut in income tax may have achieved significant increases in consumer expenditure on one occasion, but resulted in higher levels of savings or debt repayment on another. The first time round, factors as ephemeral as good weather and national success in an international football championship could have created a 'feel good' factor that was absent the next time round.

13.4 The business cycle

From the discussion in the previous sections, it should become quite apparent that national economies are seldom in a stable state. The situation where injections exactly equate with withdrawals can be described as a special case, with the normal state of affairs being for one of these to exceed the other. An excess of injections will result in economic activity increasing, while the opposite will happen if withdrawals exceed injections. This leads to the concept of the **business cycle**, which describes the fluctuating level of activity in an economy. Most developed economies go through cycles that have been described as:

- recession–prosperity
- expansion–contraction
- stop–go, and
- 'boom and bust'.

Business cycles vary in their length, and also in the difference between the top of the cycle and the bottom. Sometimes a fall in economic activity may be hardly noticed and rapidly self-correcting. At other times, such as the Great Depression of the 1930s, the depression can be long and deep. The descent into a recessionary phase can be quite rapid, as occurred in many western countries in 2008. Figure 13.5 shows the pattern of the business cycle for the UK, as measured by fluctuations in the most commonly used indicator of economic activity – gross domestic product (described below). Of course, it is relatively easy to draw such a graph with hindsight, but much more difficult to predict which way the graph is going to move next. In 2008, many economists were predicting a very long recession, but within two years, many indices of economic prosperity had already begun to improve.

13.4.1 Measuring economic activity

Gross domestic product (GDP) is just one indicator of the business cycle. In fact, there are many indicators of economic activity that may move at slightly different times to each other. Some 'leading' indicators may be used as early warning signs of an approaching economic recession or boom, with other indicators – if not corrected by government intervention – following a similar trend in due course. Some of the more commonly used indicators of the business cycle are described below.

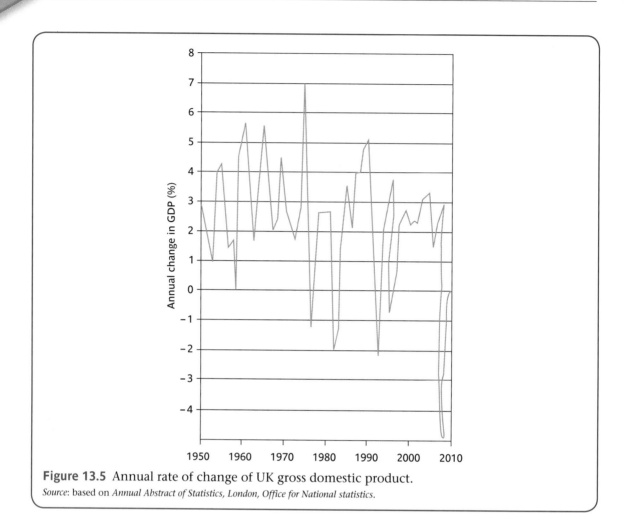

Figure 13.5 Annual rate of change of UK gross domestic product.
Source: based on *Annual Abstract of Statistics, London, Office for National statistics.*

Gross domestic product

This index measures the total value of goods and services produced within the economy, and can be used to compare economic performance over time and to compare performance between countries (see Figure 13.6). In a typical year, the economies of western European countries may expand by 2–3 per cent per annum, although this has reached 4–5 per cent in boom years, while GDP has fallen during recessionary periods. Much more rapid growth in GDP has been seen in emerging economies, such as China, where annual growth in GDP in the early years of the twenty-first century was averaging about 9 per cent a year. One derivative of the crude GDP figure is a figure for GDP per capita. Therefore, if GDP is going up by 2 per cent a year and the population is constant, it means that, on average, everybody is 2 per cent better off. Whether this is true in reality, of course, depends not only on how the additional income is distributed but also on an individual's definition of being better off (GDP takes no account of 'quality of life'). Since GDP depends on both prices and quantities, an increase in prices will also increase GDP (this is also referred to as nominal GDP). This is not a particularly good measure of economic well-being, so a GDP deflator removes the effects of price changes by calculating real GDP, expressed using a constant set of prices.

Unemployment rates

Because of the profound social and economic implications of high levels of **unemployment**, governments normally monitor changes in unemployment levels closely. Unemployment

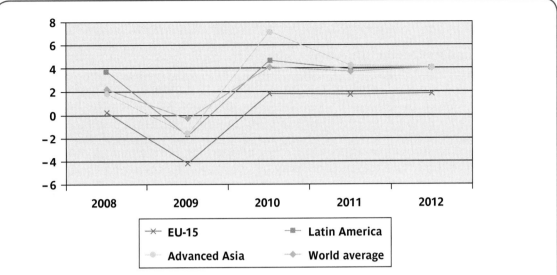

Figure 13.6 A comparison of GDP percentage annual growth rates for selected regions 2008–2012.

Source: IMF World Economic Outlook Database, October 2010; Eurostat; World Bank staff calculations.

Note: Advanced Asia refers to Korea, Hong Kong, Taiwan, and Singapore. Latin America refers to Latin America and the Caribbean. Figures for 2010, 2011 and 2012 are estimates made in 2009.

tends to rise as the economy enters a general economic recession and falls as it enters a period of recovery, although it typically lags behind changes in GDP. Unemployment occurs where firms are unable to sell their output and seek to scale back their workforce, either by laying off existing workers or not recruiting new ones. This results in less spending by the growing number of unemployed people, thereby exacerbating firms' sales difficulties. Actually measuring trends in unemployment over time can be difficult, as definitions used by governments frequently change. Cynics would say that this is done to hide the true level of unemployment – for example, by excluding people that are on job-training schemes.

Output levels

The output of firms is an important indicator of the business cycle, and is closely watched because of its effects on employment, and the multiplier effects of firms producing less and therefore spending less with their suppliers. In the UK, the government's Business Monitor publishes regular indicators of outputs for different sectors. Another widely quoted source of data on output is the Confederation of British Industry (CBI), which publishes monthly and quarterly surveys on industry's output, investment and stock levels. This provides a good indication of changes in different sectors of the economy, and possible future business trends. In addition to these widely used and formalized methods of measuring output, a number of ad hoc approaches have been used, which it is claimed give early indicators of an economic recovery or downturn. Examples include the following.

- Sales of first-class tickets by train operating companies, where a fall in sales is often an early indication of firms cutting back expenditure ahead of major cuts in output.
- The number of commercial vehicles crossing the Severn Bridge between England and Wales has been correlated with the output of the manufacturing sector in general.
- Rising sales of Ford Transit vans have been associated with a revival in fortunes by the small business sector, and rising sales of heavy trucks with growing confidence by firms to invest in capital equipment.

Stocks

During periods of boom, companies may be able to sell very quickly everything that they produce – indeed, waiting lists for some sought-after goods may by common. When the economy goes into recession, firms may continue their previous levels of production, and may not reduce output until they can be reasonably confident that the fall in demand for their products is not just a transient blip, but indicative of a more general slowdown in the economy. An example of this was seen with Scania trucks, which during the boom years of the 1990s and early 2000s had a waiting list of buyers. However, when recession set in from 2008, buyers reduced their orders and the company was left with stocks of unsold trucks.

The existence of stocks can affect the timing and extent of recovery in output. Even if demand from consumers increases, there may be no immediate increase in output by firms that may initially meet customer demands from stocks and increase their output level only when stocks decline to a normal level.

Average earnings

Unemployment figures record the extreme case of workers that have no employment. However, underemployment can affect the national economy just as significantly as unemployment, as workers are put on short-time working or lose opportunities for overtime working. Conversely, average earnings may rise significantly during the early years of a boom as firms increase overtime working and bid up wage rates in an attempt to take on staff with key skills. As the economies of many developed economies went into recession from 2008, there is a suggestion that many employers and trades unions agreed to reduce working hours, and hence the earnings of workers, rather than reduce the total workforce. One advantage of this approach is that companies could rapidly expand when demand improved, rather than having to wait to recruit new staff.

Disposable income

Average **disposable income** refers to the income that individuals have available to spend after taxation. It follows that, as taxes rise, disposable income falls. A further indicator of household wealth is discretionary income, which is a measure of disposable income less expenditure on the necessities of life, such as mortgage payments. Discretionary income can be significantly affected by sudden changes in the cost of mortgages and other items of expenditure, such as travel costs, which form a large component of household budgets.

Consumer spending

Trends in consumer spending may diverge from trends in discretionary income on account of changes in consumers' propensity to borrow or save. When consumer spending runs ahead of discretionary income, this can be explained by an increase in borrowing. Conversely, spending may fall faster than discretionary income, indicating that consumers are repaying debts and/or not borrowing additional money. There are numerous indicators of consumer spending, including the government's Family Expenditure Survey. More up-to-date information is supplied by the Credit Card Research Group (CCRG), an organization representing the main UK credit card issuers. After making a number of assumptions about changing card-using habits, CCRG is able to monitor changes in the volume of consumer spending using credit cards. It is also able to monitor consumer borrowing using credit cards and net repayments of credit card debts.

Savings ratio

The **savings ratio** refers to the proportion of individuals' income that is saved rather than spent. Saving/borrowing levels are influenced by a number of factors, including the distribution of income in society (poorer people tend to save less, therefore any redistribution of income to this group would have the effect of reducing net savings) and consumers' level of confidence about the future (see below). During periods of high consumer confidence, savings ratios tend to fall as consumer borrowing rises. During the period 1970–2008, the average household savings ratio was 7.6 per cent. It had fallen steadily during the boom years of the 2000s and reached 2.0 per cent in 2008, before rising again as the economy went into recession and households became reluctant to take on new debt and repaid old debt. Businesses look to a fall in savings ratios as an early indicator of increasing consumer confidence.

Confidence levels

Private individuals and businesses may have a high level of income and savings, but there is no guarantee that they will spend that money or take on new debt in making purchases of expensive items. They may only be happy about making major spending decisions if they feel confident about the future. Higher **confidence levels** may result, for example, from consumers feeling that they are not likely to be made unemployed, that their pay is going to keep up with inflation and that the value of their assets is not going to fall. A number of confidence indices are now published – for example, by Chambers of Commerce and the CBI, covering both private consumers and businesses. The organization GfK publishes a monthly Consumer Confidence Barometer for the European Commission.

Inflation rate

Inflation refers to the rate at which prices of goods and services in an economy are rising. It is not easy to measure inflation , as the effect of rising prices affects different groups of people in different ways. In the UK, there are two commonly used measures of inflation: the Consumer Prices Index (CPI) and the **Retail Prices Index (RPI)**. The CPI is derived from a European measure of inflation. Like the RPI, it is based on information collected about the prices of goods and services consumed by an average household. These are commonly used 'headline' rates of inflation, which are frequently used by employees as a basis for wage negotiations and by the UK government for adjusting the value of a number of social security benefits.

A problem with general indices such as the CPI and RPI is that they may be too general to be of relevance to the spending patterns of specific groups of individuals. An average figure may mask differences in component elements, resulting in different groups of consumers experiencing quite different levels of inflation. For example, during a period of rising property prices, rising property rental fees and falling interest rates, the inflation rate of home owners may be quite different to that experienced by those who rent their property. To provide more detail about what is happening to inflation, there are numerous alternative indices covering specific sectors. Many building societies, for example, produce indices of house price inflation, while specialized indices are available for new car purchases and construction costs, among others. The government publishes a monthly producer prices index, which measures changes in the prices of goods bought by manufacturing firms. A rise in this indicator can signal later increases in the CPI when the components are incorporated into finished goods bought by households.

A 'normal' level of inflation is often considered to lie in the range of 1–3 per cent per annum. Where prices are falling, the opposite case of **deflation** occurs, which can have economic consequences just as serious as very high inflation. For several years from the mid-1990s, the Japanese economy experienced deflation, resulting in a reluctance of people to invest. Why invest today in an asset that will be cheaper in a year's time? Such attitudes can lead to a self-fulfilling prophecy. During the early years of recession from 2008, deflation occurred briefly in a number of west European countries.

Interest rates

Interest rates represent the price that borrowers have to pay to a lender for the privilege of using their money for a specified period of time. Interest rates tend to follow a cyclical pattern, which is partly a reflection of the level of activity in the economy. During periods of recession, the supply of funds typically exceeds demand for them (caused, for example, by consumers being reluctant to spend, thereby building up their savings, and by the unwillingness of consumers and firms to borrow to pay for major expenditure items). In these circumstances, interest rates have a tendency to fall. During a period of economic prosperity, the opposite holds true, and interest rates have a tendency to rise. Rates are also influenced by government intervention, as governments have frequently used them as a tool of economic management. In general, low interest rates are seen as desirable because they reduce the cost of firms' borrowings and increase consumers' level of discretionary income, especially through lower mortgage costs. However, during periods of unhealthily excessive demand in the economy, governments use high interest rates to try to dampen down demand from firms and consumers.

Overseas trade figures

The monthly overseas trade figures indicate the difference between a country's imports and exports. A lot of attention is given to the 'current account', which measures overseas transactions in goods and services but not capital (discussed further in Chapter 14). In general, a current account surplus is considered good for an economy, suggesting that an economy's production sector is internationally competitive. A detailed analysis of overseas trade figures indicates trends that can often be related to the business cycle and can be used to predict future levels of activity in the economy. At the height of a boom cycle, imports of manufactured goods may rise much faster than corresponding exports, possibly suggesting unsustainable levels of household consumption. Rising imports of capital equipment may give an indication that firms are ready to invest in additional domestic productive capacity following the end of a period of recession.

Exchange rates

The **exchange rate** is the price of one currency in terms of another (e.g. an exchange rate of £1 = $1.55 means that £1 costs $1.55). A number of factors influence the level of a country's exchange rate, but as an economic indicator the rate is often seen as an indication of the willingness of overseas traders and investors to hold that country's currency. Falling rates of exchange against other currencies may be interpreted as overseas investors losing their confidence in an economy or its government, leading them to sell their currency holdings and thereby depressing its price. The theory of exchange rate determination and the implications for business are discussed in more detail in Chapter 14.

Government borrowing

During periods of economic prosperity, government income streams from taxation tend to be buoyant, while many of its costs in respect of social welfare payment may be reduced, on account of lower levels of unemployment. The reverse tends to be true during periods of economic recession. In this sense, government **borrowing** is not so much an indicator of the business cycle, but rather a consequence of it. In the UK, national debt as a percentage of GDP fell steadily from 40 per cent in 1997 to 29 per cent by 2002, helped by buoyant tax receipts during a period of economic prosperity, which allowed the government to pay off debt. It then rose to 37 per cent in 2007, reflecting the government's decision to increase expenditure on health and education. Then, national debt as a percentage of GDP increased from 30 per cent in 2002 to 37 per cent in 2007. After 2008, government debt increased to a historic high of 64 per cent of GDP. This sharp increase was brought about by a combination of normal increases in expenditure associated with the onset of recession (higher spending on unemployment and welfare benefits, lower taxation revenue, etc.), but, exceptionally in this case, by government borrowing to rescue private-sector banks (Northern Rock, Lloyds TSB and Royal Bank of Scotland).

13.4.2 Tracking the business cycle

It is easy to plot business cycles with hindsight. However, businesses are much more interested in predicting the cyclical pattern in the immediate and medium-term future. If the economy is

sector and workers' skills are quite specific to that sector, the effects of structural employment can be quite severe, as can be seen in the former shipbuilding areas of Tyneside or coal-mining areas of South Wales. Governments have tackled structural employment with economic assistance to provide retraining for unemployed workers and to attract new employers to areas of high unemployment.

2 Cyclical unemployment is associated with the business cycle and is caused by a general fall in demand, which may itself be a consequence of lower spending levels by firms. Some business sectors, such as building and construction, are particularly prone to cyclical patterns of demand, and hence cyclical unemployment. The long-term cure for cyclical employment is a pick-up in demand in the economy, which governments can influence through their macroeconomic policy.

3 Technological unemployment occurs where jobs are replaced by machines; it has had widespread implications in many industrial sectors, such as car manufacture, banking and agriculture. Governments have to accept this cause of unemployment, as failure to modernize will inevitably result in an industry losing out to more efficient competition. For this reason, attempts to subsidize jobs in declining low-technology industries are normally doomed as overseas competitors gain market share, and eventually lead to job losses that are greater than they would have been had technology issues been addressed earlier. Where a low-technology sector is supported by import controls, consumers will be forced to pay higher prices than would otherwise be necessary. Where the goods or services in question are necessities of life, consumers' discretionary income will effectively fall, leading to lower demand for goods and services elsewhere in the economy. Although technological unemployment may be very painful to the individuals directly involved, the increasing use of technology usually has the effect of making necessities cheaper, thereby allowing consumers to demand new goods and services. One manifestation of this has been the growth in services jobs, as consumers switch part of their expenditure away from food and clothing (which have fallen in price in real terms) towards eating out and other leisure pursuits.

Stable prices

Rapidly rising or falling prices can be economically, socially and politically damaging to governments.

Rapidly rising prices (inflation) can cause the following problems.

- For businesses, it becomes difficult to plan ahead when selling prices and the cost of inputs in the future are not known. In many businesses, companies are expected to provide fixed prices for goods and services, which will be made and delivered in the future at unknown cost levels.

- Governments find budgeting difficult during periods of high inflation. Although many government revenues rise with inflation (e.g. value added tax), this may still leave an overall shortfall caused by higher costs of employing government workers and higher contract costs for new capital projects.

- Inflation can be socially divisive as those on fixed incomes (e.g. state pensioners) fall behind those individuals who are able to negotiate wage increases to compensate for inflation. Inflation also discriminates between individuals that own different types of assets. While some physical assets, such as housing, may keep up with inflation, financial assets may be eroded by inflation rates that exceed the rate of interest paid. In effect, borrowers may be subsidized by lenders.

- High levels of inflation can put exporters at a competitive disadvantage. If the inflation level of the UK is higher than that of competing nations, UK firms' goods will become more expensive to export, while the goods from a low-inflation country will be much more attractive to buyers in the UK, all other things being equal. This will have an adverse effect on UK producers and on the country's overseas balance of trade (assuming that there is no compensating change in exchange rates).

High levels of inflation can create uncertainty in the business environment, making firms reluctant to enter into long-term commitments. Failure to invest or reinvest can ultimately be damaging for the individual firm as well as the economy as a whole.

This is not to say that completely stable prices (i.e. a zero rate of inflation) are necessarily good for a national economy. A moderate level of price inflation encourages individuals and firms to invest in stocks, knowing that their assets will increase in value. A moderate level of inflation also facilitates the task of realigning prices by firms. A price reduction can be achieved simply by holding prices constant during a period of price inflation. Where price inflation causes uncertainty for firms purchasing raw materials, this uncertainty can often be overcome by purchasing on the 'futures' market. Such markets exist for a diverse range of commodities, such as oil, grain and metals, and allow a company to pay a fixed price for goods delivered at a specified time in the future, irrespective of whether the market price for that commodity has risen or fallen in the meantime.

The opposite of inflation is deflation, and this too can result in social, economic and political problems.

- Individuals and firms that own assets whose value is depreciating perceive that they have become poorer and adjust their spending patterns accordingly. In Britain during 2008/2009, many individuals saw their most important asset – their house – falling in value as part of a general fall in property prices. In extreme cases, individuals felt 'locked in' to their house as they had borrowed more to buy it than the house was currently worth. They therefore had difficulty trading up to a larger house, thereby possibly also creating demand for home-related items such as fitted kitchens. More generally, falling property prices undermined consumer confidence, in sharp contrast to the early 2000s when rising house prices created a 'feel good' factor, fuelling spending across a range of business sectors.

- Individuals and firms will be reluctant to invest in major items of capital expenditure if they feel that, by waiting a little longer, they could obtain those assets at a lower price.

- Deflation can become just as socially divisive as inflation. Falling house prices can lead many people who followed government and social pressures to buy their house rather than rent to feel that they have lost out for their efforts.

Economic growth

Growth is a goal shared by businesses and governments alike. It was suggested in Chapter 9 that businesses like to grow, for various reasons. Similarly, governments generally pursue growth in GDP for many reasons.

- A growing economy allows for steadily rising standards of living, when measured by conventional economic indicators. In most western economies, this is indicated by increased spending on goods and services that are considered luxuries. Without underlying growth in GDP, increases in consumer spending will be short-lived.

- For governments, growth results in higher levels of income through taxes on incomes, sales and profits. This income allows government to pursue socially and politically desirable infrastructure spending, such as the construction of new hospitals or road improvements.

- A growing economy creates a 'feel good' factor in which individuals feel confident about being able to obtain employment and subsequently feel confident about making major purchases.

Economic growth in itself may not necessarily leave a society feeling better off, as economic well-being does not necessarily correspond to quality of life. There is growing debate about whether some of the consequences of economic growth, such as increased levels of pollution and traffic congestion, really leave individuals feeling better off. There is also the issue of how the results of economic growth are shared out between members of a society.

 Thinking around the subject

Gross domestic product or gross national happiness?

A fairly universal indicator of how 'well' a country is doing is based on its index of gross gomestic product (GDP). There can be many adjustments to this figure – for example, by expressing it as GDP per capita or adjusting it for inflation. But, in recent years, there has been more fundamental questioning about whether the pursuit of higher levels of wealth expressed as GDP actually results in greater happiness for the citizens of a country. Even the newly elected UK Prime Minister, David Cameron, suggested that it was time the country concentrated not just on GDP but on GWB (general well-being).

The 'economics of happiness' has emerged as a new area of economics to challenge some of our assumptions about the performance of national economies. Naturally enough, when you get a group of economists together, you are likely to get as many views on the subject as there are economists. There is just as much debate about how you actually measure happiness, with suggestions for items to include in a National Happiness Index ranging from life expectancy to number and severity of mental illnesses and self-reported measures of happiness.

One question that is frequently asked is whether having more money makes people happier. One study reported in 2010 suggested that people's satisfaction with life generally increased as their income increased, but their day-to-day emotional well-being only rose with earnings up to an annual income of $75,000; beyond that level there was less effect (Holmes 2010).

One of the paradoxes of western developed economies is that, despite increased prosperity, people appear to be more stressed and increasingly unhappy. Despite better healthcare, rising incomes and labour-saving devices, surveys repeatedly show that people are no happier than they were in the 1950s. This seems far from the economist John Maynard Keynes' prediction in the 1930s that once the 'economic problem' of satisfying basic material needs was achieved, people would not have to work so hard and would devote their spare time to trying to live well.

People appear to be inconsistent in their statements about what would make them happy. They may say that a shorter travelling time to work would make them happy, yet more and more people travel longer distances to their place of employment in order to work harder to earn more money for more goods that, in the end, do not make them feel any better.

One explanation for this apparent paradox is that people compare themselves to others. If everyone is getting richer, people do not get happier – they do so only if they get richer relative to their peers. A BMW 3 series car can be a status symbol only if few people can afford it. When incomes rise and more people can afford the luxury brand, individuals become motivated to work harder to afford an even better model. This mechanism is a driving force behind economic growth, but it has the effect of constantly undermining the underlying benefit of economic progress.

Politicians tend to focus on economic growth figures, but should they instead be concentrating more on indices of happiness? Indices of depression and mental illness have been rising sharply in most western countries in the past couple of decades, and seem to be closely correlated with economic growth, and it has been argued that investment in therapy can yield more happiness than conventional economic investments (Boyce and Wood 2010) . According to Lord Layard, author of a book on happiness, one in six people in the UK is thought to suffer from some form of mental illness. He has argued that a course of cognitive behavioural therapy (CBT) can alleviate depression in 60 per cent of cases and typically costs about £1000. Is £1000 spent on relieving someone's depression, so they benefit in terms of happiness, a better investment by the government than £1000 spent increasing the competitiveness and efficiency of manufacturing industry?

Distribution of wealth

Left to market forces, it is likely that inequalities in wealth will be exacerbated as the wealthy use their dominant position to gather even more wealth, while the poor become relatively powerless and even poorer. This seems to have been true historically, and even today, countries with newly marketized economies, such as those of eastern Europe, appear to become more divided between a small very wealthy group and the large mass of people who own very few assets. In the past, inequalities of wealth and power have resulted in revolution, when the masses have risen in revolt against the few who have the dominant wealth and power. It could be argued that, in order to avoid tensions within society, governments – overtly and covertly – have objectives relating to the distribution of economic wealth between different groups in society. In the UK, the trend since the Second World War has been for a gradual convergence in the prosperity of all groups, as the very rich have been hit by high levels of income, capital gains and inheritance tax, while the poorer groups in society have benefited from increasing levels of social security payments. During periods of Labour administrations, the tendency has been for taxes on the rich to increase, tilting the distribution of wealth in favour of poorer groups. However, the period of the Conservative governments in the 1980s saw this process put into reverse as high-income groups benefited from the abolition of higher rates of income tax and the liberalization of inheritance taxes. At the same time, many social security benefits were withdrawn or reduced in scope or amount, leaving many lower- or middle-income groups worse off. Actually measuring distribution of wealth has been difficult with a variety of possible indicators. There has been argument about whether the post-1997 Labour government in the UK actually managed to redistribute wealth from the rich to the poor, and many indicators suggested that the reverse had actually happened.

The effects of government policy objectives on the distribution of income can have profound implications for an organization's marketing activities. During most of the post-war years, the tendency was for mid-market segments to grow significantly. In the car sector, this was associated with the success of mid-range cars such as the Ford Focus and Mondeo. During periods of Labour administration, the sale of luxury cars had tended to suffer. The boom of the late 1980s and early 2000s saw the rapid rise in income of the top groups in society, resulting in a significant growth in luxury car sales. Manufacturers such as BMW, Mercedes-Benz and Jaguar benefited from this trend.

Improving productivity

Productivity growth, alongside high and stable levels of employment, is central to long-term economic performance and rising living standards. Increasing the productivity of the economy has become a key objective of successive UK governments. Government approaches to improving long-term productivity have followed two broad strands: maintaining macroeconomic stability to enable firms and individuals to plan for the future, and implementing microeconomic reforms to remove the barriers that prevent markets from functioning efficiently. These microeconomic reforms address historic weaknesses in competitiveness, investment, research and development, innovation and entrepreneurship.

Stable exchange rate

A stable value of sterling in terms of other major currencies is useful to businesses that are thereby able to predict accurately the future cost of raw materials bought overseas and the sterling value they will receive for goods and services sold overseas. Stable exchange rates can also help consumers – for example, in budgeting for overseas holidays. It is, however, debatable just what the 'right' exchange rate is that governments should seek to maintain (this is discussed further in Chapter 14).

An important contributor to maintaining a stable exchange rate is the maintenance of the balance of payments. Governments avoid large trade deficits, which can have the effect of

a car over ten years old would receive a grant of £2000 towards a new one – half paid directly by the government and the other half by the industry. For government, the scheme was seen as a way of reviving economic activity in car dealers, manufacturers and component suppliers, and at the same time helping to get older, fuel-inefficient cars off the road and replaced with more efficient, environmentally friendly ones.

The scrappage scheme appeared to be a success with buyers, with over 400,000 old cars being traded in for new ones during 2009, bringing much needed activity back into car dealers' showrooms. Sales of small, fuel-efficient models were particularly popular with buyers. However, critics argued about just how successful the car scrappage scheme had been for the national economy, and even for the environment. It was pointed out that a high proportion of new cars purchased would have been manufactured in the Far East, bringing little benefit to the British economy. International trade rules prevented the government restricting grants to vehicles made in Britain or the EU. Environmentalists also challenged the green credentials of the scheme, pointing out that somebody could trade in a ten-year-old Ford Fiesta and buy a new gas-guzzling 4 × 4 vehicle.

The car scrappage scheme certainly helped to stimulate some aspects of the car industry that were facing a sharp decline in revenue and, in stimulating new car sales, generated some multiplier benefits through dealer networks and parts suppliers. However, critics pointed to the blunt nature of fiscal instruments such as the car scrappage scheme. Surely it had not been the intention of governments to encourage some buyers to purchase foreign-built 4 × 4 vehicles? Would many buyers of cars have purchased a new one anyway, therefore was the scrappage grant an unnecessary incentive and a waste of government money? And what was the cost of the paperwork associated with handling hundreds of thousands of claims? To the critics, this demonstrated the limitations of fiscal policy, compared to the simplicity of monetarist approaches to getting the economy going again.

Monetary policy

An alternative approach to managing the economy is through monetarist policies. Advocates of monetarism, including Adam Smith, Milton Friedman, Robert Lucas and Paul Samuelson, see money supply as the vital tool for managing the economy. The basic proposition of **monetarism** is that government need only regulate the supply of money in order to influence the circular flow of income. From this, adjustments in the economy happen automatically by market forces without the need for intervention by government in the running of business organizations. If government wishes to suppress demand in the economy, it would do this by restricting the volume of money in circulation in the economy. It could achieve this by raising interest rates, or by restricting the availability of credit. If it wished to stimulate the economy, in other words speed up the circular flow of income, it would increase the volume of money in circulation. Following the financial crisis of 2008, many governments adopted the monetarist strategy described as '**quantitative easing**', but to some people it sounded more like 'printing money'. By this method, the central bank creates new money, which it uses to buy financial assets, including government bonds, mortgage-backed securities and corporate bonds, from banks and other financial institutions. The purchases give banks the excess reserves required for them to increase their lending capacity, and ultimately this leads to stimulation of the economy.

Monetarism appeals to free market purists because of the limited government hands-on intervention that is required. However, governments have found it politically unacceptable to pursue monetarist policies to their logical conclusion. For example, during a period of boom, suppressing demand by controlling the availability of money alone could result in unacceptably high levels of interest rates.

13.5.3 Limitations of government intervention in the national economy

At a practical level, critics of both monetarist and fiscal approaches to economic management have pointed to their failure to significantly influence the long-term performance of an economy. More recently, the fundamental concept of government intervention has been challenged in an emerging body of theoretical and empirical research, which is commonly referred to as rational expectations theory. Proponents of the theory claim that it is too simplistic to regard government economic intervention in terms of simple stimulus–response models. It is naive, for example, to assume that private companies will take an increase in government capital spending as a cue to increase their own productive capacity. Instead, firms rationally assess the likely consequences of government intervention. Therefore, an increase in government capital expenditure may lead to an expectation of eventually higher interest rates and inflation. Faced with this rational expectation, firms may decide to cut back their own expenditure, fearing the consequences for their own business of high inflation and interest rates. This is the opposite of the government's intended response. The theory of rational expectations holds that business people have become astute at interpreting economic signals and, because of this, government's ability to manage the national economy is significantly reduced.

13.5.4 The central bank

A nation's **central bank** plays an important role in the management of the national economy. In the UK, the Bank of England has responsibility for regulating the volume of currency in circulation within the economy. It was noted above that, following the credit crunch of 2008, the central banks in many countries intervened through a process of quantitative easing to create additional liquidity in national economies. The central bank has a duty to protect the stability of the banking sector. In 2007, the Bank of England was faced with the prospect of a major bank – Northern Rock – having to close down because it could not obtain ongoing credit to fund mortgages that it had lent to its domestic customers. This would have seriously affected the stability of the banking sector, and the reputation of the City of London as a financial centre, so the Bank of England intervened with emergency loans to the UK banking sector, effectively taking many of the banks into state control. When further banks failed, the Bank of England, along with the US Federal Reserve Bank and the European Central Bank, injected additional capital into the banking system in an attempt to lessen the effects of a credit shortage.

The central bank also has a role in maintaining the value of the nation's currency, which can be done by open-market operations – for example, selling the country's currency to keep its exchange rate low. Issues of exchange rate determination are discussed further in Chapter 14.

Countries differ in the extent to which the powers of the central bank are separated from those of government. In the USA, for example, granting the central bank quasi-autonomous status and allowing it freedom to make decisions on monetary policy has for a long time been regarded as a means of guaranteeing prudent management of the money supply against political intervention for possibly short-term opportunistic objectives. Against this, the argument is put forward that central banks should be politically accountable, and should be influenced by the social and political implications of their actions and not just the more narrowly defined monetary ones. In the UK, the Bank of England has traditionally been influenced by the Treasury, and seen to be effectively a branch of government decision making. However, the incoming Labour government in 1997 decided to give autonomy to much of the Bank's activity through a newly formed **Monetary Policy Committee (MPC)**, made up of a panel of eight economics experts plus the Governor of the Bank of England, who acts as Chair. The MPC is free to set interest rates at a level that it considers prudent and in the best interests of the country. Opinion remains divided on the relative merits of a politically influenced central bank and one that is above sectional political interests. While there is evidence that the MPC has acted with integrity, business leaders have sometimes accused it of being dominated by academics and financiers, who are unable to empathize with the problems faced by businesses. Employers' pressure groups, such as the CBI, feel less able to put pressure on the MPC than they previously could on Treasury ministers.

Throughout the EU, the development of a single currency has placed much greater control over monetary policy in the hands of the European Central Bank (ECB). The power of individual member states to determine their own interest rates and monetary policy is handed over to the ECB, which also handles member-states' currency reserves. The subject of the single European currency is discussed further in Chapter 14.

13.6 The international macroeconomic environment

So far, we have looked at the macroeconomic environment largely within the confines of a single national economic system. In reality, the economies of individual countries are becoming ever more closely linked with one another as goods, money and people pass between them. To understand the bases for these flows, we need to look at the underlying factors that cause them, leading some countries, such as China, to export more goods than it buys from foreign countries, leaving it with a cash surplus that it then invests in other countries. On the other hand, some countries, such as the USA, buy more goods from foreign countries than they export, and need to borrow money from foreign countries. The model of the circular flow of income that we looked at earlier in this chapter can be applied to flows between countries, so if country A reduces its purchases from country B, householders and firms in country B will have less income to buy goods from other countries, including imports from country A, whose producers pay less in wages to their employees, who in turn cut back their purchase of goods from country B.

During periods of worldwide recession, the slowdown in the flow of trade and money between countries can have serious consequences, in just the same way as a slowdown in the domestic circular flow of income can ultimately lead, through a vicious circle, to everybody being worse off. If one country's government sees the income of its firms fall, it may be tempted to keep more of its household incomes within the national economy by restricting imports from foreign companies. This can lead to retaliatory action by other countries, and the net result of this is that the flow of trade around the world is reduced. In recognition of this, a number of international institutions exist to facilitate the flow of trade, capital and people between countries, including the World Trade Organization, the World Bank and the International Monetary Fund (IMF). To give an example of where international institutions may be needed, the IMF came to the rescue of Ireland in 2011, when the Irish government found itself unable to repay the loans it had built up during the previous decade. The IMF provided an emergency loan (commonly referred to as a 'bail-out'), which restored some confidence to the companies and governments that traded with Ireland, and also to households and firms within Ireland.

The global economic environment is complex and is considered in more detail in Chapter 14.

Case study:
How sustainable is the Chinese economic boom?

Photo: Shanghai Skyline © Nikada

During the 1990s and 2000s, China's rate of GDP growth had astonished the rest of the world. While a growth rate of between 2 and 4 per cent would be considered normal for most western countries, the average annual growth rate of GDP for China during the 1990s was about 9 per cent. It had reached a peak of nearly 13 per cent in March 2007, before slowing down to a low point of 6.2 per cent in March 2009. This would have still been a very credible performance by most western countries' standards. However, this slowdown seemed to be short-lived, because GDP growth started climbing again, reaching 12 per cent by March 2010. More worryingly, other indicators were suggesting that the boom may ultimately be unsustainable. Property investment in China in 2009 was 10 per cent of GDP, up from 8 per cent in 2007. Much of this seems to be speculative investment by investors who simply thought that property prices would go even higher, therefore creating a self-fulfilling prophecy of rising prices. One survey in 2010 estimated that over 64 million apartments were standing empty, owned by investors who simply wanted to make a capital gain on their investment in a rising market. This was potentially very worrying, and analogies were drawn with the Japanese property bubble, which

many blamed for the subsequent long period of recession in Japan.

China has managed to combine very tight centralized political control by the Communist Party with thriving capitalism in its Special Economic Development Zones. Would this centralized control by the Communist Party be strong enough to prevent a western-style boom -and-bust cycle? Or had the country gone down the route of economic liberalization, which laid it open to the type of economic cycle that the West had experienced repeatedly during the previous century?

China traditionally adopted the sort of approach to economic management favoured in the West in the 1950s and 1960s, when currencies were fixed to the dollar and credit controls were used to regulate unemployment and inflation. As a result, China has been less prone to economic or financial crises than those emerging countries where financial liberalization allowed hot money to flow in and out of the country quickly, precipitating a currency crisis that eventually impacts on the rest of the economy.

China has a very high level of savings by households, which are typically invested in government-owned banks. But these state-run banks lend mainly to state-run firms without being subject to market-based disciplines. As a result, there was an evident massive overinvestment in productive capacity, with little regard for return on capital. It seemed that the Chinese economy, where state planning co-exists with market forces, had difficulty in adjusting to change. In the case of privately owned companies, when demand begins to fall (for example, in response to a fall in demand from western countries), the companies cut their investment. However, in the case of state-controlled companies, political factors can dominate and investment is not necessarily cut back when demand falls.

China's growing trade surplus – $183 billion in 2010 – has made its tightly managed currency the target of persistent complaints from the USA and Europe. At the G20 summit meeting in Seoul in November 2010, many countries accused China of using an artificially low exchange rate as a trade weapon to gain unfair advantage in overseas markets. Although the renminbi was depegged from the US dollar in mid-2005, and rose in value

Chapter 14

The Global Business Environment

We cannot escape the globalized world business environment, even in our mundane daily activities. Consider a typical day in the life of Jessica, who lives in a small town in the English Midlands. She has just received her quarterly bill from her electricity supplier EDF Energy, part of the state-owned Électricité de France. There seems to be a problem with the payment from her bank account, which is held with Santander, based in Spain. She speaks to someone in a call centre somewhere in India, using her mobile phone connected to the O_2 network, now owned by the Spanish company Telefonica. She leaves the house and catches a bus operated by the French firm Veolia, then goes to London on a train whose operator is owned by German DB Railways. In the part of London that she is visiting she sees a street cleaner wearing the uniform of the French company, GDF Suez. She is visiting a hospital for a routine scan, and finds that this has been outsourced by the NHS to the South African-based company Netcare. After all that, she stops for a spot of lunch at a fancy Italian restaurant, Zizzi. Actually, it is owned and operated by a British company – Gondola Holdings – but the waiters and waitresses are mainly from eastern Europe. She then heads to Oxford Street to do some shopping, where she finds an array of foreign-owned retailers, and relaxes in an American-owned Starbucks coffee shop. In the space of just a few hours, Jessica is made aware that globalization isn't just about big business, affecting 'somebody else' – we encounter the globalized economy in almost everything we do.

 ## Learning Objectives

This chapter will explain:

☑ The underlying reasons for the globalization of business.

☑ The benefits to nations and individual firms from engaging in international trade.

☑ Trends in world trade.

☑ Barriers to international trade.

☑ The role of currency exchange rates.

☑ Methods of undertaking research in foreign markets sources of risk in foreign markets.

14.1   The trend towards a global business environment

In an increasingly globalized business environment, 'going global' is no longer an additional activity that companies may decide to become involved in. The reality for more and more companies is that they are already part of the globalized business environment. Even if they are not taking their products to overseas customers, they are quite likely to be facing competition from companies that are based abroad.

A number of factors have contributed to the globalization of the business environment.

- There has been a tendency for barriers to international trade to be removed, facilitated by the efforts of the **World Trade Organization**.
- A tendency towards cultural convergence has reduced the differences between national market characteristics, thereby reducing the cost of adapting products to specific national markets.
- Improved communications (e.g. the telephone, air travel and the internet) have reduced the cost of dealing with faraway places.
- The growth of large multinational corporations has facilitated the process of seeing the world as one global market.

Nevertheless, new challenges face companies doing business internationally. According to Naomi Klein, global service brands such as Shell, Wal-Mart and McDonald's have become metaphors for a global economic system gone awry, as evidenced by growing concern about the pay and conditions of Third World workers. She believes that brands and their multinational owners, rather than governments, will increasingly become the target for activists (Klein 2000). Some have also pointed to individuals' need for a distinctive identity in an increasingly global world, which may be manifested in purchasing products that are culturally specific (e.g. buying Qibla Cola instead of Coca-Cola in order to make a statement about Muslim values).

Success in international trade can help to explain the emergence and growth of many of the countries that have achieved economic pre-eminence in the world, during both modern and ancient history. The Venetians, Spaniards and later the British, Americans and Japanese all saw periods of rapid domestic growth coincide with the growth of their trade with the rest of the world. Today, many see the emerging 'BRICs' countries (Brazil, Russia, India and China) as key driving forces in the globalized business environment.

International trade is becoming increasingly important, representing not only opportunities for domestic producers to earn revenue from overseas but also threats to domestic producers from overseas competition. Taking the UK as an example, while the value of GDP increased by 49.8 per cent between 1998 and 2006, the value of exports increased by 59.4 per cent. The international trade of a nation is made up of the sum total of the efforts of its individual producers and consumers who decide to buy or sell abroad rather than at home. To gain a general overview of the reasons why trade between countries takes place, explanations can be found at two levels:

1 at a micro level, individual firms are motivated to trade overseas
2 at a macro level, the structure of an economy and the world trading system can either inhibit or encourage international trade.

We will consider first the micro reasons that lead firms to enter international trade, and then the aggregate macroenvironmental reasons why international trade takes place.

14.1.1 Firms' reasons for going global

For an individual company, exporting to overseas markets can be attractive for a number of reasons. These can be analysed in terms of 'pull' factors, which derive from the attractiveness of a potential overseas market, and 'push' factors, which make an organization's domestic market appear less attractive.

- For firms seeking growth, overseas markets represent new market segments, which they may be able to serve with their existing range of products. In this way, a company can stick to producing products that it is good at. Finding new overseas markets for existing or slightly modified products does not expose a company to the risks of expanding both its product range and its market coverage simultaneously.

- Saturation of its domestic market can force an organization to seek overseas markets. Saturation can come about where a product reaches the maturity stage of its life cycle in the domestic market, while being at a much earlier stage of the cycle in less developed overseas markets. While the market for fast-food restaurants may be approaching saturation in a number of western markets – especially the USA – it represents a new opportunity in the early stages of development in many eastern European countries.

- As part of its portfolio management, an organization may wish to reduce its dependence upon one geographical market. The attractiveness of individual national markets can change in a manner that is unrelated to other national markets. For example, costly competition can develop in one national market but not others, world economic cycles show lagged effects between different economies, and government policies – through specific regulation or general economic management – can have counterbalancing effects on market prospects.

- The nature of a firm's product may require an organization to become active in an overseas market. This particularly affects transport-related services such as scheduled airline services and courier services. For example, a UK airline flying between Manchester and Paris would most likely try to exploit the non-domestic market at the Paris end of its route.

- Commercial buyers of products operating in a number of overseas countries may require their suppliers to be able to cater for their needs across national boundaries. As an example, a multinational manufacturing company may wish to engage accountants that are able to provide auditing and management accounting services in its overseas subsidiaries. For this, the firm of accountants would probably need to have created an operational base overseas. Similarly, firms selling in a number of overseas markets may wish to engage an advertising agency that can organize a global campaign in a number of overseas markets.

- There are also many cases where private consumers demand goods and services that are available internationally. One example is the car hire business, where customers frequently need to be able to book a hire car in one country for collection and use in another. To succeed in attracting these customers, car hire companies need to operate internationally.

- Some goods and services are highly specialized and the domestic market is too small to allow economies of scale to be exploited. Overseas markets must be exploited in order to achieve a critical mass, which allows a competitive price to be reached. Specialized aircraft engineering services and oil exploration services fall into this category.

- Economies of scale also result from extending the use of brands in overseas markets. Expenditure by a fast-food company on promoting its brand to UK residents is wasted when those citizens travel abroad and cannot find the brand that they have come to value. Newly created overseas outlets will enjoy the benefit of promotion to overseas visitors at little additional cost.

In addition to gaining access to new markets, individual firms may enter international trade to secure resource inputs. The benefits of buying overseas can include lower prices, greater consistency of supply, higher quality or taking advantage of export subsidies available to overseas suppliers. Manufacturing has become a highly specialized business, and the traditional approach of companies attempting to make as much of their product locally in-house has long since gone. Today there is increasing separation of the assembly of products from the manufacture of components, which are likely to be outsourced to other subsidiaries within the same multinational company, or to other specialized businesses. With global communications and reliable logistics, outsourcing is a global activity that seeks out suppliers based on factors such as low cost, high skills or manufacturing capacity. In the case of raw materials that are not available in the domestic market, a firm may have little choice in its decision to buy from overseas.

14.1.2 Macroenvironmental reasons for globalization

From the perspective of national economies, a number of reasons can be identified for the increasing importance of international trade.

- Goods and services are traded between economies in order to exploit the concept of comparative cost advantage. This holds that an economy will export those goods and services that it is particularly well suited to producing and import those where another country has an advantage.

- The removal of many restrictions on international trade (such as the creation of the EU single market and the activities of the World Trade Organization) has allowed countries to exploit their comparative cost advantages. Nevertheless, restrictions on trade remain, especially for services.

- Increasing household disposable incomes result in greater consumption of many categories of luxuries, such as overseas travel, which can only be provided by overseas suppliers. Against this, economic development within an economy can result in many specialized goods and services that were previously bought in from overseas being provided by local suppliers. Many developing countries, for example, seek to reduce their dependence on overseas banking and insurance organizations by encouraging the development of a domestic banking sector.

14.1.3 Cultural convergence?

It has often been claimed that a major driver of international business is cultural convergence, implying that individuals are becoming more alike in the way that they think and behave. Improved communications and increasing levels of overseas travel have undoubtedly led to increasing homogenization of international market segments. Combined with the decline in trade barriers, convergence of cultural attitudes allows many organizations to regard parts of their overseas markets as though they are part of their domestic market. A 25-year-old upwardly mobile professional female living in Hamburg may have more in common with a 25-year-old upwardly mobile professional living in Manchester than with fellow Germans in general. Advocates of the concept of cultural convergence remind us that needs are universal and therefore there should be no reason why satisfaction of those needs should not also be universal. If a Big Mac satisfies a New Yorker's need for hygienic, fast and convenient food, why should it not satisfy those similar needs for someone in Cairo? Against this, many observers have noted individuals' growing need for *identity* in a world that is becoming increasingly homogenized. Support for regional breakaway governments (e.g. by the Kurdish and Basque peoples) may provide some evidence of this. During the build-up to the Iraq War in 2003, many consumers in Arab countries used purchases of Muslim products to identify themselves with an anti-American cause. Many western service brands have become despised by some groups as symbols of an alien identity. Banks in many Muslim countries have reported increased interest in syariah-based banking services, which do not charge interest based on the traditional western banking model.

Figure 14.1 For many developing countries, such as Indonesia, there is a long tradition of fast food provided by hawkers' stalls, such as this one, which provide traditional, low-cost food. As economies develop, hawkers' stalls have tended to decline, but where will the growing number of wealthy consumers choose to spend their money? Will they patronize new western-style fast-food outlets? Or will they invest in home cooking equipment that allows them to store food and prepare a wider selection of food quickly and efficiently? The introduction of fast-food restaurants has not always been an immediate success in developing countries, and even in the developed economy of Singapore, cultural traditions have led to a continuing role for organized 'hawkers' markets'.

⟳ Thinking around the subject

Looking for less saturated burger markets?

A saturated domestic market is often the spur for companies to seek new foreign markets. But is there a moral case against companies seeking to promote a Western style of service consumption in countries with well-established and sustainable lifestyles? Fast-food companies have stepped up their efforts to develop new foreign markets as western markets for fast food become saturated. Is it responsible to promote burgers, which are high in saturated fats, to people whose diets are inherently healthier? Is it right that fast-food companies should develop low-fat burgers for the American market, partly out of fear of litigation, while selling higher-fat burgers to less developed countries where legislation and consumer awareness of health issues are more lax? Defenders of fast-food companies point to the fact that they are providing hygienic food prepared in conditions that may be far superior to the norm in many developing countries. It is claimed that they have offered jobs to individuals, which can be the envy of peer groups. Should the solution be greater education of consumers in healthy eating, rather than more regulation? Is greater education a realistic prospect in a culture where fast food has become a cultural icon?

14.2   Theory of international trade

Today, the UK, like most industrialized countries, is dependent on **international trade** to maintain its standard of living. Some products that buyers have become accustomed to, such as tropical fruits and gold, would be almost impossible to produce at home. For products such as these, the UK economy could overcome this lack of availability in three possible ways.

1 By using alternative products (which can be produced at home) in place of those that cannot be produced domestically. For example, faced with a domestic shortage of aluminium, many users could switch to domestically produced steel.

2 The domestic economy could try to produce the product at home. This is often impossible where key elements of production are missing (e.g. uranium cannot be produced in the UK because it is not a naturally occurring substance). In other cases, such as the production of tropical fruits, domestic production may be achieved, but only at a very high cost.

3 The third alternative is to import goods from a country that is able to produce them cost effectively.

A similar analysis could be made of the options facing all other countries, not just the UK. Rather than producers in the UK growing bananas at great expense for domestic consumption, while a producer in a tropical country attempts to grow temperate fruits, both could benefit by specializing in what they are good at and exchanging their output. This is the basis for the theory of comparative cost advantage.

14.2.1 Comparative cost advantage

The theory of **comparative cost advantage** can be traced back to the work of Adam Smith in the late eighteenth century and broadly states that the world economy – and hence the economies of individual nations – will benefit if all countries:

- concentrate on producing what they are good at and export the surplus
- import from other countries those goods that other countries are better able to produce than themselves.

The principles of comparative cost advantage can be illustrated with an example. For simplicity, the following example will assume that there are only two countries in the world: Britain and the 'rest of the world'. A second assumption is that only two products are made in the world: food and coal.

It is possible to draw up a table showing the hypothetical food and coal production possibilities of the two countries.

- If Britain used all of its natural resources to produce coal, then it could produce 40 tons per year, but no food. It could, on the other hand, use all of its resources to produce 40 tons of food per year, but no coal.

- By contrast, the rest of the world could produce 160 tons of food a year or 40 tons of coal. The different ratios reflect the fact that Britain and the rest of the world possess different combinations of resources and capabilities.

- The maximum possible world output of food is therefore 200 tons or 80 tons of coal.

This can be summarized in a production possibility table (Table 14.1).

Table 14.1 Production possibility table: food and coal.

	Food	or	Coal
Britain	40	or	40
Rest of world	160	or	40
World production total	200	or	80

Neither country is likely to produce solely coal or food. For Britain to give up 1 ton of coal production will result in an increase in food production of 1 ton. However, if the rest of the world gives up 1 ton of coal production, it can increase food production by 4 tons. In this example, Britain should continue to produce coal, because the comparative cost of giving up food production is lower than that for the rest of the world. For Britain, the cost of 1 ton of food is 1 ton of coal. For the rest of the world, the cost of 1 ton of coal is 4 tons of food foregone. The rest of the world has a comparative cost advantage in the production of food (because the 'opportunity cost' of the resources used is lower than in Britain).

The next stage of analysing comparative cost advantages is to consider how production of coal and food may actually be divided between Britain and the rest of the world, and, from this, the pattern of trade that could take place. It is again assumed that there are only two countries in the world, that these are the only two goods traded and that total world production equals total consumption (i.e. stocks are not allowed to accumulate). An additional assumption will be made here that coal is more valuable than food. For the moment, it is assumed that 1 ton of coal is worth 5 tons of food.

Table 14.2 illustrates two situations:

1 where both countries divide their resources equally between food and coal production, without engaging in trade
2 a revised trade pattern where each country specializes in the product for which it has a comparative cost advantage.

Table 14.2 Effects on a national economy of specialization based on comparative cost advantage.

	Original production pattern – no trade Food	Coal	Revised production pattern – specialization Food	Coal
Britain	20	20	0	40
Rest of world	80	20	160	0
World production total	100	40	160	40
Value of 1 ton of food = 1 unit 5 ton of coal = 5 units	100	200	160	200
Total wealth	300 units		360 units	

On the basis of the assumptions made, Table 14.2 indicates that the world as a whole is better off as a result of the two countries specializing in doing what they are good at. Total wealth has gone up from 300 units to 360 units. This pattern would hold so long as the relative costs of production and the terms of trade remained the same. Of course, both of these could, in practice, change. Increased costs in Britain could change its comparative cost in producing food compared to the rest of the world. The pattern would also change if the value of coal went down in relation to the value of food – for example, if 1 ton of coal was worth only half a ton of food, and not 5 as in this example.

Of course, this has been a very simple example using quite unrealistic assumptions. However, it does show how international trade can benefit all nations. In reality, substitutions take place between large numbers of countries and an almost infinite range of products. Nevertheless, the underlying principles of exporting what a country is good at and importing those products that can be made more cheaply elsewhere still hold true. To give modern examples of what this actually means for the UK economy, Britain is good at producing high-value pharmaceuticals, which are sold abroad in large volume. It is not so good at producing low-value labour-intensive textiles, which are imported in large amounts from the relatively low-wage countries of the Far East.

Although the example above was based on goods, the concept of comparative cost advantage can also be used to understand trade in services. In this way, a favourable climate or outstanding scenery can give a country an advantage in selling tourism services to overseas customers. Another basis for comparative cost advantage for services can be found in the availability of low-cost or highly trained personnel (cheap labour for the shipping industry and trained computer software experts for computer consultancy, respectively). Sometimes the government of a country can itself directly create comparative cost advantages for a sector, as where it reduces regulations and controls on an industry, allowing that industry to produce goods and services for export at a lower cost than its more regulated competitors (e.g. Ireland charges lower rates of taxes on company profits than apply in the UK).

14.2.2 Limitations to the principle of comparative cost advantage

Unfortunately, the principles of comparative cost advantage may sound fine in theory, but it can be difficult to achieve the benefits in practice. In reality, the global ideals described above can become obscured by narrower national interests. Consequently, the full benefits of comparative cost advantage may not be achieved.

- Imports can be seen as a threat to established domestic firms. Short-term political pressure to preserve jobs may restrict firms' and individuals' ability to import from the country that is best able to produce specific products.

- Governments seek to pursue a portfolio of activities within their economies in order to maintain a balanced economy, and may therefore protect selected industries from foreign competition. Also, governments may protect industries in order to create greater employment opportunities for particular social or regional groups of the population.

- Governments may seek to protect temporarily fledgling new industries during their development stage in the hope that they will eventually be able to become strong enough to compete effectively in world markets. Competition early on could kill such infant industries before they are able to develop.

- Trade may not take place in some products – or may be made more difficult – because the requirements of different markets vary. National regulations on matters such as food purity and electrical safety may make it uneconomic to produce special versions of a product for a small foreign market.

- Transport costs act as a deterrent to international trade. Although it may be cheaper to produce building materials in southern Europe than in the UK, the very high transport costs of getting them to the UK market will limit the amount that actually enters international trade.

- National governments often artificially stimulate exports by giving export subsidies, allowing domestic producers to compete in world markets against more efficient producers. The EU, for example, has frequently been accused of subsidizing the export of agricultural products such as grain and meat to protect European farmers against competition from more efficient and less subsidized American and Australian farmers.

- International politics may limit the trade that a country has with the rest of the world. Although the trade barriers that existed within Europe are now disappearing, there is increasing concern that the creation of the EU and other **trading blocs**, such as the North American Free Trade Agreement area, will have the effect of increasing within-bloc trading at the expense of between-bloc trade.

- Sometimes governments have defence considerations in mind in restricting international trade (for example, by restricting the sale of technologies that could be used in weapons by hostile countries).

- Imports may represent a threat to the culture of a country, and governments seek to prevent their import. This particularly affects films and publications (e.g. the governments of many Muslim countries can make it difficult for films made in the West to be imported).

Despite a plethora of international agreements to facilitate trade between nations, minor, and sometimes major, trade disputes occur. The countries involved may agree that the benefits of open markets and comparative cost advantage leading to benefits to all are fine in theory, but the actual short-term implications for them are too harmful. It could be that the government in one country is facing an election and restrictions on imports could gain rapid approval for the government. However, if one country is tempted to introduce some sort of control on imports from another country, it will invariably result in retaliation by the other country. This can spiral, resulting in progressively declining world trade levels. The precise methods by which trade is restricted can take a number of forms.

- The extreme form of import control is for a country to ban imports of a product or class of products from one or more countries. For example, during 2011 Russia banned imports of all fruit and vegetables from the EU, citing health worries associated with EU produce.

- A tariff can be imposed on goods of a specified type. Governments have imposed tariffs on imports where they believed the product was being 'dumped' by the exporting country at below its production cost, thereby threatening domestic producers with unfair competition. As an example, in 2006 the EU introduced tariffs on shoes imported from China and Vietnam, following an investigation into allegations of 'dumping' on European markets at below cost prices by Chinese and Vietnamese manufacturers.

- A quota on the volume of imports of a particular product can be imposed – imports of cars to the UK from Japan were restrained for a long time on the basis of a voluntarily agreed quota.

- Governments sometimes impose covert controls as an alternative to more formal controls, in order to try to diffuse attention and avoid retaliation. 'Health' concerns may appear to legitimize efforts to protect domestic producers. For example, the EU has banned many categories of food containing genetically modified organisms (GMOs). Although the World Trade Organization approved such bans where GMOs could have an adverse effect on human health or biodiversity, many sceptics have suspected that the ban was also motivated by a desire to protect EU farmers. At other times, import documentation or licensing procedures can be made so complex that they can significantly increase the costs of importers relative to domestic producers.

14.2.3 Multinational companies and the exploitation of comparative cost advantages

Multinational companies (MNCs) have been at the forefront of efforts to exploit comparative cost advantage differences between countries. There has been a tendency for MNCs to focus manufacture of one product line (e.g. a car model) in just one or a small number of factories, to serve the whole world. Such factories typically also benefit by being located in a country where production costs (e.g. wage rates or taxation) are comparatively low.

Companies in fiercely competitive markets often calculate that it is cheaper to manufacture a product in a low-cost country such as China and to ship the finished product to the country where there is demand for it. Most British clothes companies now manufacture the bulk of their clothing in less developed countries where wages paid to staff can be a fraction of those that would be paid to UK staff. This can more than offset higher transport costs and allow the company to compete on price, especially where there are significant price points above which buyers will not buy an item. However, locating manufacturing facilities a long way from customers extends the time between a market need being identified and the delivery of goods to meet that need. While fashion for basic underwear and socks may not change much over time, outerwear tends to be much more volatile, with preferred styles and colours changing frequently. If it takes several weeks or months to get the latest 'hot' fashion from China to Chichester, it might just arrive in the shops as customers have moved on to a new 'hot' fashion. For this reason, manufacturers supplying goods to highly volatile markets are more likely to favour manufacturing facilities closer to home. In the world of consumer electronics, Sony surprised many people when it brought production of camcorders back from China to Japan (Nakamoto 2003). Digitization had made the product life cycle even shorter than before. Previously, because the market was growing, Sony could sell just about anything that it produced. But, by 2002, the market had matured and it became necessary to adjust product configuration as closely as possible to market demand, something Sony felt was easier to achieve in Japan. Furthermore, this move helped to reduce the company's electronics inventory from ¥923.4 billion in the third quarter of 2000 to ¥627.5 billion in the third quarter of 2001, and again to ¥506.5 billion in the third quarter of 2002. To a company such as Sony, inventory is a business risk in a fast-changing market.

In general, greater distances between factories and end users lead to greater transport uncertainty, increasing the need for 'buffer stocks' to be held in the supply chain. The need to obtain customs clearance can contribute to delays and variability. Also, breaking down bulk from a large centralized factory to individual national markets can be expensive. Options include shipping direct from each source to the final market in full containers; or consolidating from each source for each general geographic area, with bulk broken down into intermediate inventory ready for specific markets.

Some companies, such as the computer manufacturer Dell, have examined their value chain and calculated that there are opportunities for delaying the final configuration of a product until it is as close to the customer as possible. They can then achieve lower costs by shipping generic sub-assemblies to the local operation which typically provides finishing, local language packaging, and direct customer delivery. Dell therefore sources many of its components from China and Thailand, among other places, and serves its European markets by assembling them at a plant in Limerick, Ireland.

14.2.4 Exchange rates

Nation-states generally have their own currency system, which is quite distinct from the currency of their international trading partners. It follows, therefore, that the currency a buyer wants to use as payment may not be the currency that a seller wants to receive as payment for goods or services. If a British customer buys a Japanese-built car, they would expect to pay for their car in pounds sterling and not Japanese yen. So the Japanese manufacturer must become involved in foreign exchange transactions by converting the sterling it has received back into yen, which it will need in order to buy components and to pay its workforce. The fact that different countries have their own currencies makes life for an exporter more complex and risky than for a company that serves only its domestic market.

The biggest problem arising from the use of multiple currencies for trade is that their value in relation to each other fluctuates through time. The value of one currency in terms of another currency is known as its exchange rate. The exchange rate of the yen to sterling will determine how many yen a Japanese car maker will receive for the sterling that it has received from its customers in the UK.

Currencies are just like any other commodity that is traded in a market. If the demand for a currency is great relative to its supply, then its 'price' (or exchange rate) will rise. The opposite will happen if there is excess supply of that currency. These are exactly the same principles of market forces that were discussed in Chapter 11, and their application to exchange rate determination is illustrated in Figure 14.2.

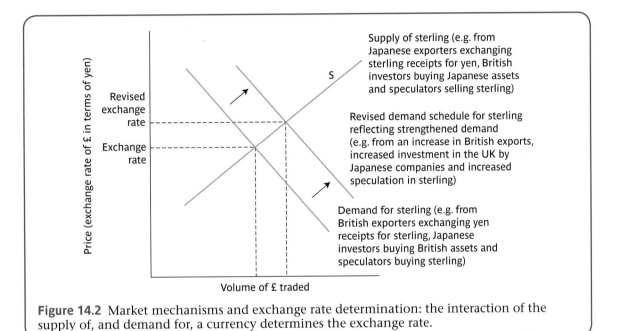

Figure 14.2 Market mechanisms and exchange rate determination: the interaction of the supply of, and demand for, a currency determines the exchange rate.

Changes in the supply of, or demand for, a currency can come about for a number of reasons.

■ Changes in demand for a nation's currency can result from a significant change in exports from that country. If UK exports to Japan suddenly increase, UK firms would be left holding large volumes of yen from their Japanese customers. When the UK exporting company goes to the currency markets to exchange its yen for sterling, its demand for sterling would have the effect of pushing up the price of sterling in terms of yen. While one company on its own may not have much impact on an exchange rate, the combined effects of many companies cause exchange rates to fluctuate.

■ An increase in imports by UK firms from Japan would have an opposite effect. Japanese firms would seek to change the sterling payments they have received into yen. Their supply of sterling will increase relative to demand for it and its price will fall. Of course, in this and the previous example, the actual transactions would normally be handled routinely by the companies' bankers, and most trading firms' transactions would be too small on their own to significantly affect exchange rates. Large overseas orders or the collective effects of many buyers and sellers could, however, have a significant effect on exchange rates.

■ Demand for foreign currencies can similarly arise from transactions involving the purchase of assets overseas and the remission of profits and dividends overseas.

■ As in many commodity markets, demand for a currency at any given time is influenced by individuals' expectations about future price levels for a currency. Traders in currencies may use their reserves to buy currencies that they consider are likely to rise in value, and sell those that they expect to fall. Expectations about changes in currency values can be based on factors such as the inflation rate in a country (which has the effect of reducing the purchasing power of its currency), growing imbalances between a country's imports and exports, and general government macroeconomic policy.

- Intervention by government can affect the supply of, and demand for, its currency. For example, if a government seeks to raise the value of its currency in terms of other currencies (or at least prevent it falling), it can use its gold and foreign currency reserves to buy up its own currency, thereby raising its exchange rate.

From an importer's or exporter's point of view, fluctuations in exchange rates cause considerable uncertainty. Companies selling goods or services abroad will not know for sure what revenue they will actually receive if they invoice in a foreign currency, since a change in the exchange rate – between agreeing the price and receiving payment – can earn them more or less than anticipated. Where imports are priced in a producer's currency, importers of goods or services may be uncertain about the final price of their purchases.

From a national government's perspective, a falling exchange rate creates inflationary pressures, since imports become relatively expensive (e.g. it takes more pounds to buy any given yen's worth of imported Japanese products). However, a falling exchange rate helps exporters to achieve overseas sales, because their products effectively become cheaper in foreign markets. It also has the effect of making imports more expensive. Through both of these effects, employment opportunities in the domestic economy are enhanced by a relatively low exchange rate. Governments must balance the stimulus to companies that a low exchange rate brings against the inflationary pressure that it generally entails.

Individual companies can minimize their exposure to risks arising from exchange rate fluctuation in a number of ways.

- Where it is important for a firm to be certain of the future cost of materials imported from overseas, it can enter into forward currency contracts that provide it with a specified amount of foreign currency at an agreed time in the future, at an agreed exchange rate. So even if the value of a currency changes in the meantime, a company can buy its materials from overseas at its budgeted price, using an overseas currency whose value was fixed during its budgeting process.

- Where the buyer's or seller's currency has a history of volatility, they may decide to use a third currency that is regarded as a relatively stable, or 'hard', currency. Many sectors of international trade, such as oil and civil aviation, are routinely priced in US dollars, regardless of the nationality of the buyer and seller.

- The impact of currency fluctuations on large multinational companies can be reduced by trying to plan for expenditure (on components, etc.) in one currency to roughly equal the revenue it expects to earn in that currency. Any change in exchange rates therefore has an overall broadly neutral effect on the organization.

- Fluctuating exchange rates can become an opportunity for companies that can rapidly shift their resources to take advantage of imports from countries that have suddenly become advantageous. Commodity traders operating in 'spot' markets may be able to switch supply sources according to changes in exchange rates.

14.2.5 Fixed exchange rates

An alternative to market-based fluctuating exchange rates is a fixed exchange rate system. Here, a country or group of countries agrees to maintain the value of its currency in terms of another currency, or at least to keep fluctuations within a very narrow range. Where necessary, governments take action to manage the currency in order to maintain the agreed rates of exchange.

An example of a managed exchange rate is the Chinese renminbi. The Chinese government has maintained a target exchange rate for its currency in terms of the dollar. Some have accused the Chinese government of trying to maintain an artificially low value of the renminbi in order to help its exports and to provide a barrier to imports. Within the EU, some countries that are not members of the common euro currency have nevertheless sought to maintain a stable exchange rate between their currency and the euro, with a view to eventually joining the Eurozone.

Countries aim to manage their exchange rate using a number of policy measures. If a country sought to increase the value of its currency, it could increase interest rates (which in the short term can attract 'hot money' into a currency, thereby pushing up its value), carry out open market operations where the government uses gold and foreign currency reserves to buy up its own currency, and generally increase speculators' confidence in its economy (e.g. by reducing inflation or a balance of payments deficit).

14.2.6 European Monetary Union

In 1999, most of the major economies of the EU agreed to replace their own currencies with the euro. Important aims of the euro were to reduce the costs of trade between EU member-states by reducing exchange transaction costs and risks associated with currency volatility. It was also hoped that the euro would become a 'hard' currency backed by substantial reserves, able to match the US dollar as a world currency. The UK did not join in the launch of the euro, arguing, among other things, that a single currency reduces the scope for national governments to manage their economies. For a common currency to be stable over the longer term, it is important that all economies converge in terms of such factors as inflation rates and government spending. Without being able to adjust exchange rates and interest rates, national economic policy may be unable to tackle economic problems that are specific to a nation-state. Despite the UK's reservations about joining the single European currency, UK companies trading with other EU companies may nevertheless use the currency for their transactions. For some, this may be a requirement of their EU trading partners, while others will see benefits in using a strong currency, in much the same way as the US dollar is used. The first few years of the euro saw its value gradually fall against major world currencies, suggesting that traders lacked confidence in the currency and/or the strength of the European economy. In 2010 the euro appeared to be in trouble as a number of weaker countries, notably Greece, Ireland and Portugal, whose governments had taken on debt denominated in euros, faced difficulties in repaying those debts and had to be rescued by stronger Eurozone countries. Many sceptics claimed that the euro would remain unsustainable as long as economies within the Eurozone had failed to converge.

Opinion has been divided about the effects of the euro on UK business organizations. Advocates of the euro point to the greatly reduced transaction costs involved in trading with other EU countries and the reduced risk of adverse currency movements between agreeing a price and actually completing a transaction. In the early days of the euro, many UK exporters were keen to join the euro area, as sterling was perceived as being overvalued relative to the euro, putting their exports at a competitive disadvantage. Against these arguments, many businesses in the UK were initially disappointed by the failure of the euro to become a strong and stable reserve currency and, for many businesses, the US dollar retained this role. Many businesses also recognized that a large currency area does not in itself guarantee a strong and stable economy, and critics of the euro have pointed out that some of the smallest currency areas, such as Singapore and Switzerland, are among the most dynamic.

⟳ Thinking around the subject

A common currency, so will there be a common price?

Will the development of the single European currency eventually lead to uniform prices for a product throughout Europe? Advocates of the euro claim that this will be one of the currency's benefits, as price discrepancies become blatantly obvious and consumers shop around in the cheapest market. But what about the price discrepancies that exist between different regions of the UK? The going rate for petrol in one town can be between 5 and 10 per cent different compared to a town just 20 or 30 miles away. The website www.petrolprices.com collects data on petrol prices around the country and continues to report marked regional price variations. This may seem remarkable considering the mobility of buyers and the ease of shopping around for petrol. Similarly, there is no immediately obvious reason why the price of used cars should vary between different regions of the UK. Similar price variations are present in the USA, which has much longer experience of a single currency. There, prices of most consumer goods tend to be higher in the affluent north-east and are lowest in the relatively poor areas of the deep south. Why should this be? And what hope is there of the single European market harmonizing prices when there are such discrepancies of commodity-type products within a single country?

14.3   Overseas trade patterns

The existence of comparative cost advantages and variations between countries in the types of goods and services demanded results in each country having its own distinctive pattern of overseas trade. The nature of a country's overseas trade can be described with respect to:

- the items that it imports and exports
- the countries it trades with.

Trade patterns throughout the world change in response to changes in the economic, political, technological and social environments. For example, during the first years of the twenty-first century, the rising GDP per capita of China has resulted in Chinese consumers purchasing increasing numbers of overseas holidays. At the same time, developments in telecommunications have allowed new forms of trade in data and call handling, purchased by western companies from companies in relatively low-cost countries.

14.3.1 Measuring international trade

The difference between what a country receives from overseas and the amount it spends overseas is referred to as its **balance of payments**. Countries differ in the way in which they break down their overall balance of payments, but these can be broadly divided into:

- the purchase and sale of goods and services (usually described as current account transactions), and
- the acquisition and disposal of assets and liabilities abroad (referred to as capital account transactions).

Although it is common to talk about a country's overall balance of payments being in surplus or deficit, they must technically be balanced (Figure 14.3). If, for example, a country has a deficit in its current account, this has to be made up by running down one of its assets (e.g. by using holdings of foreign currencies to reduce a capital asset or borrowing from overseas and thereby increasing a capital liability). The opposite would be true if a country produced a current account surplus (holdings of foreign assets would increase or foreign liabilities would reduce).

Current account:	Credits	Debits
Visible trade	Exports	Imports
Invisible trade (including services, interest, profits and dividends)	Payments received from foreign countries	Payments made to foreign countries
Capital account	Inflow of capital	Outflow of capital

Figure 14.3 Components of a country's balance of payments.

Media headlines that describe a 'trade deficit' or 'surplus' generally refer to the current account element of the balance of payments. The components of the current and capital account elements are described below.

- The current account is generally divided into two components: a visible trade balance and an invisible trade balance. **Visible trade** includes transactions in manufactured goods, raw materials and fuel products. **Invisible trade** is made up of services including government services (e.g. payments to overseas armed forces and diplomatic missions), and interest, profit and dividends receivable from or payable abroad.

- The capital account records outward and inward flows of capital for investment purposes (i.e. it excludes routine trading transactions). It includes payments made for long-term investment in tangible assets (e.g. new factories and equipment) and intangible assets (such as the purchase of shares in an overseas company). It also includes short-term movements of money between traders in the money markets (sometimes referred to as 'hot money').

14.3.2 Measuring international transactions

Traditionally, the value of manufactured goods has been measured as they pass through Customs, and from this information, the total value of imports and exports has been calculated. In the case of capital transactions, governments generally make provisions for large transactions to be reported (e.g. many countries restrict the free movement of capital to a specified maximum amount per transaction). However, it is becoming increasingly difficult to measure the value and volume of overseas trade.

- It is very difficult to accurately measure trade in services, which are transacted through a variety of means (e.g. the sale of insurance and banking services sold using the internet). In the case of earnings and expenditure on tourism, it can be difficult to measure the total expenditure of tourists, whose spending can be dispersed through a variety of business sectors. Governments estimate such figures using various survey techniques. However, initial estimates frequently have to be subsequently revised.

- Within the EU, border controls on trade have been removed, so it is now more difficult to get an accurate indication of the volume of imports and exports between EU member-states. Again, overseas trade within the EU is measured using various survey techniques.

Having made these caveats, recent trends in the UK overseas current account are shown in Table 14.3. The table shows trade data for recent years, and for previous turning points in worldwide business cycles.

Table 14.3   Key UK overseas payment figures (£000,000)

Year	Net trade in goods	Net trade in services	Current account balance	Capital account	Net errors and omissions
1960	−404	39	−205	−6	218
1970	−16	455	819	−22	21
1980	1,329	3,829	1,740	−4	421
1990	−18,707	4,337	−22,281	497	6,701
2000	−32,976	13,615	−24,833	1,703	10,526
2001	−41,212	14,423	−21,884	1,318	3,063
2002	−47,705	16,830	−16,513	932	8,379
2003	−48,607	19,162	−14,921	1,466	−7,052
2004	−60,893	25,918	−19,328	2,063	11,624
2005	−68,783	24,309	−29,165	1,491	−2,631
2006	−76,313	33,108	−45,031	713	8,950
2007	−89,754	46,798	−36,482	2,566	9,126
2008	−93,116	55,356	−23,776	3,241	−5,276
2009	−81,875	49,852	−15,506	3,219	6,690

Source: based on *Annual Abstracts of Statistics*.

Notes:

Net trade in goods and services is the difference between imports and exports; a negative figure indicates a deficit.

Current account balance includes net trade in goods and services plus other current account transfers (e.g. investment income payments to UK employees overseas).

Capital account includes payments for fixed assets.

The 'Net errors and omissions' column is necessary to make the balance of payments balance.

14.3.3 Trends in UK international trade

A number of immediate observations can be made about the changing pattern of UK overseas trade, including the following.

- During the recent past, the UK has run a deficit in its visible balance, but partly made up for this by having a surplus in invisibles. Although the visible trade balance has deteriorated in recent years, growth in the invisible balance has not been sufficient to counteract the decline in visible exports.

- The UK balance of payments has been influenced over the past few decades by North Sea oil. High prices and volumes in the 1980s greatly helped the balance of payments, but declining reserves and a falling world oil price had a negative effect in the late 1990s, which has been offset only partly by the sharp rises in world oil prices that have occurred since 2007.

The overseas trade balance of a nation is very much influenced by the structure of its domestic economy. For the UK economy, the deterioration of the visible balance is symptomatic of the declining competitiveness of its manufacturing industries. Indices of competitiveness reached a low point during the late 1980s as many industry sectors became dominated by products from low-cost producers, especially those in the Far East and, from 2004, in the newly joined EU member-states of eastern Europe.

Some indication of the importance of international trade in services for the UK can be seen by examining trade statistics. In 2009, the UK had a surplus (£49.3 billion) in services, compared with a deficit in goods and raw materials (£81.8 billion) (ONS 2010). A closer examination of trade statistics indicates the relative importance of the main service sectors. The most important is financial services, which made a net contribution to the UK balance of payments of £3.7 billion in 2004.

The year-to-year pattern of overseas trade is influenced by business cycles at a national and international level. The downward phase of the world business cycle has the effect of reducing the total value of world trade (or at least slowing down its rate of growth). The business cycles of individual countries may lead or lag the general cycle, or various local reasons may mean that a country is not significantly affected by the worldwide business cycle. The economic downturn that occurred in 2008, following the 'credit crunch', initially had an impact throughout the world, but many of the world's developing economies recovered much faster than those in western developed countries, many of which suffered a period of prolonged austerity.

A consumer boom in a domestic economy often has the effect of sucking in manufactured imports. The economic boom in the UK during the early 2000s, coupled with a high exchange rate, resulted in a very large increase in manufactured imports. At the same time, the domestic manufacturing sector was becoming increasingly uncompetitive, leading to a capacity reduction that further limited its opportunities for exports. This contributed to rising visible trade deficits, which were corrected only as downturn in the economic cycle caused a reduction in consumer goods imports, while a falling exchange rate further dampened imports and encouraged exports.

An indication of the changing relative competitiveness of UK business sectors can be found by examining ratios of:

- imports as a proportion of home demand, and
- exports as a proportion of manufacturers' sales.

In the case of imports, recent UK government statistics indicate a particular weakness in office machinery and data-processing equipment, and instrument engineering, but relatively low levels of penetration by imports in the case of food, drink and mineral products. For exports, transport equipment and chemicals performed strongly, while furniture, timber and paper products have achieved low proportions of exports.

Trade patterns can also be analysed in terms of the origin and destination of a country's transactions. Recent years have witnessed a number of changes in the pattern of the UK's trading partners.

- UK trade has become increasingly focused on the EU, accounting for 57 per cent of all balance of payments credits and 59 per cent of all debits in 2009. Except for 2001, the UK has had a current account deficit with the EU every year since 1999.
- Trade with the USA has gradually become a smaller proportion of the UK's international trade, representing 18 per cent of current account credits and 16 per cent of debits in 2009. There has been a current account surplus with the USA in most post-war years.
- The share of imports accounted for by oil-exporting countries has fluctuated with the growth and subsequent fall of North Sea oil production.

It must not be forgotten that market mechanisms in themselves have a tendency to correct trade imbalances. A country with long-term trade deficits based on structural weaknesses in its economy will experience a weakening in the value of its currency, which will have the effect of making exports cheaper and imports dearer. Through a substitution effect in its domestic markets, domestic manufacturers will gain competitive advantage over importers, thereby reducing a trade deficit. Similarly, exports will become cheaper in overseas markets, again reducing a trade deficit. For countries that run continuing trade surpluses (such as China), market forces will tend to reduce the surplus. Continuing surpluses will cause a rise in the value of a country's currency, making exports more expensive and imports cheaper. Eventually, exports may become so expensive (when priced in buyers' currencies) that the country's exporters will establish factories overseas, and may even find it cheaper to assemble products overseas for import to its domestic market.

14.3.4 Prospects for UK international trade

The post-war years have generally been disappointing for the UK's balance of trade, with a worsening deficit in visible trade being only partly offset by surpluses in services and North Sea oil. In view of its extensive ownership of overseas assets, the UK can afford to continue running a moderate trade deficit, but governments have sought to keep deficits within tolerable limits. Very high deficits would probably lead to a fall in the value of sterling, which itself would be inflationary and may lead to an increase in interest rates. Governments would prefer to avoid the social, economic and political consequences of a large trade deficit.

League tables of international competitiveness have shown the UK slipping. The World Economic Forum regularly produces league tables of competitiveness, based on such factors as resource costs, flexibility of resources and taxation. The top ten list of most competitive countries (Table 14.4) shows the UK behind a number of countries, including the USA, Japan, Singapore and many of the Scandinavian nations.

Table 14.4   Ranking of the top 20 most competitive countries for business.

World competitiveness ranking 2010			
Country		Country	
Switzerland	1	Hong Kong	11
Sweden	2	UK	12
Singapore	3	Taiwan	13
USA	4	Norway	14
Germany	5	France	15
Japan	6	Australia	16
Finland	7	Qatar	17
Netherlands	8	Austria	18
Denmark	9	Belgium	19
Canada	10	Luxembourg	20

Source: based on data presented to the World Economic Forum, Davos, 2010.

Prescriptions for the UK's future prosperity in international trade have focused on a number of issues, including the following.

- Continuing to improve the productivity of UK industry, especially through deregulation of the economy and improvements in the flexibility of labour.
- Exploiting service-sector competitive advantages, especially within the fields of banking and insurance. However, although the UK has historically achieved surpluses in these fields, competition from newly developed countries has intensified.
- The UK should exploit opportunities in new and emerging sectors when they arise – for example, biotechnology.

- Many have pointed to the valuable role played by governments, such as Japan's, in promoting a country's exports. In the UK, the emphasis of government policy has tended to lie in improving supply-side efficiency rather than promoting specific sectors overseas.

- It has been argued by some that UK companies have failed to invest in new capacity during periods of recession in order to meet an upturn in the world economy.

- The proportion of GDP spent by the UK on research and development is low by international standards, casting doubts on the ability of its manufacturers to become world leaders in new product fields (refer back to Chapter 4).

- Finally, some commentators have suggested that the poor training in marketing and management skills of UK managers has left them badly placed to tackle aggressively overseas markets, or even to protect their domestic markets from import competition. Worse still, many people suspect an anti-industry culture in which the best talent finds its way to the professions, such as law and consultancy, rather than management. Of course, there are notable exceptions to this bleak picture – for example, the entrepreneur James Dyson used innovation and good marketing successfully to launch electrical appliances in overseas markets.

14.4 International trade institutions and agreements

The exploitation of comparative cost advantages through free trade may sound fine in theory, but is often difficult to achieve in practice, for the reasons described earlier in this chapter. There have therefore been many attempts to develop international agreements for the free movement of trade. At their simplest, international trade agreements comprise bilateral agreements between two countries to open up trade between the two. Sometimes, groups of countries join together to form trading blocs in which trade between member states is encouraged at the expense of trade with non-bloc members. There are also multilateral agreements between nations to develop free trade. Some of the more important are described below.

14.4.1 The EU and the Single European Market

A principal aim of the EU has been the removal of **barriers to trade** between member-states. The most significant step towards this was achieved through the EU's Single European Market programme and the development of the European Economic Area, which extended the principles of the single market to include members of the European Free Trade Area (EFTA). Since 1993 there has been a progressive easing of trade within the European Economic Area and some of the benefits achieved are:

- the removal or reduction of institutional barriers to trade (e.g. reduced import/export documentation)
- the technical harmonization of product standards, allowing for greater economies of scale and competition using a standardized product that is able to compete in multiple domestic markets
- the ability for companies with licences to operate in their home market to be able to extend these rights to other EU markets
- the liberalization of capital movements
- the removal of discriminatory public purchasing policies
- establishment of the euro currency.

The benefits of the single market are achieved through a combination of reduced costs and increased competition, which will have the effect of reducing the local national monopoly power enjoyed by some suppliers. A number of UK sectors have been identified as beneficiaries of more open markets, able to exploit their comparative cost advantages. These include pharmaceuticals, the food and drink industry, insurance and civil aviation.

Despite the efforts of the Single European Market programme, a number of barriers to trade within the EU remain.

- There is debate about the extent to which cultural variations within Europe will eventually be homogenized. Some of these variations are based on geographical factors (e.g. the lifestyles and attitudes of people living in hot, southern-climate countries differ markedly from those of northern countries) and may be difficult to change.

- Although harmonization of product standards has proceeded a long way, some problems remain. For example, the UK's non-standard design of electrical plugs or its practice of driving on the left may never be harmonized to a European standard.

- It is still often necessary for individuals or firms to obtain licences before they can operate in another member-state. Although removal of such barriers is on the EU agenda for reform, free trade in services has generally been harder to open up to cross-border trade than dealings in manufactured goods. For example, in 2005, Germany and France rejected a proposed Services Directive that would have allowed any service provider that is registered in its home country to practise its trade or profession in any other EU member country.

Nevertheless, the single European market has become a major trading bloc, which has made trade within the bloc easier, while creating common policies with respect to trade with the rest of the world.

14.4.2 Other regional trading blocs

A number of other trading blocs exist in the world with aims similar to those of the EU. These include the North American Free Trade Agreement (NAFTA), the Gulf Cooperation Council (GCC) and the Association of South East Asian Nations (ASEAN). In the case of NAFTA, the USA, Canada and Mexico have sought to reduce barriers to trade between their countries so that each can exploit its comparative cost advantage. Some measures are already in place, but the creation of the single market will have increasing effect in the future. Inevitably, while trade is made easier within the free trade area, there is a danger of other outside countries being disadvantaged.

⟳ Thinking around the subject

Are the French taking the piste?

When does a requirement for rigorous staff training amount to a restrictive international trade practice? The French authorities have insisted that all guides accompanying groups on the country's ski slopes should take a test that is one of the toughest in Europe, citing the increased safety of groups that results. British tour operators have in the past provided their own ski guides, who are generally assessed by companies for their basic mountain awareness abilities. They have also taken on a social role. British tour operators claim that their customers prefer the social informality of their guides rather than the formality of the French ski instructors.

Is this an example of a covert restriction on international trade by the French authorities, keen to give preference to their own politically important local guides? Or does their action represent a genuine concern for safety (if not consumer preferences), which is neutral in terms of its effects on the different nationalities of guides?

14.4.3 The Organization for Economic Co-operation and Development (OECD)

The OECD was originally set up in 1947 to administer America's Marshall Aid programme in Europe, but subsequently turned increasing attention to the developing world. The OECD now has 21 members, including most European countries, the USA, Canada and Japan. It works by trying to coordinate the economic policies of members and programmes of economic aid, and by providing specialized services, especially information.

14.4.4 The World Bank

The World Bank (officially known as the International Bank for Reconstruction and Development) acts as an adviser to governments in the provision of international finance. The main role of the World Bank is to provide capital on favourable terms to aid the economic reconstruction of countries. In cases where it advances loans to overseas governments, it may require its advice to be incorporated into government policy as a condition of its loan.

14.4.5 The International Monetary Fund (IMF)

The IMF shared its origins with the OECD and World Bank in that all three institutions were created in the immediate post-Second World War period and were seen as a means towards world economic regeneration. The IMF is essentially a world forum for international negotiations on governments' fiscal policies. Its original aims of regulating and stabilizing exchange rates have been somewhat undermined by the ability of traders and multinational companies to influence exchange rates, often having a bigger impact on markets than policies agreed by the IMF. During the problems faced by the euro in 2010, the IMF was instrumental in arranging emergency financial support to 'bail out' the economies of Greece, Ireland and Portugal.

14.4.6 The World Trade Organization (WTO)

The WTO has its origins in the General Agreement on Tariffs and Trade (GATT) of the early post-war period. The signatories to the agreement sought to achieve greater international economic prosperity by exploiting fully the comparative cost advantages of nations by reducing the barriers that inhibited international trade. All the signatories agreed not to increase tariffs on imported goods beyond their existing levels, and to work towards the abolition of quotas that restricted the volume of imports. The WTO, successor to GATT, has continued to reduce tariffs and quotas through several negotiating 'rounds'. It has also tried to redress the distortion to world trade and the unfair competitive advantage given to subsidized exporters of agricultural products. More recently, it has sought to remove the distortion to world trade caused by government monopoly control of key services, for which foreign companies are unable to compete.

Many critics of the WTO's attempts to liberalize trade in goods and services claim that they create disadvantages for developing countries. As an example, it may be plausible for FedEx to run a privatized Indian Post Office, but could there really be much chance of the Indian Post Office challenging FedEx on its home ground?

14.4.7 Other international agreements and institutions

There are many examples of bilateral agreements between countries that can influence the operations of business organizations. Agreements between countries on how the taxation of multinational companies should be handled can have serious implications for businesses, leading to the possibility of double claims for taxation where this possibility is not specifically excluded by a bilateral government agreement.

There are also very many agreements and institutions covering specific industries. An example of an institution that has a direct effect on an industry is the International Civil Aviation

Organization (ICAO) to which most countries belong and which has agreed international safety standards for civil aviation. In other cases, agreements between countries can have an indirect effect on a market, as with an international agreement signed to restrict international trade in ivory.

↻ Thinking around the subject

When Should A Firm Expand Overseas?

In emerging markets, timing can be crucial for success. In the past two decades, major opportunities for hotel operators have emerged as the economies of China, India, eastern Europe and Latin America have grown rapidly. When these economies emerged as centres for economic growth, one of their first requirements has been for hotels to accommodate the army of architects, engineers and business people who headed out to these countries to create new infrastructure and trading links. The result was that in the early stages of rapid growth, hotels were very scarce, and operators could charge premium prices. As an example, China and eastern Europe are associated with low costs of labour, and many manufacturers and service businesses have moved operations there to exploit these low costs. However, their capital cities often had some of the highest hotel prices in the world, reflecting their scarcity at a time of rapid economic growth. This has been a signal for more hotel chains to move into the market, but eventually the steam would go out of the economic boom, probably just at the time when the additional hotel capacity is becoming available. The result is greater pressure on prices, and a less attractive overseas investment opportunity for newly arrived hotel companies, compared with that achieved by earlier arrivals (Figure 14.4). Of course, it is easy with hindsight to spot the right time to invest, but much more difficult to predict which economies are going to grow, when, and by how much.

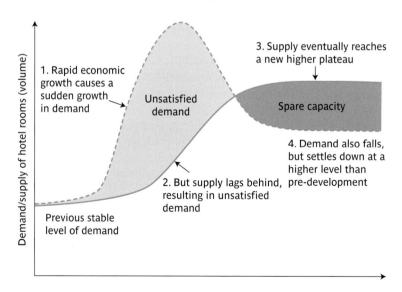

Figure 14.4 Timing of market entry can be crucial.

14.5 Evaluating overseas business opportunities

Overseas markets can represent very different opportunities and threats compared to those that an organization has been used to in its domestic market. Before a detailed environmental analysis is undertaken, an organization should consider in general terms whether the environment is likely to be attractive. By considering in general terms such matters as political stability or cultural attitudes, an organization may screen out potential markets for which further analysis cannot be justified by the likelihood of success. Where an exploratory analysis of an overseas environment appears to indicate some opportunities, a more thorough analysis might suggest important modifications to a product format that would need to be made before it could successfully be offered to the market.

This section first identifies some general questions that need to be asked in assessing the business environment of overseas countries, and then considers detailed and specific research activities.

◆ Thinking around the subject

A hotel for lunatics?

Hilton International, owner of many of the world's most prestigious hotels, has joined the race to build the first hotel on the Moon. It has developed a project called the Lunar Hilton, which would comprise a complex with 5000 rooms. Powered by two huge solar panels, the resort would have its own beach and sea as well as a working farm. Experts disagree on the practicalities of life on the Moon, but barriers seem to be diminishing as new discoveries are made.

'Space tourism' received a boost in April 2001 when the determined multimillionaire Dennis Tito paid $20 million for a round-trip ticket to the International Space Station. Such is the interest in exploiting the Moon for tourism that there is now a Space Tourism Association, and a lot of national pride is at stake. The Russians placed the first man in space and now the first tourist in space. In Japan, the Kinki Nippon Tourist (KNT) Company, the country's second largest wholesale tour operator, set up a space travel club in 2002. Back in 1998, KNT helped a Japanese Pepsi franchisee launch a sweepstake for a sub-orbital flight. The company received 650,000 applications for five tickets, each valued at $98,000. The company is convinced that excursion-class spaceships will become a driving force for the travel industry in the twenty-first century. The entrepreneur Sir Richard Branson shares this vision too, with plans for his Virgin Galactic to be launched from Spaceport America in New Mexico.

Three Japanese companies have between them already spent £25 million on development work for their own Moon projects. Compared to this, Hilton's expenditure to date of £100,000 looks quite modest. Is the company mad in believing that people will want to visit the Moon? Or is this just the kind of long-term strategic thinking that so many businesses lack? With the world becoming seemingly smaller, and increasingly saturated with goods and services, does the Moon offer a unique opportunity for expansion?

14.5.1 Macro-level analysis of a foreign business environment

The combination of environmental factors that contributed to success within an organization's domestic market may be absent in a foreign country, resulting in the failure of export attempts. In this section, questions to be asked in analysing an overseas business environment are examined under the overlapping headings of the political, economic, social and technological environments.

The political and legal environment

- Is the government of the country stable? While radical change rarely results from political upheaval in most western countries, the instability of governments in some less developed counties can lead to uncertainty about the economic and legislative framework in which goods and services will be traded.
- Is a restrictive system of licensing used in an attempt to protect domestic producers?
- Do regulations governing product standards require expensive reconfiguration of the company's products?
- Are there controls on the import of manufactured goods, requiring the company to create a local source of supply, leading to possible problems in maintaining consistent quality standards and also possibly losing economies of scale.
- What are the effects of employment legislation, such as minimum wage levels and conditions of service? These can be important in determining the viability of an overseas operation – for example, many countries restrict the manner in which temporary or seasonal staff can be employed.
- Are there any restrictions on currency movements, making it difficult to repatriate profits earned from an overseas operation?
- If supplying to an overseas government, does that government formally or informally give preference in awarding contracts to locally owned organizations?
- If the company has strong brands, how effective is legislation at protecting trademarks and patents?

The economic environment

- What is the GDP per head of the target country? How rapidly is this figure rising?
- What is the distribution of income within the country? Even if the GDP per head is low, are there any significant niches of affluent consumers?
- What are the future prospects for the economy?
- Where is the economy in its development life cycle? Are new markets just emerging, or becoming saturated?
- What is the level of competition within the market?

The social and cultural environment

An understanding of cultural differences between markets is very important for businesses contemplating entering foreign markets. Individuals from different cultures not only buy different products but may also respond in different ways to similar products. Attitudes towards work can affect production efficiency. Examples of differing cultural attitudes and their effects on international trade in goods and services include the following.

- Are there any important differences in buying processes compared to those in the domestic market? For example, does the role of women in selecting a product differ in the target market compared to the domestic market?

- Does the social structure of the country impose constraints or opportunities for the product? For example, extended family structures common in some countries have the ability to produce a wide range of services within the family unit, including caring for children and elderly family members.

- Even though the product may be taken for granted in the domestic market, could it be seen as socially unacceptable in an overseas market? Frequently encountered examples include pork products in Muslim countries and beef in Hindu countries.

- Are there differences in how buyers in the target market respond to promotional messages? The choice of colours in advertising or sales outlets needs to be made with care because of symbolic associations (e.g. the colour associated with bereavement varies between cultures).

- What is deemed to be acceptable activity in procuring sales? This varies between cultures – for example, in Middle Eastern markets a bribe to a public official may be considered essential, whereas it is unacceptable in most western countries.

⟳ Thinking around the subject

China – a lot of people, but a lot of differences

Many western companies have set their sights on the potential of China, the world's most populous country and one that can bewilder westerners. But is it good enough to simply lump all of China together as one homogeneous business environment? With 22 provinces (23 if Taiwan is included), three municipalities and five autonomous regions, there is tremendous diversity in business environments. Exporters seeking success in China must analyse the country carefully and choose the most promising area as their point of entry.

There is a significant income difference between urban and rural areas and between coastal and inland areas, with cities (especially the coastal cities) generally being much richer than rural areas. Examples of cities at the top of this purchasing power list are Shenzhen, Guangzhou, Shanghai, Beijing, Tianjin, Hangzhou and Dalian.

Exporters are particularly interested in the distribution of 'trigger' levels of income, above which an individual's needs for necessities are satisfied and they can become purchasers of imported western luxury goods. It has been suggested that a per capita purchasing power of US$1000 per annum is the critical figure above which Chinese people typically start buying colour TVs, washing machines and imported clothing.

Rapid economic growth is bringing a wide variety of goods within reach of a growing number of consumers. China's per capita GDP was $3744 in 2009, having risen sharply from just under $1000 in 2000. By 2010, it was expected that 40 million households would earn more than 48,000 renminbi ($6000) per year, enough to qualify a household as middle-class by US standards. Income varies widely, however, with the GDP per capita average in Shanghai more than five times higher than in Chongqing, in the interior of the country.

However, care needs to be taken in interpreting official figures about wealth in China. The actual purchasing power of a dollar in China compared to the West is higher because many Chinese do not report all their income. There are also distortions caused by hidden savings and allowances received from family members living abroad. Furthermore, the Chinese typically pay very low or no rent, spend little on healthcare and education due to subsidies, and are allowed to have only one or two children. There is also a booming black market in labour, goods, services and foreign exchange, which further distorts official statistics of wealth.

⟳

For exporters to China, getting their product to the market, at the right time and at the right place, can be very difficult, given the limitations of the communications infrastructure. This is especially true of the inland provinces and emphasizes the need for exporters to focus their marketing and distribution efforts on just a few of the richest areas. It has been observed that not even the largest multinational companies have attempted to take on the whole Chinese market at once.

The technological environment

An analysis of the technological environment of an overseas market is important for organizations that require the use of a well-developed technical infrastructure and a workforce that is able to use technology. Communications are an important element of the technological infrastructure – poorly developed telephone and postal communications may inhibit attempts to make credit cards more widely available, for instance.

14.6 Sources of information on overseas markets

The methods used to research a potential overseas market are in principle similar to those that would be used to research a domestic market. Companies would normally begin by using secondary data about a potential overseas market that are available to them at home. Sources that are readily available through specialized libraries, government organizations and specialist research organizations include reports of international agencies such as the Organization for Economic Co-operation and Development (OECD), local and national Chambers of Commerce, and private sources of information such as that provided by banks. Details of some specific sources are shown in Table 14.5.

Initial desk research at home will identify those markets that show the greatest potential for development. An organization will then often follow this up with further desk research of materials available locally within the shortlisted markets, often carried out by appointing a local research agency. This may include a review of reports published by the target market's own government and specialist locally based market research agencies.

Just as in home markets, secondary data have limitations in assessing market attractiveness. Problems in overseas markets are compounded by the greater difficulty in gaining access to data, possible language differences and problems of definitions that may differ from those with which an organization is familiar. In the case of products that are a new concept in an overseas market, information on current usage and attitudes to the product may be completely lacking.

Primary research is used to overcome shortcomings in secondary data. Its most important use is to identify cultural factors that may require a product format to be modified or abandoned altogether. A company seeking to undertake primary research in a new proposed overseas market would almost certainly use a local specialist research agency. Apart from overcoming possible language barriers, a local agency would better understand attitudes towards privacy and the level of literacy that might affect response rates for different forms of research. However, the problem of comparability between markets remains. For example, when a Japanese respondent claims to 'like' a product, the result may be comparable to a German consumer who claims to 'quite like' it. It would be wrong to assume on the basis of this research that the product is better liked by Japanese consumers than German consumers.

Table 14.5 Sources of secondary information on foreign markets.

Government agencies
UK government overseas trade reports (DTI/DBERR)
Overseas governments (e.g. US Department of Commerce)
Overseas national and local development agencies
International agencies
EU (e.g. Eurostat)
Organization for Economic Co-operation and Development (OECD)
World Trade Organization (WTO)
United Nations (UN)
International Monetary Fund (IMF)
Universal Postal Union
World Health Organization (WHO)
Research organizations
Economist Intelligence Unit
Dun & Bradstreet International
Market research firms
Publications
Financial Times country surveys/FT.com
Business International
International Trade Reporter
Banks' expert reviews
Trade associations
Chambers of Commerce
Industry-specific associations (e.g. ICAO)

Primary research is generally undertaken overseas when a company has become happy about the general potential of a market, but is unsure of a number of factors that would be critical for success – for example, whether intermediaries would be willing and able to handle their product or whether traditional cultural attitudes will present an insurmountable obstacle for a product not previously available in that market. Prior to commissioning its own specific research, a company may go for the lower-cost but less specific route of undertaking research through an omnibus survey. These are surveys regularly undertaken among a panel of consumers in overseas markets (e.g. the EOS-European Omnibus Survey Gallup Europa) which carry questions on behalf of a number of organizations.

⟳ Thinking around the subject

Guiding customers through international cyberspace

The internet can be a jungle. Getting a next-door neighbour to visit your website may be difficult enough, but how do you get a potential customer from the other side of the world to visit?

In principle, a company with a product to sell should put it on the internet and search engines used by buyers will find it. This cheap form of promotion would allow small businesses around the world to promote themselves without the need to print and distribute expensive brochures.

Of course, life is not so simple. Type into the search engine Google a term that describes many common consumer products and you will probably get thousands, or even millions, of hits. So firms often resort to paying intermediaries to try to raise their ranking in Google's listing, or selling through the site of an intermediary that has already achieved a high ranking.

Being close to the top of a search engine's listing has become an important part of international business strategy. Consider the case of a company that specializes in buying redundant manufacturing machinery from factories that have closed down, and reselling it to buyers looking for second-hand equipment. Addressing global markets is often the key to success here. After all, if a shoe factory that has just closed down in Leicester is selling off its injection moulding equipment, it is unlikely that there will be many potential buyers for the equipment in Leicester or indeed the UK. If one company in the UK couldn't profitably use the equipment, then it is likely that no UK companies will be able to. But the equipment may be just what an entrepreneur in Romania is looking for. How can a UK-based trader in second-hand equipment get its site to the top of the list that the Romanian is looking at? Relying on searches for 'machinery' or even 'second-hand machinery' is unlikely to be very fruitful – after all, there are likely to be thousands of sites in this category across the world. But including market-specific terms such as 'injection moulding' and 'shoes' in the web page text and meta-tags will help to put a company's site higher in a specialized search category. Having several pages with different titles, text and meta-tags provides more opportunities to target specific international market segments. And there's another trick that many companies use to get overseas buyers to their site. It costs relatively little to produce a foreign-language version of the main pages of a company's site. If a Romanian entrepreneur entered ' ecc o   ' in a search engine instead of 'injection moulding' or 'shoes', the seller's site would probably come very close to the top of the search results.

Case study:
Indian call centres create new international trade

© *Mash Audio Visuals Pvt. Ltd. Agency*

Dial an 0800 customer helpline in the UK and your call may be answered not in Birmingham or Manchester, but quite likely in Bangalore or Mumbai. Operating call centres on behalf of western clients has become an important new source of international trade for some less developed countries that have previously been associated with manufacturing cheap clothes and electrical items. In September 2010, over 250 call centre providers from around the world exhibited at the UK Call Centre Expo to try to sell their services. In India alone, the value of handling overseas clients' telephone calls was estimated by Datamonitor to be $4.64 billion in 2004. Such international trade would have been almost unthinkable only 20 years ago.

Handling customer service requirements emerged as a new international trade sector in the 1990s. Organizations of all kinds found increasing need to enter information into computerized databases – records of customer sales, services performed, details of vehicle movements, to name but a few. In the early days, most firms regarded this as a back-room function, which they could perform most cost effectively by using their own staff at their own premises. With time, an increasing volume of data to be analysed, the growing popularity of customer telephone support services and the growing sophistication of data analysis systems, many service companies emerged to take the burden of data processing away from client companies.

At first, most data-processing and call-handling companies operated close to their clients.

However, by the late 1980s, data processing began entering international trade, to be processed by companies in foreign countries where costs were lower, working regulations more relaxed and trades unions often non-existent. An important factor accounting for this development in international trade was the rapid pace of technological developments. Processed data and voice calls could now be transmitted very quickly and cheaply using satellites and fibre-optic links. Data processing and customer telephone support has established a firm foothold as an exportable service in areas such as India, the Caribbean and the Philippines. Each of these countries is characterized by relatively low wage rates, with skills that are at least as good as those of workers in many more developed countries.

In India, the outsourced call centre industry has been growing at double-digit rates from the late 1990s. According to a 2009 report by Ernst & Young, the whole business process outsourcing BPO sector in India's domestic BPO market was expected to reach $6 billion in size by 2012. Furthermore, the industry has shown an annual growth rate higher than for any other industry sector in India.

The development of Grecis illustrates the way in which international trade can be developed. Grecis started as a customer support centre for US-based General Electric in 1997. The company was looking for ways of cutting the cost of its customer support operations and back-room operations. In 2004, the company employed about 18,000 people worldwide, including more than 12,500 in India, and also had customer-contact centres in China, Hungary, Mexico and Romania. Although General Electric accounted for 93 per cent of Grecis sales in 2004, the company has had an expansion strategy to increase the proportion of third-party client work that it undertakes.

Wages at Indian call centres such as those operated by Grecis are much lower than they would be in the USA or UK. It is reported that many staff in 2004 would have earned as little as £2.90 a day and the total pay for an eight-hour shift could be below the minimum wage for one hour's work in Britain. Handling calls often involves anti-social hours, with night-time shifts a common feature of employment. National holidays such as Republic

Day and religious festivals like Diwali and Holi are usually ignored by call centre companies working for UK- and US-based clients. As for trades unions, these are rarely found. Although wages may be considered very low by western standards, a job in a call centre has been seen by many as highly prized. It has been reported that call centre wages are typically double what a fully qualified local teacher can earn, allowing individuals to buy previously unattainable luxuries.

Despite the rapid growth of call centres in India, many challenges are emerging. Most importantly, costs are rising, and appear to be following the pattern of developing countries gradually losing their competitive edge in a sector to even lower-cost countries. Staff turnover has become a major issue, with reports of it reaching 60 per cent annually. The UK's Financial Services Authority (FSA), in a study in 2005, found that the staff turnover level at Indian call centres was approaching that in the UK, and that managers were beginning to demand comparable wages to their UK counterparts. Retaining women after they marry is a problem not generally encountered in the UK. Some staff have been deterred by the abuse they can face from callers, who may hold them personally responsible for the delay in getting their computer repaired or their insurance claim settled.

The FSA also warned that overseas call centres posed 'a material risk' to its aim of cutting financial crime, protecting consumers and retaining confidence in Britain's financial markets. The industry was not helped by the arrest in 2006 of an Indian call centre employee of HSBC who was accused of stealing customers' details and selling them on to third parties. Overcoming these problems will inevitably involve more regulation, further forcing up Indian call centre operators' costs, and cutting their international competitive advantage.

Some UK companies, such as the insurer Aviva, have enthusiastically extended their support operations in India. But it seems that polarization has been occurring, with Datamonitor suggesting that, in 2008, over half of those companies that already used overseas call centres planned to increase their use, while the majority of companies would not consider sending any of their operations overseas. Some, such as NatWest Bank, have proudly proclaimed in their advertising that all of their telephone calls are actually answered in the UK.

India, like most developing countries, has a long way to go before it becomes a predominantly service-based, rather than an agricultural- or manufacturing-based economy. Meanwhile, the development of India's domestic economy has led to growing domestic demand for call centre services. Indian call centres have acquired a momentum of their own and, according to Ernst & Young, domestic buyers go through a learning curve on outsourcing. In the first phase, they become aware of the outsourcing through market hype. In the second phase, they learn about the potential benefits of outsourcing and begin pilot projects. In the third phase, they explore this option for better quality and for cost reasons. In the final stage, mature adopters use outsourcing to enable corporate strategies such as increasing business flexibility, bringing products to market faster and at a lower cost, accessing new markets or creating new business. Although much of the West is using call centres for the latter reasons, Ernst & Young found that, in 2009, the majority of Indian clients were still in the first or second phase of this process.

Further evidence of India's maturity as a call centre provider occurred when Indian companies began taking their services overseas. In a 'coals to Newcastle' scenario, a leading Indian call centre operator, ICICI OneSource, announced in 2007 that it was setting up two new call centres in Northern Ireland. Having gained expertise in handling calls for European customers, it was following these customers back to where many now preferred to have their calls answered, and responding to changes in the comparative cost advantage of Europe and India.

Source: based on Ernst & Young (2009) *Domestic BPO in India: Trends and Challenges*, London, Ernst & Young; Datamonitor (2009) *Trends to Watch: Contact Center Outsourcing and Services*, London, Datamonitor; Datamonitor (2008) *Trends in Global Contact Center Outsourcing Pricing and Attrition Report* (Strategic Focus), London, Datamonitor.

QUESTIONS

1 Why has data processing and call centre handling emerged as a major new activity in world trade?

2 What are the advantages and disadvantages to a western European-based insurance company of outsourcing its call centre operation to a supplier in India?

3 What are the advantages to the Indian economy of developing its call centre industry? Are there any disadvantages?

Summary

This chapter began by discussing the reasons why international trade takes place. Despite the theoretical benefits of the free movement of goods and services between countries, barriers to achieving such benefits remain. Currency fluctuations remain a major risk for international traders, although the single European currency alleviates this risk for traders within the EU. The overseas business environment is likely to be very different to that experienced at home, and therefore it is essential that appropriate exploratory research is carried out. This chapter has discussed methods of overseas market entry that balance the need for risk reduction against the need to maintain control over an overseas venture.

This chapter has brought together many of the issues discussed in previous chapters and applied them specifically to the needs of an overseas market. For any market, it is important to study its competitiveness (**Chapters 11** and **12**), the state of its national economy (**Chapter 13**), its political system (**Chapter 2**), its social and cultural values (**Chapter 3**), and attitudes towards social responsibility (**Chapter 5**).

Key Terms

Balance of payments (464)

Barrier to trade (469)

Comparative cost advantage (456)

International trade (456)

Invisible trade (465)

Trading bloc (459)

Visible trade (465)

World Trade Organization (WTO) (452)

Online Learning Centre

To help you grasp the key concepts of this chapter, explore the extra resources posted on the Online Learning Centre at *www.mcgraw-hill.co.uk/palmer*. Among other helpful resources there are chapter-by-chapter test questions, revision notes and web links.

Chapter review questions

1 Critically assess the advantages and disadvantages to a British capital goods manufacturer of possible UK adoption of the euro.

2 Discuss the possible advantages and disadvantages of greater liberalization of world trade. Who are the main winners? Who may be losers?

3 Critically evaluate the methods that a bank might use to go about researching market potential for offering business development loans in a less developed country.

Activities

1 Choose two or three international service providers from the following sectors: hotels; airlines; fast food; car rental; accountancy services. Go to their websites and click through to a selection of their national sites in countries with a different socioeconomic profile from your own. Analyse what is common between the service offer and the promotional messages between the different countries in which the company operates. Then try to identify ways in which the service offer has been adapted to meet local conditions.

2 Go to the website of an international hotel chain such as Hilton or Holiday Inn. Check out the price of a standard room on a particular date for a selection of the company's hotels in different capital cities. What dispersion of prices for a basically similar room do you observe between cities? What factors may explain the differences in prices that you observed? Do you think such price differences are likely to persist?

3 Go back to Chapter 2 and revisit Table 2.1, which gives information about GDP per person and the level of corruption and economic freedom in a selection of countries. If you were a European hotel operator seeking international expansion for its budget hotel format, how would this information influence your choice of target country to expand into? What specific additional information would you need to further guide your choice between those countries listed?

Further reading

The following references offer a general review of the factors that influence firms' foreign expansion decisions.

Keegan, W.J. and Green, M.C. (2007) *Global Marketing*, 5th edn, Upper Saddle River, NJ, Prentice Hall.

Lee, K. and Carter, S. (2009) *Global Marketing Management: Changes, Challenges and New Strategies*, 2nd edn, Oxford, Oxford University Press.

Doole, I. and Lowe, R. (2008) *International Marketing Strategy*, 5th edn, Andover, Thomson.

For a general overview of trends in international business, consult the following.

Overseas Trade, a DTI–FCO magazine for exporters, published ten times per year by Brass Tacks Publishing Co., London.

World Trade Organization, *Annual Report*, published annually.

World Trade Organization, *Trade Policy Review* (serial).

For statistics on the changing pattern of UK trade, the following regularly updated publications of the Office for National Statistics provide good coverage.

Economic Trends, a monthly publication that includes statistics relating to international trade performance.

Overseas Direct Investment, detailed breakdown of UK overseas direct investment activity, outward and inward, by component, country and industry.

For a review of the development of the European Economic Area, the following are useful sources.

Bulletin of Economic Trends in Europe (published by Eurostat).

Bulletin of the European Commission.

McCormick, J. (2008) *Understanding the European Union: A Concise Introduction*, 4th rev. edn, Basingstoke, Palgrave Macmillan.

References

Klein, N. (2000) *No Logo*, New York, Flamingo.

Nakamoto, M. (2003) 'A speedier route from order to camcorder', *Financial Times*, 12 February, p. 11.

ONS (2010) *Statistical Bulletin*, 30 March, London, Office for National Statistics.

World Bank (2008) *World Development Report, 2007/2008*, online at: www.worldbank.org/wdr/wdr98/contents.htm (accessed 17 June 2010).

World Factbook (2009) online at: https://www.cia.gov/library/publications/the-worldfactbook/ (accessed 17 June 2010).

Part

5

Bringing it Together: Environmental Analysis

Part contents

Chapter 15

The Dynamic Business Environment

It is relatively easy to analyse the past, but of course businesses need to understand their business environment in order that they can have a better picture of what their future environment will look like. A paradox of the business environment is that although managers of business organizations now have vastly more data available to them than their predecessors could have dreamed of, the future still remains very unpredictable. During recent years, the terrorist attacks of 9/11, political revolutions in the Middle East and rapidly rising commodity prices have taken many businesses by surprise. Some organizations have suffered from change, others have seized the opportunities. In this chapter, we explore approaches to analysing a dynamic business environment so that an organization can be better prepared for the future.

 ## Learning Objectives

This chapter will explain:

✔ How to bring together the analysis of various elements of a company's business environment in a way that is actionable by managers.

✔ The role of information in allowing managers to understand their operating environment.

✔ Models used to try to forecast future environmental change and strategies by which companies can respond to such change.

✔ Frameworks for assessing risk in the business environment.

15.1 Introduction

This final chapter brings together the themes of the previous chapter, and presents them within the context of actionable frameworks. At the start of Chapter 1, it was noted that companies seek to understand their business environment in order that they can be better prepared for the future. It is relatively easy to study the business environment with hindsight, but much more difficult to predict what it will look like in one year's time, or five years' time. Although this book has broken the business environment down into a number of component parts, in reality, these interact with each other, and modelling this interaction in order to make projections for the future can be very difficult. You may recall from Chapter 4 that predictions were made at the start of the 'dotcom' boom that have proved to be quite inaccurate – virtual conferences have not led to the disappearance of face-to-face conferences, as some predicted; online shopping has been growing, but 'real' shops have remained very popular; 'teleworking' from home has not spread as widely as many had expected. Of course, it is possible that each of these predictions could eventually come true, but it is difficult to understand the complexity of factors that may cause this to happen.

This chapter starts by considering the role of information and knowledge within an organization. We can never have full information about the future – only information about the past and present, which we can use to infer about the future. But in making inferences, judgements have to be made about the validity of data, and the frameworks within which the data will be analysed and predictions made. Often, when it comes to predicting the future, there is a wide range of views about how current data should be interpreted, and the appropriateness of different frameworks. We will review the bases for such diversity in this chapter.

15.2 The importance of environmental knowledge

Information represents a bridge between the organization and its environment and is the means by which a picture of the changing environment is built up within the organization. Managers are responsible for turning bits of information into knowledge that can be used to inform business plans.

According to Nonaka, 'In an economy where the only certainty is uncertainty, the one sure source of lasting competitive advantage is knowledge' (Nonaka 1991). A firm's knowledge base is likely to include, among other things, an understanding of the precise needs of customers; how those needs are likely to change over time; how those needs are satisfied in terms of efficient and effective production systems; an understanding of competitors' activities, and the impacts of technology, political and social trends. We are probably all familiar with organizations where knowledge seems to be very poor – the over-optimistic sales forecast that results in unsold stockpiles, the poorly designed product that doesn't appeal to buyers, or 'junk mail' that is of no interest to the person to whom it is sent. On the other hand, customers may revel in a company that delivers the right products at the right time, and clearly demonstrates that it is knowledgeable about changes in consumers' preferences. The small business owner may have been able to achieve all this quite single-mindedly, but in large organizations, the task of managing knowledge becomes much more complex. Where it is done well, it can be a significant contributor to a firm's sustainable competitive advantage.

Let us define the terms 'knowledge' and 'information'. Even though in some senses they may be used interchangeably, many writers have noted that the two concepts are quite distinct. In fact, knowledge is a much more all-encompassing term, which incorporates the concept of beliefs that are based on information (Dretske 1981). It also depends on the commitment and understanding of the individual holding these beliefs, which are affected by interaction and the development of judgement, behaviour and attitude (Berger and Luckmann 1966). Knowledge has meaning only in the context of a process or capacity to act. Drucker noted that, 'There is no such thing as knowledge management, there are only knowledgeable people. Information only becomes knowledge in the hands of someone who knows what to do with it' (Drucker 1999). Knowledge, then, is evidenced by its association with actions and its source can be found in a combination of information, social interaction and contextual situations, which affect the knowledge accumulation process at an individual level.

Here we need to distinguish between knowledge at the level of the individual, and at the level of the organization. Organizational knowledge comprises shared understandings, created within the organization by means of information and social interaction. Organizational progress is made when knowledge moves from the domain of the individual to that of the organization.

Two different types of knowledge about the environment can be identified. First, there is knowledge that is easily definable and accessible, often referred to as 'explicit' knowledge. This type of knowledge can be readily quantified and passed between individuals in the form of words and numbers. Because it is easily communicated, it is relatively easy to manage. **Knowledge management** is concerned with ensuring that the explicit knowledge of individuals becomes a part of the organizational knowledge base and that it is used efficiently and contributes where necessary to changes in work practices, processes and products. This, however, is not the limit of knowledge management. The second type of knowledge comprises the accumulated knowledge of individuals, which is not explicit, but can still be important to the successful operation of an organization. This type of knowledge, often known as 'tacit' knowledge, is not easy to see or express, it is highly personal, and is rooted in an individual's experiences, attitudes, values and behaviour patterns. This type of tacit knowledge can be much more difficult to formalize and disseminate within an organization. If tacit knowledge can be captured, mobilized and turned into explicit knowledge it would then be accessible to others in the organization and enable the organization to progress rather than have individuals within it having continually to relearn from the same point. The owner of a small business could have all this information readily available to him in his head. The challenge taken on by many large corporations is to emulate the knowledge management of the small business owner. One outcome of a knowledge-based organization has often been referred to as the **learning organization**, in which the challenge is to learn at the corporate level from what is known by the individuals that make up the organization.

The transition from individuals' information about the business environment to corporate environmental knowledge requires sharing of knowledge by all concerned. The extent to which this is achieved is influenced by internal environmental factors, which were discussed in Chapter 10. A knowledge management programme is needed to break down a *laissez-faire* attitude, and would typically include the following elements:

■ a strong knowledge-sharing culture, which can only emerge over time with the development of trust

■ measures to monitor that sharing, which may be reflected in individuals' performance reviews

■ technology to facilitate knowledge transfer, which should be as user-friendly as possible

■ established practices for the capture and sharing of knowledge – without clearly defined procedures, information technology is of only limited value

■ leadership and senior management commitment to sharing information – if senior management doesn't share information, why should anybody else bother?

Information allows management to improve its strategic planning, tactical implementation of programmes and its monitoring and control. A practical problem is that information is typically much more difficult to obtain to meet strategic planning needs than it is to meet operational and control needs. There can be a danger of managers focusing too heavily on information that is easily available, such as internal information or information from the internet, at the expense of that which is needed but may be harder to find and interpret.

Information and knowledge have to be seen in the context of the inter-functional dynamics of an organization. A timely supply of appropriate information provides feedback on an organization's performance, allowing actual performance to be compared with target performance. On the basis of this information, control measures can be applied that seek – where necessary – to put the organization back on its original targets. Organizations also learn from the past, in order better to understand the future. For making longer-term planning decisions, historical information is supplemented by a variety of continuous and ad hoc studies, all designed to allow better-informed decisions to be made. Information cannot in itself produce decisions – it merely provides data that must be interpreted by managers. As an interfunctional integrator, a management information system draws data from all functional areas of an organization, and increasingly from other members of an organization's value chain.

As information collection, processing, transmission and storage technologies improve, information is becoming more accessible, not just to one particular organization, but also to its competitors. Attention is therefore moving away from how information is collected, to who is best able to make use of the information. It is too simple to say that managers commission data collection by technical experts and make decisions on the basis of these data. There has been research interest in the relationship between managers and market researchers, focusing on the role of trust between the two and how its presence helps to reduce risk (Moorman, Zaltman and Deshpande 1992).

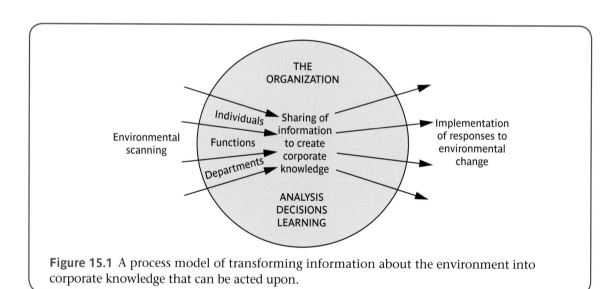

Figure 15.1 A process model of transforming information about the environment into corporate knowledge that can be acted upon.

15.3   Information systems

Many analyses of organizations' knowledge-creating activities take a systems perspective. The sub-components of a management information system typically include marketing, production, financial and human resource management systems. In a well-designed **management information system**, the barriers between these sub-systems should be conceptual rather than real – for example, sales information is of value to all these sub-systems, to a greater or lesser extent (see Figure 15.2).

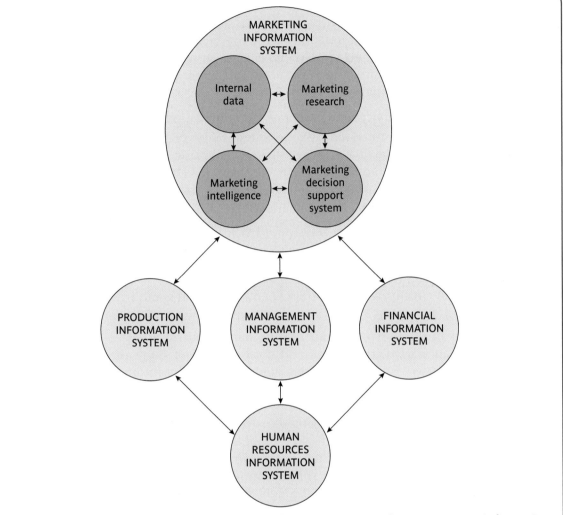

Figure 15.2 A marketing information system within the context of a management information system.

For most organizations operating in a competitive environment, a crucial role is likely to be played by the marketing information system. This can conceptually be seen as comprising four principal components, although in practice they are operationally interrelated.

◐ Thinking around the subject

Drowning in social media?

The traditional methods by which business people have kept in touch with their business environments have been described using a number of metaphors – 'keeping your ear close to the ground', 'keeping your finger on the pulse' and 'keeping a weather eye out'. These have suited business people well in a world dominated by face-to-face networks, casual conversations at trade shows and newspaper cuttings services. But with the internet offering potentially huge amounts of information about the business environment, what is the modern-day equivalent of keeping your ear close to the ground?

There are now many tools to 'push' electronic data about the business environment to key decision makers, including:

- RSS feeds from news services and corporate communications sites
- Google Alerts – programmed repetitive searches, weekly or monthly
- iGoogle – a customizable web interface that can be set as a home page and allows the user regularly to display updated news from preselected channels
- e-newsletters – subscriptions to email newsletters can provide a regular source of news about competitors, suppliers, intermediaries or the business environment in general
- listservs – this is similar to getting an e-newsletter, but in addition provides the user with a digest of important news connected to particular topics or communities; relevant listservs can be found at http://groups.google.com
- blogs are a great source of information, and by identifying active and relevant bloggers, a company can effectively leave the task of environmental scanning to an independent blogger.

This sounds like an impressive amount of information, but of course a key challenge is to separate relevance from irrelevance, and ensure that you don't drown in irrelevant information. If a listserv or an e-newsletter produces no useful information, it should be dropped. Three or four items in a newsfeed from a source is great; 300 items is probably insufficiently selective and may become unworkable. Some RSS feeds may repeat one another, so purging the duplicates is essential to avoid information overload.

Then there is the question of what to do with all the data once they have been gathered. If data are just left to pile up, finding those gems of information again might be like looking for a needle in a haystack. Companies should consider tagging their data with key words. An advantage of using tags – assigned through online services such as delicious (http://delicious.com), is that a company can put an item in several 'folders'.

Finally, information must be disseminated to key people who are able to act on it. Some companies use blogs, email and podcasts to spread information around the organization. Who decides how the vast amount of information available through social media should be separated into relevance and irrelevance so that staff inboxes are not bursting with information overload?

1 Much information is generated internally within organizations, particularly in respect of operational and control functions. By carefully arranging their collection and dissemination, internal data can provide a constant and up-to-date flow of information at relatively little cost, useful for both planning and control functions.

2 Marketing research is that part of the system concerned with the structured collection of marketing information. This can provide both routine information about marketing effectiveness – such as brand awareness levels or delivery performance – and one-off studies, such as changing attitudes towards diet or the pattern of income distribution.

3 Marketing intelligence comprises the procedures and sources used by managers to obtain pertinent information about developments in their marketing environment, particularly competitor activity. It complements the marketing research system, for whereas the

former tends to focus on structured and largely quantifiable data collection procedures, intelligence gathering concentrates on picking up relatively intangible ideas and trends. Marketing management can gather this intelligence from a number of sources, such as newspapers, specialized cutting services, employees that are in regular contact with market developments, intermediaries and suppliers to the company, as well as specialized consultants. Figure 15.3 shows some commonly used secondary (i.e. previously collected) sources of information which are used for **environmental scanning**.

- National media – e.g. *Financial Times* industry surveys
- Trade, technical and professional media – e.g. *Travel Trade Gazette, Marketing Week*
- Government departments and official publications – e.g. *Annual General Household Survey*, transport statistics
- Local chambers of trade and commerce
- Professional and trade associations – e.g. Association of British Travel Agents, Law Society
- Yearbooks and directories, e.g. *Dataquest*
- Subscription services, providing periodic sector reports on market intelligence and financial analyses, such as Keynote, MEAL, Mintel
- Subscription electronic databases, e.g. Mintel OnLine
- Competitors' websites and publications

Figure 15.3 Secondary sources of information commonly used for scanning the marketing environment.

---

4 **Decision support systems** comprise a set of models that allow forecasts to be made. Information is both an input to such models – in that data are needed to calibrate a model – and an output, in that models provide information on which decisions can be based. Models are frequently used by companies when deciding on where to locate new distribution outlets. Historical data may, for example, have established a relationship between one variable (e.g. the level of sales achieved by a particular service outlet) and other variables (e.g. pedestrian traffic in a street). Predicting the sales level of a proposed new outlet then becomes a matter of measuring pedestrian traffic at a proposed site, feeding this information into the model and calculating the predicted sales level.

⟳ Thinking around the subject

Is the glass half full or half empty?

The chairman of Bata, the shoe manufacturer, is famously quoted for his analysis of a potential foreign market for his firm's shoes. Two employees were despatched to research the market and noticed that very few people were wearing shoes. 'No hope here – the people don't wear shoes' was the response of one. But the other saw it quite differently 'What an opportunity – just think what this market will be worth when these people start wearing shoes!'

Facts alone will not make marketing decisions – the facts must be interpreted, and this interpretation can lead to quite diverse conclusions.

For those organizations that have set up marketing information systems, a number of factors will determine their effectiveness.

- *The accuracy with which the information needs of the organization have been defined*: needs can themselves be difficult to identify and it can be very difficult to draw the boundaries of the firm's environments and to separate relevance from irrelevance. This is a particular problem for large multi-product firms. The mission statement of an organization may give some indication of the boundaries for its environmental search; for example, many banks have mission statements that talk about becoming a dominant provider of financial services in their domestic market. The information needs therefore include anything related to the broader environment of financial services rather than the narrower field of banking.

- *The extensiveness of the search for information*: a balance has to be struck between the need for information and the cost of collecting it. The most critical elements of the marketing environment must be identified, and the cost of collecting relevant information weighed against the cost that would result from an inaccurate forecast.

- *The appropriateness of the sources of information*: information for decision making can typically be obtained from numerous sources. As an example, information on changes in social trends can be measured using a variety of quantitative and qualitative techniques. Companies sometimes rely on the former when only the latter can give the depth of understanding that makes for better management decisions. Companies should use a variety of appropriate sources of information.

- *The speed of communication*: the information system will be effective only if information is communicated quickly to the people capable of acting on it. Deciding what information to withhold from an individual and the concise reporting of relevant information can be as important as deciding what information to include if information overload is to be avoided.

- *Distribution of information by the organization's intranet*: information may be relayed around an organization instantly via its intranet. This poses a number of challenges about who has authority to publish or upload information on to the organization's intranet, control of access for editorial or viewing, issues of security, possible information overload, misuse of information and accuracy of information.

15.4   Forward planning with research

It should never be forgotten that the overriding purpose of all the material that has been presented in this book is to allow an organization better to understand its future. The organization will not normally be able to change the external environment that it faces, but at least it can try to understand the likely change and be prepared for it. But even the best informed companies have had difficulty knowing how to respond when there are so many uncertainties in their business environment. Consider some recent cases of business plans that failed to accurately predict the future.

- Initial take-up of cable television services in the UK was very slow, and forecasts based on American models of consumer take-up failed to take account of the quality of alternative media available in the UK, among other things.

- Many tourist attractions, such as London's Millennium Dome, have attracted far fewer visitors than originally expected, due to a misunderstanding of the attractiveness of competing attractions and the general state of the economy (see Figure 15.4).

Figure 15.4 London's Millennium Dome (now known as the O_2 Arena) was open to the public as an exhibition for just one year in 2000, but proved to be a disappointment in terms of visitor numbers. Against forecasts of 12 million paying visitors, only about half this figure actually visited. Forecasts were made difficult because of so many uncertainties in the business environment and the absence of comparable previous projects, which might give some idea of the likely take-up. What other 'millennium' projects would be launched to compete with the Dome? In fact, the London Eye, a competing attraction, beat its forecast of visitor numbers and doubtless took day-trip visitors away from the Dome. What would be the effects of the limited local transport infrastructure? Would visitors be prepared to use public transport to get to the Dome? What would be the state of the national economy during the millennium year and how would this impact on visitor numbers? And what would be the effects on public perceptions of press reviews after the Dome was opened?

On the other hand, some organizations may have been too cautious in their interpretation of the business environment, and underestimated likely demand for their new products.

⟳ Thinking around the subject

Knowledge from the shop floor?

This chapter has described a number of formalized approaches to bridging the gap between senior management and the external environment. Many of these techniques build up a picture through reports containing numbers, or sometimes verbal descriptions of the environment. But could large organizations learn from the knowledge-gathering techniques used by typical small business owners?   ⟳

A small business owner, such as a self-employed decorator or builder, is in a good position to understand their business environment – and customers' perceptions of the environment – from the comments they receive back directly from customers. In the large multi-outlet corporation, this opportunity for direct feedback is not available on a regular basis to key corporate decision makers. Many large organizations have therefore developed programmes for sending their senior staff back to the 'front line' in order that they can understand at first hand the expectations of customers and the actual performance of the company.

'Management by walking about' has become a popular method by which senior executives try to gain knowledge about aspects of their operations that are not immediately apparent from structured reporting systems. Archie Norman, when head of the retailer Asda, is reported to have introduced a number of innovations learnt during his regular visits to the company's shop floors. Some companies have adopted a formal system of role exchanges, where senior executives spend a period at the sharp end of their business. Even the vice chancellors of some universities have taken the bold step of trying to live the student life for a day or a week, and experiencing classrooms and lectures at first hand. Many have hoped that this would give vice chancellors a better understanding of the day-to-day issues that are of greatest concern to students. Although many organizations have developed similar programmes for their senior management, others have been critical of the idea. Is 'management by walking about' no more than a gimmick? Are supporters of the scientific management approach correct in their claim that the time of a highly paid executive is spent more cost effectively in the boardroom rather than doing relatively unskilled work on the shop floor?

- When the online Egg bank account was launched, it experienced an unexpectedly high level of take-up, resulting in delays and frustration for potential customers. With internet banking then being a new phenomenon, the company had very little knowledge about how consumers would react to doing their banking online. Would they be worried about security? Would they take the trouble to log on and find out?

- Many people in the industry expected the launch of Freeview digital television services in 2002 to be a flop, following the previous low levels of take-up of satellite and cable television services. In fact, Freeview quickly became very popular, with reports of shortages of set-top adapter boxes.

As a planning tool, marketing research provides management with market- and product-specific information, which allows it to minimize the degree of uncertainty in planning its business activities. This risk minimization function can apply to the whole of the business operations, or to any of its constituent parts, such as advertising. At a macroenvironmental level, simple extrapolation of trends may be acceptable where the business environment is stable. However, extrapolation often proves inadequate where major economic, social, political or technological change occurs. For example, extrapolation breaks down when events such as wars, new health scares and medical discoveries dramatically change the price and availability of a product or of competing products.

For some products, markets have historically shown very little turbulence and are unlikely to alter dramatically in the future. The market for undertakers' services will probably remain stable and simple demand **forecasting** techniques may be appropriate. However, many industries involving high technology are extremely turbulent, with rapid changes in technology occurring, sometimes overshadowing existing products. As an example, typesetting and telex bureaux saw steady growth during the 1980s but then saw a rapid contraction following the widespread advance of low-cost personal computers. Historical trends could not be relied upon to predict the future.

When it comes to forecasting demand for completely new products, simply asking potential buyers whether they would buy something can be fraught with difficulties. In the case of intangible services, it can be difficult to present potential customers with a mock-up of the product in a way that manufacturing companies often do to test likely reaction to a new product. Around the year 2000, for example, there was a lot of discussion about just what features and benefits customers would use when high-speed mobile internet services became widely available and affordable. Simply asking somebody what they would use such a service for is likely to be limited to the scope of respondents' imagination. In the context of developing a low-cost car, Henry Ford is reported as saying that if he had asked people what type of transport they wanted, they would have simply replied 'faster horses', rather than being able to imagine ever owning a car. For intangible services, the problem of consumers' limited vision can be even greater, requiring more sophisticated research methods that seek to understand deep-seated needs and motivators. Where possible, companies have sought to experiment with new goods and services targeted at trial groups, before committing themselves to large-scale provision. This may be a valid approach where capital commitments are high and the market is relatively stable, but in fast-moving markets, too much time spent understanding consumer behaviour may lead competitors to gain a lead in an emerging new service sector. In the early days of the internet, many new online services were developed with very little research; indeed, in those days, the problem of Henry Ford's horses was even more present, with most consumers having little idea of how they might use the internet. So, in order to be first to market and have a 'first mover' advantage, the process of understanding customers and forecasting demand was often based more on intuition and judgement than a rigorous analysis.

15.5 Frameworks for analysing the business environment

We now move on to consider frameworks within which the changing business environment can be studied, in order to make sense of the information presented so far and, from this, to improve the reliability of forecasts. There are two aspects to be considered when describing an analytic framework with which to analyse the business environment:

1 a definition of the elements that are to be included in the analysis, and

2 the choice of methods applied to these elements to predict the future state of the business environment, as it affects an organization.

The nature of the framework used bears a relation to the nature of the dominant business environment at the time. In the relatively stable environment that existed during the middle years of last century, management could control its destiny by controlling current performance. However, as the business environment has become more turbulent, control becomes dependent upon management's ability to predict the future and respond to change.

Diffenbach (1983) has argued that detailed environmental analysis became important only from the mid-1960s. Prior to that, the business environment was analysed primarily for the purpose of making short-term economic forecasts. As frameworks for analysis have developed in sophistication, so has the paradox that, by the time sufficient information has been gathered and analysed, it may be too late for an organization to do anything about the opportunities or threats with which it is faced. Ansoff (1985) has put forward a framework that helps to overcome this decision-making dilemma. His model allows the firm to respond rapidly to problems whose precise details are a surprise, but whose general nature could have been predicted. Ansoff's model of strategic issue analysis is shown in Figure 15.5. The central feature of the model is the continued monitoring of the firm's external and internal environments for indicators of the emergence of potentially strategic issues that may significantly influence the firm's operations in future. The focal point for Ansoff's analysis is the issue, such as the emergence of ecological awareness, rather than the conventional headings of the economic, technological environments, etc. The model allows for a graduated response: as soon as weak signals are picked up, steps are taken to allow for the possibility of these issues developing further. Responses become more precise as the signals become more amplified over time. In other words, Ansoff's model avoids the need for a firm to wait until it has sufficient information before taking a decision; it responds gradually as information emerges.

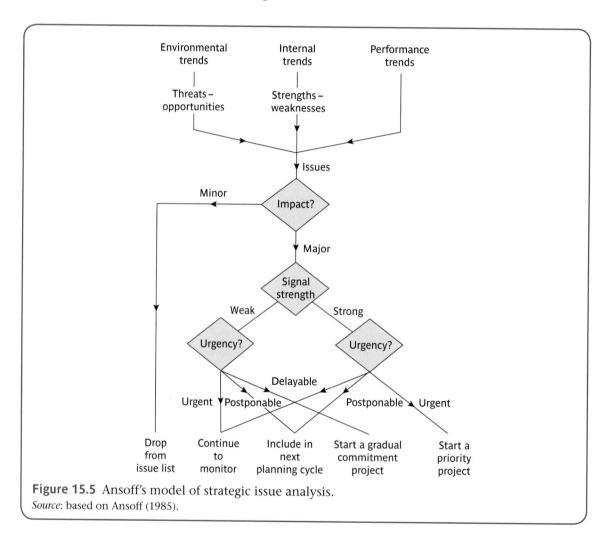

Figure 15.5 Ansoff's model of strategic issue analysis.
Source: based on Ansoff (1985).

15.5.1 Choice of framework

A range of analytic frameworks is available for companies to use in analysing their business environment and for making strategic decisions. The choice of framework will depend upon four factors.

1 The level of turbulence in the marketing environment will vary between firms operating in different markets. For example, the marketing environment of an undertaker has not

been, and in future is even less likely to be, as turbulent as that of an electronic goods manufacturer. An extrapolation of recent trends might be adequate for the former type of business, but the latter must seek to understand a diverse range of changing forces if it is to be able to predict accurately future demand for its products.

2 The cost associated with an inaccurate forecast will reflect the capital commitment to a project. A clothing manufacturer can afford to trust his or her judgement in running off a small batch of jackets. The cost of making a mistake will probably be bearable, unlike the cost of building a chemical refinery on the basis of an inaccurate forecast. The latter situation calls for relatively sophisticated analytic techniques.

3 More sophisticated analytic techniques are needed for long-timescale projects where there is a long time lag between the planning of the project and the time it comes into production. The problem of inaccurate forecasting will be even more acute where an asset has a long life span with few alternate uses.

4 Qualitative and quantitative techniques may be used as appropriate. In looking at the future, facts are hard to come by. What matters is that senior management must be in the position to make better-informed judgements about the future in order to aid decision making and planning.

We begin our discussion of frameworks with a basic building block used by many organizations to describe where they are now: the SWOT analysis. We will then look at frameworks for trying to predict the future.

15.5.2 SWOT analysis

A method widely used in marketing audits is a grid used to plot internal strengths and weaknesses in one half of the grid and external opportunities and threats in the other half. The terms opportunities and threats should not be viewed as 'absolutes' for, as Johnson, Whittington and Scholes (2010) point out, what might appear at first sight to be an opportunity may not be so when examined against an organization's resources and the feasibility of implementing a strategy. One organization's opportunity may be another's threat.

A **SWOT analysis** summarizes the main environmental issues in the form of opportunities and threats (O&T) facing an organization. With this technique, these are specifically listed alongside the strengths and weaknesses of the organization (S&W). The strengths and weaknesses are internal to the organization and the technique is used to put realism into the opportunities and threats. In this way, the environment may be assessed as giving rise to a number of possible opportunities, but if the organization is not capable of exploiting these because of internal weaknesses then they should perhaps be left alone.

The principles of a SWOT analysis are illustrated in Figure 15.6 by examining how an airline that has an established reputation as a holiday charter carrier could use the framework in assessing whether to enter the scheduled service market between London and Paris.

The strengths and weaknesses can be specified in more detail by analysing each element of the macroenvironment. This is often referred to as PESTEL analysis (Political, Economic, Social, Technological, Environmental, Legal). The previous chapters have reviewed methods of analysing each of these elements of the macroenvironment.

15.5.3 Trend extrapolation

At its simplest level, a firm identifies a historic and consistent long-term change in demand for a product over time. Demand forecasting then takes the form of multiplying current sales by a historic growth factor. In most markets, this can at best work effectively only in predicting long-term sales growth at the expense of short-term variations.

Trend extrapolation methods can be refined to recognize a relationship between sales and one key environmental variable. An example might be an observed direct relationship between

Strengths	Weaknesses
Strong financial position Good reputation with existing customers Has aircraft that can service the market	Has no allocated take-off or landing 'slots' at main airport Poor network of ticket agents Aircraft are old and expensive to operate
Opportunities	Threats
Market for business and leisure travel is growing Deregulation of air licensing allows new opportunities Costs of operating aircraft are falling	Channel Tunnel may capture a large share of market Deregulation will result in new competitors appearing Growth in air travel will lead to more congestion

Figure 15.6 SWOT analysis for a hypothetical airline considering entry to the scheduled London–Paris air travel market.

the sale of new cars to the private buyer sector and the level of disposable incomes. Forecasting the demand for new cars then becomes a problem of forecasting what will happen to disposable incomes during the planning period. In practice, the task of extrapolation cannot usually be reduced to a single dependent and independent variable. The car manufacturer would also have to consider, among other things, the relationship between sales and consumer confidence, the level of competition in its environment, the cost of borrowing, and the varying rate of government taxation.

While multiple regression techniques can be used to identify the significance of historical relationships between a number of variables, extrapolation methods suffer from a number of shortcomings. First, it can be difficult to identify the full set of variables that have an influence. Second, there can be no certainty that the trends identified from historic patterns are likely to continue in the future. Trend extrapolation takes no account of discontinuous environmental change, as was brought about by the sudden increase in oil prices in 1973 or the effects on world business confidence following the terrorist attacks of 11 September 2001. Third, it can be difficult to gather information on which to base **trend analysis**; indeed, a large part of the problem in designing a business information system lies in identifying the type of information that may be of relevance at some time in the future. Fourth, trend extrapolation is of diminishing value as the length of time used to forecast extends. The longer the time horizon, the more chance there is of historic relationships changing and new variables emerging.

Trend extrapolation as applied by most business organizations is a method of linking a simple cause with a simple effect. As such, it does nothing to try to understand or predict the underlying variables, unless extrapolation is applied to these variables too.

At best, trend extrapolation can be used where planning horizons are short, the number of variables relatively limited and the risk level relatively low. A retailer may use extrapolation to forecast how much ice cream will be demanded in summer. A historic relationship between the weather (quantified in terms of sunshine hours or average daily temperatures) may have been identified, on to which a long-term relationship between household disposable income and the domestic freezer population has been added. The level of demand for ice cream during the following month could be predicted with reasonable accuracy; with input from the Meteorological Office on the weather forecast, from the Treasury's forecast of household disposable incomes (relatively easy to obtain if the forecast period is only one month), and from statistics showing recent trends in household freezer ownership (available from the *Annual General Household Survey* office for National Statistics).

15.5.4 Expert opinion

Trend analysis is commonly used to predict demand where the state of the causative variables is known. In practice, it can be very difficult to predict what will happen to the causative variables themselves. One solution is to consult **expert opinion** to obtain the best possible forecast of what will happen to these variables. Expert opinion can vary in the level of speciality, from an economist being consulted for a general forecast about the state of the national economy to industry-specific experts. An example of the latter are the fashion consultants that study trends at the major international fashion shows and provide a valuable source of expert opinion to clothing manufacturers seeking to know which types of fabric to order, ahead of a fashion trend.

Expert opinion may be unstructured and come either from a few individuals inside the organization or from external advisers or consultants. The most senior managers in companies of a reasonable size tend to keep in touch with developments by various means. Paid and unpaid advisers may be used to keep abreast of a whole range of issues, such as technological developments, animal rights campaigners, environmental issues, government thinking and intended legislation. Large companies may employ MPs or MEPs (Members of the European Parliament) as advisers, as well as retired civil servants. Consultancy firms may be employed to brief the company on specific issues or monitor the environment on a more general basis.

In today's economy, it is essential that businesses monitor not only the domestic environment but also the EU and the international environment: as much legislation affecting UK companies comes from the EU as from the UK government. Legislation passed in the USA can have an indirect effect on UK companies, even though their products may not be intended for sale in America. What is happening in America today may be happening in Europe next year.

Relying on individuals may give an incomplete or distorted picture of the future. There are, however, more structured methods of gaining expert opinion. One of the best known is probably the Delphi method. This involves a number of experts, usually from outside the organization, who (preferably) do not know each other and who do not meet or confer while the process is under way. A **scenario** (or scenarios) about the future is drawn up by the company. This is then posted out to the experts. Comments are returned and the scenario(s) modified according to the comments received. The process is run through a number of times with the scenario being amended on each occasion. Eventually a consensus of the most likely scenario is arrived at. It is believed that this is more accurate than relying on any one individual because it involves the collected wisdom of a number of experts who have not been influenced by dominant personalities.

15.5.5 Scenario building

Scenario building is an attempt to paint a picture of the future. It may be possible to build a small number of alternative scenarios based on differing assumptions. This qualitative approach is a means of handling environmental issues that are hard to quantify because they are less structured, more uncertain and may involve very complex relationships.

Often the most senior managers in a company may hold no common view about the future. The individuals themselves are likely to be scanning the environment in an informal way, through conversations with colleagues and subordinates within the organization and through business acquaintances and friends outside. The general media, and business and technical publications, will also shape a person's 'view' of the future. Individuals will vary in their sensitivity to the environment. Such views may never be harnessed in any formal way, but they may be influencing decisions taken by these individuals. Yet the views each person holds may never have been exposed to debate or challenge in a way that would allow the individual to moderate or change his or her view.

Scenario building among senior management will help individuals to confirm or moderate their views. A new perspective may be taken on issues or forthcoming events. A wider perspective may be taken by individuals, who may become more sensitive to the environment and the impact it can have on business. A more cohesive view may be adopted by senior management, which may help strategy formulation and planning. The scenarios may be built up over a number of meetings, which may be either totally unstructured or semi-structured, with each meeting focusing on different aspects of the environment. The approach may be used at different levels of management in a large organization; a multinational company may build scenarios at the global, regional and country level. For example, Shell UK Ltd is widely reported to have used this approach on a number of occasions. In the early 1980s it was used as part of the company's methodology for attempting to assess the demand for oil depending on a number of alternative scenarios (see 'Thinking around the subject', about the Shell oil company). Chapter 4 discussed the UK government's Foresight Programme, which aims to bring together experts from industry, academia and government in an attempt to identify and evaluate trends in technological developments.

Thinking around the subject

Shell draws up likely future oil supply scenarios

How do you predict the future demand for oil products? Simple techniques based on extrapolation of previous trends have been revealed as lacking by events such as wars in the Middle East. The traditional approach used by Shell, like most of the major oil companies, was to forecast the amount of refinery capacity it would need to meet consumer demand for refined oil-based products by extrapolating recent patterns of demand. It assumed that recent trends would by and large continue, and was caught largely unawares in 1973 by the actions of the Organization of Petroleum Exporting Countries (OPEC). OPEC, a cartel of Middle Eastern oil producers, had used its monopoly power to reduce the supply of crude oil and thus force up crude oil prices threefold. This represented a very severe discontinuity in recent trends, and left most oil companies facing much lower levels of demand than they had previously planned for. Most oil companies were not much better prepared for the second sudden OPEC price rise that occurred in 1983.

Today, Shell tries to manage its future by developing a range of possible scenarios of future business environments. From these scenarios, managers can develop plans of action to meet each eventuality that could be envisaged. Identifying the nature of scenarios can present a challenge to management's creativity.

One example quoted by Shell to justify its scenario-based approach to planning is the oil price collapse that occurred in 1986. In 1984, crude oil prices stood at $28 a barrel. Other oil companies using trend extrapolation predicted that oil prices would stabilize over the next two years at the $25–$30 a barrel level. The prospect of it falling to $15 may have seemed far-fetched to many planners yet, in February 1986, the world market price of oil fell first to $17 a barrel, before drifting down to a low point of $10 two months later.

Shell claimed it was much better prepared for this price collapse as it had envisaged a scenario in which this occurred and developed a contingency plan of action in the event of it taking place. This covered, for example, alternative plans for investment in new energy sources and renewal plans for its shipping fleet. For most of its activities, Shell was trading in commodity markets in which product differentiation was either very difficult or impossible. The ability to learn and react rapidly to environmental change gave Shell its only major advantage over its competitors.

More recently, Shell's approach to scenario building demonstrated its value during the 2003 Iraq War. Although Shell had not foreseen the details of the conflict that followed the invasion of Iraq by Allied Forces, it had envisaged a scenario in which there was a serious disruption to oil supplies in the Gulf region, whether this was caused by war, accident or another cause. Contingency plans allowed the company to rapidly replace oil supplies from alternative sources and to redeploy its tanker fleet. The speed with which the company could adjust the forecourt price of petrol to the consumer in response to volatile spot market prices had been increased with improved internal communications.

For the future, Shell has stated that attitudes towards the ecological environment represent an opportunity for alternative scenario building. The company has developed two scenarios. In the first scenario, the world moves towards sustainable growth, with a change in attitudes towards consumption among consumers throughout the world and increasing controls on pollution-creating processes. The second scenario envisages a drop in environmentalism as an issue, with increasing emphasis on the need to generate economic wealth at a national level. Governments may seek to stimulate employment even if this results in greater environmental damage, while concern for worldwide approaches to the control of pollution may give way to increasing trade barriers as countries struggle for short-term economic survival. The contingency plan for the 'sustainable' scenario might include shifting resources to increase production of wind-generated electricity or biodegradable packaging. For the 'economic stimulation' scenario, expanding output and reducing production costs may be more appropriate.

The development of scenario-building methods has seen increasing importance attributed within Shell to the forecasting of business environments. The company has attributed its high and stable level of profits to this approach. The first business environment planners at Shell were seen by many as eccentric mavericks whose conclusions were relatively marginal to achieving the short-term aims of most managers. Today, the findings of the business environment planners at Shell are communicated within the organization more effectively and managers attach much more significance to the scenarios presented by drawing up their own response plans. In an increasingly turbulent environment, imagining the unimaginable can make a company more prepared. Following an explosion on one of its oil rigs, in the Gulf of Mexico in 2010, many observers commented that BP had not been well prepared for the nature of public and political reaction that followed, much of which could have been foreseen in a scenario.

15.5.6 Influence diagrams and impact grids

A more applied approach is to assess the likely impact of specific aspects of environmental change on the business. One method is to construct influence diagrams (Narchal, Kittappa and Bhattacharya 1987) so that a better understanding of the relationships between environmental forces can be obtained. If the price a company has to pay for raw materials is a critical factor then the forces that influence the price of raw materials will be of interest to it. By monitoring these it will have an earlier warning about price rises than if it were to wait until its supplier told it of the price increase. In an influence diagram (Figure 15.7), a positive relationship means that if the value of one force rises then the pressure on the dependent factor will be in the same direction. A negative relationship means that if the value of the environmental force rises then the pressure on the dependent factor is in the opposite direction, downwards.

A number of specific influence diagrams may be used to improve understanding of how forces in the environment may influence particular aspects of the business. To gain a broader

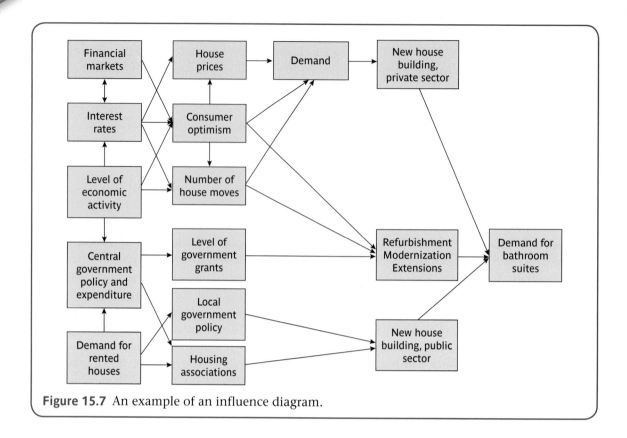

Figure 15.7 An example of an influence diagram.

view, **environment impact grids** can be constructed. Specific environmental forces or events are identified and their impact on particular aspects of the business assessed. Weighting the assessment on a simple scale, say 0 equals no effect and 10 equals substantial or critical impact, will help decision making. A simple grid can then be constructed (Figure 15.8).

Environment change / Impact on UK car market	UK government raises VAT	EU directive to limit exhaust emissions	EU announces plans for single currency	Japanese car markers abandon voluntary limits on imports to Europe	Technological breakthrough for battery car
UK demand	8				
EU demand	0				
UK production levels	4				
Prices	8				
Production costs					
Marketing costs					

Figure 15.8 An environmental impact grid, where 0 = no effect and 10 = substantial or critical impact.

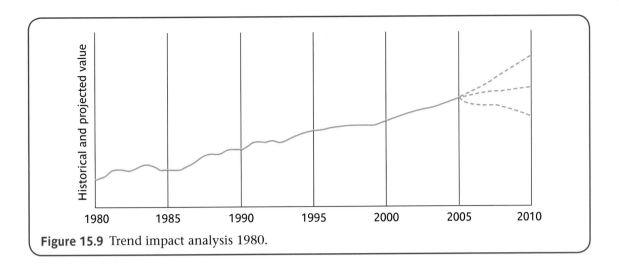

Figure 15.9 Trend impact analysis 1980.

For those companies that wish to structure the environmental analysis in a more detailed way, there are two different but complementary methods of impact analysis. The simplest is trend impact analysis (TIA), where the movements in a particular variable are plotted over time and the projected value is assessed (Figure 15.9).

A further development of trend impact analysis is cross-impact analysis (CIA), which is used in an attempt to assess the impact of changes in one variable on other variables. This is much more difficult to do but at the minimum it will help managers to understand the possible relationships between forces in the environment. At best, it will provide key information in order to aid strategic decision making (see Figure 15.10).

Wild cards \ Possible events	OPEC forces price of oil to $200/barrel	OPEC falls out: oil drop to $40/barrel with oversupply	Economic downturn becomes recession and lasts 5 years	Government increases car and petrol taxes
Clean-burn petrol engine developed				
Japanese launch first mass-produced battery-powered car				
Environment deteriorates suddenly; car drivers in western world limited to 30 miles per day				

Figure 15.10 Cross-impact analysis.

15.5.7 Environmental threat and opportunity profile (ETOP)

A marketing opportunity is an attractive situation for a company, and opportunities should be assessed for their attractiveness and success probability. Attractiveness can be assessed in terms of potential market size, growth rates, profit margins, competitiveness and distribution channels; other factors may be technological requirements, degree of government interference, environmental concerns and energy requirements. Set against the measure of attractiveness is the probability of success. This depends on the company's strengths and competitive advantage in relation to the opportunity; such issues as access to cash, lines of credit or capital to finance new developments. Technological and productive expertise, marketing skills, distribution channels and managerial competence will all need to be taken into account. A simple matrix (Figure 15.11) can be constructed to show the relationship between attractiveness and success probability.

An environmental threat is a challenge posed by an unfavourable trend or development in an organization's environment that could lead to the erosion of the organization's sales or profitability. In this case the threats should be assessed according to their seriousness and the probability of occurrence. A threat matrix can then be constructed (Figure 15.12).

In order for the environmental analysis to have a useful input into the business planning process, a wide range of information and opinions needs to be summarized in a meaningful way. This is particularly so if a number of the techniques described in this chapter have been used in a wide-ranging analysis. The information collated from the detailed analysis needs to be simplified and summarized for planning purposes. The environmental threat and opportunity profile (ETOP) provides a summary of the environmental factors that are most critical to the company (Figure 15.13). These provide a useful report to stimulate debate among senior management about the future of the business. Some authors suggest trying to weight these factors according to their importance and then rating them for their impact on the organization.

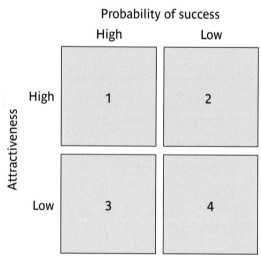

Figure 15.11 An opportunity matrix:

1 attractive opportunity that fits well with company's capabilities
2 attractive opportunity, but with low probability of success
3 high probability of success; poor fit with company's capabilities
4 let's forget this one

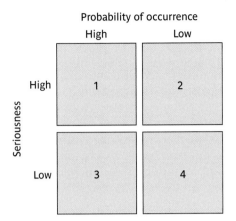

Probability of occurrence

Figure 15.12 A threat matrix:

1 competitor launches superior product
2 pound sterling rises to $3
3 higher costs of raw materials
4 legislation to cover 'environmentally friendly' claims on labels

Factor	Major opportunity	Minor opportunity	Neutral	Minor threat	Major threat	Probability
Economic						
Interest rates rise to 15%					✓	0.8
£ falls to $1.40	✓					0.4
Disposable incomes do not rise for 5 years				✓		0.3
Political						
Change in political party – more spending on education and public transport			✓			0.9
Legal						
EU bans flavouring additives in snacks				✓		0.1
Market						
Competitor launches major TV campaign				✓		0.5

Figure 15.13 Environmental threat and opportunity profile (ETOP): probability scale from 0.1 (very unlikely to happen) to 0.9 (very likely to happen).

15.6   Forming a view of environmental influence

The pace at which senior managers believe the environment is changing and the nature of that change is likely to influence their decision making and planning. Four broad patterns of environmental change may be considered, as shown in Figure 15.14. In part (a) of the figure, senior management believes that there is a stable environment with little change. In part (b) senior management believes that there is incremental change at a known and predictable pace. In part (c) the pace of change is quickening and becoming harder to anticipate. In part (d) the environment may be subject to sudden change as a major factor has a dramatic impact on other environmental forces – for example, sudden steep increases in oil prices.

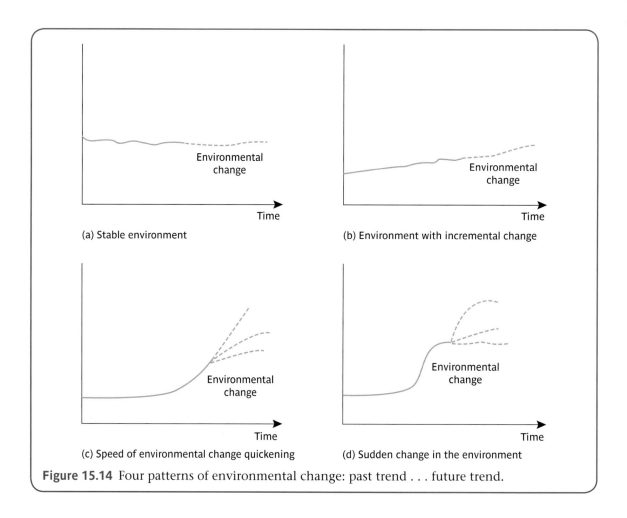

Figure 15.14 Four patterns of environmental change: past trend . . . future trend.

Other considerations for senior management are whether the environment is simple or complex and stable or dynamic (Figure 15.15). Here it is the relationship between the company and its environment that is in question and whether this is changing. Is the environment moving from being simple to becoming more complex, for example? Or is it moving from a period of stability into one of dynamism? The same environmental change may be seen as an opportunity by one company and a threat by another. The view taken will be influenced by the analysis undertaken, the views of senior management and the ability of the company to respond. For example, the UK rail industry used to be a nationalized industry owned and controlled by the UK government, which paid direct subsidies to British Rail. The industry could be said to have been simple and stable and therefore predictable. The industry was broken up from the 1980s and sold off to private companies. Railtrack managed the track and charged train operators for using it. Train operators bid for a franchise to run passenger services. Other companies owned rolling stock and leased it to train operators. Other companies ran freight services. The industry moved into a complex and dynamic environment with high levels of risk and uncertainty.

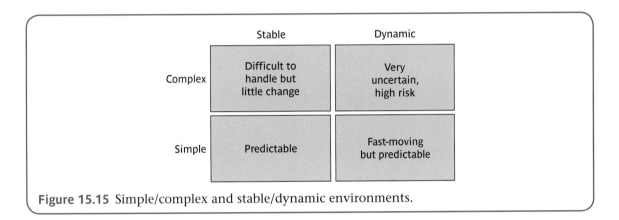

Figure 15.15 Simple/complex and stable/dynamic environments.

In the process of developing plans for the future, management needs to be able to answer the questions 'Where are we now?' and 'Where are we likely to go?' given the present performance and future environment. The SWOT summary provides a key input to the planning process. If we assume that we are preparing a business plan for a strategic business unit (an SBU may be a subsidiary or division of a larger organization), then the chief executive officer (CEO) has to set the business objectives for the coming financial year. In arriving at a decision the CEO has to balance a number of conflicting demands. The parent organization and the board of directors will have expectations regarding the performance of the SBU. These will be expressed in financial terms such as return on capital employed (ROCE), sales revenue, profit as a percentage of sales and rate of growth. The chief executive of the SBU is involved in negotiations during the setting of these objectives. During the process the CEO is conscious of the recent performance of the business (from the internal audit) and the threats and opportunities presented from the SWOT analysis. In accepting the financial objectives from the parent organization the CEO needs to ensure that they are realistic and achievable, given the current and future business environment. This may seem obvious, but remember that the parent organization may be a multinational with a head office in another country or continent. The environmental forces to which the head office managers and directors are exposed may be quite different from those influencing the local SBU.

In negotiating the objectives with the parent and in setting the SBU objectives it is beneficial to state explicitly the key assumptions made. Therefore, if the growth rate of the economy will directly influence the performance of the business it is necessary to state what level of growth you have assumed over the planning period; likewise for interest rates, levels of disposable income, business confidence indices and exchange rates etc. These would all be primary assumptions. If the business is dependent on others then some secondary or derived assumptions may need to be stated. If 80 per cent of the company's business is sales to the automotive industry, then specifying the assumed level of car sales would be important. Assumptions about the growth rate of the automotive sector may be derived – in part at least – from assumptions about growth in the national economy. Similarly, if a company

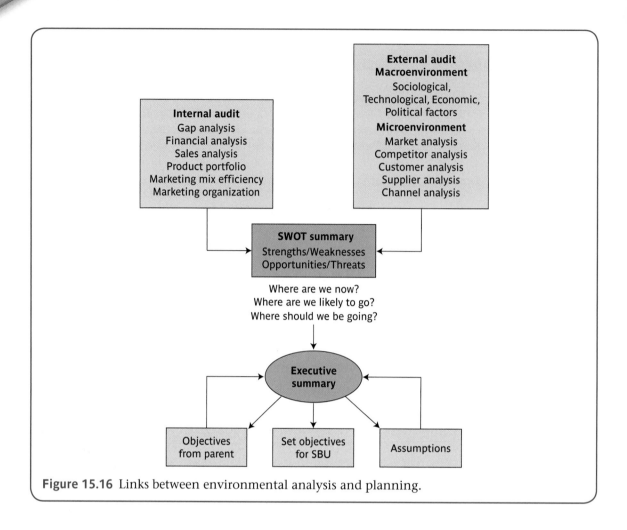

Figure 15.16 Links between environmental analysis and planning.

manufactures bathroom suites and fittings, its business is directly dependent on sales of new housing and the refurbishment of existing housing stock, both of which are influenced by the level of interest rates and consumer confidence.

Planning in larger businesses is a complex activity. If the business operates over a number of product groups, industries and international markets, then an environmental analysis needs to be conducted at the local level as well as the SBU and corporate level. Forming a cohesive view about the environment becomes much more difficult. In managing a business, senior executives have to balance the immediate requirements of existing operations against the longer-term requirements of shaping and developing the future business. Where does the organization wish to be in five and ten years' time? Since the organization cannot change the business environment it would be wise to attempt to monitor and predict it and then to shape the business to maximize the opportunities and minimize the threats posed by the environment.

15.7 Managing operational risk

So far, risk and uncertainty have been discussed at a strategic level. But in addition to making decisions at a macro level, businesses must increasingly address the issue of risk at a much more operational level. While operational risks may not normally pose such a threat to the survival of an organization as strategic risks, they can nevertheless have serious consequences for an organization. The subject of **risk assessment** has become an increasingly important item on businesses' agenda, and there are now numerous consultants that undertake, for a fee, risk assessments of an organization's activities.

Risk assessment has become increasingly important at an operational level for a number of reasons.

- Western societies have become more litigious (see Chapter 6), with consumers' rights increasingly being enshrined in legislation. Consumers now have more grounds for obtaining legal redress against a company that has failed to deliver its promises, in contrast to previous times when organizations might have been able to get away with their failings. In the field of financial services, for example, a series of mis-selling scandals has changed the focus from buyers who bought wrongly to sellers who sold wrongly, and organizations must increasingly bear the risk of mis-selling.

- The volume of government regulation of business has increased. We saw in Chapter 10, for example, that organizations are increasingly required to protect the ecological environment, and risk increasingly heavy fines if they fail to do so.

- The rights of employees have tended to increase, and organizations must assess the risk of disadvantaging individual employees or groups of employees who could potentially have a claim against the organization.

- With the growing importance of consumer brands, it has become increasingly important for an organization to preserve its image. Even though a company might not have broken any law, its association with unethical practices may do incalculable harm to the organization.

- Threats of terrorism have increased in recent years and pose a challenge for the continuity of business operations. Sometimes a terrorist group may be campaigning against a company specifically. This has been the case, for example, with the direct action taken against organizations that supplied goods and services to Huntingdon Life Sciences, a company that undertakes experiments on live animals. At other times, an organization may simply represent the values of a group that terrorists are opposed to, and an attack is a means of making this point publicly and with maximum impact. When a group bombed a branch of the British-owned HSBC Bank in Istanbul in January 2004, it probably did not have any particular grudge against the bank, but the bank symbolized a set of Western values and intervention in the world that the group was opposed to.

How should organizations respond to operational risk? They need to reconcile the potential benefits of an activity with the downside risk of certain undesirable events happening. Many approaches to risk assessment seek to develop a risk profile of an activity, and estimate the cost to the company if an event occurs and the probability that it will actually occur. An organization can therefore choose between alternative courses of action on the basis of their expected cost (defined as the total cost of an event happening, multiplied by the probability of it happening). Of course, calculating these values can be quite speculative. For a food manufacturer, for example, how does it estimate the probability of terrorist groups sabotaging its factories or environmental campaigners blockading its distribution depots? It may be even more difficult to calculate the cost to the organization of such events occurring. The costs of physical damage may be relatively easy to assess, and may possibly be covered by insurance. But it is much more difficult to assess the damage to a company's reputation. Would the activities of a protest group provide a negative association with the company that will live on in people's minds? Or would an attack on the company promote sympathy from its customers?

In choosing between alternative operational plans, organizations must take into account a number of considerations.

- Should the organization be taking part in this type of activity at all? If a service process or manufactured good offers too many opportunities for the company to make mistakes, it may be better for the organization to drop that line of activity completely. Should a train operator provide a left luggage service at its stations, when the risk of injury from a terrorist bomb is great in relation to the revenue generated? Many airlines have discontinued taking 'unaccompanied minors' on their flights, because the risk of failing to provide an adequate service is too great relative to the profitability of this type of activity.

■ Will reconfiguration of a product in order to reduce risk make it unattractive to some consumers, who will no longer buy it? For example, there has been a suggestion that increased delays at airports due to security screening have led some people to believe that the hassle of flying is too great, and so they have chosen other means of transport, or not travelled at all.

■ By contrast, rigorous measures may be perceived by some customers as a price worth paying in order to ensure that they can consume the product without fear (for example, the Israeli airline El Al is acknowledged to have the strictest security of any airline, and this has been used by the airline to promote reassurance to consumers).

■ Terrorist attacks can affect manufacturers as well as service organizations, but their effects on service organizations can be very much greater. Manufacturing companies can take steps to protect the security of their production facility by limiting access only to employees. Cases of deliberate damage to manufactured goods are rare, and manufacturers have taken steps to reduce this risk throughout their distribution channels – for example, by introducing tamper-evident packaging. This is in contrast to service organizations, where customers typically enter the production process and cannot easily be screened out in the way that unauthorized entry to a factory can be prevented. Indeed, the whole point of most services is for customers to enter the service 'factory', so, with relatively open access, risks are much greater.

Case study:

Strategic challenges and opportunities at Thomas Cook

© ilbusca

Thomas Cook has been around a long time, since 1874 in fact, when it became one of the first companies in the world to organize tours. Few organizations can have more experience in package tours than Thomas Cook. However, the holiday market has been changing and the traditional package-holiday market is stagnant, with about 19 million British people buying package holidays every year between 1997 and 2007. Although the size of the total market for holidays has been increasing during this period, more people have been making their own independent travel arrangements without the need for a tour operator such as Thomas Cook. With a cheap flight booked online with easyJet, a hotel booked through Expedia.com and a rental car booked through Holidayautos.com, the package holiday often offers few advantages to the experienced traveller. As a result of increased competitive pressure from specialists selling online, the tour companies have had to cut costs and seek new ways to generate growth in revenues.

The response by Thomas Cook to its changing business environment has taken a number of forms. One line of defence against the onslaught of 'do-it-yourself' web-based providers was to join them. Thomas Cook developed its own online booking facility where customers could book flights, hotels and a wide range of extras online, and effectively create their own package. Some commentators had accused Thomas Cook of doing too little, too late, after allowing new start-ups such as Expedia.com and opodo.com to steal a march in this sector. But Thomas Cook was hoping that its good reputation, and

widely recognized slogan of 'Don't just book it – Thomas Cook it', would give it a strong position in this sector. The company's position in the online independent travel sector was further consolidated in 2008 when it announced the acquisition of Hotels4U, which, according to the company's website 'sells exclusively via the internet, is the UK's largest independent bed bank, providing accommodation and resort transfers to over 500,000 customers per year and has access to in excess of 30,000 hotels internationally'.

A second strand to Thomas Cook's strategy has been to move into expanding product areas, such as travel insurance, foreign currency exchange and credit cards. Some of the company's developments in these areas have been in conjunction with other specialist providers – for example, the Thomas Cook credit card was launched in partnership with Barclaycard. According to Matthew Goodman, writing in *The Sunday Times*, Thomas Cook was looking nearly to double revenues from financial services, from €215 million in 2006 to €370 million by 2009–10, representing a rise in the share of group revenue from 2 per cent to 3 per cent. The share of revenue from the mainstream business of package holidays was expected to drop from 80 per cent to 72 per cent of group sales during the same period, according to Goodman.

A third part of Thomas Cook's strategy was to seek growth in overseas markets. While the holiday market was becoming increasingly saturated in the company's western Europe heartland, new opportunities were arising in the rapidly expanding economies of Asia. The company had previously sold off many overseas operations, although many continued, by agreement, to trade under the Thomas Cook brand name. The company now sought to buy back control of many of these in high-growth markets. In March 2008 the company announced that it was acquiring Thomas Cook India Limited and Thomas Cook-branded businesses in Egypt, as well as licences for the Thomas Cook brand in a total of 15 Middle East countries. The Indian purchase resulted in Thomas Cook owning India's largest foreign exchange business.

Finally, although the company had many initiatives for capitalizing on growing markets, it should never forget that although the package-holiday market may be at best stagnant, it is still a very large generator of revenue. Too many companies have focused their strategy on aspects of their activities that are never likely to be anything other than peripheral, while allowing their core business to drift along aimlessly. Thomas Cook was determined that the package-holiday business, which was still expected to account for over three-quarters of the company's revenue, should not suffer this fate. The strategic approach adopted here has been to grow the core package holiday business through merger and acquisition in order to achieve economies of scale. A stagnant market makes organic growth difficult, and therefore the most sustainable form of growth would come from a merger or acquisition of other companies, in order to achieve economies of scale. In 2007, Thomas Cook adopted this approach when it merged its operations with those of MyTravel, giving a combined company valuation of £2.8 billion. The benefits of the merger would derive from being able to negotiate better deals in contracts with travel and accommodation suppliers. There would also be possibilities for improving operational efficiencies – for example, by closing travel agency branches where the two companies had branches close to each other. In fact, in the year following the merger, the company closed 144 travel shops to cut costs.

The chief executive, Manny Fontenia-Novoa, saw the package holiday market as stable and resilient but realized that profits would have to come from expanding other parts of the business. According to the company's web page:

" The strategy of Thomas Cook Group plc is to continue to deliver benefits from existing cost saving and margin improvement plans already adopted by MyTravel and Thomas Cook; to grow revenues in existing and new market segments; and to deliver efficiencies from being part of a larger group. In particular, the strategy focuses on the following key objectives:

- *integrating the businesses of the enlarged group and delivering the planned synergies;*
- *strengthening the packaged tour operating businesses through continued operational and product improvements;*
- *growing its business in the independent travel segment through tailored products and services delivered through an asset-light business model; and*
- *extending the financial services offering of the enlarged group through the introduction of new products and services and by building on the reputation and capabilities of Thomas Cook in this area."*

Source: Goodman (2008); www.thomascookgroup.com (2008) (accessed 3 March 2011).

QUESTIONS

1 If the package holiday market is stagnant, why is Thomas Cook buying rival high-street travel companies such as MyTravel?

2 One can understand a travel company offering travel insurance and foreign exchange services to its customers, but what are the opportunities and threats of moving into a different industry such as credit cards?

3 How well does the acquisition of Hotels4U fit with the existing business? What synergies would you expect to accrue between the existing package business, financial services and internet businesses such as Hotels4U?

4 How has Thomas Cook fared since the case was written? Research Thomas Cook and its divisions/subsidiaries. Look particularly at the balance of its business between the traditional package holiday sales sold through retail travel agents/stores and sales revenue from other sources.

Summary

Information is becoming increasingly important as a means by which organizations gain advantage in a competitive business environment. With recent advances in a firm's ability to collect data, greater attention is now paid to the effective use of information. This chapter has explored the ways in which an organization can create knowledge to build up a picture of what its business environment may look like in the future. Numerous frameworks are available for analysing the business environment. The choice of framework will depend, among other things, on the complexity of the environment, the speed of change and the cost of inaccurately predicting change in the environment.

There are close linkages between this chapter and **Chapters 11** and **12**, where we discussed the nature of competition. In all but the most 'perfect' markets, understanding competitors and developing a position in relation to them is crucial to market success. An important consideration in predicting the future is the likely consequence of any change in the political and legal environments (**Chapters 2** and **6**), where change sometimes occurs quite suddenly. Change in the social and demographic environment (**Chapter 3**) tends to be more gradual. Finally, **Chapter 4** discussed developments in information technology, which are improving organizations' ability to gather and analyse information about their business environment.

Key Terms

Audit (499)

Decision support system (493)

Environmental impact grid (504)

Environmental scanning (493)

Expert opinion (501)

Forecasting (496)

Knowledge management (489)

Learning organization (489)

Management information system (490)

Risk assessment (511)

Scenario (501)

SWOT analysis (499)

Trend analysis (500)

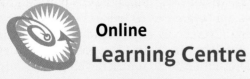

Online Learning Centre

To help you grasp the key concepts of this chapter, explore the extra resources posted on the Online Learning Centre at *www.mcgraw-hill.co.uk/palmer*. Among other helpful resources there are chapter-by-chapter test questions, revision notes and web links.

Chapter review questions

1 Identify the factors that typically make an organization's environment so complex. Using an industry example, critically discuss relevant sources of information that might help an organization understand the complexity of its environment.

2 Critically discuss methods that a producer of fast-moving consumer goods could use to reduce the possibilities of inaccurate demand forecasts for its products.

3 Choose an industry and look ahead about three to five years; build three scenarios for the future.

Activities

1 It is easy with hindsight to judge a scenario, but much more difficult to justify it at the time as a basis for planning the future. Business is essentially about preparing for the future, and previous editions of this book have tried to describe possible future business scenarios. In 1998 we outlined the following scenarios:

> *A scenario for the mid-2000s may be that the use of personal phones is set to grow very rapidly as the technology improves and prices continue to fall. Will young single professional people decide that they do not need a traditional fixed phone in their apartment? One mobile phone may be all they need. Newly married couples are likely to have his-and-hers personal phones rather than install a fixed phone in the home. A cross-impact study undertaken by British Telecom may reveal a serious threat to its traditional domestic fixed-line business. What is more, it is likely that the high-income, high-use customers will be the first to desert traditional suppliers.*

> *An alternative scenario is that while the personal mobile phone becomes the dominant mode for voice and text communications, the domestic fixed-line business will be used mainly for internet connections.*

To what extent have these scenarios become reality more than ten years later? If they haven't, why is this the case? Have there been any unexpected factors that have changed the nature of the actual scenarios?

2 Construct an influence diagram for a product category of your choosing. Some ideas are:

    (a) retirement apartments (private sector for sale or rent)

    (b) children's bikes

    (c) conservatories

    (d) fabric/material (used for curtaining and furniture coverings)

    (e) computer-controlled document handling machinery (for handling, collating and folding documents or leaflets, and stuffing envelopes)

3 Cars propelled by traditional fuels such as petrol and diesel are claimed to pollute our cities and damage the environment. Investigate the alternative fuels under development and evaluate their benefits and limitations. What environmental forces may speed up or slow down the introduction of alternative fuels? It may be technically possible to produce cars that run on alternative fuels but how could you persuade the market to accept them?

Further reading

There are many texts on the subject of marketing management that focus on how an organization can implement measures to respond to a changing external environment. The following are useful.

Johnson, G., Whittington, R. and Scholes, K. (2010) *Exploring Corporate Strategy*, 9th edn, London, FT Prentice Hall.
Kotler, P. (2011) *Marketing Management*, 14th edn, Englewood Cliffs, New Jersey, Pearson Education.
Piercy, N. (2008) *Market-led Strategic Change: Transforming the Process of Going to Market*, 4th edn, Oxford, Butterworth-Heinemann.

For a general discussion of the principles of marketing research, the following texts are recommended.

Bradley, N. (2010) *Marketing Research, Tools and Techniques*, Oxford, Oxford University Press.
Wilson, A. (2006) *Marketing Research: An Integrated Approach*, 2nd edn, London, FT Prentice Hall.
Zikmund, W.G. and Babin, B.J. (2009) *Essentials of Marketing Research*, 4th edn, Andover, Thomson.

The important role played by information in business planning is discussed in the following texts.

Byrne, D. (2008) *Web of Knowledge: Essential Knowledge Management for Those Working with Information*, London, Facet Publishing.
Hislop, D. (2009) *Knowledge Management in Organizations: A Critical Introduction*, Oxford, Oxford University Press.

References

Ansoff, H.I. (1985) *Marketing Strategy and Management*, London, Macmillan.
Berger, P.L. and Luckmann, T. (1966) *The Social Construction of Reality*, Garden City, NY, Doubleday.
Diffenbach, J. (1983) 'Corporate environmental analysis in US corporations', *Long Range Planning*, Vol. 16, No. 3, pp. 107–116.
Dretske, F. (1981) *Knowledge and the Flow of Information*, Cambridge, MA, MIT Press.
Drucker, P.F. (1999) *Management Challenges for the 21st Century*, New York, Harper & Row.
Goodman, M. (2008) *The Sunday Times*, 16 March, p. 11.
Johnson, G., Whittington, R. and Scholes, K. (2010) *Exploring Corporate Strategy*, 9th edn, Hemel Hempstead, FT Prentice Hall International.
Moorman C., Zaltman, G. and Deshpande, R. (1992) 'Relationships between providers and users of market research: the dynamics of trust within and between organizations, *Journal of Marketing Research*, Vol. 29 (August), pp. 314–328.
Narchal, R.M., Kittappa, K. and Bhattacharya, P. (1987) 'An environmental scanning system for business planning', *Long Range Planning*, Vol. 20, No. 6, pp. 96–105.
Nonaka, I. (1991) 'The knowledge-creating company', *Harvard Business Review*, Vol. 69, No. 6, pp. 96–104.

Chapter 16

Case Studies

Five case studies are presented here that bring together a number of issues discussed in previous chapters. All the cases focus on organizations or industry sectors that have faced significant changes in their business environments. Their challenge has been, first, to identify the change that was occurring, then to understand its impact on their business and to make decisions about how they could most effectively respond to the change. For each case study, a number of discussion questions are posed. The cases represent a range of different business environments, as outlined below.

- *Farming* *is generally associated with land-based activities for growing crops and raising cattle. However, farming is also becoming an important focus for service-based activities, and the case study demonstrates how farmers have become major consumers and producers of services. The case study picks up on the point made in Chapter 13, that developed economies tend to be increasingly dominated by services.*

- *Hewlett-Packard* *has a long history of innovation in the field of computer peripherals. But should it spread its research and development (R&D) efforts among lots of small innovations or concentrate its resources on one big project that could transform the company, in the way that the iPod transformed the Apple computer company?*

- *The* *UK's National Health Service* *is going through a period of rapid change, as the healthcare environment comes to rely less on centralized planning and more on competition between service providers. This case study explores some of the intended and unintended consequences of the internet in this sector. While there have been clear advantages, such as more efficient reservation and utilization systems, there have been unintended consequences, such as the 'worried well' using internet-based medical information to challenge their doctor's expertise.*

- *The pricing of* *rail services* *in the UK has become increasingly complex as rail operators try to reconcile the sometimes conflicting demands of market-based competition and government regulation. The case study explores some of the practical issues that affect pricing in the sector.*

- *Loyalty cards* *have become a common feature in many people's wallets as they seek rewards for dealing with a retailer, and retailers are keen to reward loyal customers in return for providing a lot of personal information about themselves and their spending habits. The case study builds on Chapter 4 by exploring some of the practical and ethical issues that arise from computerized loyalty programmes.*

16.1 Case 1: Farming becomes part of the services sector

By Paul Custance, Harper Adams University College

In Chapter 13, we looked at the structure of national economies and made a general observation that services have become the dominant element of most developed economies. In the UK and USA, for example, the services sector accounts for about three-quarters of GDP. But what exactly do we mean by the services sector? And how have individual organizations adapted to the service-dominant economy?

There are many examples of companies that have made the transition from being predominantly manufacturing based to being predominantly service based. WPP, one of the world's largest advertising agencies and perhaps the best example of a 'pure' intangible service industry, actually started life as a manufacturer of shopping baskets (WPP originally stood for Wire Plastic Products). However, it soon understood the needs of its customers, and the fact that they were buying its shopping baskets and trolleys in order to boost sales. From there it was a small step to selling in-store promotional displays and then on to advertising. WPP moved from being an essentially manufacturing-based company to a service-based company.

Service companies have emerged not just from the manufacturing sector, but also from the agricultural sector. By 2002, 58.3 per cent of UK farmers were engaged in some form of diversified activity, to the extent that nearly one in five diversified holdings now had no conventional agricultural production (Centre for Rural Research 2003).

Being a farmer in Britain was not generally a happy experience during the last years of the twentieth century, with numerous food scares such as 'mad cow' disease, and increasing pressure on margins from the supermarkets that bought their produce. It seemed that customers were not prepared to pay high enough prices to make it attractive for farmers to grow crops, raise animals, and produce milk and eggs. Admittedly, there had been some bright spots in the quest to improve profit margins, with farming becoming ever more intensive from the 1960s onwards, with larger farms using land, machinery and chemicals intensively. But even organic farming – seen as a hope of the 1990s – lost some of its glamour as competition forced down farmers' margins. It hardly seemed surprising therefore that farmers should seek to diversify into services.

The idea of adding value was nothing new to farmers; after all, many had undertaken some processing of the food that they had produced, such as turning milk into cheese. Many more had ventured into services by selling the produce that they had grown through their own farm shops. These had developed from simple roadside stalls that operated only at harvest time, to become fully fledged service activities in their own right. It was no longer good enough simply to have the right fruit and vegetables, but also opening hours, car parking and customer facilities that met buyers' rising expectations. Some farm shops

© Dmitry Kalinovsky

have even developed into mini out-of-town visitor destinations, which families visit to eat, go shopping partake of entertainment for children. In an attempt to get a higher price for their produce, some farmers have developed innovative service-based methods of delivery. Vegetable box schemes have become very popular with some segments of food buyers, who prefer to pay a premium price for freshly delivered local produce. Barcombe Organic Nurseries, in Lewes, Sussex, is typical of many farms that have developed a vegetable box scheme by offering buyers internet-based ordering, home delivery and food preparation advice. Getting closer to customers is also achieved by selling produce from the farm at the farmers' markets that have sprung up in many towns and cities since the late 1990s.

Increasingly, farmers have diversified into even more wide-ranging service sectors, reflecting the nature of consumer demand. Many farms have diversified into various aspects of tourism, ranging from caravan parks and paintball competitions to bed and breakfast accommodation, 4 × 4 driving courses and concert venues. Some have opened their doors as visitor centres, giving urban visitors an insight into life on a farm. Most farm attractions offer a standard range of 'unthemed' activities, such as animals, countryside access, museum/exhibition events, arts and crafts, children's entertainment, retail and catering. Some are thematically linked to the activity on the farm, such as cider farms and vineyards. Nearly one-quarter of diversified farms provide accommodation and catering services to the general public.

Moving the emphasis from growing crops to selling services can demand big changes in the way farmers run their business. No longer is the emphasis on a tangible product that can be quality-controlled through increasingly sophisticated growing methods. No longer do farmers simply sell their produce to a merchant, giving them no direct contact with the consumers who eat their food. Having customers coming on to their farm poses new challenges, and farmers must now 'design in' customers to their production processes. If customers want to come on Sundays or in school holidays, farmers will have to change their working patterns to suit the needs of these customers. Understanding what makes customers satisfied with a service can be much more complex than assessing the quality of crops against easily defined benchmarks. Farmers must now get inside the mind of customers to try to understand the often complex needs that they seek to satisfy through service-based activities. Understanding why and how a customer decides to take part in a paintball competition can be much more difficult than understanding how they buy an apple, and calls for a more thorough understanding of needs, expectations and the process of evaluating and selecting a service.

It is not only consumers who have seen the results of farmers' diversification into services. Behind the scenes, a wide range of new business-to-business services have developed. The days when a farmer would retain staff and equipment to undertake all farming tasks himself are disappearing, as specialist service suppliers are brought in. True, farmers have always relied on bought-in administrative services, such as those provided by accountants and solicitors. Today, even basic agricultural operations such as crop spraying and harvesting are likely to be bought in from a specialist service supplier. Many farmers have come to realize that it is more cost effective to get a contractor to harvest their wheat and barley, rather than keep a combine harvester for their own use. Farm labour has been increasingly casualized as many farmers rely on the services of employment agencies to source gangs of workers to cope with the harvesting of fruit and vegetables.

Even the business of applying fertilizer and pesticides has been turned into a service activity. Some pesticide manufacturers, for example, offer farmers an 'integrated pest management' service. They claim to save up to 50 per cent of pesticide costs and at the same time increase yields by the timely application of pesticides. In a more developed version the pesticide provider could even offer a crop insurance service, guaranteeing the farmer that certain pests and diseases will not affect yield. The whole pesticide application would be carried out by the service provider. For a few farmers, all of their farm operations are now undertaken by contract services providers. Farmers are not just buyers of business-to-business services such as crop spraying. Many have spotted the opportunities of doing other farmers' work for them, and have given up their own farming to become farm services suppliers.

Source:

Turner, M., Winter, M., Barr, D. et al. (2003) *Farm Diversification Activities: Benchmarking Study 2002*, report to DEFRA, Report No. 2003–02, Centre for Rural Policy Research, University of Exeter.

Questions

1 In the context of this case study, discuss the reasons why there has been a tendency for western developed economies to become more service based in the make-up of their economic activity.

2 Using examples from this case study, identify and discuss the role of business-to-business relationships in transforming an economy to one that is service based.

3 What are the principal challenges that farmers are likely to face as they develop new consumer services to supplement their basic agricultural output?

16.2   Case 2: How many winning ideas can you back?

It is often said that about three-quarters of all new product launches fail. Some fail because they are essentially yesterday's product dressed up as something new, and offer no real advantages to customers in a crowded marketplace (think of a new brand of confectionery that fails to make the mark after a year). Other new products may be technologically very advanced, but fail because they are simply ahead of their time for consumer adoption (think of early WAP mobile phones). Every company wants to back a winner, but inevitably faces a dilemma. Should it back lots of small new product ideas, or put all its resources into developing just a small number of really big ideas? Backing lots of small ideas may reduce the company's exposure to risk, but the likely consequence is a series of low-profile new product launches, which will not be transformational points for the company. Backing one big idea that becomes a winner could transform a company, as it did with the then struggling Apple Computer company, which was transformed following the launch of its iPod music player.

Sadly, expenditure on R&D has been falling in Britain and many other western countries. According to the OECD, the UK's expenditure on R&D between 1981 and 2008 declined from 2.4 per cent of gross domestic product (GDP) to 1.79 per cent (ONS 2010). This compares with an EU average of 2.25 per cent of GDP. Of course, it is not just the level of expenditure that goes into the R&D process that is important, but the number of patents that come out of it and, more importantly, the number of patents that can be commercialized.

How should a company spend its R&D budget? What percentage of the research budget should be spent on researching completely new ideas and innovations that represent the 'next generation' of products available in a market? This type of expenditure – sometimes referred to as 'blue skies research', 'ideas factories', 'hot house', etc. – typically accounts for only a small percentage of a company's total research and development budget. Some might dismiss such departments as 'pie in the sky', with little tangible outcome from a lot of effort, but as the case of Apple demonstrates, it can take just one idea resulting from blue-sky thinking to transform a company's fortunes.

Rather more of a company's research effort is typically involved in more mundane commercialization of existing technologies – for example, developing new variants of iPod players. The risks may be lower and the outcome more predictable, but this level of R&D is less likely to give a company its big break.

In the world of computing peripherals, the decision whether to invest in new applications, or new fundamental technologies is ever present. According to James Aston writing in *The Sunday Times* (16 March 2008), Hewlett-Packard (HP) spends only about 5 per cent of its research budget on 'blue skies'-type activity. It is difficult to evaluate value for money and the financial contribution of such research. Many ideas and projects do not make it as far as becoming usable products. According to Aston, HP in 2008 was 'slimming down the work in its Bristol research centre from 150 small projects to no more than 30 large ones'. The Bristol centre, one of seven globally, employed about 150 people in five labs. Their job is not only to come up with the ideas but to get them to work. But that is just part of the story. An idea needs to be tested against customer need and market demand, and finally the idea needs to be commercialized so that the manufacturing costs and market price will produce a financial return on the estimated sales volume. According to Ashton, the changes taking place in HP were designed to give the labs 'more of a venture-capital approach, zeroing on commercial potential sooner'. The hard part is knowing when to stop tinkering with the idea and when to take it to market.

Sources:

James Ashton (2008), *The Sunday Times*, 16 March, p. 14, http://www.hpl.hp.com/bristol/index.html (accessed 19 March 2008); **Office for National Statistics** (2010), *UK Gross Domestic Expenditure on Research and Development*.

Questions

1 What are the advantages and disadvantages of funding 150 small projects as against 30 large projects?

2 Should researchers be encouraged to be entrepreneurial in thinking about the commercial opportunities of their ideas, or would it be best to let them focus solely on the new ideas?

3 What are the implications of taking new technological/software ideas to market too soon or leaving it too late?

4 What are the new technologies underpinning products and services likely to be launched over the next five years?

16.3 Case 3: Health services go online in an increasingly competitive environment

The operating environment of health services is becoming ever more competitive and at the same time business managers are increasingly having to face the challenges and opportunities of the internet within their sector. Health services may be considered to be the last place where you would expect the internet to be playing a big role in improving the efficiency and effectiveness of service delivery – after all, most health services necessarily involve the physical interaction between patient and healthcare professional. Wouldn't it be difficult to imagine how the internet would change the way a dentist drills a tooth, a physiotherapist exercises muscles or an optician examines a patient's eyes? But, away from these intense professional–client encounters, the internet is changing the environment of health-service delivery. As healthcare becomes increasingly marketing orientated, efficient and effective use of the internet can become crucial to successful financial performance.

The internet can be a wonderful information source, and sites listing medical information have grown in number, reflecting significantly increased demand from the public for health information. Reasons for this growth in interest include demographic changes (especially the increasing number of elderly people in the population), a higher level of education and literacy levels, and increased demand for informed choice. Also, in many western countries, the focus of healthcare has moved towards participative healthcare models, which has encouraged individuals to take responsibility for their own health and well-being, rather than rely on professionals to tell them what is good for them. While patients' desire for more information has increased, the ability of professionals to deliver that information face to face has been increasingly challenged, with doctors' consulting times being constrained. In Britain, with patients increasingly able to exercise choice, rather than having to take what health professionals give them, the internet has become an important tool for patients making informed choices between competing public- or private-sector health providers.

From the mid-1990s, government policy in the UK has emphasized the need to provide greater health information, in a belief that providing patients with good-quality information will reduce pressure on an overburdened National Health Service. There is also evidence that well-informed patients have better health outcomes and generally make less use of health services (Murray *et al.* 2003). To this end, a plethora of health websites are available in the UK, produced by the Department of Health, the National Health Service, professional bodies such as the British Medical Council, charities specializing in particular conditions, support groups, commercial organizations and pharmaceutical companies. One estimate put the number of health sites available to the public in 2002 at 70,000 (Benigeri and Pluye 2003).

A number of surveys have sought to provide a picture of the typical online medical information service user. For example, Dolan *et al.* (2004) concluded, on the basis of a study by CIBER in the UK and Pew in the USA, that women sought health information more often than men, and younger people aged 24–44 sought health information online significantly more than those aged 55 and over.

Organizations have for some time produced leaflets on specific aspects of healthcare, but the internet opened up a new medium for distributing a much greater volume of information on more specialized subjects to a much larger audience. More importantly, the internet allows interactivity in a way that was not really possible with printed leaflets. The internet developed just at a time when growing awareness of personal health issues meant that specific answers could be provided in response to individuals' questions. An individual concerned about breast cancer, for example, can visit the breast cancer charity Breast Cancer Care (www.breastcancercare.org.uk) and undertake a guided self-test to identify any possible problems. Suffering from tinnitus? The British Tinnitus Association website (www.tinnitus.org.uk/) will guide the visitor through a checklist of symptoms, and suggest support and advice.

It has been an assumption that providing more information to patients will reduce their need to visit a doctor and take up less of their valuable time. However, it has also been suggested that web-based health information services may also have the effect of generating additional demands on doctors' time, by patients whose anxiety has been raised by the information they have seen on a website. Of course, many doctors would be glad that their patient used a website to diagnose a problem early on, at a stage when it could be treated, rather than wait until a solution was much more difficult. At the same time, it has been suggested that doctors' time is taken up with a growing number of 'worried well' patients, who simply seek reassurance and, moreover, want to spend more time with a doctor discussing points that they have read about on websites (Hogg, Laing and Winkelman 2003). The availability of online information has undoubtedly had an effect on professional–patient relationships, where the previous blind trust in a professional has now been qualified by an educated and informed group of patients who are not prepared simply to accept what the doctor says. There is an old saying that a patient who is unsure about their doctor's diagnosis would seek another doctor's second opinion. Now they can get a second, third and fourth opinion from different websites, and go back to their own doctor to challenge any diagnosis that they make.

It is not just through additional information that the internet is transforming the nature of doctor–patient relationships. 'Telemedicine' has allowed highly specialized consultants to make their knowledge available at geographically remote locations. The recent trend of the National Health Service has been towards larger, specialist units, which means that the availability of specialists may be difficult in remote areas. In the extreme case of North Sea oil platforms, it would be unrealistic to maintain anything more than basic healthcare coverage, and time-consuming, impractical and expensive to fly a patient to a mainland hospital, or fly a healthcare specialist to the oil platform. So, instead, remote delivery systems have sought to emulate the practices of many other service sectors by making specialist knowledge available through the use of telecommunications. A specialist consultant can be based in a large hospital, and give advice using a webcam or view a patient being operated on in a small-scale facility on the oil platform.

The internet has also been used by the National Health Service to make appointments systems more efficient and effective. Rather than relying on slow, expensive telephone-based systems, some trusts have introduced online bookings by which patients can choose an available slot, in much the same way as they would choose a delivery slot for their online grocery shopping to be delivered. With individual NHS Trusts facing competition from other NHS Trusts (and increasingly also from private-sector providers), an efficient booking system can be just as important to financial success as an online booking system is to a hotel or airline.

In the longer term, the National Health Service has undertaken one of the world's biggest software projects, with its plans to integrate the information systems of all health service professionals in the country. In theory, the medical records of any patient will be available online to any authorized professional at any time in any location. A visitor from London who is suddenly taken ill in Manchester would have their records made available immediately through the internet, rather than having to wait for telephone calls or letters to bring answers to questions about crucial preconditions. Unfortunately, like many large computer projects, the scheme has taken longer and cost much more than originally planned. Although medical professionals have generally been strong in their support of a unified system that allows patients' information to be made easily available, sceptics have been strong in their criticism of the system. Many remain concerned about possible breaches of security, and the loss of privacy in a system that would have hundreds of thousands of healthcare professionals authorized to access data in some form. Some healthcare professionals have been sceptical about government intentions, which might also include exerting more centralized control over their activities. The system, which brings together data from all parts of the health service, could easily be used to monitor performance and impose hospital-specific standards from the centre – something that would have been much more difficult in an environment where hospital trusts' own computer systems were not linked through the internet.

Sources:

Benigeri, M. and Pluye, P. (2003) 'Shortcomings of health information on the internet', *Health Promotion International*, Vol. 18, No. 4, pp. 381–386.

Dolan, G., Iredale, R., Williams, R. and Ameen, J. (2004) 'Consumer use of the internet for health information: a survey of primary care patients', *International Journal of Consumer Studies*, Vol. 28, No. 2, pp. 147–153.

Hogg, G., Laing, A. and Winkelman, D. (2003) 'The professional service encounter in the age of the internet: an exploratory study', *Journal of Services Marketing*, Vol. 17, No. 5, pp. 476–494.

Murray, M., Bodenheimer, T., Rittenhouse, D. and Grumbach, K. (2003) 'Improving timely access to primary care: case studies of the advanced access model', *Journal of the American Medical Association*, Vol. 289, pp. 1042–1046.

Questions

1 Summarize the ways in which the internet has had impacts on the business environment of health services providers.

2 Discuss the ethical issues likely to be involved in the use of information technology by health services providers.

3 In an increasingly competitive healthcare marketplace, critically evaluate the ways in which the internet can be used to create a competitive advantage.

16.4 Case 4: UK rail fares move to market-based pricing

The pricing of train fares in Britain has evolved over the past 40 years in response to changes in the operating environment of railways. As it has evolved from a centrally planned public service to a more competitive private-sector industry, new forms of pricing have emerged.

Gone are the days when there were just a handful of tickets available between any two points – typically full-price single and return fares, a cheap off-peak day-return fare, a child fare and a season-ticket fare for commuters. One constant theme in the development of railway pricing has been the proliferation of different types of fares. For a return journey from Manchester to London, no fewer than 23 different fares were available in April 2010. The pricing of train tickets is complicated by the existence of 'regulated' and 'unregulated' fares.

A number of market segments have been identified by train operators. The business traveller typically has a need for the flexibility of travelling at any time of the day and, because an employer is often picking up the bill, this segment tends to be relatively insensitive to the price charged. Some segments of the business market demand higher standards of quality and are prepared to pay a price of £399 for a flexible first-class ticket from Manchester to London. Some rail companies have added dedicated car-parking facilities and business lounges to their offer aimed at business people. Leisure segments are on the whole more price sensitive and prepared to accept a lower level of flexibility. Those who are able to book their ticket one week in advance can pay just £23 for the same journey.

A keen eye is kept on the competition in determining prices. Students are more likely than business travellers to accept the coach as an alternative, and therefore the Manchester to London Student Saver rail fare of £28.30 is pitched against the equivalent student coach fare of £22.10, the higher rail fare being justified on the basis of a superior service offering. For the business traveller, the comparison is with the cost of running a car, parking in London and, more importantly, the cost of an employed person's time. Against these costs, the flexible first-class fare of £399 may be perceived as good value. For the family market, the most serious competition is presented by the family car, so a family discount railcard allows the family as a unit to travel for the price of little more than two adults.

The political environment has had an important effect on rail pricing policies. Before the 1960s, railways were seen as essentially a public service and fares were charged on a seemingly equitable cost-per-mile basis, with a distinction between first and second class, and a system of cheap same-day returns, which existed largely through tradition. From the 1960s, the state-owned British Rail moved away from social objectives with the introduction of business objectives. With this came recognition that pricing must also be used to maximize revenue rather than to provide social equality. However, government intervention occasionally came into conflict with British Rail's business objectives – for example, British Rail was instructed to curtail fare increases during the 1980s as part of the government's anti-inflation policy and again, in the autumn of 1991, it was instructed to reduce some proposed Inter-City fare increases on account of the poor quality of service on some routes.

The underlying cost of a train journey is difficult to determine as a basis for pricing. Fixed costs have to be paid by train operating companies to Network Rail for the use of the track and terminals. In addition, trains and staff represent a fixed cost, although many companies have sought to make these more flexible. Companies recognize that trains operating in the morning and evening peak periods cost more to operate as fixed costs of vehicles used solely for the peak period cannot be spread over other off-peak periods. The underlying cost of running commuter trains has been publicly cited by train operating companies as the reason for increasing season ticket prices by greater than the rate of inflation during recent years.

The privatization of British Rail in the mid-1990s led to further developments in pricing. In principle, the government sought to facilitate competition, which would have the effect of reducing prices charged to passengers. Other service sectors, such as buses, electricity supply and telecommunications, had been privatized and deregulated, and price-based competition had followed, so why shouldn't the same happen with railways? Train operators have had some success in attracting passengers away from other modes of transport, especially the car and coach, by offering cheap advance booking fares. In some cases,

© *Stephen Morris*

completely new demand has been generated among people who could now afford to go away for the weekend, because a previously expensive fare was now affordable. Some competition between railway companies has occurred – for example, Chiltern Railways has competed with Virgin Trains between Birmingham and London. But competition between rail operators has generally been limited to a small number of busy routes where there are either two different lines or two operators running over the same line.

For most passengers, the prospect of competition leading to lower prices has been no more than a dream based on the idealistic principles of economic theory. Competition between rail operators has been the exception rather than the rule, and many passengers have effectively been captive, with no realistic alternative form of competition, and for whom making their journey to work in the first place is absolutely essential. Commuters into the main cities of Britain would probably feel that competition is fine in theory, but cannot benefit them in practice. For this reason the government has retained some regulation of fares where competitive pressures alone cannot be relied upon to protect the interests of passengers.

Certain standard-class rail tickets are regulated by government, including standard-class weekly season fares, and most commuter fares in and around London. The amount by which the cost of an individual regulated ticket can be increased by a rail company is usually capped at Retail Price Index (RPI) plus a maximum of 1 per cent. In January 2010, rail operators were forced to reduce many regulated fares because inflation (measured by the RPI) in the previous year was minus 1.4 per cent, so the maximum average increase was -0.4 per cent. Fares charged by the rail operators Southeastern and Northern Rail in the West Yorkshire Passenger Transport Executive area were exceptions, as they are allowed to raise individual fares by up to RPI plus 3 per cent, in recognition of those operators' commitments to additional investment.

Regulation has also been necessary to ensure a national network of ticket prices that allows a passenger to buy just one ticket for use on the trains of multiple operators who may be involved in a journey – for example, a journey from Cardiff to Newquay would involve a minimum of two train operators, and it would be unreasonable to expect passengers to buy separate tickets for each part of their journey. Furthermore, many sections of route are shared by two or more operators, and the rail network becomes more attractive to passengers if they can travel on the trains of any operator, rather than the operator that issued a ticket. A complex system exists to allocate revenue to operators where the tickets can be used on the trains of more than one company.

Interchangeability of tickets between train operators has been a key element in the retention of an integrated national rail network. However, there has been a proliferation of tickets issued by operators for use only on their own services. For the issuing train operator, there are a number of advantages arising from selling these restricted tickets. They are easy to implement, because they do not require negotiation with other rail operators, or the government's rail regulator. The operator gets to keep all of the revenue for such restricted tickets, rather than sharing it with other operators, as happens with tickets available on the trains of any operator. Many train operators that are part of larger transport networks have introduced restricted tickets that also allow use on the company's local bus services (for example, the First South Wales Bus Railcard is restricted to trains and buses operated by First Group within South Wales). Inevitably, the ever finer segmentation of markets with specialized tickets has led to more confusion among customers, and even staff. A discussion thread on the website 'railUKforums' discussed the subject of 'tickets you would never want to buy' and identified a number of apparently special-offer, restricted tickets that were actually more expensive than comparable, unrestricted tickets.

Many critics have argued that the move to market-based pricing on Britain's railways has not served users or the country well. They point out that train fares are still among the highest in Europe, despite the level of subsidy given by government increasing steadily since privatization (in 2008, the eight leading rail franchise operators received a total of more than £800 million in government subsidies (Webster 2009). As an example, the first-class fully flexible ticket price of £399 for a return journey between London and Manchester compares very unfavourably with a fare of €163 (about £143) for a first-class flexible ticket between Paris and Dijon, a similar distance but faster journey. Critics argue that fiddling about with price-based competition is relatively unimportant in ensuring competitive advantage for railways, compared with investment in new infrastructure.

At a time of increasing ecological concerns, railways should be seen as good for the environment, but critics have argued that market-based pricing has at best been of only marginal benefit. Competitive fares might have attracted a lot of young and elderly people from competing coach services, and Britain's coach network has suffered as a result. However, coaches could also claim to be good for the environment. Outside of the main urban areas, a frequent complaint is that peak-hour train fares work out as very expensive compared to driving to work, and many people may find the high fare too much of a barrier to forgoing the convenience of their car. Another common complaint is that railway pricing has done nothing to stop the growth of travel by air. Since privatization, the network of UK domestic air services has grown rapidly, with low-cost airlines such as Ryanair and easyJet selling tickets that often cost much less than a comparable train journey. On some routes, such as London – Scotland, the market share of airlines has been increasing, and reached an estimated 85 per cent of the rail/air traffic total in 2009 (DfT 2010). For a person travelling on business at peak periods, flying is often a cheaper option than using the train. Can pricing get such people back on to the ecologically more friendly train, or are market forces fundamentally incapable of making resource allocation decisions that really require long-term, centralized planning?

Sources:

DfT (2010) *Regional Transport Statistics, Department for Transport*, online at www.dft.gov.uk/pgr/statistics, (accessed 18 May 2010); **Webster, B.** (2009) 'Train companies demand bigger subsidies to protect falling profits', *The Times*, 21 January.

Questions

1 Identify and discuss the ways in which the political environment has had an impact on the pricing of railways. Should there be more or less government regulation of railway pricing?

2 To what extent would you describe the pricing of train tickets as being based on the principles of competitive markets? Is it desirable that the markets of train operators should be made more competitive?

3 Discuss ways in which the pricing of rail services may be linked to issues of ecological sustainability. What are the challenges and opportunities for establishing a link?

16.5   Case 5: Retailers drown in information about their customers

By Steve Worthington, Monash University

"*Jane is 53 years old and lives with her cat in a northern suburb of Melbourne, Australia. She works full-time on the other side of town, so she prefers to drive rather than use public transport. At the weekend Jane likes to do some gardening, and she is also fond of red wine. In fact, she drinks so much that it makes financial sense for her to buy her wine by the case. Jane's daughter lives a few kilometres away and has an 18-month-old daughter. Jane likes to buy clothes and toys for her granddaughter, even though she has more than enough already.***"*

How do we know all these things? Because, some time ago, Jane applied for a loyalty card at her local supermarket so that she could earn frequent-flyer points every time she goes shopping. She now hands over her card whenever she is at the checkout.

Although her identity is kept confidential by the supermarket chain, Jane would probably recognize herself from the 'profile' it has built from its database. The supermarket knows that she is a *pet owner*, because she buys cat food. It knows that she *drives to work*, because she buys fuel at a petrol station owned by the same company. From her regular purchases, it also knows that she is a *gardener* and a *wine drinker*. From her occasional purchases of baby products, it has even deduced that there is a baby in the family, but that it isn't hers. Given her age, it has assumed that Jane is a *new grandmother*.

Jane now receives regular mail from the supermarket chain (and affiliated companies) with advertising and promotions that are specially designed to appeal to her. After doing extensive survey and focus-group research with people like Jane, the supermarket chain has developed a sophisticated segmentation that allows it to target different kinds of customers with different messages. Like Jane, many people who hold a loyalty card do not realize just how valuable their personal information can be, even when it is aggregated with that of their fellow customers.

Loyalty programmes take a number of forms. The simplest comprise cards that are stamped each time a customer makes a purchase; then, after so many stamps are obtained, a reward is given. This is popular with simple, low-value purchases – for example, many coffee-shop chains give their customers cards that allow them to earn a free cup of coffee after they have purchased six coffees. More usually, the customer is given a credit card-style plastic card with a magnetic strip, chip or bar code containing a unique member identification number and perhaps the name of the customer. There is usually no payment facility associated with a loyalty card; its sole purpose is to monitor transactions in order to reward customers in proportion to their spending. Whenever a purchase is made, information about the purchase (such as the price, product, place of purchase and date) is recorded alongside the customer's number. Over time, therefore, the information about consumer behaviour gathered through loyalty card data can be substantial.

Loyalty programmes have often been confined within an organization, so that the company that a customer spends their money with is the company that gives the rewards. In many cases, however, loyalty programmes incorporate more than one company. Airlines that belong to one of the global alliances, such as Oneworld or Star Alliance, have for some time allowed customers of one airline to accumulate points when travelling with another, and also to take rewards on another airline or service provider. Airline programmes have also been extended to cover related businesses – for example, car rental and hotels. There are many other examples of collaborative loyalty programmes – for example, in the UK, the Nectar card combines among others the supermarket chain Sainsbury's, car-rental company Hertz, travel company Expedia.co.uk, electricity supply company EDF and optician Dollond and Aitchison.

Increased customer loyalty is just one benefit of setting up a loyalty programme; in addition, such programmes can generate a wealth of commercially valuable information about purchasing behaviour. In fact, this aspect of a loyalty programme can be just as important for a company as any increase in sales due to customer's spending to earn reward points. For this reason, the term 'loyalty programme' is something of a misnomer; a better term would be 'rewards and information exchange programme', because that is a more accurate description of the transaction between customer and company. In return for providing information about themselves and their spending patterns, members of a loyalty programme receive rewards in proportion to their spending. The company operating the programme can then use the information that these programmes generate to more accurately target offers to customers, refine their marketing approaches, and potentially to also then sell aggregated information and 'insights' about consumer behaviour to their suppliers.

The costs of running a loyalty programme can be substantial when spread across millions of members. For instance, it has been estimated that the cost to the Australian retailer Woolworths of purchasing Qantas frequent-flyer points accrued through its Everyday Rewards scheme is between A$60 and A$80 million per year, and 'lifts the cost of customer loyalty by 0.4c to 3c for every dollar spent by customers'.

There are a number of ways that retailers can recoup these costs. The first and most obvious is to raise prices. If a retailer with a loyalty programme did this, it would mean that members of the loyalty programme, who receive benefits in the form of reward points, are being cross-subsidized by customers who are not members, and therefore do not receive any rewards.

Another way to recover the costs of running a loyalty programme is to generate more revenue by increasing sales volumes. This is the ostensible purpose of a 'loyalty' scheme – to encourage people to spend their money at one store rather than another so as to earn reward points. But an even more effective way to increase sales is to turn the purchasing data from a loyalty programme into commercially valuable information. Such information might be used to refine the range of products sold to match customers' habits, or to develop offers or deals targeted at particular types of shopper. For example, it has been reported that, in Australia, Woolworths uses postcode data from its Everyday Rewards members to evaluate possible locations for new supermarkets and petrol outlets.

In addition, programme operators can partially offset the cost of their loyalty programme by aggregating member data and selling this in 'de-identified' form to suppliers or other corporate entities. UK retailer Tesco provides a telling example of how this can be done; its customer database is based on the behaviour of the 13 million households that hold a Tesco Clubcard. Information on who buys which products, when and where they buy them, and how much they spend, can be seen at the level of individual products. This information can help manufacturers and suppliers to understand the purchasing decisions and habits of customers, and to design products and marketing campaigns accordingly. The information that suppliers purchase from Tesco is aggregated, so there are no breaches of privacy law. By 'collaborating' with the retailer in this way, partners also strive to reach or retain a position as a preferred supplier, further strengthening Tesco's market power.

Customers may not realize how much information they are giving away about themselves. Some may not care, but others may be so concerned about privacy issues to the point where they would not use a loyalty card. It would be a significant problem for companies if a large group of customers who were hard to reach through conventional market research techniques also became hard to reach through their lack of participation in loyalty programmes.

In order to better understand how loyalty programmes are perceived by customers, a study was undertaken in Australia during July 2009 by the Australia Institute, in collaboration with the Department of Marketing at Monash University. It involved an online survey of 1000 people. Some of the findings are summarized below.

Four in five survey respondents (83 per cent) reported having at least one loyalty card; this figure is probably higher than for the population as a whole because of the nature of the survey sample. When looking at the average number of loyalty cards (up to a maximum of five in this survey), it is possible to see distinct differences between men and women, and between people of various ages. Women held an average of 2.02 loyalty cards, while for men this was only 1.29. Average numbers of loyalty cards increase more or less consistently with increases in age. Whereas 18–24 year olds had only 1.55 cards, those over 60 reported having 1.76 cards.

Around two in three loyalty card holders surveyed (70 per cent) said they had redeemed awards or points from a loyalty card scheme. By far the most common type of redemption was for vouchers to spend at a particular store or group of stores. Three in four of those who had made a redemption (73 per cent) estimated its value at A$100 or less, while just under half (46 per cent) made redemptions worth A$50 or less. The mean value of redemptions was A$113.

The survey asked which aspect of a loyalty card scheme was most important to respondents – keeping their personal information confidential or getting more rewards. Around half of respondents (49 per cent) said privacy was more important, while 45 per cent preferred getting more rewards (with another 6 per cent not sure about this question). Women were slightly more concerned about privacy compared to men. However, there were major differences in attitudes to privacy across the age spectrum. People aged between 18 and 24 years were much more likely to regard rewards (63 per cent) as more important than privacy (28 per cent). Respondents aged between 35 and 44 years were divided roughly evenly between preferring privacy (50 per cent) and preferring rewards (48 per cent). Among the oldest age group (65 years and over) there was an overwhelming preference for privacy (58 per cent) over rewards (35 per cent). In other words, concerns about privacy are associated with increasing age and, to a lesser extent, with women. This finding is notable, given than women and older people tend to have more loyalty cards on average than men and younger people.

A minority of respondents said they had opted out of receiving marketing materials from their loyalty card schemes – between 15 and 20 per cent depending on the type of programme. Those who had opted out almost invariably did this when they were joining the scheme, by ticking a box on the application form; there were very few who had made a request by phone or in writing after they had joined. The number of people opting out of receiving information, or allowing the information to be shared with other companies, has been a growing concern for companies keen to get the maximum value out of their database. But are people showing unreasonable concern for privacy? The study suggested that someone who is not a member of a loyalty programme would typically forgo A$123 per year in loyalty benefits to shop at a retail outlet that offers a loyalty programme, but not actually take part in it.

Sources:

Based on **Worthington, S.** (2000) 'A classic example of a misnomer: the loyalty card' *Journal of Targeting, Measurement and Analysis for Marketing*, Vol. 8, No. 3, pp. 222–234 and **Worthington, S., and Fear, J.** (2009) *The Hidden Side of Loyalty and Programs*, The Australian Centre for Retail Studies within the Department of Marketing of Monash University.

Questions

1 Discuss the role of technology in enabling companies to track their customers and learn more about their individual buying behaviour? What are the trends for the future development of customer databases?

2 What practical issues are likely to arise where a company seeks to extend a company-specific loyalty programme to embrace other collaborating service providers?

3 What ethical issues are raised by the use of loyalty cards? How should companies seek to overcome the reluctance of some groups to share their personal information?

Glossary

A

Accelerator effect – When a small change in demand for consumer products has a much larger effect on demand for capital goods manufacturers

Acquisition – When a company acquires the share capital of another company

Act of Parliament – A law passed by the UK Parliament

Age structure – The composition of a population, defined in terms of the proportions contained within defined age ranges

Anti-competitive practices – Actions by companies that have the effect of reducing the amount of competition in a market

Article numbering – An industry-wide standardized system for allocating a unique number to each product

Attitudes – An individual's consistently favourable or unfavourable feelings about an object, person or idea

Audits – Evaluation of an activity, e.g. a financial audit checks the accuracy and integrity of a company's accounting procedures

B

Balance of payments – A record of all transactions between domestic consumers and firms and those based overseas

Barriers to trade – Formal and informal obstacles that prevent trade taking place between countries

Beacon Council – A UK government scheme that identifies selected local government organizations as examples of good practice

Best value – Obtaining supplies of goods or services for the best ratio of benefits to costs

Birth rate – The number of births in a population, per 1000 members of the population

Borrowing – Temporarily having the use of somebody else's financial resources

Building societies – Organizations registered under the Building Societies Acts that are owned by their savers and borrowers

Business cycle – Fluctuations in the level of activity in an economy, commonly measured by employment levels and aggregate demand

C

Cabinet – The senior executive of the UK government, headed by the Prime Minister

Cash flow – The amount of cash available to a business at any particular time

Cellular household – A household unit in which the members of the household live their lives with a significant amount of independence from other members

Census of population – A ten-yearly survey of population characteristics

Central bank – In the UK, a lender of last resort, and responsible for setting monetary and interest rate policy; in the UK, this is the Bank of England (the European Central Bank for the EU)

Channels of distribution – A 'route to market' for a company and a means of getting its goods and services to the final consumer

Charities – In the UK, organizations registered in accordance with the Charities Acts, whose primary aim is to benefit a good cause, rather than profit-seeking shareholders

Charter Mark – A UK government scheme to recognize excellent quality in public services

Circular flow of income – The means by which money circulates in an economy between households and firms

Civil service – Paid government officials who are responsible for implementing government policies

Closed system – A system that is isolated from its surrounding environment

Codes of practice – A set of rules, usually drawn up by an industry or trade association specifying behaviour expected of members

Common law – A law that emerges through precedents created in previous judgments by courts

Companies Acts – Legislation governing the creation and operation of limited liability companies

Comparative cost advantage – When it costs a company fewer units of resources compared with its competitors to produce a unit of output

Competition Commission – UK regulatory body responsible for ensuring that markets remain competitive and in the long-term interest of consumers

Competitive cost advantage – A firm has a marketing mix that the target market sees as meeting its needs better than the mix of competing firms

Computer-aided design (CAD) – The use of IT in the design of new products

Computer-aided manufacturing (CAM) – The use of IT to make better-quality products at lower unit cost

Confidence level – In the context of consumer expenditure, the confidence felt by individuals about their personal future welfare and/or national economic prosperity

Consolidation – Reduction in the number of companies within an industry sector

Contract – An agreement between two or more parties

Control – Taking action to ensure that outcomes are in accordance with plans

Cooperative society – UK organization owned by customers

Cooperatives – Associations of producers or consumers to share benefits of cooperation

Corporate governance – Procedures adopted for the internal management of an organization

Corporate social responsibility – When an organization takes into account the interests of all stakeholders who may be affected by its activities

Credit crunch – A term used to describe the sudden reluctance of banks to lend to one another, and which had direct and indirect effects on consumers and business organizations during 2007–08

Cultural convergence – The idea that distinctive characteristics of different cultures are becoming less significant

Culture – The whole set of beliefs, attitudes and ways of behaving shared by a group of people

Customer loyalty – When the customer buys repeatedly from a company; this may be because they like the company so much, or there is simply no suitable alternative available to purchase

D

Debentures – Loans secured against the assets of a company

Decision support systems – Techniques and processes used to facilitate better decisions by managers

Deflation – A falling level of prices

Demand – Consumers' ability and willingness to pay for a product

Demand-technology life cycle – A demand-technology life cycle will have a history of emergence, rapid growth, slower growth, maturity and decline, but over a shorter period than the more sustainable longer-term demand cycle

Demography – The study of population characteristics

Directives – Instructions by the EU to member-states to introduce changes to their domestic legislation

Directors – Members of a limited company who have responsibilities for governing the company

Discrimination – Making a distinction between two or more otherwise similar phenomena

Diseconomies of scale – When unit costs increase as output increases

Dismissal – The ending of an employment relationship, other than by reasons of mutual agreement or redundancy

Disposable income – Income available to individuals after they have made allowance for essential, non-discretionary spending

Diversification – An organization enters new markets and/or launches new products that are not closely related to its current activities

Duty of care – The legal responsibility of an individual or a company not to harm others

E

Ecological impacts – The effects of organizations' activities on ecological systems

Economic structure – The composition of an economy in terms of the number and types of buyers and sellers it comprises

Economies of scale – Costs per unit fall as output rises

Elasticity of demand – The change in volume of demand for a product in response to a change in some parameter, e.g. the price of the product

Elasticity of supply – The extent to which the amount supplied to a market varies following a change in price

Electronic commerce (e-commerce) – Transactions of goods or services for which payment occurs over the internet or other wide area networks

Electronic data interchange (EDI) – Proprietary systems for transferring data between organizations

Electronic point of sale (EPOS) – A system for recording details of individual sales

Employee involvement – Making employees feel a sense of ownership in their job

Empowerment – Expecting employees to use their own discretion to solve a problem, rather than closely following instructions

Environmental impact grids – A method of assessing the impact of combinations of external events on an organization's activities

Environmental scanning – A systematic method of monitoring changes in an organization's business environment

Environmental set – All of the organisations and individuals within an organization's micro business environment

Equity capital – The shareholders' interest in a business, representing risk capital

Ethics – A culturally determined sense of what is right and wrong

Ethnic minorities – Small groups in a population who are distinctive in terms of their racial and cultural background

European Commission – Administrative executive of the EU

European Council of Ministers – Ministers representing each of the EU member-states

European Court of Justice – The supreme court within the EU

European Economic Area (EEA) – A common market area comprising the EU plus affiliate nations

European Union (EU) – The 27 states of Europe that belong to an economic and political union

Exchange rate – The price of one currency expressed in terms of another

Executive – Part of an organization given the task of implementing policy

Expert opinion – Consulting experts in a subject area to advise on a subject where the knowledge base of an organization is weak

External costs – Product costs that are borne by individuals or firms who are not compensated for the costs they incur

Externalities – Costs that are not borne by the organization that causes them

F

Factoring – When a company with money owing to it sells these outstanding debts to a third-party company, which then collects them; in return, the company receives an immediate, discounted amount based on the value of the debts

Family roles – Expectations of the behaviour of different members of a family unit

Financial community – Companies involved in lending and borrowing money, and circulating it between companies, customers and other agencies

Fiscal policy – Government policy on public borrowing, spending and taxation

Five Forces model – Porter's model of the competitive environment of any firm, which comprises the threat of new entrants and substitute products, the bargaining powers of customers and suppliers, and competition among current competitors

Flexible workforce – A workforce that is expected to be flexible in its working practices, and also possibly to be hired and laid off at short notice

Flotation – When a company seeks to raise capital on a stock market

Forecasting – Estimating the future value of a given phenomenon

Franchising – When a company sells the right for another organization or individual to use its business processes and brand name

Functional organization – An organization that structures its internal management around the functions that they perform

G

Geodemographic analysis – The study of consumer behaviour based on an individual's area of residence

Globalization – A tendency to treat the world as though it were part of an organization's domestic market

Gross domestic product (GDP) – A measure of the value of goods and services produced in an economy during a specified period

H

Horizontal integration – Merging of firms' activities at a similar point in a value chain

Household structure – The composition of a household unit in terms of the number and relationship of its members

Human resource management (HRM) – Management activity related to the effective and efficient recruitment, training, motivation, reward and control of an organization's employees

Hype cycle – The tendency for the potential benefits of new ideas to be exaggerated in the short term, until a more realistic assessment becomes mainstream

I

Ideology – A guiding set of beliefs

Imperfect competition – A market that is competitive, but does not meet the criteria for perfect competition (e.g. because of variations in product features and information availability)

Incentive – Something that motivates an individual to achieve a goal

Industrial relations – Relationships between employees and their employers, often mediated through trades unions

Inflation – A rise in the general level of prices of goods and services

Information environment – The volume and quality of information within the business environment of an organization, and the means of collecting, analysing and disseminating it

Injections – Money received by households that does not come from firms, and money received by firms in the circular flow of income

Intellectual property rights – Ownership of the rights to intangible ideas

Interest rates – The cost of borrowing money (or the return from lending money)

Intermediaries – Individuals or organizations who are involved in transferring goods and services from the producer to the final consumer

Internal environment – The processes and structures internal to an organization that facilitate or impede its response to change in its external environment

Internal marketing – The application of the principles and practices of marketing to an organization's dealings with its employees

International trade – Imports/exports to/from other countries

Internet – Computers connected through a common platform

Invisible trade – Overseas trade in services, as distinct from 'visible' goods

Invisibles – Imports and exports to/from a country that comprise intangible services

J

Joint ventures – An agreement between two or more firms to exploit a business opportunity, in which capital funding, profits, risk and core competencies are shared

Judicial review – An appeal to a court to judge as to whether correct governmental procedures were followed

Judiciary – Legal structures and processes

'Just-in-time' relationships – A customer relies on a supplier to deliver goods or services at precisely the time that they will be incorporated into the customer's production processes, thereby allowing a lower level of stocks to be kept

Just-in-time (JIT) systems – Reliably getting products to customers just before they need them

K

Knowledge management – Processes for collecting, analysing and distributing information to people in an organization, who can act upon it

L

Leadership – The ability to take charge effectively and direct a team

Learning organization – An organization that learns about its environment and adapts to change through effective information-sharing and decision-making activities

Legislature – The body responsible for passing legislation

Life stages – Distinctive patterns of behaviour associated with periods in individuals' lives

Lifestyle – A set of distinctive attitudes and behaviours

Limited company – An organization that has a separate legal personality from that of its owners

Liquidation – A company is broken up and its assets sold in order to pay off creditors and to return any surplus to shareholders

Lobbying – Seeking to influence decisions by other individuals/organizations

Local government – Government at the level of town or county

M

Macroeconomic analysis – Aims to show how the economic activities of households and firms, and the economic policies of government, can influence output, employment, price levels and rate of economic growth in an economy

Macroenvironment – The forces in an organization's environment that have an indirect impact on it (e.g. demographic and legislative change)

Management buy-out – When the management of a company agree to buy all or part of a business from the owners

Management information system – A systematic method of collecting, analysing and distributing information that can be used by management decision makers

Market structure – A definition of a market in terms of the number of sellers relative to the number of buyers

Markets – A place (actual or virtual) where buyers and sellers meet to exchange things of value

Matrix organization structures – An organization structure that relies on coordination of management functions, rather than a strict hierarchical functional control

Mergers – The amalgamation of two or more organizations

Microenvironment – The immediate environment of an organization, with which it comes into direct contact (e.g. its customers and suppliers)

Migration – Movements of people from one country/region to another

Misrepresentation – When a false representation is made about goods or services

Mission statement – A statement of the essential purpose of an organization

Models – A representation of reality, which identifies key variables and relationships between the variables

Monetarism – A view of the national economy that attributes instability in the economy to issues of money supply

Monetary Policy Committee – UK committee of the Bank of England responsible for developing and maintaining monetary policy

Monopoly – A market in which there is only one supplier; rarely achieved in practice, as most products have some form of substitute

Motivation – The desire to achieve personal goals

Multinational company – Company operating in multiple markets/countries

Multiplier effect – The addition to total income and expenditure within an economy resulting from an initial injection of expenditure

N

Nationalized industry – State-owned trading organization

Negligence – Harm caused to others through failure to exercise a duty of care

Networks – Connections between several organizations in some form of community, characterized by communication and formal or informal relationships between them

New product development (NPD) process – A sequential (sometimes concurrent) process for getting ideas for new products, developing, testing and launching them

Non-departmental public bodies (NDPBs) – Organizations that are essentially owned by the government and are part of the public sector, but operate at 'arm's length' from their sponsoring government department; also commonly referred to as 'quangos' (see below)

O

Oligopoly – A market dominated by a few interdependent suppliers

Open system – A system that continuously interacts with its surrounding environment

Organic growth – A virtuous circle of business growth in which success leads to growth, which leads to further success and further growth

Organizational culture – Shared values within an organization that help to distinguish one organization from another

Organizational life cycle – The stages that organizations go through, from initial launch, through growth and maturity, and eventually to decline and possible closure

Organizational objectives – A statement of where an organization wants to be at some defined point in the future (e.g. in terms of sales levels and profitability)

Outsourcing – When a company engages another organization to provide services (e.g. IT maintenance, office cleaning)

P

Partnership – An agreement between individuals to operate a business together, and to share risks and rewards, usually in agreed proportions

Patents – A right for a company to prevent others copying a product whose unique intellectual property has been recognized by the Patent Office

Perfect competition – A market in which there are no barriers to entry, no one firm can dominate the market, there is full information available to all buyers and sellers, and all sellers sell an undifferentiated product

Political parties – Groups of people who share a political ideology and seek to advance their cause through an organization referred to as a political party

Pressure groups – Groups that are formed to promote a particular cause

Price determination – The method of determining prices in a marketplace through the interaction of supply and demand

Private Finance Initiative (PFI) – When private-sector capital, risk and management expertise is brought in to manage government assets and/or services

Privatization – Transferring the assets and/or the operations of public-sector organizations to the private sector

Product life cycle – The stages that a product goes through from initial launch, through growth, maturity, and eventually to decline and possible deletion from a company's product portfolio

Profit maximization – When firms seek to achieve the maximum possible level of profit

Prospectus – An official document issued by a company seeking to raise fresh capital

Public limited company (plc) – A company owned by its shareholding members, which has to satisfy additional criteria regarding capital, membership and reporting, compared with an ordinary limited company

Public–private partnership (PPP) – A general term to cover joint agreements between public -and private-sector organizations, including private finance initiatives (see above)

Public sector net borrowing (PSNB) – The amount of money owed to lenders, less the amount that government has lent to others

Q

Quango – A governmental organization that operates at 'arm's length' from its sponsoring department (stands for quasi-autonomous non-governmental organization); also known as a non-departmental public body (see above)

Quantitative easing – A central bank increases the volume of money in circulation within an economy

R

Receivership – When a company is no longer a going concern and a process is initiated of breaking it up and distributing its assets to creditors (as well as shareholders if there are sufficient funds)

Recession – A period when the size of the national economy is declining, or at least not growing

Reference groups – Groups that an individual makes reference to when making decisions about their own behaviour

Regional government – In the UK, government for Scotland, Wales and Northern Ireland

Regulation – Restricting the freedom of operators in

a market to protect the interests of users and/or the community in general

Relationship marketing – Marketing to consumers or businesses that takes account of the history of dealings with a particular customer, and considers a customer's specific likely future requirements

Research and development (R&D) – Investment in new products, or new methods of making existing products

Retail Prices Index (RPI) – A measure of the percentage change in prices charged by shops for a basket of goods during a specified period

Rights issue – Used when a company seeks to raise additional equity capital from its existing shareholders

Risk assessment – An analysis of the probability of an event happening and the seriousness of its effects

Role – Behaviour that is expected of an individual

S

Satisficing – Performing to a satisfactory level, rather than the highest achievable level

Savings ratio – The proportion of households' available income that is saved rather than spent

Scenario – A hypothetical picture of an environment, which may occur in the future

Share capital – The equity capital of a company, representing owners' interests in the business

Shareholders – Investors who take a risk in purchasing a company's shares

Social class – A method of dividing a population into groups based on their social background

Social exclusion – When groups of a society are prevented by formal or informal barriers from taking a full part in the life of the community

Social objectives – Objectives pursued by an organization that will benefit the wider community at large, and not just its own members

Sole trader – A business, the identity of which is indistinguishable from that of its owner

Staff development – Investment in employees that is aimed at developing their general abilities, rather than specific skills

Stakeholders – Any person with an interest in the activities of an organization (e.g. customers, employees, government agencies and local communities)

Statute law – Legislation created by government

Stock Exchange – A market in which a company's shares are bought and sold

Strategic alliances – An agreement between two or more companies to share their resources, e.g. operational resources and access to customers

Subculture – Element within a culture with a distinctive set of values and behaviours

Suppliers – Members of a value chain who sell goods and services to other companies, who subsequently add value to them

Supply – The volume of a product that firms are prepared to bring to a market, at a given price and within a specified time period

SWOT analysis – An organization's internal strengths and weaknesses, matched against its external opportunities and threats

T

Takeover – When one company seeks to acquire control of another

Task force – Team focused on tackling a specific problem

Technological fusion – The merging of different technologies

Technology transfer – The process of disseminating new technologies between sectors and products

Tort – Law relating to the liability of individuals and organizations to others in respect of their negligent actions

Trademarks – Legal protection given to an organization for its distinctive logos and brand names

Trading blocs – An agreement between a group of nations to make trade between members easier than trade with other countries

Training – Development of skills in a workforce

Transformation process – When low-value inputs are turned into relatively high-value outputs

Tribal marketing – A type of marketing which recognizes that many individuals' purchase decisions are made with reference to the values, attitudes and lifestyles of their peer group

Trend analysis – Studying past trends as a basis for predicting future activity (e.g. of sales or costs)

Turning point – A point in a business cycle when recession turns into expansion, or vice versa

U

Unemployment – Unused or under-utilized potential workers in a population

V

Value chain – The sequence of activities and organizations involved in transforming a product from one that is of low value to one that is of high value

Values – A deep-seated set of beliefs

Vertical integration – The extension of a firm's activities to prior or subsequent points in a value chain

Visible trade – Overseas trade in manufactured goods

W

Withdrawals – Money in the circular flow of income that should flow from households to firms, or vice versa, but is instead withdrawn from circulation (e.g. through savings or taxation)

World Trade Organization (WTO) – An international organization that seeks to facilitate trade between nations, by, among other things, removing trade barriers

Index